The Sex of Things

*Gender and Consumption
in Historical Perspective*

EDITED BY

Victoria de Grazia,
with Ellen Furlough

INTRODUCTIONS BY

Victoria de Grazia

UNIVERSITY OF CALIFORNIA PRESS
Berkeley   Los Angeles   London

University of California Press
Berkeley and Los Angeles, California

University of California Press, Ltd.
London, England

© 1996 by
The Regents of the University of California

Library of Congress Cataloging-in-Publication Data

The sex of things : gender and consumption in historical perspective / edited
   by Victoria de Grazia, with Ellen Furlough; introductions by Victoria de Grazia.
      p.   cm.
   Includes bibliographical references and index.
   ISBN 0-520-20034-9 (alk. paper). — ISBN 0-520-20197-3 (pbk. : alk. paper)
      1. Consumer behavior—Sex differences—History.   2. Consumption
   (Economics)—Social aspects—History.   I. De Grazia, Victoria.   II. Furlough, Ellen, 1953–.
   HF5415.32.S49   1996
   658.8'348—dc20   95-37354

Printed in the United States of America
9 8 7 6 5 4 3 2 1

An earlier version of chapter 11 was published in Rob Kroes, Robert Rydell, and Kurt
Bosscher, eds., *Cultural Transmissions and Receptions: American Mass Culture in Europe*
(Amsterdam: VU University Press, 1993), 84–99. A shorter version of chapter 13
appears in Rachel Bowlby, *Still Crazy after All These Years* (London: Routledge, 1992).

CONTENTS

ILLUSTRATIONS

ACKNOWLEDGMENTS

The completion of this volume offers a welcome occasion to reiterate my gratitude to Rutgers University, where I taught from 1977 to 1993, and especially to thank its administration for its collective wisdom in supporting the foundation of the Center for Historical Analysis in 1988 at the initiative of the history faculty. The volume was conceived at the center from 1991 to 1993 in the course of the project under my direction on the theme of consumer cultures in historical perspective. Most of the essays were originally presented and discussed in the weekly seminars. On those occasions, the authors all agree, they profited much from the advice of visiting fellows, colleagues, and the graduate and undergraduate student body. On behalf of the contributors, I especially want to thank Ellen Furlough, a senior fellow at the center from 1992 to 1993 who edited the volume with me, together with Joe Broderick, John Gillis, David Glover, Alan Hyde, Cora Kaplan, Alice Kessler-Harris, T. J. Jackson Lears, James Livingston, Diane Neumaier, Leonardo Paggi, Bonnie Smith, and Mick Taussig. To the continuance of this humane and imaginative collective enterprise, one wholly in keeping with the university's public mission, this volume is dedicated.

Let me also reiterate my thanks to Rudolph Bell, who, as the center's executive director from 1989 to 1994, turned his boundless inventivity to supporting this undertaking, to Lynn Shanko, the center's expert administrator, and to Jan Lambertz, whose generous intellect lay behind the organization of the workshop at which the papers were discussed all together. That workshop was subsidized by grants from the Western Area Committee of the Social Science Research Council and the Council for European Studies, whose support I gratefully acknowledge. In completing the introductions to the volume, I benefited from cogent and gracious criticisms from Andreas Huyssen,

Atina Grossmann, Temma Kaplan, Kirstie McClure, and members of the Jean Howard Reading Group at Columbia University. Barbara Kruger kindly permitted us to use her work for the cover. For their prodigious and patient labor to produce this volume, my warm thanks to Sheila Levine and the production and copy editors, Dore Brown and Carlotta Shearson.

Victoria de Grazia
Fall 1994

Introduction

Victoria de Grazia

The adage "Consumption, thy name is woman" resonates with such venerable authority that one might expect to find it cited in *Bartlett's Familiar Quotations,* attributed to some Victorian savant or to an eminent critic of modern frippery. In Western societies, acts of exchange and consumption have long been obsessively gendered, usually as female. As the speculative bubbles of early-eighteenth-century capitalism burst, pamphleteering moralists excoriated the feminine volatility of nascent credit schemes and decried the foppish new rich. In scenes set in late-nineteenth-century French, British, and American department stores, novelists imagined that goods enraptured buyers, who fantasized about and fondled them before finally taking possession. Modernist intellectuals disparaged commercial mass culture as venal and vaporous, bewitching its customers with mercenary blandishments. Commercial artists sprawl idealized female figures across twentieth-century advertising copy, designing their forms and faces to elicit desirous gazes. And marketing agents probe the calculations and caprices imputed to Mrs. Consumer to survey the entity of household spending.

What more precisely is the nature of the identification of femininity, of the female sex, of womankind generally with sumptuary laws, shopping sprees, and domestic display, not to mention the mundane chores of purchase and provisioning with which women are familiarly associated? Is this identification only a timeworn trope of patriarchal culture? Or does it bear on deeper social processes? If women figure not only as the proverbial shoppers, the *Ur*-decorators, the perennial custodians of the bric-a-brac of daily life but also as objects of exchange and consumption, what then can be inferred about the relationship of man, males, and masculinity to the world of commodities? And why, skeptics might ask, should these issues concern us at all? Why should contemporary investigations into the history of consumer society be so concerned to explore the workings of gender?

The essays gathered here endeavor to respond to these questions. From the outset, they confirm what readers might already suspect. Sexualized metaphors applied to the circulation and consumption of goods may be taken to stand for elusive social relations. Sexual difference lends itself to being talked about in deceptively self-evident polarities. Often these can reveal deep levels of conceptual discomfort, the kind that people experience in the face of inexplicable changes in their material life and new inequalities. If there is a perplexing constancy in the references to sexuality and gender, there is an equally baffling variety. Both the continuities and the variations are most susceptible to explanation by firm grounding in historical context.

That writing about the meaning of consumption requires writing its history may seem obvious, even banal. Yet the consumption of goods and services is one of those human activities, like sex, leisure, or family life, that is usually taken for granted. So much so, that although the development of consumption under capitalist exchange is relatively recent, many of the suppositions about why and how we consume remain unquestioned. In the mid–eighteenth century, with Adam Smith, François Quesnay, and other Enlightenment thinkers, it became axiomatic that man was born acquisitive. Suffice it for free rein to be given to commerce and the division of labor, and civilized people would trade, truck, and barter. Later ideologues of the capitalist order averred that people instinctively sought variety and pleasure, the only constraint on their desires being scarcity. Variety was most easily achieved by acquiring possessions, and acquisition occurred mainly through market exchange. Some time in the mid–twentieth century, it also became axiomatic that access to consumer goods was a fundamental right of all peoples, that this right was best fulfilled by free enterprise, and that free enterprise operated optimally if guided by the profit motive unimpeded by state or other interference.

All of these assumptions can be challenged. We used to do so by contrasting our contemporary acquisition and use of goods with an earlier, more rural, less commodified way of life. It was common, too, to turn to the experiences studied by anthropologists: the gift giving, barter, and other exchanges of so-called primitive peoples. It was also possible to envisage alternative notions of needs and other ways to satisfy wants through the prism of socialistically planned economies. But there is skepticism now whether any of these other experiences are relevant to late-twentieth-century consumer practices. This skepticism is not necessarily a healthy one, for the loss of these critical vantage points has diminished the capacity to construct a narrative about the advent of modern consumption habits and narrowed the imagination about the motives and meaning behind today's use of goods.

This collection presents a complex of issues related to what might usefully, if not prettily, be called the sexual division of labor around consumption to show that there was nothing natural or inevitable about the development of modern consumption practices. The authors, to recall an archeological metaphor, have excavated mounds of truisms, verities, and antinomies: commonplaces about fickle femininity and dutiful female domesticity; the antonyms production and consumption, luxury and necessity; the dichotomized relationship between Mr. Breadwinner and Mrs. Consumer. They examine the forces that shaped these conventions of thinking, and they trace the often elusive linkages between discursive practices and social, political, and economic structures.

Thus we learn that in eighteenth-century Paris, public opinion indicted shop girls and female dress merchants as the embodiments of disorderly luxury, moreover, that these metaphoric disturbances were linked to the quarrels of Enlightenment thinkers, who, in the face of quickening urban commerce, were in their own way disputing definitions of the superfluous and necessary and casting about for new terms to express their uneasiness. We are piqued with curiosity, even a little appalled, at the immense economic and psychic investment in domesticity made by the mid-nineteenth-century bourgeois *maîtresse de maison*. How Proustian her agonizing over codes of decoration and etiquette! In this volume, we go beyond viewing her elaborately cultivated taste as symptomatic of a stultifying bourgeois home life to consider its multiple functions in preserving family lines, embellishing national hierarchies of taste, and eventually contributing to her own sense of individuality. Labor history has familiarized us with the making of the modern male wage earner who, with the support of militant trade unions and under the pressure of middle-class cultural norms, strove to provide wife and dependents with a decent standard of living. What a mythic and precarious figure he turns out to be once we know something of the accumulation of laws and social norms that persecuted workers who deserted their families as menaces to the "public purse," that adjudicated domestic squabbles over money, and that assisted impoverished families with collective social services, while simultaneously exalting the females of the household as modern and expert consumers and homemakers. By the time we finish, we will question the truism that women dress *up* and will wonder what is really happening when they put *on* their faces in the morning with makeup. But we will equally ask why Western men dress *down*, and, perhaps, wonder why, since the first decade of this century, they have scrupulously scraped *off* their faces by shaving daily with safety razors.

To make sense of the accretion of sexual meanings and gender identities around practices of consumption the authors could not be wedded to any single definition of the polymorphous term *consumption*. Within a collection that moves broadly from the late seventeenth to the late twentieth century and spans Western Europe and the United States, readers will find assorted behaviors designated with the verb *to consume,* the subject *consumer,* the concept of *consumer sovereignty,* and the diverse forms of *individual* and *social,* or *collective, consumption,* together with the various movements and ideologies that go under the name of *consumerism.* Thus, consumption is discussed here in terms of processes of commodification, spectatorship, commercial exchanges, and social welfare reforms, processes that involve the desire for and sale, purchase, and use of durable and nondurable goods, collective services, and images.

These variegated practices of consumption are examined with a collective eye to a larger historical problematic, namely, the development of what is familiarly called consumer society. This concept is intended here to identify the emergence of a peculiar type of market society, the Western capitalist system of exchange, and especially to probe the ever more identifiably *modern* aspect of its development. This modernity lies first in carrying out acts of consumption within capitalist exchange networks and then in the organization of institutions, resources, and values around ever larger flows and accumulations of commodities. It also lies in the transformation of goods from being relatively static symbols around which hierarchies were ordered to being more directly constitutive of class, social status, and personal identity.

The time frame for this development embraces the transition from Old Regime to bourgeois institutions, a transition that started with the dual industrial and political revolutions of the late eighteenth century. It bridges the transformations of the age of fordized mass production starting in the early twentieth century, and it extends into the present to analyze the huge changes that have occurred globally since the 1970s, which go under the name of postfordism, postindustrialism, or postmodernity. Underlying all of the contributions are the beliefs that the development of consumer society bears interpretation in light of the inequalities in and intense conflict over the appropriation and use of commodities; that gender roles have inflected this dynamic of change and have been significantly inflected by it; and finally, that this tension around the meaning of gender is especially visible at the moments of transition—from aristocratic to bourgeois society, from bourgeois to mass consumption—and in times of scarcity and social distress.

Our central interest is the myriad conflicts over power that constitute the politics of consumption. This politics could have many specific objects— pornographic picture cards and movie melodramas, cosmetics, food staples, and the standard set of home appliances (refrigerators, vacuums, radios, and televisions). It could reside in the subtlest indicators of social station, such as the cut and fabric of a dandy's suit, which decisively marked the gulf between aristocratic gentleman and bourgeois bounder in eighteenth-century England. It lay in the makeup recommended for modern women, in the palette of skin colors squirted from a cosmetics tube that signaled the uneasy coexistence of ethnic identities in race-riven, socially mobile America.

Conflicts of power attached to the legal disputes that brought harrying shop-keepers and harassed husbands, along with portionless wives, before magistrates in Victorian England. They were especially visible and threatening to the constituted order in consumer-driven mass movements, like that spear-headed by famished civilians in World War I Berlin's breadlines, which challenged the legitimacy of Kaiser Wilhelm II's rule.

To assess the nature of the politics of consumers' demands—as a means of measuring economic well-being, as a way to examine hierarchies of social place, or as a test of political consensus—the authors have been attentive to three interpretative contexts. The first context regards the Euro-American framework within which the volume is cast; the second and third reflect two specialized fields of research, the history of consumer culture and the methods and purview of feminist analysis. By and large, the conflicts over consumption that are variously investigated occurred in Western societies in which the struggle for subsistence was largely (but not entirely or evenly) won. Moreover, starting in the nineteenth century, the application of technology to production and the democratization of consumption through economic growth and social reform promised ever greater abundance. Always in the background looms what was to become the dominant model by the mid–twentieth century, that advanced by the United States. This model established the predominance of individual acquisitiveness over collective entitlement and defined the measure of the good society as private well-being achieved through consumer spending.

To establish a critical perspective on this Euro-American model, all of the contributors to this volume could be said to stand at the confluence of two relatively new streams of historical inquiry. One, the study of consumer cultures, is still a mere rivulet compared to the other, a veritable torrent with headwaters in feminist studies of women and gender. In their sources, however, the two are not unrelated. Both have arisen since the 1960s as a new cycle of rapid and pervasive economic change has shaken a secular fixity of class, national, and sexual identities, along with the canons of analysis that since the nineteenth century were propounded to analyze them. Both originate from the attempt to translate new social concerns and cultural identities into new paradigms of research.

In particular, the more intense study of the symbolic and social dimensions of consumption responds to the disorienting new profile of the material world. In a scant thirty years, perhaps even more visibly in European society than in industry-scarred America, the balance between production and consumption has shifted strikingly. The assembly-line worker is fast going the way of the cottage spinner and craft worker of earlier centuries, service labor has become the predominant occupation, and pristine nature, perennially under threat from chronic industrial waste, has become extinct. Deindustrialization in the West has whisked away factories to the fields of China, rural Mexico, and the Newly Industrializing Countries, while commercial malls and chains offering deep discounts, as well as tourist facilities of all kinds, crowd into the remaining open spaces of rural America and proliferate within view of the medieval towers of ancient Mediterranean townscapes. Not only the sheer profusion of objects but the commodification of things such as fetuses and of services such as reproduction, public education, and prisons, which formerly seemed excluded from market truck, casts doubt on what, if anything, exists outside of commodity exchange. These trends make it seem passé to think that labor and work time are the major determinants of our passions and interests. With commodities looming so large as principles of pleasure and pain, the question arises whether the asceticism and ambivalence about goods so deeply rooted in Western culture has not caused scholars to ignore the power of things to shape human subjectivities and social life.

Though the current impetus to study consumer society seems to come from common sources, the subject has not generated a unified field of inquiry. Generally speaking, current research shares some key words in common, such as "consumer culture." But on the one side, there are studies that work within the well-trod conventions of liberal historical paradigms on industrialization; these recapitulate debates about how early to date the "consumer revolution," emphasizing the demand for goods rather than innovations in the supply, and they add an important subjective-cultural dimension to the study of social-economic criteria. Thus, they emphasize the quality of life as opposed to the standard of living; instead of the structures of primary accumulation, such as the rural banks, they highlight the emergent institutions of retailing, first and foremost the department store. What they have not revised is their assumptions about how people in the past made decisions about consumption and what goods might have meant to their collective outlooks. Interpretations of motivation remain surprisingly wedded to the individualist conceptions of behavior common to present-day Western society.

On the other side, there are theoretically conceived cultural studies that challenge productivist perspectives on historical trends. These are especially concerned with cultural meanings and often use textual analysis applied to literature, film, and other cultural artifacts to delve into the psychical mechanisms as well as the social drives that shape and were shaped by consumption activities. Much of this study is present-minded, and some is influenced by psychoanalytic categories that are basically ahistorical. Hence it often lacks what the historian Marc Bloch, in his stimulating 1928 essay on comparative history, called "the sense of difference, of the exotic which is an indispensable condition for any sound understanding of the past." Some is also signally antagonistic to modernist, which is to say Marxist and Weberian, efforts to explain the social world with generalizable laws, on the grounds that these deny important sources of difference and complexity. Such approaches have tended to discourage analysis of processes of signification in the light of varying historical legacies, such as might be shaped by diverse processes of state building, or by the relative power of the market, or by varying patterns of accumulation of what French sociologist Pierre Bourdieu has familiarized as "cultural capital." For our purposes, however, such interactions are central, for they may account for politically significant differences in the evolution of the responses to changes in consumption habits within and across societies, and the diverse play of institutions, state, market, and family that affect the outcomes.

In contrast, feminist inquiry has brought to the study of consumer practices an agenda of politically compelling issues as well as sound intuitions about method. From the 1960s, if not earlier, feminist thinkers have recognized the importance of consumption to the question of what processes transform a female into a woman. Feminist inquiry has identified commercial culture as an especially totalizing and exploitative force, to which women are more vulnerable than men because of their subordinate social, economic, and cultural position and because of the patriarchal nature of the organization and the semiotics of mass consumption. By the same token, feminist researchers have long been aware of the conventional association of women with consumption, as a consequence of their role in the household division of labor and as reified objects in the commodity exchange system.

This sensitivity to the impact of mass consumption on women has not been unproblematic from the point of view of research. Like students of consumer culture generally, feminists have been entangled in a moralizing debate about whether commercial culture, and consumption more broadly, is emancipatory or stultifying, liberating or repressive. Given the stakes, the quarrel can be ferocious. One side asserts that mass consumption victimizes women. Fashion codes and beauty standards are denounced as akin to purdah, foot binding, or the veil—public sexual impositions on women, which, beyond domesticating women's drive toward liberation, constrain them physically and violate their authentic selves. The other side argues that mass consumption liberates women by freeing them from the constraints of domesticity. Accordingly, they argue that women, out shopping or otherwise practicing what has been called "style politics," use the rituals of consumption in dress, cosmetics, hairstyle, and gesture to bend the norms ordained by the market and to flout family and other authority.

The essays here, though not indifferent to such debates, advance a different set of concerns. First, they focus on the construction of gender roles rather than on an unexamined acceptance of the category of "woman" and thus construe the process of gendering broadly, in terms of male as well as female identities. This expanded focus recognizes the capacity of commodities to move between the customarily female spaces of the market and the household, between the world of production and the world of reproduction, wreaking havoc with the very polarities—of public and private, calculation and desire, commercial sphere and domestic space, male and female—that have forged modern definitions of womanhood in Western society, as well as the terms for interpreting women's subordination. The preeminent concern here is thus not with moral dilemmas, at least not as defined or resolved by judgments uncritically committed to the antinomies of private and public and of market and state—and which place oppression or freedom on one side of the equation or the other. Instead, the common task, in addition to establishing the claims and counterclaims of women and men, is precisely to capture the immense transformative powers of capitalist-driven consumption as it constantly refashions notions of authentic, essential woman- and mankind.

Second, these essays highlight not only gender but also the class relations embodied in consumption practices, an issue to which recent study of consumer cultures has been surprisingly indifferent. One can concur that an understanding of social relations requires that the realm of consumption be considered on a par with forces of production. But there is a risk here of subscribing to a couple of new fallacies. One is an aesthetic bias toward the object-laden as opposed to the object-less, toward those with the most attractive and abundant symbolic capital, often the rich and powerful, as against the dreary and "tasteless," who are usually the poor and powerless. The second fallacy is the interpretation of consumer desires as largely individual choices, motivated by the consumer's wish for self-actualization or therapeutic uplift. The gendered study of consumption brings class back through the front door. The changing meaning of consumption habits in successive forms of social stratification highlights very different roles for women and men, over time and from class to class. From an analysis of consumption styles, as practiced in households and played out in public spaces, we obtain another significant perspective on social reproduction.

The centrality of class is related to a third concern, the importance of the family. From the perspective of the history of changing consumption habits, this institution is astonishingly multiform. As a central institution of civil society, it is the site where resources derived from one form of power—purchasing power acquired and expended in the market—are recombined to shape self-identities, sense of status, and demands for entitlement. Most of what was consumed was once internally produced in the household; however, in the last two centuries, market-supplied goods and services have largely replaced homemade ones. Women have occupied a strategic place in this changeover, being positioned at the intersection of the household's three functions: reproduction, production, and consumption. Yet the process of negotiation among persons with an affective as well as material stake in this joint enterprise—usually wife and husband, but also older and younger generations—is as yet little explored, though it would seem to shape profoundly what kinds of goods are purchased, what services are delegated to or re-appropriated from the market, and what values are attached to goods in the pursuit of family well-being.

Finally, this volume brings the state back into the study of consumption. It is a bias in Anglo-American studies that consumption is generally construed as individual rather than social, to the neglect of the numerous ways in which ruling institutions define practices and standards of consumption. Yet states ration goods and services even in peacetime; they govern credit and retailing practices; they define appropriate standards of consumption with statistics and property laws; they provide the framework of private consumption through social spending on infrastructure, housing, health, education, and pensions. Indeed, it could be said that the state, in the process of allocating resources, legitimating property, and defining social obligations, establishes the very notion of private as opposed to public consumption. By the same token, the state is central to the activity of gendering consumption. In the emergent credit economy we see this process at work in the laws formulated to shield businesses and family property against the less creditworthy members of society, who, often, given family and social structures, have been propertyless females. Under authoritarian regimes, as in fascist Italy, we see the state, in the name of autarchic command economies, appealing to patriotic housewives to exploit household resources to reduce demand on the market and state, staunching the flow of foreign commodities to contain the feminized symbolic world of mass culture, and demonizing high-spending bourgeois women as "luxury mammals." In the welfare state, we see governmental legislation to regulate access to the "public purse," reinforcing the division of labor between male producer-breadwinners and female consumer-providers.

In the last analysis, the gendered study of consumer practices offers a critical stance on the wide consensus in U.S. society that material abundance, procured by individual acquisition through market-driven systems of exchange, yields the "good" society, whether judged in terms of social equity, humane values, or the efficient management of societal resources. This consensus has only been reaffirmed by the failure of so-called Eastern utopias to guarantee a decent standard of living for their citizens. Yet the Western model of mass consumption hardly offers a solution to how to build, much less sustain a "good" society. In the first place, fledgling market systems don't deliver the goods without engendering immense new inequalities, with predictably turbulent social consequences. Even if they were able to deliver commodities on a mass scale to a historically unprecedented degree, the prospect of billions of people on earth consuming in the Western style—instead of the only eight hundred million who are forecast to be able to do so at the end of the century—seems unlikely. One obvious reason is that the advanced countries are unlikely to relinquish their monopoly over global resources.

Even if by some political miracle they did, the environmental effects of individualistic mass consumption on a global scale would be unconscionable. In the United States, meanwhile, the economic restructuring underway since the 1970s has produced huge income inequalities greatly magnified in socially-differentiated consumption practices and unparalleled since the early twentieth century. Disoriented by the rapidity of change in their material existence, people struggle against the sense of historical depthlessness. But the nostalgic and contrived images most profusely available through commercial culture form a kind of retro-pastiche that seems only to intensify their confusion.

In the hope that historical analysis can help people brave this sense of disorientation, we offer here some experiences of others, women and men, who have had to contend with an equally baffling proliferation of goods. We have tried to explain the meaning of these experiences, in the first section, by offering several perspectives on the great transition from an aristocratic to a bourgeois mode of consumption; in the second section, by framing the immensely complex set of issues involved in the sexual division of labor around consumption practices in families and households; and, finally, in the third section, by addressing the significance of a politics of consumption in the era of mass politics. With new axes of interpretation in place, we can anticipate a history that better responds to the imperative to know about material needs, wants, and desires.

PART ONE

Changing Consumption Regimes

The essays in the first section locate the origins of modern ways of relating consumption to gender in the long transition from aristocratic to bourgeois society. Acts of consumption acquired entirely new meanings during the great shift from a society of orders to one dominated by capitalist exchange. Under the Old Regime, princely rule apportioned goods according to age-old hierarchies, and religious symbolism offered a central axis of meaning. Under bourgeois society, old and new classes contended the meaning of goods, that fetishistically, as Karl Marx observed in *Capital*, volume 1, appeared to move by themselves to market. In clusters of change occurring from the late seventeenth century until the outset of the twentieth—changes in the relationship of consumption to production, of abundance to scarcity, of household to workplace, and of state to market—there lie the origins of new ways of thinking about material life and human nature, which in turn yielded new ways of linking gender and consumption.

In each case, the linkages were intense and subtle. What motivated the public animus against the so-called minister of modes of Louis XVI, namely, Rose Bertin, stylist and dressmaker to the queen? In her study of Old Regime Paris, Jennifer Jones suggests that the growing commercial, but also political, prominence of women in the second half of the eighteenth century generated considerable anxiety. Male fears that confused the material longings manifest in rapid fashion turnover with physical lust were aggravated by worries that sexual and social disorder might be unleashed if lower-class females mixed with the elites in the shops and byways of commercial Paris. These fears were compounded by new scientific beliefs that argued for a physiological basis for psychological differences between men and women. Thus sharp eyesight, deft touch, and physical passivity accounted for women's innate gifts of taste and style, qualities that if not channeled into proper domesticity could present a real social disturbance.

David Kuchta also takes up the question of style politics during the transition, though in terms that reflect England's very different trajectory of development. From the late seventeenth century, British aristocrats stood down bourgeois upstarts in contests of fashion. By dressing down, they removed the stigma of effeminacy exploited elsewhere by reformers to discredit the sumptuous behavior at the courts. In Britain at least, a long reformation of manners went hand in hand with the coalescing of aristocrats and middle classes in modern constitutional politics.

How was a bourgeois mode of consumption instated? Taking the example of France, Leora Auslander catalogues the intense investment of bourgeois women and men in domesticity, the former in household adornment, the latter in collecting. Although these practices largely complemented each other, embellishing the roles prescribed for contemporary women and men, they tolerated some sexual and social eccentricity in the hands of the outré new woman or the dandified man. More generally, the fine arts of furnishing turned style into state power, legitimating the bourgeoisie's ambition to inherit the French nation's legacy of refinement.

Abigail Solomon-Godeau asks how the erotized female body became the signifier of modernity. She identifies this pictorial convention with the rise of a new patriarchal visual economy originating in the passage from classicism to realism during the mid–nineteenth century and the veritable media explosion that occurred with the commercialization of the lithographer's art at midcentury. But the tenacity of pornographic images and their centrality to modern modes of representing Eros, the body, and femininity were inconceivable without the joining of bourgeois and bohemian, commerce and art, and high and low culture in a common idiom objectifying the female body.

The entity of the changes underlying these episodes is better grasped if linked to the broader shift in the meaning of consumption itself during the seventeenth and eighteenth centuries. Whether transformations in the quality and level of material life actually merit the label "consumer revolution" can be debated. The basic social science questions of who got what, how, when, and where are only beginning to be addressed.[1] Still, the many people whose lives were touched by the rich cross-Atlantic trade acted as if they had moved from a material world of finite resource to one pivoting around the exchange of new, sometimes exotic commodities. Or so it seems from the fact that between the seventeenth and the eighteenth centuries the English word "consumption" became charged with entirely new meanings. By the early 1700s, consumption had lost much of its old pejorative significance of "to waste," "to devour," or "to use up." New definitions turned on the

antonymic distinction not between squander and employ but between production and use. Accordingly, to better estimate the national wealth, political arithmeticians called for accounts of "manufacture, importation, and consumption," where the latter had to do not with the destruction but with the
utilization of the products of human labor. Similarly, individuals became
"consumptioners," or users of commodities, the latter being objects, both
necessary and convenient, circulated through monetized exchange. As an
aggregate category, consumption became the amount of goods "consumed,"
while the "consumer" became "one who used up an article produced, thereby
exhausting its exchange value."[2]

During this same period, two inveterate prejudices that identified consumption with femininity acquired a new resonance. One, far antedating the
rise of capitalist economic relations, associated mother/mater with vile or
fertile matter and reflected an ambivalence about abundance with roots deep
in Western intellectual traditions. When men dreamed of mastering the elements with technology, their visions of dominance often depended on the
success of mastering the chaotic energies of a metaphorically female nature.
As the promise of abundance came nearer to hand, the tension, lest it seduce but not be subduable, became more acute.[3] A second prejudice associated femininity with treacherous inconstancy and change. At least since
Greco-Roman times, fluctuations in the meaning, style, and quantity of material culture were discussed in terms of luxury, a term usually associated with
effeminate men or lustful women. Under Europe's Old Regime, it was a central prerogative of princely power to rule over standards of taste and the sites
of luxury production and consumption. Since monarchs ruled over their subjects through hierarchies of taste, positioning objects to reflect rank and function, law and custom regarded unbridled consumption as profoundly destabilizing. Consequently, sumptuary laws designed to restrict exchange and
access were closely bound up with controls over women's freedoms.[4] It was
this medieval worldview of economic and sexual constraints that early-eighteenth-century mercantilist thinkers turned topsy-turvy to argue that even
the luxury trades, indeed the luxury trades first and foremost, were an impetus to the accumulation of national wealth.[5] Bernard Mandeville, in particular, is remembered for his disquieting and very funny satire *The Fable of
the Bees* (1714), in which he scolds the moralists and lauds the new "Mutability of Objects."[6] To drive home the point that luxury is economically useful to "operose manufacture," hence to the nation's good, in *A Search into
the Nature of Society* Mandeville even pardons the wanton ways of whores and
courtesans, championing the "Fickle Strumpet that Invents new Fashions
every Week; the haughty Duchess that in Equipage, Entertainment, and all
of her Behavior would imitate a Princess," together with the "sensual
Courtier," the "profuse Rake," and the "lavish Heir."[7]

With the shift in political economy from mercantilism to laissez-faire, the aristocratic rentier made way for the capitalist entrepreneur, and new premises were laid for thinking about the economic, social, and sexual connotations of consumption.[8] Consumption stood at the heart of modern market society, being "the sole end and purpose of all production," Adam Smith affirmed in book 4 of the *Wealth of Nations* (1776). That the producer existed to promote the well-being of the consumer was, he wrote, a "maxim . . . so perfectly self-evident, that it would be absurd to attempt to prove it." In the interest of specifying the nature of demand, namely, investment (or delayed consumption) and immediate consumption, Smith identified two different functions in consumption, one of which was economic, to stimulate capital investment, the other social, for sustenance and the reproduction of the social system. The former he identified in the person of the capitalist profittaker, the latter in its most conspicuous forms with the profligate habits of aristocratic landed wealth. This neat division enabled Smith to indict, on the grounds that they obstructed wealth making, the myriad sumptuary laws of his epoch, like the ones that regulated the number of flounces, ribbon lengths, or the fall of wigs. At the same time, there was no intellectual need for him to pass judgment on spendiferous aristocrats, much less condone the profligacy of the "fickle strumpets" and their unsavory companions, whose reputations Mandeville had salvaged in the interest of national manufacture.

Though Smith welcomed the rapid accumulation of capital, he was clearly ambivalent about the rapid accumulation of material goods. In *The Theory of Moral Sentiments* (1759), we find him wondering at the disproportion between the utopian promise of technology harnessed to the division of labor and the picayune wants that the products seemed designed to satisfy; wondering why it was that "enormous and operose machines contrive to produce a few trifling conveniences to the body." Smith's writings don't specifically identify this apparently universal human passion for objects of "frivolous utility" with women. However, his indictment of the "baubles and trinkets" of modern commerce and his perplexity that such great inventions turned out goods that were "fitter for playthings of children than the serious pursuits of men" hinted at a feminized definition of consumption.[9] When Smith imagined the benefits to society of consumption, it was in terms of the sound wants of industrious craftsmen and frugal peasants, as opposed to the frippery of foppish hangers-on at court or femininized male servants. In this reasoning, as well as in his worry that abundant goods could deceive with the false promise that wealth would bring happiness, Smith foreshadowed a conflict that still exists between two different visions of economic development: speculative expansion on the one hand, systematic organization on the other. Ever since the eighteenth century, admiration for the new sciences of productivity has gone hand-in-hand with fear of carnivalesque excess, one identified with imperturbable maleness, the other with an out-of-control femininity.[10]

The propensity to feminize the realm of consumption, arising in the early stages of capitalist accumulation, was reinforced by two other structural changes that became visible in the course of the nineteenth century. The first was the division of labor in the work process, and the simultaneous identification of wage labor with male labor. This division reinforced the differentiation between the household and the workplace, between female provisioners and male workers, and between consumption and production. The second change was the advent of liberal politics and public space. This change was premised on a reconceptualization of needs. In particular, it involved distinguishing those needs that were defined as irrational, superfluous, or so impassioned that they overloaded the political system from those that were rationally articulated and cast in terms appropriate to being represented and acted on through normal political processes. The former, not unexpectedly, tended to be identified with the female population, who by and large were excluded from electoral representation, whereas the latter were identified with enfranchised males.

The first structural change reflects the fear that political-economic paradigms that arose in the early nineteenth century to calculate the value of labor were profoundly shaped by and shaping of prevailing conceptions of gender.[11] Economists struggling to make sense of the industrial revolution identified the production process as the activity that gave value to things, transforming them from simple matter into items of exchange. Their calculations of the cost of labor put a price not only on the actual manufacture of the goods, meaning the amount of labor invested in them, but also on the reproduction of human capital needed to resupply the labor force. But to calculate these costs, political economists focused exclusively on the male wage. This was estimated as the amount required for the worker himself to survive, together with that required for the support of offspring until they were able to work. Not only did this calculation impute to the male worker the costs of reproduction but it passed over the female's contributions to the bearing, nurturing, socializing, and provisioning of the children.

The asymmetry in the calculation of wages—whereby men's wages included subsistence and reproductive costs, whereas women's wages required family supplements even for individual subsistence—reverberated in the way in which contemporaries conceptualized the realm of consumption and the role of men and women within it. The concern that the wage not exceed subsistence lest it be wasted in vice was fed by shocking images of the female denizens of the new manufacturing centers, independent working women, whose "unnatural" existence as wage earners (but also as prostitutes) exemplified the debauched habits induced by modern urban life. Moreover, in a world where all values turned on production, consumption was also damned as "nonwork." For early-nineteenth-century political economists, to recall Jean-Baptiste Say's aphorism, supply created its own demand. Not being work, not being production, consumption lay in a theoretical limbo.

Given that consumption was not conceptualized as a discrete problem, the household was in theory a mere receptacle for commodities, and circuits of distribution were regarded as parasitical excrescences on the economic body. Typically, the earliest empirical studies of consumption, undertaken by reform-minded statisticians in northwestern Europe starting in the 1850s, were based on family budgets, their scope being to calculate scientifically minimum subsistence standards in order to defend minimum levels for male wages. Though reformers such as Ernst Engel and Frédéric Le Play based their estimates of the total family income on the wages of male heads of household, they naturally relied on the housewives' calculations of spending to determine expenditure.[12] Yet nowhere did they calculate the value added to the household by this accounting service, much less the numerous other labors performed by female householders.

Not until the end of the nineteenth century, when neoclassical economists revised the principles of classical political economy, did the problem of demand become a prominent issue. The analysis of marginal utility was gender neutral or, better, aseptic, since it did not give a physiognomy to consumers except to presume they were capable of rational calculations about money, prices, and their own desires. The modal figure was *homo oeconomicus*, or the "average man." It would be seventy-five years before neoclassical economics would try to account for demand in terms not of (male) individuals but of the "utility function" of the entire family unit. Though much evidence attests to the diverse interests of family members and the often conflictual nature of intrahousehold relationships, as well as to the relative powerlessness of women, the traditional "new household economics" skirted the question of how contrasts might arise within a household and how these were ultimately resolved.[13] One response has been to devise new concepts, such as "well-behaved nuclear family utility function," which identifies the family with the unified optimizing consumer, whose utility function ostensibly reflects the interests of the rest of the household. But this approach still skirts the question of interests and power. For example, it doesn't take into account different estimates of the promise of goods to the purchasers. Yet calculations about their value often depend on the effort needed to use goods, which in turn involves some combination of time, skill, physical capacity, knowledge, and motivation. Different estimates of these factors in turn pivot around differences of power between the male and female (and adult and child) members of the household.

The second structural transformation relevant to examining the linkage between gender and consumption was the development of the modern public sphere. This development, as political theorists have often pointed out, was associated with the spaces, inventions, and sociability of the commercial revolution.[14] Printing houses, markets and bourses, salons, and cafés had as their common characteristic that they arose outside of the rule of absolutism and acted more or less independently of the canons of courtly taste and religious authority. Accordingly, the public sphere comprised the societal institutions in which modern public opinion was formed, as distinct and separate from the sites of private activity, namely, the household and the workplace. Expanding with industrialization and democratization in the nineteenth century, the public sphere, according to some theorists, offered the space in which citizens could mount a critique of the social system. It was this capacity, originally generated by commercial culture, that was then destined to be occluded in the twentieth century as the public sphere was overrun by highly manipulated mass commodity and mass communication systems.

The paradox here is that at the moment people were recognized as having the right to demand necessities, the notion of the necessary was narrowed, and the right to representation was denied to those who were most closely identified with the interests of the household in providing for basic social wants, namely, women. This paradox is not merely not recognized in liberal political theory but in a sense justified as indispensable to the development of a healthy modern civic culture.[15]

In tantalizing passages from one of the most frequently cited accounts of this development, Jürgen Habermas's *The Structural Transformation of the Public Sphere*, the German political theorist locates the origins of the bourgeois politics in the reinvigoration of households under the Old Regime as they became at once more privatized with respect to medieval community and more integrated into the market. Thus the first form of publicness arose, to quote Habermas, when "broad strata of population in the towns were affected in their daily existence as consumers by the regulations of mercantilist policy."[16] However, the critical stance of liberal politics did not arise, it seems, until these primitive and parochial claims for subsistence "on behalf of the reproduction of life" had passed through some sort of ill-defined political filtering process. In the event, some claims went on to be articulated through the press, coffeehouses, and salons. There they acquired the dignity of critique, becoming demands for general rights against absolutist authority. The sphere of modern politics was thereby constituted and was implicitly identified with the male voice. But what of the needs of the household that were not given legitimate voice within the public sphere? These apparently fell into the realm of particularized interests and were reclassified as mundane private desires.

According to this narrative, a civilizing politics of rights out of which constitutional government and modern political systems eventually evolved operated against a moral economy, one ruled by a primitive politics of needs and desires, that was irrelevant to or in any case outside of the evolution of modern representative politics. Arguably, the food riot was a manifestation of the politics of this earlier moral economy: the march of the women of Paris during the French Revolution to bring back the king and his family, "the Baker, the Baker's Wife, the Baker's Son," speaks to the unmediated connection between politics and consumption in the transition from the Old Regime. In the wake of the French Revolution, the liberal vision of politics justified an austere vision of needs on the part of ruling elites, as well as the exclusion of women and the propertyless, whose baser wants or private concerns lay outside of the public sphere proper.[17]

Having put forward the argument that changes in the concept of market, public space, and the division of labor that started with the industrial and political revolutions of the late eighteenth century were accompanied by significant changes in the meaning of consumption, we are ready to advance another hypothesis relevant to considering the new relations of gender and consumption, namely, that the shaking of the Old Regime transformed goods from being relatively static symbols around which social hierarchies were ordered to being more fluid and directly constitutive of social status. In other words, the making of nineteenth-century class society was not only about transformations in the relations of people to the means of production but also about their massively changing relations to systems of commodity exchange and styles of consumption.

To bring these relations into focus, more work needs to be done to develop the notion of a bourgeois mode of consumption, as integral to the bourgeois mode of production and distinct from both an aristocratic mode and, later, a mass mode of consumption. Evidence from France and England suggests that it was not before the mid–nineteenth century that the bourgeoisie was transformed from a purchasing class—or a group merely provisioning for its needs—into a consuming class that constituted its identity through a shared pattern of acquiring and using goods and a common structure of taste. Once in place, however, the bourgeois constellation endured, its elaborate and mystifying codes shaping the pyramidal social stratifications of European society, at least through the Great Depression and World War II, perhaps even down to the huge economic transformations of the 1950s and 1960s.[18] As a way of life, the bourgeois mode of consumption was historically unique, precisely because, as befitting its individualist outlooks, its ethos of progress, and the greatly varying income of its protagonists, it tolerated an unusual variety and turnover of models of self and social deportment.

To illuminate its working-class counterpart would involve investigating the vast realm of subsistence, both among the still largely self-sustaining rural households that persisted in the European countryside until the 1950s and among urban working-class families, the bulk of whose income went to food and shelter. The working-class standard of living presented very limited opportunities for the kinds of discretionary spending that we associate with modern styles of self-expression.[19] For the nineteenth century at least, when we speak of the expression of individuality, as opposed to collective belonging through goods, by definition, we are referring to the lifestyles of the bourgeoisie, bohemians, or the still extant aristocracy.

By and large, the development of bourgeois consumption pivoted around the feminized world of the home.[20] To make a home in the bourgeois manner, female heads of household not only performed tasks of nurturance and sociability but also spent money for food, clothing, and furnishings, both to provide for their own establishments and to set up their adult children. These efforts served to define their family's history, to signal their social position to other bourgeois, to differentiate their class from that of aristocrats and workers, and to lay claim to the nation's grand past. As Leora Auslander shows, bourgeois consumption practices also established a form of public presence for the *maîtresse de maison*, who was charged with managing a significant cultural capital. With little or no disposable income of her own, she had to develop enough expertise and autonomy to stand up to taste professionals, distributors, and sometimes craftsmen as well.

In their purchase and use of commodities, bourgeois women also had to balance their own sense of individuality against the interests of their family and class. It may be that these interests converged. However, sensitive to the tensions that could ensue, we have to question any bald assertion, such as that made by Colin Campbell in his provocative book *The Romantic Ethic and the Spirit of Modern Consumerism* (1987), that the origins of contemporary consumer outlooks should be traced to an individualistic, romantic "structure of feeling" or that women in the act of consumption quickly or easily tread the "hedonic treadmill" combined of "anticipatory pleasure and consummatory disappointment" that allegedly fed the modern consumerist imagination.[21] That Campbell imputes to the male psyche, as well as to the female, outlooks derived from the sensualist individualism that Rousseau and other Romantics invented to explain the natural susceptibility of women to the allure of commodities does not redeem his argument.

Clearly, the role that women were portrayed as playing in the construction of taste, style, and power under bourgeois rule was at least as complex as the role they may have actually played day-to-day. In general, works of political theory undertheorize the role of women. However, when consumption has been taken as a central axis of analysis, the conspicuousness of the female figure, in contrast to her real powerlessness, has resulted in a kind of overtheorization. This, at least, is the conclusion that one might draw from two signally important works of turn-of-the-century sociology on contemporary bourgeois society. The first of these works is the renowned *Theory of the Leisure Class* (1899) by the notoriously eccentric Thorstein Veblen.[22] The second is a lesser known study, *Luxury and Capitalism* (1913), by the equally prominent and idiosyncratic German sociologist Werner Sombart. Both men were mordant critics of bourgeois society. Veblen, a radical populist, excoriated the contemporary bourgeoisie for renouncing the modern craft spirit to revel anachronistically in the invidious hierarchies of the chivalric past. Sombart, a one-time reformer with deeply reactionary instincts, idealized the aggressive deeds of a heroic aristocratic society to belabor the German middle classes for lacking the refinement and courage to safeguard German society and culture from the dire forces of modernity.[23]

Veblen is of course remembered for his damning portrait of the lady consumer of the leisured class. She was central to the performance of conspicuous leisure. With no gainful employment, she busied herself in "painstaking attention to the service of the master," dedicating herself to unproductive undertakings such as collecting household paraphernalia and shepherding charitable societies that testified to her spouse's wealth and status.[24] Her decorativeness was tangible evidence of his purchasing power and demonstrated his dominant position in the hierarchy of invidious distinction and emulation that ruled the social pecking order.

Sombart, by contrast, is remembered for making the courtesan central to his argument that the industrial revolution was driven by the growth of the luxury trades rather than by overseas trade or wider domestic markets. Behind this development was a new sexual economy powered by the secularization of love, which, starting in the Middle Ages, eventually freed the "cosmic love instinct" from the strictures of church and marriage. The "emancipation of the flesh," timid at first, gradually gave way to an epoch of strong natural sensuality, followed by "a certain refinement, then debauchery, finally perversion." Thus not puritan virtue, as Sombart's contemporary Max Weber would have it, but the "erotic ambitions" of gallants spurred capital accumulation. Not heroic entrepreneurs but wanton courtesans stimulated invention by playing aristocrats against parvenu bourgeois in a grand struggle of emulative spending. To quote Sombart, "Luxury, itself a legitimate child of illicit love . . . gave birth to capitalism."[25]

If Veblen is read conventionally, he seems to support the view that women are cogs in the wheel of the male status mill. They are the keen-eyed neighbors and the ambitious shoppers in the battle to keep up with the Joneses.[26] By contrast, Sombart would seem to be arguing for a historical role for the free sensuality of women and insisting that behind consumer desire there is a subtle sexual unconscious at work. In other words, Veblen seems to argue for a female complicity, whereas Sombart seems to be speaking on behalf of a female agency. In reality, Veblen was a deeply committed feminist who regarded female conspicuous consumption as unfree activity.[27] Sombart, though not notably misogynist, was distinctly antimodernist. His emancipated courtesan was the figment of an intellectual strategy designed to turn the usual contrast between aristocratic luxury and bourgeois austerity on its head, and to lay the blame for the sensualist disorder in values of Europe on the debauched French, mercenary Jews, and inept German middle classes.

What prejudices Veblen's analysis is not antifeminism but his idolization of the sphere of production. Poor Veblen, who, to recall Theodor Adorno's critique, saw the fullness of life only in fulfilling the work instinct.[28] Whatever obstructs this end is "cultural lag," to recall his famous expression. That includes culture itself, a real problem for Veblen because culture prides itself on its ostentatious disutility, its goallessness. Distinguishing between the productive and nonproductive, Veblen targets the irrational mechanisms of distribution and is equally distrustful of the complex nature of household consumption. As we saw earlier, productivist outlooks are a dead end if the goal is a gendered analysis of consumption. By their drudgery, women, in Veblen's account, are immune to the predatory spirit. However, drudgery is not the spirit of workmanship Veblen admires. That women can be redeemed is thus problematic, since all of their activities occur within the sphere of consumption, as "trophies of barbaric culture." Conceivably, they could redeem themselves through self-abnegation. If that were the goal, Veblen would be a hard taskmaster, for he ill-tolerated any behaviors or poses that seemed regressive, whether the flamboyant dress, feathered hat, or phony fur. Far be it from him to see these, as would later cultural critics, as imaginary worlds or attempts to compensate through human inventivity for the loss of experience resulting from advanced capitalist technologies. In contrast, Sombart's study is seductive in its recognition of sensuous pleasures, and particularly that these have operated historically to refine and multiply the taste for consumer goods.[29]

That the female figure should lend itself to such diametrically different interpretations of the meaning of consumption, and of bourgeois society more generally, returns us to the complex problem of relating metaphor and meaning to social change, of linking the imaginary world around consumption with the structural changes giving rise to modern consumer society. Studying the transition between old and new regimes from the perspective of relations around consumer practices underscores that capitalist society is a semiotic as well as an economic system. The expansion of a modern visual economy of signs preceded the commodification of many aspects of material life, greatly magnifying the intricate and often occult relations of women to things. If we are not simply to group all of the images thereby produced as "constructions of reality," or to confine analysis merely to distinguishing visual image or verbal allusion from statistical reality, we need to study the fluent repertoire of emerging consumer society as it resonated with new systems of production, changing styles of consumption, and emergent modes of modern political representation.

NOTES

1. The problem of dating the consumer revolution has not been sufficiently discussed, though some of the arguments for an early dating are implicit in Neil McKendrick, John Brewer, and J. H. Plumb, *The Birth of a Consumer Society: The Commercialization of Eighteenth-Century England* (Bloomington: Indiana University Press, 1982). For an even earlier dating, highlighting early print culture, see Chandra Mukerji, *From Graven Images: Patterns of Modern Materialism* (New York: Columbia University Press, 1983). Simon Schama implicitly argues for a consumer revolution coinciding with the height of Dutch power; see *The Embarrassment of Riches: An Interpretation of Dutch Culture in the Golden Age* (New York: Alfred Knopf, 1987). New criteria arguing on behalf of this early dating are suggested in John Brewer and Roy Porter, eds., *Consumption and the World of Goods* (London, Routledge, 1993); and Colin Campbell, *The Romantic Ethic and the Spirit of Modern Consumerism* (Oxford, Basil Blackwell, 1987).

2. See *The Compact Edition of the Oxford English Dictionary* (Oxford, Clarendon Press, 1971), 1:532, s.v. "consumer" and "consumption."

3. Carolyn Merchant, *The Death of Nature: Women, Ecology, and the Scientific Revolution* (San Francisco: Harper and Row, 1980). See also T. J. Jackson Lears, *Fables of Abundance* (New York: Basic Books, 1994).

4. John Sekora, *Luxury: The Concept in Western Thought, Eden to Smollett* (Baltimore: Johns Hopkins University Press, 1977), 51–62, 226–27, 246–47, 256–65.

5. Eli F. Heckscher, *Mercantilism*, trans. Mendel Shapiro, rev. ed., edited by E. F. Söderlund (New York: Macmillan, 1955), 2:110, 169, 285–93.

6. Cited in Bernard Mandeville, *The Fable of the Bees, or Private Vices, Public Benefits* (1714; reprint, Oxford: Clarendon Press, 1957), 1:13.

7. Ibid., 1:355.

8. Joyce Appleby, "Consumption in Early Modern Social Thought," in Brewer and Porter, eds., *Consumption and the World of Goods* (London, 1993), 168 ff.

9. Adam Smith, *The Theory of Moral Sentiments,* ed. D. D. Raphael and A. L. Macfie (Oxford: Clarendon Press, 1976), 183; and idem, *Wealth of Nations* (Hammondsworth, England: Penguin, 1986), 16. On Smith's ambiguous attitude toward material wealth, see Albert O. Hirschman, *Shifting Involvements: Private Interest and Public Action* (Princeton: Princeton University Press, 1982), 48–50, in addition to his recent, "Industrialization and Its Manifold Discontents: West, East, and South," *World Development* 20, no. 9 (September 1992): 1225–32.

10. This is a major theme of Lears, *Fables of Abundance.*

11. Joan Wallach Scott, "'L'ouvrière! Mot impie, sordide . . .': Women workers in the discourse of French political economy, 1840–1860," in *Gender and the Politics of History* (New York: Columbia University Press, 1988), 143–45; and idem, "The Woman Worker," in *History of Women in the West IV: Emerging Feminism from Revolution to World War,* ed. Geneviève Fraisse and Michelle Perrot (Cambridge: Harvard University Press, 1993), 399–426.

12. George J. Stigler, "The Early History of Empirical Studies of Consumer Behavior," *Journal of Political Economy* 62 (1954): 95–113. For a review of early family budget studies, see also Maurice Halbwachs, *L'Evolution des besoins dans les classes ouvrières* (Paris: Félix Alcan, 1933), 1–152.

13. Gary S. Becker, "A Theory of the Allocation of Time," *Economic Journal* 75, no. 299 (September 1965): 493–517; and idem, *A Treatise on the Family* (1981; enlarged edition, Cambridge: Harvard University Press, 1991). For a critique, see Marianne Ferber and Bonnie Birnbaum, "The 'New Home Economics': Retrospects and Prospects," *Journal of Consumer Research* 4 (1 June 1977): 19–28; Jeffrey James, *Consumption and Development* (New York: St. Martin's Press, 1993); and Kathleen Blee, "Family Patterns and the Politicization of Consumption Relations," *Sociological Spectrum* 5 (1985): 295–316.

14. The two classic works are Jürgen Habermas, *The Structural Transformation of the Public Sphere: An Inquiry into a Category of Bourgeois Society*, trans. Thomas Burger with the assistance of Frederick Lawrence (1962; reprint, Cambridge: MIT Press, 1991); and Norbert Elias, *The Civilizing Process* (New York, 1978). See also Richard Sennett, *The Fall of Public Man* (New York, 1977); and especially Hannah Arendt, *The Human Condition* (1958; reprint, Chicago: University of Chicago Press, 1969).

15. Some of the implications of Habermas's conceptualization of the public sphere for history and theories of needs are discussed in Craig Calhoun, ed., *Habermas and the Public Sphere* (Cambridge: MIT Press, 1991). See in particular the contributions of Nancy Fraser, "Rethinking the Public Sphere: A Contribution to the Critique of Actually Existing Democracy," 109–42; and Geoff Eley, "Nations, Publics and Political Cultures: Placing Habermas in the Nineteenth Century," 289–330; as well as the response by Jürgen Habermas, "Further Reflections on the Public Sphere," 421–61.

16. Habermas, *The Structural Transformation of the Public Sphere*, 23–24.

17. Joan B. Landes, *Women and the Public Sphere in the Age of the French Revolution* (Ithaca: Cornell University Press, 1988). In several suggestive passages, E. P. Thompson highlights the linkage between a moral economy of consumption and egalitarian eighteenth-century politics. See *Customs in Common* (New York: The New Press, 1991), 304 ff. By and large, political theorists revising liberal paradigms still don't address the problem of needs embodied in consumption, even when it could be implied from their approach that the making of civil society is derived from the growth of private-market relations, one source surely being growing needs, as manifest in new demands for consumer goods and services.

18. This point is compellingly made by Henri Mendras with Alastair Cole, *Social Change in Modern France: Toward a Cultural Anthropology of the Fifth Republic* (Cambridge: Cambridge University Press, 1991).

19. The major study to draw implicit as well as explicit comparisons between class patterns of spending remains Maurice Halbwachs, *La Classe ouvrière et les niveaux de vie: Recherches sur la hiérarchie des besoins dans les sociétés industrielles contemporaines* (Paris: Félix Alcan, 1913). However, recent studies, in particular Paul Johnson, *Saving and Spending: The Working Class Economy in Britain, 1870–1939* (Oxford: Clarendon Press, 1985), also suggest class-based peculiarities in spending habits that were socially determined as opposed to merely reflecting diverse income levels.

20. Leonore Davidoff and Catherine Hall, *Family Fortunes: Men and Women in the English Middle Class, 1780–1850* (Chicago: University of Chicago Press, 1987). See also Whitney Walton, "Feminine Hospitality in the Bourgeois Home of Nineteenth-Century Paris," *Proceedings of the Western Society for French History* 14 (1987): 197–203; and idem,

"The Triumph before Feminine Taste: Bourgeois Women's Consumption and Hand-methods of Production in Mid-Nineteenth-Century Paris," *Business History Review* 60, no. 4 (1986): 541–63.

21. Colin Campbell, *The Romantic Ethic and the Spirit of Modern Consumerism.*

22. Thorstein Veblen, *The Theory of the Leisure Class: An Economic Study in the Evolution of Institutions* (1899; reprint, New York: New American Library, 1953).

23. Werner Sombart, *Luxury and Capitalism,* trans. W. R. Dittmar (Ann Arbor: University of Michigan Press, 1967). Originally published as *Luxus und Kapitalismus* (Munich and Leipzig, 1913). I am indebted to Mark Landsman of the history department of Columbia University for his illuminating reading of *Luxury and Capitalism* in the context of Sombart's other studies on the German bourgeoisie, in particular, *Der Bourgeois* (1913), *The Jews and Modern Capitalism* (1913), and especially *Händler und Helden* (1915). Cf. Warren G. Breckman, "Disciplining Consumption: The Debate about Luxury in Wilhelmine Germany, 1980–1914," *Journal of Social History* 24, no. 3 (1991): 485–505.

24. Veblen, *The Theory of the Leisure Class,* 82.

25. Sombart, *Luxury and Capitalism,* 48, 50, 171.

26. Acting according to this logic, women were major protagonists of the eighteenth-century "consumer revolution," according to Neil McKendrick, "Home Demand and Economic Growth: A New View of the Role of Women and Children in the Industrial Revolution," in *Historical Perspectives: Studies in English Thought and Society in Honour of J. H. Plumb,* ed. Neil McKendrick (London: Europa Publications, 1974), 152–210.

27. For Veblen, the logic of invidious distinction derives from the originary sexual division of labor. From the outset, human endeavors were divided into exploits and drudgery; while predatory men hunted, played, and engaged in devout observances, women assiduously and uneventfully shaped materials for productive and reproductive labor. In industrial societies, though dominant status was still conferred by the trophies of predatory exploits, these were now drawn from the hierarchies of goods. Under this system, the wife who has been the drudge and chattel of the husband, producing goods for him to consume, becomes the ceremonial consumer of goods that he produces. Nonetheless, she is still his chattel: "For the habitual rendering of vicarious leisure and consumption is the abiding mark of the unfree servant" (Veblen, *The Theory of the Leisure Class,* 83).

28. Theodor W. Adorno, "Veblen's Attack on Culture," in *Prisms,* trans. Samuel Weber and Shierry Weber (Cambridge: MIT Press, 1981).

29. Cf. Arjun Appadurai, "Introduction: Commodities and the Politics of Value," in *The Social Life of Things: Commodities in Cultural Perspective,* ed. Arjun Appadurai (Cambridge: Cambridge University Press, 1986), 36–39.

ONE

Coquettes and Grisettes
Women Buying and Selling
in Ancien Régime Paris

Jennifer Jones

In the 1770s and 1780s Marie Antoinette's relationship with her dressmaker, Rose Bertin, provoked considerable censure, earning Bertin the barbed title "minister of modes."[1] In 1782 a comedy titled *Le Public Vengé*, performed at the Italian Theater, savagely attacked the queen's sartorial excesses, laying the blame on the fictional character, Mme du Costume, transparently modeled after Rose Bertin.[2] Royal account books from the 1780s confirm contemporaries' worries: over half of Marie Antoinette's yearly expenditures on fashions were paid to Rose Bertin.[3] But Bertin's illegitimate sway over Marie Antoinette was blown out of proportion, becoming, in the popular imagination, directly responsible for the reckless spending that caused the bankruptcy of the French state and the ultimate downfall of the French monarchy. Why did Marie Antoinette's dresses and dressmaker become such charged topics? And what can this uproar over dresses and dressmakers tell us about changing understandings, on the eve of the Revolution, of the connections among aristocracy, femininity, and practices of buying and selling?

In a decade of fiscal crisis and a new simplicity of dress, it is not surprising that Bertin was attacked for her fabulously expensive dresses and elaborate hats. But what provoked the sharpest criticism were the haughtiness and artistic pretensions of this woman from a poor, provincial background who attempted to create a new kind of professional relationship between aristocratic female clients and fashion retailers. A visitor to the court in the 1780s, Baronne d'Oberkirch, complained that Bertin "swelled with her own importance and acted as an equal with princesses."[4] Bertin was a *marchande de modes*, the most elevated retailer in the fashion industry, rather than a mere dressmaker, and her status was signaled to her clients as they entered her shop, with its grand windows adorned with simulated lavender and yellow marble; and inside her shop, framed portraits of the nobility of Europe overhung her counters and worktables.[5] The *Correspondance secrète* reported sardonically in April 1778 that when an upper-class woman (*femme de qualité*) entered Bertin's shop to request several bonnets to be sent to the provinces "the merchant, lying on a chaise longue in an elegant dress, scarcely deigned to salute the woman with a very slight inclination of her head."[6] And Bertin's commercial rival, Beaulard, complained that Bertin "takes on the airs of a duchess and is not even a bourgeoise."[7]

On the eve of the Revolution, Bertin became a highly charged symbolic figure whose relationship with the queen aroused multiple fears in relation to luxury, femininity, aristocracy, and despotism. Recent scholarship examining the libels against Marie Antoinette has stressed the connection made by contemporaries between Marie Antoinette's supposed sexual corruption and political despotism.[8] Yet at the heart of critiques of the queen's relationship with Rose Bertin lay anxieties about women's *commercial* as well as *political* prominence, concerns about women's material as well as sexual longings, and fears of the disorder that might result if working-class women controlled the buying habits of upper-class women. If the public role of aristocratic women was increasingly called into question on the eve of the Revolution, surely this was connected to the growing conviction among contemporaries that all women were innately frivolous consumers of the material goods available in the public commercial spaces of Paris as well as of the political ideals available in the public sphere of salons and assemblies; female incapacity to rule—either in the realm of commerce or in the realm of politics—was increasingly believed to be grounded in women's enslavement to the despotism of *la mode*.

To understand why Marie Antoinette's dresses and dressmaker were construed by contemporaries as a social and political problem we will need to unpack the broader cultural concern over women's place as buyers and sellers in the expanding fashion culture of late-eighteenth-century Paris. Although Rose Bertin was surely the most colorful retail merchant, and Marie Antoinette the most prominent female consumer, contemporary critiques of their relationship must be understood in the broader context of the daily transactions of hundreds of female merchants and clients, in the context of the public's attempt to make sense of a new culture of consumption in which the old moorings of class and gender were being cast aside.

In the late eighteenth century many Parisians were troubled by the culture of shopping they saw developing in the luxury districts of Paris, a culture in which women played prominent roles as both merchants and shoppers. Among the critics of this new shopping culture was the lawyer and social critic Nicolas Desessarts, who described the danger posed to women and to society by the premier fashion merchants of eighteenth-century Paris, the marchandes de modes, in his monumental *Dictionnaire universel de police* (1785–87):

That numerous trade born of the luxury of women, fed by women's coquetry, and thriving as long as the taste for frivolity will be the ruling passion. To the eyes of the observer who searches to discover the causes of the corruption of morals, the infinite number of boutiques of the marchands de modes, the art with which one decorates these boutiques, the different finery that one exposes there to the eyes of passersby, are all sources of danger. Who is, in effect, the young woman who has the strength to turn her eyes, seeing each day the productions of genius of the marchands de modes? Certainly there are few such women. Almost all gladly stop in front of these sanctuaries of frivolity and coquetry, and how can they resist the attraction they feel, when they see women of all ages and all conditions entering into these enchanted places?[9]

Desessarts's concerns about the marchands de modes provide a useful starting place for examining the nature of the commercial culture of the Old Regime precisely because he pointed his finger at what he thought was new about the buying and selling practices of late-eighteenth-century women. First, although both men and women sold clothing and fashions in eighteenth-century Paris, Desessarts targeted those shops run by women, the marchandes de modes. Second, Desessarts insisted that these boutiques lured not a small social group but "women of all ages and conditions."[10] He thus reflected and contributed to the construction in the later eighteenth century of a conceptual framework that regarded the excessive desire to consume as a peculiarly feminine quality, a weakness shared by all women, from Marie Antoinette to the fishmonger of les halles. (See François Boucher's celebration of femininity and fashion in his painting La Marchande de modes, figure 1.)

When reading Desessarts's evocation of women's seduction by material goods in the luxury shops of Paris, we have to remind ourselves that he is describing Parisian commercial culture of the 1780s, not the 1880s. Fantastic and exotic settings, the sweeping appeal of commodities, the female consumer, the seduction of the shopper by the promise of beauty, youth, and luxury, the loss of self in a swirl of goods—is this not the "dream world" of mass consumption described in Zola's Ladies' Paradise and described by Rosalind Williams and others in their studies of the late-nineteenth-century department store?[11]

Although much in Desessarts's eighteenth-century diatribe against female consumption and shopping would be echoed by late-nineteenth-century social critics, his focus on the role of the female marchande de modes is wholly distinctive. For Desessarts and others, she was the principal agent of women's seduction and the main promoter of Paris's expanding commercial culture. The women who flocked to the fashionable boutiques of Paris were being seduced not by male advertisers, male merchants, or male-dominated corporations, as later commentators would claim, but by women.[12] And herein lay the source of the domestic discord and social chaos spawned by the new

Figure 1. François Boucher, *La Marchande de modes,* 1746.

practices of retailing found in the marchandes de modes's boutiques. In the realm of commerce, as in the realm of politics, when women ruled women, disorder, chaos, and folly inevitably reigned.

While social critics like Desessarts worried that the marchande de modes's boutique would lead to women's moral corruption, as if the lust for hats would provoke more dangerous desires, other contemporaries were concerned that these sanctuaries of frivolity would lead to an equally pernicious character flaw, bad taste. If not for male reason, the delirious folly of women would hold sway in the marchande de modes's boutique; left to themselves, women would, and did, don boat-shaped hats or squeeze themselves into lime-green taffeta dresses with pink spots, inspired by the visit of ambassadors from Tippoo-Saib.[13] In addition, contemporaries were equally if not more worried about the pernicious effects these boutiques might have on the young shop girls (*grisettes*) who tended the counter and stitched the elaborate creations of the marchandes de modes.[14] What would happen when the disciplined and socially useful work of cutting and sewing gave way to more dissipated desires for luxury goods?

This concern with the role of the female marchande de mode as promoter and seducer reminds us that the commercial culture of the Old Regime— despite its eerily similar preoccupation with the female consumer, "the look," the facade, the gaze, and playfully shifting signifiers—stood a world apart from the nineteenth-century department store and bourgeois consumer culture. Old Regime society was organized by orders as well as by classes. Hence consumers and producers possessed privileges rather than rights. Moreover, the commercial economy was just beginning to provide luxury goods such as calicoes, silks, and lace for a larger population. Rigid nineteenth-century notions about the propriety and naturalness of "separate spheres" had not yet taken hold, and new models of domestic womanhood were just beginning to form the values of the upper and middle classes. In other words, in the cultural milieu of the Old Regime, it was still believed that women— whether queens or female merchants—had the power to seduce as well as the weakness to be seduced.

Viewed from the perspective of the distinctive commercial space of the eighteenth-century marchande de modes's boutique, contemporaries' concern about Marie Antoinette's buying from Rose Bertin in particular—as well as women's buying and selling in the luxury boutiques of Paris in general— becomes more comprehensible. By probing the assumptions contemporaries made about the transactions that took place between male and female shoppers and female merchants, we can begin to understand the ways in which, at a pivotal moment in the second half of the eighteenth century, the rise of new models of womanhood and new practices of consumption began mutually to constitute each other.[15]

SHOPS AND SHOPPING

The period from the sixteenth century to the mid–seventeenth century is generally viewed as one of "commercial revolution" in western Europe, with its astonishing take-off in production, the growth of domestic and foreign markets, and the erection of vast networks of credit.[16] Yet, following this period, between 1650 and the French Revolution, the commercial culture of western Europe witnessed a second and related transformation that has been called a consumer revolution. Only in this second phase (especially after 1750) did the middle and lower classes of cities such as London and Paris begin to share in the traffic in material goods, trinkets, and minor luxuries that had been making life more comfortable and pleasurable for the aristocracy for over a century. And only in the second phase did the economic changes and new products that had been introduced before 1650 begin to be assimilated into the cultural fabric and mentality of early modern society.[17] As a result, the relationship of luxury consumption to aristocracy and femininity would have to be reconfigured to make sense of the participation of new classes of women in this expanding commercial economy.

The consumer revolution has been explored by charting the production and retailing of any number of items, from books and engravings to mirrors, bed linens, and pottery.[18] For contemporaries, one of the most striking aspects of the consumer revolution was the way it transformed their clothing.[19] In 1650 the privilege of dressing fashionably was restricted to a small group of elite men and women who had the resources to invest in heavy, ornate garments made from costly silks and gold and silver brocades by the few restricted corporations that controlled the clothing trades. The rest of the population possessed an extremely limited wardrobe, comprising either coarse, homemade clothing or the castoffs of the upper classes.

By the late eighteenth century, however, the Parisian fashion culture had been transformed dramatically. Fashionable dressing was no longer solely the privilege of the elite, but something in which men and women across a broader range of classes could indulge, if only by the purchase of a new ribbon or hat. The wardrobes of Parisians of virtually all classes and positions had increased significantly in value, size, and variety. Maids and shop girls sported cleaner and whiter blouses, cuffs, and stockings, while new, inexpensive, lightweight calicoes transformed the gray and brown wardrobes of the populace with splashes of color.[20] A host of new clothing trades set up boutiques displaying, and even advertising, their wares in new ways to entice Parisians and foreign visitors. And a specialized fashion press was born to publish information on the latest styles and the locations of the newest boutiques.[21]

One of the most striking features of the sartorial transformation of the Parisian population was the divergence of men's and women's consumption patterns. Around the year 1700, noblewomen's wardrobes were worth twice as much as those of their male counterparts. Female domestics and artisans also spent up to twice as much money on clothes as did their husbands. Only in the very poorest classes were men's wardrobes more valuable than women's. After the mid–eighteenth century, however, the relative value of women's wardrobes increased markedly across all classes, often five to ten times more rapidly than the value of men's. On the eve of the Revolution, a typical male artisan might have possessed fifteen items of clothing worth 38 livres, whereas his wife might have possessed as many as fifty items worth 346 livres.[22]

Transformations in the ways that Parisians consumed were as striking as the changes in what they consumed. In the seventeenth century most people did not buy their clothing in shops. The wealthy ordered clothing to measure from tailors and dressmakers, who fitted the garments in their boudoirs and then delivered them to their chambers, and the poor bought from ambulant merchants or secondhand-clothing merchants. Before the mid–eighteenth century, the shops that existed would have been unrecognizable to someone accustomed to modern-day boutiques. Like the buildings in which goods were produced, the shops in which they were sold were open to the street, usually without windows or window displays to separate the selling of goods from the life of the quarter. Even the most fashionable and celebrated shops of seventeenth-century Paris, the boutiques of the Palais de Justice or the stalls at the Saint-Germain fair, were narrow, cramped, and poorly lighted. And upon entering, one's ears were battered, one's person was jostled, and one's belongings were endangered. If there was one retail strategy merchants consistently relied on, it was to employ pretty daughters or attractive wives to tend the counter and entreat customers to examine their wares.

Without aid from the subtle and subliminal forms of persuasion associated with modern retailing and advertising, early modern merchants made shopping into a complicated and often stylized game of skill and cunning in which contemporaries believed the merchant almost invariably came out ahead monetarily.[23] The power of male merchants was said to be their shrewdness. Female merchants had an advantage, however, when enticing customers to buy: they could supplement the usual calculations and cajoleries of the merchant by hinting at more intimate commerce and future returns on the investment.

Until the late nineteenth century, contemporary accounts of shopping almost always portrayed the shopkeeper as a woman and the customer as a man. This inversion might seem odd, given that buying provisions was largely a female task. Shopping at the neighborhood market for necessities like butter, cheese, and produce was a daily occurrence for most lower- and middle-class women in Paris. However, the consumption that took place in the boutiques of the Palais de Justice or the Saint-Germain fair in the seventeenth and eighteenth centuries was highly visible, associated with aristocratic pleasures, and, in the popular and literary imagination, especially identified with men. The shops spatially linked licit and illicit pleasures; spaces for consumption of luxury goods flowed directly into spaces for drinking coffee, gambling, examining curiosities, and watching puppet shows.[24] According to Restif de la Bretonne, a libertine and novelist of the late eighteenth century, the rue Saint-Honoré was a bazaar where commerce rubbed shoulders with "all the abuses of social life."[25] In Louis-Sebastien Mercier's description of Paris in the 1780s, the mixture of fashion boutiques, cafés, clubs, and courtesans transformed the Palais-Royal into "une fête piquante," hardly a place appropriate for virtuous bourgeois wives and mothers.[26]

Shopping, then, for much of the seventeenth and eighteenth centuries was considered a form of male entertainment in which the line between the licit pleasures of luxury consumption and the illicit pleasures involved in the sexual consumption of women was often blurred. Mercier remarked, "Purchases are only a pretext; one looks at the seller and not the merchandise."[27] But references to the coquettish playfulness and sexual innuendo that occurred when men bought and women sold are found throughout seventeenth- and eighteenth-century literature and commentary.[28] According to contemporaries, in the sexual banter and commercial bargaining that occurred between female merchants and male customers, the female merchants almost always got their way. According to the German travel writer Joachim Christophe Nemeitz in his *Séjour de Paris*, the marchandes of Paris were a wily lot, who knew how to use their charms to full advantage: "Principally women know how to set a high value on their goods and to flatter the buyer so well that one must have the firmness of Ulysses to not succumb to their lures."[29] Attracted to the beauty of the female merchant and softened by her flatteries and charms, clients left the boutique surcharged with bagatelles, worth only half their price: "One is deceived in one's hopes, and at the end of the story, one has gained only the shop and not the person who works in it."[30]

In sum, when contemporaries imagined the act of retail buying, they imagined a male consumer and a female merchant. The model for shopping was courtship (although in the harsh light of its critics shopping might look more akin to prostitution), a decidedly heterosexual encounter between carefree but self-interested shop girls and desirous male customers. Unlike many other instances of monetary exchange, shopping, in this model, gives both parties satisfaction. The man might end up buying overpriced trinkets, but since he was not really shopping for material goods or looking for a bargain he did not feel cheated. According to the contemporary stereotype, the amorous grisette, as we will see, walked away from the encounter doubly satisfied, both by the sale and by the sexual flattery.

The second half of the eighteenth century witnessed tremendous growth not only in the sheer amount of goods consumed but also in the volume of shoppers. Like attending art salons, frequenting cafes, or promenading, shopping was part of the widespread expansion of public life in eighteenth-century Paris.[31] Part of the fun of shopping for the upper classes was the opportunity to be out in society and feel à la mode. One went shopping not merely to purchase clothing or accessories but to buy where all the rest of fashionable society was currently buying. The press of people could be so great that, as the Baronne d'Oberkirch remarked in the case of the celebrated jewelry shop Au Petit-Dunkerque, near the Pont-Neuf, the store had to hire a guard to keep the peace.[32]

For contemporaries, the increasing volume of female shoppers in the streets and under the arcades of Paris was a disturbing phenomenon. Whether at fairs, along the rue Saint-Honoré, or in the Palais-Royal, shopping provided an opportunity for the sexes and the social classes to mix freely in a "fête piquante." Female aristocrats were not alone in being harshly attacked for their excessive consumption. When Desessarts warned that women of all ages and all conditions could be seen entering the shops of the marchandes de modes, he was not particularly worried about aristocratic women. Shopping in public, like promenading or attending a fair or a theater, was an acceptable diversion for female courtiers and aristocrats but not for virtuous, middle-class mothers.

Beginning in the 1780s, these concerns were both allayed and aggravated by the building of new luxury boutiques that provided more acceptable spaces for middle- and upper-class female consumers. Larger, well-lit, and ornately decorated stores with exotic and aristocratic names, such as Au Grand Mogol, Au Pavillion d'Or, and Au Trois Mandarins, sprang up in the wealthiest sections of Paris along the rue Saint-Honoré and in the Saint-Germain quarter. They were outfitted with large counters to lay out the goods, wardrobes and chests in which to store them, mirrors, and rudimentary window displays. Some shops were filled with as many as thirty workers and assistants. They were large, permanent buildings, magasins, rather than boutiques.

As luxury shops acquired more permanent and elaborate structures in the 1780s, not only did the shops look different from the small-scale boutiques of the seventeenth century but the process of shopping itself changed. Prices were now more commonly set in advance by the merchant, and haggling was relegated to the lower classes. Ready-made clothing, which had existed since at least the seventeenth century, became more common, particularly suited as it was to the kinds of hats, capes, and coats made by marchandes de modes. Buying on credit, a long-standing practice for the aristocracy, became even more commonplace in the 1780s as merchants extended credit in an effort to lure new, often bourgeois, clients.

It is important to stress that late-eighteenth-century merchandising devices and interior displays were still rudimentary compared to their late-nineteenth-century counterparts. As late as 1807, Louis-Marie Prud'homme

Figure 2. "Promenade de la gallerie du Palais-Royal," ca. 1789.

found the marchandes de modes's window displays novel enough to note that "women's bonnets and hats are displayed in marchandes de modes' boutiques like hams and brains in the shops of charcutiers."[33] And even the most cursory glance at engravings of the Palais-Royal suggests that shopping still took place in the context of a festive and gallant mingling of the sexes. (See the press of promenades and shoppers in the engraving "Promenade de la gallerie du Palais-Royal," figure 2.) By shopping in the morning, one could avoid these "perils." The process of buying and selling was still an elaborate game of gesture and verbal parrying that involved flattery and pretension on the part of both males and females.

As shops became more inviting and hospitable spaces for women in the course of the eighteenth century, the relationship between client and merchant—the nature of the entertainment provided by shopping—changed. The change resulted partly from the growth of Paris and the increasingly impersonal relations between merchants and their clients,[34] partly from the growing importance of the marchandes de modes's trade and the growth of a kind of cult of celebrity around the most famous merchants in Paris, and partly from a new model for the relationship between female shoppers, merchants, and material objects. By the late eighteenth century, male consumers had by no means been banished from the fashion shops of Paris: contemporary engravings still portray them there eyeing both the merchandise and the shop girls. But the ways in which the transaction of shopping was discursively marked by gender and class in the seventeenth and early eighteenth centuries—with male aristocrats buying from poor shop girls—was transformed by the perception that retailing was conducted by haughty and pretentious marchandes de modes in transactions with submissive female clients.

THE FEMALE CONSUMER IN THE BOUTIQUE

Although foppish men were heaped with abuse in the eighteenth century, few contemporaries ever suggested that men were seduced by the shops of Paris to the same extent that they claimed female customers were. And, although writers on luxury never ceased to remark that Paris abounded with vain and frivolous men, they rarely portrayed men as irrational consumers seduced by trinkets and gloss, as they did women. The model of shopping as courtship worked to normalize, rationalize, and naturalize male shopping. Men did not shop to buy clothing, and they did not shop because they were irrationally seduced by goods and shop displays; men shopped for women.

When women did the shopping, the discourse changed: in the second half of the eighteenth century, women came to be viewed as more likely than men to be enticed and ensnared by the wily retail strategies of the merchants of Paris. In the past, French women had sometimes been accused of desiring luxurious fashions because of their vanity and their desire to proclaim (even if falsely) their position in society. Increasingly the desire for luxuries was attributed not only to their vanity but also to their desire for novelty, to their enslavement to that commercial deity, la mode. As Gabriel Sénac de Meilhan, physician to Louis XV and man of letters, phrased it in his Considerations on Riches and Luxury (1787), "The lightness of a woman's spirit ensures that all that is new has power over her."[35]

Women had for centuries been associated with inconstancy and change. But in the eighteenth century new theories were developed to explain women's love of frivolities and novelties. Arguments blaming Eve and original sin were set aside for the most part as philosophes and enlightened thinkers probed female psychology and mental capacities, seeking scientific explanations for women's love of all that glittered and all that was new. Women's attraction to novelties was held to be a product of a peculiarly feminine imaginative faculty and sense of sight, a product of the particular interaction between women and agreeable objects such as fabrics, jewels, and fashions.[36] As the popular French essayist Boudier de Villemert explained in his 1758 book, The Friend of Women: "The imagination of women continually nourishes itself on the details of jewels and clothing. These fill up their heads with so many colors that there is no room for objects which might merit their attention. Women's minds scarcely graze the surface of essential qualities and only attach themselves to the drapery."[37] The philosophe Antoine-Leonard Thomas, whose Essay on the Character, the Morals, and the Intelligence of Women (1772) provides the most extensive exploration of women's imaginative capacities of any Enlightenment text, explained that women were particularly sensitive to the appeals of commodities like fashions and jewels because of their heightened sense of sight and their lively imagination: "Everything they see hits them with a strong force; they see all with a particular vivacity. Their eyes quickly glance over all that lies before them and then seize the image." Thomas goes on to warn that "women's lively imaginations are like mirrors which reflect all but create nothing."[38]

This stress on women's ability quickly to seize and absorb the visual world around them was echoed by many eighteenth-century authors. The celebrated philosopher and social critic Jean-Jacques Rousseau spelled out the perceived difference between men's and women's sensations perhaps most clearly when he wrote that "from a very early age boys love anything which involves movement and sound whereas little girls love everything visual, mirrors, jewels, cloth, and above all, dolls."[39] Throughout *Émile*, Rousseau stressed that women excel at fine observations; he advised that if one wanted to judge material objects or anything pertaining to the senses, one should consult women, but when one wanted to judge a situation that required morality or reason, one should consult men.

Beliefs in the liveliness, yet passivity, of women's sense of sight and imagination provided a partial explanation for why women were peculiarly susceptible to the allure of commodities. In addition, the developing science of aesthetics and the lively popular debate on the nature of taste helped contemporaries understand how commodities acted on individuals, attracting them and seducing them. By the mid–eighteenth century, as part of the neoclassical reaction against the sensuous lines and decorative curves of rococo art, a new conception of art emerged that distinguished sharply between the fine arts and the agreeable arts.[40] The fine arts were defined as those works, like sculpture and historical paintings, that demanded appreciation by the mind and intellect. In contrast, the merely agreeable arts, such as fashion and other luxury goods, instilled in the viewer base passions and desires that were antithetical to purely aesthetic contemplation. The distinction was drawn between objects that worked on the eyes and objects that worked on the soul, between objects that captured the passive viewer through sensual delight and works of art that required domination by the mind and intellect. In the writings of Rousseau, Thomas, and Boudier de Villemert, women were thought to excel in all that required the senses, men in all that required the intellect. Women's psychology and sensory apparatus made them ideally suited to consume, and their passivity rendered them particularly vulnerable to capture by their sensual delight in agreeable and frivolous objects.

These new beliefs in the liveliness of women's visual senses and imagination and in the power of objects to create desires in their viewers helped recast certain suppositions about women and consumption. Alongside the traditional model, which held that the temptation to consume luxury goods derived from human sin and lax morality, arose a new model, which attributed the attraction of women to luxury goods to their specifically female psychology and attributed a new importance to the role of the commodities themselves in the process of seduction and the creation of desire. The drama of a woman in conflict with her soul doing lonely battle with her desires for luxury goods was replaced by the drama of a woman surrounded by window displays, fashion magazines, and business cards in bustling commercial cities like Paris. Temptation now came from without as well as from within, and it was a temptation to which women, with their heightened visual sensibility, were considered particularly susceptible.

As perceptions of the source of female consumers' temptation shifted from a metaphysical Satan to the earthly marchandes de modes, contemporaries' worries about the effects of female consumption were transformed as well. Concern for the woman's soul and worries that excessive expenditures would confuse the social hierarchy dominated seventeenth-century attacks on female luxury. As the author of a 1651 tract lamented, women's love of luxurious fashions was a cause of general social confusion: "Whereas clothing should serve as an infallible mark which distinguishes conditions and estates, one can scarcely tell nowadays, when walking in the Luxembourg or Tuilleries, who is a Duchess and who is a bookseller, or who is a Marquise and who is a pastry cook."[41] In the second half of the eighteenth century fears that ostentatious and luxurious dress would cause social confusion were still rampant, but they were aggravated by new fears that excessive consumption would threaten women's natural femininity and the proper ordering of relations between the sexes. As a tract from 1740 worried, women's insatiable desires for luxurious fashions threatened their domestic roles as wife, mother, and caretaker of the household: "As soon as a new fashion is invented a woman begins to long for it, never stopping to consider if it is appropriate to her position in society. She will plead that she must have it, no matter the price, even if buying it will ruin her husband. Although her children may be dying of hunger, she will take food from their bellies to feed her own insatiable desire for luxury. She will have her silk fashions at any cost."[42]

In the course of the eighteenth century a range of commentators, from Physiocrats and preachers to fashion magazine editors, helped shape new attitudes toward fashion and consumption in the process of redefining women's relationship to commercial culture. Replacing the strict seventeenth-century hierarchical model—which apportioned certain kinds of consumption to each class, reserving luxury and ostentation for the aristocracy and limiting the lower classes to necessities—a new model emerged that provided a more nuanced understanding of the ways in which both class and gender should shape what and how one consumed. According to the new model, instead of evincing the legitimacy of male aristocrats' social power and prestige, colorfully embroidered vests and fashionable wigs might make them effeminate, and garishly opulent dresses might reveal aristocratic women's lack of taste. Shop girls, however, who donned fashionable hats and pretty cotton dresses were upholding the "natural order," which sanctioned all women's feminine desire to appear pleasing and all men's masculine need to be pleased. For countess or shop girl, the pursuit of fashion was acceptable if it took place within the proper confines of pleasing a husband or attracting legitimate suitors. And whatever one's sex or station, bad taste, folly, and "unreason" were more immediate fears than the sins of vanity or upsetting the social order.

After the Revolution, the *Encyclopedia of Beauty* summed up this new attitude toward fashion when it asked, "Is the taste for fashions natural in women? and is it praiseworthy?" The author responded with a resounding yes, explaining:

> Clothes double the value of a woman. They augment men's pleasures and joys by revealing women's charms. They are the natural complement of beauty; without fashions a pretty woman is a diamond, but a diamond which is not mounted, and who awaits an artist to give her a brilliant setting. . . . Young women who neglect their appearance and who are little occupied with the cares of fashion, indicate by this a disorderly spirit little equipped to occupy the details of running a household. In showing so little taste they show their lack of care and their negligence for all.[43]

By the late eighteenth century, this new conception of the connection between women and fashion naturalized women's interest in clothing: the frenzy for fashions was no longer considered a pathological condition, harmful to the general health of society, but rather a natural aspect of femininity, necessary for marital harmony. The only remaining concern, given the female consumer's attraction to novelty and natural frivolity, was to insure that women's consumer desires be channeled into the sweet pleasures of domesticity rather than the dangerous pastime of coquetry. That is why social commentators worried about the powers of the marchande de modes.

SHOP GIRLS AND MERCHANTS

Although both men and women had styled themselves as marchands de modes since the late seventeenth century, only in the second half of the eighteenth century did contemporaries began to comment on this seemingly new and predominantly female retail merchant. From popular engravers who churned out dozens of prints of female fashion merchants and shop girls to satirists who ridiculed the illegitimate power of Rose Bertin, to libertine writers who celebrated the moral lapses of young dressmakers and linen workers, the marchande de modes's boutique became an important vehicle for discussion of women's role in an increasingly commercial culture.[44]

In part, the disquiet provoked by the marchandes de modes resulted from the novelty of their trade in an urban culture that had thitherto revolved around artisans and production; in theory, the marchandes de modes were *faisseuses de riens:* they made nothing. What they sold was their good taste and their genius for decorating dresses with lace and ribbons, finishing hats with feathers and artificial flowers, and making simple ready-made articles such as capes and neckerchiefs.[45] In an age when there were reportedly 150 different ways to decorate a dress, the marchande de modes became, in contemporaries' eyes, the true creator of fashion, that fickle deity who reigned supreme over Parisian commerce.[46] As Louis-Sebastien Mercier explained, dressmakers and tailors might be compared to masons who build buildings, but the marchande de modes, "in creating accessories, in lending grace and creating the perfect fold, is the architect and decorator par excellence."[47]

Although male mercers continued to sell fashions, by the second half of the eighteenth century female businesswomen had become the retail clothing merchants par excellence. Although no precise figures are available for the numbers of marchandes de modes practicing in Paris, let alone the number of workers they employed, what is certain is that contemporaries perceived Paris to be awash in their boutiques.[48] As Desessarts exclaimed, "The capital has seen the number of marchandes de modes multiply in an unbelievable manner."[49]

Until their formal incorporation in 1776 (and even after that), there was a great deal of fluidity to the definition of a marchandes de modes: female linen makers, mercers, and noncorporate women alike styled themselves as "marchandes de modes," "mercières en modes," "marchandes de frivolités," "faisseuses de modes," or "enjoliveuses." Many marchandes de modes were married to male mercers, but others were not. Unable to define exactly who the marchandes de modes were, contemporaries had trouble defining when and how they had emerged. Some believed that the marchandes de modes had originally been part of the linen makers' corporation and had split to form their own trade in the late seventeenth century. Diderot's *Encyclopédie* claimed that they had always been part of the mercers' corporation. And in his *Dictionnaire raisonné et universel des arts et métiers* (1773), the abbé Jaubert simply threw up his hands and claimed, "It isn't possible to give a fixed date to the origins of this art."[50]

What seems to be true is that these women, who became the principal fashion merchants of their day, rose up from within the cracks in the corporate system. Originally, some eked out a small trade from privileges granted to them as wives of mercers or linen makers; others, without aid of corporate connections, merely hung out a sign or printed business cards proclaiming themselves marchandes de modes. Indeed, contemporaries were concerned about who the marchandes de modes were, at least in part, because of the marchandes's problematic relationship to the guilds (corporations) that controlled production. Male mercers, tailors, and hairdressers—as well as female dressmakers and linen makers—wanted to know who the marchandes de modes were so that they could protect their own privileged status and prosecute the marchandes for usurping their prerogatives in clothing production and fashion retailing.[51]

But more than self-interest was at stake in this effort to categorize these female retail merchants. The marchandes de modes may have been seen as powerful examples of female agency, of women's making use of cracks in the corporate system of production and retailing for their own advantage as they helped shape the consumer desires of their female customers, but their image was also a product of eighteenth-century understandings of femininity. Contemporaries viewed the marchandes de modes and the shop girls who worked for them as a special category of female worker because it was useful for them to do so; the caricature of the marchandes de modes, found in sources ranging from libertine literature to the fashion press, provided a sense of both the promise and the perils of women's role in the commercial world of eighteenth-century Paris.

Between the late seventeenth century, when the female dressmakers of Paris petitioned for the right to form their own guild, and the Revolution, when women petitioned for the exclusive right to work in the needle trades, a cultural discourse was constructed that linked clothing production with femininity and women's work. Rousseau's assertion that "the needle and the sword should never be held by the same hands"[52] was taken up by Mercier, who argued throughout his *Tableau de Paris* that women could be granted a decent living—and saved from prostitution—if the work of the clothing trades was reserved for them.[53] And by the second half of the eighteenth century, writers such as Mercier, Rousseau, and Beaumarchais, all advocates of the most enlightened ideas of their day, held that women had a "natural right" to work in the clothing trades.[54] These authors not only argued that making fashions was naturally feminine but also believed that these trades were inappropriate for men. During the late eighteenth century, male fashion merchants and hairdressers became common targets of ridicule. The author of the *Toilette des dames* asserted that a male fashion merchant was no less a freak of nature than a female soldier and that "it should be necessary for the male marchand de modes to dress as a woman so that the metamorphosis can be completed and this rare bird can respond to his calling."[55]

The supposition that male fashion merchants, dressmakers, and hairdressers were effeminate was a product of the connection made in the eighteenth century between women and fashion. Women's supposedly innate taste for material objects like textiles and jewelry made them ideal merchants as well as consumers; their innate attraction to novelties made them the ideal creators and purveyors of the latest fashions. Increasingly, fashion production and retailing were considered altogether unmanly activities. While the sedentary activities of sewing and tending a shop counter were believed to suit and even benefit women, they were considered degrading to men. Restif de la Bretonne commented in *Les Nuits de Paris*: "How does it happen that men degenerate faster in Paris than do women . . . ? This is because a sedentary life is less harmful to a woman, whose fiber is softer. But there is another reason. It is that the moral education of Paris is less harmful to the second sex, than to the first. Everything is craft, trade, and homework in Paris—which is what degrades men, but is particularly suitable for women."[56] Of course the converse of the argument that the fashion trades were inappropriate work for men was the argument, made by writers throughout the late eighteenth century, from Rousseau to Mercier, that "men's work" was inappropriate for women. While it might horrify Mercier to see male marchands de modes, he was equally scandalized to see women out in the streets selling beef and pork, pulling wagons, and lugging jugs of water: "A woman lugging jugs of water on the hard pavement of Paris! Nothing is more shocking."[57] The exclusive privilege to work in the fashion trades may have been welcomed by many women, but the price of this privilege was high. Women would have to concede that this "natural right" derived from their "nature" as that half of mankind "to whom nature has only accorded her weakness and her charms."[58]

Underlying the belief that the fashion trades were particularly suited—even naturally suited—to women was the belief that there was a difference between what constituted virtuous work for women and virtuous work for men. Perhaps in a Rousseauean idyll the wives and daughters of artisans might have no need to work and could devote all their energy to raising their little Émiles and Sophies; but most enlightened thinkers of the late eighteenth century realized that work was in fact a necessity for many women. The task, then, was to find jobs appropriate for women, jobs consonant with their nature and morally uplifting. For many men and women, the clothing trades seemed to fit this bill perfectly.

Although many enlightened thinkers regarded work as a realm in which hardworking men could express their virtue, work had a fundamentally different meaning for women. Work did not endow women with virtue as much as it kept them from falling into ruin. The lower-class women of Paris were thought to be perched on a cliff, with one foot ready to slip over the edge into the abyss of destitution and prostitution, of physical want and moral ruin. Work in the needle trades, then, would provide these women not only a way to earn their daily bread but also much-needed moral discipline.

The connection between needlework and discipline and morality can be traced back to the Middle Ages. The Catholic Reformation in the seventeenth century institutionalized the connection between needlework and devotion and discipline in hundreds of convent and charity schools founded in and around Paris. Here, depending on the school, either the wealthy daughters of the bourgeois or the poorer daughters of the laboring class learned proper discipline as they perfected their stitching. So many of the poor girls and orphans who attended these charity schools ended up working in the clothing industry that they became de facto trade schools, where "all the works appropriate to their sex and their estate" were taught.[59]

Although within the confines of a convent, stitching dresses might lead to discipline and improved morals, in the workshops and boutiques of Paris, work that was supposed to save young women from misery and uplift them morally was instead placing them in direct contact with that most dangerous of vices, luxury. Part of the problem faced by shop girls was that, although they had traditionally worked both in the workshop sewing and behind the counter selling, increasingly in the second half of the eighteenth century, as the marchandes de modes became more commercially expert, there was a bifurcation of duties. Now, in the larger establishments some girls worked exclusively in the front of the boutique as salesgirls; contemporaries worried that, divorced from the discipline of stitching, the girls would become even more susceptible to the corrupting influence of *les modes*.[60]

For moralists, the shop girls, who were increasing in number, were problematic because they were both vulnerable and seductive; they were risking their own moral ruin and that of others.[61] Although libertine writers were more titillated than concerned about the moral lapses of shop girls, they were certainly aware of the potential for the seduction of the hundreds of young women who fell daily under the gaze of customers and passersby in the boutiques of Paris. For both moralists and libertines, the fashion boutiques of Paris were equated with harems and brothels, feminine worlds charged with sexual excitement and sexual danger. (See the representation of female merchants, female customers, and male admirers in the almanac *Les Belles Marchandes*, figure 3.)[62]

Contemporaries were as aware as modern-day social historians that the lapses of the grisettes were often motivated by dire economic need;[63] but there was a persistent suggestion that these women actively sought sexual liaisons because of their "libertine tastes" or their need for "dresses, hats, and footwear to distinguish themselves from ordinary dressmakers."[64] As the author of the *Encyclopédie méthodique* warned:

> The prodigious consumption produced by luxury strikingly multiplies the number of people occupied by these trades; and in many of these trades it would be difficult for the workers not to adopt inclinations analogous to this type of work. To succeed brilliantly one must have the taste for pretty trinkets, which forms the base of luxury. Soon, the desire to enjoy these goods replaces the desire to make them and any means to attain them are seized upon by a giddy youth, dragged into this disorder before even noticing that they are headed there.[65]

Figure 3. *Les Belles Marchandes,* 1784. Grisettes and coquettes in the
marchande de modes's boutique.

The female press, a primary proponent of a new sensibility of womanhood,
was the only place one could find the grisettes depicted as helpless victims
of male vice.[66] Most other observers assumed that the grisettes of Paris were
not passive but instead as busy looking out the window, "consuming" the men

passing by, as these men were busy looking in at the grisettes. As Mercier explained, although the grisettes might be chained to the counter with needles in their hands, they

> incessantly cast their eye to the street. No passer-by escapes them. The place at the counter closest to the street is always considered the best because of the brigades of men passing by who always offer a glance of homage.
>
> The girl rejoices at all these looks that one throws her way, and imagines them all lovers. The multitude of passers-by vary and augment her pleasure and her curiosity. Thus a sedentary craft becomes bearable when to it is joined the pleasure of seeing and being seen.[67]

If female garment workers and male passersby were a potentially dangerous mix, the dangers posed to the female bourgeois and aristocratic customers in these shops was perceived to be every bit as great.[68] The relationship between marchandes de modes and their clients was problematic on several counts. Contemporaries believed that, since both customer and merchant were women, the marchande de modes's boutique provided a kind of implicit leveling to the lowest common denominator, femininity. One might be rich and the other poor, but at the bottom line, as women, merchant and customer were sexual rivals. As Mercier fantasized, the central tension between shop girl and female customer is caused not by the price or quality of the goods but by their sexual rivalry: "Many grisettes, with their work baskets filled with pompons, pass the morning at ladies' dressing tables. It is necessary to embellish the faces of beautiful women, their rivals; they must silence the secret jealousy of their sex. Because of their estate, they must beautify all those who pay them and treat them with hauteur."[69] One way to explain, at least metaphorically, why the marchandes de modes charged so much for the trinkets and accessories they sold was that these merchants, driven by jealousy, wanted to make their rivals "pay dearly" for their pretty clothes. As Mercier explained, "The marchandes de modes punish women severely for their eternal taste for ribbons, always making them pay quadruple their worth."[70] The sexual rivalry between female consumers and female producers, critics feared, would lead to ever increasing expenditures on frivolous fashions.

A second problem arose from the elevation of the marchandes de modes's trade in the second half of the eighteenth century. This elevation blurred the line between art and craft and created an uneasy inversion of the social order, with female merchants claiming ascendancy over their female customers as the true artists and creators of *la mode*. Marchandes de modes like Rose Bertin were, as we've seen, accused of haughtiness and impertinence. When a male aristocrat complained of the cost of his wife's clothes, Rose Bertin is said to have retorted, "Oh! is Vernet [a celebrated male painter] paid only according to the cost of his canvas and colours?"[71] When marchandes de modes claimed to possess genius and imagination as well as the skills of cutting and sewing, were aristocratic female customers to be thought of as their clients or patrons? And who, ultimately, controlled fashion, aristocrats or shop girls?

Contemporaries feared that, freed from the twin pillars of male reason and aristocratic refinement, which had set the standards for French taste and excellence in the decorative arts, female marchandes de modes would not only corrupt the young women who worked in their shops and their female customers, as well as French taste, but ultimately imperil the economy. Public outrage over Marie Antoinette's relationship with Rose Bertin was merely a heightened version of broader cultural concerns about the relationship between all elite French women and their dressmakers, a version of new understandings of the connection between femininity and commerce. As the author of the *Correspondance secrète* observed in 1775, "Women's dress is becoming in this country a matter of politics because of its influence on commerce and manufacturing."[72]

CONCLUSION

By the end of the eighteenth century, the status of the marchandes de modes and the nature of shopping had changed considerably since the seventeenth century, when merchants hawked their wares along the Pont-Neuf or from behind narrow counters in the Palais de Justice. As the model of the aristocratic male consumer was joined by that of the bourgeois female consumer in the late eighteenth century, shopping seemed to become more "rational," with fixed prices and advertising. But if shopping could no longer be viewed as a kind of courtship, relations between female merchants and female customers were nevertheless mystified in new and seductive ways. The marchandes de modes were extolled as creative geniuses, and the boutiques themselves, once merely a backdrop for the merchants, took on a life of their own, setting the standards for what was fashionable and what was not, dazzling the customers, and convincing them that they had little choice but to bow down and pay homage to the creations of the marchande de modes, now ready-made and available for a fixed price.

As we have seen, these new practices of female seduction in the shops and arcades of eighteenth-century Paris caused contemporaries like Nicolas Dessarts to worry that virtuous dressmakers would be transformed into prostitutes, and good wives and mothers turned into coquettes as they pursued their untrammeled desire for novelties and frivolities. Fashion retailing, which had seemed tame when women sold to aristocratic men, appeared immoderate and dangerous when women sold to women, when grisettes sold to coquettes.

Yet, by the 1780s no serious social commentators had advocated that women should retreat from luxury consumption and from the boutiques of Paris. Shopping for luxuries had become an established part of urban life, and an interest in fashions—which, properly tamed, could be compatible with domesticity—was considered an innate characteristic of femininity. When contemporaries discussed the problems of commercial culture and excessive spending, they laid the blame not so much on middle- and upper-class female consumers as on female merchants. If by the 1780s the female shopper and consumer had become an acceptable fixture of the urban landscape, the female retail merchant—the marchande de modes—had not. By erecting female-dominated sanctuaries of frivolity, the marchandes de modes imperiled their female workers and shop girls; and, rather than purveying appropriate clothing for virtuous wives and devoted mothers, they indulged and corrupted women's unrestrained frenzy for fashions.

Contemporaries responded in two ways to the concerns, expressed by Desessarts and others, about the dangers posed by the marchandes de modes's boutiques. The male editors of the incipient fashion press and the burgeoning advice-book industry attempted to save women from the pursuit of novelties in the boutiques of Paris with advice on how to embellish one's natural grace with simple accessories rather than mask oneself with the artificial fashions dictated by the marchandes de modes. In addition, the marchande de modes's male commercial rivals, tailors, mercers, and male hairdressers, suggested a simple solution to the disorderly boutiques of the marchandes de modes: restrict the grueling manual work of cutting and stitching to women and reserve the artistry of designing fashions and the seduction of retailing for men. As the *Toilette des dames*, which had argued so strongly for the innate femininity of interest in fashion, claimed: "Should a man give advice to women on their dress? Yes, without a doubt. . . . The choice that women make of masculine artists would alone decide the question in our favor if another reason, even stronger, didn't lend support to the argument. Women dress, one says, to please men. So who could better know how women should be dressed to please us. We are the natural born judges of the toilette des femmes; it is we who pronounce fashion in the last resort and without appeal."[73]

The "problem" of women's place as consumers and producers had certainly not been solved by the Napoleonic period, but with the passing of the Old Regime, the urgency of Desessarts's diatribe against female retailers seemed to subside. In the nineteenth century, the development of new discourses on women, production, and consumption would dethrone merchants such as Rose Bertin, who had reigned as queens of fashion in the eighteenth century, and would help crown male dressmakers such as Charles-Fréderic Worth emperors of *la mode*. (From the Napoleonic period, see the engraving of a fashion boutique in the almanac *Les Délices de Paris*, figure 4.)

Just as she seized the imagination of her contemporaries, Rose Bertin, "minister of modes" to Marie Antoinette, also seizes the imagination of the

Figure 4. Almanach, *Les Délices de Paris,* 1804.

twentieth-century historian as a fitting symbol of female commercial dominance on the eve of the Revolution, at a pivotal moment when women's management of large retail enterprises was still a possibility, yet already assailed.
As surely as new eighteenth-century ideologies of womanhood helped construct a new politics of fraternity in the Revolution—which swept away the
possibility for aristocratic and working-class women alike to participate in

politics—so too did new conceptions of proper womanhood slowly begin to relegate prominent female merchants to the back room, where they could stitch and sew but never command and control. The eighteenth-century marchandes de modes, often characterized as the grandmothers of the great couture houses of the nineteenth and twentieth centuries, have a less glorious legacy as well, the poor working-class seamstresses of the nineteenth century, the grisettes. The very notions of femininity that had helped make possible the rise of both female consumers and retailers in the eighteenth century would ultimately undermine the commercial power of the marchandes de modes. Accorded excellence in matters of taste and consumption but denied the proper moral judgment to rule themselves or others, women could sew dresses or buy them but could never control the fine art of retailing.

NOTES

I owe special thanks to Suzanne Desan, who commented on a version of this essay presented at the 1993 Berkshire Conference of Women's Historians, and, as always, to Chris Rasmussen.

1. For contemporary anecdotes and comments on Rose Bertin, see Louis Petit de Bachaumont, et al., *Mémoires secrets*, 5 March 1779, 31 May 1779, and 8 September 1781 (London: John Adamson, 1777–89); *Mémoires de la Baronne d'Oberkirch* (Paris: Charpentier, 1869), 52–53; Mme Campan, *Memoirs of Marie Antoinette* (New York, P. F. Collier and Son, 1910). For secondary works on Bertin, see Anny Latour, *Les Magiciens de la mode* (Paris, R. Julliard, 1961), 3–29; Pierre de Nouvion and Émile Liez, *Un ministre des modes sous Louis XVI: Mademoiselle Bertin* (Paris, H. Le Clerc, 1911); Émile Langlade, *La Marchande des modes de Marie-Antoinette: Rose Bertin* (Paris, A. Michel, 1911); and most recently, Madeleine Delpierre, "Rose Bertin, les marchandes de modes et la Révolution," in *Modes et révolutions, 1780–1804* (Paris, Editions Paris-Musées, 1989).

2. The comedy-vaudeville *Le Public Vengé* by Prévot was produced on 9 April 1782.

3. See Archives Nationales, series O 3,793 (1785), on Marie Antoinette's wardrobe account.

4. *Mémoires de la Baronne d'Oberkirch* (Paris, 1869), quoted in Anny Latour, *Les Magiciens de la mode* (Paris: R. Julliard, 1961), 25.

5. For a fuller description of Bertin's shop, see Olivier Bernier, *The Eighteenth-Century Woman* (Garden City, N.Y., Doubleday, 1982), 126. In 1692, Florent Carton Dancourt's play *Bourgeoises à la mode* (Paris: T. Guillain, 1643) identified a character named Madame Amelin as a marchande de modes. The term did not appear in the *Dictionnaire de l'Académie* until 1815. It is often difficult to tell just who was a *marchande de modes* because they were a very loosely defined group of merchants, especially before their incorporation in 1776. Many women who might technically have been *lingères* (linen workers), *couturières* (dressmakers), or *coiffeuses de dames* (ladies hair dressers) may have called themselves *marchandes de modes*. Roslin's *L'Esprit du commerce, almanach pour 1754* lists thirteen marchandes de modes, and the *Almanach des arts et métiers* (Paris, 1774) lists twenty. One must keep in mind that only the most

prosperous shops would have been listed in almanacs. For documents pertaining to the marchands de modes in the period 1599–1692, see Archives Nationales, AD XI25.

6. *Correspondance secrète*, 6:146, quoted in Alfred Franklin, "Les Magasins de nouveautés," in *La Vie privée d'autrefois: Arts et métiers, modes, moeurs, usages des Parisiens, du XIIe au XVIIIe siècle* (Paris, E. Plon, 1894), 15:258.

7. Quoted in *Mémoires de la Baronne d'Oberkirch*, 137.

8. See Sarah Maza, "The Diamond Necklace Affair Revisited (1785–1786): The Case of the Missing Queen," and Lynn Hunt, "The Many Bodies of Marie Antoinette: Political Pornography and the Problem of the Feminine in the French Revolution," in *Eroticism and the Body Politic*, ed. Lynn Hunt (Baltimore: Johns Hopkins University Press, 1991).

9. Nicolas-Toussaint Lemoyne Desessarts, *Dictionnaire universel de police* (Paris, Moutard, 1785–87), 624–25, s.v. "marchandes de mode."

10. Desessarts, *Dictionnaire universel de police*, 624.

11. Rosalind Williams, *Dream Worlds: Mass Consumption in Late-Nineteenth-Century France* (Berkeley: University of California Press, 1982).

12. For an examination of nineteenth-century paradigms of the female consumer's seduction by male capitalists and advertising men, see Rachel Bowlby, *Just Looking: Consumer Culture in Dreiser, Gissing, and Zola* (New York: Methuen, 1985). See also Andreas Huyssen, "Mass Culture as Woman: Modernism's Other," *After the Great Divide: Modernism, Mass Culture, Postmodernism* (Bloomington: Indiana University Press, 1986).

13. According to the contemporary fashion journal *Cabinet des modes*, the state visit of the ambassadors of Tippoo-Saib in 1788 sparked a vogue for dresses of lime-green taffeta with pink spots, a style called "à la Tippoo-Saib."

14. The term grisette originally derived from an inexpensive type of cloth commonly used in the clothing of shop girls in the seventeenth century. Or, as Antoine Furetière defined the term in 1690: "Femme ou fille jeune vêtue de gris. On le dit par mépris de toutes celles que sont de basse condition, de quelque étoffe qu'elles soient vêtues." Furetière, *Dictionnaire* (Le Haye and Rotterdam: A. et R. Leers, 1690), s.v. "grisette."

15. In his recent study of gender construction in eighteenth-century Britain, Barker-Benfield provides a careful examination of the ways in which new conceptions of masculinity and femininity were linked to developments in Britain's consumer culture. G. J. Barker-Benfield, *The Culture of Sensibility: Sex and Society in Eighteenth-Century Britain* (Chicago: University of Chicago Press, 1992).

16. On the commercial revolution of 1500–1650, see John U. Nef, *Cultural Foundations of Industrial Civilization* (New York: Harper, 1958); Chandra Mukerji, *From Graven Images: Patterns of Modern Materialism* (New York: Columbia University Press, 1983); and Fernand Braudel, *The Wheels of Commerce* (New York: Harper and Row, 1982).

17. For an examination of the impact of new material goods on European culture, see Mukerji, *From Graven Images: Patterns of Modern Materialism*. On the political importance of this new consumer culture, see Colin Jones, "The Bourgeois Revolution Revivified: 1789 and Social Change," in *Rewriting the French Revolution*, ed. Colin Lucas (Oxford: Clarendon Press, 1991), 69–118.

18. See, in particular, Neil McKendrick, John Brewer, and J. H. Plumb, *The Birth*

of a Consumer Society: The Commercialization of Eighteenth-Century England (Bloomington: Indiana University Press, 1982); and Carole Shammas, *The Pre-Industrial Consumer in England and America* (Oxford: Clarendon Press, 1990). For other recent studies, see *Consumption and Culture in the Seventeenth and Eighteenth Centuries: A Bibliography*, compiled by Dorothy K. Auyong, Dorothy Porter, and Roy Porter (Los Angeles: The UCLA Center for Seventeenth and Eighteenth Century Studies, 1991).

19. Important examinations of eighteenth-century consumer culture and fashion include Neil McKendrick, "Home Demand and Economic Growth: A New View of the Role of Women and Children in the Industrial Revolution," in *Historical Perspectives: Studies in English Thought and Society in Honour of J. H. Plumb*, ed. Neil McKendrick (London: Europa, 1974), 152–210; Colin Campbell, *The Romantic Ethic and the Spirit of Modern Consumerism* (Oxford: Basil Blackwell, 1987); and Daniel Roche, *La Culture des apparences: Une histoire du vêtement, XVIIᵉ–XVIIIᵉ siècles* (Paris: Fayard, 1989), and the English translation, Roche, *The Culture of Clothing: Dress and Fashion in the Ancien Régime*, trans. Jean Birrell (Cambridge: Cambridge University Press, 1994).

20. The most in-depth study of transformations in Parisian wardrobes in the eighteenth century is provided by Roche, *La Culture des apparences*, especially 119–76.

21. The most important study of the eighteenth-century French fashion press remains Caroline Rimbault, "La Presse féminine" (thèse du troisième cycle, Ecole des Hautes Etudes, 1981).

22. Daniel Roche, "L'Économie des garde-robes à Paris, de Louis XIV à Louis XVI," *Communications* 46 (1987): 93–118; idem, *The People of Paris* (Berkeley: University of California Press, 1987), 160–94.

23. Jacques Savary's advice to apprentices on how to comport themselves with customers is telling: his lengthy admonishment that apprentices be both polite and honest in their dealings indicates that these standards of behavior were not always upheld. *Le Parfait négociant* (Paris: L. Billiane, 1675), 61.

24. On the shop as a place of entertainment, see Chanoine François Pédoue, *Le Bourgeois Poli* (Chartres: C. Peigné, 1631), cited in Braudel, *The Wheels of Commerce*, 71. The best introduction to Parisian fairs, an important site of consumption, is provided by Robert Isherwood, *Farce and Fantasy: Popular Entertainment in Eighteenth-Century Paris* (Oxford: Oxford University Press, 1986).

25. Restif de la Bretonne, *Les Nuits de Paris, ou Le Spectateur nocturne* (London, 1788–94), 2:244.

26. Louis-Sebastien Mercier, *Tableau de Paris* (Amsterdam, 1782), 10:244. For a discussion of Mercier's treatment of women in his *Tableau de Paris*, see John Lough, "Women in Mercier's *Tableau de Paris*," in *Women and Society in Eighteenth-Century France*, ed. Eva Jacobs et al., (London: Athlone Press, 1979), 110–22.

27. Mercier, *Tableau de Paris*, 6:311.

28. For an account of a dialogue that took place in 1702 in a boutique near the Charnier des Innocents between a beautiful *mercière* and the Prince d'Orléans as he tried to seduce her, see *Mémoires de Cardinal Dubois sur la ville, la cour et les salons de Paris sous la Règence*, Bibliothèque Nationale, Fol. Z Le Senne 789 (1). For visual images of *couturières* and *chapelières* flirting with male customers see *Les Belles Marchandes, almanach historique* (Paris, 1784), which contained a picture of one female merchant for each month of the year.

29. Joachim Christoph Nemeitz, *Séjour de Paris* (Leiden: Jean Van Abcoude, 1727), 339.

30. Ibid.

31. See Jürgen Habermas, *The Structural Transformation of the Public Sphere: An Inquiry into a Category of Bourgeois Society* (Boston: MIT Press, 1989); and Dena Goodman, "Public Sphere and Private Life: Towards a Synthesis of Current Historiographical Approaches to the Old Regime," *History and Theory* 30 (January 1992): 1–20.

32. *Mémoires de la Baronne d'Oberkirch,* 225.

33. Louis-Marie Prud'homme, *Miroir historique, politique, et critique de l'ancien et du nouveau Paris,* 3d ed. (Paris: Prudhomme fils, 1807), 5:238.

34. Establishing a regular clientele was considered an essential part of succeeding in one's business. Savary des Bruslons, *Dictionnaire universel de commerce* (Copenhagen: Les frères C. and A. Philibert, 1759), 891.

35. Gabriel Sénac de Meilhan, *Considérations sur les richesses et le luxe* (Considerations on riches and luxury) (Paris: Vve Valade, 1787), 143.

36. On the development of new understandings of the difference between the male and female nervous systems in eighteenth-century Britain see Barker-Benfield, *The Culture of Sensibility,* 1–36.

37. Boudier de Villemert, *L'Ami des femmes* (Paris, 1758), 79.

38. Antoine-Leonard Thomas, *Essai sur le caractère, les moeurs, et l'esprit des femmes* (Paris: Moutard, 1772), 111–12. Ibid., 113–14.

39. Jean-Jacques Rousseau, *Émile* (Paris: Garniers frères, 1961), 3:459.

40. For the development of these ideas see, *Réflexions sur quelques causes de l'état présent de la peinture en France* (Paris, 1752), 195. For a discussion of the problem of the beholder and works of art in the eighteenth century, see Michael Fried, *Absorption and Theatricality* (Berkeley: University of California Press, 1980).

41. *Les Paradoxes d'état servant d'entretien aux bons esprits* (1651), 37.

42. Bocquel, "Superiorité de l'homme sur la femme ou l'inégalité des deux sexes" (1740), manuscript, Bibliothèque de l'Arsenal, Paris, 3656, p. 101.

43. A.C.D.S.A. [August Caron], *Toilette des dames, ou Encyclopédie de la beauté* (Paris: A.–G. Debray, [1806]), 108.

44. For an entry into the libertine literature of the grisette see Pierre Jean Baptiste Nougaret, *Les Jolis péchés d'une marchande de modes,* 4th ed. (Paris, 1801); and Restif de la Bretonne, "Les Jolies femmes de commerce," in *Les Contemporains* (Paris: Vve Duchesne, 1782), 3:65.

45. Although in theory the marchandes de modes, like the mercers, sold and embellished rather than produced goods, in fact they made a number of items of apparel, including three different kinds of outerwear, *mantelets, pelisses,* and *mantilles.* In addition, after their incorporation in 1776, they were allowed to make the special attire required for formal presentation at court, the *habit de cour,* or grand habit, which was characterized by a boned corset, a train, and a voluminous dress spread out over huge *paniers.*

46. Few secondary sources examine the marchandes de modes in any detail. Daniel Roche includes a discussion of them in chapter 11 of his *La Culture des apparences.* See also A. Varron, "Createurs de modes Parisiens au XVIIe siècle," *Les Cahiers ciba* 2, no. 16 (December 1947): 542–75. For a detailed study of a marchandes de modes's boutiques in eighteenth-century Anvers, see Marguerite Coppens, "'Au Ma-

gasin de Paris': Une boutique de modes à Anvers," *Revue belge d'archéologie et d'histoire d'art* 12 (1983): 85. See also the forthcoming work of Cissy Fairchilds.

47. Mercier, *Tableau de Paris*, 11:218.

48. Of the existing bankruptcy cases for Parisian marchands de modes in the period 1748–89, seventy-nine are for women, twenty-one for men, and nine for married couples. Archive de la Seine, Paris, Series D5B6. Many marchandes de modes had a more modest commerce. Consider, for example, Demoiselle Artault, who lived on the rue Saint-Denis. When arrested for prostitution she claimed that the sale of the *robin* and the *guerluchon* (the hooded capes made by marchandes de modes) were not enough to permit her to support herself honestly. Erica-Marie Benabou, *La Prostitution et la police des moeurs au XVIIIe siècle* (Paris: Perrin, 1987), 285.

49. Desessarts, *Dictionnaire universel de police*, 625.

50. *L'Art de coiffures des dames* (1769), 3 n. 1, claims that the marchandes de modes split from the *lingères* in 1669. Denis Diderot, *Encyclopédie* (Paris: Briasson, 1751–80), 10:598. Abbé Pierre Jaubert, *Dictionnaire raisonné et universel des arts et métiers* (Paris: P. F. Didot Jeune, 1773), 90.

51. On the bazaar-like quality of the eighteenth-century urban economy and the intense competition among trades, see Michael Sonenscher, *Work and Wages: Natural Law, Politics, and the Eighteenth-Century French Trades* (Cambridge: Cambridge University Press, 1989), 137–38. For a careful examination of the relations between local corporations and the state in eighteenth-century Lille, see Gail Bossenga, *The Politics of Privilege: Old Regime and Revolution in Lille* (Cambridge: Cambridge University Press, 1991).

52. Rousseau, *Émile* (Paris: Garnier frères, 1961), 3:232.

53. Mercier, *Tableau de Paris*, 9:177–78.

54. See Pierre Augustin Caron de Beaumarchais's play *Le Mariage de Figaro*, first performed in Paris in April 1784. For a discussion of Beaumarchais's politics, see Sara Maza, *Private Lives and Public Affairs* (Berkeley: University of California Press, 1993), 290–91.

55. A.C.D.S.A., *Toilette des dames*, 202.

56. Restif de la Bretonne, *Les Nuits de Paris*, 2:246–47, quoted in Jeffrey Kaplow, *The Names of Kings: The Parisian Laboring Poor in the Eighteenth Century* (New York: BasicBooks, 1972), 85. Kaplow suggests that for a similar observation one see Maille Dussausoy, *Le Citoyen désintéressé* (Paris, 1767), 2:128.

57. Mercier, *Tableau de Paris*, 10:173.

58. Ibid., 9:179.

59. "Règlemens de la communauté des Filles de Sainte-Anne" (1698), quoted in Martine Sonnet, *L'Éducation des filles au temps des lumières* (Paris: Cerf, 1987), 251.

60. This worry remained well into the nineteenth century. See Jules Simon, *L'Ouvrière* (Paris: L. Hachette et cie, 1861), 200.

61. *Encyclopédie méthodique* (Paris, 1785), 1:135.

62. For a discussion of the connection between desire for clothes and sexual desire in industrializing England, see Thomas W. Laqueur, "Sexual Desire and the Market Economy during the Industrial Revolution," in *Discourses of Sexuality from Aristotle to AIDS* (Ann Arbor: University of Michigan Press, 1992), 185–215.

63. See Kathryn Norberg, "The Libertine Whore: Prostitution in French Pornog-

raphy from Margot to Juliette," in *The Invention of Pornography: Obscenity and the Origins of Modernity, 1500–1800* (New York: Zone Books, 1993), 225–52.

64. Mercier, *Tableau de Paris*, 11:111–12. For accusations of prostitution, see *Étrennes aux grisettes pour l'année 1790* (1790); *Encyclopédie méthodique* (Paris, 1785), 3:65; "Brevet d'Agnes Pompon, apprentisse fille de modes," Bibliothèque Nationale, Fol. Z Le Senne 4365 (1). In contemporary perceptions, the female merchants and young shop girls who attended these boutiques were seen as uniformly consumed by the love of fashions. Postmortem inventories suggest that both mistress *couturières* and *lingères* and their *ouvrières* (workers)—whether motivated by business acumen (what better way to advertise one's taste and skill in making clothing) or coquetry—did indeed spend a considerable amount of money on their wardrobes. True to their reputation, these women wore dresses sporting the brightest and loveliest colors and designs, silks in "vert, citron, blanc, violet and gorge de pigeon," and gaily striped or floral cottons. In addition, that both groups of women possessed a striking number of accessories such as bonnets, neckerchiefs, and handkerchiefs underscores the importance of accessories, particularly for women of modest means, in creating a fashionable look.

65. *Encyclopédie méthodique*, 1:135.

66. See the report of a rape and seduction of a fifteen-year-old *ouvrière en linge* (linen worker) in Marie-Anne Marchebout, *Journal dédié à Monsieur*, no. 9 (May 1777): 111.

67. Mercier, *Tableau de Paris*, 6:309.

68. Models for commerce among working-class women were available; it was assumed that working-class merchants and working-class customers would be equal matches in wiliness and bargaining prowess. See Ibid., 2:267–68.

69. Ibid., 6:310.

70. Ibid., 12:269. Contemporaries also believed that the marchandes de modes's female clients regarded their fellow female clients as rivals. See the description of the play *La Matinée d'un jolie femme* in *Journal de la mode et du goût* (20 January 1793): 2.

71. Quoted in de Nouvion and Liez, *Un ministre des modes sous Louis XVI*, 146.

72. *Correspondance secrète* (9 January 1775).

73. A.C.D.S.A. [August Caron], *Toilette des dames*, 22–25.

TWO

The Making of the Self-Made Man

Class, Clothing, and English Masculinity, 1688–1832

David Kuchta

"Let your dress be as cheap as may be without shabbiness," the Tory-turned-radical William Cobbett advised middle- and upper-class Englishmen in 1829, warning that no one "with sense in skull will love or respect you on account of your fine or costly clothes."[1] In 1829, Cobbett's advice was the standard fare of courtesy manuals. Clothing historians have labeled the late eighteenth and early nineteenth centuries the era of "the great masculine renunciation," a period of increasing modesty and simplicity in middle- and upper-class men's dress.[2] Thus Cobbett was writing during what fashion historians have seen as a key transitional period in English men's clothing consumption, the period when the three-piece suit took on its essentially modern uniformity and darkness. Cobbett's advice, then, should not be surprising. Nor should his reasons for recommending modesty sound unfamiliar, coming as they do from such a leading political reformer: "A great misfortune of the present day is, that every one is, in his own estimate, raised above his real state of life: every one seems to think himself entitled, if not to title and great estate, at least to live without work. This mischievous, this most destructive, way of thinking has, indeed, been produced, like almost all our other evils, by the Acts of our Septennial and Unreformed Parliament." For many political writers like Cobbett, political corruption was the source of personal dissolution. The personal was explicitly political: an unreformed Parliament had created an enormous debt, encouraged stock speculation, and allowed "a race of loan-mongers and stock-jobbers" to amass great fortunes and live in luxury. Industry and sobriety had been overwhelmed by an onrush of conspicuous consumption: "In such a state of things, who is to expect patient industry, laborious study, frugality and care."[3]

Because, to a great extent, Cobbett's advice and dissent can still be heard today, this essay is nothing more than a history of the obvious: for the past three hundred years, elite masculinity has been identified with the values of industry and economy. These values have become obvious, unquestioned, second nature, synonymous with masculinity itself. The personal has been depoliticized. Therefore, a history of the obvious, an analysis of the political origins of the great masculine renunciation, is precisely what is needed in order to repoliticize this construction of masculinity.

This essay argues that the great masculine renunciation was propelled by an ideology and social dynamic of men's fashion that I have called "inconspicuous consumption." Veblenite theories of consumer behavior argue that fashion changes are motivated by social emulation, conspicuous consumption, and invidious distinction (the need to keep up with, or ahead of, the Joneses), but this essay shows how men's fashion changes in the eighteenth and nineteenth centuries were driven by an increasingly inconspicuous form of consumption, a form of consumption—equally invidious, to be sure—that reconciled class demands for social distinction with the gender ideology of masculine renunciation.[4] Conspicuous consumption is merely one social dynamic that motivates fashion change: understanding the variety of systems of consumer behavior means identifying how various social and gender groups defined themselves in response to political, economic, and social changes. The great masculine renunciation was the result of a struggle for political power between middle-class and aristocratic Englishmen, both of whom linked their own personal identity to their claims to political legitimacy. Explaining men's fashion changes therefore requires looking at the ways in which questions of consumption, class, and gender were key to transformations in English political culture from the redefinition of aristocratic political culture with the Glorious Revolution of 1688 to the enfranchisement of middle-class men with the Great Reform Act of 1832. I outline here two different regimes of masculinity, two ways in which political legitimacy was expressed in masculinist attitudes toward consumption and luxury. After first discussing the great masculine renunciation, I describe the ways in which eighteenth-century aristocratic gentlemen used an ideological antipathy to luxury as a means of expressing their political leadership, and then proceed to examine the ways in which middle-class political reformers subsequently appropriated this ideology to gain access to the formal institutions of power.

THE GREAT MASCULINE RENUNCIATION

The great masculine renunciation has long been seen as the triumph of middle-class ideology in the late eighteenth century. J. C. Flugel, the original author of the term, wrote in 1930: "As commercial and industrial ideals conquered class after class, until they finally became accepted even by the aristocracies of all the more progressive countries, the plain and uniform costume associated with such ideals has, more and more, ousted the gorgeous and varied garments associated with the older order."[5] Aileen Ribeiro also attributes the growth of sartorial modesty to middle-class and democratic ideals in the late eighteenth century.[6] Certainly, as historians Leonore David-off and Catherine Hall have ably demonstrated, an ideology of modest masculinity was important in the making of nineteenth-century middle-class consciousness: rational, economical men were rhetorically opposed to luxurious, aristocratic fops.[7] While relying on Davidoff and Hall's insight that gender identity was central to the formation of class consciousness, this essay nonetheless argues that the ideology and practice of masculine renunciation began in an earlier era, and with a different class—that "plain and uniform costume" was not inherently, timelessly, or exclusively a middle-class ideal, but functioned as an aristocratic ideal as well. The ideology of inconspicuous consumption was important in fashioning the social and gender identity of eighteenth-century aristocratic men. As we shall see, the great masculine renunciation had its origins in an aristocratic response to the increasing diffusion of fashion in the eighteenth century and to the political culture that emerged after 1688—much earlier than historians have considered. The masculinist language of industry and frugality emerged as part of eighteenth-century aristocratic men's claims to political and cultural hegemony and had the intent and effect of excluding lower- and middle-class men, and all women, from the formal institutions of power. Thus the middle-class image of the self-made man was not a self-made image, but rather a hand-me-down from an earlier generation.

This earlier revolution in menswear, not coincidentally, took place immediately after the Glorious Revolution of 1688. Under the Restoration regimes of Charles II (1660–1685) and James II (1685–1688), elite men's dress was elaborate and ornamented, despite some Restoration attempts at sartorial reform (see figure 5).[8] Like their English predecessors and their French counterpart, Louis XIV, Charles II and James II linked political leadership with fashion leadership. Thus, as the Restoration court aspired to absolute rule, Restoration courtiers put on all the French finery and expense for which the English court had long been criticized, and for which the Restoration court has long been famed (see figure 6).[9] The Glorious Revolution, however, ended royal pretensions to absolutism by replacing James II with the more politically and sartorially modest William and Mary,[10] and in turn court observers began to notice the increasing tendency among upper-class Englishmen (though not women) to be "temper'd with becoming modesty" (see figure 7).[11] In 1691, the English chronicler Guy Miege wrote:

> Cloth amongst men is the general, and almost the only wear. And that with so much plainness and comeliness, with so much modesty and so little prodigality, that the English, formerly so apish in imitating foreign nations in their garb, might go now for a model. The women indeed, who value themselves most upon a fine outward appearance, cannot keep within those bounds. Whether

Figure 5. Frontispiece from *The Courtier's Calling*, 1675. One of the earliest known images of the three-piece suit. Originally introduced by Charles II as a reform measure, after 1670 the three-piece suit became more ornamented.

Figure 6. Frontispiece from *An Essay in Defence of the Female Sex,* 1696.
"This vain gay thing sets up for man, But see what fate attends him; / the
powd'ring Barber first began, the Barber Surgeon ends him."

Figure 7. Plate 1 for men, from F. Nivelon, *Rudiments of Genteel Behavior,*
1737. "The head erect and turned, as in this figure, will be right, as will the
manly boldness in the face, temper'd with becoming modesty."

it be to make a figure in the world, or out of emulation amongst themselves,
or out of design upon men, they go still in rich silks, with all the set-offs that
art can possibly invent from time to time.[12]

Traveling in England in 1698, the Frenchman Francis Misson observed that
"generally speaking, the English men dress in a plain uniform manner."[13]
The Scot John Macky journeyed through England from 1714 to 1724 and
found that "the dress of the English is like the French, but not so gaudy; they
generally go plain, . . . they wear embroideries and lace on their clothes on
solemn days, but they do not make it their daily wear as the French do."[14]
And finally, though these observations were common throughout the eighteenth century, the Portuguese merchant Don Manoel Gonzales found in
1730 that "for raiment, the common wear amongst the men is plain cloth
and drugget, without any thing of costly ornament. But the fair sex spares
for nothing to make the best appearance."[15]

The exception of women is telling (see figure 8). Promoters of this new
male modesty criticized the court's conspicuous consumption in masculinist terms—and thus tended to see modesty as a particularly masculine activity. "Whilst I seem to reprove . . . excess in men," confessed the Restoration
fashion critic John Evelyn, "[I] am so far from disobliging the brighter sex."[16]
Naturalizing women as "the brighter sex" and the fair sex—and as the
guardians of consumption—went hand in hand with the new male sartorial
modesty. The emergence of the new political definition of masculinity was
simultaneous with the appearance of a new construction of femininity, as
the next section will argue more fully.

By the early eighteenth century, then, fashions for English gentlemen had
changed dramatically, and the more modest and sober style of dress was
adopted throughout the eighteenth century.[17] In attempting to display the
modesty and sobriety that signified public virtue, aristocratic men created a
style in direct contrast with conspicuous consumption. As we will see,
throughout the eighteenth century a new aesthetic of upper-class masculinity was defined, whereby upper-class men were to lead society by refined
taste rather than sartorial splendor. At the same time, fashion became associated with women and the lower orders, and displaying wealth was no longer
equated with displaying worth: gentlemen were called on to lead the nation
by setting a moral example rather than by attempting to outspend their extravagant emulators. Aristocratic men could claim social leadership in part
by renouncing the world of fashion, by adopting "noble simplicity."[18]

In continuing the association between masculinity and simplicity, the great
masculine renunciation of the late eighteenth and early nineteenth centuries
was merely an extension of a century-old process. Thus, when James Malcolm
observed Englishmen's clothing in 1808, he used words that could have been
written one hundred years earlier: "Male dress changed almost insensibly

Figure 8. Plate 1 for women, from F. Nivelon, *Rudiments of Genteel Behavior,*
1737. "Let the eyes (being cast down, as this figure describes) discover the
humility and respect, whilst bending not too much, but moderately, you make
the curtsy properly; then rising from it gradually raise the eyes so too, and
look with becoming modesty." For Nivelon, "becoming modesty" for women
was not incompatible with elaborate dress.

from formality to ease. This was effected merely by altering the cut of the clothes: the materials are the same as they were an hundred years past; the colors however are more grave."[19] Certainly early nineteenth-century men's dress was darker, simpler, and more uniform, as fashion historians invariably agree.[20] As Elizabeth Wilson has demonstrated, "woollen cloth in quiet colours evolved into the normal day dress of modern urban man."[21] The value of masculine renunciation was nothing new, however: inconspicuous consumption had already been adopted by upper-class men as a strategy of social distinction as early as the period after 1688. What was new to the late eighteenth and early nineteenth centuries was a political and social dynamic that propelled this renunciation even further, turning noble simplicity into middle-class simplicity. While aristocratic men's disdain for the assumed effeminacy of commercial culture propelled the early eighteenth-century move toward modesty, it was a struggle between aristocratic and middle-class men for political superiority that propelled the great masculine renunciation from 1750 to 1850. If early eighteenth-century aristocratic political ideology had associated modest masculinity with political legitimacy, with the moral high ground that allowed aristocratic men to claim to speak on behalf of the nation, late-eighteenth-century and early-nineteenth-century reformers turned this very ideology against the aristocracy itself by claiming public virtue as the private property of middle-class men. It was a political struggle to control the means and meanings of consumption that motivated aristocratic and middle-class men to engage in invidious indistinction and inconspicuous consumption—a fashion dynamic, central to the great masculine renunciation, that the final section of this essay will further elaborate.

THE MANNERS OF A REPUBLIC

By William Cobbett's time, then, plainness in upper- and middle-class men's dress was nothing new, nor was Cobbett's targeting of political corruption as the source of vanity and luxury. "It might be no ill policy in a kingdom to form itself upon the manners of a republic," Bishop George Berkeley counseled in 1721. Writing after the collapse of the runaway stock speculation of the South Sea Bubble, Berkeley worried that speculation and luxury would "enervate and dispirit the bravest people."[22] Berkeley's republican language would have been familiar to Cobbett a century later, for the fear that luxury would enervate the bravest people was a recurrent theme throughout eighteenth-century political culture.[23] After the Revolution of 1688, encouraging and embodying public virtue was a prime concern of England's political elite, who feared that encouraging luxury would lead to England's moral and political decline. In an age when the court could no longer claim the political and cultural prerogative to dictate English fashions, aristocratic men's public virtue signified independence from the supposedly effeminating effects of both middle-class luxury and royal pomp. Modest dress signified the limited monarchy produced by the Revolution settlement: though a kingdom, England had the manners of a republic.

In eighteenth-century culture, luxury was among the chief "political vices,"[24] along with corruption, anarchy, effeminacy, and tyranny: luxury was the evil twin of consumption, the debased, debauched, and debilitating form of consumption that effeminated and impoverished England. Defenders of aristocracy defined luxury as the vice of middle-class upstarts who ambitiously lived above their social station but defined aristocratic men's consumption as manly, productive, and in the national interest. Likewise, in the male homosocial world of England's political elite, effeminacy created as many anxieties as femininity.[25] Both by making masculinity a prerequisite to political legitimacy and by claiming masculinity as their own, aristocratic men used the label of effeminacy to directly exclude from power all other men—lower- and middle-class men, as well as men with alternative sexual practices—and to indirectly yet doubly exclude all women from power (by associating femininity with luxury and masculinity with legitimacy).[26] The use of the label effeminacy, a third term coming between masculinity and femininity, demonstrates that gender ideals were both socially and sexually constructed in early modern England: aristocratic masculinity was defined in opposition to three groups of "others"—other genders, other sexualities, and other classes of men.[27]

As such, accusations of luxury and effeminacy were aimed at one's social or political enemies. Whigs, Tories, and Jacobites used a language of manly simplicity and public spiritedness in their pursuit of political and moral high ground, accusing each other of encouraging luxury and effeminacy through political corruption.[28] Eighteenth-century political ideology thus linked manly modesty with English liberty: "Temperance and patriotism go hand in hand," reflected Nathaniel Lancaster, writing in response to the 1745 Jacobite rebellion.

> [W]hat is so pernicious to the common weal as vice? And what vice, so much as luxury?. . . [W]e think no lot so vile as that of subjection to a despotic Lord; and yet we crouch under the most abject of all servitude, the servitude of weak and effeminate passions. . . . [W]e can, without a blush, squander away immense sums upon foreigners, and barter . . . the sinews of war for an effeminating delicacy, which would ill become us even in times of peace, and is perhaps as unsuitable to our genius and climate, as it is inconsistent with the care and solicitude which danger awakens in the patriot's breast.[29]

In contrast to the effeminacy that supposedly threatened to invade England from across the Channel, aristocratic masculinity was to be expressed by independence from the servitude of fashion. Sartorial restraint signified political liberty; the freeborn Englishman's personal self-discipline was a sign of his political self-governance and economic self-sufficiency. Thus France, as the source of absolutism and luxury fabrics, of "despotic Lords" and "effeminating delicacies," was the great political and cultural rival to English definitions of masculinity.[30]

In an age when increasing importation and domestic production of textiles made fashionable dress more widely available to the middle class, as various authors have noted, political and social leadership no longer corresponded with fashion leadership, and this situation created anxieties for England's social elite.[31] There was no longer a one-to-one correspondence between social level and level of expenditure, between social fabric and material fabric. Spurning the materiality and seeming effeminacy of fine fabrics made a gentleman's values less susceptible to being purchased by upstarts.[32] Fashionability meant following the crowds, submitting to the ruling passion; fashionability implied a lack of judgment, a lack of disinterest. In defending England's oligarchy against Thomas Paine's "libertine principles," one anonymous late-eighteenth-century author argued that those in "the fashionable world . . . [are] so much in love with their own stupidity, that, though they were capable, they could not command time for disinterested reflection. . . . If the riches of a nation were generally diffused, and all shared equally of them, or nearly so, all would devise, and none would execute: And this kingdom, after becoming enervated with luxury and the fine arts, would undergo the same or a similar fate with that of Rome."[33] In aristocratic political ideology, the greatest threat to the English commonwealth was common wealth, considered a precursor to luxury, enervation, effeminacy, and tyranny.

Thus aristocratic men's "disinterested reflection"—the moral superiority created by the permanent wealth of a landed estate—was essential to guarantee the moral well-being of the nation. As E. P. Thompson has cogently argued, "ruling-class control in the eighteenth century was located primarily in a cultural hegemony, and only secondarily in an expression of economic or physical (military) power."[34] Thus defenders of aristocracy saw aristocratic men's moral example as central to their political legitimacy. The "influence of example and perceptive counsel," as the conservative John Tinney saw it, would prevent a decline into either democratic Jacobinism (which others attributed to "the mania of foreign fashion")[35] or "that feeble, sumptuous and licentious effeminacy of royalty."[36] Even the early reformer James Burgh called on England's elite to rule as much by cultural superiority as by political power: "Upon you, my Lords and gentlemen, who hold the first ranks in the nation, whether sharers in the legislative power, or not; upon you it lies to begin the general reformation, by your superior example and influence, which, you know, cannot fail to lead the nation. Let but the quality and gentry . . . live mostly in the country upon their estates, and within their incomes; . . . and observe how long extravagance and impiety will continue in Britain."[37] In a polity led by lords and gentlemen, it was "superior example," not merely "legislative power," that held the nation together. Insubordination in dress as well as in politics would be prevented by the manly simplicity of aristocratic men. Edmund Burke looked to "the unbought grace of life, the cheap defence of nations, [and] the nurse of manly sentiment and heroic enterprize" to defend the "age of chivalry" from democratic revolutions.[38] For Burke, "manners are of more importance than laws. Upon them, in a great measure the laws depend. . . . According to their quality, they aid morals, they supply them, or they totally destroy them."[39] Or, as the antiradical John Bowles none too subtly put it, preventing "luxury and dissipation" would make the English "orderly, tractable, and easily governed. Having such powerful restraints within, they will require fewer restraints from without."[40]

A polity led by manly aristocrats was thus essential to the national welfare. Aristocratic men's political rule was legitimated by an ideology of masculine disinterest in the fashionable world, and, in turn, a polity limited to aristocratic men would help maintain England's masculinity: "There are a variety of causes which operate in forming the disposition of the people, and perhaps none more than the Constitution and form of Government under which they live. Thus the English Character has acquired a vigor and manliness from the Constitution."[41] Only an understanding of the mutually defining relationship between gender construction and political ideology allows us to comprehend John Bowles's enigmatic statement that English manliness derived from the constitution. In eighteenth-century aristocratic political culture, the political was as personal as the personal was political. By associating modest masculinity with political legitimacy, aristocratic men used a cultural construction of gender to define the character necessary for participation in the polity. Controlling the reins of power meant controlling the means and meanings of consumption.

Political participation in the nation, then, was defined in terms of a masculine renunciation of luxury, and this definition explains why vanity and luxury were such dominant definitions of femininity. If displaying masculinity was inherently tied to political legitimacy, displaying femininity was intimately linked with political exclusion. Like many writers, Jeremy Collier used a political argument to exclude women from his calls for modesty:

[Women] are by custom made incapable of those employments by which honor is usually gained. They are shut out from the pulpit and bar, from embassies, and state negotiations, so that notwithstanding (as I believe it often happens) their inclinations are generous, and their abilities great to serve the public; yet they have not an opportunity of showing it. . . . [T]herefore it's allowable for them to set a value upon their persons, for the better disposal of them. And further if they have a mind to it, they may please themselves, because they are acceptable to others, which is a generous satisfaction.[42]

Like the new masculinity, the new femininity was an explicitly political construct. Barred from "state negotiations," elite women displayed their social
station by becoming guardians of consumption, responsible for the world
of fashion. In this construction of femininity, wealth still corresponded with
worth; consumption was still conspicuous.[43]

Thus a new political culture was used to define new constructions of both
masculinity and femininity, and in turn the new femininity was used as a justification for excluding women from political culture: the personal and political defined each other. Women were excluded from political institutions
both by the equation between political legitimacy and masculine renunciation and by the naturalized equation between femininity and luxury. It was
precisely this double exclusion that posed such great obstacles to women's
claims to political participation: early feminists had to both denaturalize this
feminization of fashion and degender virtue.[44] In seeking to denaturalize
this construction of women as the fair sex, Mary Astell linked luxury not to
nature but to corruption, just as male political writers did. Thus "pride and
vanity" were not inherent in women's nature but instead

> the product of a good soil; they are nothing else but generosity degenerated
> and corrupted. A desire to advance and perfect its being is planted by God in
> all rational natures, to excite them hereby to every worthy and becoming
> action. . . . And therefore to be ambitious of perfections is no fault. . . . [W]ould
> they pride themselves in somewhat truly perfective of a rational nature, there
> would be no hurt in it. But then they ought not to be denied the means of ex-
> amining and judging what is so; they should not be imposed on with tinsel
> ware.[45]

And when women such as Mary Wollstonecraft and Catherine Macaulay
sought to gain entry into political culture by degendering virtue, by asserting that "the cold arguments of reason . . . give no sex to virtue,"[46] mas-
culinists accused them of political cross-dressing, the "affectation of manliness."[47] By naturalizing women as the fair sex—as inherently associated with
luxury, beauty, and consumption—male political writers denied women a
political voice precisely because men saw women as too beautiful for words.
At the heart of English political culture, constructing women as consumers
went hand in hand with masculine renunciation.

In eighteenth-century political culture, then, ideologies of consumption
were used to separate masculinity from femininity, and to separate the political world from the fashion world, precisely at the moment when the court
and crown no longer led the beau monde. Landed gentlemen spurned the
effeminating effects of luxury, thereby accumulating the political capital that
came with displaying public virtue. For aristocratic men, "superior example"
brought virtue and wealth, manliness and prosperity, liberty and property,

industry and refinement. In sum, it brought public benefits without private vices. It was this ideology that propelled and sustained aristocratic men's renunciation of luxury throughout the eighteenth century. The great masculine renunciation of the early eighteenth century was thus both a social response to the increasing diffusion of fashion and a political response to the new political culture that emerged after 1688.

LIBERTY, EQUALITY, MASCULINITY

By the late eighteenth century, however, aristocratic Englishmen were not the sole proprietors of their own ideology, since middle-class reformers had appropriated the language of manly public virtue for their own political ends. Throughout the period under study, the condemnation of vice, profligacy, and effeminacy was as much a critique of power as it was a justification of power. Like aristocrats, political reformers saw a revolution in character as central to a revolution in government; the radical William Godwin's assertion that "revolutions of states . . . consist principally in a change of sentiments and dispositions in the members of those states"[48] shares the same emphasis on manners as Edmund Burke's conservative argument that "the most important of all revolutions," that which occurred in 1789, was "a revolution in sentiments, manners, and moral opinions."[49] Many reformers saw a parallel between their movement and the "correct and manly" principles that had informed the Glorious Revolution of 1688.[50] Throughout the great transformation of English political culture in the late eighteenth and early nineteenth centuries, a reformation of manners went hand in hand with a revolution in politics.[51] From John Wilkes to Thomas Paine to William Cobbett, English reformers and radicals drew on the masculinist language of public virtue to redefine citizenship and claim participation in the polity.[52] This section, then, will show how middle-class reformers gained access to the institutions of power in part by appropriating and undermining aristocratic men's claims to masculinity, by using the aristocratic ideology of republican masculinity against aristocrats themselves.

While aristocratic men portrayed the middle class as vain, venal, and vicious, middle-class reformers pitted "prodigal luxurious landlords" against middle-class proponents of virtue and liberty.[53] Thus the masculinist language of modesty and public virtue was used by both aristocratic conservatives and middle-class reformers to define the political nation. Modest masculinity was still the basis of the political inclusion of men, and a naturalized feminine frivolity continued to be the basis of the political exclusion of women. William Cobbett believed that femininity itself was sufficient reason to deny women suffrage: "Women are excluded . . . because the very nature of their sex makes the exercise of this right incompatible with the harmony and happiness of society."[54] In portraying aristocratic men as "the profligates of rank, emasculated by hereditary effeminacy," middle-class reformers reproduced the double exclusion of women from the political sphere.[55]

In reformers' eyes, luxury and effeminacy were still central threats to the English commonwealth, but they originated not in the commons but in the "hereditary honors and titles of nobility [which] produce a proud and tyrannical aristocracy."[56] A titled nobility, James MacKintosh argued, was unknown to "the manly simplicity of the ancient commonwealths." A title, argued Thomas Paine, "marks a sort of foppery in the human character, which degrades it. It reduces man into the diminutive of man."[57] Whereas aristocratic men were portrayed as England's prodigal sons, "the general manners of the middle ranks of people" stood as models of virtue and true liberty.[58] Praising "that simplicity of character, that manliness of spirit, that disdain of tinsel" displayed by American colonists, Richard Price argued that it was "not in the high ranks of life, or among the great and mighty, that we are to seek wisdom and goodness. . . . They are to be found chiefly in the middle ranks of life."[59] Political reformers thus reversed eighteenth-century aristocratic men's claims to masculinity and political legitimacy by ascribing these virtues to middle-class men.

Although they agreed with aristocratic men that luxury and effeminacy undermined claims to unprejudiced disinterest, reformers turned that argument into a critique of landed wealth. Reasoned disinterest—the manly disdain for profligacy and venality—was still a requirement for political legitimacy, but the class associations had been transformed. "The commercial, or monied interest," James MacKintosh wrote, "has in all nations of Europe (taken as a body) been less prejudiced, more liberal, and more intelligent, than the landed gentry." Political legitimacy rested in the hands "of those disinterested and independent men, who are chiefly to be found in the middle classes of mankind," rather than with either the profligate aristocracy or the "submissive and venal" populace, argued suffrage reformer Christopher Wyvill. For middle-class reformers like Wyvill, universal suffrage was as dangerous as a strictly aristocratic constitution—both were susceptible to corruption by luxury, both lacked the "well-regulated spirit of manliness and humility" so necessary for defending English liberty.[60]

Middle-class men were thus between two forms of corruption, an effeminate aristocracy and a vicious working class: "The one seems to be too much encumbered with artificial imaginary necessities; the other too much encumbered with the real and natural necessities of life, to attend to its cultivation."[61] In middle-class ideology, as in aristocratic political culture, virtue was still the basis for political participation: "A parliament whose seats, through the universality of freedom, . . . shall be attainable only by public virtue, must to all parties, be equally favorable, equally acceptable," wrote one anonymous political reformer.[62] But now virtue was associated with middle-class industry, as Joseph Towers argued in his critique of "ministerial despotism:"

> Those who possess much, are desirous of obtaining more; they are solicitous to rise higher, and with this view court the favor of those above them; and are often too much enervated by luxury to be influenced by any principles of patriotism. Whilst, on the other hand, men of lower circumstances, of more moderate views and expectations, and of more regular and temperate manners, though they enjoy less property, often possess more independence of mind, and are more influenced by a virtuous affection to their country.[63]

In middle-class discourse, as in aristocratic discourse, temperance and patriotism still went hand in hand, were still threatened by luxury and enervation.

Thus aristocratic men's presumed luxury and profligacy were directly linked with political corruption, and the modesty of the middle-class electorate was seen as essential to liberty. "It is the virtue of the people that preserves their freedom," Thomas Mortimer argued. "If therefore the people are virtuous, sober, frugal, and industrious, they will choose honest representatives in parliament, and they will put them to as little expense as possible in obtaining their feats, that they may not be tempted to repair their fortunes at the expense of the liberties of the people."[64] Luxury was the source of election manipulations ("rotten boroughs"): Richard Price associated "running wild after pleasure," attending masquerades, and visiting gaming houses with "trafficking for boroughs, perjuring ourselves at elections, and selling ourselves for places."[65] Parliament was "filled with idle school-boys, insignificant coxcombs, led-captains and toad-eaters, profligates, gamblers, bankrupts, beggars, contractors, commissaries, public plunderers, ministerial dependents, hirelings, and wretches," complained Major John Cartwright.[66] When, for example, the M.P. Charles James Fox opposed freedom of the press, his opponents portrayed him as a fop, linking his extravagant lifestyle with political repression.[67] John Horne Tooke criticized what he saw as Fox's "boundless profusion and prodigality," and weighed in on the side of Fox's rival, the younger Pitt, whom he praised as "remarkably sober, prudent, moral and economical."[68]

If luxury was the source of political corruption, reformers saw political corruption as equally the source of luxury: manners and politics were mutually defining. "It is only where the magistrates are virtuous," argued Robert Evans, "that the morals of a people can be correct. But the Borough system is the root of all the corruption that exists." The abolitionist Granville Sharp believed that frequent elections were "necessary for the maintenance of public virtue." Political reform thus required "unexceptionably prudent and manly" assertions of republican liberty in the face of "the servility and corruption of elected officials," as Christopher Wyvill put it. From his cell in King's Bench prison, John Wilkes wrote to the Westminster electors who time and again returned him to his seat in Parliament, praising the "manly spirit you have exerted this day in direct opposition to every art and intrigue of a corrupt Administration."[69] Wilkes's defenders returned the compliment, lauding his "noble firmness, and manly constancy, [which] give him a just claim to being considered as a very proper man to maintain their [his constituents'] privileges in the great national assembly."[70]

Modest manliness, then, was central to middle-class, as well as aristocratic, notions of political culture. In reformers' eyes, an artificial aristocracy prevented natural, rational manliness from leading the nation. In the new politics of character, political legitimacy was still determined by manliness, modesty, and frugality, but these were now the attributes of the self-made man. To both critics and defenders of aristocracy, the issue of consumption was central to political legitimacy. Citing James Burgh, John Cartwright noted the centrality of luxury to English political culture: "Instead of counteracting the natural ill effects of luxury proceeding from wealth and prosperity, and giving it a beneficial turn by wise and humane laws; it has been the business of government (which 'in almost every age and every country,' says Burgh, 'has been the principle grievance of the people') to debauch and corrupt the manners and morals of the people, by every possible invention; in order to remove every obstacle in the way of absolute power."[71] As "the principle grievance of the people," the political corruption that emerged from luxury was a key element in English political culture in the late eighteenth and early nineteenth centuries. Thus a reformation of politics began as a reformation of character: "unnatural customs" and "gothic notions of beauty" were replaced by the natural rights of modest, middle-class, manly men.[72] New relationships between class, consumption, and masculinity helped fashion a new political culture, which simultaneously helped fashion a new social ideology of masculine consumption—in sum, a new political culture of masculinity in which, as William Cobbett argued, above all else, "superior sobriety, industry and activity, are a still more certain source of power."[73]

SUPERIOR EXAMPLE

England did not have a revolution in 1789 or 1832. Nor did middle-class Englishmen gain a stake in the political nation by overthrowing an old regime and replacing it with an entirely new political culture.[74] England's old regime had already ended by 1688, expelled by an aristocratic republican ideology, which was easily appropriated by middle-class political reformers. Middle-class Englishmen gained access to the formal institutions of power by assimilating an aristocratic language of manly virtue and cultural hegemony into their own identity. In its struggle for political power, England's bourgeoisie did not play a revolutionary role in history—as Marx would have

it—merely a reforming one. Middle class men did not put an end to all patriarchal, idyllic relations, leaving no other bonds than naked self-interest
and callous cash payment. Rather, they replaced one age of chivalry with another: their own self-interest was well-dressed in the three-piece suit of industry, frugality, and respectability. "Trade has now a chivalry of its own,"
gloated middle-class free trader Henry Dunckley, celebrating "the nobility
and dignity of industry and commerce."[75] Political reformers replaced aristocratic men's cultural hegemony with a middle-class version, appropriating
aristocratic discourse and using it to redefine public virtue and the national
interest. Thus the political triumph of middle-class Englishmen came about
not as a result of a revolution in the means of production but as a result of
a reformation of the meanings of consumption. In redefining aristocratic
men as luxurious profligates "emasculated by hereditary effeminacy," middle-class men claimed public virtue as their private property, thereby gaining a share in what James Burgh called "superior example."

Simply stated, then, the great masculine renunciation occurred as a result of this struggle for superior example in a culture where modest masculinity meant political legitimacy. Aristocratic and middle-class men attempted to outdo each other's claims to political legitimacy by displaying a
"well-regulated spirit of manliness and humility." The great masculine renunciation began in the early eighteenth century as an aristocratic response
to the political culture that emerged after 1688 and continued into the early
nineteenth century motivated by a rivalry between aristocratic conservatives
and middle-class reformers. From 1688 to 1832, a multiplicity of classes and
interests groups—Whigs and Tories, radicals and conservatives, bourgeois
and aristocrats—used a masculinist morality of public virtue for their own
ends.

Writing at the beginning of the eighteenth century, Bernard Mandeville
affronted English political morality by arguing that encouraging private vices
rather than public virtue would actually bring public benefits.[76] Mandeville
criticized the recently triumphant Whig notion of the compatibility of manly
virtue and economic well-being: he denied the possibility "of enjoying all the
most elegant comforts of life that are to be met with in an industrious, wealthy
and powerful nation, and at the same time be bless'd with all the virtue and
innocence that can be wish'd for in a Golden Age."[77] Historians have all too
often adopted Mandeville's compellingly cynical reversal of English political morality as an explanation for the birth of consumer society in eighteenth-
century England.[78] Arguing that Mandeville "anticipated Veblen," Neil Mc-
Kendrick has claimed that the early eighteenth century saw a "revolutionary
commitment to fashion" and the acceptance of "the doctrine of beneficial
luxury," since in McKendrick's account "good repute rested on pecuniary
strength." Thus "one of the best means of displaying that strength, and
thereby retaining or enhancing one's social standing, would be to indulge

in conspicuous consumption of goods."[79] Yet, as this essay argues, the Veblenite theory of conspicuous consumption cannot account for changes in men's fashion. Male fashion changes were motivated not by Mandevillian private vices but by the pursuit of public virtue. "Good repute" was divorced from "pecuniary strength," and displaying worth rather than wealth was key to enhancing one's sociopolitical standing, to gaining "superior example."

Now, "superior example" is an oxymoron: once the example is followed, it is no longer superior. It is this fundamental contradiction in terms, this unstable definition of elite masculinity, that gave the great masculine renunciation its central dynamic. Changes in male fashion were driven not by a social dynamic of conspicuous consumption, not by an attempt to keep up with, or ahead of, the Joneses, but by a politics of inconspicuous consumption, by elite understatement, by an attempt to stay away from the Joneses. Once the example of public virtue was followed, superiority was lost, and a greater degree of modesty was required. Thus invidious indistinction was central to the political ideology of "superior example": one generation's modesty became the next generation's conformity. What was once seen as informality and inconspicuousness later became conspicuous formality. Thus a century-long movement "from formality to ease," to use James Malcolm's words (1808), was propelled by a dynamic instituted after 1688; exemplary modesty was a claim to social distinction, but once modesty became fashionable it lost its ability to define a social and political hierarchy, thus motivating even greater modesty. Once identified as a fashion, antifashion lost its ability to stand outside and above the world of fashion. Mary Wray cogently identified this new fashion dynamic in the early eighteenth century: "All peoples avoiding the fashion would be only setting up another fashion."[80] Thus opposition to luxury promoted, not inhibited, fashion change. Understatement was still a fashion statement. As a political statement, then, elite men's disdain for fashion was itself the motivating dynamic to men's fashion change.

By looking at the way aristocratic and middle-class Englishmen defined their social and gender identities, we have been able to identify how fashion systems can be regulated by inconspicuous consumption and invidious indistinction. Moving beyond Mandeville and Veblen to understand the role of manly public virtue in English political culture has allowed us to better comprehend the relationship between gender and politics within the consumer society of eighteenth- and nineteenth-century England. Transformations in political culture were central to transformations in the relationships between class, clothing, and English masculinity, just as changing attitudes toward class, clothing, and masculinity were key to transformations in English political culture. "On what trifles," the Tory-turned-radical and all-around masculinist William Cobbett advised, "turn the great events in the life of man."[81]

NOTES

1. William Cobbett, *Advice to Young Men, and (Incidentally) to Young Women, in the Middle and Higher Ranks of Life* (London, 1829–1830), paragraph 21 [no pagination]. In the interests of readability, I have modernized spelling and punctuation throughout this chapter.

2. The term is from J. C. Flugel, *The Psychology of Clothes* (London, 1930), 113, and has been widely adopted by fashion historians. For recent historical surveys, see Penelope Byrde, *The Male Image: Men's Fashion in Britain, 1300–1970* (London, 1979); Diana de Marly, *Fashion for Men: An Illustrated History* (London, 1985); and Elizabeth Wilson, *Adorned in Dreams: Fashion and Modernity* (Berkeley, 1985).

3. Cobbett, *Advice to Young Men*, paragraph 21.

4. Veblenite theories of emulation are central motifs in G. J. Barker-Benfield, *The Culture of Sensibility: Sex and Society in Eighteenth-Century Britain* (Chicago, 1992); Neil McKendrick, John Brewer, and J. H. Plumb, *The Birth of a Consumer Society: The Commercialization of Eighteenth-Century England* (Indianapolis, 1982); and Harold Perkin, *The Origins of Modern English Society, 1780–1880* (London, 1972).

5. Flugel, *Psychology of Clothes*, 113.

6. Aileen Ribeiro, *Dress and Morality* (New York, 1986), 95.

7. Leonore Davidoff and Catherine Hall, *Family Fortunes: Men and Women of the English Middle Class, 1780–1850* (London, 1987), 410.

8. For a more detailed discussion of Restoration dress, see my "'Graceful, Virile, and Useful': The Origins of the Three-Piece Suit," *Dress: The Journal of the Costume Society of America* 17 (1990): 18–25.

9. See, for example, Edward Chamberlayne, *Anglia Notitia, or The Present State of England*, 6th ed. (London, 1672), 52.

10. Lois G. Schwoerer, "The Glorious Revolution as Spectacle," in *England's Rise to Greatness, 1660–1763*, ed. Stephen B. Baxter (Berkeley, 1983), 133.

11. F. Nivelon, *The Rudiments of Genteel Behavior* (London, 1737), caption to plate 1.

12. [Guy Miege], *The New State of England under Their Majesties K. William and Q. Mary* (London, 1691), 2:38–39. The French visitor Béat Louis de Muralt also asserted that the English no longer emulated the French: "They have too good an opinion of themselves, to imitate other people" (Béat Louis de Muralt, *Letters Describing the Character and Customs of the English and French Nations* [1694–5; reprint, London, 1726], 52).

13. [Francis Misson], *M. Misson's Memoirs and Observations in His Travels over England* (1698; reprint, London, 1819), 15.

14. John Macky, *A Journey through England* (London, 1722), 2:238. As Linda Colley has noted, French fashions were worn at court (Macky's "solemn days"). Yet Colley overstates the influence of French fashion on England's elite, since the court no longer regulated the everyday dress (Macky's "daily wear") of elite men. See Linda Colley, *Britons: Forging the Nation, 1707–1787* (New Haven, 1992), 165–66.

15. "The Voyage of Don Manoel Gonzales, (Late Merchant) of the City of Lisbon in Portugal, to Great-Britain", in *A Collection of Voyages and Travels* (1730–31; reprint, London, 1745), 1:188.

16. John Evelyn, *Tyrannus, or The Mode* (London, 1661), 13.

17. It is difficult to determine the extent of this sartorial revolution, especially given the sweeping claims of the observations cited above. There were certainly ex-

ceptions to this general trend: "In a country free from custom or general folly," de Muralt noted, "there's at the same time a great number of particular errors" (de Muralt, *Letters*, 52). The "particular errors" received all the attention and condemnation from their contemporaries and have received an inordinate amount of attention from fashion historians. This inordinate attention has also been noticed by Penelope Byrde in *The Male Image: Men's Fashion in Britain, 1300–1970* (London, 1979).

18. *Common Sense, or The Englishman's Journal* (London, 1738), 24.

19. James Malcolm, *Anecdotes of the Manners and Customs of London during the Eighteenth Century* (London, 1808), 449.

20. Penelope Byrde qualifies that "although black or dark-coloured cloth became fashionable at the beginning of the nineteenth century, shades of blue, green, red and white were still worn for evening wear for the first few decades" (Byrde, *The Male Image*, 72).

21. Wilson, *Adorned in Dreams*, 27.

22. George Berkeley, *An Essay towards Preventing the Ruine of Great Britain* (London, 1721), 11.

23. Paul Langford has identified the fear of luxury as a central element in eighteenth-century political culture. Paul Langford, *A Polite and Commercial People: England, 1727–1783* (Oxford, 1989), 3–4.

24. James Burgh, *Political Disquisitions* (Philadelphia, 1774), 2:17. This text was originally published in London.

25. For a general discussion of the trope of effeminacy in eighteenth-century attitudes to consumer culture, see Barker-Benfield, *The Culture of Sensibility*, 104–53. Though Barker-Benfield correctly argues that consumer capitalism created masculinist anxieties about luxury, a reaction to consumer society was only one source among many of the new masculinity.

26. For a discussion of homosexuality and homosociability in eighteenth-century political culture, see G. S. Rousseau, *Perilous Enlightenment: Pre- and Post-Modern Discourses. Sexual, Historical* (Manchester, 1991).

27. For a more general statement of how gender functions both as "a constitutive element of social relationships" and as "a primary way of signifying relationships of power," see Joan Wallach Scott, "Gender: A Useful Category of Historical Analysis," *American Historical Review* 91, no. 5 (December 1986): 1067. Like the term "luxury," then, "effeminacy" is used in this chapter to refer to cultural constructions rather than to any actual sartorial practices.

28. For an overview of the issue of public virtue in eighteenth-century political rhetoric, see J. G. A. Pocock, *The Machiavellian Moment: Florentine Political Thought and the Atlantic Republican Tradition* (Princeton, 1975); Linda Colley, *In Defiance of Oligarchy: The Tory Party, 1714–1760* (Cambridge, 1982); and Paul Monod, *Jacobitism and the English People* (Cambridge, 1989).

29. Nathaniel Lancaster, *Public Virtue, or The Love of Our Country* (London, 1746), 25, 21–24.

30. For a recent discussion of English opposition to the importation of French culture, see Colley, *Britons*, 87–92. Like many authors, Colley understates the role of gender ideology in English nationalism.

31. Neil McKendrick, "The Commercialization of Fashion," in *The Birth of a Consumer Society: The Commercialization of Eighteenth-Century England*, Neil McKendrick, John

Brewer, and J. H. Plumb (Indianapolis, 1982), 34–98; and Beverly Lemire, *Fashion's Favourite: The Cotton Trade and the Consumer in Britain, 1660–1800* (Oxford, 1991); and John Brewer, introduction to *Consumption and the World of Goods*, ed. John Brewer and Roy Porter (New York, 1993).

32. In a different context, Pierre Bourdieu has analyzed aristocratic taste as a reaction against cultural diffusion. See Pierre Bourdieu, *Distinction: A Social Critique of the Judgement of Taste* (Cambridge, Mass., 1984).

33. *An Address to the Associated Friends of the People* (Edinburgh, 1792), 29–30. Political parallels between England and Rome were made long before Edward Gibbon described Rome's fall from the "manly pride" of its republican era to the "effeminacy" and "vanity of the East" of its imperial era (Edward Gibbon, *The History of the Decline and Fall of the Roman Empire*, ed. J. B. Bury [1776; reprint, London, 1912], 2:159). As John Sekora has noted, Rome was a focal point for debates about luxury: John Sekora, *Luxury: The Concept in Western Thought, Eden to Smollett* (Baltimore, 1977), 297, n. 5).

34. E. P. Thompson, "The Patricians and the Plebs," in his *Customs in Common* (London, 1991), 43. From a different perspective, J. C. D. Clark also analyzes aristocratic claims to cultural hegemony and argues that those claims were generally accepted throughout English society. Thus Clark conflates "an examination of its [the aristocracy's] self-image" with an examination of English society as a whole (J. C. D. Clark, *English Society, 1688–1832: Ideology, Social Structure, and Political Practice during the Ancien Régime* (Cambridge, 1985). I make no such claims.

35. Peter Alley, *Public Spirit, A Lyric Poem* (London, 1793), 5.

36. John Pern Tinney, *The Rights of Sovereignty Vindicated* (London, 1809), 44.

37. James Burgh, *Britain's Remembrancer* (London, 1746), 43. See also Hannah More, *Thoughts on the Importance of the Manners of the Great to General Society*, 4th ed. (Philadelphia, 1808), 9–10. This text was originally published in London.

38. Edmund Burke, *Reflections on the Revolution in France* (1790; reprint, Indianapolis, 1955), 86.

39. Edmund Burke, "Letters on a Regicide Peace" [1796], in *The Works of the Right Honorable Edmund Burke* (London, 1826), 8:172.

40. John Bowles, *Thoughts on the Late General Election. As Demonstrative of the Progress of Jacobinism*, 2d ed. (London, 1802), 33.

41. John Bowles, *Dialogues on the Rights of Britons, between a Farmer, a Sailor, and a Manufacturer* (London, 1792), 20–21.

42. Jeremy Collier, *Essays upon Moral Subjects* ([1694]; reprint, London, 1697), 74–75.

43. To be sure, there was also a large literature prescribing female modesty, but it linked female modesty to domestic ideology and sexual chastity rather than explicitly to political legitimacy. See Nancy Armstrong, *Desire and Domestic Fiction: A Political History of the Novel* (Oxford, 1987).

44. For a discussion of eighteenth-century feminism, see Alice Browne, *The Eighteenth-Century Feminist Mind* (Brighton, 1987).

45. Mary Astell, *A Serious Proposal to the Ladies* (London, 1694), 31–33. "Fetters of gold are still fetters," echoed the anonymous author of *An Essay in Defence of the Female Sex* (London, 1696), 25.

46. Mary Wollstonecraft, *A Vindication of the Rights of Men, in a Letter to the Right Honourable Edmund Burke*, 2d ed. (London, 1790), 114.

47. *A Vindication of the Right Honorable Edmund Burke's Reflections on the Revolution in France, in Answer to all his Opponents* (London, 1791), 98. These words were written in response to Catherine Macaulay.

48. William Godwin, *An Enquiry Concerning Political Justice, and Its Influence on General Virtue and Happiness* (London, 1793), 1:202. For a general discussion of political culture in this period, see James T. Boulton, *The Language of Politics in the Age of Wilkes and Burke* (London, 1963); John Brewer, *Party Ideology and Popular Politics at the Accession of George III* (Cambridge, 1976); and Edward Royle and James Walvin, *English Radicals and Reformers* (Lexington, 1982).

49. Burke, *Reflections on the Revolution in France*, 91. English admirers of the French Revolution also made the comparison between the masculinism of 1688 and that of 1789. See *Observations on Mr. Paley's Theory of the Origin of Civil Government and the Duty of Submission* (London, 1789); and Joseph Towers, *Thoughts on the Commencement of a New Parliament* (London, 1790). For a discussion of gender ideology in the French Revolution, see Joan Landes, *Women and the Public Sphere in the Age of the French Revolution* (Ithaca, N.Y., 1988); Dorinda Outram, *The Body and the French Revolution: Sex, Class and Political Culture* (New Haven, 1989); and Lynn Hunt, "The Many Bodies of Marie Antoinette: Political Pornography and the Problem of the Feminine in the French Revolution," in *Eroticism and the Body Politic*, ed. Lynn Hunt (Baltimore, 1991), 108–30.

50. Sir James MacKintosh, *Vindiciae Gallicae: Defence of the French Revolution and Its English Admirers against the Accusations of the Right Hon. Edmund Burke* (Philadelphia, 1792), 156.

51. For a recent discussion, see Joanna Innes, "Politics and Morals: The Reformation of Manners Movement in Later-Eighteenth-Century England," in *The Transformation of Political Culture: England and Germany in the Late Eighteenth Century*, ed. Eckhart Hellmuth (London, 1990), 57–118. For a general discussion of English reform and radicalism, see Edward Royle and James Walvin, *English Radicals and Reformers, 1760–1848* (Lexington, 1982); John Cannon, *Parliamentary Reform, 1640–1832* (Cambridge, 1973); and Ian Christie, *Wilkes, Wyvill, and Reform* (London, 1962).

52. For a discussion of the role of public virtue and moral corruption in English nationalism, see Gerald Newman, *The Rise of English Nationalism* (New York, 1987). Newman, however, confuses a middle-class portrait of the aristocracy with the aristocracy's own self-image.

53. [Thomas Mortimer], *The National Debt No National Grievance, or The Real State of the Nation* (London, 1768), 60.

54. Cobbett, *Advice to Young Men*, paragraph 337.

55. Wollstonecraft, *Vindication of the Rights of Men*, 97. Wollstonecraft's masculinist critique of aristocratic vice runs contrary to her claim, cited above, that "the cold arguments of reason . . . give no sex to virtue."

56. Richard Price, *Observations on the Importance of the American Revolution, and the Means of Making It a Benefit to the World*, 2d ed. (Philadelphia, 1785), 40. This text was originally published in London. For a similar argument, see MacKintosh, *Vindiciae Gallicae*, 42.

57. MacKintosh, *Vindiciae Gallicae*, 40; Thomas Paine, *The Rights of Man: Being an Answer to Mr. Burke's Attack on the French Revolution*, 8th ed. (London, 1791), 70.

58. Mortimer, *National Debt,* 57.

59. Price, *Observations on the Importance of the American Revolution,* 44; and idem, *Additional Observations on the Nature and Value of Civil Liberty, and the War with America* (London, 1777), 25.

60. MacKintosh, *Vindiciae Gallicae,* 41; Rev. Christopher Wyvill, *A State of the Representation of the People of England* (York, 1793), 44, 43; idem, *Papers and Letters, Chiefly Respecting the Reformation of Parliament* (Richmond, 1816), 18.

61. [Frances Reynolds], *An Enquiry Concerning the Principles of Taste, and of the Origin of Our Ideas of Beauty* (London, 1789), 44.

62. *An Address to the Gentlemen, forming the several Committees of the associated Counties, Cities, and Towns, for supporting the Petitions for Redress of Grievances, and against the unconstitutional Influence of the Crown over Parliament* (London, 1780), ix.

63. [Joseph Towers?], *Observations on Public Liberty, Patriotism, Ministerial Despotism, and National Grievances* (London, 1769), 27–28.

64. Mortimer, *National Debt,* 47.

65. Richard Price, *Observations on the Nature of Civil Liberty, the Principles of Government, and the Justice and Policy of the War with America* (London, 1776), 98.

66. [John Cartwright], *Take Your Choice!* (London, 1776), x.

67. Valerie Steele, "The Social and Political Significance of Macaroni Fashion," *Costume: The Journal of the Costume Society* 19 (1985): 89–101.

68. John Horne Tooke, *Two Pairs of Portraits, Presents to All the Unbiassed Electors of Great Britain, and Especially to the Electors of Westminster* (London, 1788), 13, 3. Later, William Cobbett also referred to the "squandering and luxurious habits" of Fox (Cobbett, *Advice to Young Men,* paragraph 19).

69. [Robert Evans], *Three Letters of Publicola, On The Expediency of A Reform in Parliament* (London, 1811), 30; Granville Sharp, *A Declaration of the People's Natural Right to a Share in the Legislature, Which Is the Fundamental Principle of the British Constitution of State* (London, 1775), 160; Christopher Wyvill, *A Defence of Dr. Price, and the Reformers of England* (London, 1792), 5; John Wilkes, *A Collection of All Mr. Wilkes's Addresses to the Gentlemen, Clergy, and Freeholders of the Country of Middlesex* (London, 1769), 33.

70. Towers, *Observations on Public Liberty,* 9.

71. Cartwright, *Take your Choice!* xix.

72. Wollstonecraft, *Vindication of the Rights of Men,* 10.

73. Cobbett, *Advice to Young Men,* paragraph 40.

74. For a discussion of the "constitutionalist" rather than revolutionary nature of English radicalism, see especially James Epstein, *Radical Expression: Political Language, Ritual, and Symbolism in England, 1790–1850* (New York, 1994); and James Vernon, *Politics and the People: A Study of English Political Culture* (Cambridge, 1993).

75. Henry Dunckley, *The Charter of the Nations* (London, 1854), 25, cited in Asa Briggs, "The Ideology of 'Class' in Early-Nineteenth-Century England," in *History and Class: Essential Readings in Theory and Interpretation,* ed. R. S. Neale (Oxford, 1983), 17.

76. For brief discussions, see M. M. Goldsmith, "Public Virtue and Private Vices: Bernard Mandeville and English Political Ideologies in the Early Eighteenth Century," *Eighteenth Century Studies* 9, no. 4 (summer 1976): 477–510; and Thomas A. Horne, "Envy and Commercial Society: Mandeville and Smith on 'Private Vices, Public Benefits,'" *Political Theory* 9, no. 4 (November 1981): 551–69.

77. Bernard Mandeville, *The Fable of the Bees, or Private Vices, Publick Benefits* (1714; reprint, Oxford, 1924), 6.

78. See Barker-Benfield, *The Culture of Sensibility*; and McKendrick, Brewer, and Plumb, *The Birth of a Consumer Society*.

79. McKendrick, Brewer, and Plumb, *The Birth of a Consumer Society*, 52, 40, 19, 52.

80. Mary Wray, *The Ladies Library* (London, 1722), 60–61.

81. Cobbett, *Advice to Young Men*, paragraph 21.

THREE

The Gendering of Consumer Practices in Nineteenth-Century France

Leora Auslander

It has become a truism in the historiography of nineteenth-century France that bourgeois women were excluded from paid labor and ensconced within the home.[1] It has been claimed that the social identity "producer" became a constitutive element of masculinity and that the social identity "consumer" became a constitutive element of femininity.[2] I will argue, in contrast, that the production/consumption dichotomy is misleading, that the bourgeoisie of both genders were cast as consumers, albeit consuming to different ends. All acts of consumption were also acts of production, but some kinds of consumption produced things defined as feminine and others produced things defined as masculine.[3] The gendering of these products of consumption was not stable across the century, however, nor were the boundaries between the masculine and the feminine impermeable at any given moment.

Over the course of the nineteenth century, both the gendering and the meanings of bourgeois consumption changed. In the first part of the century, the focus for women's consumption was the making of the family and the class. To these tasks, representing the nation was added at about mid-century, and representing the self was added during the 1880s. After the turn of the century, single women started to use their interiors to create and represent themselves and to write about their creation of these interior spaces. The tasks of constitution and representation of family, class, nation, and self through domestic consumption were cumulative rather than sequential. Women continued to be defined as responsible for the social representation of family and class throughout this period but had the projects of making the nation and the self added onto their earlier obligations and possibilities.

Contemporaneous with the development of the bourgeois housewife's consuming activities in the 1830s were the elaboration and expansion of two forms of consumption associated with men: collecting and dandyism. Consumption, like many other social activities, tended to be deemed appropriately masculine when it was productive of self and of a durable legacy beyond the self.[4] Collecting could, therefore, be characterized as appropriate masculine behavior, whereas dandyism was seen by contemporaries as threatening to their masculinity. Therefore, it would appear at first glance that although consumption was not an exclusively feminized activity, it did simply mirror and reproduce stereotypes of masculinity and femininity. But the story is more complicated than that, for the appropriate always bears the seeds of its opposite.[5] Collectors could also be dandies, and dandies collectors. Women could create collections and could also construct a self and a legacy through their consumption. All was not always equally fluid, however. Masculine forms of consumption became more accessible to women only at the end of the nineteenth century, whereas men had been playing with feminine forms since the 1830s. The changing gendered meanings of the acquisition and use of goods both reflected and produced changing meanings of femininity and masculinity.

Many of these dynamics of the gendering of consumption, and the making of gendered subjects, were similar across Europe and in the United States. But the gendering of consumption is, in many ways, a very French story. The essay, therefore, opens with a brief discussion of the particular dynamics of consumption in postrevolutionary French bourgeois society and then follows the changing uses of domestic objects in men's and women's lives and in the definitions of masculinity and femininity from the 1820s to the early years of the twentieth century. Through an analysis of the discourse on the obligations and behavior of women, collectors, and dandies, I hope to demonstrate the variability in the definitions of the masculine and the feminine and to indicate points of divergence and of intersection. The essay concludes with some speculative thoughts suggesting that the explanation for why and how the gendering of market behavior changed over the course of the nineteenth century must be linked to the changing gendering of the polity.

FRANCE: THE BOURGEOISIE AND CONSUMER SOCIETY

Historians have argued that consumer society—in which subjectivities, identities, and solidarities are created by commodities—was born in England and the United States in the eighteenth or even the seventeenth century. France, however, did not become a modern consumer society until the nineteenth century.[6]

Before the French Revolution the crown had played a fundamental role in creating new styles and in structuring relations of production, distribution, and consumption of goods. The nation and the state were embodied in the king, and the ruler and the state were represented by the king's things. With the destruction of absolute monarchy, this system of political and social representation and economic organization ended.

The definitive repeal of sumptuary legislation, the expansion of new forms of retailing, the urbanization of society, and the growth of a population with disposable income all meant that more people were able to buy more things from a wider variety of merchants. Even more significantly, perhaps, the acquisition of goods came to have new meaning in this consumer society: goods came to represent and even constitute people, groups, and institutions in a new way. That is, class, gender, nation, and even self were constructed through the acquisition and use of goods.[7]

The explosion of new institutions and discourses devoted to analyzing goods, as well as to providing advice on appropriate consumption, bear witness to the new centrality of goods. To the institutions of the market were added the institutions of the state. The texts included decorating magazines and books, etiquette books, and advertisements. The authors included architects, interior decorators and designers, philanthropists, collectors, writers, and civil servants. Most were men, a few were women. Many of them earned their living through their role as taste professionals, although not by actually selling objects. Through midcentury most worked in the private sector; under the Second Empire and especially the Third Republic, the state became an important employer. These discourses and institutions, as much as the practices of consumption themselves, form the basis of the analysis here, for it is in those discourses—concretized in novels, etiquette books, treatises, magazines, and memoirs—that the changing perceptions of the use of goods for the constitution, and the representation, of society are manifest.

Although many of these taste professionals expressed anxiety about working-class consumers, consumer society in France was at first inhabited by the bourgeoisie and middling classes.[8] While working people could participate in some of the new recreational activities and buy a few more clothes, very few had enough disposable income for consumer durables, enough domestic space to contain them, and enough time to shop, even by the end of the century.[9] Thus, as historian Marguerite Perrot has argued, ownership of appropriate goods became defining of membership in the bourgeoisie (and perhaps the new petite bourgeoisie) but not in other classes.[10] The focus of bourgeois production through consumption was the home. Homes and the goods they contained were the reflection of the individuals and collectivities that inhabited them.

Domestic goods, therefore, occupied a particular location in this nineteenth-century bourgeois world of goods. Furniture, paintings, silverware, and rugs, unlike food and clothing, were often intended to last at least one lifetime. The acquisition of an objet d'art, even for the very rich, represented something different than the purchase of a new spring suit. Clothing could be changed according to the social occasion. One had, in contrast, only one living room in which to receive, and that living room was not only one's own but also the family's. And, no matter what one's income, furniture was almost always a major purchase and was intended as an investment for use in the future as well as in the present. Furthermore, furnishings were not simply a financial investment like stock or a savings account; family histories were inscribed in the domestic objects. These objects were, therefore, situated at a very different point along the border between individual and family than clothing was. However, it was not only the family but also the state that was interested in matters of furnishings.

The Revolution transformed the relation between the state and consumer goods.[11] The principle of the free market—along with its necessary corollary, the end of sumptuary legislation—was established. The role of the state in the production and exchange of goods, as well as in the determination of their meaning, was redefined. The state became less important as a direct patron of domestic goods and style as the legitimation of its power came to reside more and more in other places. The liberal state defined both the workshop and the home as private spaces, in theory beyond the reach of the state. Yet, all of the varied nineteenth-century political regimes cared about the production and consumption of French style and taste. The health of the French economy was understood to depend on its capacity to export tasteful luxury goods, and, equally important, the unity and stability of the nation was understood to depend on the establishment of French style in domestic goods. The nation, if not the state, could, through style, be made manifest in the everyday lives of the nation's inhabitants. By midcentury, therefore, the state had resumed an intense interest in what its citizens bought and used and had started to create institutions intended to improve consumers' taste. The first among these were the world's fairs and exhibitions, which began in the 1850s and were followed by the new museums, libraries, and schools of the 1880s and 1890s.[12] These state efforts were a response, however, to the forces of the freer market of the early nineteenth century, in which stores, markets, and goods proliferated and in which consumers attempted to reorient themselves in a postrevolutionary world. The first bourgeois relations to be consolidated through consumption were those of family and class.

BOURGEOIS HOUSEWIVES, 1820–1914: CONSTITUTING AND REPRESENTING FAMILY AND CLASS

By the second decade of the nineteenth century,[13] wives and daughters of Parisian large manufacturers, professionals, and civil servants had largely been excluded from paid labor, including that in the family business.[14] The bourgeois "home" (the English word was borrowed by the French in 1816) was invented along with the housewife.[15] Part of the very definition of the bourgeoisie, part of what distinguished it from the working class and especially the petite bourgeoisie, became that the wife and daughters of the household did not work outside the home, and that they had at least one servant to give them managerial status within the home.[16] The separation of workplace from home was not absolute; professionals—doctors, lawyers, notaries, and architects—often still worked out of an office at home. But even when the dwelling was physically segregated from the workplace, the location, cost, and appearance of the home were far from irrelevant to the professional success of the husband/father and to the economic well-being of the family.

Bourgeois women, as consumers, had two tasks; they were to adorn themselves and they were to constitute and represent the family's social identity through goods.[17] Bourgeois daughters, when on the marriage market, were encouraged to increase their value through the cultivation of their beauty and the acquisition of clothing, jewelry, and culture. That obligation did not end with marriage, for in the bodies and talents of wives, and in the homes they created, inhered the position of the family. Therefore, bourgeois wives not only had to produce themselves as cultural objects but also needed to acquire, arrange, and use those goods—especially furnishings—defined as necessary for representing and constituting the family's social position. Consequently, although the home was characterized as a "feminine sphere," as a haven from the outside world, that home and the women supposedly contained within it were fully a part of the world outside. Historians have recently analyzed the degree to which homes were not fully private, familial spaces, as well the degree to which bourgeois women were not in fact protected from the fierce world of capitalism and exchange. Wives received their extended families, a wide social circle, and their husband's business acquaintances. Social and business networks overlapped; the workday, therefore, did not necessarily end when the man of the household crossed the threshold but rather when the last guest departed. Likewise, wives' afternoons were not merely for pleasure and friendship but also for the consolidation of relationships with economic implications.[18] Women needed sophisticated social skills and literary, musical, and artistic culture in order to be successful wives.

The importance of bourgeois wives' domesticity for their families' economic well-being may be seen in Mme Pariset's *Manuel de la maîtresse de maison, ou Lettres sur l'économie domestique*, published in multiple editions in the 1820s, which used the epistolary form to sketch a wife's obligations and responsibilities. Mme Pariset outlined how it was crucial to keep careful and exact accounts of household expenditures so as to be able to show them, on a moment's notice, to one's husband.[19] Through her condemnation of boudoirs and her advocacy of account books, she located her audience in the wealthy bourgeoisie rather than the aristocracy. Furthermore, the decorative style was to be motivated by "comfort" (the code word in this period to distinguish bourgeois from aristocratic taste—the objects in question were not necessarily actually comfortable): "Real good taste involves buying useful, practical, durable goods which should, above all, go together. I think that this harmony is the essential aspect of what the English express in the word *comfortable* [in English in the text]."[20] Mme Pariset's suggestion of the English as models would become much more problematic later under the Third Republic as the web connecting style, taste, and the national was spun. The bourgeois world in the first half of the century was conceived of as explicitly transcendent of national boundaries, linked by the shared values embedded in the word "comfort." Bourgeois interiors were not luxurious (to distinguish them from aristocratic dwellings) but harmonious (unlike the chaotic world outside the home), and they were modeled on the avant-garde of European bourgeois society—the English. In *Manuel de la maîtresse de maison*, readers were offered entry into a bourgeois International; the salient category was class rather than nation or self.[21]

These guides to appropriate bourgeois consumption were a response to the rapid expansion of commercial culture, to the makings of a new elite society after the upheaval of the Revolution, and to the rapid changes in political regime in the first thirty years of the nineteenth century. Women in the 1820s were already facing a more diversified and expanded network of retailers, and new conventions of shopping were emerging. The first stores with fixed (as opposed to negotiated) prices opened in this period; displays of goods became more important and shops more comfortable.[22] The new institutions of distribution were supported and sustained by an expansion in the media of advice. By this period, a model of domesticity, with the woman/wife as consumer, was already becoming quite apparent in the developing genres of women's magazines, etiquette books, marriage manuals, and furnishings guides—genres largely, although not entirely, controlled by men.[23] This literature was dominated by discussions of fashion, style, society news, and women's responsibilities. Primary among those responsibilities was buying the right goods for the family's social position, a topic discussed in great detail.

Beyond generally advocating furnishings that conveyed comfort, durability, and utility, Mme Pariset provided extremely precise instructions—in fact a formula—for furnishing the various rooms of the house, down to the color of paint, number and kind of furnishings, and placement of pictures: "A middling size living room is adequately furnished with a three-place sofa, two high-backed upholstered arm-chairs [*bergères*], six arm-chairs and four chairs. One may add to this a few very clean straw chairs and a few matching pillows may be arranged on the sofa. . . ."[24] Although she offered such exact advice, she urged that her reader not even attempt to choose her furniture herself: "Consult a decorator/upholsterer [*tapissier*] with a well established reputation based upon recognized sensibility [*probité*]. Explain to him your plans and your taste, and let him take care of the purchasing."[25] All of this was said in the context of urging women to accept their confinement at home and not to strive for individuation and accomplishment in the world beyond the home.[26]

Women were to exist only as representatives of their families; the self and the family were coterminous. This focus on familial representation, the importance of tasteful consumption, and the encouragement of self-abnegation through consumption was not limited to etiquette books and was both very durable (lasting through the end of the century) and also widely diffused through women's magazines, and novels. Contemporaneous with this discursive focus on housewives' consumer duties were discussions of two consumer practices deemed masculine—collecting and dandyism.

THE STATE AND MEN AS CONSUMERS: COLLECTING, 1830–1914

> *It [collecting] is the hunt for the masterpieces! . . . one finds oneself face to face with adversaries who defend the quarry! it's trick against trick! . . . it's like in fairy tales, a princess guarded by sorcerers!*
>
> BALZAC, *LE COUSIN PONS*

Balzac's classic description of collecting suggests how certain forms of consumption were characterized to make them male and compatible with definitions of masculine individuation and citizenship.[27] For Balzac, collecting was a challenge, a proving ground, a hurdle separating the boys from the men and the men from the women.[28] While bourgeois wives and mothers were to make families through their activities as consumers, bourgeois men were to make themselves into individuated men through theirs.[29] While no systematic study of the collecting practices of women and men in nineteenth-century France has been done, it does appear that the vast majority of collections were assembled by men. Certainly masculine models of collection dominated in literature; most collectors were depicted as men, and the activity of collecting was compared to the hunt and to conquest.[30] But the story was more complicated than this, for when collectors went too far and sought their individuation, emotional satisfaction, and immortality *exclusively* through their collections they were calumniated by critics and incorporated into the category "dandy." In nineteenth-century France, collecting was conceptualized as a properly masculine activity if it did not emotionally replace the family, if it could be conceptualized as investing, if it could be understood as knowledge producing.

Collecting, in its modern form, is largely an invention of the 1830s.[31] Individuals had had large collections in their *cabinets de curiosités* since the Renaissance, but the phenomenon at that time was much more limited than it was during the nineteenth century.[32] In the seventeenth century, the vast majority of collectors specialized in specimens—geological or biological— from the natural world or relics of the ancient world.[33] By the first half of the eighteenth century, contemporary painting had become a common object of collection, often by painters themselves. The ideology of collecting, in this period, in contrast to the nineteenth century, held that pictures were to be judged on their beauty alone; their content, attribution, and provenance were essentially irrelevant. Old handmade objects, unless they were Greek or Roman, had little appeal; medieval and even Renaissance sculptures and objets d'art found few buyers.[34] After 1750, auction houses expanded their operations and catalogues multiplied. In this early period of collecting, mastery, completion, and social and political power were all already at stake. However, the institutional structuring brought by the development of art history as an academic discipline—museums, art criticism, and the expansion of the art market—was not yet in place. In the nineteenth century, far more people started to collect; there was a new preoccupation with authenticity and a new interest in the old.

In the 1830s expertise came to play a new role in collecting. With the development of art history as an academic discipline, preoccupation with attribution and with the creation of a canon increased among collectors.[35] This new development led to an expanded role for the picture merchant and the art expert, who could assess attribution.[36] Historian Kryzsztof Pomian has argued that collectors, through the creation of categories and because of the collaboration of experts, came to control a domain of knowledge.[37] Creating a respected collection may have given a recently wealthy consumer more prestige than investing the same amount of money in other commodities.[38] A corollary of the utility of collecting for establishing social position was the status of collecting as a creative act, an act of taste.[39]

Appropriate consumption for bourgeois men was deemed to be highly individual and often authenticity-based, a creative, self-producing, order-making activity—one best enacted in collecting. The sites at which collectors consumed provide some insights into the differences between masculine and feminine consumption. In the fantasies of Balzac and others, collectors, rather than shopping in the banal department stores or specialty or custom shops frequented by female consumers, were to, with great ingenuity and intrepidness, hunt down and uncover unexpected, unrecognized treasures at auctions and flea markets and in antique stores.[40] Finding and acquiring the object of one's desire was understood to require different talents in each of these places. Buying at auction required persistence, guile, quickness, and a willingness to take risks.[41] Flea markets were characterized as exotic, dangerous places, in which unexpected treasures, offered by dubious characters, lay amidst heaps of junk and stolen objects. Lastly, buying furniture from antique dealers also required the pitting of wits; the collector by bluff would try to persuade the dealer that an object was worth less than it was. Many of the innovations of the department and specialized stores, innovations that developed simultaneously with the elaboration of bourgeois women's roles as consumers, were absent in collecting; there were no fixed prices, and advice represented as expert was as often a challenge as a help.[42]

In auctions, the hunter did have some information before entering the contest; auctioneers published catalogues detailing, and whetting the appetite for, the goods for sale. But once in the auction room, the collector had to mobilize all his wiles to corner his quarry. In bidding auctions, the auctioneers took a percentage of the total sales, so the challenge was not only to defeat the other bidders but also to force the auctioneer to accept a lower price. Collectors were competing against each other but also against antique dealers trying to acquire goods for their stores. In auctions, unlike other markets, the buyers competed with each other for the right to buy what were often unique objects.

Perhaps paradoxically, just as the taste professionals were critical to the place of consumption in bourgeois women's lives, so they were critical to the elaboration of collection as a masculine activity. Modern collectors depended on authentication of their goods to establish the legitimacy and value of their collections. While the taste professionals and distributors attempted to dictate to female consumers what they should buy, the experts upon whom the collectors relied were employed to confirm that an object was what it was claimed to be. Experts did not get to define either what objects were appropriate material for a collection or what the categories should be. An expert could not say that a collection of Chinese porcelain was inappropriate for a collector occupying a particular social position, he could only state that a vase that claimed to be from seventeenth-century China really was. It was then up to the collector to decide if he wanted it. But collecting functioned in a complicated way in the establishment of social position, for many collectors were extremely unwilling to show others their collections. Collections were often known about but secret, that is, never seen. It is possible, however, that their invisibility and their mystery increased their power, for unseen, the collection could be fantasized about and discussed; its potential was boundless. A new class of male experts worked with a new class of male collectors to reinforce a preoccupation with the authentication, acquisition, organization, and classification of goods. But collections were not understood simply as demonstrating mastery and affording social prestige; collections were works of art and mirrors of the soul.

Collections were understood to be the reflection and the creation of their possessors; they represented the fantasy of immortality. The major function of the objects acquired for collections, as opposed to the function of the collection as a whole, was to take their place in the collection, to contribute to the collection's wholeness. Thus, for example, a chair acquired for a collection of Louis XIII chairs did not serve the usual function of providing seating, blending in harmoniously with the other furnishings of the salon or dining room, or even representing the personality of the purchaser and the status of the family to the outside world. The objects composing a collection did not even have to be beautifully displayed to function well. They had to suit the collection, to fill some gap in the search for completeness and perfection.[43] The use of consumer goods that were not a part of a collection was very different. A Louis XIII chair purchased to be used in a dining room had to match the other chairs and furniture, be judged reasonably comfortable (or acceptably uncomfortable) to sit on, convey the tastes of the mistress of the house, and be an accurate indicator of the wealth and social position of the family.

Assembling a collection was understood to be an individualistic act, more akin to sculpting or painting than to decorating a living room. The Baron J. de Pinchon, in the forward to the sale of the collection of his friend M. de la Béraudière, insisted strongly on the individuality of collections:

> A collection like the one assembled by M. de la Béraudière fits only the person who made it. I often hear regretted the sale of certain collections. I must admit that I rarely share that opinion. A collection made by one man for and by him rarely suits, in its entirety, another man. It is the clothing of the spirit, of a soul which has now died; the collection was made to the measure of that spirit and not to that of another. The dispersion of the collection sends to each the piece which suits him the best.[44]

Clearly something similar could be said about the furnishings acquired gradually across a lifetime by a noncollector: that they suited their owner and no one else. But the individuality of a collection was thought to be different from that of an ordinary interior, however beautiful. Objects in a collection were thought to have been denatured and transformed into something new. Their economic and aesthetic value was thereby also transformed. While the collection represented the individual who possessed it, objects used as part of interior decoration were representative of the family, not of the individual. When the husband died, the wife kept the furniture and vice versa; when both members of the elder generation died, the furniture was divided among the family. It lived on, but as an emblem of the family, of the immortality of the family, not as a means to immortality for the individual creator of the collection. An understanding of the collection as the mirror of the soul was not, of course, incompatible with its preservation after the death of the collector. Although Pinchon argued that his friend's collection should be dispersed, as he was now dead, and that his soul, as embodied in the collection, should be liberated with his body, others who believed equally passionately that the collections *were* their owners, argued equally strongly for keeping collections unified after the death of their creator.

Normative collecting allowed domestic consumption, normally encoded as feminine, to be recoded as masculine and manly. One could be a manly consumer if in consuming one was really hunting (as in Balzac), liberating captive princesses (and putting them in one's own cave), creating an immortal chef d'oeuvre, creating oneself, or competing with other men for the love of women. One could care about beauty if one controlled it, or used it to control others. The qualities of the collector were like the qualities of the active citizen. It was not, as is sometimes claimed, that men were not conceptualized as consumers. Men were to consume to acquire the objects of their desire: wealth, control, knowledge, and mastery.[45] They were, however, to do so responsibly, as heads of households entitled to govern because they had dependents. The definition of responsible masculine consumption was that it contribute to the family's patrimony.

In this period, however, it was not only the family's patrimony that was to be established through collecting but also the state's. From the founding of the Louvre as a national museum under the Directory through the founding of the Decorative Arts Museum in the late nineteenth century, the state became increasingly preoccupied with producing organized, classified displays of the national heritage. The intent was both pedagogic and preservationist. Museums, like schools and the army, became sites outside the home for the making of the nation. It is not surprising, perhaps, that the form of private consumption most closely resembling state consumption should have been the one defined as appropriately masculine. But this appropriateness bore within it the possibilities for transgression; collecting could be appropriated by women, as it was more and more often toward the end of the century. But the fetishization of objects necessary for a successful collector could also carry men away from their social, political, and familial obligations.

The definition of collecting was permeated with paradoxes, paradoxes that mirrored and reproduced those of bourgeois masculinity. Bourgeois men were to simultaneously assure their immortality and their family name through reproduction. Through their sons they were to live into the future. But they were also to acquire immortality through their work, through a business, a book, even a painting with their name. Furthermore, their political voice depended on their possession of dependents. Collections could both reinforce and seriously disrupt this bourgeois relation to time, reproduction, and property: "The true collector is he who seeks to satisfy a complicated need, both cerebral and sensual. He experiences physical joys which are among the most noble which we may ask of our organism. Furthermore, the beautiful objects which surround us distract us from the idea of death, and give to the spirit the idea of eternity, through the past."[46] In this text, the novelist Elisabeth de Gramont characterized the collector as seeking escape from mortality in the past, rather than in the future, and as experiencing a mysterious physical joy (orgasm?) through the acquisition of objects rather than the production of children. The arguably most famous collectors of the nineteenth century, the Goncourt brothers, were also dandies. Neither of them ever married, and Edmond de Goncourt was explicit about the incompatibility of love and collecting:

> For our generation, art collecting is only the index of how women no longer possess the male imagination. I must admit here that when by chance my heart has been given, I have had no interest in the objet d'art. . . . This passion . . . gives immediate gratification from all the objects that tempt, charm, seduce: they provide a momentary abandon in aesthetic debauchery. . . . These are some of the causes that invest an almost human tenderness in objects; they have made me in particular the most passionate of collectors.[47]

Edmond, furthermore, created a bedroom for himself which was "an authentic room of a château, where I become a sleeping beauty from the era of Louis XV."[48] Needless to say, the sleeping beauty he had in mind was not a man; the bed in this supposedly authentic room had been made for the Princesse de Lamballe, a French noblewoman. The boundary between the collector and the dandy was thus highly permeable.

DANDIES AND *FLÂNEURS*, 1820–1914:
"DEVIANT" MASCULINE CONSUMPTION

Dandies appeared in England at the end of the eighteenth century with Beau Brummell and in France during the 1820s. Although they continued to be a presence in French society until the end of the century, they were especially significant in the period before midcentury.[49] All were men for whom living elegantly was essential. They dressed carefully, expensively, and distinctively. They furnished their apartments with like extravagance and attention. They also cultivated their bodies, disciplining their gestures, their gaits, and their stances. Some were heterosexual, some were homosexual. A few married, most did not. Many had to work to support their style; all acted as if they were men of leisure.[50] A very few were dandies for a lifetime, far more were dandies only for a while. Dandies appear to have had a highly complex relation to artistic production. Many novelists of the nineteenth century were dandies, and yet there was a perceived contradiction between producing art and living as art. Literary analysts Patrick Favardin and Laurent Bouëxière argue, for example, that when the Comte d'Orsay and Eugène Sue (among others) turned their attention to serious literary and artistic work, they had to "kill their dandyism."[51]

Dandies were men who engaged in extensive self-adornment with clothing or jewels and created for themselves alone beautiful, expensive, and carefully chosen interiors. In dressing with great care, the dandy embodied the inappropriately narcissistic man, or perhaps more accurately, the model of a man who commodified himself as an object for the consumption of others—

either women or men. In creating an elegant home for himself (and his friends) the dandy disrupted the logic of the home as the sacred site of the production and reproduction of the family. Dandies, in their clothing and interiors, seemed to parody bourgeois feminine roles.

The *flâneur* offered other possibilities for disruptive masculine consumption.[52] *Flâneurs* occupied public space without a tangible purpose, lingered in cafés, promenaded on Baron Haussmann's new avenues, and frequented the fashionable public parks. And, as cultural critic Rachel Bowlby eloquently argues, *flâneurs* were definitively men.[53] *Flâneurs* could not be accompanied by women, nor could they be women; women, like the goods in store windows, were the objects of the *flâneur's* gaze. Women could window-shop but could not shop for men. Men could both window- and women-shop. But I would argue that *flâneurs*, within the bourgeois political economy of nineteenth-century France, were not unproblematic men. *Flâneurs* consumed the streets and the scene with their eyes and feet rather than with money; they did not even come to possess the objects of their attention. The *flâneur*, who by definition occupied public space "unproductively," was considered an embarrassment to his gender and class.[54]

Many historians have argued that the dandies who appeared in England toward the end of the eighteenth century and in France in the early decades of the nineteenth century were reacting against the new bourgeois domination of society. These were men who refused to play their assigned male bourgeois role of living economically productive, or at least artistically creative, lives. Rather, dandies made the aesthetic pursuits of life their job. Dressing appropriately and finding the right furnishings for their homes, the right posture and the right tilt of hand, and the right horses and carriages consumed practically all of their time and money. They have been described as attempting to sustain an aristocratic lifestyle in a bourgeois world.[55] This analysis is only partially right.

Dandies were trying to make their lives their art and their work, but in doing so they more closely paralleled their contemporaries, the moral and social economists whom they no doubt despised, than they did the aristocrats of the Old Regime. On the one hand, Old Regime aristocratic investment in style, in form, and in beauty had to do largely with power and politics. One bought certain things, dressed in certain clothes, and carried oneself in a certain way in relation to the king and the court.[56] There was no integrity to the posture, in the sense that it was entirely instrumentally and externally driven. Dandies, on the other hand, really did turn their bodies and their surroundings into art for art's sake. They made a morality of the aesthetic, of the everyday. The social and moral economists were saying that if the working class would only live appropriately as defined by bourgeois norms—that is, in a house that looked as the commentators thought it should, with the right number of people (no more than two) to a bed—

and eat the correct food with proper table manners all would be well. The dandies took style and beauty as seriously as the taste professionals and social reformers, albeit to different ends. They were not seeking political power or social stability. They were on a quest for social prestige, but social prestige only as part of the art of living, not as a source of increased income or job mobility. Thus, the dandies divorced style from power—political or social—and in that they were very far from the Old Regime.

They also divorced style from reproduction and from anxieties concerning social harmony and the class conflict sparked by the conjuncture of industrialization and repressive postrevolutionary monarchies, and in that they were, indeed, in protest against the bourgeois society in which they lived.[57] Ephemeral beauty for its own sake was a deeply troubling concept in this period. Women indulged in beauty not for the sake of beauty but rather for higher ends—the welfare of their husband and children, the family's social standing. Even collectors were more acceptable than dandies; for while they, like the dandies, in a sense acquired beauty for the sake of beauty, they created order, rationality, and a kind of purpose, however elliptical and complex. They also left a legacy. Although most collections were dispersed upon the death of the collector, they did not have to be, and they were potentially far more durable, far more cumulative, than the beautiful ties, silk hats, and vests of the dandy. Dandies accepted mortality; they lived in the ephemeral, in the transient, in the mortal. Collectors and housewives both fought mortality—collectors by creating a legacy and a sense of control, completion, and totality, housewives by assuring the reproduction of the family. Dandies were not simply rebelling against the strictures of a nascent bourgeois society. It is not an accident that they came into existence at a moment that lay in the interstices between courtly and bourgeois societies, in a society in which style no longer had political meaning but did not yet have an established social meaning.

Dandies were terrifying in their nonreproductivity, their denial of the illusion of immortality, and they were therefore subject to much abuse:[58] "In making himself into a dandy, a man becomes a fixture in a boudoir, an extremely ingenious mechanical doll [*mannequin*] that one can set on a horse or on a sofa, who gracefully nibbles or sucks the head of a cane [*tête . . . le bout*]; but a thinking being . . . never."[59] Balzac argued that in becoming a dandy a man transformed himself into a demasculinized, inanimate thing. Balzac's portrayal was even more insulting in its infantilization; the words he chose, "sucking the head of a cane," more usually used to mean nursing at the breast, typified the derogatory commentary of contemporaries. The accusations derided the dandies' intelligence, utility to society, masculinity, maturity, and sexuality.

Dandies differed from the taste professionals in that they were not particularly interested in influencing, except by example, how others dressed themselves or furnished their houses. They were also certainly not interested in developing a bourgeois aesthetic or inventing an aesthetic for the working class. They put themselves outside and above the social fray. They did, however, set an important nineteenth-century, that is, modern, precedent for masculine involvement in the decorative arts. They also created a link between masculine engagement in matters of decorative beauty and a rejection of bourgeois society and reproductive responsibility. In nineteenth-century discourse they were seen as men who, by turning their lives into art, abdicated their class and their gender and normative heterosexuality. By contrast, when men made art—fine art, not decorative art or industrial art—they remained men, for the creation of fine art was a matter of genius.[60] The fine arts came to be understood as transcending the everyday, the domestic. The great sin of the dandies, therefore, was not their interest in Art, which was a perfectly acceptable interest for a bourgeois man, but their interest in their own adornment and the adornment of their domestic space.

BOURGEOIS HOUSEWIVES, 1848–1914: CONSTITUTING AND REPRESENTING THE NATION

Initially as a result, perhaps, of both contemporaries' perception of increased economic competition as well as the reification of taste as an exportable commodity, from midcentury on bourgeois housewives found the task of representing their nation added to that of representing their family and their class. The first movements toward this notion of constitution and representation of the nation through the goods of everyday life appeared following the Revolution of 1848 and were further fostered under the authoritarian Second Empire established in 1851. Women were to contribute to social peace by buying tasteful French products. Their purchases would both help the luxury trades prosper in the domestic market and, by encouraging the production of tasteful, distinctive products, assure French industries a place in the international market. Finally, under the Third Republic, the obligations of republican mothers came to include not only biological but also social and cultural reproduction; women were to raise patriotic children by surrounding them with Frenchness. Furthermore, the French language and French consumer goods came to be seen as a means of integrating an influx of foreigners into the French nation, as well as a means of unifying the diverse regions of the hexagon itself.

The first hint of consumption for the sake of the nation can be seen in a series of articles published in the woman's magazine *Le Conseiller des dames [et des demoiselles]: Journal d'économie domestique et de travaux d'aiguille*, a monthly published between 1847 and 1854. Its founders intended *Le Conseiller des dames* to be an "intelligent" women's magazine, different from the fashion magazines. Nearly every issue contained household advice; menus;

poetry; historical anecdotes; obituaries; discussions of literature, theater, and fashion; and embroidery and needlepoint designs to copy. It took women and their domestic lives as profoundly serious, making comparisons between domestic economy and the state budget and emphasizing that the magazine was carrying on the tradition of the salons.

The editorial in the April 1848 issue of *Le Conseiller des dames* opened with words of praise for the Revolution and the provisional government and continued with a discussion of women's place in this new regime. As "the voice of women, the newspaper of the home, the echo of the elegant world, the guide to domestic economy," *Le Conseiller des dames*, the editors felt, had no obligation to "occupy [itself] with political affairs." It was not that the editors were indifferent to the transformations of their world: "Like our subscribers, we wish for the progress of civilization, the gentling of mores, the relief of the needy classes, the extinction of resentments and the union of all parties, for these principles are those of the first legislator of the world, our Lord Jesus Christ." But they identified women's interests and concerns as charitable and religious rather than political; women were to seek social peace rather than social justice. It was men who were to worry about politics: "Whether women are the wives of republicans or the wives of royal subjects, their mission remains the same— . . . to preserve France's old reputation of distinction, by their taste and their spirit, to encourage the beautiful in arts and letters, to teach their families love of country and fear of God. . . ." The dominant trope in this editorial is continuity. "France," "love of country," and "the beautiful" were unchanged by revolution or transformation in political regime. The nation, the country, and the tasteful were, for these authors, transcendent and interconnected qualities whose protection from politics was women's task. Consequently, the encouragement of the appreciation of beauty was deemed equivalent to and part of teaching patriotism and Christianity.

In any case, according to the editors, society had changed little since the first excitement of the Revolution. The salons were reopened, and it was people's obligation, in fact, to continue to throw large parties: "The Government itself, in the interests of the laboring population . . . wants parties . . . a precious source of work for all industries. To continue one's habits of yesterday, therefore, is to serve more seriously than one would have thought, to come to the effective aid of national commerce. The elegant woman, who tastefully and intelligently composes her attire, the mistress of a house who organizes a dinner-party properly [according to the rules], is using her fortune nobly."[61] Women were to serve the nation through their employment of others, through their practices of sociability, and through their taste.

The divisions and the connections made in this editorial, between the domestic and political worlds, between the feminine and the masculine, between the religious and the secular, are telling. At one moment the editors implied that the world could turn upside down and backwards but nothing would (or should) change in everyday practice—women were to continue to educate their children, give dinner parties, give to charity, worship God, and patronize beauty; the personal was conceived as very distant from the political. But at other moments in the text, the personal was construed as profoundly political and therefore had to remain unaltered.[62] Elite women were obliged to consume luxuriously because, through that consumption, they provided women workers with labor, they encouraged beauty, they served God, and they brought up the next generation. The editorial was conscious enough of the Republic of Labor brought into existence by the Revolution of 1848 to insist on the contribution consumption made to the welfare of the laboring classes, but it was equally clear that matters of taste and style belonged in the feminized home, away from politics. The implication was that although the state must assure the possibility for the cultivation of good taste in domestic objects, the cultivation of appropriate domestic style, the state need no longer make a style, as it did during the Old Regime. Style and taste were the affair not of the state but of women and of the nation. State-supported style creation turned into state fostering of good taste as matters of everyday aesthetics moved from the state to the nation. Women could not vote, could not participate in politics, but they could, through their taste, participate in the making of the nation.

By the 1850s, then, the task of the housewife was to represent her husband, class, and nation through the acquisition and use of appropriate goods. The idea of fostering national as well as class-based taste in domestic goods was becoming more widespread, both out of fear of economic competition and in the hopes of disseminating Frenchness. The Second Empire saw a new round of discussions concerning the role of the state in the fostering of taste, and numerous schemes for drawing courses, museums, and libraries intended to improve the taste of the consumer were offered to the government. Little institutional change actually occurred during this period, but the notion of the importance of bourgeois women's role in the making of the nation through tasteful consumption was born.

This theme was to continue and gain in importance through the Third Republic.[63] As the staunch republican and arts administrator Edmond Bonnaffé stated in his argument for the importance of learning the history of art: "We will make the Old Masters known and understood, especially our own Old Masters, who brilliantly practiced French art. We can best assimilate the works of these artists, for they were of the same flesh, the same blood and the same land as us."[64] Taste and beauty were at the same time transmitted through the body, through the land, *and* taught. The nation was made, in part at least, of French goods. From the 1880s, however, domestic objects were asked to serve yet another service of production and representation. For the family, the class, and the nation to be produced through things, the self itself had to be adequately represented in domestic goods.

BOURGEOIS HOUSEWIVES, 1880–1914: CONSTITUTING AND REPRESENTING THE SELF

You are too good a French woman to think that you have accomplished your duty in giving a lot of money and a free hand to a decorator.

American women do that cheerfully; it's so convenient! But you are certainly enough behind the times *to prefer your* home *[in English in the text] to the most luxurious furnished dwelling.*

GEORGES DE LANDEMER, *LE CARNET DE FIANÇAILLES*

By the third and fourth decades of the Third Republic, the task of adequately representing family, class, and nation was defined as necessitating the representation of the self. According to etiquette-book writer Georges de Landemer, writing around 1910, a "real" French woman, unlike her American sister, had enough taste and self-confidence to furnish her home herself.[65] The home was now a woman's canvas, and furnishings were her palette. Through the interior she constructed, a woman could (and should) express her individuality, her personality, her taste, and her quality. For example, Mme Hennequin, the etiquette-book writer, explicitly identified the home as one of the few places women had to "express their personalities" without danger of indiscretion.[66] A catalogue from the Trois Quartiers department store had a rather threatening tone:

> The wife's task is to create an agreeable interior. There her personality can express itself in all of the details that make up the home. Her tastes and her character will be so clearly reflected there, that without even knowing her, a visitor with some skills at observation could represent to himself the mistress of the house as she really is, "careful and flirtatious, attentive and artistic," all of these qualities will emerge in the furniture and the things. . . . Of course, all the faults of laziness, of lack of taste, of inattention will also leave their mark.[67]

According to this catalogue, women had the obligation to furnish their homes, but in fulfilling that obligation they could express, and would inevitably reveal, themselves. However, this advertisement threatened that just as a woman's home could reveal her personality, so too could it betray her weaknesses and her deviations from the norm. In the terrorist vision of the advertisers who wrote this ad, dwellings had become reflections less of the family than of the individual woman. Dwellings always bore witness to the innermost qualities of mind and soul.[68]

The taste expert Henri de Noussane, in his guide to decoration published in 1896, emphasized the fact that tastes were necessarily multiple because personalities were unique, and therefore one should not worry about having an interior that differed from that of one's neighbor: "Tastes cannot be made in the same mould any more than intelligences. . . . all tastes are [to be found] in nature. One should cultivate them in such a manner as to cause them to bear abundant fruit, without being put off by startling differences."[69] Other writers and advertisers avoided the democraticizing implications of this pluralist, nonnormative definition of taste by insisting that good taste was born simultaneously of nature and of culture, and a specific culture at that: "Good taste is, simultaneously, an intuition and the result of education. This education is more or less ubiquitous in good society, where women devote themselves to benefiting from the lessons of history."[70] Good taste, like a sense of belonging to the nation, was a product of both nature and nurture. But this last advertisement indicated that the task of representing the class, though supplemented by the newer tasks of expressing the self and the nation, was far from dead. Since, according to this advertisement, everyone in "good society" had the education necessary to decorate tastefully and elegantly, failure to do so would indicate that one lacked innate good taste, that one did not belong to "good society."

Both the advertisers and the taste professionals agreed on the division of the home into public and private spaces, each with different needs and possibilities. In the private space one could express individuality, while in the public space one had to produce a representation of oneself, as well as of one's family: "We will pass little time on the living and dining rooms, because given the very nature of their purpose and their importance from the point of view of representation, I am sure that you will have already devoted all of your attention to them."[71] The theme of individuation of the mother carried over to the other members of the family by the end of the century. Each person was to have his or her own room, decorated in a style appropriate to that person's social location, coloring, age, and personality.[72] This theme of representation of the self did not eradicate the other tasks of representing the family, the class, and the nation. For example, in a book published in 1912, Mme Hennequin argued: "Is not the question of the home one of the multiple aspects of the question of happiness? It is in the home, if one is careful to make it what it ought to be, . . . that family bonds will be tied. The influence of the home is immense, and more far-reaching than one can say. The home can be uplifting, but if it is conflict-ridden then it will be depressing and demoralizing."[73] The expensive store Cerf, in its advertisements, also emphasized the crucial importance of the home. One advertisement stated that, after becoming engaged, the young woman although tired and disoriented "should give care and thought to the important act of furnishing, for the happiness of a life often depends on the comfort of the *home* [in English in the text]. We, having thought of this matter . . ."[74] The implication of this advertisement, that the happiness of the couple depended largely on the wisdom of the young woman in her choice of decor, was a theme found not only in advertisements of this period but throughout the discourse on women's role. Émile Zola, in 1876, for example, had his protagonist in *Son Excellence Eugène Rougon* state that he had acquired a wife as a commodity who would know how to buy other commodities simply in order to assure his class position.[75] Madame de l'Alq, a writer on matters of decoration, trod a thin line between irony and seriousness concerning women's role in the home in an otherwise rather staid decorating/etiquette book published around 1890: "The home . . . occupies such a large place in life . . . that it deserves to always be taken into serious consideration, especially by a woman, for whom it is the prison, or rather the nest, to use a less harsh expression."[76]

The intensity and ambivalence of statements like this in the 1880s and 1890s about the relationship between women and the home were perhaps a response to the threat posed by the notions that women could achieve individuation through their homes and that women were, in any case, inevitably going to express their *own* personalities. Married bourgeois women in the Third Republic were instructed not only to find the home an adequate site for the expression of their personalities and creativity but to consider having that personality and creativity as part of the job. It had become essential that each bourgeois home look different from every other, but not too different. Women, even respectable married women, could, and were even obliged to, express their individuality through their consumption practices. This notion represented a considerable shift from the attitudes of the early and middle years of the century and was commonsensical enough to be part of the advertising language. Why this change should have occurred—how it was that bourgeois women's individuation came to be a reality, and a reality to be expressed through domestic commodities—and the implications of that change are questions that cannot be fully addressed here, but some speculation is possible.

I suspect that the change came about as a result of the increased focus on the domestic market for consumer goods and the need, therefore, to increase demand. As long as consumers were simply representing their husbands and their class, there was little need for frequent renewal of goods, and as long as there were etiquette books to tell one exactly what to buy, there was little anxiety. After midcentury, the multiplication of advice, increased competition among producers and distributors, and more sophisticated advertising—as well as the idea that one was revealing one's soul in one's things—made consumers more likely to replace their purchases more often. In a very different domain, the nineteenth century also saw the elaboration of the ideology of individualism and the critique (especially in Britain and the United States) of the exclusion of women from full individuality.

Women seem to have acted on the taste professionals' and advertisers' instructions to "be themselves." Married women's construction of aesthetic palettes through commodities became less limited to their homes than it once had been. Historian Whitney Walton has found that proportions of expenditures on clothing and jewelry compared with expenditures on linen and silver in the period from 1869 to 1870 were markedly higher than the same proportions from 1828 to 1830. This shift could be read to indicate that bourgeois wives were becoming increasingly concerned with their personal appearance and less concerned with their family's image.[77] By the 1890s, bourgeois women's preoccupation with self-validation had spread from diversion of the family's money from furnishings to clothing to demands for education and suffrage.[78] As historian Debora Silverman has argued, efforts to elevate the status of women within the home and to persuade them of the importance of the domestic activities and potential of those domestic activities for their self-realization may have been a response to the threat posed by the "New Woman."[79] By the early years of the twentieth century that threat was becoming more and more real. The number of women who did not marry or who divorced increased.[80] Consumption by divorced and single women at the turn of the twentieth century made clear the complexity of consumption's gendering, for in many ways these women resembled collectors and dandies more than they did their married sisters.

SINGLE WOMEN'S INTERIORS AND COLLECTIONS, 1890–1945: OVERLAPPING GENDERS

—*I'm having all of the divan cushions re-covered, you know. And then I'm pushing the divan itself right into the corner, and I'm going to have an electric lamp fixed above it.*

—*Splendid! It'll look just like a brothel, says Brague gravely.*

—*Silly ass! And besides that, oh well, I've heaps of things to do. It's such ages since I paid any attention to my home.*

—*It certainly is! agrees Brague drily. And who are you doing all this for?*

—*What d'you mean, who for? For myself, of course!*

COLETTE, *LA VAGABONDE*

In 1911, Colette had her protagonist in *La Vagabonde* express many of the complications of being an independent woman in the early twentieth century. Her protagonist enthusiastically describes creating an interior for herself that broke with bourgeois conventions, only to be faced with a double put-down, accused of not being woman enough to be interested in interior decoration and of having the taste of a prostitute. Such a room could only be for a prostitute because a woman could not create an interior only for herself.[81] The motif of the independent/divorced artist/writer who created her own home, a home that reflected the liminality of her independence, was repeated in the memoirs (published in 1967 but describing here events of the teens) of the writer Camille Marbo:

These women opened their apartments . . . which usually had only two rooms, to their friends. For example, Mme Mantelin, the divorced wife of the musician Groviez, rue du Bac, welcomed her guests in a mauve tunic, her gray hair worn "à la garçonne" above an androgynous body. In each of the rooms, there was a large divan covered with black, yellow, and blue cushions. The furniture consisted of a Norman wardrobe, a round table, and straw chairs, and a piano reserved for the composer Florent Schmitt.[82]

The women writers Camille Marbo described lived modestly, dressed androgynously, and were surrounded by furniture whose color scheme, style, and quantity would have been deemed singularly inappropriate for their bourgeois households of origin. Indeed, Marbo used the description to mark the distance between these women and other women of their class. The only comfortable seating consisted of two large sofas strewn with pillows in a combination of colors associated with prostitutes in the etiquette books of the period. The straw chairs and Norman wardrobe were also out of place in a Parisian apartment—those were country, not city, furnishings. Lastly, the piano, the fixture of every bourgeois salon, here waited for a visiting composer rather than a cultured daughter of the bourgeoisie. Even if this description was entirely a figment of the memoirist's imagination, it is significant that the representation of autonomous women should include a radically different decor. According to Marbo's image, these women bought what they wanted to create interiors that suited them. They were not chosen to represent a husband or to assure a social place within the bourgeoisie. By the early years of the twentieth century, divorced women were expressing their right to have a home even though they were alone.

Furthermore, independent women not only furnished their homes for themselves and chose to play on styles associated with prostitution but also took up collecting in more significant numbers. A 1946 description by the actress Cécile Sorel demonstrates the distance decorating advice had traveled since Mme Pariset advised women in the 1820s:

> Our furnishings are our friends. Works of art are extensions of ourselves. Near them, I ennobled my personality.
> . . . the perfect art of the Regency inspired in me an obsessive passion. I loved this style. . . . How many times have I gotten up during the night, to see, to touch, a unique piece of furniture which I had just purchased? As I looked at it, my eyes filled with voluptuousness. I knelt before its perfect forms to caress it with devotion.
> . . . I went into my bedroom. There, on a platform, reigned the bed of the "Dubarry" [the mistress of Louis XV], in gilded wood, crowned with roses, with its four columns topped with incense burners. I slid into bed, as the favorite once had, finally liberated from her court dress, waiting for her royal lover. The room breathed, beat, like a heart. Was it not Louis XV who wandered

amidst the scented smoke? And I pursued this vision which evaporated slowly in the dreams of the night.[83]

Like the Goncourts, discussed above, Sorel was nostalgic for an earlier, courtly world. She, however, dreamed of a world where fine artisans made beautiful objects for lovely women, a world in which she could have had a royal lover. In the last paragraph, Sorel is transformed into Mme du Barry waiting for Louis XV to come into her bed. Yet, this is the bed that she, Cécile Sorel, has bought, and it is she who, at night, rather than passively waiting to be caressed, actively caresses the furniture she has acquired. She uses her power to acquire these goods to allow herself fantasies of both dominance and submission. Sorel is "unwomanly" in acquiring and enjoying objects for herself, "unwomanly" in her fetishistic and active relation to her furniture, but "womanly" in imagining herself as a woman waiting for a male lover.

Colette, Marbo's writers, and Cécile Sorel were perhaps exceptional in their autonomy and in their choice of careers. But their behavior as consumers, and as writers who used the tropes of consumerism, was also the logical outcome of the final addition to the panoply of obligations a bourgeois woman incurred as a consumer—that of expressing herself. By the interwar years and especially after World War II, when France moved into a society of mass consumption in which women had the vote, the gendering and meaning of consumer practices in the making of the nation and the state would change again. But that is another story.

REPRESENTATION: NATION, STATE, AND THE EVERYDAY

In conclusion I would like to suggest that to adequately explain the gendering of consumer practices in the nineteenth century one ultimately must locate that process within the dynamics of the making of nation and state and of capitalist expansion in the postrevolutionary era. I would argue further that it is the simultaneous interdependence and parallelism of the political and the social that explains the complexity of debate on the practices of everyday life, including the acquisition, use, and disposal of goods—that is, consumption—throughout the nineteenth century. Thus, deciphering consumption's logic provides a key to understanding the changing forms of representation and the new definitions of the individual and the citizen.[84]

Nineteenth-century France inherited from the Revolution a productive chaos concerning the fundamental concept of "representation." With the destruction of absolute monarchy came the end of a system of political and social representation and economic organization in which the nation and the state were embodied by the king and the ruler and the state were represented by the king's things.[85] Determining what it meant to be represented politically and socially was a dominant problem of the century, dominant because the determination was essential to definitions of citizenship, state, and nation.

The state came to be understood as a constructed object (man-made, quite literally), while the nation was equated with the natural, feminized, domestic world.[86] Men were members of the state—citizens representing themselves, their families, and other men politically. The definition of the French state was, therefore, relatively clear because the boundary between inclusion and exclusion was legally explicit.

The definition of the French nation was much more problematic, however, because marking its outer (generally physical) boundaries was but the first step in specifying its crucial essence. Those included must exhibit "Frenchness," and it was perceived that many people living within the hexagon still needed to be made French. For the state to function, some degree of consensus on the appropriate organization of political process was needed; for the nation to function, some degree of consensus on the appropriate organization of the everyday was needed. This division of labor was part of, perhaps a precondition for, the hyphen in "nation-state." The hyphen was not there accidentally; contemporaries thought that for the state to be secure, for the votes of its male citizens to be properly cast, nation was also necessary. Women were to be members of the nation—"nationals" representing their families (and sometimes themselves) socially.

The gendering of consumption served, reflected, and reproduced this dynamic. Legitimate feminine consumption was initially defined as consumption that produced the constitutive elements of the nation: family, class, and Frenchness itself. Legitimate masculine consumption was initially defined as consumption that produced the constitutive elements of the state: autonomous, responsible, reasoning heads of family. But the story of the building of nation and state cannot fully explain the gendering of consumption, for consumption was embedded not only within a political narrative but also within a growing and changing capitalist economy.

Consumption's simultaneous location in the economic, political, and social worlds necessarily produced historically specific contradictions and paradoxes—within as well as between each of these domains. In the world of the economy, the ideal was sometimes maximum consumer expenditure, which would stimulate production, and sometimes limited consumer spending, which would liberate capital for investment or taxation. In the political world, both universalized Frenchness and strong class differentiation among the French through goods were perceived as necessary to the stability of the state.[87] In the social world, women's and men's different forms of simultaneous economic and political dependence and independence produced conflicting goals for, and patterns of, consumption. Bourgeois women were to consume appropriately for their family, class, and nation, and yet, by the end of the century, they were expected to do so through the expression of their individuality. Bourgeois men were supposed to marry, to have children; they were to acquire immortality through their name and their lineage. Yet that was not enough; they were also expected to be innovative and creative, to achieve immortality through the work they did. They were to represent their families in the outside world and yet inhabit a domestic space that they paid for but did not directly manage. These tensions, contradictions, and paradoxes were produced by efforts to negotiate the complex relations of state, nation, and capitalism in the postrevolutionary period.

Conflicts also arose between social, political, and economic worlds. The fetishization of goods was both necessary and dangerous for the family and for the nation. Bourgeois women were supposed to desire objects; department stores were explicitly designed to create desire, yet women were not to desire too much. The labeling of women who stole as mad (victims of the new disease of kleptomania), as overcome by the excesses of desire, illustrates how terrified contemporaries were of women's desire.[88] Likewise, when men appeared to be overcome by desire in their acts of consumption, when they appeared to detach consumption from the reproduction and representation of the family and the nation, they were perceived as dangerous and attacked as unmanly. Consumption, while necessary to the economic health of the country, was understood as potentially profoundly disruptive of the libidinal economy, capable of deregulating and destabilizing the family and the society.

Consumption was perceived as capable of producing unfettered individualism incompatible with the survival of the state, which was composed of individuals whose independence rested on the dependence of others, and of the nation, the stability of which depended on the localization of individuals in families and classes. And yet, postrevolutionary French society was also based on the rights of the individual and egalitarianism. The end of the corporate order, the end of the society of estates, and the development of political economy enabled (and perhaps necessitated) the concept of the sovereign, ungendered, autonomous, universal subject. There was, in other words, tension between the concept of a society and polity composed of individuals and the concept of a society and polity composed of dominant and dependent members of households. These tensions were expressed and transformed through changing articulations of the roles of nation and the state. The state needed the nation as much as the nation needed the state, and the nation was made as much within the spheres deemed private and social as within the public and political spheres of the state itself.[89]

I would like to suggest that bourgeois housewives occupied a pivotal position at the intersection of state and nation, of public and private. As consumers they gave substance to the nation; as intimate yet excluded citizens they shaped the meaning and value of the state. The complexity of their roles and the paradoxes within the interstices of state and nation can be understood, however, only when contrasted with two contemporaneous categories of consumer—collectors and dandies. Housewives were to represent their families through their homemaking practices. Collectors were to represent themselves, create a new object, and leave a legacy. Dandies defied both masculine and feminine models of consumption, thereby moving into a marginal location in the gender, political, and social orders. By the late nineteenth century, however, the tensions between consumption in the polity and consumption in the economy became more acute. Capitalism encouraged women's individuation through goods; the state needed women to subordinate those needs to the needs of the nation. But the claim to individual rights was also part of the political heritage. One may, perhaps, argue that the political and economic legacies of liberalism were united in the person of the "New Woman."

NOTES

Some of the research for this project was funded by the Social Science Research Council and by Tocqueville, Chateaubriand, and Fulbright fellowships.

1. On bourgeois women's sphere in France see Bonnie Smith, *Ladies of the Leisure Class: The Bourgeoises of Northern France in the Nineteenth Century* (Princeton: Princeton University Press, 1981); James Macmillan, *Housewife or Harlot: The Place of Women in French Society* (New York: St. Martin's, 1981); Anne Martin-Fugier, *La Bourgeoise* (Paris: Grasset, 1983); Michelle Perrot, ed., *De la Révolution à la grande guerre*, vol. 4 of *Histoire de la vie privée*, ed. Philippe Ariès and Georges Duby (Paris: Seuil, 1987); Anne Martin-Fugier, *La Vie élégante: Ou la formation du Tout-Paris, 1815–1848* (Paris: Fayard, 1990), especially chaps. 3, 4; Adeline Daumard, *Les Bourgeois de Paris au XIXe siècle* (Paris: Flamarion, 1970); and Louise A. Tilly and Joan Wallach Scott, *Women, Work, and Family* (New York: Methuen, 1987). On the critical importance of domesticity in the making of the bourgeois family and class elsewhere in Europe see Leonore Davidoff and Catherine Hall, *Family Fortunes: Men and Women of the English Middle Class, 1780–1850* (Chicago: University of Chicago Press, 1987); and Marion Kaplan, *The Making of the Jewish Middle Class: Women, Family, and Identity in Imperial Germany* (Oxford: Oxford University Press, 1991).

2. Rosalind H. Williams's *Dream Worlds: Mass Consumption in Late-Nineteenth-Century France* (Berkeley: University of California Press, 1982) is a path-breaking study on consumerism. Whitney Walton's *France at the Crystal Palace: Bourgeois Taste and Artisan Manufacture in the Nineteenth Century* (Berkeley: University of California Press, 1992) is an insightful study of the importance of bourgeois women's consumer demands in the dynamic of the French economy. The classic essay on Germany is Karin Hausen, "Family and Role-Division: The Polarization of Sexual Stereotypes in the Nineteenth Century—An Aspect of the Dissociation of Work and Family Life," in *The German Family*, ed. Richard Evans and W. R. Lee (New York: Barnes and Noble, 1981). See also Sibylle Meyer, "The Tiresome Work of Conspicuous Leisure: On the Domestic Duties of the Wives of Civil Servants in the German Empire," in *Connecting Spheres: Women in the Western World, 1500 to the Present*, ed. Marilyn Boxer and Jean H. Quataert

(New York: Oxford University Press, 1987), 156–66; Sandra Coyner, "Class Consciousness and Consumption: The New Middle Class during the Weimar Republic," *Journal of Social History* 10 (1977): 310–31.

3. Michel De Certeau makes the argument that consumption is a form of production. Michel De Certeau, *The Practice of Everyday Life*, trans. Steven F. Rendall (Berkeley: University of California Press, 1984). While Jean Baudrillard's argument in *The Mirror of Production* (St. Louis, Mo.: Telos Press, 1975) is very different, I have found it useful in conceptualizing the relations of production and consumption.

4. It is striking that when consumption became the basis for organized political action in the nineteenth century, it became as much a masculine domain as a feminine one. Ellen Furlough, *Consumer Cooperation in France: The Politics of Consumption, 1834–1930* (Ithaca: Cornell University Press, 1991).

5. See Emily Apter's analysis of fin-de-siècle "cabinet fiction," in which the dandy and the collector merge. Emily Apter, "Cabinet Secrets: Peep Shows, Prostitution, and Bric-a-bracomania in the Fin-de-Siècle Interior," chap. 3 in her *Feminizing the Fetish: Psychoanalysis and Narrative Obsession in Turn-of-the-Century France* (Ithaca: Cornell University Press, 1991), 39–64.

6. Some have argued that consumer society emerged much earlier in Holland and England. See for example Simon Schama, *The Embarrassment of Riches: An Interpretation of Dutch Culture in the Golden Age* (Berkeley: University of California Press, 1983); Margaret Spufford, *The Great Reclothing of Rural England: Petty Chapmen and Their Wares in the Seventeenth Century* (London: Hambledon Press, 1984); Joan Thirsk, *Economic Policy and Projects: The Development of a Consumer Society in Early Modern England* (Oxford: Clarendon Press, 1978); Lorna Weatherill, *Consumer Behavior and Material Culture in Britain, 1660–1760* (New York: Routledge, 1988); Carole Shammas in, *The Pre-industrial Consumer in England and America* (Oxford: Clarendon Press, 1990).

7. Central to my analysis here are Jean Baudrillard, *La Société de consommation: Ses mythes, ses structures* (Paris: Denoël, 1970); and Thomas Richards, *The Commodity Culture of Victorian England: Advertising and Spectacle, 1851–1914* (Stanford: Stanford University Press, 1990).

8. Examples of expressions of those anxieties may be found in *Exposition universelle (de 1855): Galerie de l'économie domestique* (Paris: J. Claye, 1855), 44; *Exposition universelle de 1855: Rapports du jury mixte internationale* (Paris: Imprimerie Impériale, publiés sous la direction de Son Altesse Imperiale le prince Napoléon, 1856), 1402–3; M. A. Cochin, "Classe 91: Meubles, vêtements, et aliments de toute origine, distingués par les qualités utiles, unies au bon marché," in *Exposition universelle de 1867 à Paris: Rapports du jury international*, edited by Michel Chevalier (Paris: Imprimerie administrative de Paul Dupont, 1868), 13:775–77; Alfred Picard, *Exposition universelle internationale de 1889 à Paris: Rapports du jury international* (Paris: Imprimerie Nationale, 1891), 3:6–7. For a fuller discussion of these texts see my "After the Revolution: Recycling Ancien Régime Style in the Nineteenth Century," in *Re-creating Authority in Revolutionary France*, ed. Bryant T. Ragan and Elizabeth Williams (New Brunswick, N.J.: Rutgers University Press, 1992), pp. 144–74.

9. The slowness of the extension of consumerism to the working class was largely a matter of their limited disposable income. A study in 1907 demonstrated that families headed by unskilled or service workers spent more than 80 percent of their yearly income on food and rent. Artisans in the same period spent about 65 percent of their

income on perishable necessities. Cited in Lenard Berlanstein, *The Working People of Paris, 1871–1914* (Baltimore: Johns Hopkins University Press, 1984), 46. Another study from 1907 gave an even bleaker image of the disposable income of a Parisian *menuisier-ébéniste*'s (cabinetmaker's) family: they were in debt at the end of the year without buying any durables at all. Gaston Cadoux, "Contribution à l'étude des salaires réels et du coût de la vie des ouvriers des grandes villes," *JSSP*, no. 12 (December 1907): 414. Finally, see also Maurice Halbwachs, "Revenus et dépenses de ménages des travailleurs: Une enquête officielle d'avant-guerre," *Revue d'économie politique* 14 (1931): 55–57.

10. Marguerite Perrot, *La Mode de vie des familles bourgeoises, 1873–1953* (Paris: Presses de la Fondation Nationale des Sciences Politiques, 1961). Adeline Daumard confirms the importance of goods to the constitution of the nineteenth-century French bourgeoisie. Adeline Daumard, *Les Bourgeois et la bourgeoisie en France depuis 1815* (Paris: Aubier, 1987), esp. 32, 214.

11. This is not to say, of course, that people in Old Regime France did not own or care about things. Annik Pardailhé-Galabrun, *La Naissance de l'intime: 3,000 foyers Parisiens XVIIᵉ-XVIIIᵉ siècles* (Paris: Presses Universitaires de France, 1988); and Daniel Roche, *Le Peuple de Paris* (Paris: Montalban, 1986), provide extensive documentation of ownership in prerevolutionary Paris. I am arguing, however, that both the people's and the state's relation to objects changed in a fundamental way with the Revolution. For a fuller discussion of this point see part 1 of my *Taste and Power: Furnishing Modern France* (Berkeley: University of California Press, forthcoming).

12. Different parts of this story may be found in Walton, *France at the Crystal Palace;* Patricia Mainardi, *Art and Politics of the Second Empire: The Universal Expositions of 1855 and 1867* (New Haven and London: Yale University Press, 1987); idem, *The End of the Salon: Art and the State in the Early Third Republic* (Cambridge: Cambridge University Press, 1993); Debora L. Silverman, *Art Nouveau in Fin-de-Siècle France: Politics, Psychology, and Style* (Berkeley: University of California Press, 1989); and my *Taste and Power.*

13. I have used 1914 as my closure date for the nineteenth century throughout. I do not mean to imply that the phenomena being described ceased after 1914; I am simply using the date to mark the end of the study. The opening dates are more telling than the closing dates.

14. Tilly and Scott, *Women, Work, and Family,* 77, 149–51; Smith, *Ladies of the Leisure Class,* passim.

15. *Le Petit Robert,* 1987 ed., 933, s.v. "home".

16. Martin-Fugier, *La Bourgeoise,* esp. pp. 10–14.

17. I have developed some arguments presented rather sketchily here in greater detail and with different emphases in my "After the Revolution," 144–74.

18. See especially the contributions to Perrot, ed., *De la Révolution à la grande guerre,* vol. 4 of *Histoire de la vie privée;* Davidoff and Hall, *Family Fortunes;* Walton, *France at the Crystal Palace;* Geneviève Fraisse, "L'Éducation ménagère et le métier de femme au début du XIXᵉ siècle," *Pénélope,* no. 2 (1980), special issue entitled Éducation des filles. Enseignement des femmes; Leonore Davidoff, *The Best Circles: Women and Society in Victorian England* (Totowa, N.J.: Rowman and Littlefield, 1973).

19. Mme Pariset, *Manuel de la maîtresse de maison, ou Lettres sur l'économie domestique,* 3d ed. (Paris: Gudot, 1825), 8–9.

20. Ibid., 22.

21. Whitney Walton has made a similar argument in *France at the Crystal Palace*, 28, 47–48.

22. Michael B. Miller, *The Bon Marché: Bourgeois Culture and the Department Store, 1869–1920* (Princeton: Princeton University Press, 1981); Philip Nord, *The Shopkeepers of Paris* (Princeton: Princeton University Press, 1986).

23. I am following the discussion of Evelyne Sullerot, *La Presse féminine* (Paris: Armand Colin, 1966).

24. Pariset, *Manuel de la maîtresse*, 33–34.

25. Ibid., 52.

26. Ibid., 197–98.

27. Honore de Balzac, *Le Cousin Pons* (Paris: Gallimard, 1973), 75. Susan Stewart's work on the self and the collection is fascinating, although she does not analyze the gendering of the processes. Susan Stewart, *On Longing: Narratives of the Miniature, the Gigantic, the Souvenir, the Collection* (Baltimore: Johns Hopkins University Press, 1984), esp. 158–59.

28. For other, similar descriptions of collectors, see Leo Larguier, *Au vieux saint de bois* (Avignon: Aubanel, 1944), 18, 20, 55.

29. Historian Steven Gelber has argued that women and men in nineteenth-century America had different collecting practices. He argues that men tended to organize their collections "scientifically"—in recognized classificatory categories—while women tended to organize theirs aesthetically. Steven M. Gelber, "Free Market Metaphor: The Historical Dynamics of Stamp Collecting," *CSSH* 34, no. 4 (October 1992): 748. Walter Benjamin also emphasizes the order-making aspect of collecting. Walter Benjamin, "Unpacking My Library," in *Illuminations: Essays and Reflections*, ed. Hannah Arendt, trans. Harry Zohn (1988; reprint, New York: Schocken, 1969), 60. Gelber argued further that as goods entered the commodity state—as they acquired value on the market—they came to be collected by men rather than women. Historian Paula Findlen has argued that from as early as the late sixteenth century men used collections to masculinize domestic space. Paula Findlen, "The Museum: Its Classical Etymology and Renaissance Genealogy," *Journal of the History of Collections* 1, no. 1 (1989): 59–78, esp. 69–71. Steven Mullaney's analysis of the contemporaneous German *Wunderkammern*, or "chamber of wonders," provides an interesting contrast to those of Gelber and Benjamin. Mullaney argues that the point of these collections was their lack of order. Steven Mullaney, "Strange Things, Gross Terms, Curious Customs: The Rehearsal of Cultures in the Late Renaissance," *Representations* 3 (summer 1983): 40–67.

30. This, in some sense, continues the eighteenth-century pattern of scientific voyages organized to "collect" the world. That is, samples were brought back to be classified and displayed, and they, thereby, produced mastery and order. This interpretation may be found in Daniel Defert, "The Collection of the World: Accounts of Voyages from the Sixteenth to the Eighteenth Centuries," *Dialectical Anthropology* 7, no. 1 (September 1982): 11–20. James Clifford's work supports and extends these conclusions. See his "On Collecting Art and Culture," in his *The Predicament of Culture: Twentieth-Century Ethnography, Literature, and Art* (Cambridge: Harvard University Press, 1988).

31. Gerald Reitlinger argues that even in the 1860s, the value of antiques had not yet been firmly established. Gerald Reitlinger, *The Economics of Taste: The Rise and Fall*

of Objets d'Art Prices since 1750 (London: Barrie and Rockliffe, 1963), 2:13. Paul Eudel insisted that it was Victor Hugo who convinced the French that antiques had value. Paul Eudel, *Le Truquage: Altérations, fraudes, et contrefaçons dévoilées* (Paris: Librairie Molière, [late 19th century]), 296–97.

32. See Oliver Impey and Arthur MacGregor, eds., *The Origins of Museums: The Cabinet of Curiosities in Sixteenth- and Seventeenth-Century Europe* (Oxford: Clarendon Press, 1986).

33. Krzysztof Pomian, *Collectionneurs, amateurs, et curieux* (Paris: Gallimard, 1987), 50.

34. Reitlinger, *The Economics of Taste,* 2:20; and August Luchet, *L'Art industriel à l'exposition universelle de 1867: Mobilier, vêtements, aliments* (Paris: Librairie internationale, 1867), 94.

35. See especially, Pomian, "Marchands, connaisseurs, curieux à Paris au XVIIIᵉ siècle," in his *Collectionneurs, amateurs, et curieux* (Paris: Gallimard, 1987).

36. Pomian, *Collectionneurs, amateurs, et curieux,* 185.

37. Ibid., 51–52.

38. Janine Capronnier, *Le Prix des meubles d'epoque 1860–1956* (Paris: Armand Colin, 1961), 15; Maurice Rheims, *The Strange Life of Objects: Thirty-Five Centuries of Collecting and Collectors* (New York: Atheneum, 1961), 23.

39. Rheims, *The Strange Life of Objects,* 25.

40. André Warnod, *La Brocante et les petits marchés de Paris* (Paris: E. Figuiere, 1914); Larguier, *Au vieux saint de bois.*

41. The best discussion of the auction dynamic is Charles W. Smith, *Auctions: The Social Construction of Value* (New York: Free Press, 1989). There were three major auction houses in Paris—Drouot, Petit, and Charpentier—which sold a wide range of goods, either in complete lots or as individual items.

42. For a detailed discussion of transformations in the organization of distribution see Miller, *The Bon Marché;* Williams, *Dream Worlds;* and my *Style, Taste, and Power.*

43. See for example the room of "the collector" in Eugène Atget's photographs. The rooms of the collector were filled with series. A row of almost identical pitchers sat on a mantelpiece. A glass case was filled with butterflies and other exotic species in boxes. Eugène Atget, *Intérieurs Parisiens, début du XXᵉ siècle: Artistiques, pittoresques, et bourgeois* (Paris: Chez l'auteur, 1910).

44. Introduction by Baron J. de Pinchon to the sale of the possessions of M. le comte de la Béraudière, vente en son hôtel, 12, rue de Poitiers, 18–30 mai 1885. *Catalogue . . . riche mobilier XVIIIᵉ siècle,* Bibliothèque Forney, Paris.

45. Although not specifically concerned with consumer practices, the following sources are useful works on masculinity: Colette Guillaumin, "The Masculine: Denotations and Connotations," *Feminist Issues* 5, no. 1 (1985): 65–73; C. Church, "Victorian Masculinity and the Angel in the House," in *A Widening Sphere: Changing Roles of Victorian Women,* ed. Martha Vicinus (Chicago: University of Chicago Press, 1982); Paul Willis, "Shop-Floor Culture, Masculinity, and the Wage Form," in *Working-Class Culture: Studies in History and Theory,* ed. John Clarke, Chas Critcher, and Richard Johnson (London: Hutchinson, 1979); Ava Baron, ed., *Engendering Labor* (Ithaca, N.Y.: Cornell University Press, 1992); Michael Roper and John Tosh, eds., *Manful Assertions: Masculinities in Britain since 1800* (London: Routledge, 1991).

46. Elisabeth de Gramont, *Mémoires: Les Marronniers en fleurs,* 25th ed. (Paris: Grasset, 1929), 185.

47. Edmond de Goncourt, *La Maison d'un artiste* (Paris: Charpentier, 1881; new ed., Paris: Charpentier, 1904) 1:2–3, quoted in Silverman, *Art Nouveau in Fin-de-Siècle France,* 36.

48. Goncourt, *La Maison d'un artiste,* 2:200, quoted in Silverman, *Art Nouveau in Fin-de-Siècle France,* 36.

49. This discussion has emerged from readings of Jules Barbey d'Aurevilly, *Du dandysme et de George Brummell,* edition presented and annotated by Marie-Christine Natta (1845; Paris: Plein Chant, 1989); Marylène Delbourg-Delphis, *Masculin singulier: Le Dandysme et son histoire* (Paris: Hachette, 1985); Patrick Favardin and Laurent Bouëxière, *Le Dandysme* (Paris: La Manufacture, 1988); Anne Martin-Fugier, *La Vie élégante;* Arnould de Liedekerke, *Talon Rouge: Barbey d'Aurevilly, le dandy absolu* (Paris: Oliver Orban, 1986); Ellen Moers, *The Dandy: Brummell to Beerbohm* (Lincoln: University of Nebraska Press, 1978); Thomas Spence Smith, "Aestheticism and Social Structure: Style and Social Network in the Dandy Life," *American Sociological Review* 39 (1974): 725–43; Williams, *Dream Worlds;* Robert Kempf, *Dandies: Baudelaire et Cie.* (Paris: Seuil, 1984); Michel Lemaire, *Le Dandysme de Baudelaire à Mallarmé* (Montreal: University of Montreal Press, 1978); and Sima Godfrey, "The Dandy as Ironic Figure," *SubStance,* no. 36 (1982): 21–33.

50. It was very expensive to maintain a dandy lifestyle. *L'Entracte* of 10 January 1839 estimated the annual budget of a dandy at 94,500 francs. Cited in Martin-Fugier, *La Vie élégante,* 355.

51. Favardin and Bouëxière, *Le Dandysme,* 70–71.

52. Still the most eloquent on *flâneurs* are Walter Benjamin and Charles Baudelaire. See Benjamin, *Illuminations.*

53. Rachel Bowlby, *Still Crazy after All These Years* (London: Routledge, 1993), 9 and passim.

54. Jerrold Seigel, *Bohemian Paris: Culture, Politics, and the Boundaries of Bourgeois Life, 1830–1930* (New York: Viking, 1986); Eugen Weber, *France, Fin-de-Siècle* (Cambridge, Mass.: Belknap, 1986).

55. Williams, *Dream Worlds;* Martin-Fugier, *La Vie élégante.*

56. I am, to some extent, following the argument of Martin-Fugier, *La Vie élégante,* 355. However, Martin-Fugier mentions aristocrats' *obligation* to consume but emphasizes the fact that aristocratic consumption was *authorized* by rank and position, whereas dandy consumption was not.

57. For a discussion of the relation between bohemia and the bourgeoisie see Michael Wilson, "'Sans les femmes, qu'est-ce qui nous resterait?': Gender and Transgression in Bohemian Montmartre," in *Body Guards,* ed. Julia Epstein and Kristina Straub (London: Routledge, 1991), 195–222.

58. Stendhal, *De l'amour;* Eugène Ronteix, *Manuel du fashionable;* and Jules Janin, *Journal des débats,* all cited in Martin-Fugier, *La Vie élégante.*

59. Honoré de Balzac, *Traité de la vie élégante,* cited in Anne Martin-Fugier, *La Vie élégante,* 351.

60. This point is elegantly elucidated by Naomi Schor in her *Reading in Detail: Aesthetics and the Feminine* (New York: Methuen, 1987).

61. Z. Bourkey, *Conseiller des dames [et des demoiselles]: Journal d'économie domestique et de travaux d'aiguille* (April 1848), 161–62.

62. The story is a bit more complicated than it appears. Tucked into the middle of the article cited, and while saying that, given the separation of women and politics, the *Conseiller des Dames* does not need to change its format, the editors go on to say that they will use the freedom from censorship to discuss "special questions within its competence, like the increase in work and of wages of women workers; the protection for nurseries and orphanages to be demanded from the government, changes in the rules of admission for women teachers . . ." (ibid., 161). But this explicit discussion is muffled underneath the business-as-usual stance.

63. On this issue see Marie-Claude Genet-Delacroix, "Esthétique officielle et art national sous la Troisième République," *Le Mouvement social* 131 (April-June 1985): 105–120; Silverman, *Art Nouveau in Fin-de-Siècle France*, pt. 3.

64. Edmond Bonnaffé, *Etudes sur l'art et la curiosité* (Paris: Société Française d'éditions d'art, 1902), 227.

65. Georges de Landemer, *Le carnet de fiançailles* (Paris: Fédérlé, c. 1910), no pagination.

66. Mme Hennequin, *L'Art et le goût au foyer* (Paris: Armand Colin, 1912), 10.

67. Trois Quartiers furnishings catalogue, n.d., Archives de la Seine D 12 Z1, Paris.

68. An additional example of this kind of discourse may be found in *La Femme chez elle et dans le monde par madame Marie de Saverny* (Paris: Au bureaux de journal la revue de la mode, 1876), 41–42.

69. Henri de Noussanne, *Le Goût dans l'ameublement* (Paris: Firmin-Didot, 1896), 245–46.

70. Trois Quartiers furnishings catalogue, n.d.

71. Mme la comtesse Drohojowska, *Conseils à une jeune fille sur les devoirs à remplir dans le monde comme maîtresse de maison à Paris,* 4th ed. (Paris: Perisse Frères, [1870s]), 206. Work approved by Monseigneur the bishop of Rodez.

72. For a fuller explication of this argument, see my "After the Revolution," 144–74. Whitney Walton also documents the fine divisions of space within the household. See her *France at the Crystal Palace*, 78–79.

73. Mme Hennequin, *L'Art et le goût au foyer* (Paris: Armand Colin, 1912), 7.

74. 120-Ameublement, C, Cerf, n.d., Bibliothèque Historique de la Ville de Paris. The very high price of twelve hundred francs for a Louis XVI dining room set given in this advertisement attests to the luxuriousness of this store.

75. Émile Zola, *Son Excellence Eugène Rougon* (Paris: Charpentier, 1876), 151–52. See also Paul Nizan, *Antoine Bloyé,* trans. Edmund Stevens (1933; reprint, New York: Monthly Review Press, 1973).

76. Mme de l'Alq, *Le Maître et la maîtresse de la maison* (Paris: Bureaux des Causeries Familières, [ca. 1890]), 14.

77. Walton compared the expenditures of sixteen bourgeois households from the Restoration (1828–30) with sixteen from the Second Empire (1869–70). She defined "bourgeois" households as those having goods worth at least three thousand francs. Walton, *France at the Crystal Palace*, 72–73, 101.

78. For feminists' use of the liberal tradition of individualism, see Laurence Klejman and Florence Rochefort, *L'Egalité en marche: Le Féminisme sous la Troisième République* (Paris: des femmes, 1989)·

79. Silverman, *Art Nouveau in Fin-de-Siècle France*, 198–206.

80. The shifting relationship between the individual and the family can also be seen in a very different kind of source—the labor census. The 1872 census divided the labor statistics as follows: (1) "Individuals really engaged in the trade"; (2) "Relatives of all degree living off of the labor or fortune of the previous"; (3) "Domestic servants engaged in personal service of the preceding"; (4) "Total number supported directly or indirectly by each of the trades" (*Statistique de la France: Résultats généraux du dénombrement de 1872* [Nancy: Imprimerie Administrative, 1874], 125–128). In other words, the census tracked not just the number of workers in each trade, as it did later, but also the number of dependents each worker's employment supported. After the 1872 census, the family as an economic structure completely dropped out, never to return. It was replaced by individual workers, who were categorized according to their relation to the means of production.

81. Colette, *The Vagabond*, trans. Enid McLeod (New York: Farrar, Straus, and Young, 1955), 69. I am grateful to Ellen Furlough for calling this text to my attention.

82. Camille Marbo, *A Travers deux siècles, souvenirs, rencontres, 1883–1967* (Paris: Grasset, 1967), 197.

83. Cécile Sorel, *Les Belles heures de ma vie* (Paris, 1946), 127, 129, 130, respectively, cited in Margaret Nesbit, "Atget's *Intérieurs Parisiens*, the Point of Difference," in the catalogue for an exhibit at the Musée Carnavalet, 19 October–21 November 1982, 8–9. Although the date of publication of Sorel's memoirs makes this citation seem anachronistic for this discussion, the memoirs were written at the end of a long life. Atget had already photographed these rooms by 1910.

84. I have found Gillian Brown's *Domestic Individualism: Imagining the Self in Nineteenth-Century America* (Berkeley: University of California Press, 1990) very helpful in conceptualizing this issue.

85. This essay presents in some detail part of a larger project that traces the changing political and social meanings of domestic objects under the different political regimes in France from the Old Regime to the late nineteenth century. Some of the points (such as the one in the text) are, therefore, simply asserted rather than fully argued here. For a fuller discussion and more complete documentation see my forthcoming *Taste and Power*.

86. A great deal of work has been done in the last twenty years on nationalism, and more recently scholars have started investigating the gendering of the nation and the state. I have found the following theoretical discussions grounded in other parts of the world especially helpful: Lauren Berlant, *The Anatomy of National Fantasy: Hawthorne, Utopia, and Everyday Life* (Chicago: University of Chicago Press, 1991), which contains a very concise and elegant discussion of the concept of the "national symbolic" (see pp. 20–22); Elaine Scarry, *The Body in Pain: The Making and Unmaking of the World* (New York: Oxford University Press, 1985); Benedict Anderson, *Imagined Communities: Reflections on the Origins and Spread of Nationalism* (London: Verso, 1983); Eric Hobsbawm and Terence Ranger, eds., *The Invention of Tradition* (Cambridge: Cambridge University Press, 1983). In a different register, recent work on the gendering of the welfare state is essential to reflections on the gendering of the nation and the state. See for example, Seth Koven and Sonya Michel, eds., *Mothers of a New World: Maternalist Politics and the Origins of Welfare States* (New York: Routledge, 1993). On France, Eugen Weber's *Peasants into Frenchmen: The Modernization of Rural*

France, 1870–1914 (Stanford: Stanford University Press, 1976) remains very useful; the three volumes of Pierre Nora, ed., *Les Lieux de mémoire* (Paris: Gallimard, 1986), contain some fascinating articles, although there are telling omissions. On the later period, see Stanford Elwitt, *The Making of the Third Republic: Class and Politics in France, 1868–1884* (Baton Rouge: Louisiana State University Press, 1975).

87. In addition, not all the French were to be French in the same way; because the security of the state was understood to depend on (changing) class orders, Frenchness was a category strongly inflected by class. Tension between a fantasy of unity and homogeneity and a reality of inherited (historically produced) and contemporary (politically produced) fractures and heterogeneities permeated French nineteenth-century society and polity. But the terms "fantasy" and "reality" are obviously too simple. The French understood themselves to be like other French people, because of their common nationality, yet at the same time to be very unlike many of those with whom they shared citizenship.

88. Patricia O'Brien, "The Kleptomania Diagnosis: Bourgeois Women and Theft in Late-Nineteenth-Century France," *JSH* 17, no.1 (fall 1983): 65–77. For kleptomania in the United States, see Elaine S. Abelson, *When Ladies Go A-Thieving: Middle-Class Shoplifters in the Victorian Department Store* (New York: Oxford University Press, 1989). For a wonderful primary text on the erotic dangers of consumption see Gaetan Gatian de Clérambault, *Passion érotique des étoffes chez la femme* (Paris: Les Empêcheurs de Penser en Rond, 1991 [texts originally 1908 and 1910]). On the representation of women (and the desire to control women's desire) in realist novels, see Naomi Schor, *Breaking the Chain: Women, Theory, and French Realist Fiction* (New York: Columbia, 1985).

89. For an analysis of the simultaneous making of the middle class and of the nation in Sweden, see Jonas Frykman and Orvar Löfgren, *Culture Builders: A Historical Anthropology of Middle-Class Life*, trans. Alan Crozier (New Brunswick, N.J.: Rutgers University Press, 1987).

FOUR

The Other Side of Venus

The Visual Economy of Feminine Display

Abigail Solomon-Godeau

"Money has sex appeal" one hears, and this formula itself gives only the crudest out-lines of a fact which reaches far beyond prostitution. Under the domination of com-modity fetishism, the sex appeal of [every] woman is tinged to a greater or lesser degree with the appeal of the commodity.
WALTER BENJAMIN, *DAS PASSAGEN-WERK*

The commodity, like the sign, suffers from metaphysical dichotomies. Its value, like its truth, lies in the social element. But the social element is added on to its nature, to its matter, and the social subordinates it as a lesser value, indeed as a nonvalue. Participation in society requires that the body submit itself to a speculation, that trans-forms it into a value-bearing object, a standardized sign, an exchangeable signifier, a "likeness" with reference to an authoritative model. A commodity—a woman—is divided into two irreconcilable bodies: her "natural" body and her socially valued, exchangeable body, which is a particularly mimetic expression of masculine values.
LUCE IRIGARAY, "WOMEN ON THE MARKET"

One of the most conspicuous features of commodity culture is its sexual-ization of the commodity, its eroticization of objects, which in turn inflects, if not determines, the psychic structures of consumer desire. Within the cul-tural forms of what W. F. Haug has so suggestively termed "commodity aes-thetics,"[1] it is the image of desirable femininity that is central, having become in the course of more than a century a supplementary emblem of the com-modity itself. In becoming not only the commodity's emblem but its lure, the feminine image operates as a conduit and mirror of desire, reciprocally intensifying and reflecting the commodity's allure. The bikinied model adorning a Harley Davidson is in this respect the direct descendent of Alphonse Mucha's femme fatale, whose sinuous form announced the supe-riority of Job cigarette papers or Peugeot bicycles. The apparent inevitabil-ity of this coupling of eros and commodity, and indeed its global ubiquity, should not however blind us to its historicity, its roots in social as well as sex-ual relations. Accordingly, a double analysis is required, whereby the signi-fying codes of commodity culture are genealogically investigated in both their material and their psychic instrumentalities. In this respect, we may recall Roland Barthes's injunction that "the analysis of codes perhaps allows an easier and surer historical definition of a society than the analysis of its signifieds, for the latter can often appear as trans-historical, belonging more to an anthropological base than to a proper history."[2] In other words, in considering the role of femininity in the shaping of commodity culture, we need also to examine the historical shaping of femininity itself.[3] It is in fact a certain cultural articulation of femininity—what I have elsewhere called its "spectacularization"[4]—that is the necessary precondition for the connotative linkage of the erotics of femininity with the commodity and its assimilation to the structure of commodity fetishism. Furthermore, it is the ideological naturalization of the feminine-as-spectacle, or what Griselda Pollock has called "woman-as-image," that is the precondition for the apparently self-evident homology between the seductive, possessable feminine and the seductive, possessable commodity.[5]

Connections between a visual economy of feminine display, the psychic mechanisms governing Guy Debord's society of the spectacle, and the hydralike forms of commodity fetishism would accordingly seem obviously there to be made, but what exactly is to be made of them? From our postmodernist (or late-capitalist) perspective, we now understand that capitalism is as much a semiotic as an economic system. Indeed, one of the significant motifs in postwar critical theory is precisely its rereading of Marx in terms of semiology.[6] And as scholars such as Thomas Richards have pointed out, the cultural forms of consumerism came into being well before the consumer economy did.[7] For other scholars of early modern Europe, "consumers," "commodities," and "mass culture" are already recognizable as such in pre-Renaissance towns and cities.[8] In this regard, there is good reason to invoke the notion of uneven development insofar as the component elements of a fully realized commodity culture, along with its symbolic representations, do not emerge simultaneously or in fully evolved form.

What is at work therefore in the complex social, psychic, and material processes that collectively foster connotative associations between femininity, modernity, and the commodity is an economy of desire operating on the register of the visual, which is itself commodity culture's primary and privileged mode of address. This libidinal economy, needless to say, is gendered. Thus while images of femininity may be consumed by women as well as men— think here of any fashion magazine—their material production and ideological underpinnings are unambiguously patriarchal, manifesting the deep structures of what Martin Jay has termed "phallogocularcentrism."[9] It is for this reason that analyses of the structures of commodity culture made by Frankfurt School critics, situationists, and their various progeny seem so imprecise, if not flat-footed. For example, in W. F. Haug's elaboration of "the ambiguity of commodity aesthetics exemplified by the use of sexual illusion," the operative assumption is that the sensual investment in the commodity, and the concomitant abstraction and reification of human sensuality are sexually indifferent:

> The suppression of instincts plus the simultaneous illusory satisfaction of instincts tend towards the general sexualization of the human condition, called by Max Scheler *Gehirnsinnlichkeit* or "sensuality on the brain." The response of the commodities is to reflect sexual images from all sides. Here it is not the sexual object which takes on the commodity form, but the tendency of all objects of use in commodity form to assume a sexual form to some extent. That is, the sensual need and the means by which it is satisfied are rendered nonspecific.[10]

What Haug neglects to consider in this formulation is that human sexualization and the sexually reflective properties of the commodity are themselves structured by the hierarchical terms of sexual difference, and these have different consequences for male and female subjects precisely *as* subjects. In some cases, the growth of consumer culture—as in the social activity of shopping—had emancipatory possibilities for women of various classes.[11] The same phenomena instated its own perversions—kleptomania, for instance. Consequently, any investigation of the mechanisms of commodity fetishism and commodity culture that fails to acknowledge the imbrication of gender ideologies within them is inevitably partial.

In this essay I want to look at a particular moment in French visual culture that on the one hand predates the fully evolved commodity culture of the late nineteenth century but on the other can be seen to have provided one of its characteristic tropes; namely, the equivalence between the imagery of eroticized feminine display and the allure (or threat) of modernity. Once this equivalence was secured, at a historical moment already consumed by the Baudelairean "cult of images,"[12] it was at least doubly determined that the distinctive forms of modern mass consumer culture would adapt the image of feminine desirability as its most powerful icon.

For this reason, I want to examine one of the early manifestations of nineteenth-century France's "media explosion," namely, the large-scale production of lithographic imagery in which these associations were given their characteristically modern form. In this respect, it is important to take note of the fact that the ubiquity and prominence of images of eroticized femininity within French visual culture are of such magnitude that art historians have tended to accept their ubiquity as a given rather than a question. In fact, the dominant visual place of femininity in nineteenth-century French culture itself constitutes a historical mutation, during which the idealized and erotically invested male body was effectively eclipsed by the female.[13] Traditionally, it had been the *male* body that had occupied the central place in art theory, pedagogy, and academic practice. The substitution of the female body for the male body—occurring between the French Revolution and the later years of the Restoration—is thus part of a larger shift in *mentalité,* signaling the increasing consolidation of new—that is to say, bourgeois—ideologies of gender and sexuality.

Moreover, the eclipse of antique subject matter and its overarching context of the beau ideal additionally implied the eclipse of the male body as the container of ideals of corporeal as well as moral perfection. It thus happened that as femininity progressively became the primary signifier for the sexual and the erotic, as well as the new vehicle for the ideal, it became a battleground between a defensive (and effectively defeated) classicism and the stylistic ideologies of realism or, later, naturalism. Hence, the female nude was recruited by those who still adhered (in principle) to classical paradigms (that is, critics and theorists such as Victor Cousin and Charles Blanc and academic artists as well as more complex figures such as J. A. D. Ingres) and by those who appropriated the female nude under the banner of a defiant realism, such as Gustave Courbet. In addition, the female nude became a widely employed motif in all aspects of decorative arts and architectural ornamentation. The point, therefore, to emphasize is that the image of femininity as image of desire is a fully modern one—not because there were not numerous prototypes for such articulations of the feminine (obviously there were many) but because its masculine analogue was now for all intents and purposes foreclosed. Significantly, what Beatrice Farwell has designated the "display nude" has no equivalent in the imagery of masculinity in nineteenth-century French culture.[14] Although there are occasional exceptions, visual culture from the Restoration period and after has relatively little to do with the celebration of masculine beauty. Fops, *fashionables,* dandies, and *beaux* were more frequently mocked than admired, in keeping with the new imperatives of masculine subjectivity.[15] Furthermore, the foreclosure of an exhibitionistic and narcissistic variant of masculinity was by no means a phenomenon limited to the visual arts. In theater, in opera, and, above all, in the ballet, masculinity was reconfigured and reconstructed as femininity became the gender elected to exclusively represent the erotic, the beautiful, and indeed corporeality itself.[16] It is therefore the female body's monopoly of the role of image of desire that is characteristically modern.

However, in the process of becoming the unique cultural locus of aesthetics, sexuality, and difference, the female body became the bearer of other contemporary meanings, especially, but not limited to, the concept of modernity. From the 1820s on, the large-scale production of engraved and lithographed nudes, pinups, images of demimondaines and other female celebrities, fashion plates, titillating erotica purveyed in print shops and by *colporteurs,* and, as I will argue, even the illegal pornographic imagery (both graphic and photographic) sold under the counter are thus the harbingers of a visual culture in which the notion of modernity and the manufacture of desire on which commodity culture depends are jointly secured by the linchpin of a femininity explicitly put on display. And to the degree that the concept of the modern could be viewed as alternately (or simultaneously) seductive and threatening, figures of femininity could be inflected in either direction, mobilized and animated to figure, to "sublimate," and to psychologically "manage" the conflicts and contradictions of industrial capitalism and their effects on psychic and social life. Hence, on one side of the divide, we confront the textual and graphic prevalence of the prostitute (figure 9)—commodity and labor collapsed into one—as a major trope of nineteenth-century French culture;[17] on the other side a growing corpus of imagery of the modern Parisienne (figure 10), which sprung from lithography and was later adopted by painters as a high art subject. In this respect, the progressive isolation of femininity as a motif—the disappearance of narrative, mythological, or classical allusion—and the distillation of the female figure, nude or clothed, to a subject in and of itself (even for ambitious salon painting) signals the ways in which femininity, display, and spectacle became visually collapsed into one another. It is this representational collapse that aligns the structures of (male) psychic fetishism with Marx's "metaphysical subtleties" of the commodity fetish.

I shall have more to say about this relationship, but at this point I would note that the iconographic dominance of femininity is even more evident in nonelite forms of visual culture: photography, lithography, wood engraving, book illustration, *imagerie parisienne,* and so forth. Accordingly, the historical questions to be asked about the demise of an idealized and erotically cathected masculinity in visual culture and the concomitant rise of feminine iconography have two components: what were the meanings—cultural, social, and sexual—carried by this profuse dissemination of feminine imagery (and an accompanying prolix discourse on "Woman"), and how does this latter production of feminine iconography intersect with the burgeoning culture of modernity? In this regard, midcentury France, while far behind England in conventional indices of modernization (that is, industrialization, urbanization, development of railroads, and so on), can be viewed as the vanguard culture with respect to the terms of the visual culture of commodity capitalism. This was indeed Walter Benjamin's perception of July Monarchy France, and it was for this reason that he placed such emphasis on the arcades and their innovative display of goods, soliciting the mobile gaze of the *flâneur.*[18]

Even before the advent of the camera in 1839 and *its* contribution to France's media explosion, mass-produced imagery of the feminine was itself a quasi-industrial production of considerable scale. It is as though the real absence of women as actors in the bourgeois civil sphere was filled by compensatory fantasies—or constellations of fantasies—about femininity. And where law, medicine, the church, and the state all operated to "contain" women and to police female sexuality, the image world of high and

Figure 9. Nicolas Emmanuel Péry, "Comment trouves-tu la nouvelle mode, Fany?" from the series *Les Cocottes*. Lithograph, ca. 1850.

Tassaert pinx.^t   Léon Noël delin.

LE PIANO.

A Paris, chez Neuhaus, rue Saint Honoré, N.º 123.   Lith de Villain.   Et chez Ostervald ainé, quai des Augustins, N.º 37.

Figure 10. Octave Tassaert, *Le Piano*. Lithograph by François Le Villain, ca. 1830.

mass cultural forms conversely manifested femininity's untrammeled expansion even as it demonstrated the radical instability of the epistemology of containment.[19]

It is one of my arguments that the formation and emergence of what I will be calling "mass culture" and the prominence of images of femininity within it are themselves integrally related phenomena.[20] However, before returning to the imagery of femininity itself, I must justify the designation "mass culture" applied to graphic, and particularly lithographic, production from the late 1820s on. Indeed, invoking the term "mass culture," as opposed to the term generally employed in art history, that is, "popular culture," is to risk the charge of anachronism. Definitions of the two terms are themselves debated, nowhere more so than in the field of cultural studies. On one side of the debate are those, such as Robert Muchembled, who would argue that the denomination "popular culture" is rightly limited only to that part of culture that not only emanates directly from the people but, more important, expresses values, behaviors, and beliefs that are more or less explicitly oppositional to those of the dominant culture.[21] In this Bahktinian interpretation of popular culture, it is the upside down world of carnival, the transgressive speech (songs, curses, billingsgate) of fair, marketplace, and tavern, and in the realm of religion, the "people's religion" of witchcraft that collectively constitute the domain of the popular. For historians such as Muchembled or Robert Mandrou, cultural forms such as the *imagerie d'épinal* or the *bibliothèque bleue* of Troyes, far from being paradigms of popular culture, are rather the impositions of a cultural and class elite. Insofar as such artifacts are generated by the lettered and disseminate values in conformity with the ideology of church and town, they may be said to operate as "colonizing" arms of a centralized (and centralizing) culture. Moralizing and Christianizing, didactic or patriotic, such forms are permeated by the values and ideology of the dominant and are thus to be fundamentally differentiated from authentic, antihierarchical, and local expressions of popular culture.[22]

Mandrou and Muchembled's models are perhaps somewhat extreme formulations and do in fact represent a minority view within the field.[23] Nonetheless, such arguments have the merit of providing at least some kind of model for a conceptual distinction between the very different compass of popular and mass cultural forms. For my purposes this is a crucial distinction, inasmuch as the artifacts produced by the media explosion of early-nineteenth-century France can only with difficulty be factored into a model of popular culture. Thus, the quantum increase in print media, such as newspapers, *revues*, journals, *canards*, broadsides, and of course, affordable books; the emergence of characteristically modern forms such as publicity; and the massive output of visual imagery through the media of lithography, wood engravings, and by the Second Empire, photography, do not in and of themselves translate into an unmediated expression of *le peuple*.

The justification for adopting the label mass culture is obviously not predicated on a purely quantitative definition of mass culture, although by the 1840s the economic status of both daguerreotype production and the lithographic industry might well justify such a definition.[24] Rather, the sense in which I employ the term relates to specific characteristics that distinguish mass culture from both elite and popular forms. Most important, mass cultural forms, like those of elite culture, disseminate values, beliefs, and ideologies generated by dominant class fractions from a centralized point, although these meanings may be variously negotiated and even transformed by their consumers. A division of labor is also implied, whereby producer and consumer are not the same (a distinction not necessarily the case with popular or folk art). Because mass culture is considered to be one of the hallmarks of modernity, inseparable from the commodity culture that it serves to purvey, it is therefore a crucial shaping factor in the culture of modernity *tout court*.[25] As a corollary feature mass cultural forms reflect, articulate, and to a certain extent actively construct the culture of urbanism and modernity, countering regional, local, or rural specificity with the cosmopolitanism and sophistication of the city, its entertainments, its commodities, its individualism, and its mobility. Influence thus tends to run in one direction only, from center to periphery, city to country, Paris to provinces.

Although the world of print culture that existed at the advent of lithography was divided into several distinct ranks, lithography, in keeping with the democratizing tendency of the century, exploded the once-clear boundaries of the "classes" of print production. Centuries earlier, the printed book had similarly functioned to link elite and nonelite cultures; lithography was therefore the second reproductive technology to bridge different classes, regions, and nations. Hierarchically, the intaglio print production of old masters continued to occupy the highest cultural rung and descended through the master printers of the eighteenth century down through the Parisian manufacture of the *imagerie* of the rue St. Jacques. Parallel to the upper tiers were the reproductive uses of prints; engraved translations of paintings were exhibited in the salons and collected as works of art in themselves. In the class structure of print production, there was consequently an acknowledged distinction between the kinds of prints that belonged to elite visual culture and those that occupied the lower strata.

Lithography, however, was a print medium that almost immediately overarched the spaces of both elite and nonelite culture. Invented in 1798 by the Viennese Alois Senefelder, lithography was introduced in France in 1817, where it was first classified as an industrial product. By 1824, however, it had been repositioned as a fine art medium and had its own section in the *Salon livret*. By 1828 there were 223 lithographic establishments in the Department of the Seine alone, with 180 presses operated by five hundred workmen producing three million francs worth of prints per year. Needless to say, an industrial enterprise of this magnitude did not escape government control and surveillance.

Like books and newspapers, presses were controlled; printers and publishers were bonded, proofs needed to be submitted to the government censors before the prints could be legally sold or even published, registration in the government Dépôt Légal was mandatory, and fines and even prison sentences were levied for political and moral offense. Although there were changes and variations in print and press control legislation throughout the Napoleonic, Restoration, and July Monarchy periods, some form of control was always in place.[26]

What the advent of lithography signaled within print technologies had first to do with quantity; a lithographic stone could generate a far greater print run than any previous print technology. It was this attribute that made lithography affordable, even for a working-class clientele. Second, because a lithographic drawing was produced directly on the stone, it provided for a degree of spontaneity of execution unrivaled by any other print media. This was itself a factor in its adoption for immediately topical and political purposes (Honoré Daumier is of course the towering figure). Third, by the late Restoration, the period when lithography had achieved technical perfection, lithography was capable of rendering a broad range of aesthetic effects, from the most linear and detailed effects of pen drawing to dramatic chiaroscuro and sfumato effects, which augmented both its artistic and its commercial applications. Consequently, lithography was almost from the beginning divided into three principal uses: a medium of translation by which existing images (including high art ones) could be translated into lithography, either by the artist or the lithographer; a commercial medium for the printing of handbills and other commercial products; and an image-making technology adapted to either Salon, bourgeois interior, garret, or brothel. In its imaginative, as opposed to transcriptive, applications, lithography therefore encompassed a range of genres from the archetypal romantic views exemplified by the *Voyages pittoresques* (a multivolume compendium of vistas, ruins, sites, and locales) to the hard-core pornographic fare for which Paris was famous. And insofar as the print industry also represented itself visually (often for publicity purposes), there exist numerous depictions of passersby crowded in front of printsellers' window displays, looking at the newest prints. These remind us that the public display of images constituted one of the spectacles of urban life, and until 1835, it was used as a form of political speech.

In all these respects, it seems legitimate to situate the birth of mass culture with the explosion of cheap and topical imagery, some of which reiterated traditional motifs and forms, some of which constituted new ones. Unlike traditional "popular" prints, which can be considered a conservative form (owing to their themes, conventionality, and relatively fixed formats), lithographic prints—in keeping with their own modernity and rapidity of production—specialized in fashion, topicality, ephemerality; their references were to up-to-date styles, fads, and decor. To the extent that print culture repetitively, ceaselessly staged its erotic feminine display—indeed femininity *as* display—in direct contiguity with the modern and the modish, the eroticism of the feminine infused its setting and, by extension, the new world of consumption of which the print itself was itself a talisman.

A good and quite typical example of these processes of imbrication is provided by Achille Devéria's 1828 *Le Roman du jour* (The Fashionable Novel, figure 11). As is the case with many of Devéria's lithographs, the motifs in the print have eighteenth-century prototypes. For example, the woman-with-book motif is featured frequently in eighteenth-century iconography. In part, this motif was fostered by the linkage of the novel (many of whose producers and consumers were women) with femininity. Furthermore, as a leisured activity, novel reading was associated with wealth and (feminine) idleness. Consequently, the young-woman-with-a-book figured not only in the form of what I will provisionally call the "legal erotic," as in the *Le Roman du jour*, but in pornographic representation as well.[27]

Le Roman du jour elicits a narrative reading in several ways. Its mise-en-scène is instantly recognizable; the swathe of curtain, silk-covered sofa, embroidered foot cushion, and carved table declare the print's setting as the bourgeois home. The dishabille of the girls, their ambiguous relation to each other (lovers? sisters? friends?), are narrativized by the presence of the book immediately identifiable to the British consumer, to whom the print was equally addressed, as a "French" novel. Simultaneously a corrupter of innocent morals and an entrée to worldly knowledge and pleasure, the book thus serves as a narrative "prompt" to justify the erotic display.

This display has two components: on the one hand, the corporeal display of breasts and shoulders, on the other, the provocative and coquettish gaze of the girl in the nightcap directed out to the viewer. While narrative is relatively minimal, an important aspect of that narrative is the solicitous look at the viewer, presumed male by artist, lithographer, printer, and publisher. This solicitous look is a staple feature of the legal erotic, and to state the obvious, it retains its currency to this day. Although it would be wrong to entirely discount a female consumer or viewer (and there were certainly both), it is nonetheless fair to say that *Le Roman du jour*'s address is deliberately pitched to the male consumer who is interpolated by the blonde woman's look. While here too there are prototypes for this spectatorial address going back as far as the Renaissance, these newer gazes are addressed to a potential purchaser and emerge from objects that make no aesthetic or intellectual claims. Compliant, chic, titillating, these icons of femininity are significant because they are the first mass-produced commodities designed exclusively to purvey "the feminine" and because they offer to the purchaser more than the fantasy of possession of the woman (or women).

Figure 11. Achille Devéria, *Le Roman du jour/The fashionable novel*. Lithograph, 1829.

Figure 12. Eugène le Roux, untitled lithograph, 1848.

In other words, what is equally on offer is the fantasy of possession of the world the print depicts—*mondaine* but private, fashionable but not oppressively aristocratic, "realistic," and thus of this world. In this it presages the mechanisms of modern advertising in which desire is provoked not merely or only for the commodity but for the ambiance or lifestyle that the commodity represents.

Finally, *Le Roman du jour* provides as good an example as any of the linking of the feminine to the modern; novel, decor, and the girls themselves are all unambiguously *du moment,* and this is undoubtedly part of such prints' appeal. This combination of elements—eroticized femininity, book, seductive gaze, and modern decor—is frequently encountered throughout the century; obviously it was a popular motif. Devéria and his brethren could have depicted nymphs and goddesses had they wanted; it was, on the contrary, the contemporaneity of such images that heightened their eroticism even as it modernized them. There were, of course, a substantial number of prints published that *did* feature nymphs, sylphides, bathers in landscapes, and the like, vestiges of the classical motifs that elite official culture struggled to preserve (figure 12). What is significant, however, is that even in the form of *nudités,* hairstyles and ornament still intentionally and explicitly declare the con-

Figure 13. Charles Landelle, *Aujourd'hui/Today*. Lithograph, 1850.

temporaneity of their subjects, signaling that the scene is fully as modern as those situated in interiors.

In effect, what is being purveyed is the familiar lure of the commodity, "figured" by femininity but laden with the even more potent implications of "having." Although not yet explicitly linked to the commodity as such (a process that begins in the Second Empire and fully develops in the Third Republic), lithographic imagery of the 1820s and 1830s appears on the basis of its sheer scale to have played a crucial role in securing (and naturalizing) associations among femininity, eroticism, modernity, and consumption, whose epitome—a fetish monument to capitalism and patriarchy—was the monumental statue *La Parisienne*, erected, as it were, on the occasion of the triumphant festivities of the 1900 Exposition Universelle.

Another suggestive feature of this genre of print is its function as a kind of theater of erotic spectacle where femininity is literally put on display. While this was quite literally the lot of certain classes of women (for example, street-

Figure 14. Becquier and Bettanier, *Les Cocottes en 1867.* Lithograph, 1867.

walkers, marriageable bourgeois and upper-class women—goods on the market in the social spaces of the city and its entertainments), print culture allegorizes this social fact through its presentation of femininity, like a precious object, ensconced in cushions, draperies, luxurious clothing, and so forth (figure 13). Using the iconographic repertoire of their elders and betters (for example, Watteau, Fragonard, and Boucher and master printers such as Moreau le Jeune, Pierre Antoine Baudouin, Nicola Lavreince, and so on),[28] virtuosic young draftsmen like Devéria applied their skills to naturalizing a vision of femininity whose allure was heightened by its banal possessability, by its appeal to their bourgeois consumers' fantasies of social mobility. The numerous variations in the imagery of display were further naturalized within a visual rhetoric of realism, whereby scenes of feminine display were plausibly situated within the actual spaces of feminine display—opera, theater, ball, certain parks and promenades, places of commerce (figure 14).

Here it is useful to reintroduce Griselda Pollock's distinction between image-of-woman and woman-as-image. Implicit in the notion of woman-as-image is not only the separation of signifier and signified that underpins my distinction between "femininity" and "woman" but also, particularly important, the notion that the construction of modern femininity is itself aligned with a condition of exaggerated specularity, a condition hypothesized by Luce Irigaray and famously described by Laura Mulvey as "to-be-looked-at-ness."[29] But the solicitation of the look that can be identified in the emergence of new iconographies of the feminine—iconographies that are effectively *about* the feminine as spectacle—needs to be historicized as well as psychoanalyzed. Grandville's extraordinary lithograph entitled *Venus at the Opera* (figure 15) suggests both avenues of investigation. Grandville here explicitly and literally renders the aggressively phallicized terms of the male gaze while situating it within the historic and material specificity of the social and cultural spaces where feminine specularity was both promoted and enacted, in this instance, the Opéra loge where society women, marriageable daughters, and courtesans participated in intricate rituals of exhibition and display. This (feminine) condition of pure specularity suggests numerous parallels with the emerging culture of commodity fetishism. From the 1830s on, the open display of goods, the construction of the commercial arcades, the invention of the department store, new apparatuses of publicity and promotion, the invention of ready-made clothing, the new public spaces of leisure and consumption—all these historic developments tend to reinforce a visual culture premised on appearance, display, exposure, and spectacle.[30] Specularity and spectacle, we might say, are in any case a priori inflected on the side of femininity, an inflection established at least as early as Rousseau's "Lettre sur les spectacles." And to the extent that the evolution of gender ideology precluded a comparable position for nineteenth-century men, there were as few masculine equivalents of the pinup as there were contemporary representations (painted or printed) of men sleeping, disrobing, or reclining naked, indoors or out.

Comparison of rococo prints featuring themes of gallantry with those of Devéria (or Pierre Numa, or Antoine Maurin, or a host of more or less gifted lithographers) reveals another significant shift from eighteenth-century iconography, namely, the diminished importance of the gallant. Even where these various scenes involve a male protagonist—husband, lover, old lecher, and so forth—the men are there as props; in effect, they function as supernumeraries to the display of femininity rather than as equal foci of the image (figure 16). While it could be argued that the masculine presence within such prints still functions as a surrogate for the implied male viewer, the more important observation is that men tend to play supporting roles. Eighteenth-century scenes of flirtation between equally attractive men and women are often as much social as private, evidence of a culture in which the erotic is

Figure 15. Grandville (Jean-Ignace-Isidore Gérard), *Venus at the Opera,* 1844.

still inseparable from a courtly notion of *sociabilité* and has not yet become
fully privatized. Furthermore, where rococo prints often feature attractive
men as lovers, escorts, or as equal accessories to the feminine, lithographic
production gradually narrows the focus to boudoir or sitting room and con-
centrates increasingly on the feminine alone.[31]

The structural correspondences between the iconography of femininity
as fetish (which is also a fetishized femininity) in the image world of capitalism, and the commodity form in which it circulates are therefore important ones. These correspondences are vividly apparent in the *feminités* so
deftly purveyed by Devéria and a host of other *imagiers.* "To desire the fashionable, purchasable woman-as-thing is to desire exchange-value itself, that
is, the very essence of capitalism," Walter Benjamin observed.[32] Psychic and
commodity fetish are thus unified, mutually implicated (from the Latin *im-
plicare,* "to be folded within") in the erotic spectacle of a reified femininity
itself produced in commodity form.

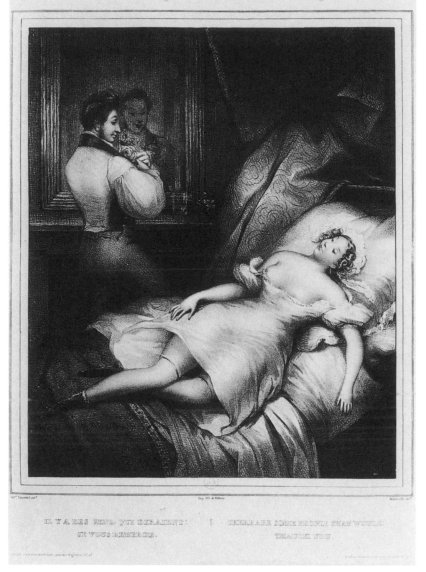

Figure 16. Octave Tassaert, "Il y a des gens qui diraient: je vous remércie," from the series *Les Amants et les époux*. Lithograph, 1829.

LE RÊVE | DREAMING.

Figure 17. Achille Devéria, *Le Rêve*, 1829.

The attempt to think the commodity fetish in relation to the imagery of fetishized femininity disseminated in commodity form is further prompted by consideration of one of the distinctive motifs in early-nineteenth-century print culture; specifically, the kind of image clearly recognizable as the prototype of the modern pinup.[33] By pinup, I am referring to an image type that could be relatively deluxe, as in figure 17, or relatively crude, as in figure 18, but in either case was predicated on the relative isolation of its feminine motif through the reduction or outright elimination of narrative, literary, or mythological allusion. As we have seen, this decontextualization, reduction, or distillation of the image of femininity to a subject in and of itself had a venerable lineage with immediate precursors in the rococo. But as we have also seen, in its July Monarchy graphic and mass media incarnations, such imagery trades less on its high art or classical prototypes (even

LA BELLE DE NEW–YORK

à Paris, chez Clericetti, rue Galande N.º 41.   Déposé.

Figure 18. *La Belle de New-York,* anonymous lithograph, ca. 1830.

when they provide the pose or influence the formal treatment) than on its modernity, ephemerality and status as an affordable commodity.

Whether or not we are yet able to determine if the relation between commodity fetish and psychic fetish is best conceived as one of homology, analogy, or correspondence (in both the Baudelairean and Benjaminian senses), we can in any case acknowledge a similar structural logic at work. For example, the psychic fetish, like the commodity fetish, is not to be understood as the thing in itself, but as a veiled sign, or better, a hieroglyph (Marx and Freud both employ the term). What distinguishes the commodity from the commodity fetish, what enables the latter to be apprehended as separate from its conditions of production, to be detached from its use value, to take on "a life of its own," what enables commodities to "speak to each other," "to share in their own life world," in short, to be both mystified and reified, is moored in the commodity fetish's ability to conceal its constituent relations of production, thereby veiling its own structure of contradiction. Insofar as the commodity fetish historically becomes not only eroticized but expressed as a desire *for* the feminine, we therefore need to examine the nature of the role played by sexual relations, as well as that played by the (occulted) relations of production in the commodity fetish's fully evolved form. Just as a historicized inquiry into the mechanisms of psychic fetishism requires attention to its hidden social as well as sexual relations, an examination of the commodity fetish requires consideration of the psychic zone of production at work in the shaping of the fetish. In this respect, it would seem that psychic and commodity fetish are secondary sign systems detached and transformed from their psychic and social origin, and it is for this reason that an investigation of either form devolves more on structure than on content. Accordingly, the historical debut of the pinup commodity, like the ubiquity of the eroticized imagery of femininity itself, attests to historical transformations on the level of psychic as well as social relations.

Consistent with their fetishistic structure, these early pinups observe the same conventional protocols governing the representation of the female nude—the elision of sex organs, elimination of body hair (these are to be found only in pornographic representations), and often a phallic figuration of the entire body itself.[34] Insofar as both image and commodity promise and withhold satisfaction while endlessly provoking desire, there is further justification in mapping their shared psychic purview. Furthermore, the chimerical illusion of erotic plenitude, in conjunction with the semiotic excess of both image and commodity, additionally suggests the need to grant an enlarged purview for fetishism, one that would incorporate these libidinal mechanisms into the Marxist model while integrating the role of economic and social relations into the Freudian one. As Anne McClintock has written: "Far from being a purely sexual icon fetishism is a memorial to contradictions in social value that can take a number of historical guises. The fetish stands at the crossroads of a crisis in historical value, as the symbolic displacement and embodiment in one object of incompatible codes in social meaning, which the individual cannot resolve at a personal level. The fetish is thus destined to recur with ritualistic repetition."[35] As a "memorial to contradictions" psychic fetishism and commodity fetishism both operate by means of elision and displacement; both are structured by the rhetorical logic of metonymy (paralleled by the rhetorical logic of the unconscious, structured, as the French psychoanalyst Jacques Lacan insisted, like a language). In the former instance, the unconscious repression of the (visual) perception of an (imagined) castration denies the material fact of sexual difference while in a corresponding operation, the material social value of the commodity is transubstantiated into the magical—that is, imaginary— commodity fetish. "The object that had been an accidental means to achieving some desired end becomes a fixed necessity, the very embodiment of desire, and the effective, exclusive power for gratifying it."[36]

With the advent of photography—specifically the production of deluxe daguerreotype erotica in the late 1840s, much of it stereographic—there subsequently emerged new figurations of the sexual body, as in the invention of the beaver shot (figure 19). I have discussed this type of production elsewhere, but a few points may be made here.[37] What is especially interesting in photographic as opposed to graphic erotica is the way it augments and ratifies the tendency, already apparent in lithographic prototypes, to articulate the sexuality of femininity in terms of specularity rather than activity. Whereas traditional graphic pornography conceives of the sexual as active, frequently featuring a male participant as the viewer's surrogate, photographic pornography, more often than not, devolves on the sight of the female body alone. Moreover, and with specific respect to the beaver shot, the medium of photography can be said to technically foster a radical fragmentation of the body, even as it attests to a fascination with female genitalia that makes the implicit fetishism of the legal erotic unmistakably explicit.

Interestingly, French judicial language did not utilize the word *pornographie* in designating this genre of imagery. The criminality of such pictures was legally defined as "offenses to good morals," the imagery characterized as obscene or licentious. Insofar as state censorship recognized only three categories for its intervention—religious, moral, and political—and no distinction was drawn prior to 1806 between the criminality of works considered heretical, sexually obscene, or politically and philosophically objectionable, what we now consider as pornographic was in nineteenth-century France merely part of a continuum of the transgressive or subversive per se.[38] Even more suggestive, there was no contemporary legal description clearly defining the boundary between the legal erotic and the illegal pornographic. On the evidence, it would appear that what defined the (visual) difference for juridic purposes resided exclusively in the depiction of genitalia

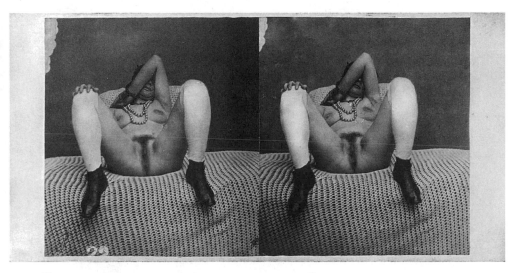

Figure 19. Anonymous wet plate stereo carte, ca. 1855.

or the depiction of specific sexual activity. In some cases, legal prints that were already sexually suggestive, such as Nicolas Maurin's *J'en veux, j'en veux encore* (figure 20) or his *Enfin, je te tiens!,* were reworked into explicitly porno-graphic equivalents (figure 21). In other instances, the censors seem to have tolerated prints whose sexual innuendoes remained on the level of double entendre, or connotation. But since the sexual suggestiveness of the legal prints leaves little to the imagination anyway, we may observe in the print and photographic production of the period the same meanings circulating whether legal or not. Nowhere is this discursive mobility clearer than in the photographs of female nudes, where the legal *académie*—that is to say, a nude figure ostensibly produced for the use of artists (figure 22)—requires only the most minor of accoutrements or modifications in pose to be transformed into the illegal and prosecutable image. In terms of our own contemporary debates on pornography, it seems evident that juridicating between one class of imagery arbitrarily designated as pornographic and another that is deemed unobjectionable is ultimately untenable.

While it is impossible to establish empirically what proportion of litho-graphic imagery was consecrated to erotica, on the basis of the many sur-viving examples it seems evident that it was substantial. To be sure, there were also massive numbers of topographic views produced—lithography was very much a medium of the Romantic picturesque view—and there was a sub-stantial commerce in religious, historical, and portrait subjects. Many of the most successful lithographers covered all these genres. Devéria, who in this and other respects exemplifies the diversity of the lithographic industry, pro-

Figure 20. Nicolas Maurin, "J'en veux, j'en veux encore." Lithograph, ca. 1830.

duced in great numbers religious, patriotic, and moralizing subjects as well as illustrations from popular literary sources.[39] These were in many cases far less distinguished in either sophistication or virtuosity. Devéria clearly functioned within several discrete print markets. But the sheer number of lithographs in which the image of explicitly eroticized femininity is central is the point of departure for all my arguments. Moreover, while politically

Figure 21. Anonymous lithograph, ca. 1830s.

provocative—that is to say, republican, Bonapartist, or antigovernment—propaganda lithographs were carefully monitored, and frequently prosecuted,
the overwhelming impression produced by an examination of lithographic
production of the period 1820–1848 is that government censorship was far
more lax or dilatory in prosecuting sexually suggestive (or explicit) prints
than political ones.

For example, on the basis of the kind of lithographic prints that *did* legally

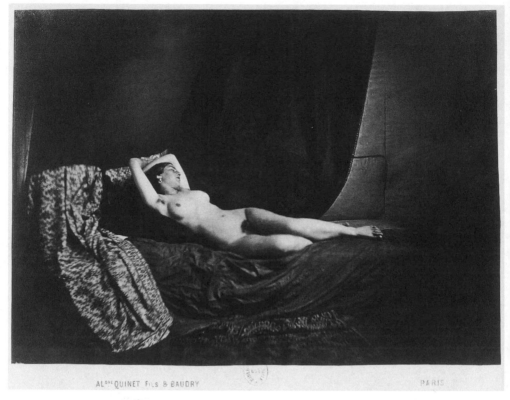

ALᵍⁿᵉQUINET Fₗₛ B BAUDRY   PARIS

Figure 22. Alexandre Quinet and Paul Baudry, wet plate photograph, ca. 1855.

pass muster (that is, approval by the government censor, registration in the
Dépôt Légal, authorized sale by licensed booksellers, print sellers, *colporteurs*,
and *bouquinistes*), it seems evident that erotic, if not pornographic, imagery
was basically tolerated through the Restoration and July Monarchy. (See, for
example, the three duly registered lithographs by Octave Tassaert [figures
16, 23, and 24], part of the series *Les Amants et les époux* and *Boudoirs et
mansardes*.)

    Second, while the archives of the police and other dossiers preserved in
the Archives Nationales are filled with letters from irate citizens deploring
the open display and sale of licentious prints, there seems to have been remarkably little follow-up on the part of the authorities, and there were, in
fact, relatively few prosecutions in relation to the number of complaints. For
example, on 18 March 1832, ten deputies wrote a letter to the prefect of the
Seine protesting the display of obscene and licentious engravings and lithographs displayed "avec profusion" in the most frequented streets, quais, and
boulevards. This protest received a sympathetic but formulaic response, and

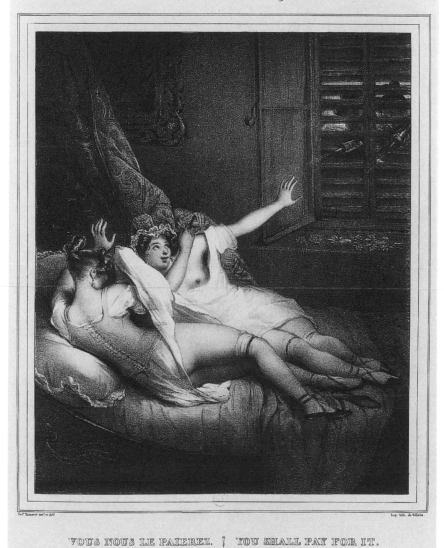

VOUS NOUS LE PAIEREZ. | YOU SHALL PAY FOR IT.

Figure 23. Octave Tassaert, "Vous nous le paierez," from the series *Boudoirs et mansardes*. Lithograph, 1828.

Figure 24. Octave Tassaert, "Ah, mes belles dames . . . ," from the series *Les Amants et les époux.* Lithograph, 1828.

there is no indication in the file that this complaint with its influential signatories received any more attention than those made by ordinary citizens.
Lastly, the sheer scale of erotic—and pornographic—lithographs extant in
the Cabinet des Estampes (and in the Réserve Libre, when it concerns
pornography) suggests that production on such a scale would not have been
possible had the government seriously attempted to curtail it.[40]

There is some reason to think that the proliferation of more or less eroticized imagery of the feminine follows the rhythms of overtly political censorship. Thus, for example, when the government of King Louis Philippe
imposed the draconian press laws of September 1835, political caricaturists
such as Daumier and Grandville had little recourse but to shift from explicitly political targets to more generalized social commentary, often devoted
to the category of *moeurs*. What I am tentatively suggesting is that the repression of political discourse, in combination with the traumatic stresses
and conflicts of both modernity and modern capitalism, may play a role in
both the hypostatization of the feminine and the terms by which it is discursively defined.

In this respect, it is significant that artists like Paul Gavarni, who had not
been much involved in political commentary in the first place, went on to
specialize in the popular avatars of femininity of the July Monarchy—the
Parisienne, the *grisette* (a young working-class woman, such as a seamstress,
who took lovers but was not paid for her favors), the *lionne* (a type of courtesan), and, last, but not least, the *lorette*. Gavarni's enormous success and
renown were based in part on the appeal of these typologies and stereotypes.
These types, moreover, are instances where femininity is either directly connected to the venal (love for sale) or where the sexualization of the feminine is explicitly classed; that is, associated with working-class women. The
lorette, for example (thus named by Nestor Roqueplan, after the new quarter of Paris developing around Notre Dame de Lorette supposedly populated
by prostitutes) was imagined as a pretty working-class woman who, unlike
the *grisette*, sold her favors.[41] As such, she provides a good example of the
way sex, class, and desirability were configured as instances of the modern.
In keeping with an already highly developed typological iconography, de-
riving from John Caspar Lavater, from the so-called *physiologies*, from *cris-de-
Paris* imagery, and the like, the *lorette* was instantly recognizable *as* a type.[42]
Thus, an already highly elaborated system of typologies and stereotypes was,
by the 1820s, adapted to the form of the *physiologie:* a literary or graphic representation that mimicked the forms of natural history description and classification, a reading of appearance that, like phrenology, professed to read
inner essences via external physical signs.

As the repertory of types grew, particularly in the first decades of the century, so too did its feminine cast of dramatis personae; accompanying mass-
produced imagery of more or less eroticized types of femininity, such as the

lorette and *lionne,* were specific working-class types as well: the *rat* (the young dancers in the Opéra corps de ballet, figure 25), the laundress, the flower seller, the modiste, and so forth. These types, originating in graphic media, were later translated into photographic equivalents, and ultimately into the paintings of realists and Impressionists. At the upscale end of the spectrum was the courtesan, the *grande horizontale*—the expensive and extravagant creature who became one of the most visible modern icons of Second Empire and Third Republic feminine mythology. Well before these types would appear in the high art production of realists and impressionists—that is to say, after the middle of the century—they were staples of this mass cultural production, both textual and graphic. Such types operated culturally to eroticize working-class women while disavowing the reality of working-class women's economic and material circumstances. Another important feminine type developed in the 1820s was, as we have seen, the Parisienne—unlike the others, not necessarily working class and not necessarily associated with prostitution. Pretty, fashionable, fickle, desirable, but venal, the Parisienne might well be described as an emblematic figure for that Paris being constructed through capitalism as the capital of desire. In one sense, the consumable, possessable aspects of the fetishized image of femininity could therefore be said to offer the palliative of "having," a visual plenitude that masks lack. But in keeping with the dialectics of fetishism, they could equally connote castration and evoke the threat and corruption associated with commodified sexuality while augmenting an anxious perception of the breakdown of traditional social (and sexual) relations. In this regard, the nineteenth-century French obsession with prostitution, its nuances and its gradations; French culture's elaborate distinctions between forms of prostitution and its harlots high and low; its sexualized working-class women (modiste, *serveuse,* flower seller, dancer, laundress), and its fantasy figures of bohemian sexuality (*grisette, lorette, débardeuse,* and so on) are not only the obvious symbolizations of a capitalist society where everything has a price, nor are they merely the expression of patriarchal alarm at the lawlessness and uncontrollability of female sexuality. Rather, the range of fantasies about femininity that occupy such a conspicuous place within cultural production operate to contain—or exceed—complex and ambivalent responses to large-scale social transformations. Equally seductive images of femininity could thus be relatively anodyne in their manifest content (the chicly dressed Parisienne, the Good Mother, the Venuses and Andromedas of the official Salon) or more ambivalently incarnated (the prostitutional continuum from courtesan to *fille publique,* the representational continuum from fashion plate to beaver shot). This Janus face of femininity, most familiar to art historians in its Second Empire incarnations, was fully institutionalized by 1840. In all instances, however, it is part of the raison d'être of such imagery, a crucial part of its func-

Une chambre de rats.

Figure 25. Albert (or Wilhelm) Teichel, *Une chambre de rats.* Lithograph, 1851.

tion, that it operates actively to produce certain concepts of modernity for which the image of femininity is often a kind of scrim, a screen on which is projected a constellation of desires and anxieties that are themselves constitutive of the social psychology of modernity.

By the beginning of the 1850s, positive/negative photographic processes and the attendant mass production they enabled transformed the cult of images into a veritable flood tide. Photographic pornography itself passed from the status of luxury object to mass-produced commodity, from an artisanal mode of production to a fully industrialized one, from the province of male elites to that of working-class men. While lithographic imagery of femininity continued to be produced and disseminated—including the reissue of

July Monarchy classics like Achille Devéria, Charles Bargue, and their ilk—photographic icons of femininity, of all sorts, of all formats, effectively constituted another quantum leap in numbers and breadth of dissemination.

Consequently, there exist in the first decades of the nineteenth century an already existing schema for the manufacture of types, new visual technologies for their quantitative expansion and dissemination, and, well before the July Monarchy, a demonstrable proliferation of images of femininity in both high and mass culture. Schema, technology, and motif come together at a historical moment in which, to use Raymond Williams's useful terms, emergent and residual forms of social and sexual identity alike are subjected to the twin juggernauts of capitalism and modernization, punctuated by cycles of political revolution and reaction.

Hence, the heightened visibility of femininity, like the profusion of image technologies that both fostered and disseminated it, established—definitively, it seems—the libidinal economy of commodity culture, which retains, in both Marx's and Freud's characterizations, its essentially fetishistic attributes and structures. And insofar as femininity was everywhere seen and "spoken" by midcentury, we do well to look not only at all sides of Venus but at all aspects of visual representation. As Frank Mort and the late Nicholas Green have written: "Visual representations need to be seen as a part of an interlocking set of histories which involve multiple relations and dependencies across a range of social fields and practices. It is no longer a question of analyzing an internal field of visual imagery in its relation to a set of external determinations . . . but of understanding the interdependence and interchange of discourses and practices, with mutually reinforcing results."[43] It is precisely for this reason that any hard and fast distinctions between mass cultural production and our cherished icons of avant-gardism and modernism, or moralizing distinctions between acceptably sensual and unacceptably pornographic imagery, are neither tenable nor desirable. Which is not to say that there are no differences between, say, Manet's *Olympia* and Cabanel's *Birth of Venus,* but rather to say that these differences need to be reformulated in the light of feminist work on representation itself. Once it is admitted that both mass cultural and high cultural forms are instrumental in the construction of lived subjectivities, there seems little justification in maintaining discursive boundaries between the mass-produced imagery pumped out by the millions and the production of the modernist avant-garde, or, for that matter, the official and sanctioned production of elite culture. It is not then simply a question of examining how femininity is discursively produced by, for example, both Manet and Cabanel but, more historically speaking, a question of examining this discursive production in a range of different sites, none of which are independent of one another. Furthermore, if Venus can be said to prevail in the salons of midcentury

France, we are all well acquainted with her other side; not goddess but whore, not ennobled in easel painting or marble but reduced to banal lithograph or photograph, not the vehicle of the ideal but the emblem of carnality and corruption. While both classes of imagery are equally fantasmatic and reciprocally dependent on each other's terms, what needs to be explored is the traffic between them. For if one orthodox account of modernism insists on the absolute and irreducible difference between forms of mass and high culture, another perspective, one more attentive to the nature of subject matter —and, furthermore, attentive to femininity as itself a crucial term within modernity—reveals a complex web of interdependencies and relationships. Finally, and in conclusion, it would seem that an inquiry into the genealogy of the mass-produced imagery of eroticized femininity provides us with a way—pace Grandville's emblematic *Venus at the Opera*—to historicize the psychic fetishism underpinning the production of woman-as-image with the commodity fetishism that has been so seamlessly merged with it. For insofar as we are enabled to grasp the historicity of forms that have been so effectively naturalized, we may be better enabled to denaturalize them.

NOTES

1. Wolfgang Fritz Haug, *Critique of Commodity Aesthetics: Appearance, Sexuality, and Advertising in Capitalist Society*, trans. Robert Bock (Minneapolis: University of Minnesota Press, 1986).

2. Roland Barthes, "The Photographic Message," in Barthes, *Image, Music, Text*, trans. Richard Howard (New York: Hill and Wang, 1977), 31.

3. In using the term "femininity," I am referring to a social and psychosexual concept, which I largely dissociate from its ostensible referent—biological women. I take "femininity" and "masculinity" to be historically shifting and mobile models and roles, forged on the level of the symbolic, which collectively represent a culture's gender ideology. The antifoundationalist, anti-essentialist, social constructivist position taken here has now a substantial bibliography. See for example, Judith Butler, *Gender Trouble: Feminism and the Subversion of Identity* (New York: Routledge, 1990); Denise Riley, *Am I That Name? Feminism and the Category of "Women" in History* (Minneapolis: University of Minnesota Press, 1988); Joan Wallach Scott, *Gender and the Politics of History* (New York: Columbia University Press, 1988).

4. Abigail Solomon-Godeau, "The Legs of the Countess," *October* 39 (winter 1986): 87–105.

5. Griselda Pollock, "What's Wrong with 'Images of Women'?" in *Framing Feminism: Art and the Woman's Movement, 1970–85*, ed. Rozika Parker and Griselda Pollock (London: Pandora Press, 1987), 132–38.

6. This is an enterprise most closely associated with the earlier work of Jean Baudrillard and Roland Barthes. See, for example, Baudrillard, *The Mirror of Production*, trans. Mark Poster (St. Louis, Mo.: Telos Press, 1975); idem, *For a Critique of the Political Economy of the Sign*, trans. Charles Levin (St. Louis, Mo.: Telos Press, 1981); Roland

Barthes, *Elements of Semiology*, trans. Annette Lavers and Colin Smith (New York: Hill and Wang, 1986); idem, "Myth Today," in Barthes, *Mythologies*, trans. Annette Lavers (New York: Hill and Wang, 1972.)

7. Thomas Richards, *The Commodity Culture of Victorian England: Advertising and Spectacle, 1851–1914* (Stanford: Stanford University Press, 1990).

8. For example, Chandra Mukerji, *From Graven Images: Patterns of Modern Materialism* (New York: Columbia University Press, 1983); Neil McKendrick, John Brewer, and J. H. Plumb, *The Birth of a Consumer Society: The Commercialization of Eighteenth-Century England* (Bloomington: Indiana University Press, 1982); Arjun Appadurai, ed., *The Social Life of Things: Commodities in Cultural Perspective* (Cambridge: Cambridge University Press, 1986); and Edwards, *Commodity Culture of Victorian England*.

9. Martin Jay, *Downcast Eyes: The Denigration of Vision in Twentieth-Century French Thought* (Berkeley: University of California Press, 1993).

10. Haug, *Critique of Commodity Aesthetics*, 55.

11. For discussions of the implications of new forms of consumption for women in the European city, see Rachel Bowlby, *Just Looking: Consumer Culture in Dreiser, Gissing, and Zola* (London: Methuen, 1985); Ann Friedberg, *Window Shopping: Cinema and the Postmodern* (Berkeley: University of California Press, 1993); Rosalind H. Williams, *Dream Worlds: Consumption in Late-Nineteenth-Century France* (Berkeley: University of California Press, 1982); Elizabeth Wilson, *Adorned in Dreams: Fashion and Modernity* (London: Virago, 1985).

12. In this regard, see the exhibition catalogue for the exhibition organized by Beatrice Farwell, *The Cult of Images* (Santa Barbara: Santa Barbara Museum of Art, 1977).

13. See Solomon-Godeau, "Male Trouble: A Crisis in Representation," *Art History* 16, no. 2 (June 1993): 23–42.

14. Beatrice Farwell, *Manet and the Nude: A Study of Iconography in the Second Empire* (New York: Garland Editions, 1981).

15. A link may be made here between the satirical eye cast by illustrators and printmakers on the "effeminacy" of the dandies, and those contemporary history paintings that thematized the collision of ancien régime and bourgeois masculinities such as the encounter between Dreux-Brezé, the king's delegate to the Estates General, and Mirabeau, the representative of the Third Estate (a subject painted, for example, by both Delacroix and Delaroche).

16. For a discussion of how ballet reflected (and also constructed) these changes in gender ideology see Solomon-Godeau, "The Legs of the Countess."

17. The dominating position of the prostitute in nineteenth-century imagery hardly requires demonstration, either in its numerous literary incarnations or within visual culture. Some recent discussions of this powerful symbol are as follows: Charles Bernheimer, *Figures of Ill Repute: Representing Prostitution in Nineteenth-Century France* (Cambridge: Harvard University Press, 1989); Hollis Clayson, *Painted Love: Prostitution in French Art of the Impressionist Era* (New Haven: Yale University Press, 1991); Alain Corbin, "La Prostituée," in *Miserable et glorieuse: La Femme au XIXe siècle*, ed. Jean-Paul Aron (Paris: Éditions Complexe, 1900); Jann Matlock, *Scenes of Seduction: Prostitution, Hysteria, and Reading Difference in Nineteenth-Century France* (New York: Columbia University Press, 1994); Susan Buck-Morss, "The Flâneur, the Sandwichman, and the Whore," *New German Critique* 13, no. 39 (fall 1986): 99–140.

THE OTHER SIDE OF VENUS   *147*

18. Walter Benjamin, *Charles Baudelaire: A Lyric Poet in the Age of High Capitalism,* trans. Harry Zorn (London: Verso, 1983).

19. See in this regard, Rachel Harrison and Frank Mort, "Patriarchal Aspects of Nineteenth-Century State Formation: Property Relations, Marriage and Divorce, and Sexuality," in *Capitalism, State Formation, and Marxist Theory: Historical Investigations,* ed. Philip Corrigan (London: Quartet Books, 1980); Louis Devance, "Femme, famille, travaille, et morale sexuelle dans l'ideologie de 1848," *Romantisme,* nos. 13–14 (1976): 79–103; Yannick Ripa, *La Ronde des folles: Femme, folie, et enfermement au XIXe siècle* (Paris: Aubier, 1987); Erna Olafson Hellerstein, "French Women and the Orderly Household, 1830–1870," *Proceedings of the Western Society for French History* 3 (1976): 378–89; Robert Deniel, *Une image de la famille et de la société dans la Restauration (1815–1830): Etude de la Presse Catholique* (Paris: P.U.F., 1989); Jean-Paul Aron, ed. *Miserable et glorieuse.*

20. There is by now a substantial critical tradition that acknowledges femininity as an important emblem of and for the modern. This linkage is made quite explicit in literary sources ranging from Balzac through Baudelaire's poetry and prose poems (notably *Paris Spleen*) through to Zola's *Nana* on up through Victor Margueritte's *La Garçonne.* Femininity has also been traditionally associated with mass culture, itself negatively characterized as feminine. In this latter context see Andreas Huyssen, "Mass Culture as Woman: Modernism's Other," in *After the Great Divide: Modernism, Mass Culture, Postmodernism* (Bloomington: Indiana University Press, 1986); Tania Modleski, *Feminism without Women* (New York: Methuen, 1991).

21. Robert Muchembled, *Culture populaire et cultures des elites dans la France moderne* (Paris: P.U.F., 1977). See as well Peter Burke, *Popular Culture in Early Modern Europe* (London: Maurice Tempe Smith, 1978).

22. This model of cultural hegemony has been implicitly countered by, among others, Natalie Zemon Davis and Carlo Ginzburg. Davis's work on literacy and reading in early modern Europe focuses on the "negotiations" of oral culture that occur when, for example, written texts are read aloud to nonliterate auditors. Carlo Ginzburg has explored how literate culture can be altogether transformed and idiosyncratically interpreted by any one "user." See Davis, *Society and Culture in Early Modern France* (Stanford: Stanford University Press, 1975); and Ginzburg, *The Cheese and the Worms* (New York; Penguin, 1980).

23. See for example, the useful anthology *Rethinking Popular Culture: Contemporary Perspectives in Cultural Studies,* ed. Chandra Mukerji and Michael Schudson (Berkeley: University of California Press, 1991).

24. The growth of the lithographic industry in France has not yet been the subject of an inclusive study (nor, for that matter, does there yet exist a history of mass media in France), but Jeffrey Rosen's dissertation on the firm of Lemercier provides an indispensable overview that gives a good idea of the industry's scale. In 1819, for example, there were 2 lithographic print establishments in Paris; by 1839, there were more than 90. In 1847 the number of lithographic printers in Paris tripled, to 3,305. In that same year, 305 Parisian establishments sold products worth nearly 8 million francs. Classified under the economic rubric *imprimerie, papetrie, et gravure* (printing, paper, and engraving), lithography was part of an industry that was then rated eleventh in terms of economic importance. By 1860, the volume of sales for all lithographic products (*ouvrages de commerce* and *ouvrages d'art*) had grown to 12.6 million francs per annum. Rosen further points out that the growth of the lithographic

industry was fostered by its modern—what he terms "proto-industrial"—mode of production. The rationalization of labor in lithographic printing establishments such as Lemercier's led to a division of labor whereby the lithographic print was produced by several hands. While not precisely assembly-line production, this division and diversification of labor made lithography not merely the medium by which the iconography of modernity was widely purveyed but a medium-cum-technology that was itself one of the prototypes for modern capitalist forms of commodity production. As well, the lithographic print was a new form of commodity. In 1851, for example, the Catalogue Renaissance (the mail-order print listing for the editor Jean-Baptiste François Delarue) was advertising individual lithographic prints for anything between Fr 1.6 to Fr 4. A weekly salary for a manual laborer in 1848 averaged Fr 2 per week. See Jeffrey Howard Rosen, "Lemercier et campagnie: Photolithography and the Industrialization of Print Production in France, 1837–1859" (Ph.D diss., Northwestern University, 1988).

25. The transformation to modernity has been itself identified with image production and consumption:

> Feuerbach observes about "our era" that it "prefers the image to the thing, the copy to the original, the representation to reality, appearance to being—while being aware of doing just that." And his premonitory complaint has been transformed in the twentieth century to a widely agreed-on diagnosis: that a society becomes modern when one of its chief activities is producing and consuming images, when images have an extraordinary powers to determine our demands upon reality and are themselves coveted substitutes for firsthand experience. . . .

Susan Sontag, *On Photography* (New York: Farrar, Straus, and Giroux, 1977), 153.

26. A useful survey of censorship of imagery can be found in Robert Justin Goldstein, *Censorship of Political Caricature in France* (Kent: Kent State University Press, 1989). See as well Irene Collins's standard study, *The Government and the Newspaper Press in France, 1814–1881* (Oxford: Oxford University Press, 1959).

27. For example, in the pornographic print series that comprises the *Passe-temps de Julie*, ca. 1830s, Réserve Libre, Bibliothèque Nationale.

28. Differences between rococo easel painting and inexpensive prints are, of course, inherent in their forms. But aside from the obvious contrast between the painting's status as a unique luxury object (which includes its attributes of scale, color, facture, texture, and demonstration of the artist's virtuosity and style), there are also the differences in the spectator's perception that correspond to the shift from object to image. In this respect, the term *imagerie* serves to remind us that, print connoisseurship notwithstanding (and in the case of nonintaglio processes especially), responses to prints tend to be more focused on motif than on formal attributes. This doubtless explains why prints could be sold through catalogs, where the only information provided was the name of the artist, the subject or title, and the price. The second, and equally obvious, distinction is to do with the contrasting conditions of consumption. While the price of a Devéria lithograph put it well beyond the means of working-class purchasers, it was entirely affordable for the bourgeois patron, to whom, moreover, it was directly addressed.

29. Laura Mulvey, "Visual Pleasure and Narrative Cinema," in Mulvey, *Visual and Other Pleasures* (London: Macmillan, 1988).

30. See in this regard Rachel Bowlby's chapter on Zola's *La Bonheur des femmes* in

her *Just Looking: Consumer Culture in Dreiser, Gissing, and Zola*; Michael B. Miller, *The Bon Marché: Bourgeois Culture and the Department Store, 1869–1920* (Princeton: Princeton University Press, 1981); Benjamin, *Charles Baudelaire;* Jennifer Jones, "*Coquettes* and *Grisettes:* Women Buying and Selling in Ancien Régime Paris," in this volume.

31. I am distinguishing here between prints that are functionally erotic icons as opposed to the more "sociological" or satirical work of an artist like Gavarni, let alone an artist like Daumier, who is largely uninterested in eroticism or femininity as a subject. Thus, Gavarni's print series that deal with feminine types and typologies—*lorettes, lionnes, débardeuses,* etc.—are more concerned with social relations and rarely reduce to the pinup or simple icon.

32. Walter Benjamin, *Gesammelte Schriften,* ed. Rolf Tiedemann and Hermann Schweppenhauser (Frankfurt am Main: Suhrkamp Verlag, 1972–1989), 5:435. I use Susan Buck-Morss's elegant and illuminating gloss on the *Passagen-Werk,* "The Flaneur, the Sandwichman, and the Whore," 121. See as well her full-length study *The Dialectics of Seeing: Walter Benjamin and the Arcades Project* (Cambridge: MIT Press, 1989).

33. See in this regard: Beatrice Farwell, "Pinups and Erotica," in vol. 4 of *French Popular Lithographic Imagery, 1815–1870* (Chicago: University of Chicago Press, forthcoming).

34. Cf. the now-classic essays by Laura Mulvey, "You Don't Know What's Happening, do you Mr. Jones?" and "Visual Pleasure and Narrative Cinema," both of which detail the ways in which the female body can be figured as fetish. Both essays in Mulvey, *Visual and Other Pleasures.*

35. Anne McClintock, "Screwing the System: Sexwork, Race, and the Law," *Boundary 2* (summer 1992): 72, in a special issue on feminism and postmodernism edited by Margaret Ferguson and Jennifer Wicke.

36. William Pietz, "Fetishism and Materialism: The Limits of Theory in Marx," in *Fetishism as Cultural Discourse,* ed. Emily Apter and William Pietz (Ithaca: Cornell University Press, 1993), 119–51, quote on p. 147. See as well Pietz's excellent series of articles on fetishism, "The Problem of the Fetish," *Res* 9 (spring 1985): 5–17; *Res* 13 (spring 1987): 23–45; and *Res* 16 (autumn 1988): 105–23. I am greatly indebted to his work as well as to discussions on the subject with Avery Gordon and Lawrence Rickels.

37. Cf. Abigail Solomon-Godeau, "Rethinking Erotic Photography: Notes towards a Project of Historical Salvage," in Solomon-Godeau, *Photography at the Dock: Essays on Photographic History, Institutions, and Practices* (Minneapolis: University of Minnesota Press, 1991).

38. See Robert Darnton, *Edition et sédition: L'Univers de la litterature clandestine au XVIIIe siècle* (Paris: Gallimard, 1991). With respect to some of the implications of this discursive organization, see Lynn Hunt's eloquent introduction, "Obscenity and the Origins of Modernity, 1500–1800," in the anthology *The Invention of Pornography: Obscenity and the Origins of Modernity, 1500–1800,* ed. Lynn Hunt (New York: Zone Books, 1993).

39. There is still only one monographic biography devoted to the life and works of Devéria, which is also about his brother, Maximilien Gauthier. *Achille et Eugène Devéria* (Paris: H. Floury, 1925). I have drawn as well on the exhibition catalogue *Achille Devéria: Témoin du romantisme Parisien, 1800–1857* (Paris: Musée Renan-Scheffer, July–September 1985). Other information has been provided by Farwell, *The Cult of*

Images; and idem, *The Charged Image* (Santa Barbara: Santa Barbara Museum of Art, 1989). Devéria is in many respects an ideal figure for a discussion of nineteenth-century mass culture, given, among other factors, his prolific output (over three thousand extant lithographs and over three hundred books for which he provided the illustrations).

40. My assumption that the traffic in sexual, as opposed to politically provocative, imagery was less strenuously policed and prosecuted is based on my reading of the following archives: Archives de la Police, Carton 229, Service des Moeurs 1829–1878; Archives Nationales F18*VI-48, Dépôt des Estampes et Planches Gravées Presentées et Non-autorisé (through September 1835); Archives Nationales F18, 39, and 40, Correspondance, mémoires et rapports sur les ouvrages censurés par la police, rapports des censeurs, hommages d'ouvrages, 1803–1828.

41. For a good discussion of these distinct types of erotized femininity see Novelene Ross, *The Bar of the Folies Bergères* (Ann Arbor: UMI Press, 1978).

42. For a discussion of the assimilation of typology and physiology into French visual culture, see Judith Wechsler, *A Human Comedy: Physiognomy and Caricature in Nineteenth-Century France* (Chicago: University of Chicago Press, 1982). See as well Anne Coffin Hanson, *Manet and the Modern Tradition* (New Haven: Yale University Press, 1977).

43. Frank Mort and Nicholas Greene, "Is There Anyone Here from Education (Again)? Radical Art History and Education for the 1990s," *Block* 3 (winter 1987–88): 20–27.

PART TWO

Establishing the Modern Consumer Household

The essays in this part examine the obligations of families as consumers and providers. Obligations to provide subsistence to children and pay creditors, to purchase up-to-date household appliances, and to plan for insurance and savings were central to establishing the modern Western consumer household. Many forces were active in establishing what these obligations should be. States were active in establishing contractual obligations not only through consumer legislation but also through laws on credit, property, and social entitlement. Reform movements were active in prescribing the obligations of wives to husbands and vice versa and of both toward their offspring. Advertisers were active in pitching their slogans to family values at the same time as they pandered to individual desire. Ultimately, families themselves determined how these obligations were fulfilled, though still little is understood about how such intimate negotiations over desires and needs were carried out, often in the face of implacable economic pressures.

The context for these essays is the rise of the modern consumer household, which we can define schematically as one dependent on market exchange for most of its supplies and services, by way of contrast with the so-called producer household, one that relies mainly on its own resources and labor. In the accounts of some historians of the family, the passage from one kind of household to the other reads like a linear development. Accordingly, the demise of the extended producer family started during the industrial revolution and was the outcome of urbanization, the spread of the factory system, and the modernization of retailing systems. These developments in turn fostered the household's growing dependency on market-provided goods and services. As the household became more involved in market transactions, family life was exposed to new domestic ideologies, housework was gradually mechanized, and female labor was redeployed within a smaller household to respond to new standards of child rearing, nutrition, and hygiene, as well as to gain access to government-provided social services.[1]

This transition has as its conventional point of departure the British rural cottage circa 1800. There, the story goes, men and women worked side by side; the many children nearby helped intermittently and were educated under the tutelage of their parents, through apprenticeships, or by the local parish. The household economy was largely self-sufficient, relying on barter and gift arrangements with kin networks for what could not be obtained from its own husbandry. The conventional end point is the American suburban homestead circa 1960. There, while the father worked away from home, commuting by automobile to an office job, the mother, isolated from relatives, friends, and even neighbors, operated a self-contained, all-equipped establishment-cum-decorative garden. Household comanager with Mr. Breadwinner, Mrs. Consumer was an astute and mobile shopper, bringing her expertise to all aspects of consumer choice—from the schools for her children and the pet's veterinarian to the family's health insurance plan.

The essays here suggest that this development was anything but rapid or straightforward. Nothing about modern family attitudes toward consumption seems to have come naturally, least of all the sex-based division of labor between Mr. Breadwinner and Mrs. Consumer. If studies of the eighteenth-century consumer revolution are right and if the increased participation rates of European women at the moment of transition to mass consumption in the 1960s are read correctly, significant changes in household consumption patterns have been just as likely to push women into the labor market as to shunt them off into domesticity.[2] The studies here suggest too that there was no unitary or cross-class model of modern consumer household, at least not until after World War II. From the nineteenth century through the interwar years in the United States and through the 1950s in continental Europe, family standards of living varied profoundly according to class, so much so that in early-twentieth-century Europe, bourgeois and working-class families were separated by castelike differences in tastes and needs, and several million rural abodes still resembled the eighteenth-century producer households in their self-sufficiency.[3] These profound differences of class were in turn played out in the very different demands made on the male and female members of the household.

Family budget studies suggest that the most remarkable difference between working-class and bourgeois households in the early part of this century regarded expenditure on food and lodging.[4] In working-class families, expenditure on food did not decline proportionately as income grew, nor did expenditure on lodging increase, contrary to what might be predicted from Engel's laws on consumption.[5] When real wages went up, which occurred rarely, the extra pay went to more food and clothing purchases as well as to sociable pastimes outside of the home, such as drink and games.[6]

The fact that income was both low and unpredictable only reinforced these tendencies. By contrast, even when the incomes of bourgeois families declined, the families rarely allowed the share allotted to lodging to diminish, and they equally maintained their outlays on servants, toiletries, clothing, and other marks of status, signally education, even if this meant cutting down on the costs of food. In the bourgeois case, it seems, the women of the family with the help of servants compensated for cheaper cuts and ersatz ingredients by more imaginative but also more laborious food preparation.

What these spending choices meant for defining class lifestyles has been at least hypothesized, whereas what they meant for defining gender roles has not. The French sociologist Maurice Halbwachs, who invented the notion of "lifestyle" (*genre de vie*) in pioneering research on working-class consumption, strongly emphasized the socially determined nature of working-class expenditures. By and large, Halbwachs had household choices reflecting the preferences of the men, who, he argued, to compensate for their atomized work experience, favored all occasions of sociability. This preference suggested that the meaning of domestic space differed according to class. Thus, working-class families (which changed lodging with astonishing frequency in the first part of the century) played down the value of domestic space, not only because they had huge difficulties finding cheap and decent housing but also because they preferred forms of consumption that gave a sense of collective life, such as large midday meals, clothing, and public entertainment. In this highly sociable, if primitive, form, consumption reinforced working-class subcultures. Needless to say, Halbwachs's pessimistic assessment of the animality of working-class needs sharply contrasts with the high-minded vision of working-class cooperativists. In many areas of Europe, as well as the western United States, working-class households were embedded in tight networks of socialist consumer cooperatives and mutual aid associations in recognition both of the shared needs of their members and of their common political goals.[7]

By contrast, the characteristic sign of living in the bourgeois style was to maintain a dignified residence and a full array of hired labor—whose wages were minuscule and rarely showed any increase. A bourgeois woman simply did not do laundry, scrubbing, food provisioning, or other menial labor. It was also crucial that household operations at least pretend to be conducted with the same rationality as business enterprise, according to accounting rules that were codified in household ledgers.[8]

Prescriptive literature, as well as some historical studies, pretty much ignore that class differences entailed significant differences in housewifery. However, the different functions respectively of the working-class and bourgeois household in reinforcing class solidarity imply very different roles for the working-class and the bourgeois woman consumer. The pattern of expenditure for the bourgeoisie reflected considerable individuality, especially with regards to socially strategic commodities such as home furnishings, education, and charity, even when the family fortunes were in decline. To manage this expenditure in turn demanded the exercise of huge expertise, taste, and power with respect to the servants, shopkeepers, and craftsmen. In this sense, to come back to a point made in the previous section, the bourgeois house mistress was the indispensable and highly visible backbone of the bourgeois social constellation.

In comparison, working-class consumers faced significant constraints on their purchases, not only because of low income but also as a result of class-rooted social routines. There was virtually no discretionary spending: family expenditures, consciously or not, were largely regular and customary. Mostly, families accepted the patterns laid down for them by their community.[9] Poverty must also have deterred efficiency, since consumer efficiency depends on the ability to shop around. Given the relatively unspecialized operations of provisioning, it is not surprising that male-female roles could be interchangeable, a point that Susan Porter Benson makes compellingly in her essay here on interwar working families in the United States.

In social systems in which needs were still class-categorized and spending was carefully controlled, consumer credit was a vexing issue. It would be difficult to speak of consumer credit for the working classes in any formal sense until the 1920s in the United States and a decade after World War II in Europe. But it had long been customary in family routines for the chief provisioner, usually the mother, to hock the family sheets or candlesticks at the pawnshop or to cozy up to local storekeepers to obtain credit in order to tide the family over from one payday to the next.[10] Even before delayed payment and installment purchasing were formalized, the middle classes had begun to avail themselves of the informal credit arrangements that individual shopkeepers had traditionally extended to aristocratic customers.

Though credit purchases offered a kind of freedom to middle-class women, momentarily delivering them from dependency on their husbands' purse, it also exposed their lack of contractual freedom, feeding what one of our authors, Erika Rappaport, delicately phrases as "tensions around purchasing." That term could usefully embrace the episodes of kleptomania among female shoppers in British, U.S., and French department stores at the turn of the century, as well as the thousands of legal disputes over property ownership and indebtedness involving tradesmen, women customers, and spouses in England in the wake of the married women's property acts of the 1870s and 1880s.[11] Near the end of the century, these conflicts, insofar as they involved property rights, patriarchal oppression, and moral dilemmas, had become the stuff of high drama, as Henrik Ibsen's feminist tragedy *A Doll's House* (1879) captured. Nora makes her stage entrance returning from Christmas shopping. Her hidden sin turns out to be the theft of credit: she forged her dead father's signature to a loan to pay for her husband's rest cure in Italy. Her striving spouse reveals himself to be a consummate hypocrite. Nora's drastic, irrevocable response, one that Thorstein Veblen would have appreciated, is to abandon her family.

Even lesser family dramas created legal dilemmas for local justice systems. If the courts ruled in favor of the creditors, as Erika Rappaport shows, they created a form of complicity against the husband. If they favored the husband, they disregarded the sanctity of private property. Since property laws made husbands and wives liable for different types of debts, husbands for their families' necessities, wives for their own luxury purchases, they put the courts in the intrusive position of having to interpret the nature of goods and interpret family needs.

At a later moment, credit, as it became widespread, may have freed women from some of the constraints they experienced, either from lack of control over property or for want of a personal income. Surely, it curtailed some of the arbitrariness of credit relations, which, if novels and movie melodrama contain any truth, could be exploited by bullying shopkeepers to seduce hapless female customers. When installment buying, "funny money," the "never-never," eventually became part of household budgeting, it surely modified family negotiations over purchases. Whether in fact consumer credit actually redressed some of the asymmetries of power in household getting and spending is doubtful, though we cannot ignore that the classic dupe of mid–twentieth century comic literature is not the old-fashioned cuckold but the long-suffering spouse of modest means, the white-collar Dagwood whose leisured wife, Blondie, is perpetually out shopping with the girls, joyfully dissipating his salary.

But to think that any individual freely disposed of his (or her) salary according to his (or her) individual lights is a fallacy. As the austere economy of the nineteenth century gave way to relatively higher wages as well as to enticing amusements and cheap goods on which to spend them, mechanisms of advice and constraint proliferated. Social reformers had no problem arguing that a man's wage was a social rather than a personal matter, and that the working class man in particular could not be trusted to spend it in the best interest of the family and society. By the turn of the century, as Anna Igra shows, welfare reformers in the United States reasoned that the interests of the "public purse" were paramount. Irresponsible consumption on the part of workingmen who valued their own pleasures—gambling, drink, and "other" women—over their wives' and children's well-being amounted to welfare fraud when it threw women and children onto the relief rolls. By the same token, social workers kept a vigilant eye on mothers to assure that welfare payments were consumed for the purposes intended by the law.

More needs to be said about the invention of the male breadwinner. Although the modern sexual division of labor dates back to the mid-nineteenth-century factory system, with roots even earlier, the notion of a scientifically efficient division between the wage-earning half of the family and the consuming half is purely an invention of the early twentieth. If a date can be identified for this invention, it is 1908, when Henry Ford decided, in the context of launching the Model T, to promote the five-dollar, eight-hour day as a means to widen markets for the standardized goods of mass production. For Ford, the unit of consumption was not the individual but the family. The five-dollar day was intended for family men not wastrel single males, much less women. To secure that pay packets were appropriately spent by families, the company established a huge system of social service and surveillance.[12] The ideal family was analogous to the firm: it was based on a clear-cut division of labor and mechanized with a standardized set of consumer durables. Its members thereby achieved an equality of sorts, a consumer democracy, through shared access to mass-manufactured goods.

In effect, with rising incomes and in the absence of European-type social stratifications, consumer spending in the United States eventually yielded a convergence around a new middle-class pattern of consumption. Retailers and advertising targeted the family as the primary consumer unit. Government services facilitated this development by linking households to modern services such as gas, electrical, and sewage lines and to the national market by means of transport subsidies, rural postal services, national radio broadcasting, and telephone lines. The household management movement—playing on the notion that the household was analogous to the firm, that there was a "one best way" in domestic equipment and administration—devised strict managerial precepts to accompany household mechanization, invoking the name of the engineering genius F. W. Taylor, while business, foreseeing a vast middle market in home furnishings, pioneered the growth of low-cost consumer durables. In the new consumer household, characterized initially by very low labor participation rates among married women, women occupied a highly visible role, acquiring the know-how to mix discretionary spending with household provisioning. In time, the sharp class distinctions between the survival-oriented proletarian household and the genteel bourgeois home with its servants, house mistress, and heirlooms gave way to a more diffuse and subtle set of distinctions, based on income and reinforced through a wide variety of social, educational, and cultural acquisitions.

True, the fordist paradigm hardly does justice to the constrained choices of the gamut of working-class families; in particular, it fails to illuminate the exclusion of many African-Americans from mass consumption, including almost all those in the rural South. Moreover, Susan Porter Benson shows that during the Great Depression especially, gender roles were out of necessity fluid, at least so far as procuring household basics, and that strategies of survival called forth unceasing inventiveness, haggling, and self-deprivation on the part of women.

The modernization of the household in the context of the relative success of fordist strategies of modernization in the United States also returns us to the issue of why mass consumption took so long to make inroads in Europe and, specifically, to the implications this delay had for adopting machinery for household use. Sue Bowden and Avner Offer recognize that low income may have been one impediment to the consumer durables revolution in interwar Britain, but not the only one. Electrical domestic appliances would appear to have found a receptive middle-class market, in that they promised to diminish women's hard physical labor within the home and save time. And during this period, appliances related to domestic leisure (such as radios) did indeed enjoy a rapid diffusion rate. Yet appliances targeted for housework purposes (such as vacuum cleaners) spread slowly, the effect, the authors argue, of women's limited employment opportunities outside the home, inferior earnings, and low bargaining power inside the family. Even within the English middle class, mechanization was slow. Advertisements emphasized that home appliances would offset the loss of domestic servants, as well as improve standards of cleanliness. In reality, mechanization did not compensate for the precipitous decline in the availability of hired labor. Housework for middle-class women may even have increased to achieve new standards of food preparation, home hygiene, and child care. At the same time, working-class women were effectively shut out of the market for home appliances because of their high price, their big operating expenses, and the lack of deferred payment facilities. With middle-class housewives doing more drudge work, the result, ironically, was some equalization of labor burdens among women across classes.

Many of the trends in family consumption discernible for the United States starting in the early 1920s appear in continental Europe starting in the mid-1950s. In 1960, to suggest the contrast, practically every urban American family had access to a mechanical washing machine, whereas in England, only 27 percent of the households did, and in France, only 12 percent did.[13] In the course of the "economic miracle" starting in the mid-1950s, family budgets began to be expended differently: outlays on food, clothing, and lodging dropped significantly while expenditure on the household (furnishings, but also gas, electricity, and so on), leisure, transportation, and culture rose.[14] Even in relatively backward countries and across all classes, there was a convergence of purchases around a standard set of household equipment, from indoor toilets to the most recent commodity on the market, namely, television. Unlike studies of household budgets from only three decades before, European studies from the 1960s took for granted that there were overarching standards of household hygiene and comfort, common to all classes and eventually to be shared by all Western Europeans.[15] This vast change in the notion of standard of living was tied not only to rising income, as a result of big productivity increases and government spending on social services, but also to urbanization, the huge shift of rural workers into town-based occupations, and, last but not least, to new housing.

However, once initiated, the changes in household spending proceeded so rapidly as to suggest not only increased income but also radically changed values as well. It is plausible that families were persuaded to purchase a refrigerator or gas stove on the basis of time-worn calculations about the marginal costs of replacing female labor in the home with equipment. For families to decide, say, that a refrigerator was a priority purchase seemed to depend on a whole new decision-making process, one based on giving new weight to the value of female labor, to household comfort and nutrition, and to achieving social status within the new middle-class social constellation by subscribing to the new common standard of living. Such decisions would thus imply a changed consensus among generations within the family (which was especially important if there was a rural-urban shift) as well as between the male and female heads of household about the importance of the quality of life in the home.

As households became equipped with modern communications goods such as radios, television, and telephone, they underwent a real revolution with respect to their links with the outside: the modern homemaker was socialized not so much with respect to neighborhood or class-hierarchical standards, as might have occurred in the past, but with an eye to wider, more socially diffuse national standards of well-being. Women themselves simply by virtue of being the major users of consumer durables in the home acquired a leadership of sorts in setting new standards of comfort. In Italy, where rural landflight was especially precipitous, women in search of "modern comforts" contributed to the rapid depopulation of the countryside by refusing peasant men as marriage partners.[16] As they handled more discretionary income and credit, working-class provisioners educated themselves to become shoppers, the instruction manuals, so to speak, being their exposure to national advertising and their experiments with the new pricing and display systems in operation at self-service stores. More and more, old-fashioned retailers came under pressure from the new wholesaling systems, their capacity to arbitrate taste as well as to control pricing—up or down—diminished as manufacturers pushed branded products onto the market.

These developments were accompanied, as we have seen in the United States, by the rallying of household members around powerful familist ideologies. In the Catholic countries especially, Italy, France, and West Germany, these ideologies were promoted by Christian democrats, with an anticommunist scope. Though governments in Europe generally made more provision for social spending than the United States government did, resulting in the growth of full-fledged welfare states by the 1970s, the ethos underlined was family-oriented consumption. This was the consumerism imputed to the austere Prime Minister De Gaspari of Italy. By the early 1950s, with re-construction well under way, European households began to glimpse a world of satisfactions akin to the consumer promises that Herbert Hoover had held out to the American people in the 1920s with his pledge of a "chicken in every pot." In Italy, it would have been utterly rash for a politician to make extravagant claims for what the consumer revolution could deliver. As late as the mid-1950s, few working-class families believed that they would ever own a refrigerator, and a small-cylinder Fiat car was a mirage. Nonetheless, as early as 1950, De Gaspari could safely see the day that there would be a Vespa on every door stoop.

Whether we can speak of a full-fledged European Mrs. Consumer in the postwar context is nonetheless debatable. In most European countries there was never any lengthy period that women were not significantly active in the labor force: indeed, the boom in mass consumption was accompanied by the massive reentry of women into the labor force. Moreover, the consumer revolution was not preceded, much less quickly accompanied, by any profound reform in the status of women in the family or the workplace. On the European continent, outside of the Scandinavian states, this did not occur until the 1970s. Nevertheless, as households from all classes converged in their spending around a single middle standard, observers agreed that the bell had tolled for the old bourgeois standard of life. By the early 1950s in France, the male heirs to the old bourgeois lines were becoming salaried professionals and income from property had begun to be taxed. The chief signs of the demise of the bourgeois household from the point of view of consumer mores, were the disappearing servant class, the rise in expenditure on automobiles (which would soon grow for workers as well), and the passing of the meticulously kept accounts of household expenditures.[17]

NOTES

1. Joan Wallach Scott and Louise A. Tilly, "Women in the Family Consumer Economy," in *Women, Work, and Family,* 2d ed. (New York: Methuen, 1987); Ruth Schwartz Cowan, *More Work for Mother: The Ironies of Household Technology from the Open Hearth to the Microwave* (New York: BasicBooks, 1983); Christina Hardyment, *From Mangle to Microwave: The Mechanization of Household Work* (New York: Basil Blackwell, 1988). See too Elaine Tyler May, *Homeward Bound: American Families in the Cold War Era* (New York: BasicBooks, 1988).

2. This flexible deployment of female labor in economies of transition is well illuminated in Anna Cento Bull and Paul Corner, *From Peasant to Entrepreneur: The Survival of the Family Economy in Italy* (Oxford: Berg, 1993).

3. For late 1930s France, André de Cambiaire estimated that 20 percent of the total national output of goods and services was consumed within the households in which it was produced, without passing through the market (*L'Autoconsommation agricole en France* [Rennes: Imprimerie Réunies, 1952], 184). In Italy, which was some-

what more rural than France and where household autarchy was pushed by the fascist regime, autoconsumption was estimated at one-third the total national product (Victoria de Grazia, *How Fascism Ruled Women: Italy, 1922–1945* [Berkeley: University of California Press, 1992], 83–84). In far more industrialized Germany, too, even urban families had recourse to home production. According to Michael Wildt, the number of garden plots (*Schrebergarten*) within the Hamburg city limits grew from 4,200 in 1917 to 47,422 in 1933 (Michael Wildt, *Am Beginn der "Konsumgesellschaft": Mangelerfahrung, Lebenshaltung, Wohlstandshoffnung in Westdeutschland in den fünfziger Jahren* [Hamburg: Ergebnisse Verlag, 1994], 23).

4. Maurice Halbwachs, *La Classe ouvrière et les niveaux de vie: Recherches sur la hiérarchie des besoins dans les sociétés industrielles contemporaines* (Paris: Félix Alcan, 1912); *L'Evolution des besoins dans les classes ouvrières* (Paris: Félix Alcan, 1933).

5. These laws, formulated in the 1860s by the German statistician Ernst Engel on the basis of household budget studies, estimated the changes that certain items of family expenditure, e.g., food, clothing, and lodging, were estimated to undergo as proportions of total expenditure if income was increased. For a good introduction, see George J. Stigler, "The Early History of Empirical Studies of Consumer Behavior," *Journal of Political Economy* 62, no. 2 (April 1954), esp. 98–100.

6. See Henry Delpech, *Recherches sur le niveau de vie et les habitudes de consommation (Toulouse, 1936–1938)* (Paris: Librarie du Recueil Sirey, 1938).

7. See Lynn Abrams, *Worker Culture in Imperial Germany* (London: Routledge, 1992); Dana Frank, *Purchasing Power: Consumer Organizing, Gender, and the Seattle Labor Movement, 1919–1929* (Cambridge: Cambridge University Press, 1994); Ellen Furlough, *Consumer Cooperation in France: The Politics of Consumption, 1834–1930* (Ithaca: Cornell University Press, 1991), 193–224.

8. On the bourgeois family, see Marguerite Perrot, *Le Mode de vie des familles bourgeoises, 1873–1953*, 2d ed. (Paris: Presses de la Fondation Nationale des Sciences Politiques, 1982).

9. Hugo E. Pipping, *The Standard of Living: Its Conceptualization and Place in Economics* (Helsingfors: Societas Scientarum Fennica, 1953), 178.

10. On the United States, see the excellent study of Martha L. Olney, *Buy Now, Pay Later: Advertising, Credit, and Consumer Durables in the 1920s* (Chapel Hill: University of North Carolina Press, 1991). For European societies, there is no comparable study, though for England, Ellen Ross's *Love and Toil: Motherhood in Outcast London, 1870–1918* (New York: Oxford University Press, 1993), 40–55, contains pertinent information on the use of credit among working-class women.

11. Patricia O'Brien, "The Kleptomania Diagnosis: Bourgeois Women and Theft in Late-Nineteenth-Century France," *Journal of Social History* 17 (fall 1983): 65–77; and Elaine S. Abelson, *When Ladies Go A-Thieving: Middle-Class Shoplifters in the Victorian Department Store* (New York: Oxford University Press, 1989).

12. On fordism, specifically, see Stephen Meyer: *The Five-Dollar Day: Labor Management and Social Control in the Ford Motor Company, 1908–1921* (Albany: State University of New York Press, 1981). Lawrence Glickman studies the pressures internal to the labor movement and male working-class culture that shaped the breadwinner ethos, even earlier than the turn of the century. See in particular "Inventing the 'American Standard of Living': Gender, Race, and Working-Class Identity, 1880–1925," *Labor History* 34, nos. 2–3 (spring–summer 1993): 221–35.

13. This periodization is captured in two important books: Michael Wildt's *Am Beginn der "Konsumgesellschaft,"* which dates the beginning of the new period from 1950, technically 1948, with the currency reform; and Perrot's *Le Mode de vie des familles bourgeoises,* which treats the early 1950s as the point at which the bourgeois family ceased to exist in any socially meaningful sense. Statistics on washing machine diffusion in England and France are from, respectively, F. Graham Pyatt, *Priority Patterns and the Demand for Household Durable Goods* (Cambridge: Cambridge University Press, 1986), 38; and Paul-Marie de la Gorce, *La France Pauvre* (Paris: Grasset, 1965), 181.

14. François Gardes, "L'Evolution de la consommation marchande en Europe et aux U.S.A. depuis 1960," *Consommation: Revue de socio-economie* 30, no. 2 (April–June 1983): 3–32. Also Louis Levy-Garboua, "Les modes de consommation de quelques pays occidentaux: Comparaisons et lois d'evolution (1960–1980)," *Consommation: Revue de socio-economie* 30, no. 1 (January–March 1983): 4–52.

15. Dominique Badault, *Equipment du logement et demande de biens durables en Bretagne, 1962–1968* (Rennes: Centre Regional d'Etudes et de Formations Economiques, 1971), 293.

16. See on this Franco Alberoni, *L'integrazione dell'immigrato nella società industriale* (Bologna: Il Mulino, 1965).

17. Andre Siegfried, "Budgets d'hier et d'aujourd'hui," in Perrot, *Le Mode de vie des familles bourgeoises,* 262–63.

FIVE

"A Husband and His Wife's Dresses"

Consumer Credit and the Debtor Family in England, 1864–1914

Erika Rappaport

On 5 August 1892, a Mr. Charles Portier, trading as "Mme Portier, dress-maker," brought an action in the City of London Court against a Mr. and Mrs. Lewin to recover twenty pounds. Although all agreed that Mr. Portier had not been paid for the dresses he had made for Mrs. Lewin, both husband and wife denied responsibility for the bill. Mrs. Lewin pleaded that she owned no property and therefore could not be held liable for any debts. Mr. Lewin testified that he gave his wife a sufficient dress allowance beyond which he forbade her to spend. His attorney then argued that a husband was not legally accountable for his wife's debts "unless the wife had the direct authority of her husband to pledge his credit."[1]

The question of liability thus turned on proof that this privately bestowed authority had been given. For that purpose the court explored the couple's domestic arrangements, examining both their economic and emotional relationship. The judge speculated that "the fact that they are living together, eating and drinking at the same table is evidence that he sees the dresses on his wife" and implied that Mr. Lewin approved of his wife's purchases. Mr. Lewin, however, rebutted this argument, asserting that "he never knew what dresses his wife wore or where they came from." This contention was apparently cause for acquittal: the judge released him from all financial responsibility, with an admiring nod to the fact he was one of the "few men of sense in this world . . . who don't care a farthing for what their wives wear." Although judgment was entered against the separate estate of Mrs. Lewin, recovering money from a married woman was a drawn-out and generally unsuccessful endeavor. Mr. Charles Portier probably never saw his twenty pounds. In addition to his financial loss, "Madame Portier" suffered the indignity of being referred to by the judge as "a man carrying on business as a woman."[2]

More than money was at stake in this courtroom drama. Throughout the second half of the nineteenth century, thousands of others found that their financial entanglements brought them before England's county courts each year.[3] In settling their debts, debtors, creditors, and judges were active participants in a wider debate concerning the meaning of "family," "property," and "consumption," as well as the extent of women's legal agency.[4] Because the struggles around consumer debt involved confrontations within and between the home, the shop, and the courts, their history suggests that the family and the economy can hardly be regarded as separate spheres. As Leonore Davidoff and Catherine Hall have shown, the reproduction of the middle classes depended upon the linkages between these spheres.[5] Yet, if gender ideals, the social organization of the family, and the economy were mutually reinforcing, the same ideals and social arrangements could also undermine each other.

Indeed, married women's debts, incurred through purchasing on credit, pointed out an irreconcilable conflict between bourgeois domestic ideology and the growth of an advanced capitalist economy. The increasing impersonality of the market, coinciding with the cultural prescription that purchasing was a female activity, collided with shifting definitions of property ownership to produce a volatile and problematic relationship between retailers and their customers, and between husbands and wives. The social and cultural practices of buying and selling clashed with the laws that governed these activities. Wives shopped, but husbands generally paid for and legally owned the purchased goods. During the last decades of the nineteenth century, the English legal system wrestled with this inconsistency while reforming both married women's property rights and creditor-debtor law. While a husband's liability for his wife's consumption decreased steadily, a wife's legal responsibility increased slowly and unevenly. Into the twentieth century, who was responsible for a wife's debts remained unclear, and family discord and unpaid debts were frequently the result.

Whatever the precise locus of these financial and emotional conflicts, they ultimately turned upon a pervasive fear that the expanding consumer culture unleashed female desires that would bring financial and personal ruin upon both husbands and shopkeepers. These conflicts also called into question the integrity of the law and the morality of the family. Both husbands and retailers turned to the legal system to protect their economic well-being from female consumption, but the courts and legislature tended to favor the interests of husbands over those of retailers. Regardless of the husband's social class or the amount of debt, the legal system buttressed his economic authority against the dangers of credit, advertising, large luxurious urban shops, and itinerant hawkers of finery. Legal authorities interpreted women's shopping as immoral, since it potentially conferred on women power over their husband's economic and social position. Common and statutory law reflected this fear of women's power by limiting men's liability for their wives' consumption. These laws had the effect, enhanced by tradesmen's legitimate grievances, of further damaging women's credit and discrediting their autonomy as consumers.

CREDIT: "THE SHOPKEEPER'S TEMPTATION"

Purchasing on credit was as much a "cultural transaction" as a simple financial exchange in that it involved moral judgments about class, gender, consumer practices, and particular commodities.[6] Standardized and impersonal forms of credit such as the installment plan and credit card have been seen as contributing to the expansion of consumer society in the nineteenth and twentieth centuries by facilitating both the purchase and production of expensive consumer durables.[7] For most of the nineteenth century, however, consumer credit was still informal and was based on personal trust and a financial and moral assessment of the buyer.[8] From studies by Melanie Tebbutt and others, we know how informal store credit and the pawnshop forged social relations and sustained working-class families.[9] That consumer credit also occupied a prominent role in the middle- and upper-class family economy has not been sufficiently emphasized. Few studies have explored these diverse forms of consumer credit or how and why they changed during this period, much less their social and cultural meanings.

Selling on credit, which always created problems for small retailers, was a widespread practice throughout the nineteenth century, as it had been earlier.[10] Yet as the shopping population became more mobile in the second half of the century, informal store credit seemed increasingly risky, particularly for the urban shopkeeper selling expensive goods. Buying and selling, especially in an urban context, often involved strangers rather than neighbors and relations. Large shopping districts such as London's West End transformed the personal relations between buyer and seller into fleeting contacts between strangers. The ever more spectacular transformation in late-nineteenth-century consumption—the advent of advertising, monumental architecture, store services, and lavish displays—encouraged women to consume and to perceive consumption as a leisure activity.[11] In order to limit its risks, the business classes regularized the use of credit. Wholesalers turned to newspapers and trade papers to learn about the creditworthiness of their customers; local papers printed notices in which husbands publicly renounced their wife's agency. The larger firms also restricted the extension of credit and ultimately insisted upon cash, legitimating this practice by stressing the resulting reduced prices.[12] These options were not readily available to small urban retailers, who were therefore faced with all the risks attendant on the expansion of a credit economy.

At the same time, male householders were losing some of their authority

over family expenditure. Until the 1860s, the male head of household, as
the owner of the family's property, was considered to have a legal duty to
maintain that family and was assumed to have a direct knowledge of all familial consumption.[13] Since few married women owned property, most wives
could not enter into a contract of any kind, including a credit purchase.[14]
When they and other dependents bought goods, they traded on the basis of
the householder's credit, essentially acting as his agent. Wives frequently
bought goods trading on their husband's credit, but they usually did so in
local shops and markets, and wealthier families had basic provisions delivered directly to their home and paid for them at the end of the year.[15]

From the second half of the century on, however, the growth of new commodities and occasions for shopping, the relocation of markets, and the physical separation of workplace and home disrupted this system. Working-class
and middle-class husbands were no longer present when itinerant tradesmen
came to their homes to hawk their wares.[16] Middle- and upper-class women
were buying more and doing so further from their homes; for example, by
the 1860s, untold numbers of women traveled from the suburbs and provinces
for a day's shopping in the West End of London.[17] As male supervision waned
or became more impersonal, husbands, traditional retailers, and moralists
equated these consumer practices with seduction.[18] In this view, easy credit
aided the conquest of the female shopper.[19] When a woman pledged her husband's credit, she betrayed him by jeopardizing his economic and personal
well-being. Ideally family and market were separate spheres, but women's
shopping brought the market to the home and women to the market. The
female shopper thus inherently disrupted the supposedly separate spheres
and thus was accused of a moral crime akin to adultery.

Retailers played the well-worn trope of the extravagant woman possessed
of an insatiable appetite for all it was worth in their criticism of trading on
credit. A writer in an early trade journal, *The Drapier and Clothier,* for example, warned that the "hundreds of hawkers" vending "tawdry finery and vulgar ornaments" to the wives of farm laborers and weavers on credit empowered wives at their husband's expense. "It would be fearful," he asserted,
"to consider the number of persons in the country who have been imprisoned in respect of goods supplied to their wives during their absence from
home."[20] Wealthy husbands in London's metropolitan suburbs were made
to worry too, since it was common practice for London's retailers to send
"false representations and puffs" when the male head of the family was away
from home. Of course, readers were not supposed to doubt that female shoppers were "accustomed . . . to lives of purity, economy, and domestic privacy,
and truth." But women's "love of dress and great bargains" caused them to
be "far more easily ensnared by men than men are ensnared by each
other."[21] The sexualized effects of buying on credit were similarly conjured
up in the homilies of mass magazines, household manuals, and fiction.[22]

Legally excluded from most "honorable" means of making money, the female debtor was portrayed by these texts as particularly vulnerable to male attentions. This image of the female debtor was not unlike that of the kleptomaniac or the prostitute. All three female types represented the social and moral collapse resulting from women's immersion in the mires of the economy. Indeed, they stood for the loss of control that many individuals feared in a consumer society.[23]

In middle-class prescriptive literature, a wife's purchases on credit were thus a major source of infection of the home, weakening the man financially and morally.[24] Not surprisingly, credit, the "shopkeeper's temptation," was the focus of the jeremiads of the middle-class moralist Samuel Smiles.[25] Responding in part to a pervasive sense in the 1860s and 1870s that the cost of living had risen, Smiles defended "traditional" notions of thrift and domestic and political economy.[26] Although specifically writing for the working classes, in the mid-1870s he criticized all classes for living beyond their means in order to appear respectable and successful. This desire, he argued, led to ruin rather than success by encouraging people to "spend their money before it is earned—run into debt at the grocer's, the baker's, the milliner's, and the butcher's . . . [to] entertain fashionable friends at the expense of the shop-keepers." Smiles especially worried that women's "rage for dress and finery . . . [which] rivaled [that in] the corrupt and debauched age of Louis XV of France," would ruin husband and draper alike. "No woman," he asserted, "is justified in running into debt for a dress without her husband's knowledge and consent. If she do so, she is clothing herself at the expense of the draper." Husbands were cautioned that allowing wives to purchase on credit gave another person "power over [their] liberty."[27] The still common use of the debtors' prison underscored the reality of this threat.[28] However, Smiles believed buyers, not sellers, needed to be reformed. The solution was simple: "When pleasure tempts with its seductions, have the courage to say 'No' at once."[29]

Despite these negative images of consumer credit, many of the commodities that filled the Victorians' homes and adorned their bodies were bought with its help.[30] Credit allowed working-class families to make ends meet and helped middle-class families on limited incomes set up households.[31] Credit also served the aristocracy, as evidenced by the fact that approximately 80 percent of all sales in the small, elite shops of metropolitan districts such as the West End were offered on credit.[32]

In the case of aristocrats, credit was clearly the vestige of an older client economy, in which retailers were viewed more or less as retainers and their services were extended on the basis of the aristocratic customers' social position rather than their financial solidity. By definition quality establishments extended credit. Lady Jeune, a prominent female journalist, wrote of shopping in the 1870s that we "dutifully followed in the steps of our forefathers, paying for the things we had at the end of the year, for no well-thought-of firm ever demanded or expected more than a yearly payment of their debts."[33] Even in the late nineteenth century, many aristocrats still regarded cash payment as demeaning, especially if the sums were regarded as small. As an exclusive London boot maker, for example, testified of the gentleman who casually dropped by for a pair of boots and a couple of pairs of shoes and then disappeared, "If I do find him out, when I press him for the money, he feels angry, because the sum is so small."[34] One Edwardian fashion designer found that "the richer people are the more difficult it is to get them to pay their bills."[35] Accounts, therefore, sometimes stood for as long as several years. Although wealthy customers may have been poor credit risks, the so-called carriage custom was nonetheless difficult to refuse, since their patronage, in addition to affording business, gave a certain luster to the house. In a commercial economy in which credit was part aristocratic deference system, part modern financial incentive, shopkeepers walked a fine line. They relied on their customers for both payment and patronage, for too little of either could lead to bankruptcy. Indeed, middle-class women also tried to exploit this uncertainty. They too partook of society's ambivalent attitudes toward property and money that were inherent in commerce with the aristocracy. However, ambivalence about dealing with middle-class women resulted largely from their dependent legal status rather than class privilege.

THE WIFE'S AUTHORITY AND HUSBAND'S LIABILITY

The legal system expressed and furthered anxieties about the transformation of distribution systems, women's appetites, and definitions of property. In the later decades of the nineteenth century, to decrease the risks of selling to married women, retailers sought reforms of the laws governing women's property rights and liability for debt. Although creditors eventually acquired great power over male customers, they were thwarted in their attempts to control female credit by judges and legislators, who, in violation of a strict construction of laissez-faire ideology, were reluctant to overturn conventional assumptions about class and gender roles.

In the 1860s, both the laws regulating credit and debt and those governing married women's property concurred on the husband's liability for debts incurred by the wife. In the next decade, however, the laws pertaining to this liability actually grew more inconsistent. These inconsistencies were compounded when Parliament passed the Married Women's Property Act of 1870, its 1874 amendment, and the more sweeping 1882 act, which recognized married women as property owners without making them fully liable for the debts they incurred. The confusion was only heightened by common-law treatment of family debt, an issue that retailers seized on. Knowledge of these anomalies put married women in an unusually strong position to avoid paying for what they purchased.

Although most men paid their spouse's debts with little complaint, disagreements over domestic expenditure commonly led to family quarrels, violence, divorce, or a summons from the county courts.[36] Part of the larger reformation of the antiquated legal system, these courts had been established in 1846 to aid in the recovery of small debts. However, according to the legal historian G. R. Rubin, the judges' cultural and social prejudices often defeated this purpose.[37] He argues that county court judges disliked their role as debt collectors, bore a great deal of animosity towards the small traders and traveling drapers who made up the majority of the plaintiffs, and believed that selling on credit, especially to women, was morally questionable. They therefore often found for the debtor husband, despite the straightforward nature of the original sale.[38] Although Rubin suggests these decisions were the result of class prejudices against small traders, the judges' attitudes towards gender, marriage, and consumption also played a central role. Indeed, county court practice and the developing case law were built upon the same images of threatened masculinity and frivolous femininity that figured in the writings of Samuel Smiles.

The courts' work to protect male control over the family purse by diminishing a husband's liability for his wife's debts began in 1864 with a precedent-setting case in the Court of Common Pleas. The decision made it legal for a husband to deny liability for his wife's debts if he could prove that the purchased goods were not "necessary" and that he had forbidden her to pledge his credit. *Jolly v. Rees* addressed the questions of whether a wife was a legal agent of her husband and whether and how he could revoke this agency.[39] The fashionable draper Jolly and Sons claimed it had sold goods to Mrs. Rees with the legitimate presumption that she had the authority to pledge her husband's credit. When payment time came, Mr. Rees, "a country gentleman," protested that he had explicitly forbidden his wife to act as his agent and that, therefore, he should not be liable for the debt.

After hearing the case, the justices concluded for the defendant. The decision stated that though it could be presumed that "a woman living with a man as his wife had his authority to pledge his credit," the man always had the right to revoke this agency without any public notice to retailers. Denying a husband "this right" might lead to "domestic discords" and cause tradesmen to speculate "on enforcing payment for goods sold to a wife on such presumed authority." It was the court's "duty simply to say that a wife derived her authority from the husband's will, and that she had no right to pledge his credit from any presumption as his wife."[40] These words remained the basis of the common law regarding familial consumer responsibility until the mid–twentieth century. More or less explicitly, the court determined that women's agency in respect to family property was not an absolute right derived from marriage but a conditional one derived from the husband's authorization. In so ruling, the court reaffirmed the husband's final authority over expenditure on family consumption. From then on, creditors had to presume that men could in *private* forbid their wives to purchase on credit—in sum, not buyers but creditors beware.

Whereas husbands' financial liability decreased, wives' liability increased only very slowly and haltingly. The Married Women's Property Act of 1870 bestowed women with only limited property rights and did not make them fully liable for their debts.[41] The act removed some of a wife's property from her husband's control, adopting the concept of a "separate estate."[42] Originally a legal device developed in early modern equity courts, the separate estate was a trust that had permitted wealthy families to keep some of a woman's property out of the control of her and her husband's creditors, thus guaranteeing the maternal property line.[43] In effect it prevented the wife too, by means of a "restraint on anticipation," from disposing freely of her property or charging it with debts. The 1870 act, by adopting the concept of a separate estate, created a situation in which a married woman's property was "protected" from both her husband's creditors and her own.[44] The wife could sue or be sued but was only liable for the amount of her estate at the time she entered the contract. Even then, a woman could not be held personally liable, that is, could not be imprisoned, when she refused to pay her debts. The 1870 act thus made a married woman "less liable for her debts than other citizens were for theirs."[45]

The 1870 act also effectively absolved a husband from responsibility for his wife's prenuptial debts even when, as in certain cases, he had acquired her property. This legal anomaly regarding prenuptial debts led to the passage in 1874 of an amendment to the 1870 act. Also known as the Creditors' Bill, this amendment once again made husbands liable for their spouse's prenuptial debts up to the amount corresponding to the value of the property they had acquired from the wife.[46] Husbands were, however, still technically responsible for debts determined by a court to be "necessaries." Debts for luxuries could be avoided if the husband pleaded, as Mr. Rees had, that he had forbidden his wife to incur them. What was necessary and what was a luxury were based on the nature of the goods relative to the perceived social status of the couple. Drapers were particularly uneasy, since they primarily dealt with women; and clothing and related goods were not easily categorizable. Drapers thus stood to lose considerable sums if the court followed the *Jolly v. Rees* precedent.[47]

An 1878 case involving a notorious demimondaine and a West End milliner might be characterized as a logical outcome of this legislative morass, notwithstanding the huge sums involved and its rogue's gallery of characters. The case involved Laura Bell, a former prostitute, who, on her road to respectability, married Augustus Frederick Thistlethwayte, an army ensign who had inherited a considerable fortune. The couple constantly quarreled about money, and eventually Mr. Thistlethwayte warned tradesmen that his wife no longer had the authority to pledge his credit. Mrs. Thistlethwayte, nonetheless, continued to run up bills, which her husband refused to pay. Finally, a firm of West End milliners (owned by a Mr. Aaron Schwaebe) trading under the name Madame Rosalie sued Mr. Thistlethwayte for one thousand pounds for "bonnets and shawls and other feminine fripperies."[48]

Women's "natural" extravagance, the nature of luxury, and patriarchal authority became the questions argued in this case. Mrs. Thistlethwayte stated that her dress allowance of five hundred pounds was far too low for her requirements and that her purchases were necessary for her social position. To test this claim the court sought to establish what "ladies of fashion" usually spent on their "feminine fripperies." When asked, Mr. Schwaebe had to admit that "he knew several ladies of fashion who actually had as little as £500 a year to spend on cutting a dash." Defending the husband, the attorney-general exploited assumptions about women's extravagance by telling the jury that "Mrs. Thistlethwayte appears to have a passion for such wretched vanities, and it is most improper that her husband should be expected to meet the bills thus incurred." He then condemned Schwaebe for pandering to this "frivolous and shocking expenditure of money." The jury agreed with this moral conception of buying and selling and absolved Mr. Thistlethwayte from all responsibility.[49]

Given that these moral attitudes evinced in court decisions had such profound economic repercussions, retailers were determined to shift the legal basis on which such decisions rested. For that reason, the drapery trade backed litigation to the Court of Appeal undertaken by the West End firm of Debenham and Freebody in its pursuit of over forty-three pounds from a Mr. Mellon, the manager of a large hotel in Bradford. Debenham and Freebody had lost its claim in a lower court on the defense, established in *Jolly v. Rees*, that Mr. Mellon had privately forbidden his wife to pledge his credit beyond her dress allowance. The trade hoped the Court of Appeal would overturn this precedent, which they argued sacrificed the needs of the economy to private arrangements between husband and wife.[50]

The Court of Appeal first sought to define the always ambiguous concept of "necessaries." The justices confronted the difficulty of defining needs in a consumer society by attempting to resurrect some mythic correlation between class status and the level of commodity consumption.[51] Since English aristocrats had little knowledge of the material practices of everyday life, this proved quite complicated. Although reputed to be a formidable legal thinker, Lord Bramwell, one of the justices, was notably imprecise in his affirmation that necessary goods were "such as the wife would require—articles of dress suitable to her station, but not necessary in the sense that she stood in need of them, she either having a sufficient supply of them, or having sufficient funds from her husband to supply herself with them." While a couple is cohabiting, he suggested, "she may have authority to pledge his credit for articles of necessity, usually supplied on credit, or by weekly bills, as butchers' meat, or the like, where that is the convenient course. But here it is not so."[52]

Drawing a line between clothing and other consumer goods, Bramwell showed his ignorance of the nature of clothing retailing by stating "there is neither general usage (that we are aware of) nor convenience in favor of having articles of dress on credit." It is not clear whether he was unaware of this practice or simply refusing to recognize it when he announced, "The Courts cannot take judicial cognizance of any practice of wives to pledge their husband's credit for such articles. . . . Why should she have such authority?" A husband, stated Bramwell, may say to his wife "go and pledge my credit to any extent your love of finery may prompt you to." However, it is the husband and not the law who possesses this "right." Summing up, the lord justice stated: "It would be very mischievous if the law enabled a foolish woman and any tradesman eager for profit to combine together to impose serious liabilities on the husband contrary to his orders, without his knowledge and against his will. Consequently, this judgement must be affirmed."[53] The other two justices agreed, and the lower court's decision stood.

The ruling had widespread reverberations. The drapery trade was outraged; the editor of the *Warehouseman and Drapers' Trade Journal* protested that "it was all very well to say that they [tradesmen] might conspire with wives to make husbands liable, but it is equally fair to retort that married people can now conspire together for the purpose of defrauding the tradesman." The lord justice's remedy, that retailers should ask ladies "for their husband's authority before trusting them" was "absurdly impracticable."[54] A county court judge, in a letter to the *Times,* likewise affirmed that the law "had been and will continue to be exceedingly difficult to apply particularly since there was a deeply rooted impression amongst the parties involved" that a wife had special agency with regard to pledging her husband's credit. Among the lower classes especially, the wife was "practically her husband's agent in almost all the daily affairs of life." It was she who bought "all articles of domestic consumption . . . appear[ed] for him, if any one [did], in the county court, and agree[d] on his behalf to the monthly installment by which the debt [would] be discharged." No amount of "judicial decisions would change this basic division of labor," as it was "incident to the conditions of rural labouring life."[55] Besides ignoring prevalent conceptions about the division of labor, the law, others argued, failed to acknowledge the deferential relationship between elite buyers and sellers. Only the "boldest" of shopkeepers, claimed one writer, would "put to a lady of fashionable appearance the interrogatory: 'Does your husband know that you are shopping, and if so, does he approve of your engaging in that amusement?' . . . such conduct would soon drive away customers from any shop."[56] Given the state of the law, this *Daily Telegraph* editorialist quipped that retailers were lucky that "mankind" and "womankind" were "basically honest, that husbands generally were a complaisant and forgiving race," and that few would "care to hold their wives up to public gaze as virtually repudiated agents in order to save themselves from monetary loss."[57]

Unplacated, the firm of Debenham and Freebody was determined to take its case before England's highest court, the House of Lords. But the Lords, like the lower court, stumbled over the complexities of defining "fripperies," female agency, and family relations. Queried by one lord as to whether a wife had a greater authority to pledge her husband's credit than a sister acting as a housekeeper, the appellant's attorney responded that wives did hold "greater authority than a servant or other relative." However, if "the husband found that his wife used her authority indiscreetly . . . he should give public notice of the revocation of that authority."[58] But what if, the perspicacious Lord Watson asked, the wife "takes an express train and orders goods from a tradesman at a distance who has not had notice of the revocation. Would the husband still be liable?" Mr. Mellon's attorney answered that a woman's traveling by express train to London to do her shopping "would of itself be notice that she was doing something improper."[59] The Lords agreed that such shopping was disobedient behavior and that husbands should not be held liable for its consequences.

Specifically referring to *Jolly v. Rees*, the lord chancellor affirmed that in the present case "nothing had been done by the husband which would justify the assumption that he had given any authority to this wife to pledge his credit." Under no circumstances did Mrs. Mellon act as purchasing agent for her husband. He felt this was quite clear, since the couple lived in the hotel "where all the usual necessaries of a household were supplied to them, and there was no domestic management at all."[60] The Lords, then, confirmed that marriage itself did not legally make a wife the husband's agent. Rather it was the husband who created the agency. With this ruling the Lords acknowledged that wives shopped, but they insured that this activity would not give them any access to family resources beyond what husbands expressly wished.

The Lord's decision sparked a national discussion on the nature and propriety of women's shopping. An editorial in the *Times* supported the decision, criticizing Debenham and Freebody's business practices: "The very fact that their customer came from a distant town like Bradford should have put them on their guard." However, the editorial also acknowledged that it seemed "too much . . . to require a tradesman to question every unknown customer" about her marital arrangements and admitted the decision would probably lead to a "panic" among "West-end Milliners, who relied on credit trading." The editorialist then noted that such a panic would be beneficial, since it would lead to the extension of the "ready-money system."[61] Debenham and Freebody defended the soundness of the transaction. Mrs. Mellon had received credit based on the firm's long relationship with her mother, who had always promptly and regularly paid her bills. "Although the husband resided at Bradford, which for all purposes of business is no further than Bayswater, we were perfectly acquainted with his position." The firm wished to relate these facts because, it said, "It is obvious that a very large proportion of the credit usually given to wives rests upon no firmer basis than that given in this case; and, as society is so constituted, we fail to see how it can be otherwise."[62] The firm thus represented the belief that the legal restrictions on women's agency were inconsistent with their considerable freedoms as consumers.

Yet through the 1880s legal innovations did not echo this belief. Early in 1880, before the final decision against Debenham and Freebody, Parliament debated another married women's property bill. Retailers once again hoped that if women were granted free use of their property, they could also be made to pay their debts. Credit traders wholeheartedly supported the bill, although for very different reasons than feminists and legal reformers, and hoped it would "settle the vexed question as to the wife's authority and husband's liability." However, they soon recognized that this particular bill ignored the debts of propertyless wives and was "somewhat vague" on the extent to which credit could be pledged with reference to a woman's separate estate. Although they longed for some "provision to prevent that juggling between man and wife" the effect of which was to "defraud creditors," they worried that if the bill passed it would not address their needs.[63] By limiting a married woman's contractual rights, Parliament, retailers complained, had the wronged husband not the cheated trader in mind.

The debates did indeed suggest that many M.P.'s were more concerned with husbands' liabilities than creditors' losses. One member's protestation that he would not support the law unless it "made provisions to protect the husband from the extravagance and dishonest dealing of his wife" seemed to be a popular position.[64] When the new Married Women's Property Act finally passed in June of 1882, it was applauded by feminists as "'the Magna Carta' of women's liberties."[65] Yet the 1882 act preserved some of the 1870 act's restrictions on women's property, and wives still lacked full and equal contractual rights and responsibilities.[66] Since restrained property could not be charged with debts and wives remained responsible only for debts equal to their separate property at the time they entered the contract, the question of the agency of married female customers was as confused as ever.

Although originally in favor of allowing married women to become property owners, creditors violently criticized the 1882 act.[67] As it was put in one journal, "the legal position of husbands and wives is just now in a transition state, and hence the muddle." Shopkeepers were warned to be wary about extending credit to married women, since "ancient rules still cling to their new position."[68] As an editorialist in another journal complained, "it requires a strong imagination to grasp the idea of a time when paying, as well as purchasing, will be done by married women."[69]

The property acts together with the Lords' ruling on *Debenham and Freebody v. Mellon* thus caused uncertainty about women's credit, which persisted for at least the next decade. Those retailers who incorrectly believed that they could hold women fully responsible for their debts were deluded. According to an 1890 editorial in *The Drapers' Record,* some retailers, in the erroneous belief that the 1882 act "greatly enlarged the capacity of married women to contract," had extended easy credit to married women only to discover later that they could not legally collect from these customers.[70]

It seems ironic that as married women became property owners, they came to be regarded as less creditworthy individuals. Yet restrictions on contractual rights and the degree of proof required to collect debts worked in this direction. A county court judged explained the process: "In attempting to recover from a married woman certain matters have to be proved most conclusively. . . . first, that the defendant had a separate estate; secondly, that she had it at the time the contract was entered into, and could bind it; and thirdly, that she intended to bind it."[71] When sued, women often pleaded coverture, stating that they possessed no separate estate.[72] Those who had such an estate but still refused to pay could not legally be imprisoned.[73]

Shopkeepers interpreted their legal defeats in class and gender terms. They blamed their predicament on "the movement in favor of the so-called 'emancipation of women,'" and mourned the loss of the time when "in the eyes of the law husband and wife were one."[74] They felt cheated by a legal system that failed to recognize their needs. "If we are a nation of shopkeepers, is it not time that the Legislature should throw its aegis over the shopkeeper instead of over the social vultures who are ready enough to prey upon him?" *The Drapers' Record* plaintively asked.[75]

Although judges slowly began to find women liable for their debts, married women did not gain full contractual rights and liabilities until 1935.[76] The history of wives' credit is not, however, a simple story of class struggle between a still aristocratic legal system and the middle-class retailers. Anti-trade bias within the legal system, fear of women's potential power as consumers, and Parliament's ignorance of shopping practices collectively fed tensions between retailers and female customers. We cannot discount a certain emancipationist zeal on the part of women themselves, who, in these legal loopholes, found a way to flout the authority of not only their spouses but also the retailers, and, in certain measure, the legal system as well.

WOMEN'S CONSUMPTION ON TRIAL

In practice, many married women turned a real disability—their lack of full contractual responsibilities—into an opportunity. When brought to court, wives consistently protested that they bought on credit because they disagreed with their husband's limited perception of their material needs. Buying on credit in diverse stores, perhaps far from home, became a weapon that some women used to circumvent the social and legal restrictions on their property rights. Both poor and wealthy women found purchasing on credit gave them limited, if informal, access to property. Women whose husbands would not give them control over household or personal expenditure, who had no money of their own, or whose property was in some way restrained used their assigned role as consumers to gain a measure of economic control otherwise denied to them.

The tensions surrounding purchasing brought the economic and emotional life of families into the public arena as county court judges were charged with sorting out the rights and liabilities of retailers and consumers. Court decisions ultimately rested on the concept of extravagance, with each party involved articulating a different conception of extravagant consumption. Throughout these years the law consistently required husbands to pay for debts for goods determined to be "necessaries."[77] The meaning of necessary, however, varied "with the rank and station of the parties, from the merest means of daily subsistence to comparatively luxurious living, which [might] include a carriage and jewellery of considerable value."[78] When sued, husbands nearly always insisted they were the victim of an extravagant wife who had a passion for luxuries. To settle these cases, county court judges had to consider several factors: the connection between the social class of the purchaser and the type of commodity purchased, the relationship between the husband and wife, and that between the shopkeeper and the customer.

The first issue to be settled, as the following case suggests, regarded the relation between the commodities bought and the family's social class. In June of 1880, a Mr. Sharpe successfully avoided paying for a debt owed to Whiteley's department store. Whiteley's sought to recover twelve pounds for a sealskin jacket sold to Mrs. Sharpe. Mr. Sharpe, who earned about three hundred pounds a year as the keeper of the records at the guildhall, argued that this jacket was an extravagant purchase for which he should not be held liable. Mrs. Sharpe, however, testified that she had warned her husband that if he did not supply her with the money for her winter things she would purchase them without his consent. Mr. Sharpe denied having heard this threat and said he had assumed the new jacket had been part of her trousseau. Clearly, Mr. and Mrs. Sharpe disagreed about what goods were necessary. According to the judge, the jacket "may be perfectly 'suitable' . . . but it cannot be called necessary, and, if the husband is not generous enough or rich enough to indulge his wife in the luxury, she must go without."[79] Mr. Sharpe was absolved of this debt, and Whiteley's had to go without. The law, in recognizing that there was no absolute morality regarding consumption, rested on the judges' determination of the social construction of needs. They determined that men were legally required to pay for women's needs but not for their desires.[80]

In contrast to husbands, both retailers and wives could benefit if they could argue that even quite costly purchases were not extravagant. In 1896, for example, the marital and economic problems of a Mr. and Mrs. Hallmann resulted in their being sued in the Queen's Bench Division.[81] The plaintiff, Miss Vivian Floyd, a Savile Row court dressmaker, sued Mr. Edward Hallmann for £113, the cost of dresses and other goods that she had supplied to Mrs. Hallmann in 1894. Miss Floyd defended her extension of credit to Mrs. Hallmann by claiming that the goods were reasonably priced and appropriate for someone of Mrs. Hallmann's status. Miss Floyd had made careful inquiries before filling any orders and knew that Mr. Hallmann held "an exceptionally good position" as a clerk in a banking firm, for which he earned about one thousand pounds a year and that Mrs. Hallmann was the daughter of a baronet. She therefore had sold Mrs. Hallmann a plum-colored velvet gown for twenty guineas, some less expensive dresses, and two silk blouses.[82]

Attempting to establish whether such purchases were necessary, Justice Grantham asked Miss Floyd what she considered a fair amount for a husband with Mr. Hallmann's salary to "allow his wife to spend on her dresses?" Aware that if the purchases were considered extravagant she would lose her claim, Miss Floyd suggested that two hundred pounds a year was a very reasonable sum, but she also insisted that she could not possibly estimate whether Mrs. Hallmann would exceed this amount.[83] The judge, however, expected this retailer to make inquiries into her customer's financial status and then to interpret the appropriate level of expenditure relative to her family's position. He assumed that sellers should essentially tell buyers when they had bought enough. Shopkeepers were thus expected, indeed legally encouraged, to become aware of quite intimate familial details. In essence, the law asked the market to intrude into the home.

When Mr. Hallmann was called to give evidence, he made his private life public in order to win the case. He presented himself as a long-suffering husband whose financial difficulties were worsened by an extravagant wife who acted as though "he were made of money." Although she was the eldest daughter of Sir Digby Murray, she had no money of her own. When they were first married, "they had moved in what is known as good society."[84] However, he had not been able to support this lifestyle, and they had been forced to drop their old acquaintances. In 1892 they had had to give up their house in Park Street and move to a less expensive one in Sutton, Surrey, but "his wife's extravagance compelled him to move to a yet smaller one." His next step had been to advertise in the local Sutton paper that he would not be responsible for his wife's debts. After Mrs. Hallmann found her credit "put an end to in Sutton," she had gone to London to do her shopping without her husband's knowledge. He agreed to pay some of her accounts, but when he received Miss Floyd's bill he was astonished at the prices of certain items, such as lace at forty shillings a yard and buttons at over seven shillings each. After he spoke to his wife about it there was "a scene," and he decided to place the matter in the hands of his solicitors rather than pay the bill.[85]

To win his case Mr. Hallmann had to prove that the goods purchased were extravagant and that he was ignorant of these particular purchases. He consistently denied any knowledge of his wife's shopping and insisted that he had never seen the goods in question, with the exception of the two blouses. When asked why he had not sent these things back to the shop, he complained that his wife had locked them in her wardrobe. Under cross-examination, Mr. Hallmann insisted that he had "nothing to do with the ordering of the things, and he declined in any way to interfere with them." He concluded his testimony by saying that "if West-end tradespeople chose to supply things to married ladies on credit behind their husband's back they must not find fault if the husband refused to pay for them."[86]

Like many couples, the Hallmanns diverged in their attitudes toward expenditure. Mrs. Hallmann felt her husband could afford to and should give her more than the sixty to ninety pounds a year he gave her to dress herself. These economic disagreements were perhaps a result of their class positions. With her aristocratic background, Mrs. Hallmann might very well have had different expectations than her husband did. Although portrayed as irrationally given to overspending, she may have been trying to uphold the standards and maintain the acquaintances of her life before marriage. She may have believed that a twenty-guinea velvet gown was necessary to her station in life, even if her husband thought such an item to be extravagant. Her motives were not relevant in the eyes of the law, however. When a husband and wife disagreed about expenditure, the law almost always sided with the husband. Accordingly, Miss Vivian Floyd lost her action.

Even if a propertied wife was found liable for her "extravagant" purchases, it could be difficult to force her to settle on claims. Burberry's discovered this when they tried to collect a debt from a Mr. and Mrs. Mayer.[87] Mr. Mayer, a picture dealer with an income of between four and five thousand pounds, had married a Danish countess who owned a home and forty acres in her native country. Not long after Mrs. Mayer bought the goods in question, the couple divorced, and neither party would pay the bill. According to Mrs. Mayer, the £156 debt was for "articles of ladies' wear, except two coats and a hat," which she said were presents for the "old man." She evidently no longer wished to give him these presents. Mr. Mayer claimed he had provided his wife with an ample allowance to run their household, but she argued that the fourteen hundred pounds a year was both inadequate and irregular. When asked to support this charge, she detailed their housekeeping expenses and asserted that they were so great that they left her only three hundred pounds for her dress. She then argued that, since her allowance did not meet these expenses, her husband should pay this bill. The jury disagreed and found against her. However, the firm had difficulty actually recovering, since her separate property was "restrained from anticipation." As she could not sell this property, she had little means of actually raising capital.[88] Legal restrictions on married women's use of their property as well as the couple's emotional and economic disagreements added up to a large loss for Burberry's.

If, however, plaintiffs could prove that the husband was aware of his spouse's consumption, he could usually be found liable. For example, in the 1891 case of *Jay v. Annesley*, a noted Regent Street firm sued Mrs. Annesley for a debt of fifteen guineas. She was the object of the summons because they knew she had her own property and she usually paid her own bills. The plaintiff's counsel argued that she ordered the "costume" and generally paid for orders herself with her own checks.[89] But Mrs. Annesley used an interesting subterfuge. She claimed that in this particular instance her husband had accompanied her to the shop and exclaimed, "I will give you a present of a dress for Ascot!" Thus it was not her credit that had been pledged. To be consistent, the judge absolved Mrs. Annesley from the debt; after all, if the husband was present, he had given his pledge. In general, shopkeepers felt more comfortable extending credit to wives who brought their husbands shopping. But in this case, Jay's misinterpreted the wife's economic power and lost the claim.[90]

Husbands discovered that shopping with their wives could be a costly affair. Mr. Clement Stanley, for example, was required to pay the two-guinea bill for a coat his wife had bought from Thomas Wallis and Company of Holborn Circus. Although he tried the usual defense that shops should not give a wife credit without her husband's permission, the judge reminded Mr. Stanley that he had accompanied his wife on her expedition to the West End: "If I went with my wife into a shop I should expect to have to pay for all she bought. . . . You have given yourself away by going shopping with your wife."[91] Ironically, it could be in the husband's financial interest to avoid shopping with his wife, that is, to forego the supervision that had been traditionally regarded as his right and duty. Men's and women's places in the consumer sphere thus depended on the financial and emotional arrangements negotiated in the family, the courtroom, and the shop.

Designed to protect husbands who could not control their wives' consumption, the law actually contributed to distancing husbands from shopping. Judges admonished husbands for shopping with wives and praised them, as in the case of Mr. Lewin, for not caring "a farthing for what their wives wear." Many husbands did not conceive of their wives' "conspicuous consumption" as establishing their own social position, as Veblen had implied.[92] To the contrary, legislatures, judges, and husbands perceived female consumption as a threat to class position and male financial status. No legal authority ever suggested that wives should not buy goods for their family. However, the authorities tried to limit the financial ramifications of that buying for husbands, but not for retailers. Ultimately, the legal treatment of wives' debts tended to fix shopping as a female practice, and as one that was threatening to husbands and retailers. Nonetheless, the legal system was open to disputes, and these disputes reshaped conceptions of family debt, credit, property, and consumption.

From the 1860s, at the very moment of the spectacular increase in the presence of women in the public sphere of shopping, the law embodied the paradoxical nature of this activity. These women were the most prominent actors on the consumer scene, yet their financial liability was the legacy of a precapitalist order. Armed with an understanding of the cultural, social, and legal practices that governed buying and selling, certain women may have indirectly gained access to goods. To what extent women deliberately manipulated retailers, spouses, and judges deserves further study. In the end, retailers' inability to find legal means to force families to pay for what they bought curbed women's chances of receiving credit, furthered the use of cash trading, and fixed the image of the female shopper as extravagant and dangerous to both the household and national economy. The slowness of the separation of the English family into the individual economic actors of contemporary society ensured that, for several decades at least, wives, even as consumers, continued to have an unequal position in the economy.

NOTES

I would like to express special thanks to John Gillis, Bonnie Smith, Cora Kaplan, Margot Finn, Scott Sandage, Victor Uribe, and Jordan Witt.

1. The quote appears both in "A Husband and His Wife's Dresses," *The Times* (London), 6 August 1892, 6; and in *The Warehouseman and Drapers' Trade Journal* (hereafter *WDTJ*), 13 August 1892, 747.

2. *WDTJ*, 13 August 1892, 747.

3. In 1881 over a million proceedings were heard in the county courts. The majority involved drapers seeking unrecovered debts (*WDTJ*, 17 June 1882, 414). Although many of the original records no longer exist, the decisions and testimonies of cases were reprinted every week in the trade journals and newspapers. My article is based on these weekly reports and editorial material in both national newspapers and the major journals of the drapery trade from the 1860s to 1914. Further research on other trades such as jewelry and household furnishings would provide a useful comparison.

4. "Female agency" has taken on a very general meaning in feminist scholarship. However, in nineteenth-century legal discourse, it specifically referred to a woman's

ability to act as a financial agent or representative for her husband, father, brother, or employer.

In the second half of the nineteenth century, the notion of family was undergoing a major cultural, social, and economic reevaluation. This reevaluation was especially visible in the debates over divorce and married women's property reform. See Mary Poovey's discussion of these debates in *Uneven Developments: The Ideological Work of Gender in Mid-Victorian England* (Chicago: University of Chicago Press, 1988), esp. 51–88.

5. Leonore Davidoff and Catherine Hall, *Family Fortunes: Men and Women of the English Middle Class, 1780–1850* (Chicago: University of Chicago Press, 1987).

6. I have borrowed this term from Scott Sandage, who is presently working on a cultural and social analysis of credit in nineteenth-century America.

7. Rosalind H. Williams, *Dream Worlds: Mass Consumption in Late-Nineteenth-Century France* (Berkeley: University of California Press, 1982), 92–94. However, in some industries, standardized credit was introduced not to serve as a marketing tool but to solve problems in financing production. For the use of credit in the U.S. auto industry, see Martha L. Olney, *Buy Now, Pay Later: Advertising, Credit, and Consumer Durables in the 1920s* (Chapel Hill: University of North Carolina Press, 1991).

8. For an analysis of the social meaning of credit, see Craig Muldrew, "Interpreting the Market: The Ethics of Credit and Community Relations in Early Modern England," *Social History* 18, no. 2 (May 1993): 163–81. Scott Sandage has argued, however, that the moral assessment involved in face-to-face lending actually remained as credit became supposedly "rationalized" by modern credit reporting; see Scott Sandage, "'Small Man, Small Means, Doing Small Business': Credit Reporting and the Commodification of Character, 1840–1880" (paper presented at the Warren I. Susman Memorial Graduate History Conference, New Brunswick, N.J., April 1993).

9. Melanie Tebbutt, *Making Ends Meet: Pawnbroking and Working-Class Credit* (New York: St. Martin's and Leicester University Press, 1983); Paul Johnson, "Credit and Thrift and the British Working Class, 1870–1914," in *The Working Class in Modern British History: Essays in Honour of Henry Pelling*, ed. Jay Winter (Cambridge: Cambridge University Press, 1983), 147–70; Gareth Stedman Jones, *Outcast London: A Study in the Relationship between Classes in Victorian Society* (New York: Pantheon Books, 1984), 87–88; Ellen Ross, *Love and Toil: Motherhood in Outcast London, 1870–1914* (New York: Oxford University Press, 1993), 81–84.

10. The widespread use of retail credit stemmed from the shortage of coin in the eighteenth century. Dorothy Davis, *Fairs, Shops, and Supermarkets: A History of English Shopping* (Toronto: University of Toronto Press, 1966), 185. See also John Brewer, "Commercialization and Politics," in *The Birth of a Consumer Society: The Commercialization of Eighteenth-Century England*, Neil McKendrick, John Brewer, and J. H. Plumb (Bloomington: Indiana University Press, 1982), 208–9.

11. See, for example, Michael B. Miller, *The Bon Marché: Bourgeois Culture and the Department Store, 1869–1920* (Princeton: Princeton University Press, 1981); Williams, *Dream Worlds*; Rachel Bowlby, *Just Looking: Consumer Culture in Dreiser, Gissing, and Zola* (New York: Methuen, 1985); Susan Porter Benson, *Counter Cultures: Saleswomen, Managers, and Customers in American Department Stores, 1890–1940* (Urbana: University of Illinois Press, 1986); William Leach, *Land of Desire: Merchants, Power, and the Rise of a New American Culture* (New York: Pantheon Books, 1993); Thomas Richards, *The Com-*

modity Culture of Victorian England: Advertising and Spectacle, 1851–1914 (Stanford: Stanford University Press, 1990); Anne Friedberg, *Window Shopping: Cinema and the Postmodern* (Berkeley: University of California Press, 1993). The transformations in shopping in late-nineteenth-century England have been explored in my "The West End and Women's Pleasure: Gender and Commercial Culture in London, 1860–1914" (Ph.D. diss., Rutgers University, 1993); and my "'A New Era of Shopping': The Promotion of Women's Pleasure in London's West End, 1909–1914," in *Cinema and the Invention of Modern Life*, ed. Leo Charney and Vanessa R. Schwartz (University of California Press, forthcoming).

12. Gareth Shaw has argued that the decreased use of credit in the drapery shops improved their performance and was one of the factors that contributed to their expansion into department stores. Gareth Shaw, "The Evolution and Impact of Large-Scale Retailing in Britain," in *The Evolution of Retail Systems, c. 1800–1914*, ed. John Benson and Gareth Shaw (Leicester: Leicester University Press, 1992), 137. See also, Peter Mathias, *Retailing Revolution: A History of Multiple Retailing in the Food Trades Based upon the Allied Suppliers Group of Companies* (London: Longmans, 1967), 47. Department stores eventually reestablished limited forms of credit, but accounts were only given to select customers. See, Benson, *Counter Cultures*, 90.

13. P. S. Atiyah, *The Rise and Fall of the Freedom of Contract* (Oxford: Clarendon Press, 1979), 182–83.

14. Even wives with separate property had only very limited power to make a contract with reference to it. C. A. Morrison, "Contract," in *A Century of Family Law, 1857–1957*, ed. R. H. Graveson and F. R. Crane (London: Sweet and Maxwell, 1957), 121–22.

15. Few women shopped alone outside of their neighborhood before the 1860s. See Davis, *Fairs, Shops, and Supermarkets*; Alison Adburgham, *Shops and Shopping: 1800–1914: Where and In What Manner the Well-Dressed English Woman Bought Her Clothes*, rev. ed. (London: Barrie and Jenkins, 1989); David Alexander, *Retailing in England during the Industrial Revolution* (London: Athlone Press, 1970); Molly Harrison, *People and Shopping: A Social Background* (London: Ernest Benn, 1975); Lorna H. Mui and Hoh-Cheung Mui, *Shops and Shopkeeping in Eighteenth-Century England* (Kingston, McGill-Queen's University Press, 1989). On nineteenth-century retailing see, for example, James Jefferys, *Retail Trading in Great Britain: 1850–1950* (Cambridge: Cambridge University Press, 1954); Michael J. Winstanley, *The Shopkeeper's World, 1830–1914* (Manchester: Manchester University Press, 1983); Hamish W. Fraser, *The Coming of the Mass Market, 1850–1914* (Hamden, Conn.: Archon Books, 1981).

16. On these traveling drapers, see Gerry R. Rubin, "From Packmen, Tallymen, and 'Perambulating Scotchmen' to Credit Drapers' Associations, c. 1840–1914," *Business History* 28 (April 1986): 206–25.

17. On the development of urban shopping districts see, Gareth Shaw, "The Role of Retailing in the Urban Economy," in *The Structure of Nineteenth Century Cities*, ed. James H. Johnson and Colin G. Pooley (London: Croom Helm, 1982); Hermione Hobhouse, *A History of Regent Street* (London: Macdonald and Jane's in association with Queen Anne Press, 1975); and Rappaport, "The West End and Women's Pleasure." On the practice of traveling to London to shop, see "Ladies Shopping," *WDTJ*, 12 July 1873, 374; Henry Mayhew, *The Shops and Companies of London and the Trades and Manufactories of Great Britain* 1 (1865): 86; and G. A. Sala, *Twice around the Clock,*

or The Hours of Day and Night in London (1859; reprint, New York: Humanities Press and Leicester University Press, 1971), 161–63.

18. T. J. Jackson Lears argues that in American culture the itinerant peddler personified the emerging market and was frequently portrayed as seducing wives with his salesmanship. T. J. Jackson Lears, "Beyond Veblen: Rethinking Consumer Culture in America," in *Consuming Visions: Accumulation and Display of Goods in America, 1880–1920,* ed. Simon J. Bronner (New York: W. W. Norton, 1989), 78–80.

19. Samuel Smiles, *Thrift* (London: n.p., 1875), 261.

20. *The Drapier and Clothier* 1, no. 1 (May 1859): 11.

21. "Puffing Impostors—A Few Words to All Ladies Making Purchases," *The Drapier and Clothier* 1, no. 3 (July 1859): 86–87.

22. For examples of household manuals, see J. H. Walsh, *A Manual of Domestic Economy: Suited to Families Spending from £100 to £1000 a Year,* 2d ed. (London: Routledge, 1857); Mrs. Warren, *How I Managed My House on Two Hundred Pounds a Year,* 4th American ed. (Boston: Loring, 1866); Florence Stacpoole, *Handbook of Housekeeping for Small Incomes* (London: Walter Scott, 1897); *Cassell's Household Guide: Being A Complete Encyclopedia of Domestic and Social Economy,* 3 vols. (London: Cassell, Petter, and Galpin, 1869–71); Mrs. C. E. Humphrey, *The Book of the Home: A Comprehensive Guide on All Matters Pertaining to the Household* (London: Gresham Publishing, 1910). On the centrality of debt in the narrative structure of Dickens's fiction, see C. R. B. Dunlop, "Debtors and Creditors in Dickens' Fiction," *Dickens Studies Annual: Essays on Victorian Fiction* 19 (1990): 25–47. The popular press as well as novels and household manuals hinted that a woman's financial debts would bring about her moral ruin. See, for example, Coralie Stanton and Heath Hoskin, "Everyone Must Pay," *The Ladies Home Paper: A Weekly Journal for Gentlewomen* 1 (13 February 1909): 8; Violet Lady Greville, "A Lady Dressmaker," *The Queen, The Lady's Newspaper* 134 (4 October 1913): 614.

23. For an analysis of the invention of kleptomania and its social and cultural meanings, see Elaine S. Abelson, *When Ladies Go A-Thieving: Middle-Class Shoplifters in the Victorian Department Store* (New York: Oxford University Press, 1989), 31. Among the studies of the central place of the prostitute in contemporary critiques of consumer society, see Mariana Valverde, "The Love of Finery: Fashion and the Fallen Woman in Nineteenth-Century Social Discourse," *Victorian Studies* 32, no. 2 (winter 1989): 169–88; Susan Buck-Morss, "The Flâneur, the Sandwichman, and the Whore: The Politics of Loitering," in *New German Critique,* no. 39 (fall 1986): 99–140; Walter Benjamin, *Charles Baudelaire: A Lyric Poet in the Era of High Capitalism,* trans. Harry Zohn (London: Verso, 1983), 119–25; and Elizabeth Wilson, *The Sphinx in the City: Urban Life, the Control of Disorder, and Women* (Berkeley: University of California Press, 1991), 55–57.

24. Henry Mayhew, *London Labour and the London Poor* (1851; reprint, London: Frank Cass and Co., 1967), 1:333.

25. Smiles, *Thrift,* 261.

26. This sense was more a result of increasing consumer expectations than of inflationary pressures. See, for example, W. R. Greg, "Life at High Pressure," *The Contemporary Review* 25 (March 1875): 632–34; "The Cost of Living," *Cornhill Magazine* 31 (January–June 1875): 412–21.

27. Smiles, *Thrift,* 252–53.

28. Although imprisonment was abolished with the 1869 Debtors Act, until 1970, small debtors could be and were jailed. Nearly ten thousand a year were imprisoned

just before World War I, and the number was still averaging seven thousand persons, or 14 percent of the prison population, annually between 1961 and 1964. See O. R. McGregor, *Social History and Law Reform* (London: Stevens and Sons, 1981), 36–38. See also Gerry R. Rubin, "Law, Poverty, and Imprisonment for Debt, 1869–1914," in *Law, Economy, and Society, 1750–1914: Essays in the History of English Law*, ed. Gerry R. Rubin and David Sugarman (Abingdon, Great Britain: Professional Books, 1984): 241–99. Well into the twentieth century, legal manuals advised solicitors and creditors how and when to imprison reluctant debtors. See *County Court Practice Made Easy, or Debt Collection Simplified*, 5th (revised) ed. (London: Effingham Wilson, 1922), 65–67, 115.

29. Smiles, *Thrift*, 274.

30. J. A. Banks, *Prosperity and Parenthood: A Study of Family Planning among the Victorian Middle Classes* (London: Routledge and Kegan Paul, 1954), 54.

31. Johnson, "Credit and Thrift"; Tebbutt, *Making Ends Meet;* Banks, *Prosperity and Parenthood.*

32. Alexander, *Retailing in England*, 176.

33. Lady Jeune, "The Ethics of Shopping," *Fortnightly Review* 57 (January 1895): 123.

34. Quoted in Alexander, *Retailing in England*, 176. Dorothy Constance Peel presented a similar image of the difficulties of collecting payment from the aristocracy in *Life's Enchanted Cup: An Autobiography* (London: John Lane and The Bodley Head, 1933), 129–34.

35. Lady Lucile Duff-Gordon, *Discretions and Indiscretions* (London: Jarrolds, 1932), 54. The same difficulties plagued shopkeepers who served lower-class customers. John Birch Thomas, *Shop Boy: An Autobiography* (London: Routledge and Kegan Paul, 1983), 7–8.

36. In practice most working-class husbands relinquished control of family monies to their wife, but further up the social scale, wives traditionally had less direct control over domestic expenditure. See Viviana A. Zelizer, "The Social Meaning of Money: 'Special Monies,'" *Journal of American Sociology* 95, no. 2 (September 1989): 342–77. On financial tensions within the working-class family, see Ellen Ross, "'Fierce Questions and Taunts': Married Life in Working-Class London, 1870–1914," *Feminist Studies* 8, no. 3 (1982): 575–602; Pat Ayers and Jan Lambertz, "Marriage Relations, Money, and Domestic Violence in Working-Class Liverpool, 1919–39," in *Labour and Love: Women's Experience of Home and Family 1850–1940*, ed. Jane Lewis (Oxford: Basil Blackwell, 1986), 195–219; Tebbutt, *Making Ends Meet*, 37–38; A. James Hammerton, "Victorian Marriage and the Law of Matrimonial Cruelty," *Victorian Studies* 33, no. 2 (winter 1990): 278.

37. Going to court was usually a last resort, and frequently the summons would lead to a settlement rather than a formal trial. Melanie Tebbutt discusses the trader's reluctance to turn to legal remedies. Tebbutt, *Making Ends Meet*, 121. On the power of the summons to settle the debt, see *The County Courts* (London, 1852). See also Brian Abel-Smith and Robert Stevens, *Lawyers and the Courts: A Sociological Study of the English Legal System, 1750–1965* (London: Heinemann, 1967), 32–36. The social implications of both the civil law and the operation of the small courts have received very little attention from scholars. For a discussion of the literature, see David Sugarman and Gerry R. Rubin, introduction to *Law, Economy, and Society*, esp. 43–47. For a more detailed social history of debt enforcement, see Rubin, "The County Courts

and the Tally Trade, 1846–1914," in *Law, Economy, and Society*, 321–48; and idem, "Law, Poverty, and Imprisonment for Debt." According to one critic, the courts actually operated "as a stagnation to trade in provincial districts" (*Our County Courts: The Practice Contrasted with that of the Superior Courts; with suggestions for the Improvement of Both* [1857], quoted in W. L. Burn, *The Age of Equipoise: A Study of the Mid-Victorian Generation* [London: George, Allen, and Unwin, 1964], 138). For early modern England, see Craig Muldrew, "Credit, Market Relations, and Debt Litigation in Seventeenth-Century-England" (Ph.D. diss, Cambridge University, 1990); idem, "Credit and Courts: Debt Litigation in a Seventeenth-Century Urban Community," *Economic History Review* 46 (February 1993): 23–38; Margot Finn, "Victorian Women as Consumer Debtors: Theory and Practice" (paper presented at the North American Conference on British Studies, Montreal, October 1993).

38. On the county court judges' attitudes towards small traders, see Rubin, "The County Courts and the Tally Trade, 1846–1914," 321–48.

39. Atiyah, *The Rise and Fall of the Freedom of Contract*, 485–86.

40. *The Times* (London), 2 February 1864, 9.

41. On the legal treatment of wives' debts, see Morrison, "Contract," 116–21. For a history of married women's property law, see Lee Holcombe, *Wives and Property: Reform of the Married Women's Property Law in Nineteenth-Century England* (Toronto: University of Toronto Press, 1983); Mary Lyndon Shanley, *Feminism, Marriage, and the Law in Victorian England, 1850–1935* (Princeton, Princeton University Press, 1989); Caroline Norton, *Caroline Norton's Defense: English Laws for Women in the Nineteenth Century* (1854; reprint, Chicago, Academy Chicago, 1982); Mary Poovey, "Covered But Not Bound: Caroline Norton and the 1857 Matrimonial Causes Act," in Poovey, *Uneven Developments*; and Amy Louise Erickson, *Women and Property in Early Modern England* (London: Routledge, 1993). For the history of women's property rights in the United States, see Norma Basch, *In the Eyes of the Law: Women, Marriage, and Property in Nineteenth-Century New York* (Ithaca: Cornell University Press, 1982), 124–26. While these are all valuable studies, more work needs to be done on the connection between these laws and changing ideas about women's place in the market.

42. On the alterations by the Lords of the original bill, see Shanley, *Feminism, Marriage, and the Law*, 49–78. Only earnings, investments, and property coming from someone who died intestate and legacies of less than two hundred pounds became a married women's separate property. Proponents complained that money a woman earned before marriage or before the act passed would not become her separate property, nor would money deposited in savings banks or similar institutions, unless she made a special application for her account to be so registered. See Shanley, *Feminism, Marriage, and the Law*, 70–75.

43. Erickson, *Women and Property in Early Modern England*, 107.

44. Shanley, *Feminism, Marriage, and the Law*, 71. Further work is needed on the role of debt in the debate surrounding these laws. The importance of ideas about women's debt and the reform of married women's property and the precise impact of the laws on debt litigation are still unclear.

45. Ibid., 70.

46. Ibid., 105–7.

47. "Husbands and Other Debtors," *WDTJ*, 4 April 1874, 151. It was estimated that nine out of ten cases involving a dispute over a husband's liability for a wife's pur-

chasing involved drapery goods. *The Drapers' Record*, 5 October 1889, 424. A systematic analysis of these cases based on the husband's income and the size of debt would be particularly illuminating. My general impression is that, although poor men could successfully prove their wives had bought extravagant purchases without their knowledge, they were less successful than wealthy men in proving this in court.

48. Laura Bell began her career as a draper's assistant. She then became a prostitute and later married an aristocrat. She eventually became a well-known lay preacher. She is mentioned in various Victorian memoirs, and her life is described in Horace Wyndham, *Feminine Frailty* (London: Ernest Benn, 1929), 36–45.

49. Ibid., 44–47.

50. "Debenham and Freebody v. Mellor," *WDTJ*, 27 March 1880, 199. There is some confusion about the defendant's name. It was originally reported as "Mellor," but once it reached the House of Lords it was spelled "Mellon."

51. On the social and cultural construction of "needs," see Jean Baudrillard, *Selected Writings*, ed., with an introduction, by Mark Poster (Stanford: Stanford University Press, 1988), 37–45; William Leiss, *The Limits to Satisfaction: An Essay on the Problem of Needs and Commodities* (Toronto: University of Toronto Press, 1976).

52. "Debenham and Freebody v. Mellor," *WDTJ*, 27 March 1880, 199.

53. Ibid.

54. "A Husband's Liability," *WDTJ*, 3 April 1880, 213.

55. Reprinted as A County Court Judge, "Debenham v. Mellor," *WDTJ*, 3 April 1880, 216.

56. Reprinted as "Liability of Married Women," *The Drapers' Journal*, 10 June 1880, 3.

57. Ibid. A few years later, tradesmen worried that this fear of publicity was lessening and that husbands were beginning to prefer spending "a few minutes in the witness-box" to paying "fifty or a hundred pounds." *The Drapers' Record*, 28 October 1893, 1027.

58. "Debenham and Freebody v. Mellon," *The Times* (London), 25 November 1880, 4.

59. Ibid.

60. "Debenham and Freebody v. Mellon," *The Times* (London), 29 November 1880, 4.

61. Ibid., 9.

62. *The Times* (London), 30 November 1880, 5.

63. "The Married Women's Property Bill," *WDTJ*, 19 June 1880, 386–87.

64. Dr. Cousins, quoted in *The Drapers' Journal*, 17 June 1880, 7.

65. *Women's Suffrage Journal* 13 (September 1882): 131, quoted in Shanley, *Feminism, Marriage, and the Law*, 124.

66. Shanley, *Feminism, Marriage, and the Law*, 126–30.

67. *WDTJ*, 9 September 1882, 633.

68. *WDTJ*, 22 April 1882, 280.

69. *WDTJ*, 14 August 1883, 530.

70. "Married Women's Contracts," *The Drapers' Record*, 17 May 1890, 653.

71. *The Drapers' Record*, 1 November 1890, 643.

72. "Important Decision under the Married Women's Property Act," *The Drapers' Record*, 11 May 1889, 562. In 1854 Caroline Norton described the same situation. She

pointed out that the laws allowed her husband to defraud her creditors and that as a married woman she had only to plead coverture: "Because I am Mr. Norton's wife I can cheat others, the tradesmen who have supplied me would (by the law of England) utterly lose their money" (Norton, *Caroline Norton's Defense*, 96).

73. "Married Women's Rights," *The Drapers' Record*, 2 August 1890, 139; "Married Women's Liability," *The Drapers' Record*, 24 May 1890, 694; 2 May 1891, 7.

74. "Married Women's Debts," *The Drapers' Record*, 13 April 1895, 75.

75. *The Drapers' Record*, 2 May 1891, 792.

76. Morrison, *Century of Family Law*, 121–126.

77. For example, in *Thomas Wallis v. Grossmith*, the judge found Mrs. Grossmith's purchases quite reasonable, so Mr. Grossmith was found liable. *The Drapers' Record*, 5 October 1889, 428.

78. "Law for Ladies," *The Lady*, 12 March 1885, 138.

79. *The Times* (London), 5 June 1880, 6; *The Drapers' Journal*, 10 June 1880, 3.

80. After the decision of *Debenham and Freebody v. Mellon* in the Court of Appeal, there was a great deal of discussion in the trade press as to whether any clothing could be considered necessary. *WDTJ*, 3 April 1880, 212.

81. Their case was heard in this court rather than in the county court because of the size of the debt. There was some inconsistency as to the debt limits for cases heard in the county courts during this period, but the generally accepted limit was fifty pounds.

82. "Floyd v. Hallmann and Wife," *The Times* (London), 20 March 1896, 14; *WDTJ*, 28 March 1896, 363.

83. *The Times* (London), 20 March 1896, 14.

84. Ibid. Moving in society had profound social, political, and economic importance and did require a great deal of conspicuous consumption. See Leonore Davidoff, *The Best Circles: Women and Society in Victorian England* (Totowa, N.J.: Rowman and Littlefield, 1973), 68.

85. *The Times* (London), 20 March 1896, 14.

86. Ibid.

87. "Burberry's v. Mayer and Another, High Court of Justice, King's Bench Division," *The Times* (London), 20 January 1909, 3.

88. Ibid. Occasionally tradesmen found themselves at a loss, for example, when a couple separated and the wife, who owned all the property, gave the husband an allowance. A West End jeweler sued a husband for one hundred pounds for a pearl necklace the jeweler had sold to the wife. During the trial it became clear that the wife, a daughter of successful West End draper Peter Robinson, had all the money in the family. The jeweler sued the husband and lost his claim. "Halford & Sons v. Price and Another, High Court of Justice, King's Bench Division," *The Times*, 19 April 1910, 3.

89. "A Wife's Liability," *The Drapers' Record*, 1 August 1891, 217.

90. Ibid.

91. "A Husband's Responsibility," *The Retail Trader*, January 1913, 16.

92. Veblen, of course, argued that a wife's "conspicuous consumption" helped "establish the good name of the household and its master." Thorstein Veblen, *The Theory of the Leisure Class: An Economic Study in the Evolution of Institutions* (1899; reprint, London: Penguin, 1979), 81.

SIX

Male Providerhood and the Public Purse

Anti-Desertion Reform in the Progressive Era

Anna R. Igra

Dear Editor,

This is the voice of thirty-seven miserable men who are buried but not covered over by earth, tied down but not in chains, silent but not mute, whose hearts beat like humans, yet are not like other human beings. . . .

We feel degraded and miserable here. And why are we confined here? For the horrible crime of being poor, not being able to satisfy the mad whims of our wives. . . . Even during the worst times of the Russian reaction people didn't suffer as the men suffer here in America because of their wives. For a Jewish wife it's as easy here to condemn her husband to imprisonment as it is for her to try on a pair of gloves. . . .

. . . As soon as the wife tastes an easy and free dollar, as soon as she discovers that the "charities" won't let her starve, she doesn't care that her husband is condemned. She lives a gay life, enjoys herself . . .

Therefore, it is your duty as editor of the *Forward,* the newspaper that is read mainly by the working class, the class that furnishes more than all others the candidates for the workhouse and for grass widowhood, to warn all Jewish women not to take such revenge on their husbands. . . .

Thirty-seven inmates of Blackwell's Island Prison workhouse, 1910[1]

Dear Mr. Edelson,

I am appealing to you for your servicies in regard to the trouble with my husband. I have always led a miserable life for my husband but always tried to meet the obsticles with a smile. I was always content of denying myself of proper clothing although he could afford it. The last straw came when he left me for the second time destitute. My rent and other bills were long over due and I had the choice of leaving the rooms or being put out. I feal in no way to become a public charge. . . .

Applicant to the National Desertion Bureau, 1923[2]

An urban landscape beckoning with the promise of consumer goods and mass entertainments lay behind the struggles waged by working-class men and women over meager familial resources. In their petition, the thirty-seven prisoners accuse their wives of preferring consumer pleasures—clothing ("gloves") and cheap amusements (the "gay life")—to husbands of limited means; in her appeal, the deserted woman complains that her husband refuses to pay for necessary household expenses, "although he could afford it." The limited employment available for married women with children in early-twentieth-century American cities left many women, like our letter writer, substantially dependent on their husbands for access to needed goods. That some men resisted the expectation that they would provide is evidenced by the letter of complaint to the *Forward*. Coming recently from an eastern European Jewish milieu in which women were expected to be breadwinners—sometimes the sole supporters of families, including husbands—the thirty-seven Jewish prisoners may have sharply resented that in the United States the law, the charities, and their wives expected them to be the primary household providers. Their bitterness reflects their rapid transition from a culture in which wives were valued as breadgivers to one in which a central index of manhood was breadwinning.[3]

The confrontation of Jewish immigrants with new gender norms was but a heightened case of a wider transformation that had been underway in the United States for decades. Over the course of the nineteenth century, the economic center of the American household had shifted from production to consumption. Although still not complete by the turn of the century, this gradual transformation shaped the gender expectations and behaviors of husbands and wives, as well as the conflicts that afflicted their marriages.[4] Men, who in an earlier time might have derived a sense of identity from their work, increasingly experienced it as the source of a paycheck rather than as a sign of competent manhood. Organized labor registered this shift by redefining virtue for workingmen as providing their families with a "respectable" standard of living.[5] The consumerist turn made breadwinning more central to normative masculinity and highlighted men's connections to families and households. The complaints of wives, the resistance of husbands, and the anxieties of family reformers who feared that the lure of consumer pleasures could erode men's motivation to provide demonstrate that this transition was neither smooth nor comprehensive.

The anti-desertion movement, spearheaded by lawyers, judges, and social workers, sought to regulate male breadwinning.[6] Reformers defined desertion as a problem of economic distribution within the family and linked judgments about a man's use of his wages to notions of respectable manhood and responsible consumption. In a debate over the causes of marital dissolution, social reformers pitted working-class men's responsibilities as providers against their desires as consumers.[7] The proliferation of household-budget studies in the Progressive Era signaled the assumption that women should and did control household consumption. Anti-desertion reformers emphasized men's responsibility to support women as household managers, both by providing the necessary funds and by refraining from personal spending.

Legal and social welfare professionals contended that responsible providerhood among working-class men would also benefit the middle class. The institutions the professionals created—domestic relations courts and legal aid arms of charitable agencies such as the National Desertion Bureau (N.D.B.)—were designed to protect the public purse. In a provocative article, Carol Brown argues that around the turn of the century many men came to view wives and children as burdens, rather than as assets, and a "class struggle" ensued between "the private family and the public system" over who would bear the costs of support.[8] Indeed, by reducing the numbers of poor women and children eligible for public funds, anti-desertion measures aimed to ensure that middle-class resources would not be consumed by working-class dependents. The new socio-legal agencies and their policies became integral parts of public assistance programs such as mothers' pensions, limiting public liability for poor women and children. Class and gender anxieties about workingmen's spending, so prominent in anti-desertion rhetoric, thus exposed the disruptive potential of male consumption for both the familial and the social order.

By analyzing the anti-desertion rhetoric about male spending, I hope to underscore the familial and social dimensions of the emerging mass consumer society. These are not fully explored in studies that frame consumer culture in terms of the production of desire, self-actualization or expression, and the "therapeutic ethos."[9] Anti-desertion reformers sometimes sounded like opponents of release and self-gratification through consumption. However, they had no moral objection to consumption per se, provided it was directed to certain ends. They sought to achieve their goals through the use of various state apparatuses—domestic relations courts and welfare programs—institutions that, although contemporary developments, are rarely discussed in studies of consumer culture in the United States. In these endeavors, we encounter not images of feminine frivolity and extravagance but serious anxieties about male consumption and misspending.

The geographic focus of this article is New York City, the center of the anti-desertion movement in the Progressive Era. The movement was national in scope, however, and material is drawn where appropriate from reform documents from around the country. Many of the reformers cited here were Jewish because in a number of respects Jews led the anti-desertion movement. Their involvement was in part a response to fears that antisemitism and immigration restriction might be fueled by Jewish desertion and welfare dependency.[10] But it was also one aspect of the middle-class American Jewish movement to acculturate working-class immigrants to new familial norms and patterns of consumption. The letters from the thirty-seven family deserters and the abandoned woman thus emerge from a rich intersection of gender, class, ethnic, legal, and social welfare dynamics with a Progressive reform movement anxious to regulate male breadwinning and, hence, male consumption.

THE "DISCOVERY" OF DESERTION

In 1909, the author of a manual for charity workers observed: "Fifteen years ago the deserted family was hardly differentiated from any other instance of poverty; it was a family in want, and the mere fact that that want was caused by the desertion of the natural breadwinner did not seem to the philanthropists of the day to have any material bearing on the situation. . . . a deserted family was supposed to occupy the same position as a family which had lost its head by death." By 1909, however, desertion had been "discovered": "The subject is discussed at almost every national or state conference . . . and it is rapidly developing a literature of its own." Charity workers were now advised to track down nonsupporting men and enlist the aid of the law in prosecuting them.[11]

Because deserted women were classed with widows in the 1880s, there was little discussion among charity workers about legal remedies for deserted women until the late 1890s. Beginning in the 1880s, the United Hebrew Charities (U.H.C.) occasionally acknowledged the existence of desertion, but it was not until 1897 that deserted wives were specified as a group requiring special attention.[12] In annual reports of social agencies, as in manuals for charity workers, deserted women were grouped with widows both in statistical compilations and in discussions of their treatment. The New York Charity Organization Society (C.O.S.), for example, kept no separate statistics for deserted women in the 1880s. Although deserted women occasionally appeared in the annual reports' appendix of "illustrative cases," intended both to raise funds and to instruct C.O.S. agents, prosecution of deserters was not recommended as a course of action. Instead, successful resolutions of desertion cases included finding paid work for the woman, sending her children to institutions, or sending both woman and children to a (female) relative.[13] The C.O.S. treated widows the same way.

The disaggregation of widows from deserted wives laid the groundwork for increased attention to the prosecution of nonsupporting husbands and fathers. Distinctions between the two groups of women emerged with increasing frequency as the movement to remove children from institutions and to return them to their mother's care gained ground in the 1890s. One of the earliest pieces of legislation in New York designed to accomplish this purpose was a mothers' allowance bill introduced into the state legislature in 1897. The bill, which applied to the city of New York, instructed the city comptroller to pay to a destitute mother the amount normally expended by an institution for the care of a child in order to keep the child at home. It covered any destitute mother who was compelled by poverty to seek the commitment of her children, whether she was widowed or deserted, whether or not she had a wage-earning husband or wage-earning children. The bill passed both houses of the legislature in 1898 but was vetoed by the governor under pressure from New York City social agencies opposed to public outdoor relief.[14]

Those who had opposed the mothers' allowance legislation raised an issue that would shape the policy of social agencies toward deserted women. The bill's opponents labeled it the "shiftless fathers' bill," arguing that giving aid to women with living husbands would encourage desertion because men could rest assured that the public would support their children.[15] Social agencies, also concerned about "shiftless fathers," advocated a policy of withholding relief from deserted women as a "preventative" measure. C. C. Carstens of the Society for the Prevention of Cruelty to Children (S.P.C.C.), for example, warned that "to treat the deserted wife . . . as if she were a widow is giving unbegrudging aid but is also giving a cowardly husband encouragement."[16]

"Cowardly husbands" and "shiftless fathers" who allegedly defrauded the charities evoked different anxieties than did the able-bodied unemployed of the nineteenth century. Deserters were assumed to have incomes, and the movement to prosecute them reflected anxieties about working-class men's access to cash wages. Anti-desertion reformers defined a man's use of his wage as a social, rather than a personal, matter, one that involved simultaneous obligations to his family and to society. A "shiftless father" treated his wage as his own personal property, to be spent on his own consumer pleasures— drink, gambling, "other women"—thereby reneging on his civic duty to support his family.

THE POOR MAN'S VACATION, OR WHY BREADWINNERS WENT AWOL

The conviction that desertion reflected men's irresponsible use of their wages solidified over time. In the early years of the century, many prominent commentators on desertion tended to assume an equivalency between male wage earning and breadwinning; therefore, they believed that unemployment was the main cause of nonsupport. In 1905 attorney Charles Zunser, then an agent for the Committee for the Protection of Deserted Women and Children and later chief counsel of the N.D.B., cited only two causes for desertion: "defects of the woman" and "the far more important reason . . . bad industrial conditions. Lack of work . . . has driven more men away from their families than any other single factor."[17] As U.H.C. director Morris Waldman recalled, "To take legal measures against such men was considered harsh."[18]

The discovery of desertion, however, stimulated research into its "causes," resulting in a different interpretation.[19] As social worker Mary Conyngton observed in 1909, the former "vivid pictures of the man driven by stress of poverty to abandon his family, finding himself unable to support them" were deemed inaccurate; "the deserter of this kind, if he exists at all, is in a small minority, and . . . ordinarily the man who abandons wife and children is influenced by frankly selfish motives."[20] Charles Zunser changed his earlier opinion about the connection between desertion and unemployment and, by 1931, was convinced that economic hard times instead kept men at home. He argued that men were less likely to take up with other women when unemployed, and he predicted that the Great Depression would cause some deserters to return to their families. He reasoned: "In hard times 'other women' are expensive. It feels good to come back to the real wife who has a home and often credit from local tradesmen to tide over a bad economic spell. . . . In hard times, the old wife will have to do."[21]

The shift in explanation away from unemployment signaled the recognition by anti-desertion reformers that male wage earning and breadwinning were not equivalent: men's personal consumption could disrupt the connection between the two. The search for alternative explanations for men's failure to provide resulted in lists of what could be characterized as "gender disorders": a lack of "manliness" in husbands and fathers and inadequate "womanliness" in mothers and wives. The two disorders were related in reformers' minds: a man with an insufficiently feminine wife was likely to desert; a woman whose cowardly husband left her might lose her womanly virtues. Manliness was defined as responsible providerhood, womanliness as efficient housekeeping and physical attractiveness.

"Defects of the woman" believed to contribute to desertion were in effect inadequate femininity. Keeping house according to middle-class American standards, attending to her appearance, being sexually available, and assuming a posture of dependence were all necessary if a woman wanted her husband and his paycheck to stay home. Deserted wives were suspected of having "a disinclination to marital intercourse" or of suffering from "sexual anaesthesia."[22] Michael Francis Doyle of the Society of St. Vincent de Paul attributed desertion to the failure of married women to preserve their looks: "The wife loses her attractiveness after a few years of marriage and trouble, she becomes untidy and lacks neatness," so the husband departs.[23]

Housekeeping, like sex, was viewed by anti-desertion reformers as part of the marriage bargain. They cited domestic "inefficiency" and a woman's inability to create an attractive and peaceful refuge at home as disincentives for male breadwinning. In Progressive Era budget studies, domestic "efficiency" was defined as the ability to attain an "American standard of living."

A family's standard of living was measured not only by the size of its income but also by the way in which a wife allocated it.[24] Solomon Lowenstein, superintendent of the Hebrew Orphan Asylum, suspected that deserted women lacked adequate training in the "domestic sciences," and this lack resulted in "the unattractiveness of the average tenement home" and "the unpalatable, ill-cooked food" served in it. Other reformers agreed, recommending that deserted women receive instruction in directing the household budget toward making the home more attractive to their husbands than cafés, other women, and nonfamilial amusements.[25]

Immigrant women received more than their share of criticism for failing to Americanize their domestic habits and personal appearance. Social worker Kate Claghorn pictured the foreign-born woman as "a plain, hard-working, slow-thinking domestic drudge," far less attractive than the "more sophisticated, better-dressed" American woman. N.D.B. president Walter Liebman recounted the story of a man who had tried, unsuccessfully, to "Americanize" his wife: "She could not depart from the slovenliness of her home and her person. Result—desertion." A wife's lack of deference, anti-desertion reformers feared, might sap a man's will to provide. Joanna Colcord, superintendent of the C.O.S., warned that women should guard against "a tendency to dominate or try to control." Morris Waldman found it "alarming" that some deserted women were older than their husbands and thus were not subordinate in the family age hierarchy. "The theory is," explained Lilian Brandt of the C.O.S., "that if the wife is decidedly older she assumes the leadership, to a certain degree, with the result that the husband's sense of responsibility remains embryonic."[26]

Even though many involved in the anti-desertion movement were aware that women made crucial contributions to the household income, they nevertheless worried that wage earning among wives might contribute to male negligence. Wifely dependence was viewed as a stimulus to male breadwinning and hence, ironically, as protection against destitution through desertion. Joanna Colcord believed that an "overefficient" woman risked desertion by impinging on male territory: "Many a non-supporter got his first impulse in that direction when his wife became a wage-earner in some domestic crisis." She advised that a woman should adopt an attitude of feminine helplessness when her husband lost his job—she should sit down and cry until he found a new one. Probation officer John J. Gascoyne advised: "If the probation officer learns that the wife goes out to work by the day, his first effort should be to gradually put a stop to the same."[27] "If a woman becomes a wage-earner," Earle Eubank explained in his 1916 study of desertion, "the husband's feeling of responsibility for providing for her may be lessened. . . . The woman, in turn, from the fact of being economically independent, may be led to assert her independence in ways which will in themselves be provocative. . . ."[28]

While worried about the "provocative" behavior of women, anti-desertion reformers only infrequently accused them of extravagance. In contrast to the thirty-seven incarcerated men who laid the blame for their desertion on the "mad whims" of their wives, anti-desertion reformers were relatively unconcerned about this kind of misspending. They commented with approval on men who turned their pay packets over unopened to their wives and viewed with suspicion and trepidation the man who controlled his own paycheck. Weighing the risk of housewifely inefficiency against the risk of male irresponsibility, anti-desertion activists generally regarded the former as posing the lesser danger.

Reformers' statements revealed what would be a lasting tension between viewing deserted women as victims and stigmatizing them as guilty parties. A widow was clearly not responsible for her plight, but it was not easy for charity workers to admit that a deserted woman was abandoned through no fault of her own. Commenting on the growing support within charity societies for giving privately funded regular stipends to widows, Mary Breed of the C.O.S. argued, "The deserted wife is distinctly below the [moral] standard of the widow deprived of her husband by death. . . . There seem to be, then, few deserted wives to whom we can apply the character test necessary for a pension plan."[29]

Although most descriptions of deserted wives and their homes were distinctly unflattering, the "defects" of the women were not seen as justifying the complete abandonment of children by men. Men who deserted had their own faults, reformers believed. They lacked the "manliness" necessary to lead a proper family life. Domestic Relations Court Judge Jonah Goldstein believed that the man who deserted his family was "hardly worthy of the name 'man.'" Such a father did not have the "instinct" of manhood, Max Hertzberg of the U.H.C. asserted, and was the opposite of a real man, a "coward." C. C. Carstens agreed that deserters were "peculiarly cowardly"; Walter Liebman exclaimed that they were driven by "a strange mixture of folly and cowardice!"[30]

The cowardice of deserting fathers was linked to the cowardice of a soldier who deserted in wartime. The persistent use of the term "desertion" to cover abandonment and/or nonsupport underscored the connection between obligation to one's country and the law of support. Relying on the military resonance of the term, Judge Goldstein declared, "Desertion is A.W.O.L." One reformer speculated that men who married during World War I in order to evade military service ("slacker marriages") were likely to desert their families.[31] The military branches were concerned with both types of desertion; they assisted the N.D.B. in tracking down nonsupporting, "deserting," servicemen. Like the nurturing tasks of motherhood, which were viewed not only as a private duty but also as a service to the state, a man's duty to support his family was part of his duty to his country.

Reformers argued that selfishness and self-indulgence led men to with-hold their income from their families and to spend it on themselves. They accused men of "hoarding their earnings" or of spending them on leisure consumption, including other women.[32] The middle class may have em-braced the transition from producer to consumer, but they did not encour-age a similar transition for men who could not afford both providerhood and leisure consumption.[33] The working-class man would have to choose between the two—he would have to provide for his family before he could participate in the culture of consumption—even while the professionals who enforced this principle were able to do both.

The theme of male self-indulgence appears frequently in the anti-deser-tion literature. The term did not indicate that men failed to work, but rather that they spent their wages on their own pleasures. The family deserter, re-marked social investigator Lilian Brandt, was an "irresponsible, ease-loving man" who felt "justified in making arrangements for his own comfort which [did] not include his wife and children."[34] A. S. Newman, superintendent of a Jewish aid organization, characterized the cause of desertion as male "selfishness, licentiousness, self-indulgence and a lack of a sense of duty."[35] Such "weak-willed" men unable to resist temptation were likely to withdraw their support from their families to have "a good time on Saturday night," to "spend money in saloons," and generally to seek their own "enjoyment."[36]

Anti-desertion reformers were attempting to make working-class male con-sumption responsible. Their efforts paralleled those of settlement house workers and other social reformers to encourage men to participate in fam-ily-oriented leisure pursuits rather than in all-male activities. Shared social time was thought to bind a man closer to his family, making desertion less likely. Joanna Colcord worried about men who spent their leisure time in nonfamilial settings—"in saloons and social clubs"—particularly when do-ing so gave husbands an opportunity to compare their own situation with that of their unmarried companions.[37] Men were thus encouraged to spend their wages with their families, rather than with their male friends.

Like immigrant women, immigrant men came in for more than their share of criticism. Anti-desertion reformers theorized that the transition from the repressive old country to the land of liberty and abundance had unleashed male irresponsibility. Morris Waldman decried the way such men were "mis-taking liberty for license."[38] Another reformer complained, "They take the American freedom and liberty in a different light from which it has been given."[39] Lawyer and social worker Bernhard Rabbino described the immi-grant deserter's presumed state of mind: "This was America, the Land of Free-dom. No more oppressive religious obligations. No more chafing 'Don'ts.' Life must be lived to the fullest, material enjoyment must reign supreme. . . . The self-denials of the past were to be amply balanced by the self-indulgences of the present."[40]

Anti-desertion reformers believed that men acculturated faster than did women and that this accounted for men's dissatisfaction with their marriages. "Americanization" for immigrant men, believed Eubank, meant "a taste for brighter lights, fancier clothing, more stirring amusements and less confined life." He linked immigrant men's material desires to their presumed preference for native-born women. "Plain, hard-working Francisca or Gretchen," he observed, "cannot compare in style with their modernized counterparts in the cities of America."[41] Morris Waldman agreed: "The new environment affects the immigrant husband and wife differently; the former is more open to its influence. . . ." He linked men's Americanization to the achievement of new and better standards of consumption:

> The husband is employed in some shop or factory in the vicinity of Broadway, and so is brought in contact with cleanliness and respectability. In most cases it is cheaper for the man to have his noonday meal in a neighboring restaurant . . . infinitely better cooked and better served than at home. The man becomes accustomed to his separate plates and his cloth napkin—unheard of luxuries at home. The aesthetic sense is aroused. . . . the husband's standard of living has risen above that of his wife.[42]

Anti-desertion reformers hoped that immigrant women could "Americanize" their housekeeping and thereby preserve domestic peace. At the same time, they worried about the disintegrative effects of participation in American consumer culture on immigrant families. Historian Andrew Heinze suggests that immigrants and social reformers alike understood that acculturation occurred through consumption. The equation of freedom with access to American abundance was one that, he suggests, was made especially by Jewish immigrants from eastern Europe. Heinze argues that social reformers approved of immigrants' aspirations in the arena of consumption because they viewed the desire for an American standard of living as a positive sign of acculturation.[43] But, as the comments of Rabbino and Waldman suggest, social reformers also understood the disruptive potential of consumer aspirations and of the equation of American freedom with consumer pleasures. Liberty, they contended, meant the opportunity to provide for a family, not simply the freedom to consume American goods. Consumption may have been a route to social integration, as Heinze suggests, but anti-desertion reformers believed that it also posed the danger of familial and hence social disintegration.

Historian Linda Gordon has suggested that one of the goals of family reformers was the "'modernization' of male dominance, its adaptation to new economic and social conditions." Particularly in their work with immigrant families, Gordon argues, reformers aimed to facilitate a transition from patriarchal control over children's and women's labor power to the dependence of women and children on a male wage. They sought "to reconstruct the family along lines that altered the old patriarchy, already economically un-viable, and replace it with a modern version of male supremacy" and "to im-pose a new middle-class urban style of mothering and fathering."[44]

But, as Gordon would agree, it would be incorrect to assume that the ef-forts of courts and social agencies to enforce the role of breadwinner for working-class men was simply an instance of middle-class social control. La-bor unions often assisted the N.D.B. in locating nonsupporting men. James O'Connell, president of the International Association of Machinists, insisted that organized labor and social workers shared common ground on the is-sue of desertion: "It is not generally understood that organized labor aims at any reform or any high standards of family ethics. This is indeed a great mistake." As evidence, he pointed out that he had "in hundreds of cases, been able to run down wife-deserters and men who neglected their families and [had] been able to compel them to return to their wives and their children or in case of their refusal, to strike their names from the rolls of member-ship of the Association."[45]

Members of the rank and file may have also judged fellow workers ac-cording to their fidelity to the breadwinner ideal. Historian Sherri Broder has found evidence that working-class people evaluated one another ac-cording to the performance of familial duties in ways that overlapped with middle-class definitions of respectability and manhood. By the late nineteenth century in urban working-class communities, "roughness" and "respectabil-ity" had come to define poles of manhood, with respectable manliness con-sisting of being a good provider, staying sober, and exhibiting solicitude for children. Manliness thus defined was one way that the "respectable" working-class distinguished itself from the "rough" and "degraded" poor.[46]

There is reason to believe that over the course of the nineteenth century, the locus of working-class men's own gender identity had shifted slowly away from production and toward providerhood.[47] The loss of control over the work process, accelerated by techniques of scientific management, and the degradation of skill levels undermined the old touchstone of working-class manhood—the pride of the skilled producer. Workers were developing an "instrumental view" of their jobs; they looked to the wage and what it could buy on the market for satisfaction and identity rather than to the workplace.[48] The link between income and manhood was crucial to the twentieth-century campaign for the family wage. Whereas in the nineteenth century the family wage had been viewed as a just reward for and ratification of a man's craft competence, in the twentieth century it became the reason to work and an end in itself. In the process, the family wage shifted from a de-mand based on notions of class justice to one based on gender privilege, with middle-class reformers and labor unions using it to undermine women's position in the labor market and to shore up men's position at home.[49] The tendency to emphasize breadwinning as the key to successful manhood was thus increasingly embraced by both "respectable" working-class and middle-class men.

As the normative meaning of "manhood" changed in emphasis from producer to provider in the context of an emerging consumer capitalism, charity workers detected a new form of "welfare cheat." The old specter of the able-bodied-yet-idle man who refused to join the ranks of sturdy producers was joined by the specter of the employed man who chose to spend his wages on himself rather than on his family. The welfare fraud that anti-desertion reformers claimed they had discovered was perpetrated by the man who could provide but refused to do so, thereby leaving his wife and children a burden on the public purse.

While arguing that the boundary of working-class men's obligations extended beyond themselves to include wives and children, reformers also marked out the limits of middle-class men's obligations. That boundary, too, would encompass—but not exceed—one's own family. Middle-class familial individualism was thus mirrored in the ideology of the "independent family." When anti-desertion reformers intoned that the family was "the cornerstone of the nation,"[50] they meant the "independent" male-headed household. This preoccupation was not quite the same as the earlier notion of the independent citizen as the foundation of the state; it relied primarily not on the productive citizen but on the providing father. An "independent" family was one in which a man provided for his own wife and children; "dependent" women and children were public charges.[51]

DESERTION AND SOCIAL POLICY

The debate over desertion and male self-indulgence had long-ranging consequences for the development of institutions and policies to deal with both nonsupporting men and abandoned mothers. The effects of professional concern about desertion are most easily identified in the legal mechanisms designed to deal specifically with nonsupport. After initially pursuing stiffer abandonment laws, reformers turned to building institutions, such as the N.D.B. and a system of domestic relations (or family) courts, to implement the laws. Their concerns were also incorporated into public assistance rules and procedures that relied on these new institutions to limit the reach of welfare programs, including mothers' pensions. Private charities' reluctance to assist deserted women was translated into public policy as the framers of pension legislation, fearing the taint of corruption that adhered to state spending in the Progressive Era, attempted to establish themselves as responsible administrators of the public purse.[52] In the process, what appeared to be a concern for the transfer of resources within the family from the wallet to the purse was revealed to be at least as much about the distribution of resources among classes.

Beginning around the turn of the century, social agencies began calculating how much the support of deserted women and children was costing the public.[53] The domestic relations court was seen by anti-desertion reformers as a vehicle for reducing the amount that both local government and private charities expended on poor women and children by coercing husbands and fathers to provide for their families. Although much paternalistic rhetoric about reconciling disaffected spouses accompanied the creation of the courts, the public interest in containing dependency in the family was central to the legal approach to cases of desertion. As attorney Benjamin Tuska noted, "The communal and legal standpoint is one dictated by self-interest. We must save the community expense."[54]

As a survey of opinions in the New York domestic relations courts reveals, male breadwinning was indeed treated as a public obligation, therefore subject to state regulation through legal intervention. The first full domestic relations courts in the country were established in New York City in 1910.[55] Reflecting the financial motivations for its establishment, the domestic relations court was given jurisdiction over proceedings involving "all persons charged with abandonment or non-support of wives or poor relatives."[56] Regarding nonsupport of wives and children, it specified proceedings under subdivision one of Section 899 of the Code of Criminal Procedure, which defined "disorderly persons" as "persons who actually abandon their wives or children, without adequate support, or leave them in danger of becoming a burden upon the public, or who neglect to provide for them according to their means."

This was the law under which the thirty-seven signatories to the letter to the editor of the *Forward* had been charged. They complained that they were imprisoned for not satisfying the "mad whims" of their wives. However, these disgruntled husbands were not brought to court over a dispute about whether, for example, a particular dress was a "necessary" or whether it suited the station of a woman married to a man with a certain level of income.[57] Their crime was against the public.

Although the statute appears to mandate that husbands share their class status with their wives—by supporting them "according to their means"—in fact the courts almost always ruled that violation of this clause alone was not sufficient basis for a complaint. As Judge Hazard observed in 1930 in *People ex rel. Case v. Case,* "Rather curiously all the numerous cases bearing upon the paragraph seem persistently to construe it as if the word 'or' was 'and.'"[58] Building on the decision in *Case,* another judge acknowledged, "I am aware of the fact that the disjunctive 'or' is used in this section . . . [but] an act should not be characterized as criminal unless it offends the public. . . . The act of a man in neglecting to support his family in accordance with his means is not, in and of itself, criminal in its nature because it involves a difference between the husband and wife in which the public is not interested."[59]

On the eve of the creation of the domestic relations courts, a string of decisions made clear that rulings under the "disorderly persons" law (and the almost identical Section 685 of the Greater New York City Charter) would be concerned less about a just distribution of resources within the family than about limiting the obligations of middle-class taxpayers to poor women and children. These decisions agreed that "the statute was not enacted for the settlement of matrimonial differences"[60] and that it was not intended "to enforce the performance of marital obligations and duties, beyond what was necessary to protect the community against the unnecessary imposition of the support of a man's wife and children."[61] This is how the "disorderly persons" statute continued to be construed.[62]

The statute, which allowed for complaint by a destitute woman or a welfare agent but not by a woman of any means, was thus part of the "family law of the poor."[63] The domestic relations court was in effect a kind of poor-law court, created to handle an impoverished economic class with the goal of protecting the pocketbooks of the middle class. It perpetuated what legal scholar Jacobus ten Broek has labeled the "dual system of family law," which placed the poor on a different legal track than the family of means.[64] Although the courts were often described with lofty rhetoric about repairing family life and reconciling disaffected spouses, there is compelling evidence to conclude that they were only interested in the material aspect of marriage as it affected the taxpayers. Other kinds of domestic cases, such as those involving wife battering, had no place in these courts unless the battery was accompanied by nonsupport.[65] The "court of domestic relations" was thus as much a creature of class relations as of gender relations.

The legal machinery for regulating male breadwinning defined men's obligation as the minimum required to prevent social spending on dependent women and children. Social welfare workers feared that if public assistance programs became available to deserted women, then men would shift their spending from household provision to personal consumption. Concerned that social spending on deserted families would end up subsidizing male "self-indulgence," they looked to the new socio-legal institutions for help in preventing welfare fraud by "shiftless" men.[66]

The influence of anti-desertion rhetoric and institutions on social welfare policy can be seen in the most notable Progressive Era innovation in public assistance, "mothers' pensions." Mothers' pension legislation swept the nation like wildfire, beginning in 1911; by 1920 forty states had instituted programs.[67] The principles that guided the pension movement, if not the implementation of programs, were that children should not be separated from their mothers simply because of poverty, that a good mother's care was superior to institutional care, and that motherhood was a service to the state. Mothers' pension plans varied in the definition of recipients, including any combination of widows, wives of incarcerated or disabled men, deserted women, and unwed mothers. Many states named deserted women as eligible recipients at some point, but there was considerable ambivalence regarding their inclusion. The primary recipient, and the image used to drum up support for pension legislation, was the "worthy widow," the figure least likely to arouse public opposition.

The mothers' pension movement developed alongside the campaign for domestic relations courts and for the prosecution of family deserters. The two movements shared some personnel. The General Federation of Women's Clubs and their ally William Hard, the editor of *The Delineator* and a prominent proponent of mothers' pensions, urged the passage of anti-desertion legislation. Jewish reformers were at the forefront of both movements; non-Jewish private charities emerged as the most vigorous opponents of mothers' pensions.[68] Both the anti-desertion and mothers' pension movements aimed to reduce the population of children's institutions, for both economic and ideological reasons. And both were haunted by the specter of the irresponsible male spender.

While debates over the two reforms overlapped chronologically, in New York, anti-desertion legislation and domestic relations courts preceded mothers' pension legislation by a number of years. By the time mothers' pension legislation was drafted, anti-desertion reformers had articulated rationales for disaggregating widows from deserted women and for excluding the latter. New institutions had been created that offered mechanisms for diverting deserted women away from the pension program and toward the legal system. Anti-desertion reform thus may have contributed to the narrow scope of New York's mothers' pension program.[69]

Debates about mothers' pension legislation echoed earlier discussions about private charity as an incentive for desertion by shiftless men. New York City Commissioner of Charities Robert W. Hebberd, a member of the commission that drafted New York State's pension legislation who had been actively involved in creating New York City's domestic relations courts, warned against making the program a broad one: "There are, doubtless, thousands of men in this country who would be overtempted . . . to desert their families if they could be sure that a 'pension' would be forthcoming as the result of such desertion. . . . It must be evident that society cannot afford to hold out this temptation to the weak or the shiftless heads of families." Hebberd did not want to lend men "any encouragement to waste their means in drink or in any other form of hurtful extravagance." He therefore wished to restrict pensions to "the natural objects of charity," worthy widows, whom he viewed as "a logical charge . . . upon the body politic with its adequate resources."[70]

The commission created to make recommendations on mothers' pensions to the New York state legislature included members who had been immersed in debates about desertion for over a decade, among them William Hard, Robert Hebberd, and Hannah Einstein. Their report argued for extending benefits only to widows: "The misfortune that follows upon the decease of the poorer laborer is not caused in any way by those who must suffer. Then, too, adequate relief cannot in any way increase the number of worthy families in distress as can easily be the case with other mothers whose husbands are living. To pension desertion or illegitimacy would, undoubtedly, have the effect of [putting] a premium on these crimes against society."[71] By the time mothers' pension legislation succeeded in New York with the 1915 Child Welfare Act, it had been narrowed to include worthy widows only; it was among the most conservative legislation of its type in the nation.

The New York pensions program was finally opened to deserted mothers almost a decade later, but with the stipulation that, in order to qualify, a deserted applicant must first engage in a complex and lengthy search for her husband, who, if located, was to be prosecuted. This process could take years. When a woman applied to the Board of Child Welfare for a pension after 1924, she was sent to a location agency, such as the N.D.B., to the domestic relations court, or to the district attorney. If her husband was located, she was denied a pension.[72] In the late 1920s and early 1930s, the New York City Board of Child Welfare used the legal procedures and institutions created by anti-desertion reformers to defer or deny deserted women's applications for mothers' pensions, drawing on the reformers' argument that the responsibility for support rested with the husband, not the public.[73]

An odd assumption underlay social policies regarding desertion: men would leave their families if they could. Reformers believed that if men caught wind of the possibility that charities or the state would provide for deserted women and children, many men would view it as an opportunity to gain their "freedom." The same people who extolled marriage and the family gave little sense of why men would want to stay, beyond a feeling of duty. Recall the comparisons made between tasty restaurant food and unpalatable home-cooked meals, between dating a stylish sophisticate and living with a domestic drudge, between an uninviting home and the comradery of cafés and saloons. All these comparisons add to the impression that perhaps on some level anti-desertion reformers agreed with the sentiment expressed by the thirty-seven resentful prisoners: marriage was no bargain for men.

The assumption that marriage was burdensome for men (especially working-class men), and the corollary that opportunities to escape would be seized upon eagerly, rested on a devaluation of wives' contributions to families, much of which were in the form of unpaid labor. The outraged thirty-seven letter writers saw their wives only as frivolous spenders, not as household workers and managers. The devaluation of the unpaid household labor of deserted women was also implicit in their exclusion from the mothers' pension program. Pensions were granted to widows on the principle that motherhood was a service to the state, one that benefited society, the nation, and the "race," and hence deserved compensation. Although desertion was often said to have dire consequences for the state—in that it purportedly damaged future citizens by contributing to juvenile delinquency—deserted women's maternal contribution to society continued to be treated as a private duty not eligible for public compensation. The persistent conceptualization of deserted women's motherhood in familial rather than social terms implied that the public had no social duty to support deserted families. While defining male breadwinning as a civic obligation subject to legal regulation, the state, it seems, was itself a reluctant breadwinner.[74]

In the context of a debate about the division of domestic money and consumer power between husbands and wives, anti-desertion reformers thus participated in defining the proper uses of state power and public funds.[75] Anti-desertion reformers assumed a relationship between personal spending and social spending. Concerned about irresponsible male consumption, they attempted to ensure that public assistance would not subsidize married men's personal spending. The public purse was not to be used to promote workingmen's pleasure or participation in the economy as leisure consumers. Implicitly, public funds were designated for meeting subsistence needs rather than for satisfying consumer desires and aspirations.

The fear of middle-class professionals that taxpayers and charities would be saddled with the responsibility for, as Earle Eubank emphasized, "other men's children" accounted for the way in which anti-desertion measures were designed for poor women only.[76] Public money, anti-desertion reformers claimed, should not be used to meet working-class familial obligations. Their definition of the relationship between the family pocketbook and the public purse indicated a belief that dependence and support should define the relations between the sexes, and that the middle-class segment of the population should not be responsible for working-class dependents. The rules governing nonsupport proceedings and the allocation of pensions to deserted women embodied the fear that workingmen's spending could upset these relations, resulting in illegitimate claims on the public purse and disrupting the economies of both the household and the state.

NOTES

I am grateful to Norma Basch, Alice Kessler-Harris, Jan Lambertz, Suzanne Lebsock, Megan McClintock, and Howard Oransky for their invaluable encouragement and criticism. Financial support was contributed by a Samuel I. Golieb Fellowship from the New York University School of Law and a Littleton-Griswold Research Grant from the American Historical Association.

1. *A Bintel Brief: Sixty Years of Letters from the Lower East Side to the Jewish Daily "Forward,"* ed. Isaac Metzker (New York: Schocken, 1971), 110–12.

2. Letter dated 15 May 1923, National Desertion Bureau case file B1620, Archives of the YIVO Institute for Jewish Social Research, New York.

3. It was the American normative expectation of male breadwinning and female dependence that generated conflict, not the role of women as consumers per se. As Andrew Heinze convincingly argues, women's control over household consumption in the United States continued and enhanced the Eastern European Jewish female role of "baleboste." Andrew Heinze, *Adapting to Abundance: Jewish Immigrants, Mass Consumption, and the Search for an American Identity* (New York: Columbia University Press, 1990), chap. 6.

4. Elaine Tyler May, *Great Expectations: Marriage and Divorce in Post-Victorian America* (Chicago: University of Chicago Press, 1980).

5. In the nineteenth century, organized labor promulgated "a new discourse of virtue, replacing a producerist republicanism with a consumerist one," argues Lawrence Glickman. Glickman, "Inventing the 'American Standard of Living': Gender, Race, and Working-Class Identity, 1880–1925," *Labor History* 34, nos. 2–3 (spring-summer 1993): 221–35.

6. Martha May, "The 'Problem of Duty': Family Desertion in the Progressive Era," *Social Service Review* 62 (March 1988): 40–60.

7. Recent echoes of Progressive Era anti-desertion reformers' arguments, but applied to middle-class men, can be found in Barbara Ehrenreich, *The Hearts of Men: American Dreams and the Flight from Commitment* (New York: Anchor Press/Doubleday, 1983).

8. Carol Brown, "Mothers, Fathers, and Children: From Private to Public Patriarchy," in *Women and Revolution,* ed. Lydia Sargent (Boston: South End Press, 1981), 239–67.

9. Richard Wightman Fox and T. J. Jackson Lears, eds., *The Culture of Consumption: Critical Essays in American History, 1880–1980* (New York: Pantheon Books, 1983).

10. For further discussion of Jewish involvement in anti-desertion activities, see Jean Ulitz Mensch, "Social Pathology in Urban America: Desertion, Prostitution, Gambling, Drugs, and Crime among Eastern European Jews in New York City" (Ph.D. diss., Columbia University, 1983), 20–74; Reena Sigman Friedman, "'Send Me My Husband Who Is in New York City': Husband Desertion in the American Jewish Immigrant Community, 1900–1926," *Jewish Social Studies* 44 (winter 1982): 1–18; Ari Lloyd Fridkis, "Desertion in the American Jewish Immigrant Family: The Work of the National Desertion Bureau in Cooperation with the Industrial Removal Office," *American Jewish History* 71 (December 1981): 285–99.

11. Mary Conyngton, *How to Help: A Manual of Practical Charity* (New York: Macmillan, 1909), 148, 150.

12. *Fifty Years of Social Service: The History of the United Hebrew Charities of the City of New York* (New York: Jewish Social Service Association, 1926), 80–81.

13. *Second Annual Report of the Central Council of the Charity Organization Society of the City of New York* (New York, 1884), 71–72; *Sixth Annual Report . . . for the Year 1887* (New York, 1888), 84–85; *Seventh Annual Report . . . for the Year 1888* (New York, 1889), 81–82.

14. David M. Schneider and Albert Deutsch, *The History of Public Welfare in New York State, 1867–1940* (Chicago: University of Chicago Press, 1941), 180–82; Mrs. William Einstein, "Pensions for Widowed Mothers as a Means of Securing for Dependent Children the Benefits of Home Training and Influence," in *Eleventh New York State Conference of Charities and Correction. Proceedings* (Rochester, N.Y., 15–17 November 1910), 230, 241.

15. Schneider and Deutsch, *The History of Public Welfare*, 182.

16. C. C. Carstens, "How to Aid Deserted Wives" (paper read at the New York State Conference of Charities and Correction, November 1904), reprinted in *Jewish Charity* 4 (February 1905): 141.

17. Charles Zunser, "Impressions of a Worker in a New Field," *Jewish Charity* 5 (December 1905–January 1906): 59–60.

18. Morris Waldman, "Family Desertion," in *Proceedings of the Seventh National Conference of Jewish Charities* (Cleveland, 1912), 51.

19. Marilyn Friedman comments that such research typically overlooked the significant causes of women's poverty, which lay in the "poverty of feminization," the result of inequities in the economic, legal, governmental, and social systems. Marilyn A. Friedman, "Women in Poverty and Welfare Equity," in *Poverty, Justice, and the Law* (New York: University Press of America, 1986), 91–104.

20. Conyngton, *How to Help*, 150–51.

21. "Desertion and Unemployment: An Exchange of Letters between Dr. Billikopf and Mr. Zunser," *Jewish Social Service Quarterly* 7 (March 1931): 12. Domestic Relations Court Judge Goldstein agreed: "There are more desertions in good times than in times of economic stress. In times of economic stress, the husband sticks closer to home. Wives are less expensive than lady friends." Jonah J. Goldstein, *The Family in Court* (New York: Clark Boardman Company, 1934), 165. By 1910, Morris Waldman had also become convinced that male "self-indulgence" was the main factor in desertion. "Family Desertion," in *Proceedings of the Sixth National Conference of Jewish Charities* (St. Louis, 1910), 61, 81.

22. Joanna C. Colcord, *Broken Homes: A Study of Family Desertion and Its Social Treatment* (New York: Russell Sage Foundation, 1919), 34, 38.

23. Michael Francis Doyle, Esq., address on family desertion, "Causes of Family Desertion," *City Club Bulletin* (Philadelphia) 6 (12 February 1913): 246.

24. Martha May, "The 'Good Managers': Married Working Class Women and Family Budget Studies, 1895–1915," *Labor History* 25, no. 3 (summer 1984): 351–72.

25. Solomon Lowenstein, "Jewish Desertions," *Jewish Charity* 4 (February 1905): 144. See also similar comments in Zunser, "Impressions," 59; John J. Gascoyne, "Judicial and Probationary Treatment of Cases of Non-Support of Family," *Proceedings of the Thirty-Ninth National Conference of Charities and Correction* (Cleveland, 1912), 464.

26. Kate Holladay Claghorn, *The Immigrant's Day in Court* (New York: Harper and Brothers, 1923; reprint, New York: Arno Press and the New York Times, 1969), 82; Walter H. Liebman, "Some General Aspects of Family Desertion," *Journal of Social Hygiene* 1 (April 1920): 205; Colcord, *Broken Homes*, 36; Morris Waldman, "Family Desertion," *Jewish Charity* 5 (December 1905-January 1906): 53; Lilian Brandt, *Five Hundred and Seventy-Four Deserters and Their Families* (New York: Charity Organization Society, 1905), 20.

27. Colcord, *Broken Homes*, 154; Gascoyne, "Judicial and Probationary Treatment of Cases of Non-Support of Family," 463.

28. Earle Edward Eubank, *A Study of Family Desertion* (Chicago: University of Chicago Press, 1916), 13.

29. Mary Breed, "The Difference in the Treatment of Widows and That of Deserted Wives," *Eleventh New York State Conference of Charities and Correction. Proceedings* (Rochester, N.Y., 15–17 November 1910), 79.

30. Goldstein, *The Family in Court*, 163; Max Hertzberg, "How the Jewish Charities Are Dealing with the Problem," *City Club Bulletin* (Philadelphia) 6 (12 February 1913): 248, 250; Carstens, "How to Aid Deserted Wives," 141; Liebman, "Some General Aspects of Family Desertion," 204.

31. Colcord, *Broken Homes*, 97.

32. Rebecca G. Affachiner, "The Deserted Woman," *Jewish Charity* 5 (October 1905): 24.

33. T. J. Jackson Lears, "From Salvation to Self-Realization: Advertising and the Therapeutic Roots of the Consumer Culture, 1800–1930," in Fox and Lears, eds., *The Culture of Consumption*, 3–38.

34. Brandt, *Five Hundred and Seventy-Four Deserters*, 45, 63.

35. A. S. Newman, *Proceedings of the Sixth National Conference of Jewish Charities* (St. Louis, 1910), 96.

36. William H. Baldwin, "The Most Effective Methods of Dealing with Cases of Desertion and Non-Support," *Journal of the American Institute of Criminal Law* 8 (1917–1918), 572; Nathaniel J. Walker, *Second Capital District Conference of Charities and Correction* (Albany, 1914), 1082; Gascoyne, "Judicial Probationary Treatment of Cases of Non-Support of Family," 462; Max Herzberg, in *Proceedings of the Seventh National Conference of Jewish Charities* (Cleveland, 1912), 110.

37. Colcord, *Broken Homes*, 47–48.

38. Waldman, "Family Desertion," *Jewish Charity*, 53.

39. Affachiner, "The Deserted Woman," 24.

40. Bernhard Rabbino, *Back to the Home* (New York: printed by Court Press, 1933), 29–30.

41. Eubank, *A Study of Family Desertion*, 39.

42. Waldman, "Family Desertion," *Jewish Charity*, 53.

43. Heinze, *Adapting to Abundance*, esp. 23, 30.

44. Linda Gordon, "Family Violence, Feminism, and Social Control," *Feminist Studies* 12 (fall 1986): 464–65.

45. Report of the Committee on Families and Neighborhoods, *Proceedings of the Thirty-Ninth National Conference of Charities and Correction* (Cleveland, 1912), 88–89.

46. Sherri Broder, "Informing the 'Cruelty': The Monitoring of Respectability in Philadelphia's Working-Class Neighborhoods in the Late Nineteenth Century," *Radical America* 21 (July–August 1987): 37–39, 42–43, 45. Broder suggests that working-class distinctions were subtly different from middle-class ones. For example, men who in an S.P.C.C. agent's middle-class eyes were failing to provide properly would be defended by working-class neighbors who felt it was enough that he was "struggling manfully to keep his family together." As Broder suggests, when working-class people insisted on "a father's dedication to supporting his family, their defense bespoke a first-hand knowledge of the difficult circumstances of raising children in the city's poorer wards," a kind of knowledge that did not inform middle-class outsiders' judgments. Broder, "Informing the 'Cruelty,'" 42, 43.

47. Alice Kessler-Harris, "Gender and the Construction of Culture" (paper presented at the Conference on Ideology and Resistance, Haifa, Israel, 8 January 1990); and idem, "Gendered Interventions: Exploring the Historical Roots of U.S. Social Policy," *Japanese Journal of American Studies* 5 (1993–94): 3–22.

48. Ronald Edsforth describes the attitude of workers who entered factories af-

ter the "second industrial revolution": "For them, success could be measured in terms of improved income and the things they could buy with it, and extended leisure time and the pleasure they could derive from it. As they saw it, industrial work was principally a means to this kind of individual fulfillment, not part of a craft tradition that conveyed its own standards of value." Ronald Edsforth, *Class Conflict and Cultural Consensus: The Making of a Mass Consumer Society in Flint, Michigan* (New Brunswick, N.J.: Rutgers University Press, 1987), 34, 89, 95, 114.

49. Martha May, "Bread Before Roses: American Workingmen, Labor Unions, and the Family Wage," in *Women, Work, and Protest: A Century of U.S. Women's Labor History,* ed. Ruth Milkman (Boston: Routledge and Kegan Paul, 1985), 1–21.

50. Rabbino, *Back to the Home,* frontispiece. This aphorism appears with minor variations in most of the literature on desertion.

51. As Linda Gordon notes, there is an ironic contradiction in "the rhetoric that welfare represents deplorable 'dependence,' while women's subordination to husbands is not registered as unseemly." Linda Gordon, "The New Feminist Scholarship on the Welfare State," in *Women, the State, and Welfare,* ed. Linda Gordon (Madison: University of Wisconsin Press, 1990), 14.

52. Richard L. McCormick, *The Party Period and Public Policy: American Politics from the Age of Jackson to the Progressive Era* (New York: Oxford University Press, 1986); Theda Skocpol, *Protecting Soldiers and Mothers: The Politics of Social Provision in the United States, 1870s-1920s* (Cambridge: Harvard University Press, 1992).

53. Generally, they estimated that in New York City about 10 percent of the dependent population were deserted families and that between 20 and 25 percent of children in New York City institutions had been abandoned. A survey of available statistics from the 1890s through the 1910s reveals little long-term change in these proportions. Eubank, *A Study of Family Desertion,* 22–26; Brandt, *Five Hundred and Seventy-Four Deserters,* 10; Leonard Wallstein, "Deserted and Abandoned Children: A Test of the Value of Enforcing the City's Rights against Child Deserters" (report submitted to Mayor John Purroy Mitchel, New York, 1916); Liebman, "Some General Aspects of Family Desertion," 201.

54. Benjamin Tuska, *Proceedings of the Sixth National Conference of Jewish Charities* (St. Louis, 1910), 87.

55. The first court to segregate desertion cases by setting aside special hours for them was in Buffalo, New York, in 1908. New York City was the first to create an entirely separate and distinct domestic relations court. Theodore Fadlo Boushy, "The Historical Development of the Domestic Relations Court" (Ph.D. diss., University of Oklahoma, 1950).

56. *Laws of New York* (1910), chap. 659, sec. 74.

57. These types of disputes are discussed in Erika Rappaport, "A Husband and His Wife's Dresses: Consumer Credit and the Debtor Family in England, 1864–1914," this volume.

58. *People ex rel. Case v. Case* (1930), 138 Misc. 131.

59. *People v. McAdam* (1937), 164 Misc. 800.

60. *People v. De Wolf* (1909), 133 App. Div. 879.

61. *Goetting v. Normoyle* (1908), 191 NY 369. See also *People v. Smith* (1910), 139 App. Div. 361 ("The purpose of this section is not to furnish appropriate provision for family support, but simply to prevent the family from becoming a public burden . . .").

62. *People ex rel. Case v. Case* and *People v. McAdam; People ex rel. Heinle v. Heinle* (1921), 115 Misc. 469 ("The purpose of the proceedings is not to adjust domestic relations but to prevent abandoned wives and children from becoming public charges"); *Germer v. Germer* (1938), 167 Misc. 882. In the two exceptional cases, where the statute was interpreted literally, the destitution of the woman was relevant to the decisions, both of which were written by the same judge. Thus, even as Judge Tompkins exclaimed that not to read the statute literally would be "to rate the Municipal pocketbook . . . above the well-being of its wives and children!" he repeatedly stressed the "destitution" of the wife and her children: "She is not possessed of any property; is living with a sister who is asking board, which she has no means of paying. . . ." *People v. Goodwin* (1938), 167 Misc. 627, and Tompkins' opinion in *People v. Gross* (1936), 161 Misc. 514.

63. Deserted women who were not already receiving relief, or who were deemed not to be in immediate danger of becoming public charges because they had possessions that charitable agencies believed could be sold or used for support, were excluded from the domestic relations courts but could bring an action for separation and support in the civil courts. For a woman on the borderline of poverty, this exclusion must have presented difficulties, for as one New York judge observed, "This entails considerable expense and delay and women amply justified, are sometimes restrained . . . from proceeding in civil courts even to obtain a separation or partial divorce." Nathaniel J. Palzer, *Handbook of Information on Non-Support, Desertion, and Illegitimacy* (New York: Charity Organization Society, 1916), 3; Hon. Cornelius F. Collins, "The Proposed Constitutional Amendment—Effect upon the Children's Court and Court of Domestic Relation," *The Legal Aid Review* 17 (January 1919): 13.

64. Jacobus ten Broek, "California's Dual System of Family Law: Its Origin, Development, and Present Status," *Stanford Law Review* 16 (1964): 257–317, 900–981; 17 (1965): 614–82. Further discussions of this concept can be found in Thomas P. Lewis and Robert J. Levy, "Family Law and Welfare Policies: The Case for 'Dual Systems,'" and Walter O. Weyrauch, "Dual Systems of Family Law: A Comment," in *The Law of the Poor*, ed. Jacobus ten Broek (Scranton, Pennsylvania: Chandler Publishing Co., 1966), 424–467; and Deborah Harris "Child Support for Welfare Families: Family Policy Trapped in Its Own Rhetoric" (unpublished paper presented at the PARSS seminar on work and welfare, University of Pennsylvania, 21 November 1988). My thanks to Michael Katz for providing me with a copy of Harris's paper.

65. Palzer, *Handbook of Information*, 4.

66. The legal machinery created to combat desertion became an integral part of twentieth-century welfare policy from the Progressive Era up to our own time. In the 1940s, 1960s, and 1970s, legislators on the state and national levels repeated variations of the anti-desertion strategies adopted in the Progressive Era. In the amendments to the Social Security Act of 1974 and 1975, lawmakers spurred by resurgent suspicion of welfare cheats set up a parent-locator service, resurrecting through a federal-state partnership the private services offered by the National Desertion Bureau earlier in the century. Sanford N. Katz, "A Historical Perspective on Child-Support Laws in the United States," in *The Parental Child-Support Obligation: Research, Practice, and Social Policy*, ed. Judith Cassetty (Lexington, Mass.: D.C. Heath and Co., 1983): 17–28; Harris, "Child Support for Welfare Families."

67. Mark H. Leff, "Consensus for Reform: The Mothers'-Pension Movement in the Progressive Era," *The Social Service Review* 47 (September 1973): 397–417.

68. Skocpol, *Protecting Soldiers and Mothers,* chap. 8; Roy Lubove, *The Struggle for Social Security, 1900–1935* (Cambridge: Harvard University Press, 1968), 91–112.

69. Comparisons with other states would surely strengthen the argument that anti-desertion reforms affected the scope of mothers' pension programs. Pennsylvania may be a place to start. In Pennsylvania, pension legislation including deserted women was passed in 1913; domestic relations courts were established in 1914; and the next year, in 1915, deserted women were struck from the roster of eligible recipients. Deserted women received similar treatment in Illinois, where domestic relations courts were created almost simultaneously with the passage of mothers' pension legislation. Deserted women were quickly dropped from the list of eligible pension recipients and were diverted instead to the court of domestic relations. This process is described in Joanne Goodwin, "An American Experiment in Paid Motherhood: The Implementation of Mothers' Pensions in Early-Twentieth-Century Chicago," *Gender and History* 4 (autumn 1992): 323–42.

70. Robert W. Hebberd, (address to the National Conference on the Education of Backward, Truant, Delinquent, and Dependent Children, Buffalo, N.Y., 28 August 1913), reprinted in *Annual Report of the State Board of Charities for the Year 1913,* 1914, N.Y.S. Doc. 57, 534–35, 541. Hebberd was appointed the director of investigations for the New York State Commission on Relief for Widowed Mothers, which drafted the pension legislation, and his 1913 speech was reprinted as an appendix to the 1915 Hill-McCue Bill. Commenting on Hebberd's position, charity worker Mary Breed worried about the example of Illinois, where deserted women had been removed from the pension rolls: "Even so the tide of desertion has not been stemmed and is said to be greater than before the passage of the original bill, which placed deserted women on the same footing as widows." Mary I. Breed, "Report of the Committee on Relief of the Poor in their Homes," *Proceedings of the Second Capital District Conference of Charities and Correction* (Albany, 6 March 1914), 1071.

71. *Report of the New York State Commission on Relief for Widowed Mothers* (Albany: J. B. Lyon Company, 1914), 21.

72. For example, one woman who was sent to the National Desertion Bureau by the New York City Board of Child Welfare in 1931 ended up being denied a pension because the bureau found someone in Cleveland who had spotted her husband in a store a couple of times in 1932, after which he disappeared. The woman was sent to the domestic relations court to have a warrant issued, should her husband return to New York, and to the district attorney to initiate proceedings for extradition under the Child Abandonment Law. This brought no results, and her children were placed in institutions. The woman was finally granted a pension in 1938, on the eve of her youngest child's sixteenth birthday. (Pensions were granted only to women who had children under sixteen years of age.) N.D.B. case file A8112, Archives of the YIVO Institute for Jewish Social Research, New York.

73. Mothers' pensions were intended to remove the stigma of poor relief from aid to women with dependent children, especially in New York, where separate boards, rather than the courts, were given oversight of the program. See "Senator Hill's Letter to Governor Whitman," 1 April 1915, in *The Hill-McCue Bill for the Relief of the Children of Widowed Mothers* (Albany: State Board of Charities, 1915), 12. But when pensions were extended to deserted women, the courts became an adjunct of the

mothers' pension program, supplementing the county boards; and thus mothers' pensions were brought into closer relation with the poor-law system of family liability.

74. Even in mothers' pensions, state funding did not stand in for male bread-winning, nor did it sustain full-time motherhood; as implemented, mothers' pensions were inadequate to support families. Joanne Goodwin, "An American Experiment in Paid Motherhood," 323–42.

75. Claiming to defend the public purse, they were in fact defining its social meaning as what sociologist Viviana Zelizer calls "special money." The institutionalization of rules governing the use of funds, rules that carry cultural meanings and particular conceptions of the social structure, is a crucial factor in the creation of "special money." Viviana A. Zelizer, "The Social Meaning of Money: 'Special Monies,'" *American Journal of Sociology* 95 (September 1989): 342–77.

76. Eubank, *A Study of Family Desertion*, 34.

SEVEN

Living on the Margin

Working-Class Marriages and Family Survival Strategies in the United States, 1919–1941

Susan Porter Benson

The standard of comfort can never be divorced from the question of wages.
MARY KINGSBURY SIMKHOVITCH, 1917

A study of working-class consumption quickly verifies what Mary Kinsgbury Simkhovitch concluded from her experience as a settlement-house worker: consumption—spending—cannot be neatly detached either from earning or from nonmarket behavior, such as household manufacture or scavenging, that substitutes for spending.[1] Consumption clearly cannot take place unless someone earns, inherits, borrows, or even steals the money to spend, and household production of at least some goods and services continues even in the most affluent families. These connections are especially direct in families living close to the edge economically, families whose income is insufficient or irregular or both. Between 1919 and 1941, the period on which I focus, most American working-class families remained on the margins of the emerging world of consumption because their incomes were neither large enough nor steady enough to allow the wide range of discretionary spending usually associated with mass consumption. They had only very limited access to the therapeutic aspects of consumption. All working-class families experienced the marketplace in ways shaped by their subordinate class status, but race and gender imposed further economic burdens on people of color and women. Moreover, the exigencies of survival produced a certain flexibility in the gendered division of labor—whereby men produced or earned and women consumed or spent—usually associated with the culture of consumption. For working-class people, such a division was often neither possible nor desirable. Because conventional notions about the gendering of consumption rest on a division of labor within marriage, one of the first steps in my investigation was to examine working-class marriages and gender roles within those marriages in the context of the families' economic fortunes.

In the working class I include people who worked at nonsupervisory jobs, either manual or nonmanual. Most earned hourly or piecework wages or salaries, but some independent entrepreneurs in retailing, services, and construction are included, as are some factory foremen. Although this is a relatively static, structural definition, I recognize that class was (and remains) a matter not only of absolute levels of material resources but also of culture, desire, and circumstance. One family's sufficiency was another's penury. However, in the sources I used to explore working-class marriage and the family economy, families from widely differing geographical areas and racial/ethnic backgrounds spoke a shared language of deprivation. It was as if they felt the economic squeeze so generally throughout their lives that they rarely paused to note specific woes, such as their inability to buy favorite ethnic foods.

My sources impose certain constraints on my study, constraints that are inseparable from their vivid insights into family processes. For the 1920s, I rely most heavily on the raw data from investigations of wage-earning women and their families by the Women's Bureau of the United States Department of Labor. Most useful are the home visit forms on which bureau agents recorded basic information and offered their own free-wheeling observations about women wage earners and their families. For the late 1920s and the 1930s, when the Women's Bureau documents become less revealing, my most fruitful sources are case studies—compiled by psychologists, sociologists, social workers, and settlement-house workers—of working-class families experiencing unemployment. Households studied by the Women's Bureau included at least one female wage earner—daughter, wife, or head of household—and ranged from securely prosperous to miserably poor. The family case studies typically targeted two-parent families with at least one resident child. The disadvantage of their focus on families in economic distress is offset by the advantage of their attention to the changes families experienced as they moved through cycles of relative prosperity and penury. Almost all of these accounts of working people's families are filtered through the middle-class perspective of the bureau agents and social scientists, but for the most part these observers were sensitive to the material constraints facing these families and met the families as advocates and well-wishers. They were not, of course, nonjudgmental; they condemned dishonesty, cruelty, callousness, irresponsibility, drunkenness, slovenly habits, and foolishness even as they understood the conditions that encouraged this behavior.

The sources agree in two vital respects. First, they offer qualitative evidence that gives life to the statistics on the dismal economic position of the working class. In the comparatively prosperous 1920s, as well as in the depression 1930s, most working-class families had to wrestle with the consequences of insufficient or irregular income; the difference between the 1920s and the 1930s was one of degree rather than one of kind. Far from seeing a definitive break between the two periods, I find a striking continuity of conditions and of family strategies to cope with them.

Under close scrutiny, the vaunted prosperity of the 1920s turns out to have been quite limited and unevenly distributed. Managers' longstanding concern with efficiency and productivity intensified during the 1920s and 1930s, perpetuating insecurity and instability of employment. Although some groups of workers experienced gains in real wages during the 1920s, historian Frank Stricker calculates that "35 to 40 percent of the non-farm families in 1929 were poor," using as a standard for poverty an income level roughly equivalent in real terms to the federal government's current absurdly low poverty line. In concrete terms, families at or below this income level could not afford even the minimally adequate diet devised by social workers for charity recipients. More frivolous consumption was yet farther out of reach. Even though a used car could be purchased on an installment plan for sixty dollars, fewer than one in three working-class families owned an automobile. By 1930, barely half of the nation's households had flush toilets, and only about two-thirds had electric lighting. A large proportion of the working class therefore missed out on these conveniences. And, again in 1930, very few working-class households would have been among the one out of four of the nation's homes that owned a washing machine or the one in a dozen with a mechanical refrigerator.[2] This is not to argue that working-class families were completely shut out of the mass consumption of the 1920s but to point out that they tasted its joys in a very limited way and at considerable sacrifice of other needs.

Second, the evidence suggests that gender figured in both breadwinning and consumption in ways that defied as well as confirmed conventional gender expectations. The male breadwinning ethic was far from universal among these families; men's attitudes toward the responsibility for breadwinning ranged from total acceptance to outright rejection. Many women felt an obligation to earn some or all of the family support, even when husbands and/or fathers were present and earning. Some women turned to paid work expressly to avoid household work, and some men saw housework as part of their responsibility. Male wage earners tended to consume in an individualistic, self-indulgent way, and female wage earners tended to engage in more family-oriented consumption. Because the sources made no effort to be representative or inclusive and because the family studies tended to solicit demographically homogeneous groups, it is impossible to estimate the relative prevalence of these patterns. Still, virtually every Women's Bureau study and every collection of family case studies provide examples of gender-boundary crossing, in every region of the country, in families linked to every industry studied, and in families of all origins—African, European, and (although the cases are few) Latin-American. One of the most intriguing things about this material is the degree to which the Women's Bureau agents and the social-science writers do not "take in" these gender transgressions; they invariably ignore this evidence or write it out of their analyses. Ironically, this gives me greater confidence in the evidence they did record. As historian Carlo Ginzburg said of the sixteenth-century inquisitors' accounts on which he relied, these documents are much more valuable when those who created them "did not understand" what their informants were telling them.[3]

The marriages discussed in these documents differ distinctly from the companionate marriage that was so widely touted during the 1920s and 1930s.[4] The term companionate marriage implies a strong and primarily romantic bond between marriage partners, but in these working-class relationships loyalty, obligation, and family economic survival compete with and often obscure entirely romance or sexual attraction. In this respect, their closest analog is European peasant marriages; for example, Natalie Zemon Davis's discussion of the competing forces of duty and desire in the sixteenth-century family of Martin Guerre and Bertrande de Rols has more resonance with these families than the interwar writings about modern marriage.[5] Companionate marriage, in addition, rested on rigidly segregated sex roles that cast husbands as breadwinners/producers and wives as consumers, whereas these working-class partnership marriages involved definite, if subtle and partial, breaching of the boundaries between gender roles. These breaches came about not, I emphasize, because of a belief in some abstract notion of gender equality but because the material conditions of life in the American working class reinforced some people's willingness to improvise and to put other goals above the maintenance of dominant-culture gender constructions. Working-class people made adjustments in one area of their lives in order to relieve pressures and lighten burdens originating in other areas of their lives. They sought to make the best of lives lived amidst great difficulty, lives conditioned by circumstances not of their own choosing. However, these marriages should not be idealized, just as slave marriages should not be idealized. In the latter case, any gender equity between spouses came at the price of being owned as chattel property; in the case I examine, gender equity was inseparable from want and scarcity. And in both cases, adherence to dominant-culture notions of gender did not take top priority.

THE TRAVAILS OF THE MALE BREADWINNER

Because men, by and large, could earn higher wages than women, access to a man's wage was crucial to the family economy. The ideal husband earned steady wages and contributed his entire pay envelope to the family fund.[6] Yet even for those men inclined by culture and temperament to be model breadwinners, the labor market provided as many barriers as it did opportunities. Throughout the 1920s and 1930s, families complained of longer and more frequent spells of worklessness. Skilled men were thrown out of steady work by technology. Printers and skilled carpenters were among the hard hit, and one woman said of her father, "A cooper hasn't a job these days."[7] Periodic and seasonal unemployment among semiskilled and unskilled men continued or increased. "Slack work"—short hours—was a repeated complaint, and workers who had long been accustomed to seasonal, usually winter, unemployment found those seasons of unemployment stretching from one month to three months and even to five. One month of unemployment, or even three months, could be planned and saved for, but seven months of a laborer's wages could not stretch to cover a year.[8] In early 1933, a Washington, D.C., carpenter voiced his mounting frustrations at seeing his situation go from bad to worse: "One lone salary is not enough to buy a home and support a family on. . . . It was hard when I had steady work and now I just can't do it."[9]

Like everyone, men had multiple identities, some of which could conflict with the breadwinner role. Union men, for example, asserted their manly independence through union activity. If successful, strikes and other union activities assured more regular work and higher wages and, hence, made men better breadwinners; if unsuccessful, however, strikes could seriously hamper a man's breadwinning potential. For example, a Philadelphia taxi driver, after six years of steady employment at substantial wages, joined his fellow taxi drivers in a strike for higher pay. The strike was broken and he was blacklisted for eighteen months.[10] A Memphis man was out of work for almost a year after the 1922 railroad shopmen's strike.[11] An African-American carpenter found himself out of a job when he joined the union: employers refused to hire him at white men's union wages.[12] Union militancy was a gamble under the best of circumstances, but during the 1920s, at least, it does not seem to have been a good bet for the family.[13]

Other men rebelled against the breadwinning ethic itself instead of against their employers. The transition from bachelorhood to serious wage earning seems to have been difficult. A Women's Bureau agent wrote of one Providence woman that "her husband never worked and after 3 months of marriage she left him"; the woman counted herself fortunate that he did not demand money from her.[14] The bachelor subculture of which George Chauncy has written so eloquently, which countered the male breadwinner role with its "alternative definition of manliness that was predicated on a rejection of family obligations," may have continued to exert a social and erotic pull on urban men even after marriage. Reluctance about breadwinning would have been an eloquent way to perpetuate the bachelor subculture's scorn for "the domesticating and moralizing influence of women."[15] Perhaps the best general explanation for men's rejection of their responsibilities came from a southern textile worker to whom the writers of *Like a Family* gave the pseudonym Ruth Elliot. Musing on her husband's irresponsibility and alcoholic binges, she speculated on the roots of his behavior: "When we were married we wasn't anything but kids. We had three babies, one right after the other, and somebody had to settle down. And it had to be me. Jesse never did settle down. It was too much of a load on him. If he had stayed single and hadn't saddled himself with a wife and kids, he would have sowed his wild oats and gotten over it. Instead of that, he planted a permanent garden, and it was disastrous. I know that now. But that didn't help me out a bit then."[16]

Fair-weather breadwinners balked at the rigors of the labor market and industrial work discipline. One man, a Greek-born shoe-factory worker, took being out of work quite casually; according to the settlement-house worker, "[He believes] that he is doing his best and is in no way responsible, and that if he isn't able to support his family, some one else will have to do it. . . . He searches for jobs, but he is not adaptable."[17] A fired streetcarman refused to work "unless he [could] find an easy job and so far hasn't been able to find one."[18] Other men resisted the punishing demands of available jobs: a St. Joseph, Missouri, man who could only secure jobs that required "heavy carrying" finally decided that he would "rather stay home than break his back."[19] Wives often saw such behavior as shiftlessness, as did the ex-wife of an African-American Chicagoan who claimed that her husband "would not work walking up and down the streets all day smoking cigarettes," so she "put him out."[20] But in a class by himself was the St. Paul, Minnesota, man who steadfastly refused the Armour Company's offer of a steady, year-round job at twenty-seven dollars a week: he would work only during the summer, so that he could play on the company baseball team.[21] These examples suggest that behavior that might seem to be evidence of assertive manliness on the job—union activity or rebellion against industrial time discipline and bad working conditions—could mean want and uncertainty for the family.

Husbands frequently withheld a portion of their wages from the family fund.[22] Most probably kept just enough for their daily expenses. A Boston plumber kept back between three and five dollars of his handsome weekly pay of forty-two dollars for "fares, lunches, and smokes."[23] A Kansas City tile maker withheld more but could still be counted upon to pay for the rent and groceries.[24] Expenditures on alcohol and gambling, forms of consumption that could enhance a man's position with his peers, cut his contributions to the family fund. One Chicago meatpacker so indulged himself that his only financial contribution to the family was "some food."[25] Some could not be counted on for even that much. One brazen man did not contribute a cent to the family fund for over two years; his wife finally threw him out.[26] Husbands could also control their wages by not telling their wives how much they earned. An African-American barber's wife from Oklahoma remarked, "[He] says he don't make nothin'. I don't know if he just tells me that or maybe he don't."[27] Two meatpackers, one Polish-born and one

African-American, told Women's Bureau agents that they did not know their husband's wages.[28] Whatever the complicated dynamics that determined whether a husband withheld his wages or contributed them to the family fund, his decision was not necessarily related to his wife's performance as a householder. A settlement worker portrayed a neighborhood woman in the following way: "She was plump and engaging, and often drunk. . . . She was a great scandal and aggravation to the neighbors because her husband loved her and gave her his money and was faithful to her and never beat her. As one of her next door neighbors said, 'There's Margaret next door being beaten and bullied and living right, and that Aggie Bennett with a man setting such store by her and her perfectly worthless.'"[29] A wife could not count on receiving the bulk of her husband's earnings as her "wages" for being a good housekeeper; her husband might treat her as arbitrarily as the labor market treated him.

Even during the Great Depression, husbands continued to withhold some earnings from the family fund. The occasional approving note in the National Federation of Settlements' 1932 survey of unemployment about a husband who "gave every cent he earned to his wife" suggests that this behavior was far from typical.[30] The Depression also revealed in high relief the meaning of pocket money for men. Guilt and shame, of course, plagued men who could no longer support or contribute to the support of their families, but these feelings were compounded by the anguish caused by their own financial dependency. Mr. Patterson, profiled by sociologist Mirra Komarovsky, felt such pangs intensely: "It is awful to him, because now 'the tables are turned,' that is, he has to ask his daughter for a little money for tobacco, etc. He would rather walk miles than ask for carfare money. His daughter would want him to have it, but he cannot bring himself to ask for it. He had often thought that it would make it easier if he could have 25 cents a week that he could depend upon."[31]

Other men linked their pennilessness to other aspects of the loss of male status: "The whole thing was wrong. . . . It was awful to have to ask her for tobacco, or to have to tell the landlady, 'My wife will come, and I will pay you,' or to be expected to have the dinner ready when she came home."[32] Men experienced a lack of pocket money as disempowering and feminizing. It meant dependency, insecurity, uncertainty, and public embarrassment, and being at someone else's beck and call—all feelings from which their status (however precarious) as breadwinners had insulated them, but which had been the staples of their wives' lives. Class as well as gender shaped their reactions: they missed not lavish consumption but small comforts such as tobacco, carfare, newspapers, and the occasional drink. If they had been women, their pocket change might have been termed pin money. The freedom to spend in these ways was a sign of a man's modest independence as a breadwinner and as a workingman.

Husbands held tenaciously to their right to control their wages and frequently deserted or threatened to do so when women tried to mobilize them to increase the family fund. One woman hesitated to insist that the family apply for relief, despite the "almost unbearable" strain that managing the family's budget put on her. Her husband had already deserted twice before and threatened to do so again if she pushed the relief issue.[33] Another husband was described as "a rather selfish person." The settlement-house worker went on to say, "The fact that his family is not able to have the things necessary for good health and happiness, does not seem to distress him particularly. In fact, he threatened to leave them all many times."[34] A Mrs. Adams, whose husband missed his pocket change, saw the Depression as her ally; according to the case worker, "If she had insisted on taking his wages away from him when he was earning, she is sure he would just have deserted the family and she would have been left with the two children."[35] If the loss of all support was the price of pressuring a husband either to be a better provider or to collaborate in her attempts to provide, a wife might well calculate that it was better to scrape by on what she had.

Of course, not all men were voluntarily deficient as breadwinners. Many tried diligently to support their families, only to be thwarted by the conditions of the labor market. An East St. Louis sausage maker asked a Women's Bureau agent, "Don't you think Missus if I could [make] a living for my family my wife [would not] go to work?"[36] Some felt that they could adequately support their families without their wives' earning wages. Often, such men were young and relatively newly married—naive, perhaps, about the demands of raising a family and confident in their youth and strength.[37] Prefiguring a popular argument of the post–World War II period, one husband argued that his wife's meager earnings made little difference to the family budget and that her job was undermining her health and her son's.[38] But the most bizarre example of a man's dedication to breadwinning was that of a bigamist, convicted and in prison, who faithfully turned over the nine dollars a month he earned as a prison barber to his first wife on her regular visits. His wife clearly considered his bigamy a minor sin in light of his other husbandly virtues; not only did he turn over his wages regularly but he was a good earner, making as much as forty dollars a week when not in prison. Moreover, she said that he was "very kind and good hearted—never spoke a cross word to me in his life," and she excused his bigamy because "whiskey got him."[39] Their marriage certificate, elaborately framed, held the place of honor on the mantel of her two-room home.

The rejection of the breadwinner role was, moreover, not invariably an act of self-indulgence or a privileging of another aspect of male identity. The African-American men mentioned above found themselves uniquely disadvantaged in the labor force, and one can easily imagine the succession of disappointments that led that Chicago man to pace the streets, cigarettes his only consolation. Although the sharp edges of the labor market's injustices and irrationalities cut most deeply into African-Americans' chances to establish a male-breadwinner family, European-Americans too had ample reason to become discouraged and ultimately alienated from a role they were blocked from fulfilling. The husbands who sought "easy" work and refused to break their backs might have had a lazy streak, but they might also have been mindful of the grim reality of industrial accidents and injuries. To refuse backbreaking work could conserve one's potential as an earner; to take such work might be to consign oneself to the scrap heap of industrial casualties. The evidence from working-class families, black and white, in the 1920s and 1930s, suggests that the male rejection of the breadwinner's role might not have originated, as Barbara Ehrenreich suggests, with the *Playboy* mentality of the 1950s. The crisis for the middle-class men on whom Ehrenreich focuses may have been a product of post–World War II conditions, but for working-class men the crisis was rooted in longstanding conditions of wage work. This crisis attracted special attention from middle-class observers during the interwar period.[40] Middle-class men's and working-class men's resistance to breadwinning, of course, grows out of the very different contexts of their lives. When working-class men distanced themselves from or rejected the breadwinning ethic, they did so primarily because of the material circumstances of their working lives, and only secondarily because they sought personal and consumer fulfillment outside a family context. Middle-class men, by contrast, walked away from the breadwinner role more often than they were pushed away. In both cases, of course, the result was an increasingly difficult and insecure life for the women and children left to fend wholly or partially for themselves.

THE GOOD MANAGER

The female counterpart to the male breadwinner was the good manager, a miracle worker of consumption. The world of household production having yielded much to the marketplace, women were left to make the most of very little, to create sufficiency out of inadequate materials. Mary Simkhovitch described the good manager: "As spender it is she who gives the family its tone or character. Upon her interest, skill and order the family economy depends. Around her the whole machinery of the family revolves. . . . Her economic importance is far greater than that of her wealthier sisters, for, as income increases, the proportion of it controlled by the wife diminishes."[41] Until her eldest child could enter the labor force, a mother had to rely on "her husband's wages and character, and her own strength and ability as a spender."[42] When bestowed by a social worker or reformer, the accolade "good manager" was the highest praise. A woman could be a good manager even if not supported by a male breadwinner, but these single women often lived with other adult women who helped with the support and labor of the household. One woman, who earned the rare label of "very good manager," was a mothers' pension recipient living with a second pensioner who took care of both women's children while the first worked.[43]

The good manager's skills in stretching resources seemed almost magical to middle-class observers. A New Orleans settlement worker profiled a mother of seven, wife of a worker at a bag factory: "In some hands $18 might not be productive of much comfort but in Hilda's it worked wonders. Their home was clean, their furniture was good and they had been able to achieve something near their ideal of right living. Besides this, incredible though it may seem, they had several hundred dollars in the bank and they prided themselves on being respectable, substantial people."[44] Such energetic good management was not only crucial to material welfare, but also a powerful contributor to class status, opening possibilities that might otherwise have been beyond the reach of their economic resources. Such domestic miracles were a source of pride to the women who accomplished them—a Kansas City meatpacker was described by the Women's Bureau agent as "a very close manager . . . [who] took pleasure in explaining how she managed"[45]—as well as to the husbands who benefited from them; a Philadelphia laborer boasted that his wife was "a good manager and [could] squeeze every cent out of a nickel."[46]

Even the most skilled manager, however, was limited by the material base from which she had to work. As a Philadelphia woman told a settlement worker, "I can always manage when the money is regular."[47] A good manager's mettle was put to the test when unemployment or slack work struck the family. The most successful could maximize the family's well-being in lean times, and her skills could sustain her own sense of purpose and self-esteem as well as the family's. When Hilda's husband's work at a New Orleans bag factory became irregular and then nearly dried up, the family spent its savings, dropped its insurance policies, turned off the gas and electricity, and sank into debt. As if inspired by adversity, Hilda rose to the challenge and demonstrated that good managing involved psychological as well as fiscal skills: "Hilda has shown much courage and cooperation. She sympathizes with her husband, encourages him to look for work, and does not blame him when he is unable to find it. She economizes to an almost unbelievable degree and at the same time she keeps the house neat and attractive."[48] Ironically, one woman found that the Depression provided her first opportunity to show what she could do as a manager:

> Mrs. Adams doesn't know what to say about the effect of the depression because in the last five years she has been more secure than in any other period of her life. When the family applied for relief she insisted on getting the relief check herself. She also controlled the money that was coming in from the boarders and from the children. Thus, for the first time in her life she knew

exactly how much she had instead of just getting what was left after Mr. Adams' saloon bill was paid. She doesn't feel the humiliation of being on relief and is quite well satisfied with the present status.[49]

The role of good manager, like the late-twentieth-century role of superwoman, took its toll; feelings of responsibility and tendencies toward self-blame and self-exploitation increased as financial resources shrank. Of Hilda, the settlement worker observed: "But in spite of her determination the strain is telling on her. She is losing control of her emotions and says she feels so bewildered that she can't think logically."[50] Being a good manager, far from conferring real power and autonomy, looked a lot like a stressful paid job. Women had little authority over the economic context that shaped their families but had enormous responsibilities for securing their welfare. Women who could not rise to the demands of good management were in an even more difficult position. A Boston wood finisher's wife never got the knack of it. A settlement worker described her as "spunky"; she did "her best to make both ends meet. But years of experience have not taught her how to plan her income so as to get by, and she feels that the burden falls unduly on her and she is censorious."[51] The good manager role was a socially constructed one; good managing was no more a "natural" female ability than steady breadwinning was a "natural" male inclination. But that fact did not lighten the weight of social expectations on those who performed badly the work society assigned to their gender.

The trope of the good manager to some degree obscures the process of economic decision making in the family and tends to assume that good managers both made the decisions and spent the money. An Omaha family profiled in the case files stands at one end of a spectrum ranging from full discussion and mutual agreement about the allocation of the family's money to arbitrary control by one of the spouses. These childless meatpackers in their late twenties earned about the same amount of money; the husband participated in all housework except sewing. The Women's Bureau agent wrote that the wife "wanted a new coat and a rug this fall but they talked it over and decided all extra money must go into the house payments."[52] Similarly, a St. Joseph wife told a Women's Bureau agent, "We was just sitting here planning how we were going to hit our tax bill."[53] At the other pole stands a Detroit couple brought to court in 1935 by a department store and an automobile finance company for nonpayment of bills. The husband testified that he had no idea what his wife had purchased at the department store, although he guessed that it might have been something for one of their six children. In this extreme of noncommunication, not even a court summons could provoke the husband to cross the boundary between his economic realm and that of his wife.[54]

However decisions were made, in most cases the women managed the resulting expenditures, an undertaking that amounted more to disbursing than to discretionary spending. Remarks such as "he leaves the bills and other obligations for her to handle" recur in the family case studies,[55] although the Women's Bureau data, as we shall see below, sometimes show more complicated divisions of consumption labor. But the spending role, like that of the good manager, involved more responsibility than authority. Economist Jessica Peixotto described this division of labor in the families of San Francisco typographers in 1920–21: "Occasionally the man was found to be the real purchasing agent; but here, as in most income groups, the wife had the more intimate knowledge of the way the family funds were used. It was only in the usual order of things to find that her knowledge of the man's payments for union dues, for tobacco, and for other personal expenses was vague."[56] Husbands commonly consumed for themselves, taking their needs off the top before turning their wages over to the family fund. Wives rarely had access to, influence over, or even knowledge of these expenditures. Gender dynamics, therefore, constituted an important limitation on a wife's role as the family spender. Peixotto noted further: "Most schemes of family spending are routinized. . . . according to a routine which was not so much the result of a conscious budget plan as the habit of years."[57] What seemed to be a rut was in fact a response to scarcity and want, arising out of the fact that most working-class families had very little discretionary income. The typical woman householder devoted almost all the money that came into her hands to fixed expenses such as rent, basic needs such as food, and emergencies such as medical bills. Her creativity was more likely to be exercised in deciding which bills had to be paid immediately and which could be put off than in embellishing her family's life with consumer goods. The range for choice and initiative here was narrow; class dynamics as well as gender dynamics hedged in working-class women as they spent their family's money.

Although the pattern of family spending was routinized, it varied from family to family. Some husbands shared the discomfort and shame of not being able to make ends meet; Hilda's husband, for example, met "his bill collectors himself, not leaving them to Hilda."[58] Other husbands left such humiliations to their wives, or even exacerbated their wives' problems. In this category was a factory foreman whose wife "handle[d] the family disbursements": "He did not spend much, but what he did spend was not budgeted and he sometimes left his wife with a problem on her hands to pay for his purchases."[59] Some husbands felt uneasy with their wives' disbursements but hesitated to interfere in their domain; such was the case of a Toledo construction laborer: "Mr. Whalen would like to pay his back bills promptly, but most of the financial responsibility rests with the wife after he turns over his pay."[60] Male improvidence evoked contempt from wives who considered themselves savvy consumers. Thus, a St. Louis candy-factory worker watched silently while her "very garrulous" husband held forth on the economic situation that caused his unemployment, but the woman followed the Women's Bureau agent out to the gate to say that her husband shot "craps and [did] not know the value of money."[61] Good managing, however vital to the family's economic survival, did not necessarily produce domestic peace.

FEMALE BREADWINNING AND CONSUMPTION

The good manager was only one of the roles available to married women in the family economy. Women whose husbands, for one reason or another, inadequately fulfilled the breadwinner role—a very high proportion of the husbands in the working class as I have defined it—devised compensating strategies. These included cutbacks, nonmarket transactions, domestic production, child labor, and private charity or public assistance. But some women developed a female breadwinner ethic that complemented and sometimes replaced the male version, and the Women's Bureau's focus on wage-earning women gives such women a large part in this story. Their motivations were often complex, and Women's Bureau agents too frequently reduced them to stock categories, oversimplifying the tangled web of strands making up the female breadwinning ethic. When an especially eloquent woman worker, an African-American in the sausage department at the Omaha Cudahy plant, encountered a sympathetic and dedicated Women's Bureau agent—Caroline Manning, who commented copiously on the schedule forms and appears to have had a special rapport with black respondents—we learn how many motivations could converge to send a woman into the labor force, and how even a strong matrix of such motivations could be undercut by ambivalence. The sausage maker worked, she argued, because she could get steadier work than her husband, because a family couldn't live on one wage, and because she felt an obligation to support her children from an earlier marriage. Her reasons overlap but still express distinct motivations. The first reflects a cool assessment of the job market: since she held the key to regular income, she could best hedge the family bets by holding on to her job. The second situates the family in the larger political economy: the cost of living was too high, and wages were too low, for a family to live on one pay envelope. The third taps into her vision of motherhood: she told Manning, "These are my children, not his." And yet, however deep and broad her commitment to breadwinning, she still clung to a hope that it was but a stage in her life cycle and envisioned a life without paid work. Following Manning outside at the end of the visit, she confided her "wish to give up steady work as soon as [her two teenage] boys could support themselves."[62]

A second example shows a different but equally complex constellation of reasons for working; civic obligation opened the way to expanded consumption, satisfying work, and family responsibility. A Newark mother of two—white, native-born, forty years of age—who was married to a man earning forty dollars a week injured her finger working on a press manufacturing paper containers. Interviewed in 1923, four years after the accident, she was back at the same machine on which she had been hurt. A Women's Bureau agent reported on her reasons for working: "Started to work because she wanted to 'help win the war.' Went on because she bought a player-piano & wanted to pay for it on the installment plan. Does not earn much, but likes the place where she works & thinks that she ought to help out her husband somewhat financially."[63] Her sense of responsibility as a deputy breadwinner is clear, but it is mixed with other very different motivations. Civic duty looms large, but one wonders if perhaps the war supplied this woman with the justification she had been looking for. The job had both intrinsic and extrinsic appeal; she could have her player piano, and perhaps some other consumer goods once that was paid off, and she could have these things while enjoying her work. The engaging and unusually full accounts of the sausage maker and the press operator are reminders that women had mixed and complicated feelings about their role as breadwinners.

The Women's Bureau agents' stock phrases often obscure as much as they reveal about women's motivations for working outside the home, and the two most frequently recorded responses are frustratingly opaque. First, the agents note that many of the women expressed a general sense of personal responsibility for contributing to the family fund, an obligation typically rendered in ungendered terms. One agent captured a forty-one-year-old Serbian-born woman's emphatic belief in her responsibility: "Always worked . . . felt that she had come to this country to work and took it for granted that as long as she could get work [she] would work."[64] Other responses in this category include "I gotta work," "I suppose I have to," "Feel I should."[65] Some comments indicate a feeling of permanence in the sense of responsibility: "It's always work, I need it and have to go"; "I've been the foundation of this family for six years"; "always has done her share."[66]

Not surprisingly, the breadwinning ethic seems to have been especially prevalent among African-American women (four of the six responses quoted above came from African-Americans) because of their above-average rates of labor-force participation. One woman told a Women's Bureau agent that it was a "natural thing for colored women to work after marriage."[67] That all the responses cited came from either African-Americans or immigrants from central Europe suggests that these important sectors of the working class assumed the importance of female breadwinning. However, these women did not necessarily like their jobs; a forty-five-year-old Croatian woman noted that "no woman works for fun,"[68] and a Rumanian woman nine years her junior dourly noted, "We don't work for our health."[69] The fact that these two comments were recorded in Omaha by different Women's Bureau agents visiting meatpackers within the same week gives the historian pause, suggesting that perhaps the agents' chats among themselves predisposed them to "hear" certain kinds of comments that they might have otherwise ignored.

The second frequently recorded explanation given by women for working outside the home was that their husbands didn't or couldn't earn enough, and this explanation was also difficult to read from the agents' comments. Such phrases as "husband's earnings insufficient," "husband does not earn enough," "necessary to supplement husband's wage," "husband no good job," and "could not get along on husband's pay" were probably infused with a wide range of affect—regret, blame, anger, despair, sympathy, resignation, intransigence, and more—but the agents rarely gave a clue to the emotional tone of the comments.[70] Certainly some wives understood their husbands' low earnings as reflections of systemic rather than individual problems. A Kansas City woman, for example, remarked that "they don't pay the men a living wage."[71] African-American women, even when they did not mention race explicitly, were especially cognizant of the difficulties men faced in securing steady work. Typical was the Muskogee, Oklahoma, laundry worker who asserted that it was "hard for men to get anything but 'little piddlin' jobs.'"[72] Other women placed the source of instability not in the labor market but in the husbands they married; many saw depending on a husband as a chancy thing indeed, a perception often borne out by experience. An African-American South Carolinian stated that she had "had good luck with her husband but he died."[73] A Memphis candy worker's first husband was killed in a workplace accident, and her second husband "was taken sick" shortly after their marriage, incurring such high medical bills that the spouses were forced to separate and live with their respective parents.[74] Such were the perversities of the economy in which these families were mired that a disaster might turn out to be a windfall. A New York family of Italian immigrants had come apart at the seams after years of seasonal unemployment for the laborer husband. When things looked as if they were beyond saving, he was hit by a truck and severely injured; the eventual financial settlement allowed him to establish himself as a successful fish peddler and to reunite the scattered family. His wife, aware of the ironies of their position, remarked, "I ain't wishing my husban' any harm, . . . but we could not have got up again if he hadn't been knocked down by that truck!"[75]

Wherever the blame was placed, these responses reflect a pervasive sense of the family economy as a shared enterprise, albeit one in which men play the primary earning role. When paid work was scarce for both men and women, it was not always possible to choose when one entered and left the labor force; dual wage-earning was a logical way to counter seasonality, slack work, and layoffs. An African-American meatpacking couple in Omaha plagued by the irregularity of the husband's work described their strategy to a Women's Bureau agent: "[They] never know when he is going to be laid off so both work as much as they can."[76] Women thus spoke of wanting to do their share or expressed what agents often referred to as a sense of "joint" responsibility for family support: a Czech-born woman asserted that "one can't keep all," and an African-American said that her meatpacker husband "couldn't do it alone."[77] Sometimes this sense of shared responsibility was linked to a stage of the life cycle. A pregnant woman who had just quit her slaughterhouse job said that she wanted "to help while able."[78] Many were conscious of employers' preference for younger workers and seized a fleeting opportunity to earn. Two Omaha meatpackers, one twenty-one years old and native-born and the other thirty-eight years old and Polish-born, saw themselves as maximizing their youthful earning power.[79] Others said they worked "to get established" at turning points in their lives, such as marriage, moving, or immigration.[80]

Married women's breadwinning responsibilities extended beyond the nuclear family. Frequently, they worked to support or contribute to the support of other relatives. African-Americans and immigrants from Europe and Mexico were especially likely to fall into this category, but so did many native-born European-Americans. A Women's Bureau study of married women dismissed from civil service jobs because Section 213 of the Economy Act prohibited federal employment of spouses showed that 80 of the 113 women who were studied in detail were supporting or contributing to the support of their own relatives outside their immediate families.[81]

While most women saw their breadwinning as a way of satisfying family obligations, a vocal minority used it as a route to independence within marriage and autonomy in the marketplace. A Richmond woman wrote in an essay for the YWCA Industrial Commission, "I had rather work and feal [sic] independant [sic] as I do now than stop and let him have mother and sister as well as me to support."[82] She spoke for those who did not see marriage and independence as mutually exclusive. Although their independence rested on waged work rather than on property ownership or the independent practice of a skill, it partook of the same desire to be beholden to no one as did the varieties of male republicanism. One road to independence was to build up savings; thus, a Kansas City Armour worker whose shipping clerk husband earned steady wages went to work because, in her words, "I could get along, but I could not save. I do not want to be dependant [sic] on others when hard luck comes so I shall continue to work while I am young."[83] Other women spoke of a desire to be self-supporting for the sake of their own independence, irrespective of their husbands' ability to provide. An East St. Louis woman married to a factory foreman asserted, "My husb[and] could support me but he doesn't have to."[84]

Independence also had powerful connections to consumption. By asserting that they wanted to earn their own money so that they could spend it independently, women were commenting upon the constraints they felt in ad-

ministering the family fund and the uneasiness of being a financial dependent in a market economy. That wage-earning women frequently remarked
that they controlled their own wages suggests that their jobs gave them a modicum of economic autonomy that they would not otherwise have had. For
these women, breadwinning was not just a way to have more money but also
a way to have "different" money—money that was entirely under their control. Of a Chattanooga bakery worker married to a steadily employed me-
chanic, a Women's bureau agent reported, "She does not work regularly, just
enough to make own spending money."[85] Another agent wrote of a Providence lamp-factory worker, "She used her own money for her self [sic]."[86]

From women's specific comments about what they did with their earnings, it is apparent that they focused on household improvements and clothing. A Women's Bureau agent reported that one woman who worked off and
on in meatpacking said that she worked "so as to have own money to buy
things for self and house."[87] Such comments recur frequently in the sources.
Women often spoke of devoting their earnings to their own clothing and
clothing for their children.[88] A few especially revealing comments suggest
that women sought autonomy in the marketplace because their husbands
were stingy or did not comprehend their desire to enhance the home. One
husband was described as a "selfish mortal" who not only denied his wife
money for "personal belongings" and "nice things for the house" but also
refused to allow her to adopt a child.[89] Of a Fort Dodge, Iowa, woman who
had worked as a dressmaker in an overall factory and as a dime-store sales-
woman the agent wrote: "[Her barber husband doesn't] realize all the needs
of the home, such as bedding etc. that must be replaced. Feels she needs
more than he gives her."[90] Consumption standards, then, could be gendered;
women led the push for more, and more elaborate, household goods and
clothing.

But consumption was not always gendered nor was it always linked to autonomy in the thinking of these women. Many expressed their desires for a
higher standard of living for the family in general, both quantitatively and
qualitatively. A St. Joseph meatpacker married to a steadily employed grain-
mill worker explained her reason for taking a job: "We want all the money
we can get."[91] Many women earned wages in order to move from a plane of
bare existence to a level where small extras and humble luxuries enhanced
their lives. Mere subsistence, many argued, was no longer enough; thus, a
childless African-American wife of a Pullman porter worked, she said, "to
raise standard of living,"[92] and a Kansas City Croatian woman remarked that
her family could "scrape along" on her husband's seventy-five dollar monthly
earnings but needed "money for extras."[93] A woman's wages could enhance
a family's status, as they did for a native-born Kansas City meatpacker married to a steadily employed millwright; she maintained: "Nowadays if you want
to live respectably you both have to work."[94] One woman connected her fam-

ily's plight with censorious attitudes toward working-class consumption and married women's wage earning, asserting a right to expanded consumption: "Shouldn't poor people have a little pleasure in li[f]e[?] [S]omething more than just food & shelter[?]"[95] These references to class—the one oblique, the other piquantly pointed—are among the very few recorded comments tying class and consumption together.

Lest we begin to imagine a direct relationship between the therapeutic ethic of consumption and women's wage earning in the interwar working class, it is useful to examine the findings of one of the few systematic studies of the reasons that married working-class women took jobs, the Women's Bureau's 1932 study of women employed in slaughtering and meatpacking.[96] The great majority of respondents stated that they worked for the family-oriented reasons already discussed—the insufficiency of their husband's earnings, the unsteadiness of his work, or the need to support relatives outside the immediate family. Fewer than one in four mentioned a specific spending goal for their earnings. About 10 percent of the total said they were in the labor force to enable the family to purchase a home, among them an Austrian woman who asserted, "If my house was paid I would work no more."[97] About 6 percent were working to pay expenses related to the education of children, including an African-American woman who was earning to "help school [her] little girl" and a Hungarian woman whose husband told a Women's Bureau agent, "Better for child. We give them education, they give us very much thanks."[98] Just over 3 percent were working to pay medical bills, among them a Croatian wife who said, "Lady I work just for doctor";[99] and just under 3 percent worked to buy furniture. These women were working primarily to deal with the unpredictable—medical emergencies—and to invest in the family's future—a home, education for the children, even furniture.[100] Their consumption goals, by and large, were modest and prudent. This is not to say that these families spent nothing on the sheer enjoyment of commercialized leisure or consumer goods but rather to note how limited an appearance such expenditures make in the worldview of working wives. They may have been playing to their middle-class questioners' sensibilities, but given the willingness of the Women's Bureau agents to note foolish or profligate behavior, the sober tone of the recorded answers to this question is noteworthy.

The sources tell little about how working couples divided financial responsibility, but scattered evidence reveals some clearly negotiated divisions of labor. Some wives shouldered the primary responsibility for family support. A forty-year-old food processor was dedicated to supporting an "old husband" who kept up the pretense of wage earning by doing occasional draying with his mules, who ate far more than they earned. She told the Women's Bureau agent, "He's been mighty good to me, helped me bring up my two nephews."[101] Some husbands supported only themselves and left everything else to their wives. A Keokuk, Iowa, shoe-factory worker took this situation stoically according to the Women's Bureau agent, "For three years she has had the entire responsibility of her son, her self, and the house."[102] More frequently, hostility developed, as in the case of a Virginia tobacco worker whose husband refused to contribute to the family's support and tried to throw her out of the house, which she owned. She told the Women's Bureau investigator she would "burn it before she [left] it to him."[103]

Most spouses seem to have divided up expenses in a more equitable and mutually satisfactory way. The arrangements made by the family of a Missouri clothing-factory worker are typical: "She has clothed family, given some educational advantages to children, paid insurance, kept up house furnishings and made it possible 'to live' while older husband took responsibility of food and rent. She has a very little saved."[104] Another Missouri family cut the pie differently: the husband bought food and fuel, while the wife (who worked in a Kansas City laundry) and two children paid off the house mortgage in four years flat.[105] The wife and daughter kept five dollars a week to pay for their carfare and clothes and to partially pay for the husband's and son's clothes. Evidence about such financial divisions of labor is tantalizingly rare; the Women's Bureau raw data describe seven situations fully, as does one case study compiled by the YWCA Industrial Commission. In six cases of the eight, the husband provided the food, and in five the rent or mortgage payment. Clothes, furniture, insurance, and education were always the wife's responsibility.[106] In the intriguing case of a childless Polish couple, the husband provided food and rent, while the wife's earnings went "for saving or good time."[107] Perhaps this case reflects best the spirit of other households in which the division was not so clearly specified and in which earnings allowed for more than a bare existence. The husband took care of subsistence, while the wife provided for long-term security and for something beyond the most basic needs. The addition of children to the family might well, however, wipe out the possibility for both saving and recreation and make it necessary to divert the woman's earnings to clothing, medical expenses, or education.

THE SECOND SHIFT

Just as breadwinning was equivocally gendered, so too was work within the home. Housework played an important role in working-class family economies by replacing market expenditures. Laundry, cooking, housecleaning, and child minding could all be done either on a fee-for-service basis or as unpaid work by a family member. When a wife took a job, a husband's participation in housework became an important way to conserve cash by avoiding resort to the market for household services, and, thus, a way to maximize the net effect of a wife's earnings.

A vocal minority of women linked breadwinning to their dislike of housework. A feeling of being at loose ends without enough work to keep busy was common; the women who preferred paid work over housework were not idlers or slatterns but women who wanted more to occupy their time and attention. A childless St. Paul woman living in furnished rooms told the Women's Bureau agent that she had "nothing to do,"[108] and women whose families were living as boarders frequently echoed her.[109] Two women disliked homemaking so much that they broke up their own homes and went to live with relatives. One, a Dayton woman, did so because her husband criticized the quality of her housekeeping. Primarily committed to her paying job, she simply gave up housekeeping entirely rather than try to please her husband.[110] The other, whose husband worked out of town, lived with a sister who boasted an array of appliances: electric washer, sweeper, and iron. Belying the axiom that labor-saving devices in the home raise the standards for housekeeping instead of decreasing the overall amount of time spent on housework, this woman maintained that she had ample free time to devote to wage earning.[111] Many women thus shifted the burden of housework to coresident relatives—most often mothers and children[112]—and others paid neighbors or commercial firms to do their laundry, child minding, sewing, or housecleaning.

Women contrasted the satisfactions and camaraderie of their jobs with the drudgery and loneliness of household work. Two South Carolina cotton-mill workers strongly preferred mill work to household work. One told the Women's Bureau agent, "[I like] to work in mill better than keep house. . . . work in mill is easier than housework, less running about and not so many things to do."[113] She resisted her husband's urging that she quit her job and take in boarders instead; she used her wages to hire a "good colored maid," clearing five dollars after paying the maid's wage, room, and board. No slacker, though, she spent her evenings making clothes for her children and squeaked by on six or seven hours of sleep. Even without hiring undervalued African-American labor, a Rhode Island box-factory worker expressed the same preference for factory work, although she probably relied upon her coresident mother to do at least some of the housework.[114]

For other women, the home was a lonely or depressing place from which wage earning offered a sociable escape. A Chicago candy packer found that there was "not much to keep her home" after her two daughters died; her only other child was an eighth-grader.[115] Another Chicagoan in the same occupation, childless and married a year, went out to work because "the days at home [were] long and tiresome when she [was] alone."[116] Jessica Peixotto's observations of San Francisco typographers' wage-earning wives ("They seem to be women who, finding themselves with relatively light home responsibilities, worked outside the home because they enjoyed it or, more probably, because their standard of living urged new classes of expenditure")[117] are consistent with the evidence in the Women's Bureau raw data, although the therapeutic aspects of work and consumption loom larger for Peixotto because she was studying a more uniformly prosperous group. The pleasure that the South Carolina mill worker and the Rhode Island box-factory worker took in their work, however, suggests that liking one's work was not a luxury reserved for those with a comfortable family income to fall back on.

A significant proportion of women relied on their husbands to take an active part in housework. The received historical wisdom about the gender division of labor in families is that the tendency is greater for women to take over men's work than for men to take over women's work. On farms, women worked in the fields, but men didn't work in the kitchens; on the Overland Trail, women drove wagons and hunted, but men cooked only in the most dire emergencies.[118] But in many working-class families during the 1920s and 1930s, men did carry part of the burden of household work, and their willingness to do so freed up cash for other purposes. The Women's Bureau study *Women in Slaughtering and Meat Packing* provides the most systematic information on husbands' participation in household work. The women interviewed were asked, among other things, whether and from whom they received assistance with household tasks such as dishwashing, cooking, laundry, cleaning, child care, and sewing. Among the 897 women visited, 390 were married women with husbands present and healthy enough to assist in household chores. Of those husbands, 61 did some housework. Given that this question was frequently left unanswered, and given that agents specified what tasks women received help with more often than who gave that help, I take this number—fully 15 percent of the total—to be the bare minimum number of men who actually pitched in. Central European husbands acquitted themselves particularly well: nearly two-thirds of all the helpful husbands were of central European origin, and one in six central European husbands helped with housework.[119] The other third of helpful husbands were married to native-born women and were divided about evenly between northern and western European origins and African origin; one in ten husbands of northern and western European descent and one in fifteen husbands of African descent did some housework. Three of the seven German-born wives interviewed had helpful husbands, the highest rate for any group.

Though working-class men participated in housework to a far greater degree than the conventional historical wisdom allows, their participation seems to have had an idiosyncratic and ad hoc character, to have been negotiated within the family rather than as community norms.[120] Some of the men were unemployed, some on short hours, some fully employed.[121] Some men did more housework when they were unemployed or working short hours,[122] but at least two did less around the house when they were unemployed than when they were working.[123] That most of the reports of men's household work indicate in a general way that men helped around the house perhaps indicates a task-oriented willingness to pitch in and do whatever needed to be done. Specific household tasks were mentioned a total of sixty-seven times, and men's efforts seem to have been spread across the spectrum of chores. Cleaning was most often mentioned (sixteen times), followed by child care and dishwashing (fourteen times each), laundry (twelve), and cooking (ten). Sewing was the exception: only one man sewed, an African-American who mended his clothes after his wife suffered a hand injury in an industrial accident.[124] Four men married to meatpackers worked nights and took care of children and did housework during the day while their wives were at work, using a shift-work strategy similar to that used by families studied by anthropologist Louise Lamphere in Rhode Island in the 1970s and 1980s.[125] A Chicago man, for example, worked nights repairing street-railway cars; his wife trimmed pork at Armour's during the day while he looked after their three school-age children and one preschooler.[126]

As difficult as it is to estimate the amount of housework done by men, it is even more difficult to gauge how these gender transgressions were viewed by the men and women in these families. Only one man—the Irish husband of a critically ill wife—expressed discomfort with his domestic duties. He threw himself into the heavy household work, including the laundry, but drew the line at hanging it outside where the neighbors could see him.[127] On several occasions, Women's Bureau agents found husbands preparing the evening meal when they visited the homes of woman workers. The agents gave no indication that these men were in any way embarrassed at their activities, and their matter-of-fact reporting of the husbands' cooking suggests that the men themselves acted nonchalant about it.[128] Arlie Hochschild, in *The Second Shift*, found a similar matter-of-fact sharing of earning, housework, and consuming during the 1980s in the California working-class family of Carmen and Frank Delacorte. The Delacortes developed a partnership marriage in fact even though they clung to traditional gender ideology.[129] Intriguingly, Hochschild found that the labor sharing in this working-class household was less conflictual than that in the more self-consciously egalitarian middle-class households she studied, and this finding leads to the sobering possibility that joint responsibility might evolve more easily when it is linked to logistic needs rather than to nontraditional gender ideologies.

Despite the many instances of gender transgressions, in most cases household work remained the woman's primary responsibility, just as wage earning tended to be the man's main responsibility. Much of the child care done by men, for example, was rather perfunctory and involved supervision of children who were in school most of the day. Men were typically described as "helping" with housework, although in some cases they took on major household responsibilities. A woman streetcar conductor told a Women's Bureau agent that her husband was "much help in [house]work 'good as a woman.'"[130] One man explained to the Women's Bureau agent that the "first one home starts the soup."[131] A woman praised her cattle driver husband because he was "good about helping with work."[132] And on the key question of how husbands came to do housework, the only two shreds of evidence contradict each other. One Polish-born wife had demanded that her husband take part in household chores, telling the Women's Bureau agent, "husband no help me, I quit [my job],"[133] but the husband of a Hungarian-born woman asserted his own sense of household duty when he said, "She helps me [by earning wages] so I help her."[134] Significantly, neither of these two families had children, and negotiating the household division of labor would doubtless have been more complex if children had been in the picture.

In two respects, men's housework had an unexpected spin. First, some men exhibited contradictory behavior. One of these helpful husbands evoked the Women's Bureau agent's sternest reproach: he was "n.g."—no good. He worked irregularly, a circumstance that, according to his wife, gave him a "lot of time to drink." But the wife also told the investigator that he helped with both the laundry and the housecleaning.[135] Two other men who were similarly condemned for their drinking and lackadaisical labor-force attitudes also acquitted themselves well in doing housework.[136] The Women's Bureau investigators focused on the drinking, but the wives clearly were cognizant of the men's contributions to the housework; one might imagine that a husband who drank but scrubbed the clothes and the floors was clearly preferable to one who only drank. Second, a man's participation in housework did not necessarily indicate support for his wife's wage-earning activities, and in fact two of the handful of husbands who objected to their wives' jobs helped with the housework, one of them "a lot."[137] Once again, these domestic arrangements appear to have been responses to the logistics of household survival and to have been not only unconnected to but often in contradiction with ideology.

MAKING DO: SATISFACTIONS AND DISSATISFACTIONS

These interwar marriages contained the seeds of the family strategies that Louise Lamphere found in a contemporary Rhode Island industrial city among both Colombian and Portuguese immigrant households. Arlie Hochschild, writing about the 1980s, also linked similar behavior to class rather than to ethnicity. The arrangements I have discussed were not the monopoly of any race or ethnic group, and in any event the selection of informants and the conditions under which the Women's Bureau questionnaires were administered were not systematic enough to support arguments about ethnic specificity. They appear instead to have been linked to class and immigration. It might be argued that families that had been disrupted by pulling up roots and migrating to another culture might then become more flexible in all their arrangements, more willing to experiment with new roles, more willing to respond creatively to the exigencies of their situation. Under such circumstances, male dominance and patriarchal roles, even though supported both by the cultures of origin and by the dominant culture in the United States, might become negotiable.

Not all families, of course, moved toward a less sharply defined division of productive and reproductive labor, and we may never know why some did and some did not. For many, respectability and male self-esteem demanded that women avoid wage work outside the home,[138] but since my sources are heavily weighted toward families with wage-earning women and families whose economic fortunes were scarred by unemployment, it is not surprising that such sentiments rarely surface. It is enough, however, to know that some families did blur gender distinctions and that patterns of shared family enterprise are not peculiar to the post–women's liberation family of the last three decades of the twentieth century but can be found in significant numbers among working-class families in the 1920s and 1930s.

Taking joint responsibility for the family economy could produce mutual respect. Few put it so explicitly as an Iowa man who asserted that "he and his wife were partners and both contribute[d] their wages to the support of [the] family,"[139] but many expressed more indirectly a sense of partnership that spoke of mutual pride. An Oklahoma woman whose husband was laid off a year after they were married proudly told a Women's Bureau investigator, "My husband said, he guessed we would have gone hungry if I hadn't [found a job in a food-processing plant]."[140] The husband in a more prosperous East St. Louis couple who both worked in meatpacking credited his wife for their well-being; the Women's Bureau agent noted that he maintained that "they have a comfortable home & have gotten ahead some because his wife was willing to help when she could."[141] Housework was not on this man's agenda, because his sixty-year-old mother lived with the family and took responsibility for the housework. In this household, the wife "helped" the mother-in-law just as men helped women in other households. Perhaps in this household the sense of shared enterprise included not just a husband and wife but also his mother.

In other families, a sense of partnership could rest on a woman's nonmarket efforts. A San Francisco streetcarman who said, "If Mrs. B. was not such a good mother, cook, seamstress, doctor, barber, and laundress, we could never make ends meet" respected and appreciated his wife's role in cash-replacement activities.[142] Appreciation took concrete form when families made investments to ease the woman householder's work or maximize her efficiency. Even though a Wisconsin Italian family could afford only the barest necessities, the laborer husband insisted on spending over seven weeks' wages on a washing machine, justifying his action to a settlement-house worker by arguing, "With four children there are a lot of clothes to wash and the work is too hard for my wife."[143] This wife was not a wage earner.

Just as a solid partnership could be built on the satisfactions of shared effort in family support, the refusal or inability of one partner to take part in
that effort could produce deep disillusionment about and even outright rejection of marriage as an economic partnership. Small wonder that an Italian immigrant to St. Louis, for example, questioned the worth of a husband
who hadn't worked for nearly a year, who refused to do any work around the
house even though she worked full time in a garment factory, and whose
major ambition—according to her—was "to look nice all the time."[144] All
consumer and a failure as a producer, he was a washout as a husband. A Dayton woman, writing in response to the YWCA Industrial Commission's request for opinions about married women's wage earning, counseled single
women who hoped to leave the labor force upon their marriage: "She may
now think that she will not work when she gets married but will marry a man
who can support a family, but few of us ever marry the man of our dreams.
And even if she were to marry a man with a fairly good salary, he may in a
very short time after they are married lose his job, or become a [sic] invalid
and unable to work."[145] Even in the most promising circumstances, a woman
might trust her husband but still cut the cards. A Women's Bureau agent
wrote of a Georgia clothing-factory worker, "Her husband is good to her,
helps with the work, etc. But she seems to feel that no husbands can be absolutely depended on, so she is buying the place in her own name."[146] Marriage was a risky undertaking, although not always because of the personal
failings of the partners. Indeed, given the stresses to which these marriages
were subject, the need to explain why any held together seems as pressing
as the need to explain why some fell apart.

These working-class marriages were deeply entangled in production and
reproduction, earning and spending. The insecurity of the economic context weighed heavily on them, producing misery and anger as well as mutual support and satisfaction. The therapeutic aspects of consumption made
no more than a cameo appearance in these family dramas. Consumption
was always tightly tethered to earning; close calculation and worry seem to
have overshadowed the pleasurable and escapist aspects of spending. The
classic husband-as-breadwinner/wife-as-consumer division of labor has limited descriptive power for these families because of the structural aspects of
their lives. Men had great difficulty earning a wage regular or ample enough
to fulfill the breadwinner role well, and women's efforts to be good managers were repeatedly thwarted by the insufficiency and irregularity of the
funds they had to work with. As individual consumers, husbands and wives
reacted in remarkably similar ways: both chafed under the burden of dependency, and both sought to have some money of their own as a testimony
of independence. The difference, of course, was that husbands rarely experienced utter financial dependency, as all non-wage-earning wives did;
most men enjoyed a modicum of independence as consumers, and relatively

few women did. Husbands expanded their consumption role only at the expense of their breadwinner role, whereas women's entry into breadwinning tended to give them more consumer autonomy. Understanding the complex dynamics of marriage and individual aspirations in the American working class is an important first step in developing an understanding of consumption that is not conditioned by the experiences of the middle class.

NOTES

I gratefully acknowledge the support of the National Endowment for the Humanities, the National Humanities Center, the University of Missouri Research Council, and the Weldon Spring Fund for the larger project of which this essay is a part. I also thank Jean Allman, Edward Benson, Victoria de Grazia, Ellen Furlough, David Roediger, Christina Simmons, and the members of the Feminist Women in History Group (especially Judith Bennett and Jacquelyn Dowd Hall) for helpful and perceptive comments on earlier versions of this essay.

1. Mary Kingsbury Simkhovitch, *The City Worker's World in America* (1917; reprint, New York, 1971), 53. My argument here parallels the arguments laid out in Gary Cross, "Time, Money, and Labor History's Encounter with Consumer Culture," *International Labor and Working-Class History* 43 (spring 1993): 2–17, and in the responses by Michael Rustin ("Trading Work and Pay," 18–23) and Victoria de Grazia ("Beyond Time and Money," 24–30) in the same volume. Like these authors, I assume that production and consumption must be studied in tandem, but unlike them, I focus on processes within the family. Because I pay special attention to gender and find multiple meanings and strategies in family consumption, my approach is closest to de Grazia's.

2. Frank Stricker, "Affluence for Whom?—Another Look at Prosperity and the Working Classes in the 1920s," *Labor History* 24, no. 1 (winter 1983): 5–33. My sketch of the general outlines of working-class poverty during the 1920s rests heavily on Stricker's excellent article; see esp. pp. 7, 25–29, 31–32.

3. Carlo Ginzburg, *Clues, Myths, and the Historical Method,* trans. John and Anne C. Tedeschi (Baltimore, 1989), 162–63.

4. Christina Simmons, "Companionate Marriage and the Lesbian Threat," *Frontiers* 4, no. 3 (fall 1979): 54–59.

5. A good survey of European peasant marriages is Barbara A. Hanawalt, *The Ties That Bound: Peasant Families in Medieval England* (New York, 1986).

6. For example, see Marion Elderton, ed., *Case Studies in Unemployment* (Philadelphia, 1931), 187, 333; Mirra Komarovsky, *The Unemployed Man and His Family—The Effect of Unemployment upon the Status of the Man in Fifty-Nine Families* (New York, 1940) 9, 26. The National Federation of Settlements asked member settlement houses to provide case studies of families experiencing unemployment during the winter of 1928–1929. Some 300 cases were submitted, of which 150 are published in Elderton, *Case Studies.* Seventy-six of the original case studies are in the Helen Hall Papers, and of these seventy-six, twenty-nine have not been published. Because the published versions differ minimally from the manuscript versions, I have referred to published cases in the more readily accessible Elderton collection.

7. National Archives, Washington, Records of the Women's Bureau, Record

Group 86, Raw Data for Published Bulletins, bulletin no. 88, *The Employment of Women in Slaughtering and Meat Packing* (1932), box 123, 21-43. I will subsequently refer to this series as NA, RG 86, PB [bulletin number], [box number]. Schedules for bulletin nos. 60 and 88 can easily be located by the schedule number; the folder name is not required. On some schedules, the number is absent or illegible, and the citations will use the informant's last name. For other bulletins, the schedules cited are in the home-visit folder unless otherwise noted. I will include a folder name only in the few cases where it is necessary to easily locate the cited schedule.

8. Elderton, *Case Studies*, p. 102.

9. National Archives, Washington, Records of the Women's Bureau, Record Group 86, Division of Research, Unpublished Studies and Materials, box 14, folder "Housing Survey 1933 District of Columbia—Schedules," no. 59. I will subsequently refer to this series as NA, RG 86, USM.

10. Elderton, *Case Studies*, 26.

11. NA, RG 86, PB no. 56, *Women in Tennessee Industries: A Study of Hours, Wages, and Working Conditions* (1927), box 31, Baldwin.

12. Elderton, *Case Studies*, 347.

13. The CIO, of course, was a far better bet, but none of my documents deal with the families of men involved in CIO organizing. For a discussion of the impact of the CIO on the family economy, see Lizabeth Cohen, *Making a New Deal* (Cambridge, 1990).

14. NA, RG 86, PB no. 21, *Women in Rhode Island Industries: A Study of Hours, Wages, and Working Conditions* (1922), box 8, Lombardi.

15. George Chauncy, *Gay New York: Gender, Urban Culture, and the Making of the Gay Male World, 1890–1940* (New York, 1994), 79.

16. Ruth Elliot, pseud., quoted in Jacquelyn Dowd Hall et al., *Like a Family: The Making of a Southern Cotton Mill World* (Chapel Hill, 1987), 165-66.

17. Elderton, *Case Studies*, 160.

18. NA, RG 86, PB no. 88, box 123, 26-12.

19. Ibid., 56-34.

20. NA, RG 86, PB no. 88, box 121, 17-92.

21. NA, RG 86, PB no. 88, box 117, folder "#88 Correspondence," Case Records from United Charities, St. Paul.

22. This pattern was especially common in England, more so than it appears to have been in the United States. See, for example, Ellen Ross, *Love and Toil: Mothers in Outcast London, 1870–1918* (New York, 1993), chap. 3; and Jan Pahl, *Money and Marriage* (New York, 1989), 40-42.

23. Elderton, *Case Studies*, 42.

24. NA, RG 86, PB no. 88, box 122, 36-35.

25. NA, RG 86, PB no. 88, box 120, 11-16. See also box 120, 11-46, and box 122, 36-22.

26. NA, RG 86, PB no. 88, box 122, 31-66.

27. NA, RG 86, PB no. 48, *Women in Oklahoma Industries: A Study of Hours, Wages, and Working Conditions* (1926), box 25, Rowe.

28. NA, RG 86, PB no. 88, box 122, 32-48 (African-American woman) and 36-40 (Polish immigrant woman). It is significant that these women, both meatpackers, worked in different industries than their husbands did; the former was married to a

tire builder, the latter to a foundry worker. Women who worked in the same industry as their husband were much more likely to know how much their husband's wages were. For a father who hid the amount of his wages from his daughters, see NA, RG 86, PB no. 60, *Industrial Accidents to Women in New Jersey, Ohio, and Wisconsin* (1927), box 33, 1085.

29. Social Welfare History Archives, Minneapolis, Minn., Helen Hall Papers, box 105, folder 9, Aggie Bennett. I will refer to this collection as SWHA, HHP.

30. SWHA, HHP, box 43, folder 2, Benda; see also folder 7, O'Dowd. These two studies come, respectively, from Cleveland and New Orleans.

31. Komarovsky, *Unemployed Man,* 27.

32. Komarovsky, *Unemployed Man,* 76.

33. SWHA, HHP, box 48, folder 5, Caruso.

34. SWHA, HHP, box 43, folder 14, Sciarro.

35. Komarovsky, *Unemployed Man,* 32.

36. NA, RG 86, PB no. 88, box 123, 24-42.

37. Ibid., 42-36 and 56-67.

38. Ibid., 41-1.

39. NA, RG 86, PB no. 10, *Hours and Conditions of Work for Women in Industry in Virginia* (1920), box 3, Skipper.

40. Barbara Ehrenreich, *Hearts of Men: American Dreams and the Flight from Commitment* (Garden City, N.Y., 1984). Kenon Breazeale pushes the emergence of a male consumer back to the 1930s, linking it to *Esquire* magazine, but does not make the same links as Ehrenreich does between male consumption and dereliction in the breadwinner role. See "In Spite of Women: *Esquire* Magazine and the Construction of the Male Consumer," *Signs* 20, no. 1 (autumn 1994): 1–22.

41. Simkhovitch, *City Worker's World,* 101.

42. Ibid., 95.

43. NA, RG 86, USM, box 3, folder "Mothers' Pensions, 1925–26," case 9; see also case 73.

44. Elderton, *Case Studies,* 36. For other examples of good managers, see ibid., 207, 215, 270, 296, 300, 321–22, 323–24.

45. NA, RG 86, PB no. 88, box 122, 32-16.

46. Elderton, *Case Studies,* 85.

47. Ibid., 27.

48. Ibid., 38.

49. Komarovsky, *Unemployed Man,* 31.

50. Elderton, *Case Studies,* 38.

51. Ibid., 187.

52. NA, RG 86, PB no. 88, box 123, 41-19.

53. Ibid., 56-16.

54. Sophia Smith Collection, Smith College, Northampton, Massachusetts, Mary Van Kleeck Papers, box 99, folder 1553, case 21993/21996.

55. Elderton, *Case Studies,* 207, and also 322; and Roger Angell, *The Family Encounters the Depression* (New York, 1936), 48, 63.

56. Jessica Peixotto, *How Workers Spend a Living Wage—San Francisco Typographers* (Berkeley, 1929), 164.

57. Ibid., 164.

58. Elderton, *Case Studies*, 37–38.

59. Angell, *Family*, 172.

60. Elderton, *Case Studies*, 332.

61. NA, RG 86, PB no. 25, *Women in the Candy Industry in Chicago and St. Louis: A Study of Hours, Wages, and Working Conditions in 1920–1921* (1923), box 12, folder "#25 Survey Materials Home Visits [sic] Schedules (Chicago)," Freund.

62. NA, RG 86, PB no. 88, box 123, 42-21.

63. NA, RG 86, PB no. 60, box 33, 221.

64. NA, RG 86, PB no. 88, box 123, 56-8.

65. NA, RG 86, PB no. 88, box 123, 43-8; box 120, 11-39; and box 122, 31-37 and 32-51.

66. NA, RG 86, PB no. 88, box 122, 36-10; box 121, 17-120; box 123, 21-Taylor.

67. NA, RG 86, PB no. 88, box 123, 42-16.

68. Ibid., 42-77.

69. Ibid., 42-127.

70. NA, RG 86, PB No. 88, Box 122, 36-3 and 36-30; box 121, 16-32, 16-33, and 16-36.

71. NA, RG 86, PB no. 88, box 122, 36-2.

72. NA, RG 86, PB no. 48, box 25, Pearson.

73. NA, RG 86, PB no. 32, *Women in South Carolina Industries: A Study of Hours, Wages, and Working Conditions* (1923), box 16, Dennis.

74. NA, RG 86, PB no. 56, box 31, Banks. For another case of illness so severe that a husband went to live with his parents, see NA, RG 86, PB no. 48, box 25, Saunders.

75. Elderton, *Case Studies*, 127.

76. NA, RG 86, PB no. 88, box 123, 42-25.

77. NA, RG 86, PB no. 88, box 123, 24-Dozoul; box 122, 31-10.

78. NA, RG 86, PB no. 88, box 121, 16-50.

79. NA, RG 86, PB no. 88, box 123, 42-60 and 41-77.

80. For women who said they took jobs to help out when they married, see NA, RG 86, PB no. 88, box 121, 17-114; box 122, 36-24; and box 123, 24-Hlavek and 24-Zajac. See also NA, RG 86, PB no. 10, box 3, Everett. Women who took jobs at the time of a move include NA, RG 86, PB no. 88, box 123, 42-12 and Ottumwa-16; NA, RG 86, PB no. 22, box 9, folder "Home Visit Schedules—Georgia—2," Skee; NA, RG 86, PB no. 56, box 31, Barrett. Women who entered the labor force after immigration include NA, RG 86, PB no. 88, box 123, 24-14 and 24-31.

81. NA, RG 86, USM, box 17, folder "Effects of Dismissing Married Persons from the Civil Service (Section 213 of the Economy Act) 1932–1936," Selected Cases Taken from Questionnaires Used as Basis of Report 'Effects of Dismissing Married Persons from the Civil Service' (Section 213).

82. Mary Van Kleeck Papers, box 96, folder 1503, "Why I Work." The document gives no demographic data about the writer.

83. NA, RG 86, PB no. 88, box 122, 31-55.

84. NA, RG 86, PB no. 88, box 123, 26-29.

85. NA, RG 86, PB no. 56, box 31, Stillwell.

86. NA, RG 86, PB no. 21, box 8, Wood.

87. NA, RG 86, PB no. 88, box 122, 31-32. For other examples, see Mary Van Kleeck

Papers, box 96, folder 1503, Married Women in Industry (Stories from Aurora, Illinois); NA, RG 86, PB no. 88, box 122, 31-32; NA, RG 86, PB no. 21, box 8, E. Ryan; Sophia Smith Collection, Smith College, YWCA Papers, box 31, folder 5, Mrs. Rose P. The account of Rose P. was one of the case histories collected by the YWCA's Commission on the Study of the Second Generation Girl, later called the Commission on First Generation Americans, during the late 1920s and early 1930s.

88. NA, RG 86, PB no. 88, box 123, 41-6 (Croatian) and 32-20 (African-American).

89. Mary Van Kleeck Papers, box 96, folder 1503, Married Women in Industry (Stories from Aurora, Illinois).

90. NA, RG 86, PB no. 19, *Iowa Women in Industry* (1922), box 7, Vaughn.

91. NA, RG 86, PB no. 88, box 123, 51-Whittington.

92. NA, RG 86, PB no. 88, box 121, 17-53.

93. NA, RG 86, PB no. 88, box 122, 31-71.

94. Ibid., 36-2.

95. NA, RG 86, PB no. 88, box 123, South St. Paul A-4.

96. Mary Elizabeth Pidgeon, *The Employment of Women in Slaughtering and Meat Packing*, Bulletin of the Women's Bureau, no. 88 (Washington, 1932), 126–27. The percentages in the following discussion are based on my tally of the responses on the home-visit forms. The basis for computation is the "634 women . . . who were not the sole support of themselves or others" (Pidgeon, *Slaughtering and Meat Packing*, 126). Because the responses were often vague and unspecific, the counts are approximate and should be taken only as a general indication of the numbers of women in the various categories.

97. NA, RG 86, PB no. 88, box 122, 36-1.

98. NA, RG 86, PB no. 88, box 121, 17-122, and 17-Magier.

99. NA, RG 86, PB no. 88, box 122, 31-70.

100. I argue elsewhere in the project of which this article is a part that furniture was an investment as much as an object for immediate consumption.

101. NA, RG 86, PB no. 22, box 9, folder "Home Visit Schedules—Atlanta," Smith.

102. NA, RG 86, PB no. 19, box 7, Robinson.

103. NA, RG 86, PB no. 10, box 3, Kahler.

104. NA, RG 86, PB no. 35, *Women in Missouri Industries: A Study of Hours and Wages* (1924), box 18, Tennyson.

105. Ibid., Dubark.

106. See the cases in nn. 103 and 104; see also NA, RG 86, PB no. 88, box 122, 36-7, and 32-42; and box 123, 42-129; NA, RG 86, PB no. 32, box 16, Sanders; NA, RG 86, PB no. 124, *Women in Arkansas Industries* (1935), box 219, M. Smith; Mary Van Kleeck Papers, box 96, folder 1503, Married Women in Industry, Danville, Illinois. For a partial account of a family's financial division of labor, see Elderton, *Case Studies*, 354–55.

107. NA, RG 86, PB no. 88, box 122, 36-7.

108. NA, RG 86, PB no. 88, box 123, South St. Paul A-11; see also box 122, 32-17.

109. Mary Van Kleeck Papers, box 96, folder 1503, Richmond.

110. Ibid., Woman Taking Comptometer Course.

111. Ibid., Some Reasons for Married Women Working. See also Ruth Schwartz Cowan, *More Work for Mother: The Ironies of Household Technology from the Open Hearth to the Microwave* (New York, 1983).

112. For an example of each, see NA, RG 86, PB no. 21, box 8, Howe; NA, RG 86, PB no. 88, box 121, 16-12.

113. NA, RG 86, PB no. 32, box 16, Ingram; and ibid., Martin.

114. NA, RG 86, PB no. 21, box 8, Howe.

115. NA, RG 86, PB no. 25, box 12, *Women in the Candy Industry in Chicago and St. Louis: A Study of Hours, Wages and Working Conditions in 1920–1921* (1923), folder "#25 Survey Materials—Home Visits Schedules (Chicago)," Deysch.

116. Ibid., Hawkenson. Women in St. Paul and Memphis echoed her sentiments. NA, RG 86, PB no. 88, box 123, South St. Paul S-12; NA, RG 86, PB no. 56, box 31, Dingley.

117. Peixotto, *How Workers Spend a Living Wage*, 177.

118. John Mack Faragher has made this argument; see his *Women and Men on the Overland Trail* (New Haven, 1979) and *Sugar Creek: Life on the Illinois Prairie* (New Haven, 1988).

119. The determinations of ethnicity should be viewed as approximate because of the imprecise reporting on the forms. No questions were asked about the husband's ethnicity. The forms contained blanks for wife's race and country of birth. Ethnicity was often recorded in the race blank, but this blank was also frequently left unfilled. I included in the category central European the wives whose birthplace was listed as Poland, Croatia, Serbia, Estonia, Yugoslavia, Hungary, Lithuania, Russia, Austria, Rumania, Czechoslovakia, Slovakia, or the Ukraine. Also included were thirty-five women who surnames were clearly of one of these ethnicities even though they themselves were listed as native-born. Those identified as "colored" on the forms were counted as African-American; native-born people with surnames that appear to be English, Irish, Scandinavian, or German were counted as being of northern or western European origin. I assumed that there were no interracial marriages. The necessity of relying on both the wife's ethnicity and the husband's surname to categorize ethnicity inevitably creates imprecision. The major source of error in assigning ethnicity results from putting native-born non-African-Americans with surnames of indeterminate ethnicity into the northern and western European category; it should therefore be considered something of a residual category. The errors are unavoidable given the nature of the data, but the differences between the central Europeans and all others are much larger than the probable degree of error.

120. Elderton, *Case Studies*, 139, 230, 343; NA, RG 86, PB no. 35, box 18, Barrett; NA, RG 86, PB no. 21, box 8, Jasper; NA, RG 86, PB no. 19, box 7, Bright; NA, RG 86, PB no. 32, box 16, Edwards; Komarovsky, *Unemployed Man*, 44, 45, 76, 78–79. Barrett and Jasper are cases where husbands did housework in the absence of a wife.

121. For examples of each, see NA, RG 86, PB no. 88, box 120, 11-80, and 11-48; box 121, 17-105.

122. Komarovsky, *Unemployed Man*, 45, 78–79; NA, RG 86, PB no. 88, box 123, Ottumwa-6.

123. Elderton, *Case Studies*, 100; Komarovsky, *Unemployed Man*, 44.

124. NA, RG 86, PB no. 60, box 33, 2941.

125. Louise Lamphere, *From Working Daughters to Working Mothers: Immigrant Women in a New England Industrial Community* (Ithaca, 1987), 278–88, 366–69.

126. NA, RG 86, PB no. 88, box 120, 11-79.

127. Elderton, *Case Studies*, 138.

128. NA, RG 86, PB no. 88, box 122, 31-17 and 31-70; box 123, 24-14.

129. Arlie Hochschild, *The Second Shift* (New York, 1989), 59–74.

130. NA, RG 86, PB no. 11, *Women Street Car Conductors and Ticket Agents* (1921), box 4, Lamb.

131. NA, RG 86, PB no. 88, box 122, 31-5; see also Komarovsky, *Unemployed Man,* 76.

132. NA, RG 86, PB no. 88, box 122, 32-35.

133. Ibid., 37-5.

134. NA, RG 86, PB no. 88, box 123, 56-14.

135. Ibid., 41-23.

136. NA, RG 86, PB no. 88, box 123, 56-18; box 121, 16-51.

137. NA, RG 86, PB no. 88, box 123, 56-67; box 122, 37-5.

138. This argument is made by Susan A. Glenn, *Daughters of the Shtetl: Life and Labor in the Immigrant Generation* (Ithaca, 1990), 238–39.

139. NA, RG 86, PB no. 19, box 7, Osborn.

140. NA, RG 86, PB no. 48, box 25, Koos.

141. NA, RG 86, PB no. 88, box 123, 24-26.

142. Heller Committee for Research on Social Economics, University of California, *Cost of Living Studies. IV. Spending Ways of a Semi-Skilled Group: A Study of the Incomes and Expenditures of Ninety-Eight Street-Car Men's Families in the San Francisco East Bay Region* (Berkeley, 1931), 344.

143. Elderton, *Case Studies,* 218.

144. NA, RG 86, PB no. 35, box 18, Ferranza.

145. Mary Van Kleeck Papers, box 96, folder 1503, My Ideas on Married Women in Industry.

146. NA, RG 86, PB no. 22, box 9, folder "Home Visit Schedules—Georgia," Day.

EIGHT

The Technological Revolution
That Never Was

Gender, Class, and the Diffusion of Household Appliances in Interwar England

Sue Bowden and Avner Offer

> *. . . electricity can serve in reducing drudgery, providing leisure for other things besides keeping the house comfortable and clean, and generally in raising domestic work to an altogether higher status. . . .*
>
> JOHN SNELL, IN *THE ELECTRICITY HANDBOOK FOR WOMEN* (1934)

Housework has been a permanent fixture in the lives of most married women throughout the centuries. Whether women performed the work themselves or employed and organized other women to do the work for them, the tasks of cooking, heating, cleaning, and lighting have constituted the woman's job. Because housework is time-consuming and physically demanding, electrical appliances, with their potential to alleviate the burdens of housework, should have found an immediate response from millions of housewives.

At the turn of the century, the least attractive aspects of housework were drudgery and physical labor. Cooking, cleaning, heating, and laundry were time-consuming, tiring, and frustrating. Housework presented "a picture in which monotony, loneliness, discouragement and sordid hard work are the main features."[1] In the nineteenth century, domestic servants had relieved middle- and upper-class women from the unskilled tasks of housework. By the early twentieth century, the decline in the supply of domestic servants was causing anxiety as these wealthier housewives were faced with the prospect of performing their own housework.[2] One might assume, therefore, that any domestic technology that could have alleviated the burden would have been attractive to large numbers of housewives.

On the face of it, electric household appliances should have been highly desirable, most obviously because they promised to alleviate the unskilled, hard physical labor involved in many housework tasks. The vacuum cleaner reduced the work involved in cleaning floors with broom and pan; water heaters, cookers, and irons eliminated laying and heating of stoves for water

heating, cooking, and laundry. Electric technology did not promise to eliminate or even reduce the skilled tasks of housework, that is, management tasks
of the housewife, such as menu planning and budgeting. Time saved was
time saved from manual labor.[3] The reduction of manual work involved in
a given task was also a reduction in the time spent on that task. Switching on
an electric heater took seconds; maintaining and cleaning a coal fireplace
claimed a considerable amount of time.

It follows that if domestic technology promised to alleviate the drudgery
and sheer hard work of many household tasks, it also offered the potential
for the reallocation of work. For middle- and upper-class households that
employed domestic servants, electric appliances promised to reduce dependence on full-time help in the home and, thus, to mitigate the problems
caused by the decline in availability of domestic servants. Technology also
had the potential to bring household services back to the home. For example, most women preferred to do their washing at home, and the introduction of water heaters, wash boilers, and irons promised to enable them to do
so.[4] Domestic appliances also had the potential to realize better standards
of home care and cleanliness and to allow women to reallocate their time to
the so-called caring aspects of housewifery. Time saved from cleaning and
heating could be used to prepare better meals, to look after children, and
to create a comfortable home for other household members.

Electric technology was highly desirable and should have found a ready
market among millions of housewives in Britain. It did not. Why? What was
the pattern of diffusion of electric appliances and how do we explain revealed
trends? By the end of the 1930s, electricity wires had reached out to most
British households. In 1937, the proportion of wired households (73 percent) was higher than that in the United States (67 percent). But the take-
up of electrical appliances in Britain lagged almost a generation behind.[5]
Electricity allowed most households, in principle at least, to install a wide
range of appliances designed to alleviate household tasks, but the opportunity was not taken up. How is this paradox to be explained?

We begin by considering different approaches to the study of the diffusion of household appliances. Next, we identify distinct acceptance rates, or
diffusion curves, for different appliances; in particular, there is a clear difference between housework and leisure appliances. Subsequent sections consider the influence of the low value placed on women's time; of economic
factors, such as price, income, operating costs, and deferred payments, which
largely explain why demand was limited to the more affluent members of
society; and of the existence of substitutes and other claims on family income,
which assigned a lower priority for electricity in less wealthy households. The
primary attractions of electricity turned out to be a superior quality of illu-
mination, and access to the broadcast recreation of radio. Electric light and
radio recreation were both of them non-gendered goods. Housework ap-

pliances for women had a lower priority. Finally, we consider the themes of advertising directed at women as a source of the motivation for the deployment of electricity in the household. Throughout, we consider the influence of class and gender on the diffusion of these appliances.

The diffusion of household durables has been studied by economists, marketing scientists, and historians of housework. One economic approach is adapted from epidemiology and models the diffusion of ownership on the spread of a disease through a population.[6] In this diffusion process, an appliance typically starts as a luxury. Ownership then becomes more widespread, and finally the stage of mass ownership is reached. Each of these stages marks a change in the rate of diffusion. In explaining these shifts economists consider supply and demand factors. On the supply side, technological progress pushes down production costs.[7] On the demand side, a substantial improvement in real earnings increases the demand for goods.[8] This approach is gender neutral, and it stresses revealed consumer preferences for certain goods rather than the satisfactions actually afforded by the goods. It largely treats consumer durables in isolation, thus ignoring the possibility that there are substitutes or other claims on family expenditure. In this approach, the main influence on the rate of diffusion is learning about the product and thus acquiring a desire to own it. Desire is stoked by advertising and facilitated by credit.[9] Credit in the form of deferred payment schemes influenced the diffusion of television in the United Kingdom more than the rise in real incomes or the decrease in purchase prices.[10] Credit and advertising were important in both the United States and the United Kingdom during the interwar years, but again the research in this area has largely been gender neutral, assuming that all consumer durables offered similar satisfactions to both men and women.[11]

Another strand in economics, household-production theory, relates the acquisition of appliances to the allocation of men's and women's time between paid work and the home. This approach suggests that the demand for appliances is positively related to the opportunities for women to work outside the home.[12] With more money and less time, women in paid work would purchase more time-saving appliances.

Appliance prices and family income levels do not tell the whole story. Marketing scientists have studied the satisfactions afforded by particular goods and have made a distinction between housework and leisure appliances.[13] Our own recent work suggests that since the 1920s households on both sides of the Atlantic have consistently given priority to leisure appliances over housework durables. Radios and televisions, for example, diffused at a rapid rate that appears to have been insensitive to price and income; whereas household appliances diffused much more slowly, and increases in ownership were generally in line with income growth.[14]

Historians increasingly regard women as the key to the demand for consumer durables. Women bought the new appliances and also worked on the production lines that made them.[15] Such research considers changes in housework patterns but tends to view the purchasing decision in isolation from economic variables and from the availability of substitutes and alternative claims on family expenditure.

This essay combines elements of the economic, marketing, and housework-history approaches to the diffusion of consumer durables to explore the reasons why appliances were not taken up, despite their attractions. The diffusion of these goods in England during the interwar years has to be explained not only in terms of income and price effects but also in terms of the satisfactions afforded by each of these durables, the preference given to leisure over housework, and the value of women's time.

PATTERNS AND CHARACTERISTICS OF DIFFUSION

The main electric housework appliances were introduced shortly before or after World War I. Household penetration of the electric iron began in 1909, and the vacuum cleaner followed in 1915. The 1930s saw the introduction of the clothes washer and the water heater. By 1934, these appliances had penetrated 1 percent of households.[16] Despite the introduction of a range of domestic electric appliances, which in theory should have appealed to millions of housewives, penetration levels in the 1930s were low, and most women did not own even the most basic appliances (table 1).[17]

Slow growth rates and low penetration levels cannot be explained solely in terms of the economic climate of the 1930s. We have traced the diffusion pattern for a range of consumer durables in the United States and the United Kingdom from the 1920s to the present day and have found that slow growth rates and low penetration levels for housework appliances were as much a characteristic of the postwar years as of the 1930s (table 2).[18] Irons, refrigerators, washing machines, water heaters, and vacuum cleaners all took decades to diffuse through society. Both irons and refrigerators took over two decades to enter the majority of households, while the water heater, washing machine, and vacuum cleaner reached only a 20 percent ownership level in the same time. The vacuum cleaner, the washing machine, and the water heater took 40, 30, and 33 years, respectively, to reach 50 percent ownership levels. This slow diffusion rate does not indicate a ready market for household technology. Many appliances took a long time to acquire necessity status in Britain, and some, like the dishwasher, have never achieved it.

In stark contrast, those durables that catered to leisure interests enjoyed rapid growth rates, whether household penetration began in the interwar years or in the postwar era (table 2). In 1922, less than 1 percent of all households owned a radio, but three years after household penetration began, ownership had grown to 20 percent of all households. Seven years later half the

TABLE 1 The Growth of the Market for Domestic Electrical Appliances, England, 1932–1938: Percentage of Homes Wired for Electricity and the Percentage of Wired Homes Having Selected Electric Consumer Durables

	Wired Homes	Cookers	Wash Boilers	Water Heaters	Fridges	Irons	Vacuum Cleaners
1932	31.84	4.9	—	—	—	—	19.3
1933	49.15	6.1	0.9	1.2	—	56.4	23.5
1934	49.33	9.3	1.4	1.9	—	—	28.9
1935	54.54	11.3	2.0	3.1	—	—	27.1
1936	57.75	13.4	2.4	3.8	2.3	70.9	31.6
1937	61.77	15.4	2.9	4.8	—	—	35.3
1938	65.39	16.9	3.5	5.6	2.4	—	38.6

SOURCES: Column 1: "Survey of Present and Past Annual Surveys," *Electrical Trading* (September 1938): 47, 63. All other columns: *Electrical Trading* and *Electrical Times*, Annual Market Surveys, 1932–1939, inclusive.

NOTE: Wired homes refers to the percentage of homes wired for electricity; the permeation levels described in table 1 relate to wired homes, not total homes.

TABLE 2 Diffusion Rates of Selected Household Appliances, England and Wales

	Date Penetration Began[a]	Number of Years Taken to Reach 50% Ownership Level	Date 50% Ownership Level Reached
Iron	1909	24	1933
Vacuum cleaner	1915	40	1955
Clothes washer	1934	30	1964
Water heater	1934	33	1967
Refrigerator	1946	22	1968
Radio	1923	10	1933
TV, black-and-white	1949	9	1958

SOURCE: Sue Bowden and Avner Offer, "Household Appliances and the Use of Time: The United States and Britain since the 1920s," *Economic History Review* 47, no. 4 (November 1994), table 1, 729.

[a]Defined as the date that the penetration level reached 1 percent.

TABLE 3   Attributes of Consumer Durables

Housework Appliances	Domestic Leisure Appliances
Slow take off periods	Rapid take off periods
Slow growth rates	Rapid growth rates
Low penetration levels	High penetration levels
Long product cycle	Short product cycle

SOURCE: Sue Bowden and Avner Offer, "Household
Appliances and the Use of Time: The United States and Britain
since the 1920s," *Economic History Review* 47, no. 4 (November
1994), table 1, b.

households in the country had a radio, and by the end of the interwar period penetration levels exceeded 80 percent. Black-and-white televisions diffused even more rapidly, achieving 20 percent and 50 percent ownership levels only five and nine years, respectively, after household penetration began.
Seventy-five percent ownership levels were recorded after twelve years.[19]

Consumer durables can be grouped into two descriptive categories.
Durables used for housework can be defined as "time-saving" in that they reduce the time required to complete specific household tasks and have the
potential to release discretionary time. Such goods took decades to diffuse
through society. In contrast, durables used for leisure, which require the use
of discretionary time in conjunction with the product, can be described as
"time-using" goods. They experienced rapid growth rates and achieved high
penetration levels over much shorter periods of time.[20] The growth characteristics of the two categories are summarized in table 3.

In another study, Bowden has used regression analysis to relate the diffusion trends of "time-saving" goods to owner characteristics in the 1930s.
By the end of the 1930s, ownership of housework appliances was firmly established among the middle-income groups of society in the affluent south
of the country and was spreading among this same group in the less affluent north. Working-class women, however, were not acquiring these goods
and thus did not stand to benefit from them.[21] Only a minority of women,
namely, those from the middle classes, gained from "time-saving" appliances.
Ownership patterns had important class dimensions.

THE VALUE OF WOMEN'S TIME

Why then were diffusion rates of "time-saving" electric durables so low? For
a working-class woman, the incentive to acquire electric appliances was constrained in the first place by the low "opportunity costs" of her time; that is,
the time she spent on housework cost little in terms of income she might
have earned in the labor market. Women have tended to be treated as a low-

TABLE 4   Average Weekly Wages of Men and Women, in Shillings,
Selected Industries, England, 1924–1935

	1924		1930		1935	
	Men	Women	Men	Women	Men	Women
Engineering	51.1	26.3	50.4	26.8	55.0	28.0
Textiles	51.0	28.6	48.0	26.9	49.2	27.5
Clothing and footwear	54.8	26.9	53.6	26.9	54.3	27.8
Food, drink, and tobacco	58.0	27.9	57.5	28.0	56.6	6.6

SOURCE: Elizabeth Roberts, *Women's Work, 1840–1940* (London, 1988), 70, table 5.1,
derived from A. L. Bowley, *Wages and Income in the U.K. since 1860* (London, 1937) and
N. Soldon, *Women in British Trade Unions, 1874–1976* (London, 1978).

paid, temporary, unskilled secondary labor force, one used to fulfill short-term needs in the economy.[22] Historically women have found work in the casual labor market, where hours of work varied according to the day of the week, the time of the day, and the season.[23] There was no shortage of labor during the interwar period; demographic trends and industrial restructuring did not create any stimulus for the reallocation of married women's labor outside the home.[24] In addition, women earned less than men (see table 4). Low female earnings compounded the problem. Table 4 indicates a lack of demand for female labor and the weakness of incentives for women to undertake employment in the formal labor market. Because women were excluded from many occupations and industries, and because their earnings were significantly lower than men's, they had little incentive to invest in labor-saving appliances that could have helped them to combine housework with paid work outside the home.

SUPPLY, PRICE, OPERATING COSTS, AND AVAILABILITY OF DEFERRED PAYMENT SCHEMES

The availability of electricity and the cost of installing it, the purchase price of appliances, their operating costs, and the terms and conditions of deferred payment in relation to family income levels further constrained the growth of a working-class market for domestic electric appliances.[25] Market growth in the first instance depended on the existence of electric power in the home. The provisions of the Electricity (Supply) Act of 1926 gave the Central Electricity Board the power to operate a newly constructed national grid of high-tension transmission lines. Work on the project began the following year and by the end of 1934 the grid was operating in most of the country.[26] The subsequent years witnessed a marked extension of electricity throughout the country. In 1930, just over a third of homes in England and Wales were wired;

TABLE 5   Average Annual Wage Payments per Head,
England, 1932 and 1938, Selected Industries, £ Current Prices

	1932	1938
Coal mining	143.6	171.0
Chemicals	135.6	150.0
Mechanical and general engineering	129.9	146.6
Iron and steel	140.2	171.7
Food	114.9	123.3
Paper	121.0	130.6
Clothing	94.6	100.3
Building	141.8	149.8
Commerce	116.2	130.0
Finance	74.4	81.2

SOURCE: Estimated from Agatha L. Chapman and Rose Knight, *Wages and Salaries in the United Kingdom, 1920–1938* (Cambridge, U.K., 1953).

NOTE: In the interwar years, the distinction between waged and salaried occupations had class dimensions. Three quarters of the population were manual laborers, who were employed on a weekly basis and were paid a weekly wage. Salaried income was associated with professional occupations (Noreen Branson and Margot Heinemann, *Britain in the Nineteen Thirties* (St. Albans, U.K., 1973), 165–66.

by 1938 72 percent of homes were supplied with electricity.[27] Although the supply of electricity increased dramatically in the 1930s, not all homes were wired. In 1938 more than a quarter of households were still excluded, many of these in small villages with populations of less than five hundred.[28]

Given the low average income of the majority of the population at this time, the physical access to electricity was less of a constraint on ownership than the costs of installing electric power and of buying and running appliances. Before World War II an income of £250 a year was regarded as approximately the social dividing line between the working classes and the rest of society. Households in receipt of less than £250 a year (or £5 a week) constituted about three-quarters of all households in the United Kingdom.[29] When a working-class family was dependent on the income of a sole wage earner, annual household income could be considerably less than the £250. Average annual waged income in all economic sectors was well below £250 (table 5), and average weekly income was significantly below £5 (table 6). High unemployment levels (table 6) and employment insecurity among those in work added further disincentives to investment in capital equipment for the home.

Installation costs for a modest lighting system fell from £11–£20 in 1919 to £5–£6 in the 1930s, but these prices remained beyond the budgets of most lower income households.[30] Assisted wiring schemes provided deferred payment facilities for those who could not afford to pay the costs outright. Light-

TABLE 6   Average Weekly Wages and Unemployment,
Britain, 1924–1938

	Average Weekly Wages (£)	Unemployment Rate (%)
1924	2.80	10.3
1925	2.82	11.3
1926	2.79	12.5
1927	2.81	9.7
1928	2.79	10.8
1929	2.79	10.4
1930	2.79	16.1
1931	2.75	21.3
1932	2.70	22.1
1933	2.69	19.9
1934	2.72	16.7
1935	2.75	15.5
1936	2.81	13.1
1937	2.86	10.8
1938	2.95	12.9

SOURCE: Barry Eichengreen, "Unemployment in Interwar Britain," *Refresh*,
no. 8 (spring 1989): 4, table 1.

ing could be installed for as little as twenty quarterly payments of £0.2 in the
late 1930s.[31] These schemes usually covered the installation of electric lighting and a small number of low-power sockets in the home. The installation
of heavy-power-consuming appliances—that is, cookers, heaters, and boilers, which had to be specially connected—was rarely covered. In the north-
east, for example, the assisted wiring scheme offered by the Hull undertaking consisted of two power sockets, and for each additional socket there was
a charge of £0.079 per quarter spread over ten years. In the southwest, Bath's
scheme offered six lighting sockets.[32] Although electric power became increasingly available during the interwar period, and the terms of assisted
wiring schemes were such that most households could afford to install a modest power and lighting system, many households would not have had access
to electric appliances that required special connections and additional
power.

For the large majority of households, even assuming the availability of full
electric supply, the purchase cost of appliances precluded ownership; prices
ranged from £6 for a cheap vacuum cleaner, to £8–£12 for one of the smaller,
nonthermostatic cookers (electric ovens), £5 for an instantaneous water
heater, £1–£2 for an inset-panel standard fire-bar electric fire, £20 for a washing machine and £23–£35 for a 3–4.5 cubic-foot refrigerator.[33]

Acquisition of the new technology in the interwar period did not depend
on outright cash purchase of the goods. Most of the appliances could be ac-

quired either on hire-purchase (installment purchase) terms from retail outlets, direct from manufacturers, and local electricity undertakings or by rental
from the latter. However, hire purchase allowed only a small number of families to acquire domestic electric appliances. The cheapest vacuum cleaner
sold by General Electric in 1936 was offered by that company on hire-purchase terms of £0.425 deposit and twelve subsequent payments of £0.75 a
month.[34] The most common repayment period for vacuum cleaners was one
of twelve months, incurring an average monthly charge to the purchaser of
£0.87 for a vacuum cleaner alone. Most working-class families would have
had difficulty meeting such costs. Moreover, given a choice, families used
hire purchase to acquire radios and furniture rather than "time-saving"
equipment (see the discussion of leisure appliances below).[35]

Although the terms and conditions of hire schemes varied considerably
from one area to another, the evidence does suggest that most working-class
households could have afforded to hire at least one electric appliance. At
the high end, the Poplar, Hornsey, and Plymouth undertakings in the south
charged between £0.4 and £0.5 a quarter for the smallest cookers. The cheapest terms were in Liverpool, in the north, where a small cooker could be hired
for £0.2 a quarter. Use of such schemes, however, depended in the first instance on their availability. In 1934, about two-thirds of electricity undertakings in the country offered such schemes.[36] A household in a district
served by one of the undertakings that did not offer such a scheme was, of
course, automatically excluded.[37]

A further deterrent was the high cost of running these appliances. The
evidence suggests that many women "would utilize and use electricity if the
cost of supply were not so expensive."[38] The costs are estimated in table 7.
At the end of the 1930s, the average weekly expenditure of an industrial working-class household on fuel and light was £0.321, £0.158 of which was spent
on coal.[39] Could such a family have afforded to use electricity for lighting
and other domestic uses? Weekly fixed charges were £0.033 and lighting
would have cost about £0.068 a week, thus leaving only £0.061 a week for
power for space and water heating, cooking, and cleaning.[40] If unit costs for
purposes other than lighting were one pence a unit, then cooking with electricity would have cost £0.096 a week, and hire of a cooker would have cost
about £0.002 a week. Thus, the cost of running heavy-power-consuming appliances—when combined with fixed charges, lighting costs, hire payments,
and assisted wiring charges—precluded many members of the industrial
working class from acquiring electrical appliances. Most families found the
new appliances too expensive to run. In addition, a potential consumer had
to consider installation costs, since "more than a marginal difference in cost
would be necessary to justify the cost of removing existing appliances—say
a kitchen range—and installing different ones".[41] The high cost of electric
installations could be avoided if cooking appliances already existed.

TABLE 7   Estimated Average Weekly Fuel Budget, including Use of Electricity, of an Industrial Working-Class Household, United Kingdom, 1937–1938

Fuel and light budget	£0.321
Coal for heating	– £0.158
Amount available for light, cooking, and other uses	£0.163
Lighting	– £0.068
Electric standing charge	– £0.033
Residual amount available for cooking and other uses	£0.062
Electricity for cooking[a]	£0.096
Hire of cooker	+ £0.002
Total electric cooking expenses	£0.098

SOURCES: Sue Bowden, "The Market for Domestic Electric Cookers in the 1930s: A Regional Analysis," (Ph.D diss., University of London, 1984), 254–60; Ministry of Labour, "Weekly Expenditure of Working-Class Households in the United Kingdom, 1937–1938," *Ministry of Labour Gazette* 48, no. 12 (December 1940): 505.

[a]Unit cost for purposes other than lighting assumed to be 1 pence.

These economic considerations are an important part of the explanation for the low rates of ownership of household appliances. They are not, however, the full story. The decision not to acquire electric durables was motivated not just by price and income considerations but also by the availability of substitutes—in the form of alternative household appliances—and by the presence of other claims on the family income.

SUBSTITUTES AND OTHER CLAIMS ON FAMILY INCOME

The existence of substitutes provides another part of the answer to low diffusion rates for "time-saving" goods. Electric technology was only one of several forms of domestic technology available at the time. If women were to be persuaded to acquire electric appliances in the interwar years, then they had to be motivated to replace existing appliances. Gas and solid fuel were already being used for cooking and for space and water heating.[42]

Gas was the most commonly used form of power for cooking, with nine million gas cookers in use in Great Britain at the end of the 1930s.[43] Its popularity grew, so that by 1946, 74.6 percent of households were using gas for cooking. Of the 16.4 percent who used electricity, about 5 percent used it in conjunction with other fuels.[44] Solid fuel tended to be used for heating water. In 1946, penetration levels for heating water with coal, coke, and gas were 49.2 percent, 9.5 percent, and 46 percent, respectively; the penetration level for electric water heaters was 12.5 percent.[45] Coal and coke also provided the mainstay for space heating, although the tendency was to supplement solid fuel with additional power sources for heating the main living room in the house. Electricity became the most popular of the alternative sources, with 35 percent of households sampled in 1952 having one electric fire (compared to 19 percent having one oil fire and 12 percent one gas fire); 48 percent of households had no electric fire.[46]

The popularity of gas and solid fuel did not rest entirely upon consumer inertia. Gas in particular had far more than habit to recommend it to the majority of housewives. Forty-seven percent of housewives surveyed in 1945 expressed a preference for cooking with gas. They deemed it to be clean, easy, quick, and economical. Only 33 percent expressed a preference for electricity. Electricity was disliked because it was considered to be too expensive, inconvenient, and slow for cooking.[47] Coal fires and boilers were considered to be cheap and satisfactory for space and water heating; electricity was too expensive.[48] While these preferences may embrace an element of familiarity with an existing appliance, it is doubtful that housewives would have continued to use gas and solid fuel had electrical appliances been considered vastly superior.

Gas consumers avoided installation costs if they applied for gas appliances, since they were already connected to the gas supply. In addition, there was no restriction in terms of supply nor were there any minimum charges, since the gas industry, unlike the electricity industry, was legally bound to supply any consumer with gas, even if it was uneconomical to do so. Since 1855, gas companies had been required to supply on demand without insisting that the consumer use enough gas to pay for the service.[49] It was easier for women to economize without a minimum usage charge. Therefore, it is not altogether surprising that so many women decided to stick with gas. Rising gas usage and the continued use of solid fuel indicate that both gas and solid fuel had many positive features and that women were making informed choices of cooking and heating appliances.

There were, moreover, other claims on family income. Furniture and fittings, clothing and leisure goods, notably the radio, were assigned greater priority than electric technology. Household furnishings, fittings, and equipment in particular constituted a major part of consumerism in the interwar period. Expenditure on furniture and fittings increased steadily each year, from £108.4 million in 1924 to a total of £164.4 million in 1937. Expenditure on household textiles also grew, from £14 million in 1924 to an interwar peak of £18.2 million in 1937.[50] Double sheets, pillows, woolen blankets, tea towels, bath and hand towels, curtain net, and curtain materials

TABLE 8 Estimated Annual Expenditure on Furniture, Furnishings, Household Equipment, and Clothing Purchased for Final Consumption in the United Kingdom, 1924–1938, £ Current Prices

| | Furniture, Fittings, and Household Equipment | | Clothing | |
	£m	%[a]	£m	%[a]
1924	191.5	4.98	491.3	12.77
1928	217.3	5.43	522.1	13.05
1932	208.9	5.58	439.0	11.72
1936	260.2	6.28	501.2	12.10
1938	263.7	5.92	567.4	12.73

SOURCE: Richard Stone and D. A. Rowe, *The Measurement of Consumers' Expenditure and Behaviour in the United Kingdom, 1920–1938* (Cambridge, 1966): furniture and fittings, 2:26, table 12; clothing, 2:13, table 6; total expenditure, 2:110, table 45.

[a]Percentage of estimated expenditure at current prices on all goods and services purchased for final consumption in the United Kingdom; excludes consumers' expenditures abroad.

were the most popular items.[51] Hardware and hollowware also proved to be popular items of household expenditure. The Woolworth chain, where nothing cost more than £0.025, brought a wide range of cheap cooking utensils, cutlery, and crockery to the mass market. In 1924 total expenditure on hardware and hollowware amounted to £49.4 million; by 1937 it had grown to £75.9 million.

Expenditure on the home was dwarfed by expenditure on clothing. Women's magazines and the glamorous images created by the Hollywood films of the time helped create a demand for "fashion," made all the more compelling by changes in styles and a new emphasis on comfort and practicality.[52] For a large number of working-class women, "fashion" remained a dream, and clothing was limited to mend-and-make-do. The interwar years also saw the growth of a ready-to-wear industry associated with the expansion of chains of retail outlets. Marks and Spencers and C & A sold cheap, mass-produced clothes targeted at the young working woman and lower-middle-class housewives, while the Co-Operative Society continued to be the main source of supply for working-class women's and children's wear.[53]

Synthetic materials, notably rayon, brought imitations of silk stockings and underwear within the reach of many working-class women, at between a quarter and a half of the price of natural fabrics. Expenditure on clothing far exceeded that on other household goods (table 8). Ready-made clothes for women, girls, and children were the largest items of expenditure, accounting for 37 percent of total expenditure on clothing and other personal effects in 1936. In that year, expenditure on men's and boys' wear, at £130.1 million, accounted for 26 percent of total expenditure on clothing and per-

TABLE 9   Estimated Weekly Expenditures, United Kingdom, 1938

	Furnishings, Furniture, and Household Equipment	Clothing	Food
Middle class			
Pence per head	42.6	78.0	154.5
Percentage of estimated weekly expenditure	*9.0*	*16.5*	*32.6*
Industrial working class			
Pence per head	9.5	26.0	109.1
Percentage of estimated weekly expenditure	*4.3*	*11.9*	*49.8*

SOURCE: Richard Stone and D. A. Rowe, *The Measurement of Consumers' Expenditure and Behaviour in the United Kingdom, 1920–1938* (Cambridge, 1966), 2:113, table 48.
NOTE: The estimates of percentage expenditures are based on data that exclude housing costs.

sonal effects.[54] There were, however, significant variations in expenditure patterns at this time: the middle classes spent more, both in actual and in percentage terms, on clothing and on furniture, furnishings, and household equipment than the working classes did (table 9).

Food continued to account for a large proportion of the weekly expenditure of the working classes, and as purchasing priorities were not confined to durable or even semidurable goods, there were more immediate alternatives to expenditure in the form of a greater variety of animal protein, vegetables, and fruit. Although the diets of many families in the population were inadequate from a nutritional point of view, the interwar years did witness an improvement over the prewar level.[55]

Other claims on family expenditure also existed in the form of leisure activities outside the home. The pub (largely working class), restaurants (largely middle class), and weekly outings, day trips, and holidays (by car in the middle classes and by bus, motorcycle, or train among the working classes) all enjoyed enhanced popularity, and leisure became an increasingly important feature of consumer expenditure patterns in the interwar years.[56] The increase in expenditure on entertainment and recreation largely reflected the popularity of the cinema in this period, as cinema going became a regular weekly event (or in some cases a bi- or triweekly event) and assumed a dominant role in the leisure of the working classes and in the life of the young (table 10). The cinema crossed class boundaries and came to play an increasingly important part in middle-class leisure as well.[57] By 1938, when there were 987 million annual admissions to the cinema, estimated expenditure on cinema going had reached £41.5 million and accounted for 15.8

TABLE 10   Estimated Annual Expenditure on Entertainment
and Recreation Purchased for Final Consumption,
United Kingdom, 1928–1938

	£m	%ᵃ	Number of Cinema Admissions (millions)	Number of Admissions All Entertainments (millions)
1924	186.7	4.85	—	1,090
1928	210.6	5.26	—	1,150
1932	221.7	5.92	—	1,253
1936	242.9	5.89	917	1,400
1938	262.5	5.89	987	1,497

SOURCE: Richard Stone and D. A. Rowe, *The Measurement of Consumers' Expenditure and Behaviour in the United Kingdom, 1920–1938* (Cambridge, 1966), 2:91, table 36; 2:92, table 38; and 2:110, table 45.

ᵃPercentage of estimated expenditure at current prices on all goods and services purchased for final consumption in the United Kingdom; excludes consumers' expenditures abroad.

percent of all expenditure on entertainment and recreation and nearly 6 percent of consumers' total expenditure in the United Kingdom.[58]

The evidence thus far suggests that, in this period, much of the consumption frontier was nonelectrical—with preference being given to furnishings and fittings as well as clothing, food, and leisure—and that consumers made informed choices not to replace existing sources of heating and cooking with electrical appliances.

THE PREFERENCE FOR LEISURE

Low ownership levels of goods such as the electric cooker, wash boiler, and water heater appear to be related to the existence of substitutes and of alternative claims on the household budget. In contrast, the higher ownership levels of goods such as lighting, radios, irons, and vacuum cleaners appear to be related to the lack of obvious substitutes for these items. In addition, radio and lighting were not gendered, and their acquisition was only weakly dependent on class. Gendered goods were far more difficult to establish.

To judge by diffusion levels, radio provided the most compelling satisfactions of all electrical goods (table 11), and lighting was the second most compelling good (table 12). Both goods were not gendered and only weakly class related. In the variety of drama, music, and current affairs programs, radio offered entertainment, communication with the outside world, information, and, to many, a release, an escape from the tedium of everyday life and enhanced leisure time within the constraints of limited incomes. Moreover, the

TABLE 11   The Growth of Expenditure on the Radio,
United Kingdom, 1924–1935

| | Estimated Consumers' Expenditure on Radios and Gramophones[a] | | Diffusion Level of Radios[b] |
	£m	%[c]	%
1924	7.1	6.5	7.8
1930	18.3	13.4	65.6
1935	27.1	18.1	71.5

SOURCES: Sue Bowden and Avner Offer, "Household Appliances and the Use of Time: The United States and Britain since the 1920s," *Economic History Review* 47, no. 4 (November 1994): table 5; Richard Stone and D. A. Rowe, *The Measurement of Consumers' Expenditure and Behaviour in the United Kingdom, 1920–1938* (Cambridge, 1966), 2:17, table 8.

[a] Expenditure on radios is estimated by Stone and Rowe only for the years 1924, 1930, and 1935.

[b] Diffusion level is defined as the percentage of all households in the United Kingdom with a radio license.

[c] Percentage of estimated consumers' expenditure at current prices on furniture and furnishings in the United Kingdom.

TABLE 12   The Growth of Electricity Usage in the Home,
England and Wales, 1926–1938

	Average Annual Consumption of Electricity per Domestic Customer (kWh)	Average Annual Consumption of Electricity per Domestic Customer for Purposes other than Lighting (kWh)
1926	520[a]	220[a]
1931	510[a]	210[a]
1933	468	168
1934	454[a]	154[a]
1935	457[a]	157[a]
1936	494	194
1937	541[a]	241
1938	579[a]	279[a]

SOURCE: A. J. Anscomb, "Domestic Sector Analysis, 1932/3 to 1978/9," Electricity Council, Economics and Forecasting Branch, Commercial Department, July 1990, File EF 144, p. 6.

NOTE: Average lighting usage varied from household to household. Consumption depended on a number of factors including the size of house and the number of occupants. Usage could vary between 100 and 300 kWh a year (Leslie Hannah, *Electricity Before Nationalisation* [London, 1979], 192). Consumption for lighting purposes for the above table has been estimated as 300 kWh per year.

[a] Estimated.

benefits of the radio could be shared by all members of the household. Radio played a part in the general transition from public leisure to private leisure in the home in a family setting.[59]

For working-class women leisure was a relative term: "Anything which is slightly less arduous or gives a change of scene or occupation from the active hard work of the eight hours for which she has already been up is leisure."[60] Leisure for such women usually came at the end of the day when the children were in bed, when they could sit down and deal with the sewing, the knitting, and the mending and/or listen to the wireless: "An overwhelming proportion say that they spend their 'leisure' in sewing and doing other household jobs, slightly different from the ordinary work of cooking and house-cleaning."[61] These women referred to the radio quite deliberately and specifically as a *luxury*. Although it did not eliminate or reduce housework, it may have made the work more tolerable. In these terms the satisfaction derived from the radio was far greater than that derived from any one housework-related consumer durable. When family incomes were limited and choices had to be made, the priority of a radio exceeded that of other domestic electric appliances, with the possible exception of lighting.

The interwar years saw the continuation and completion of a process of market segmentation that dates back to the late nineteenth century, wherein electricity increasingly took over the lighting market and gas was limited to the space and water heating market.[62] For lighting, electricity appeared to be a valid alternative to gas. Gas lighting gave off offensive fumes and was considered by consumers to be poor in quality, dirty, and unreliable. It was also expensive relative to electricity, since electrical utilities were able to offer differential tariffs and to reduce prices as economies of scale were realized with the extension of electric power in the 1930s. In the interwar years the increase in electricity sales derived both from the increase in the number of consumers and from the increased use of electricity by existing consumers (table 12). For many, electricity meant electric light. When an alternative to gas appeared that was relatively cheap and both reliable and free of the smell and dirt associated with gas, its market was more or less assured. But, again, lighting, like the radio, was not gendered, nor was its attraction determined by class. All members of the household could benefit from artificial lighting in the home, and assisted wiring enabled most consumers to install electric lighting.

MIDDLE-CLASS CONSUMERS, DOMESTIC SERVANTS, AND THE PRIVATIZATION OF HOUSEWORK

If, then, price and income effects, the existence of substitutes, and the preference for leisure appliances can explain low ownership levels among the working class, can they also explain the take-up of household appliances among the middle classes? Why did middle-class women acquire the new electric "time-saving" technology? The explanation may lie in the growth of real incomes in this group during the period. Salaried incomes among the professional middle classes were high and increased significantly in the interwar years. The average annual income of a general practitioner, for example, grew from £756 between 1924 and 1929 to £1,094 between 1930 and 1940.[63] Most middle-class families were not operating under the budget constraints experienced by the working classes in this period and therefore could afford to acquire the new appliances.[64] By the late 1930s, the category "other expenditure," which excluded the basic necessities of life but included items such as entertainment, travel, and holidays, constituted the largest part of the middle-class budget (table 13).

Income and expenditure patterns were, however, only part of the story. Electrical appliances facilitated this transition to discretionary consumption. This is suggested by a 1939 assessment by the electricity industry: "So far electric cookers have been sold chiefly to households where the chief income earner receives £4 a week or more and the housewife does *most* [our italics] of the housework herself."[65]

Work in cleaning, child minding, laundry, and sewing for other people's households was attractive to women who needed to supplement the family income. This casual and informal labor market was preferable to the formal labor market, since the former "meant less disruption to home routines."[66] To what extent then did electric appliances encourage an increase in informal, casual work by creating a demand for part-time, as opposed to full-time, domestic help in the home?

The diffusion of consumer durables among the middle classes was influenced by the decrease in the number of domestic servants and by the increase in the standards for child and home care. From the turn of the century, the decline in the number of women seeking domestic work had caused serious concern among the middle classes.[67] Indoor domestic service accounted for 36 percent of female employment in England and Wales in 1881; by 1931, less than a quarter of occupied women were employed in domestic service.[68] The decline in the number of women willing to accept work as full-time domestic servants meant that during the interwar period many households no longer employed domestic servants: "Whereas in the commuter areas of London, the number of servants per 1000 households had been 24.1 in 1911, by 1921 it was already 12.4 and continuing to fall."[69] The trend away from the live-in servant is supported by the fact that "few speculatively built houses . . . made provision for resident staff."[70] It was "acceptable to live in a small well-designed house with only a daily servant instead of a living-in maid. . . . it was also natural to look hopefully at the new domestic technology for positive assistance in saving labour."[71] The middle classes did not altogether forgo domestic help in this period (in 1938

TABLE 13   Average Weekly Expenditure Patterns of Middle-Class Households, Britain, 1938–1939

| | Annual Income of Head of Household | | | | | | | |
| | £250–350 | | £350–500 | | £500–700 | | £700+ | |
	£	%ᵃ	£	%ᵃ	£	%ᵃ	£	%ᵃ
Food	1.78	26.2	2.10	24.2	2.63	23.1	3.23	20.1
Housing	0.95	14.0	1.00	11.5	1.29	11.3	1.74	10.8
Clothing	0.62	9.1	0.77	8.9	1.02	9.0	1.33	8.3
Fuel and light	0.42	6.2	0.51	5.9	0.64	5.6	0.81	5.0
Coal	0.20	2.9	0.25	2.9	0.32	2.8	0.33	2.1
Electricity	0.09	1.3	0.11	1.3	0.14	1.2	0.18	1.1
Gas	0.08	1.2	0.08	0.9	0.10	0.9	0.17	1.1
Other items	3.03	44.6	4.29	49.5	5.81	51.0	8.98	55.8
Entertainments	0.10	1.5	0.13	1.5	0.20	1.8	0.26	1.6
Domestic help	0.09	1.3	0.16	1.8	0.33	2.9	0.74	4.6
Furniture	0.16	2.4	0.21	2.4	0.33	2.9	0.46	2.9
Total weekly expenditure	6.80		8.67		11.39		16.09	
Total average annual expenditure	353.60		450.84		592.28		836.68	

SOURCES: Phillip Massey, "The Expenditure of 1,360 British Middle-Class Households in 1938–39," *Journal of the Royal Statistical Society* 105, pt. 3 (1942): 181–85, table 22; Ministry of Labour, "Weekly Expenditure of Working-Class Households in the United Kingdom, 1937–1938," *Ministry of Labour Gazette* (London, 1940), 305.

NOTE: In comparison, the total average annual expenditure of an industrial working-class household was 224.25.

ᵃPercentage of total weekly expenditure.

expenditure on domestic help ranged from £4.8 a year among those with an annual income of between £250 and £350 to £38.5 among those with an annual income of over £700).[72] Instead, the full-time live-in servant was replaced with casual, informal help in the form of a "daily."

There was a ready supply of women to take up "daily" work. There are no official figures on the number of dailies in this period. Elizabeth Roberts however has found that 10.5 percent of Barrow mothers, 18 percent of Preston mothers, and 18 percent of Lancaster mothers in the interwar period went out cleaning or washing or both and that about 40 percent of women in Preston and Lancaster and 50 percent of women in Barrow worked at some point in their lives on a casual, part-time basis.[73] The part-time employment of married women with young children in unskilled and semiskilled occupations—notably office cleaning and child minding—has been described as a characteristic of the postwar era.[74] This type of employment existed in the interwar period, although it was not officially recorded. Electric appliances, by reducing the demand for the live-in servant, may have resulted in an increase in this type of employment, and, in doing so, contributed to the continued segregation of women into low paid, unskilled work.

In the nineteenth century, those who could afford to do so had the household laundry done within the home either by the domestic servant or by a washerwoman; indeed the latter was one of the principal female occupations until the twentieth century.[75] Commercial laundries were rarely used.[76] The preference for home laundry continued into the twentieth century.[77] Why did women make this choice? What part did "time-saving" technology play in this process?

When asked why they preferred to do laundry at home, 37 percent of women claimed they could not afford to use a laundry, and 49 percent claimed they "preferred to do it at home."[78] Of those who used a laundry, only 15 percent explained that they did so because washing was heavy work; 5 percent claimed that the laundry performed the task better.[79] Christina Hardyment has explained this preference in terms of the relative costs of laundries: "If laundries had become more efficient and cheaper instead of declining in the face of the mass production of small domestic machines, the household could have been relieved of a considerable burden."[80] Caroline Davidson, on the other hand, has argued: "The explanation is a moral one: if 'cleanliness was next to godliness,' women wanted to create that moral worth with their own hands, or if this was not feasible, at least in their own homes."[81] Judy Wajcman has invoked an aversion to communal facilities, which were "associated in many people's minds with back-to-back houses with their shared water supply and sanitation."[82]

During the interwar years, women with low incomes continued to do their washing at home because they could not afford to do otherwise; women on higher incomes occasionally sent the washing to the laundry but more often had washing done for them at home with the assistance of some form of domestic help. Domestic electric technology made little difference; the low penetration levels (table 1) reflect both the capital and running costs of electric wash boilers at this time.

The limited acceptance of electrical appliances among middle-class women can be understood in terms of their need to alleviate the domestic servant problem, rising standards of home and child care, and their preference for home laundry. These factors, however, were not the whole story. The development of the market for domestic electric technology was bounded by the existence of viable substitutes in the form of gas and solid fuel and by more pressing, nongendered claims on family income. Therefore, according to the Electrical Development Association, it was "necessary to create, in the face of keen competition, demand for the service provided, and this can only be done by making known by every possible form of publicity, the advantages electricity offers over other methods of light, heat and power."[83]

ADVERTISING

Since, in the view of the industry, "people could exist without electricity . . . it had to be sold."[84] In order to create a climate of consumption, to change the perception that electric appliances were luxuries rather than necessities, and to persuade women of the advantages of ownership, the electrical industry embarked on advertising campaigns designed to educate women on the advantages of its products. To this end, the Electrical Development Association was formed in 1919; its main objectives were the education of consumers and the promotion and development of applications of and, therefore, demand for electrical energy. Although it was also involved in questions of design and safety, which had some bearing on public relations, and to this end lobbied trade bodies (notably architects, builders, supply authorities, and manufacturers), its main activities lay in publicity campaigns, which involved providing lecture courses, liaising with schools, holding exhibitions, and organizing press advertising. Press advertising was seen to be the most effective mechanism and was particularly favored by the Electrical Development Association: "You don't buy space in a newspaper, you buy circulation and influence."[85]

Press advertising focused on three specific areas of the "domestic servant" problem, all of which struck a chord in contemporary middle- and upper-class concerns. First, advertising claimed that a servant who used an electric appliance would be far more productive than her unmechanized counterpart. Household technology was described as easing the transition from the live-in to the "daily."[86] Second, the industry implied that servants would rather work in a household that offered electric technology than one that did not. Third, electric appliances were less trouble than servants—they did not require time off or decent wages.[87]

A recurrent theme in advertising was the claim that electrical appliances helped a woman become a better housewife. The electricity industry saw four marketable features of electric technology: its potential to reduce the hard physical work involved in many areas of housework, its potential to reallocate time to the "caring" aspects of housewifery, its potential to raise standards of cleanliness, and its ability to reduce dependency on paid help in the home. The industry played up the extent to which electric technology could reduce the toil of given tasks. "Cut the work out of housework—use electricity," "Electricity—the light that lightens labor." Such slogans abounded in the advertising claims of the time.[88] The emphasis on time saved is less interesting than the explicit assumptions as to how that time might be used. "Use the electric vacuum and you will not fear the sunshine" and "It revolutionizes the day to day routine of [the home's] management" were two widely used slogans at the time.[89]

Time saved via the use of electric appliances could be put to the more "caring" aspects of housewifery: "With this new leisure from purely household tasks . . . the more efficient the methods she employs, the bigger the chance has she of being 'a model mother' in every sense of the word."[90] With this type of advertising, the industry invoked and contributed to the ideology of the perfect mother, increasing the expectations for and consequent responsibilities of child care and confirming the belief that a woman's place was in the home.[91]

The industry also linked its products to concerns about health and hygiene. By the interwar period, dust had been linked with disease in the popular, if not the scientific, mind, and the preoccupation with cleaning reached obsessive levels in the contemporary media. The claim that electrical appliances would make the home "germ free" was never made explicitly by the industry. It was made in the popular media. In the popular press, dust was depicted as a direct cause of illness: "Where there's dust there's danger. . . . dust is one of the greatest evils. Every particle of it may support a cargo of disease germs."[92]

Personal and domestic cleanliness, together with the strict ordering of the household, had emerged in the nineteenth century as important ways of "marking the middle class off from those below them" and were "part of the parcel of behavior and attitudes bundled together in that imprecise but vital concept, respectability."[93] Such middle-class "virtues" were emulated by working-class women.[94] In the interwar years, standards for acceptable home care rose, and part of the attraction of electric consumer durables thus lay in their potential to help middle-class women, at a time of decreased availability of domestic help, to realize the new standards of cleanliness.[95] The electrical industry, by emphasizing in its advertising the ability of its products to achieve high levels of cleanliness, not only catered to a concerned audience but also contributed to the obsession with cleanliness in the period.

For most of the period, press advertising was concentrated in local newspapers and in middle-class-women's magazines. The only national newspapers regularly used were the *Daily Mail*, the *Daily Express*, and the *Financial Times* (winning over the male householder was obviously given high priority by the industry, since women could not sign hire-purchase agreements at this time).[96] *Good Housekeeping, Woman and Home, Home and Gardens,* and *Ideal Home* were the favored magazine outlets for advertisements.[97] Electricity advertising was not taken out in the popular weeklies read by lower-class women in the 1920s. By contrast, the gas industry made a strong commitment to advertising, as even a cursory reading of the relevant weeklies read by working-class women in the 1930s demonstrates. Nearly every issue had at least one advertisement for gas appliances—frequently in a prominent position of the magazine, for example, the inside front cover. If lower-income housewives were being urged to use a labor-saving appliance, it was the modern gas appliance. Working-class women, at least until the middle of the 1930s, were to all intents and purposes ignored by the Electrical Development Association.

The electricity industry's advertisements not only influenced consumers but also resulted in "more ready co-operation of the editorial and reporting staff for insertion of electrical news."[98] This cooperation is demonstrated in the case of a local daily, the *Walthamstow Mercury and Post,* where regular articles that referred to electricity appeared in the women's section of the paper. For example, an article on germ control in the paper claimed: "The greatest safeguard is to keep the house . . . so clean that it offers no inducement to the fly as a breeding ground. . . . the home is not only cleaner but also healthier where electricity is used for every purpose to which its use can be adopted."[99]

Time saved was thus depicted not as time released for leisure or paid employment but as time well spent on achieving higher standards of cleanliness in the home. Again the message confirmed social norms that a "proper" wife and mother was to be found doing housework at home. A model middle-class housewife could achieve such objectives if armed with a variety of domestic electrical appliances. Whether she was to do all the work herself or to receive some form of paid help is less clear in the advertisements. Although washing machines and vacuum cleaners were frequently referred to as domestic servants in advertising campaigns, the industry was careful not to claim a capital investment in an appliance would or could completely replace labor. Advertisements often featured a servant using an appliance.

The electricity industry also held lectures and demonstrations. Those held by the Electrical Development Association reached a limited audience. In Manchester, for example, about two hundred invitations were usually sent out, and the average attendance normally amounted to between forty and fifty people.[100] Lectures moreover were concentrated in the Home Counties (around the capital) and were directed to trade and professional bodies. In 1934, twenty-six lectures were given to women's organizations, but sixty-two were given to trade and professional bodies. The pressure to educate working-class women in the benefits of electricity came from the Electrical Association for Women (EAW), which, in 1934, declared that its purpose was to bring electricity into the homes of ordinary women, and the resolution was followed up by an exhibition at its headquarters in London.[101] Local EAW groups were effectively social clubs for middle-class women—at least if the activities of the Hull branch are representative. The Hull program was dominated by social events, such as visits to places of interest and whist and bridge parties, events for which working-class women would have had neither the time nor the inclination.[102]

The EAW also produced literature in which estimates were made of family budgets and the costs of running appliances. The tone was optimistic, and the estimates assumed the cooperation of supply authorities and housing departments in reducing tariffs, installing full electric wiring, and offering hire and hire-purchase schemes on reasonable terms—somewhat unrealistic assumptions. This literature, however, was not widely publicized. Although it received some mention in the weekly and monthly journals, there was no mass publication of the details. The publicity campaign was ineffective in the absence of advertising and public lectures aimed at working-class women. Nor could the publicity campaign overcome budget constraints or the higher priorities given to leisure goods and nongendered durable and semi-durable goods in household expenditure patterns.

CONCLUSION

The demand for electric durables among the middle classes was based on the perceived ability of the appliances not only to alleviate the domestic servant problem but also to permit middle-class women to become "better" housewives, to permit them to do the work their grandmothers and mothers would have delegated to servants. Ironically, the true significance of electrical goods may therefore lie in their contribution to a certain equalization between the classes in the interwar period, one that came about not because working-class women did less housework but because middle-class housewives did more. Electric appliances helped to confine middle-class women in the home and to reallocate to them work the previous generation would never have done. The final irony was that middle-class women acquired electric

appliances but rarely used them, whereas working-class women did not acquire them but used them in their capacity as part-time and casual servants
in middle-class homes.

NOTES

1. Quote from Margery Spring Rice, *Working-Class Wives* (London, 1939), 94. Contemporary accounts that confirm this picture may be found in Elizabeth Roberts, *A
Woman's Place: An Oral History of Working-Class Women, 1890–1940* (Oxford, 1984),
chap. 4; Margaret Llewelyn Davies, *Maternity: Letters from Working Women* (London,
1915); and Maud Pember Reeves, *Round About a Pound a Week* (London, 1913).

2. Patricia Branca, *Silent Sisterhood: Middle-Class Women in the Victorian Home* (London, 1977); Jane Lewis, *Women in England, 1870–1950* (Brighton, 1984), 156.

3. Graham Thomas and Christine Zmroczek, "Household Technology: The Liberation of Women from the Home?" in *Family and Economy in Modern Society*, ed. Paul
Close and Rosemary Collins (Houndmills, U.K., 1985), 104–5.

4. See Caroline Davidson, *A Woman's Work Is Never Done: A History of Housework in
the British Isles, 1650–1950* (London, 1982), 163; Christina Hardyment, *From Mangle to
Microwave: The Mechanization of Household Work* (New York, 1988), 74; Judy Wajcman,
Feminism Confronts Technology (Oxford, 1991), 98.

5. Sue Bowden and Avner Offer, "Household Appliances and the Use of Time:
The United States and Britain since the 1920s," *Economic History Review* 47, no. 4 (November 1994), table AI, 745–46.

6. Angus S. Deaton, "The Structure of Demand, 1920–1970," in *The Fontana Economic History of Europe: The Twentieth Century, Part One*, ed. Carlo M. Cipolla (Glasgow,
1976), 121; Hendrick S. Houtthaker and Lester D. Taylor, *Consumer Demand in the
United States: Analyses and Projections*, 2d ed. (Cambridge, Mass., 1970); F. Knox, "Some
International Comparisons of Consumers' Durable Goods," *Bulletin of the Oxford University Institute of Statistics* 21, no. 1 (February 1959): 31–38; F. G. Pyatt, *Priority Patterns and the Demand for Household Durable Goods* (Cambridge, 1964), 1–10; Paul Stone-
man, *The Economic Analysis of Technological Change* (Oxford, 1983), 69–73.

7. R. E. Catterall, "Electrical Engineering," in *British Industry between the Wars: Instability and Industrial Development, 1919–1939*, ed. Neil K. Buxton and Derek H. Ald-
croft (London, 1979), chap. 9; Leslie Hannah, "A Pioneer of Public Enterprise: The
Central Electricity Board and the National Grid," in *Essays in British Business History*,
ed. Barry Supple (Oxford, 1977), chap. 11; Leslie Hannah, *Electricity before Nationalisation: A Study of the Development of Electricity Supply in Britain to 1948* (London, 1978).

8. Alan Jackson, *The Middle Classes, 1900–1950* (Nairn, Scotland, 1991); Philip
Massey, "The Expenditure of 1,360 British Middle-Class Households in 1938–1939,"
Journal of the Royal Statistical Society, 105, pt. 3 (1942): 159–85.

9. A. D. Bain, *The Growth of Television Ownership in the U.K.* (Cambridge, 1964);
G. J. Stigler and Gary S. Becker, "De gustibus non est disputandum," *American Economic Review* 67 (1977): 76–90.

10. Bain, *Television Ownership*, 14.

11. Martha L. Olney, *Buy Now, Pay Later: Advertising, Credit, and Consumer Durables*

in the 1920s (Chapel Hill, N.C., 1991); Sue Bowden, "Credit Facilities and the Growth of Consumer Demand for Electric Appliances in England in the 1930s," *Business History* 32, no. 1 (January 1990): 52–75; idem, "Demand and Supply Constraints in the Interwar U.K. Car Industry: Did the Manufacturers Get It Right?" *Business History* 33, no. 2 (April 1991): 241–67.

12. Gary S. Becker, "A Theory of the Allocation of Time," *The Economic Journal* 75, no. 299 (September 1965): 493–517; W. K. Bryant, *The Economic Organisation of the Household* (Cambridge, 1990).

13. K. P. Corfman, D. R. Lehmann, and S. Narayanan, "Values, Utility and Ownership: Modelling the Relationships for Consumer Durables," *Journal of Retailing* 67 (1991): 184–204.

14. Bowden and Offer, "Household Appliances."

15. Ruth Schwartz Cowan, *More Work for Mother: The Ironies of Household Technology from the Open Hearth to the Microwave* (New York, 1983); Davidson, *Never Done;* Miriam Glucksmann, *Women Assemble: Women Workers and the New Industries in Interwar Britain* (London, 1990); Hardyment, *Mangle;* Susan Strasser, *Never Done: A History of American Housework* (New York, 1982); Wajcman, *Feminism.*

16. Bowden and Offer, "Household Appliances," table 1, 729.

17. Data for ownership levels in the 1920s are not available.

18. Bowden and Offer, "Household Appliances," fig. 2, 731.

19. Ibid., table 1, 729.

20. Ibid., 728–32.

21. Sue Bowden, "The Technological Revolution That Never Was: Women and Domestic Electrical Appliances in England during the Interwar Period" (Business and Economic Studies, University of Leeds, 1987, mimeographed).

22. Sylvia Walby, *Theorising Patriarchy* (Oxford, 1990), 29–40.

23. Pat Ayers, "The Hidden Economy of Dockland Families: Liverpool in the 1930s," in *Women's Work and the Family Economy in Historical Perspective,* ed. Pat Hudson and W. R. Lee (Manchester, U.K., 1990), 271–90; Roberts, *Woman's Place;* Elizabeth Roberts, "Women's Strategies, 1890–1940," in *Labor and Love: Women's Experience of Home and Family, 1850–1940,* ed. Jane Lewis (Oxford, 1986), 223–47.

24. George Joseph, *Women at Work: The British Experience* (Oxford, 1983), 126–27; A. T. Mallier and M. J. Rosser, *Women and the Economy: A Comparative Study of Britain and the U.S.A.* (London, 1987), 47; Nick Von Tunzelmann, "Britain 1900–1945: A Survey," in *The Economic History of Britain since 1700,* ed. Roderick Floud and Donald McCloskey (Cambridge, U.K., 1981), 2:242.

25. Sue Bowden, "The Consumer Durables Revolution in England, 1932–1938: A Regional Analysis," *Explorations in Economic History* 25, no. 1 (January 1988): 42–59; Bowden, "Credit Facilities," 52–75.

26. Catterall, "Electrical Engineering," 244–45; Hannah, "Pioneer," 210–11, 216.

27. Bowden and Offer, "Household Appliances," table AI, 745–46.

28. Hannah, *Electricity,* 192.

29. Sue Bowden and Paul Turner, "Some Cross Section Evidence on the Determinants of the Diffusion of Car Ownership in the Interwar U.K. Economy," *Business History* 35, no. 1 (January 1993): 55–69.

30. Hannah, *Electricity,* 187.

31. *Epitome of Proceedings* (25 July 1935), Manchester City Council, MS 352.042.M12, no. 132, Local History Archive, Manchester City Archive, Manchester, U.K.

32. Minutes of the Hull Electricity Committee, 21 February 1933, Local Studies Library, Hull, England; Minutes of the Electricity Committee, 17 July 1928, item no. 10, Minutes of the Electricity Committee, 1929–1939, Bath City Council, Bath City Council Archive Department, Bath, England.

33. Political and Economic Planning, *The Market for Household Appliances* (London, 1945), xxix, xxxii, 54, 100, and 105.

34. *Electrical Trading*, March 1936, 60, Science Reference Library, British Library.

35. Crowther Committee, *Consumer Credit* (London, 1971), vol. 1, Cmnd. 4596, p. 42, par. 2.1.39, and p. 43, par. 2.1.42.

36. Electricity Commissioners, *14th Annual Report* (1934), Electricity Council Archive, London.

37. Prior to nationalization, electricity supply was provided at a local level by private and local-authority undertakings. Just before World War II, there were about 650 undertakings in England and Wales.

38. Electrical Association for Women, *Electrical Age*, March 1923, 39, Electrical Association for Women, London.

39. Ministry of Labour, "Weekly Expenditure of Working-Class Households in the United Kingdom, 1937–1938," *Ministry of Labour Gazette* 48, no. 12 (December 1940): 305.

40. Assuming there was no weekly charge for assisted wiring, which averaged £0.020 a week. Sue Bowden, "The Market for Domestic Electric Cookers in the 1930s: A Regional Analysis" (Ph.D. diss., University of London, 1985), 254–60 and 259, table 107.

41. T. I. Williams, *A History of the British Gas Industry* (Oxford, 1981), 68.

42. Bowden, *Consumer Durables*, 49.

43. Political and Economic Planning, *Report on the Gas Industry in Great Britain* (London, March 1939), 5.

44. British Electrical and Allied Industries Research Association, *A Large Scale Sampling Survey of Domestic Consumers: Technical Report K/T125a* (London, 1948), 9, table 1, Electricity Council Archive, London.

45. Ibid., 10, table 3.

46. P. G. Gray, *The Social Survey: Domestic Heating* (London, 1955), 4–8, Central Office of Information, Electricity Council Archive.

47. Building Research Board of the Department of Scientific and Industrial Research, *Heating and Ventilation of Dwellings*, Postwar Building Studies no. 9 (London, 1945), 151, table 18; 153, table 19A; and 154, table 21.

48. Gray, *Social Survey*, 4, 11.

49. Joint Committee of the House of Lords and House of Commons on Gas Prices, Report together with Proceedings of the Committee and Minutes of Evidence, 21 April 1937, par. 16.

50. Richard Stone and D. A. Rowe, *The Measurement of Consumers' Expenditure and Behaviour in the United Kingdom, 1920–1938* (Cambridge, 1966), 2:26, table 12.

51. W. F. F. Kemsley and David Ginsburg, *The Social Survey: Expenditure on Household Textiles, Furnishing Fabrics, Repairs to Household Articles, and the Making Up of Materials* (London, 1949), 4, table 2, Central Office of Information.

52. Elizabeth Wilson and Lou Taylor, *Through the Looking Glass: A History of Dress from 1860 to the Present Day* (London, 1989), 95–105.

53. Wilson and Taylor, *Looking Glass*, 95–96.

54. Stone and Rowe, *Measurement*, 5, tables 1 and 2; and 13, table 6.

55. John Boyd Orr, *Food, Health, and Income: Report on a Survey of Adequacy of Diet in Relation to Income* (London, 1937), 24, table 2.

56. Jackson, *Middle Classes*, 298–309; Stephen G. Jones, *Workers at Play: A Social and Economic History of Leisure, 1918–1939* (London, 1986).

57. Jeffrey Richards, *The Age of the Dream Palace: Cinema and Society in Britain, 1930–1939* (London, 1984), 18.

58. Stone and Rowe, *Measurement*, 91, table 36; 110, table 45.

59. Hugh Cunningham, "Leisure and Culture," in *The Cambridge Social History of Britain, 1750–1950*, ed. F. M. L. Thompson (Cambridge, U.K., 1990), 2:317.

60. Spring Rice, *Working-Class Wives*, 99.

61. Ibid., 103.

62. Political and Economic Planning, *Report on Gas.*

63. Jackson, *Middle Classes*, 336–37. Jackson reports similar increases for bank clerks (from an average of £280 to an average of £368) and for commercial clerks (from an average of £182 to an average of £192). Ibid.

64. Massey, "Expenditure," 159–85.

65. C. Weid, "Selling to the Artisan Consumer," *Electrical Industries*, February 1939, 57–65, Science Reference Library, British Library.

66. Roberts, *Woman's Place*, 137.

67. S. J. Kleinberg, "Escalating Standards: Women, Housework, and Household Technology in the Twentieth Century," in *Technology in the Twentieth Century*, ed. Frank J. Coppa and Richard Harmond (Dubuque, Iowa, 1983), 9; Lewis, *Women in England*, 156.

68. Lewis, *Women in England*, 156.

69. John Burnett, *A Social History of Housing, 1815–1970* (Newton Abbott, U.K., 1978), 258.

70. Ibid.

71. Hardyment, *Mangle*, 38.

72. Massey, "Expenditure," 181–85

73. Roberts, *Women's Strategies*, 236; idem, *Woman's Place*, 136.

74. Veronica Beechey and Tessa Perkins, *A Matter of Hours: Women, Part-Time Work, and the Labor Market* (Oxford, 1987).

75. Davidson, *Never Done*, 136; Hardyment, *Mangle*, 10, 56.

76. Davidson, *Never Done*, p. 163.

77. On the rarity of the use of commercial laundries, see Davidson, *Never Done*, 163. On the preference for home laundry, see W. F. F. Kemsley and David Ginsburg, *The Social Survey: Consumer Expenditure on Laundries, Dyeing and Cleaning, Mending and Alterations, and Shoe Repairing Services* (London, 1949), 3–6, Central Office of Information, British Library of Political and Economic Science, London.

78. Kemsley and Ginsburg, *Laundries*, 18, table 19.

79. Ibid., 19, table 20.

80. Hardyment, *Mangle*, 74.

81. Davidson, *Never Done*, 163.

82. Wajcman, *Feminism*, 98.

83. G. A. Proctor, "The Basis and Methods of Electricity Supply Advertising in a Large Town" (paper read at the Electricity Supply Sales Management Conference, Electrical Development Association, Electricity Council Intelligence Service, London, 25 March 1935).

84. Alex C. Cramb, "Sales Organisations of Various Kinds" (paper read at the Electricity Supply Sales Management Conference, Electrical Development Association, Electricity Council Intelligence Section, London, 8 February 1934).

85. S. G. Pike, "Functions of Different Media" (paper read at the Electricity Supply Sales Management Conference, Electrical Development Association, Electricity Council Intelligence Section, London, 8 February 1934).

86. Hardyment, *Mangle*, 113.

87. Kleinberg, *Standards*, 9.

88. Electrical Association for Women, *Electrical Age*, March 1923, Electrical Association for Women, London.

89. Electricity Development Association, *Third Annual Report*, March 1923, Electricity Council Intelligence Section, London; idem, *Fifth Annual Report*, 1925, 15, Electricity Council Intelligence Section, London.

90. Electrical Development Association, *Fifth Annual Report*, Electricity Council Intelligence Section, London.

91. Kleinberg, *Standards*, 10–12.

92. V. E. Bennett, "Homes That House Health," *Walthamstow Mercury and Post*, July 1935, Walthamstow Local History Library.

93. Leonore Davidoff, "The Rationalisation of Housework," in *Dependence and Exploitation in Work and Marriage*, ed. Diana Leonard Barker and Sheila Allen (London, 1976), 9, 27.

94. Alison Ravetz, "Modern Technology and an Ancient Occupation: Housework in Present-Day Society," *Technology and Culture* 6, no. 2 (1965): 256–60.

95. Kleinberg, *Standards*, 10–11.

96. Most families in the United Kingdom in the interwar years took at least one morning paper (the middle classes often took two) and one Sunday paper (some households took two or more). In addition, about half of all households took an evening paper. The *Financial Times* was very much the morning paper of the businessman; the *Daily Mail* and the *Daily Express* were favored by middle-class women. The *Express* was the first to reach a circulation of two million. Noreen Branson and Margot Heinemann, *Britain in the Nineteen Thirties* (St. Albans, England, 1973), 272; Jackson, *Middle Classes*, 279–80.

97. Electrical Development Association, *Ninth Annual Report*, March 1929, 20, Electricity Council Intelligence Section, London. In the 1920s, there was a great expansion in magazines aimed at the middle-class woman. *Ideal Home*, launched in 1920, portrayed quality middle-class homes; *Vogue*, launched in 1916, concentrated on fashion and was aimed at the upper- and middle-class market. *Woman and Home*, launched in 1926, and *Homes and Gardens*, launched in 1916, also reflected the lives of the wealthier middle class. The circulation of these magazines extended to most middle-class women. Nicola Beauman, *A Very Great Profession: The Woman's Novel, 1914–1939*

(London, 1983), 109; Deirdre Beddoe, *Back to Home and Duty: Women between the Wars, 1918–1939* (London, 1989), 14; Jackson, *Middle Classes*, 116–17.

98. Proctor, "Basis."

99. Bennett, "Homes That House Health."

100. Proctor, "Basis."

101. Electrical Association for Women, *Ninth Annual Report,* 31 December 1934, NAEST/33/2.2, p. 26, Institute of Electrical Engineers, London; Electrical Association for Women, *Tenth Annual Report,* 10 May 1935, NAEST/33/2.2, p. 15, Institute of Electrical Engineers, London.

102. *Electra,* 1934 and 1935, L352.91, Hull Local Studies Library, Hull, England.

PART THREE

Empowering Women as Citizen-Consumers

Much of the feminist discussion about women in consumer societies pivots around the question of whether women have been empowered by access to the goods, sites, spectacles, and services associated with mass consumption. Two lines of argument are advanced to support the view that they have been. One is basically historical, built on observations of the effects of expanding consumption. This argument holds that the invention of the department store and other centralized institutions of shopping brought women into downtown commercial districts and other spaces from which their semicloistered domesticity, as well as their lack of civil liberties, had previously excluded them.[1] In addition, consumer movements were initially largely women-oriented; poor women were at the forefront of food riots, socialist women backed consumer cooperatives, and middle-class women reformers promoted consumer legislation.[2]

The second line of reasoning moves from a general observation about the interplay between modern political and mass communication systems and commodity flows. From the vantage point of postcolonial cultural studies, especially, it has been argued that new kinds of public-commercial spaces and means of communication, by fragmenting the class-based social and political formations of bourgeois society—largely oriented to including (and excluding) male citizens and based on mobilizing men—opened the way for voices outside of the centralized and patriarchal systems of rule traditional in Western societies.[3]

The premise behind both arguments appears to be that commodity forms and market-driven networks of communication and sociability can yield a voice to subjects, specifically women, who have been disempowered by economic inequality, exclusion from democratic processes, and social and cultural discrimination. Yet those who make these arguments would not deny that patriarchal power has been unceasingly inventive in reappropriating emancipatory spaces, so that today's flaunted freedom, tomorrow, could be turned into some new form of degradation. There is no dearth of examples. The bus and subway campaign for Virginia Slims cigarettes dating from the 1970s provides one of my favorites, not just because the posters relentlessly exhibited procaciously postured, worldly-wise young women but also because the advertiser's slogan "You've come a long way, Baby" begged for comment, which somebody would occasionally supply by scrawling "yeh, baby, from a cunt to a cunt" or graffiti to similar effect.[4] In the face of this dialectic of expression/repression, questions linger: What is opposition? What is empowerment?

These queries can be reformulated as a broader question, namely, what is the relationship of what has more recently been characterized as "identity politics"—the "performance" of gender and other differences—to politics intended as collective action? Numerous acts that feminists might characterize as transgressive—from the famous bobbed hair and silk stockings of 1920s flappers and the bright-hued Sunday dresses worn by girls in traditional communities to defy the conventional mourning black to the burned bras of the sixties and the butch gear of 1980s lesbian subculture—hardly look forceful or meaningful enough to bear the weight of the main issues that need to be addressed: What kinds of collective and political identity does individual acquisitiveness give rise to? Can demands for entitlement based on consumer demands coexist with the class-based solidaristic demands that historically have yielded movements on behalf of social reform and political justice, in the interest of women as well as men? Is there a distinctively feminist politics of consumption, even if only one of style?

In answer, not a lot of help is to be had from traditional social scientific study of the impact of mass consumption on collective action. Basically, we are confronted with two kinds of interpretations. One is associated with the Marxian critique of capitalist society, the other with liberal political theory. The former is relatively familiar to feminists, in the form of the New Left's refashioning of interwar German critical theory. This critique sustains that goods are the bearer of false consciousness; commodity fetishism occludes the nature of human exploitation, and the "society of spectacle," to recall Guy Debord's term, which is in effect the highest stage of commodification, so transmogrifies the nature of human social interactions that radical social movement is preempted.[5] Even the optimists in this tradition, who believe that more leisure and higher standards of living will lead to more egalitarianism and individual freedom, anxiously equivocate as to whether these activities won't permit greater ideological manipulation and seduce people from some alternative better social relations.

Liberal theory is no less generic about the significance of mass consumption for political action. The most optimistic construction put on mass consumption is that it was the condition for building the United States' centrist political democracy. For historians, the connections are clear: Americans became a "people of plenty," to recall David Potter's history from the perspective of the Pax Americana of the mid-1950s.[6] In that context, as another much-cited U.S. historian, Daniel Boorstin, wrote, "communities of consumption" arose, crisscrossing class and territory and thereby dulling the radical ideologies, both left- and right-wing, that had hitherto been nurtured by traditional class and sectoral interests.[7]

For political theorists, the connections between plenty and political quiescence are not so obvious. If Adam Smith's image of man as eternally disquiet in his desires is taken seriously, mass consumption, not to mention any significant change in consumption regimes, can just as easily lead to discontent as to satisfaction. Consumer choices, like all others, involve passions as well as interests, to recall Albert Hirschman's famous phrase. Goods whet the appetite for more, choices engender rancor and disappointment, and satiation produces social unhappiness, at times outright protest.[8] This basically essentialist view of human behavior as ever questing has the virtue of allowing that a materially satisfied society could generate protest as much as one in which there is scarcity. From this perspective, political scientists have probed the wave of protest throughout the West in the late 1960s, attributing it to postmaterialist demands oriented to issues of identity and quality of life.[9] By the same token, it can be argued that in Eastern Europe frustrated consumerist desires brought down the Soviet empire. But the model of social behavior behind this analysis, that collectivities behave like individuals in the boundlessness of their appetites, is extrapolated from a behaviorally primitive model according to which wants are basically insatiable. The notion that needs, rights, and entitlements might be contingent on specific historical circumstances is undeveloped, as is any sustained consideration of the symbolic or communicative powers of particular goods.

With good reason then, given that the issues at stake are so large and the guiding concepts still so elusive, the essays in this section are tentative about defining what protest, much less empowerment, through acts of consumption means, coming to a more or less common conclusion that the relationship of consumption to citizenship and more generally to collective identities is a complex one, not least because the relationship has not yet been adequately conceptualized. For the moment, what historians can do, is what they do best, namely, establish the sometimes elusive connections between the fast-paced commercial-consumer sphere and new forms of gendered citizenship within specific constellations of time and place.

From that perspective, the case studied by Belinda Davis is the least equivocal. Her subjects, largely the middle- and working-class women of war-starved Berlin, milling about in the streets to protest food shortages, engaged in what by all definitions was meaningful collective action. This movement,

278   VICTORIA DE GRAZIA

though it did not include only women, was portrayed by the police and interpreted by public officials as instigated by female consumers. That it succeeded in delegitimizing Wilhelm II's militaristic regime was not only because of its disorderly presence in the streets but also because it revealed the
imperial system's patriarchal conservativism as deeply flawed in its incapacity to deliver food to the home front. Pressure from this female-consumer
home front thus generated a new notion of sovereignty that implicitly embraced women and recognized citizens' rights to basic necessities, a notion
that the Second Empire's successors, the Weimar Republic and Hitler's Third
Reich, would ignore at their own risk. Nonetheless, to conclude that women
were empowered as result of the fact that females were at the head of the
crowd in the disorders would be debatable, given that the systems of consumer entitlement enacted after World War I did nothing to redress male-
female inequality.

The results of the other cases are even more ambiguous. Kathy Peiss finds
that in the fast-changing U.S. society of the first half of the century, the significance of cosmetics was multivalent. The products themselves were devices
in a flamboyant, often anxious, politics of self-expression, and the industries
that created and manufactured them, when owned by women, earned power
and autonomy for their enterprising heads, not to mention some tidy profits. One conclusion is absolutely clear, that cosmetics are utterly misconstrued
if they are regarded merely as instruments of patriarchal oppression.

My essay on the competition between fascist and commercial cultural
models of femininity also suggests the ambiguity of women's relationship to
commercial culture, this time under an authoritarian regime, the Duce's fascism, that pretended to a total command over culture and commodities. The
most that can be said is that the sites, themes, and wares of commercial culture comprised a public space differently natured from that ruled by fascist
spectacle. Even though the messages of commercial culture were troubling
to the regime, to be a consumer or spectator hardly constituted resistance,
though it did perhaps yield alternative notions of self and social ties. Erica
Carter moves this argument some steps further to suggest that when reconstructed West Germany began to make strategic choices aimed at the development of consumer democracy in the late 1940s, conservative antennae
were far extended to probe whether full-fledged female participation in consumer society would be healthy or noxious. Through the early 1950s, at least,
official and commercial images of societal abundance went hand in hand
with images enjoining self-restraint on the part of women. This mixed message was sharply conveyed in cinematic representation of gender conflicts
over modern lifestyles, particularly in the melodrama designed for female
audiences. Finally, Rachel Bowlby, a cultural critic, underscores that feminist criticism, notwithstanding its sensitivity to the problematic of consumption, may itself run the risk of being seduced by consumption's allure.

In the very effort to do justice to the equivocality and paradoxes of meaning of mass consumption, the scholarship represented here has clearly moved beyond the Manichaean view that divides the world of goods into things that are either manipulative or emancipatory. The point is rather that in the modern period, the turnover and sheer quantity and variety of consumption practices continuously disrupt conventional boundaries of all kinds, challenging received notions of sovereignty, customary identities, and familial authority—as well as the conventional distinctions between private and public. If it seems plausible to hypothesize that this disruption has proven emancipatory, it is because these boundaries, if not originally designed to exercise patriarchal power over female subjects, have often perpetuated it.

Still, we know enough about the communicative and symbolic character of acts of consumption to move beyond simply contending that goods empower or disempower according to circumstances to ask more meaningful questions about the ways in which different consumption regimes are produced by, support, and even undermine varying political systems. Put another way, processes of forming identities through acts of consumption need to be related to definitions of the rights and obligations of citizenship under particular regimes of power: whether, for example, the regimes recognize the right to consume, and, if so, with what scope and under what "signs." If, for example, the well-to-do Italian woman flaunts a Parisian-made feather boa in xenophobic fascist Italy, does this gesture have a different significance when performed by a Parisian bourgeoise under the left-wing Popular Front or by a New York society grande dame under the New Deal? Does desiring to purchase a vacuum cleaner have the same valence for women consumers if it is purchased in deeply class-stratified society, where it is a luxury item, as opposed to a society with diminishing class differences, in which the machine is merely one in the normal cluster of household fittings? If social consumption by the welfare state is ample—that is, if the state provides ample provisions in the form of education, social security, subsidized housing, or health benefits—do not the private purchases of the household acquire a different cultural meaning and political valence? In sum, historians of consumer society still have a formidable task before them: to link particular acts of consumption to collective patterns and to examine these within the broader play of needs, expectations, and entitlements specific to different societies.

The differences of development between the United States and Europe, understood in this volume as Western Europe, are in this sense ultrasignificant. In the United States it was relatively early that what we might call in shorthand "the consumption sphere" began to compete with the political sphere as a major locus of social identities and demands for entitlement. Starting as early as the 1880s, giant corporations began to organize the market, developing highly articulated distribution systems oriented to a far-flung, rapidly growing, and ethnically diverse population. By the first decade of the century, reform-minded observers had spoken of mass consumption as providing "the new basis of civilization."[10] Cheap goods (obtained through the exploitation of a fast-growing, informal empire but especially through standardized manufacture, the market for which was a rapidly growing, decently paid workforce) were conceived as operating as a formidable mechanism of social integration. By the 1920s, at the same time that the political sphere was expanded to include many of the have-nots of liberal societies, including women and workers, the consumer sphere—greatly expanded by commercial cultural goods, for example, the radio and cinema, as well as consumer durables—promised an altogether different and more variegated mode of social integration around a broad middle class standard. Mass consumption also promoted a wholly new sense of the relationship of private to public, separating intimacy and personhood from the domestic sphere.

Subsequently, as historians have since observed, class-based demands gave way before new pressures for entitlement from broad middle- or "one-class" communities of consumption: whether consumption actually caused class identities to disintegrate thereby obliterating class-based organizations or just enabled them to be rearticulated so as to voice grievances more broadly across an ethnically divided working class is still much debated.[11] The important point here is that mass consumption promised to overcome class-based political cleavages by advancing the idea that individuals, even entire peoples, could mount a new kind of social claim, that to well-being. The American "civilization of customs," to recall how an Italian observer of the 1930s interpreted the famed U.S. standard of living (as it was projected through the cinema), stood for the "new rights of mankind," meaning the "right to a comfortable existence," "to be young, elegant, well-dressed, and to aspire to be ever more so."[12]

In this phase of development, the space of commercial culture, previously associated with the bourgeois department store and center-city shopping districts, was greatly expanded by the revolution in communications associated with the radio and cinema, so much so that it attracted a new public that was both mass and distinctively female. Unlike, say, producers of mass-market fiction, which was designed for individual consumption in private spaces, silent-movie producers and exhibitors catered to female audiences as "the subject of collective reception and public interaction."[13] This was a deeply ambivalent project, to be sure. Profit making was often at odds with patriarchal wisdom as cinema producers both recognized and absorbed female discourses. Accordingly, as women's increased importance as consumers eroded the hierarchical segregation of private and public, cinema producers sought to impose masculine forms of vision. The experiences that gave an extraordinary resonance to female subjectivity thus may also have operated as strategies for its containment. The point is that female spectatorship, which the film historian Miriam Hansen describes as forming a "feminine public sphere," had become a significant cultural sounding board, if not a social interlocutor.

At the same time, mass consumer message-makers (including manufacturers, advertisers, and advice columnists), for all of their professions of devotion to domesticity and family values, detached female consumption from its earlier identification with the home. In time, the meaning not only of domesticity but also of consumption itself was thereby fundamentally transformed. Consumer durables, together with the rise of experts outside of the home, modified household labor: the homemakers' skills, honed with advice literature, displaced the prideful craft of the housewife.[14] The growing permeability of the household to consumer culture may not have been incompatible with a growing sense of intimacy and self. It may indeed have been a source of greater self- and social confidence that the home was not cut off from but fully confluent with the mainstream of commercial relations.

More generally, the consolidation of the consumer sphere greatly contributed to what Nancy Cott, in a compelling generalization from the experience of U.S. feminists after the Great War, has identified as a "widespread 'disremembering'" of the goals of early-twentieth-century feminism.[15] On the one hand, citizenship, understood in political terms as suffrage, had not significantly empowered women. At the same time it was becoming ever more anachronistic to conceive of feminist reform in terms of old notions of sexual difference, like that which advanced women's claims to power in society by virtue of their reproductive capacities, and under the banner of "social motherhood," organized about the axis household-state and across the continuum between private and public. On the other hand, mass consumption generated what has since been characterized as "life-style feminism."[16] Which is to say, it promoted those values of personal independence, female self-assertiveness, and individual fulfillment that had in some measure been advanced by the early-twentieth-century feminist movement itself, with the overriding goal of empowering women as the equals of men through the political process.

This is the backdrop against which Kathy Peiss examines the modern American use of cosmetics. In the nineteenth century, adopting a physiognomic paradigm—that external appearance and internal self were commensurate—middle-class Americans idealized a so-called natural, unadorned face for women, a face in which beauty and moral goodness were transparently revealed. By the early twentieth century, a mass cosmetics trade, supported by advertising, women's magazines, and the "advice" industry, shifted the burden of female identity from this essential, interior self to one formed through marking and tinting the face. Makeup was to contribute to the constitution of women's identity, no longer to its falsification. Through this argument, which simultaneously prescribed feminine appearance and played upon the consumer's sense of self, the cosmetics industry attempted to make its products indispensable. At the same time, if one effect of the cosmetics industry was to represent femaleness as a kind of merchandise or objectified spectacle, another was to destabilize nineteenth-century cultural hierarchies among women. Although seemingly trivial consumer purchases, cosmetics problematized social identity, enabling women to manipulate their external appearance and, thus, to grapple with the paradoxes of being a "New Woman" in a time of extremely unstable definitions of gender.

It is not farfetched to link the often commented upon figure of the "New Woman" to a far-reaching reconstruction of the self under the pressure of commercialism. Historians, referring to male subjects, have spoken of the shift from "character" to "personality," by which they intended the reconstruction of individual identity, the shift from an individuality linked to the small property-owning bourgeois of the nineteenth century to an individuality bound up with a salaried middle-class status articulated through the appropriation of commercial cultural motifs.[17] This shift could be surmised to have wholly different meanings for women—to involve a greater clash between self and image, which is to say between old and new ideas of one's own sense of being. These conflicts seem to have been especially fraught in the United States, where—because of the fluidity of class relations, the early arrival of consumer commodities, and the pervasiveness of Protestant belief with its peculiar emphasis on appearance and authenticity of self—commodities appeared to have played an especially significant role in constructing social and individual identities. Anglo-Protestant culture, its grip on American civic life repeatedly shaken by the rapid transformations of U.S. lifestyle, also appears to spur an Anglo-American propensity to see selling as seduction. In the United States, at least, this fear, together with the quest for profits of a rapidly growing and oligopolistic marketing structure, early and intensely propelled a "constant need [on the part of preachers, advertisers, and advice counselors] to organize the meanings attached to consumption—to domesticate and moralize them."[18]

In continental Europe, and perhaps to a lesser extent in England, where the coming of mass consumption was a source of enormous political dispute, obstructed by conservative strategies of development and the hostility of entrenched elites, there was a very different interplay between political solidarities and consumer identities. This was especially visible where, as in Germany and Italy, authoritarian regimes took power and sought to deploy consumer culture politically, to use it as an instrument of political mobilization and hegemony.

The experience of Italy's fascist dictatorship, to take an extreme case, sug-

gests that notwithstanding its vaunted ability to respond to the semiotic confusion attendant on the rise of mass society, the regime was baffled in the
face of the proliferation of identities generated around new types of commodity consumption, leisure pastimes, and spectatorship. The new streams
of consumer durables and cultural artifacts (often coming from the United
States) not only challenged the symbolic order and spatial layout of bourgeois society but also, in equal measure, defied the primary organizing principles of fascist mass politics with its emphasis on hierarchies of rank and
function rather than of class. Moreover, they abided by and perhaps reinforced the old divisions between public or male space and a private or domestic female domain. Far from operating in tandem with the mass-produced
traditions of state-directed cultural systems to "nationalize" female citizens,
market-driven consumer cultures appear to have a centripetal character, un-
derwriting the creation of individual subjectivities and group identities outside of the purview of official power and authorizing definitions of female
citizenship not contemplated by an authoritarian state.

When the U.S. model of mass consumer society finally prevailed in postwar Europe, consumer citizenship arrived hand in hand with, and gave an
individualist cast to, the "social citizenship" of Western Europe's emerging
welfare states. The background of Erica Carter's essay here is indeed the so-
called German miracle, meaning the prodigiously rapid reconstruction of
the German Federal Republic, in which the coming of mass consumption
was closely bound up with economic recovery, democratization, and breaking with the Nazi past. According to Ludwig Erhard, chancellor of the GFR
from 1963 to 1966 and the so-called father of the economic miracle, mass consumption was the keystone of the new social market economy; the informed
consumer was the linchpin of freedom and democracy. "Every citizen must
be conscious of consumer freedom and the freedom of economic enterprise
as basic and inalienable rights, whose violation should be punished as an as-
sault on our social order."[19]

In principle, the citizen-as-consumer was more readily interpretable as female than male. Women exercised a new public role through the daily task
of provisioning and domestic labor. Female-led housewives' associations,
which by the mid-1950s embraced an estimated 7 percent of the female population, acted as a powerful lobby and appealed to nonorganized women
to exercise their rights—as the American housewives purportedly did—by
means of consumer boycotts. To a degree, these abstract appeals were concretized in the rebuilding of public space around new commercial districts.
For example, planning in postwar West Berlin divided the territory between
residential areas and commercial zones, the latter including the central shopping districts. Depersonalized retailing, including variety and self-service
stores, invited customers to use their "purchasing power" and "shop around,"

thereby breaking the monopoly of small shopkeepers. The new forms of retailing were especially attractive to younger consumers, freeing them to look, compare, and admire at their leisure, with no compulsion to buy.

Belying the appearance of female quiescence, deplored by Simone De Beauvoir in *The Second Sex,* female consumerism took on a quasi-activist character in this context. Given the previous political obstacles to mass consumption and the growing political visibility of consumers in the strategies of economic development during the interwar years, the recognition of the female citizen-consumer after the war had political implications of enormous moment. Contemporaries recognized that extending consumer entitlements presented an alternative to the use of mobilizing politics and nationalist appeals as the major devices for integrating the collectivity. At the same time, the path to mass consumption, which is to say the recognition of the right to well-being on a mass scale, was a different path from that to social citizenship carried forward by the reformist labor movement. Projects emphasizing consumer citizenship could claim that they favored women in their emphasis on family and individual well-being, whereas the left suffered, first, from its disbelief that consumption would ever truly be mass and, second, from its advocacy of collective as opposed to individualist forms of consumption. Though the labor movement in Europe would play an important role in widening consumption through its pressures for higher wages, by the 1960s, because of the austerity of its vision of appropriate levels of consumption and the lack of specific attention to particular segments of the consumer market, such as women and youth, it would quickly lose its capacity to sustain its political subculture through a politics of consumption around working-class communities.

NOTES

1. See in particular works on the development of commercial and public spaces in the United States: William Leach, *Land of Desires: Merchants, Power, and the Rise of a New American Culture* (New York: Pantheon Books, 1993); also Mary Ryan, *Women in Public: Between Banners and Ballots, 1825–1880* (Baltimore: Johns Hopkins University Press, 1990). Related arguments are contained in Lisa Tickner's interesting study of the turn-of-the-century suffrage movement in Great Britain, *The Spectacle of Women: Imagery of the Suffrage Campaign* (Chicago: University of Chicago Press, 1989).

2. See Ellen Furlough, "Women and Cooperation," in *Consumer Cooperation in France: The Politics of Consumption, 1834–1930* (Ithaca: Cornell University Press, 1991); Dana Frank, *Purchasing Power: Consumer Organizing, Gender, and the Seattle Labor Movement, 1919–1929* (New York: Cambridge University Press, 1994); Lester Golden, "The Women in Command: The Barcelona Women's Consumer War of 1918," *UCLA Historical Journal* 6 (1985): 5–32; and Mary McAuley, "Bread without the Bourgeoisie," in *Party, State, and Society in the Russian Civil War: Explorations in Social History,* ed. Di-

anne P. Koenker, William G. Rosenberg, and Ronald Grigor Suny (Bloomington: Indiana University Press, 1989), 158–80.

3. This has been especially sensitively illustrated outside of the Euro-American context: see, for example, Jean Franco, *On Edge: The Crisis of Contemporary Latin American Culture* (Minneapolis: University of Minnesota Press, 1992); and Miriam Silverberg, "The Modern Girl as Militant," in *Recreating Japanese Women, 1600–1945*, ed. Gail Lee Bernstein (Berkeley: University of California Press, 1991), 239–66.

4. In his "Parasexuality and Glamour: The Victorian Barmaid as Cultural Prototype," *Gender and History* 2, no. 2 (summer 1990): 148–172, Peter Bailey reminds us that in earlier periods too—such as at the turn of the century, when feminism advanced simultaneously with the commercialization of female sexuality in burlesque, vaudeville, and other theatrical entertainment—managers constructed new styles of "licit sexuality." This appears to have helped deflect anxieties over the growing presence of women in public places as well as in politics by underscoring their subaltern nature.

5. Guy Debord, *The Society of the Spectacle* (1967; reprint, New York: Zone Books, 1994). The variations in the positions commonly listed under the Frankfurt School are so significant, even for single authors over time, that the label is misleading. Readers interested in the implications of such approaches for feminist inquiry should consult, in addition to the diverse classics by Theodor Adorno and Max Horkheimer, Walter Benjamin, Siegfried Kracauer, and Herbert Marcuse, works of interpretation referring to them, notably Miriam Hansen, *Babel and Babylon: Spectatorship in American Silent Film* (Cambridge: Harvard University Press, 1991); and Andreas Huyssen, *After the Great Divide: Modernism, Mass Culture, Postmodernism* (Bloomington: Indiana University Press, 1986). A much criticized but valid study referring to this tradition is Stuart Ewen and Elizabeth Ewen, *Channels of Desire: Mass Images and the Shaping of American Consciousness*, 2d ed. (Minneapolis: University of Minnesota Press, 1992).

6. David Potter, *People of Plenty: Economic Abundance and the American Character* (Chicago: University of Chicago Press, 1954).

7. Daniel Boorstin, *The Americans: The Democratic Experience* (New York, Vintage, 1974).

8. Albert O. Hirschman, *Shifting Involvements: Private Interests and Public Action* (Princeton: Princeton University Press, 1982); see also idem, *Rival Views of Market Society and Other Recent Essays* (New York: Viking, 1986).

9. See, for example, Ronald Inglehart, *The Silent Revolution* (Princeton: Princeton University Press, 1977); and idem, *Culture Shift in Advanced Industrial Society* (Princeton, Princeton University Press, 1990).

10. As in Simon N. Patten, *The New Basis of Civilization* (1907; reprint, Cambridge: Belknap Press, 1968).

11. One of the most intriguing hypotheses, which highlights the role of communication goods (e.g., radios) and consumer appliances in constructing cross-ethnic working-class solidarities, is advanced by Lizabeth Cohen, *Making the New Deal* (New York: Cambridge University Press, 1990). This argument about "integration" and "communities" created by consumption is an argument that is substantially different from the conservative hypotheses advanced by David Potter and Daniel Boorstin.

12. Corrado Alvaro, "I cinquanti'anni del cinema," *Nuova Antologia,* 7th ser., 70, no. 1514 (16 April 1935): 603.

13. Hansen, *Babel and Babylon,* 123.

14. Glenna Matthews, *Just a Housewife: The Rise and Fall of Domesticity in America* (New York: Oxford University Press, 1987), 193–94.

15. Nancy Cott, *The Grounding of Modern Feminism* (New Haven: Yale University Press, 1989), 274.

16. Rayna Rapp and Ellen Ross, "The Twenties Backlash: Compulsory Heterosexuality, the Consumer Family, and the Waning of Feminism," in *Class, Race, and Sex: The Dynamics of Control,* ed. Amy Swerdlow and Hannah Lessinger (Boston: G. K. Hall, 1982), 93–107.

17. Cf. Warren Susman, *Culture as History: The Transformation of American Society in the Twentieth Century* (New York: Pantheon, 1984).

18. T. J. Jackson Lears, "Beyond Veblen: Rethinking Consumer Culture in America," in *Consuming Visions: Accumulation and Display of Goods in America, 1880–1920,* ed. Simon J. Bronner (New York: W. W. Norton, 1989), 73–97, esp. 79 ff.

19. Ludwig Erhard, *Well-Being for All,* cited in Erica Carter, "Alice in the Consumer Wonderland: West German Case Studies in Gender and Consumer Culture," in *Gender and Generation,* ed. Angela McRobbie and Mica Nava (London: Macmillan, 1984), 192.

NINE

Food Scarcity and the Empowerment of the Female Consumer in World War I Berlin

Belinda Davis

In turn-of-the-century Germany, "consumer" was an ill-defined term, and German consumers were a fractured group without considerable societal significance or power. It was not until World War I that the consumer acquired a prominent and positive place in national life. At this time, many among the German urban population came to identify themselves as consumers and even came to relate this identity to their Germanness.[1] Although both men and women saw themselves in this way, they envisioned the figure of the consumer as female. This more sympathetic, prominent, and focused image both enhanced the influence of the consumer and permitted beleaguered women in the streets and market squares to press public officials to respond to the needs of the civilian population while the war was on and the British blockaded goods to Central Europe. In the process, the urban public in particular came to perceive the sacrifices of the consumer as emblematic of the civilian contribution to the war effort. In return for their contribution, those acting as consumers demanded that the state recognize its obligation to its subjects. The consumer thus functioned as a catalyst for the transformation of relations between state and society: demands that were consumption-driven brought about transformations central to the prolonged metamorphosis of Bismarckian social policy (*Sozialpolitik*) into the modern welfare state represented by the Weimar Republic. This process will be traced through a case study of Berlin.[2]

Several images of the consumer coexisted on the eve of World War I. One image encompassed both the profligate parvenu and the factory worker newly arrived from the countryside alike in succumbing to the offerings of the booming mass market.[3] Another image was that of the working- or lower-middle-class mother, often new to urban life, who struggled to feed her family in the inflationary years preceding the war.[4] These personae reflect contemporary and more recent discussion concerning, respectively, "wants" versus "needs" in consumer society.[5] Yet a third image was that of the participant in the consumers' unions, usually middle- or upper-class, of the early part of the century. Although these unions formally represented consumer interests, they did so principally in narrow class-based terms; for example, the bourgeois organizations were concerned with such matters as preventing unionization of domestic servants.[6] Yet, despite the lack of a universal urban consumer identity in the years before the war, in rapidly growing cities such as Berlin, there was widespread concern, cutting across class lines, about the growing number of middlemen (*Zwischenhändler*) who stood between producers and buyers. The presence of these middlemen raised the specters of excess profit, "artificial" shortages, and dubious product quality. There was also broad-based concern about the lack of direct access to land for most Berliners, even enough land for tiny truck gardens as a buffer against hard times.[7]

These disparate consumers were all largely if not exclusively envisioned as female.[8] This perception remained throughout the war years; the feminization of the home front population served to reinforce it. In turn, the image of the female consumer served increasingly as a filter for public conceptions of actual women. These conceptions changed over the course of the war. At the outbreak of hostilities, women were cast most commonly as heedless, wasteful consumers. The concern about food scarcity fostered by the British embargo of goods gave this image enormous currency. The female consumer was a potential traitor; her purchase of luxuries in the new environment of scarcity put her fellow nationals at risk. At the same time she represented a soft, degenerate culture diametrically opposed to the clean, hard, male culture, devoid of excesses, in the name of which German men were losing their lives.

However, a more sympathetic image of the consumer had risen to prominence by early 1915: that is, the woman who, in the face of adversity, sought to fulfill her needs and those of her family rather than her own selfish desires. This role contemporary observers could condone. The image evoked concern and empathy for urban German women among other Berlin residents, particularly for those women who were impoverished by the wartime conditions. This was, in part, because the conditions of war served to reinforce the set of consumer concerns shared across class lines that had emerged in the course of the city's rapid growth. It seems that, in the war years, at the same time that the consumer was being figured as a woman, all urban residents came to identify themselves as consumers and as wronged consumers. This new image of the consumer superseded the fractionated and weak prewar class-based image. At the same time, its feminized character did not prevent men from identifying with it. Indeed, in the context of wartime scarcity, the label "consumer" was perceived as synonymous with "Berliner"—and even with "we Germans" and "we the people."

Further, the figuring of this universalized identity as a woman conferred not only rights but also social power to women as they acted in this role, power that to a significant degree defied their legal and social disenfranchisement. The role of consumer also created opportunities for women to act and interact in the public sphere: in the streets, before shops, and in market squares.[9] Women in World War I Berlin thus gained both a public role through which to express their interests and a public space in which to do so. Street protesters, unable to procure basic foods, drew broad public support and inspired condemnation of merchants, rural producers, and, ultimately, the government, which seemed to have a hand in denying this fundamental consumer "right," as it was now construed, to provide for oneself and one's family.[10] Such empathy was not extended to working-class men.[11] Indeed, the combination of the feminized image of the consumer and the sheer physical presence of masses of women standing in lines for food, particularly in poorer quarters of the city, from winter 1914 on, effectively made "women of little means" (*minderbemittelte Frauen* or simply *die Minderbemittelte*) leaders for consumer interests.

Finally, the protest of the *Minderbemittelte* played a significant role in ushering in the modern welfare state, as represented by the Weimar Republic.[12] As the war dragged on, the public called for the government to respond swiftly and forcefully to the demands of these consumer leaders, to intervene actively in the pricing, distribution, and even production of foodstuffs. This public appeal grew out of the government's own war propaganda in the context of worsening food scarcity. Officials had defended entry into the war in part by claiming the need to protect the most vulnerable elements of German society as represented by the nation's women. The public believed that by late 1915 poor women were suffering as keenly from the privations of the "economic war" as they were from the effects of the hostilities on the battle front. Public opinion across the political spectrum supported government intervention on behalf of hungry consumers, whether inspired by the ideology of "war socialism" or by the ultranationalist view that the state could not allow *Germans* to starve at the hands of the enemy. Moreover, in light of the sacrifices made by civilians, as well as their direct contributions to the war effort,[13] it was widely perceived that noncombatants could no longer be stigmatized as hindrances to the war effort. The public insisted that the contribution of civilians be recognized and be treated, like that of soldiers, with a sense of reciprocal obligation by the state. It was in this spirit that the Weimar Republic was conceived.

I

On the eve of World War I, Germany was dependent on imports for about one-third of its total food supply.[14] Therefore, as the British declared a blockade of goods to Central Europe with the declaration of war, German officials expressed concern about the effect of this blockade on popular morale.[15] Authorities were especially worried about the capital city, where popular discontent had the potential to draw widespread domestic and international attention. The German government stepped up propaganda addressing the scarcity, largely as a substitute for a coherent domestic economic policy to control existing supplies. Officials claimed that basic food reserves were adequate, but limited. They attempted to establish civilian responsibility for conservation of remaining food stocks by urging the population to exercise control over their habits of consumption. They admonished that "those who stuff themselves full, those who push out their paunches in all directions, are traitors to the fatherland."[16] Because they were particularly afraid of the reprisals that food shortages might cause among women,[17] civilian authorities addressed propaganda predominantly to the urban female procurer of food.[18] Warnings in newspapers, in public lectures, and on handbills emphasized the need for women to overcome their irrationality and lack of restraint when purchasing goods; these warnings intimated that, in their role as consumers, as in other roles, women were the point of vulnerability of the otherwise invincible German nation.[19]

Such rhetoric reflected the tensions between the two images of the female consumer: the conscientious *procurer* of supplies for her family and the vain, extravagant *user* of unnecessary goods, both transposed onto a template of civilian patriotism and contribution to the war effort. Interior ministry representatives instructed doctors in Berlin and greater Prussia to "teach housewives about the 'food question'": "implore them to use available supplies propitiously" and "warn them to curb their own intake of food."[20] Propaganda connected femaleness to prevailing public concerns that civilians were slackers, challenging women to put doubts about their contribution to rest by mobilizing themselves as a "voluntary home front army, which support[ed] the soldiers, by fighting the battle of the economy."[21] Only then might women overcome their lack of consciousness and surface from immersion in their immediate world to fulfill their patriotic obligation.[22]

These appeals, which employed existing negative images of women, were initially effective in deflecting the government's responsibility for food management onto the civilian population. Food began to grow scarce in late fall 1914, and prices rose, while unemployment still climbed in this early period of the war. The first of the "absolute most necessary foods" to suffer shortages and inflation was bread. Bread was at once a staple of the German diet and physiologically central to working-class nutritional needs. The scarcity and high price of bread thus engendered a generalized sense of deprivation, which led to widespread public sympathy for the working poor, who were particularly affected. As a large urban center, Berlin was especially badly hit by the shortage in part because it was the last stop on the line for delivery of many foodstuffs. As a result, as early as October 1914, struggling Berliners—men and women alike—began to pick up on the themes articulated in the official propaganda. A study of police reports and the press indicates that poorer capital residents singled out the figure of the soldier's wife as the immediate manifestation of the vain and thoughtless female consumer: an "inner enemy" in the "economic war," as the blockade was called.[23]

This characterization of these women came as a surprise to authorities. Because the soldier's wife had earned considerable social prestige in the 1870–71 Franco-Prussian War, on the basis of her perceived sacrifices—not least of which was the loss of the family breadwinner—officials, from the outset of the war, had allotted soldiers' wives a separation allowance. However, in the fall of 1914, Germans experiencing difficulty in obtaining bread perceived the soldier's wife, most often from the working class herself, to hold an exclusive position of privilege vis-à-vis her prewar cohorts, and even her petite bourgeois "superiors." Police reports expressed the sentiment that the scarcity of flour must result from wasteful use by consumers with special privileges. Berliner police reported what they claimed to be a general impression that soldiers' wives were living quite well, enjoying cake when their class counterparts could afford no bread. The soldier's wife thus seemed to have transcended her lowly prewar social status—and its concomitant deprivations—apparently at the expense of the basic well-being of others.[24] Her selfish behavior, police reported, also seemed to compromise the war effort.

The primacy of gender in the characterization of this profligate and traitorous consumer is transparent. The author of one police report commenting on the situation, a Sergeant Schwarz, moves easily from a discussion of "war dependents" to "the wives of active soldiers" to "the women," all applied to the same subject.[25] In the same way, Police Officer Schulz asserts in his April 1915 report, in the same shorthand fashion, that "only the women" protested a new prohibition on the production of cakes, though he referred to soldiers' wives.[26] This habit of eliding these categories reflects at once the perception of consumers as women and the notion that it was only through their gender that soldiers' wives had achieved their advantage. By the measure of police reports, it appears that Berliners expressing outrage at this injustice were far less concerned about the continued relative privilege of the prewar upper classes. Police Chief Jagow observed, "It is asserted *from all sides* that war dependents from the working class are doing considerably better than before the war."[27] Officer Diercks echoed the perception: "Also, the number of women dressed in somber clothing, claiming to be robbed of their breadwinner or other close family member, is increasing, creating a sobering image; but one must on the other hand note that the women are untouched by either neediness or despair. One can see for oneself, that it is exactly the poorer women who daily occupy the cafés of department stores, sampling delicacies that certainly don't number amongst the most necessary foods."[28]

Of course, all war dependents, including children, siblings, and elderly parents of soldiers, were eligible for separation allowances, and this did not go unnoted by the greater public. But the protest was made primarily against the figure of the soldier's wife.[29] Other exclusively female categories (or categories construed as such) that likewise appeared to profit as consumers under the war conditions and shed characteristics that defined their prewar societal status were similarly objects of protest during the early years of the war. These included mothers with many children (literally, "child-rich mothers") and wives of munitions worker. Many indicted child-rich mothers for their inability to steward the extra ration coupons they received: "There are mothers who send their children to school scantily clothed, but who can't give up their constant doughnuts."[30] Aggrieved Berliners protested that "precisely the munitions workers' wives often buy the most expensive things."[31] Capital residents condemned not the man whose wages were swollen by the war but the wife who was seen as spending these wages. Notably, together these categories made up much of the working class, as they applied to real people.

II

Although the perceived link between women and consumers held fast, and the female consumer remained a prominent rhetorical figure, the specter of women as the inner enemy in the economic war had receded by the beginning of 1915. The image of women unable to restrain themselves in the face of tempting luxuries was superseded by that of worry-worn mothers struggling to procure the most basic foods for their families.[32] New food shortages, as well as shifts in government policy and propaganda, informed this transformation. By the last months of 1914, potatoes had become extremely scarce, especially in the working- and lower-middle-class neighborhoods, where the need was greatest. By January 1915, rumors were rampant that farmers were responsible for the scarcity; they were reportedly feeding potatoes to their pigs rather than bringing them to market. Propaganda successfully encouraged the conviction that domestic food production was adequate. Police Officer Dittmann noted the popular perception that "there are quite enough potatoes to be had, as this year's harvest was abundant. . . ." Berliners concluded in turn, Dittmann observed, that ". . . the producers have held them back in order to demand truly unconscionable prices."[33]

Public outrage in Berlin and other cities was now turned against the farmer, as well as the wholesaler: both were perceived as valuing profit above patriotism, and above the well-being of the German people.[34] According to one police report, "Since this [difficulty in procuring food] concerns predominantly the population of little means and the lower civil servants, bitterness against the big, rich rural producers and business people grows daily. In general one considers the latter as the most evil enemies, who haven't the faintest glimmer of love of country, nor love for their fellow humanity."[35] Public discourse defined these new societal nemeses moreover as primarily male.[36] In turn, the press cast the conflict over access to potatoes as one of "people [that is, urban consumers] versus pigs."[37] This characterization further inflamed a wide cross-section of Berliners, stirring up civilian anxieties that they were perceived as not adequately contributing to the war effort, and that the tumultuous wartime conditions would compromise their pre-war social and economic status.

As this new explanation for inadequate food supplies gripped public imagination, the prominent image of the egregiously wasteful female consumer receded, and the element of "femaleness" lost much of its unfavorable association. Female consumers were still vulnerable, yet vulnerable not to their own wastefulness and excess but rather to the circumstances of war, circumstances that farmers and merchants unconscionably exploited. The broader urban public felt the pangs of this vulnerability. The wider press observed, " . . . defenseless are the consumers now that potato profiteering has been delivered upon them. . . . a *deep bitterness* fills millions of citizens of the German state."[38] In turn, within a matter of weeks, press and police reports came to emphasize the figure of the poor woman who strove only to secure perceived dietary necessities. Moreover, remaining charges of consumer excess, such as they existed, now targeted the (male) factory worker who stuffed his belly full of bread, potatoes, and beer or, alternately, the (male) bourgeois "waster of food," "glutton," or "gourmand," who watched bread lines in the street from a restaurant window.[39]

Indeed, Berliners from across the socioeconomic spectrum felt far more comfortable voicing sympathy for and associating themselves with financially struggling female consumers than for male producers, or, for that matter, for factory workers, whom bourgeois Germans continued to fear as the enemy of capitalism and the Wilhelmine state. At the same time, the wartime impoverishment of lower-middle-class Berliners brought them into a kind of *mariage de convenance* with working-class capital residents: both groups protested distributional "inequities," high prices, and the holding back of food. The term *minderbemittelt* (of little means) emphasized a common lot of having little to spend and, therefore, worked to smooth over production-centered class divisions. This broadening of the *minderbemittelt* population to include more socioeconomic groups also helped win support for this population's cries for greater government intervention (at least publicly) from middle- and upper-class Berliners—intervention to prevent the lower middle class, the backbone of German society, from sliding too deeply into neediness, that is, precisely into the straits of the working class. Indeed, bourgeois capital residents identified with the *Minderbemittelte* and emphasized in apocalyptic terms the battle between "the German people" and their enemies over the question of food. At the same time, this newfound influence of poorer woman consumer was informed as much by fear as by empathy: fear of the street disturbances that these consumers could create and, ultimately, fear of revolution. Thus, this poor female consumer commanded not only respect for her rationality, via her acknowledged responsibility to provide for her family, but also respect for her potential irrationality, which might be drawn out in the event that her rightful needs went unserved.

In response to both the threat posed by the *Minderbemittelte* who protested food scarcity in the streets and the public support given these actions by wider Berlin society, the German state hastened to take on the new role of defending the interests of unjustly deprived—female—consumers. Anxious to adopt the appearance of forcefulness, the state commanded the so-called pig murder of March 1915, in which officials ordered the sacrifice of some nine million of twenty-five million swine.[40] But even the symbolically significant pig murder was deemed inadequate to demonstrating the active intervention protesters called for, in terms of controlling both production and distribution. Later in the month, the High Commander in the Marks and the Imperial Council, representatives of top-level military and civilian authority, respectively, took another step: they divided the Berlin population up into those "of little means" and those who were "better off" (*wohlhabend*) and ordered the distribution of ration cards permitting the former category of consumer to purchase potatoes at a lower price.[41] In these circumstances, as the state attempted to head off the appearance of disorder and tried simultaneously to ward off international charges of "barbarism," officials now found it acceptable and even necessary to effectively redistribute wealth at some level, and to intervene explicitly on behalf of the urban consumer.

As conditions in Berlin continued to deteriorate in the first half of 1915, popular rhetoric quickly moved to include the neighborhood retailer among the nation's inner enemies. As the axis of conflict shifted from unjust privilege for certain consumers to excess profit for producers and merchants, the latter were accused of engaging in both "artificial" and "arbitrary" pricing: that is, fixing prices at levels far above what was popularly perceived as just. By these standards, producers and merchants were not acting in an economically rational fashion but rather were using the circumstances of war to exploit consumers—fellow Germans. A broad range of Berliners protested the victimization of the *Minderbemittelte* by speculation, trade through middlemen, and, by mid-1915, by profit *tout court*. These Berliners challenged the legitimacy of the state's tradition of intervening on behalf of agriculture and even of its remaining aloof from the market altogether.[42] Officials were, the capital public asserted, to stem profit specifically on behalf of the needs of impoverished women, that is, the population officials claimed Germany fought the war to protect. Police spies opined that "this shrinkage [of the purchasing power of housewives of the middle circles] would be easier to bear, if the opinion weren't so widely entertained, that the high prices [were] not a justifiable product of the circumstances, and [were], rather, for the most part, to be chalked up to the arbitrariness of producers, speculators, and shopkeepers, against which the government [had] made insufficient use of its powers."[43] Many capital residents demanded the government's effective elimination of profit for at least the period of the war: for in the terms of the economic war, profit was seen as being in direct conflict with patriotism. The merchant was now cast against "all other people."[44] And in the context of the wartime conditions, "all other people" were rhetorically represented by poorer women consumers.

Public rhetoric from many quarters of the city suggested first in the course of the war that the state was responsible for securing a minimum standard of living specifically for the nation's "vulnerable population," through active market intervention and through guaranteed subventions. Social Democrats did not exaggerate when they advanced the broad claim that "the population at home . . . consider[ed] it the most urgent responsibility of the government" to care for the nutritional needs of the people by, among other things, "distributing food equally to the entire population, at prices affordable for all."[45] The liberal *Vossische Zeitung* concurred that it was the job of the highest level authorities to tend to the nutritional needs of the broader population: "*Only the central government agencies* have the capacity to take control over all the individual goods, from production on, and to institute real regulation of goods. . . . Any other economic regulation is doomed to remain a palliative on the bigger problem."[46]

By the latter half of 1915, the greater public indicated that if imperial officials did not explicitly act in the interests of disadvantaged urban consumers, it would be perceived that they acted against these interests, and that this would not be looked upon in a positive light. The press from left to far right castigated imperial authorities for "reckless inattention" to the righteous demands of consumers, and for attending rather to the wishes of producers and merchants.[47] Thus, officials' attempts to goad women to demonstrate their patriotism were now turned back on the state, which was forced to demonstrate its own commitment to the German people and nation by acting on behalf of the impoverished, female, urban consumer. This reconceptualization of state obligations to the German consumer was clearly grounded in the immediate circumstances of the war and economic blockade. But the press and police reports suggest that in the course of the following months and years, widespread expectation grew that the state's control over the market, in the name of the consumer, would extend beyond the period of war. Support for such intervention and the notion of entitlements can be traced from the war era to the Weimar constitution, drafted following the revolution of November 1918.

III

In the environment of material scarcity that prevailed in World War I Berlin, from the serious inconveniences of the first half of the war to the subsistence crises of the second half, public discussion often turned on the image of the downtrodden female consumer. The centrality of the image in turn worked in some respects to the advantage of women who had been negatively affected by the economic circumstances of the war. The image gave such women a social niche, through which their concerns were legitimized and their social prestige elevated. But the role of the righteous consumer, as it was assumed by large groups of actual women, also provided a further benefit, at least during the course of the war: it gave these women a voice and a means for acting on behalf of their own concerns. In turn, the specific content of these women's appeals was central to the recasting of state obligation, which the new Weimar state would embody.[48]

In World War I Berlin, the chorus of poor women's voices was heard most loudly in the streets of the city. German officials had long demonstrated fear of assembly of any sort in the nation's streets and above all in the streets of the capital. This fear was intensified in the war years.[49] Since the early nineteenth century, Prussian police (and before that, military personnel) had been notorious for their activities connected with maintaining public order. From the 1890s on, their activities were explicitly extended to include the protection of the state from popular political activity.[50] Concerned that even this restraint was insufficient, officials declared a state of siege at the onset of hostilities in 1914 and filled the streets with police (who had previously been assigned to "Social Democrat" pubs) to prevent any public activity not explicitly related to a necessary task. But as crowds of women regularly grew before shops and in the marketplace as a result of food scarcity, the street became the public space in which women, acting in their assigned, legitimized role as consumers, were able to communicate their grievances as effectively as those with statutory political rights. Certainly there was nothing remarkable about bread riots in the streets. But the attention and support provided by the onlooking public was impressive; and the way in which this public cast protesting women as leaders of the urban populace was remarkable.

As food shortages grew more severe and costs rose sharply, the incidence of queuing up for food (or "dancing the polonaise"[51]) burgeoned. As the first full year of war reached its close, the image of people, predominantly women, occupying the streets and marketplaces at all hours of the day and night became a powerful symbol for Berliners, as indicated in the press and in police reports.[52] At the same time, women formed a growing majority of the civilian population as the state stepped up its conscription of men; this too raised their public prominence. And by the fall of 1915, Berliners perceived poorer women, in their role as consumers, as the most activist population, as leading the fight on the "right" side of the inner, economic war. Thus, although women remained cast as victims, they were also very much agents whose activity inspired the support of others. The perception of the activist role of working women in particular was cemented during the butter riots of October 1915, in the course of which women in working-class districts of the capital protested the practices of rural producers, wholesalers and retailers, and, finally, the government itself.

In mid-October, riots grew out of the long queues for food. Demonstrators described alternately in police reports as "the women" and *"die Minderbemittelte"* gathered before butter shops to protest retail practices that deprived them of the butter they were told was available. The rioters in Lichtenberg, Wedding, and other working-class districts were incensed above all with the practice of "chain trade" (*Kettenhandel*). The butter franchises Bolle and Assmann were rumored to be relocating butter from their stores in poorer neighborhoods to those in wealthier localities, where they could both charge a higher rate for this coveted food and curry favor with richer customers.[53] Chain trade, like foddering potatoes, was a simple strategy of profit maximization in a capitalist society; but in the context of World War I Berlin, it was interpreted by working-class consumers as indefensible. The effects were compounded by the rude and patronizing fashion in which shopkeepers were purported to treat poorer customers. The combination of the lack of butter and merchant affronts sent hungry, cold, and tired customers into dramatic spontaneous demonstrations. Crowds, described by police as consisting mostly of women, whistled, yelled, and condemned merchant practices. Along with "adolescent boys," they broke shop windows filled with unavailable goods, an incendiary symbol of merchant deception.

There were dozens of small riots between 12 October and 16 October 1915; in some cases riots grew to five thousand to six thousand participants. And, although the Lichtenberger butter riots lasted only a few days, they sparked unrest that continued unabated for the next nine months, throughout Greater Berlin, and in other big cities throughout the country. The public condemned forcible suppression of these demonstrations and called upon authorities to intervene on the behalf of protesters, protesters performing in the role of consumers. Significantly, street-level police also responded favorably to the demonstrators, as their reports to superior officers testify. In contrast, the public responded unsympathetically to merchants' complaints about the "irrationality" of "excited and feeble-minded old female persons" and about the "life-threatening press of women" that pushed its way into their shops.

However, this sympathy for the protesters was not extended to men or young boys who joined in the street protest. Public attitude toward demonstrators' behavior fell as sharply along gender lines as it did along the divide of consumer versus merchant. The public seemed to differentiate (in the press, for example) between what was conceived as reasonable, defensible, legitimate activity and activity that both engendered chaos and threatened the war effort. This differentiation was reflected as well in police reports and other internal government documents. To be sure, the actors in the October incidents appear to have been much the same as those who protested in the unrest over potatoes earlier in the year (and in food riots in the decades preceding the war). Police and other officials most commonly identified participants as "women," "women of little means," and "women of the working classes." But "adolescent boys" and, to a lesser degree, "drunken men" also frequently appear in the reports about these riots. This tableau is not surprising: in the contemporary political topos, all of these figures lacked the reason required for participation in public and formal political life, precisely as manifested by their unruliness in the street. However, after the first day or two of the protests of October 1915, assessments of the unrest differ strikingly from descriptions of the demonstrations that took place the previous February.

Youths and drunken men were described throughout the war era as wantonly and purposelessly violent, caught up in a crowd mentality and the "rabble-rousing" (*radaulustig*) tendencies associated with the "lowest masses."[54] They obeyed no reason as they roamed the streets hooting and howling, destroying show windows, and plundering goods, and were thus difficult to control.[55] But the behavior of women was described very differently. From October on, police and other officials attributed the women who comprised the majority of the participants with near rational motivation. The public and police alike believed that protesting women were expressing their rightful concerns and asserting particular demands in an understandable and even appropriate fashion. Police expressed the belief, moreover, that these women rationally ceased protest as soon as their demands were met. Thus, on 16 October, an Officer Sauer noted, "[Women] continued the tumultuous street demonstrations, which are directed against the shameless exploitation of the German people."[56] On 17 October, however, that there were "no disturbances of the peace, even in Lichtenberg" was directly tied to the demonstrators' acknowledgement of the new butter price ceiling in Berlin and Brandenburg.[57]

The attribution of a rational political voice to women indicates an important transformation in the prominent public view of female temperament or nature and, relatedly, in the view of the right of women to act politically. A wide cross-section of respectable society, from members of the press to leaders of charitable organizations to the police, now saw women as legitimate actors on the public stage. Police reports referred to these female demonstrators as "persons," and even as "the public," the term usually reserved for the citizen classes.[58] In representative fashion, Police Captain Schwarz connects "the public" and "working-class women," with the unnamed identification "consumer" serving as the effective link between the two: "Several rows between merchants and the public have already been reported. One must reckon with unrest over the high costs, because working-class women are in the absolute most agitated mood because of the ongoing food speculation."[59] In writing up the mid-October butter riots, police spies, themselves lower-level civil servants, offered the view that women were completely justified in their often violent response, that they were acting within their roles as consumers. The police not only noted that the women's acts were defensible but spoke to the greater responsibility that the government must take on their behalf.

IV

It was when women appeared to act in the role of wronged consumers that their disruption of order in the street was accepted and even condoned. And it seems that only women were accorded the privilege of responding in that fashion. Yet the deprived consumer was increasingly a public persona with which both men and women could identify. Indeed, public response to the demonstrations effectively put poor women in a position of leadership to advance consumer interests. At the same time, it is clear that it was the active support of the broader population that gave these women the power to influence official decisions. Forces across the political spectrum, and up and down the socioeconomic hierarchy, came to work together in the name of their perceived common needs as consumers, Berliners, and Germans, to forge a powerful force for pressuring the government at all levels to respond to the growing food crisis, bringing enormous pressure to bear on domestic policy, and even on foreign policy.[60]

By early 1916, public demands included confiscation of food supplies from producers, "equitable" distribution of these supplies, and price subsidies. These demands implied an enormous economic and political reorientation of the country. In the press, public speeches, and letters to officials, the broad Berlin public proclaimed the honorable status of the civilian population and the mutual obligation between state and society. Collectively, in Berlin and in other German cities, residents articulated a new concept of German sovereignty and citizenship. At the same time, they gave voice to a new notion of entitlement: an idea of what the state owed to Germans as consumers.[61] This contrasted sharply with the dominant philosophy behind social policy in the Kaiserreich up until this point. Previously, authorities had effectively cast aid to those in need, whatever its source,[62] as a gift: a gift that might be retracted at any time from a restive or otherwise undeserving population. Moreover, Bismarck's "social insurance" was predominantly directed at factory workers, that is, producers. Women were rarely direct recipients of these benefits despite their high participation in the paid workforce in the late nineteenth century. And none of the benefits was conceived of as meeting the rights of men or women as consumers, or as addressing "needs." But during the war years new shared assumptions about consumers' needs and rights developed around Germany; it was these assumptions that would inform the welfare tenets of the Weimar state.[63]

Wilhelmine authorities, as we have noted, were remarkably responsive to the demands of *die Minderbemittelte,* enacting as per demands everything from rations to price ceilings to total government control of the nation's food supplies. Yet, because of their reactive style, and because officials handled ineffectively the contradictory demands placed on them by different interests and various populations, authorities failed to prevent or alleviate crises in food distribution, which became ever more prevalent in the second half of the war. Turning official propaganda back against the state, the public declared that the state was "unreasonable," and had created the weakness in the German armor: by failing to take food matters in hand and punish the exploitative profiteer, authorities had both promoted divisiveness and prevented the civilian population from working for the war effort at full strength. This failure was a vital force in the public's loss of faith in Wilhelmine officials and must be seen, along with the military defeat, as an important spur to revolution, and to demands for a new system of government.

From early 1916, demands for drastic reform of domestic policy had spread around the country. Although demands were cast in terms of the temporary crisis of the war, the ideological transformation was, in the event, a more lasting phenomenon. This transformation did not ultimately lead to sustained political valuation of women after the war, in spite of the important universal franchise and the movement of predominantly middle-class women into the ranks of social welfare officials. But Weimar's significance as a model for the modern welfare state, one that attempted to serve the citizenship on the basis of its consumer needs, finds its most immediate and perhaps most important source in the wartime activities of urban working women, such as those in Berlin, and their image as consumers.

It must be stated that competing notions of needs and entitlement, submerged in the wartime sense of national unity, sat heavily on the shoulders of the Weimar leadership, all the more onerous under the conditions of military defeat and intractable economic and political crisis. In the face of massive popular need, the Weimar state was unable to meet demand, and arguments over the validity of varying bases for government subsidy contributed to that state's further fragmentation and loss of legitimacy.[64] But provisions for state aid for consumers would survive Weimar, although this aid would take very different forms under the various successor regimes, the Third Reich, the Federal Republic of Germany, and the German Democratic Republic. Still, a constant was attention to the needs of the German consumer citizen, a notion that first emerged with strength over the course of World War I.

NOTES

1. The specific terminology for "consumer" in German is varied. The formal designation was *Konsument* or *Verbraucher*. Those who frequented department stores or traditional small shops were described as *Kauflustige* or *Kunde*, both of which are more like "customer" (the latter was reserved primarily for the middle and upper classes). During the wartime coalescence of a consumer identity, newspapers sometimes spoke of *Wir Konsumenten* (we consumers). But more often than not, the designation was implicit, though, I would argue, nonetheless meaningful. Thus, in both oral and written discourse, designations for the German population were used regularly in combination with phrases that marked them as consumers: "we," or "we Germans," or "the people," all of whom "need to eat," "can't get enough food," and so on. Those in the streets seeking food in the war era were most frequently referred to by others as *die Minderbemittelte* (those of little means), a term that emphasized what one had to spend rather than what one earned.

2. The experience of Berliners was in many respects comparable to that of other urban residents throughout Germany; processes described here regarding transformations in relations between these populations and authorities in Hamburg, Königsberg, Breslau, and elsewhere appear to have been similar in important ways, as indicated by local press and police reports and by the monthly reports of the deputy commanders who monitored morale around the country. But, as the capital—as well as the center of national press, a premier site of war industry, and a garrison city— and for many other reasons, Berlin was certainly not typical. Berlin was carefully observed, both domestically and abroad, by German civilians and by frontline soldiers. This was one reason authorities, vulnerable by their proximity to the capital populace, were so anxious to respond positively to the demands of Berliners: to maintain domestic morale and to avoid damaging Germany's prestige in the eyes of other nations. Moreover, officials' response to food problems in Berlin tended to set in motion Reich-wide decrees.

The experience and interests of rural Germans were of course different, as discussed below, and representatives of rural interests put pressures on authorities at odds with urban demands. For a comparison of circumstances in Berlin with those of the capitals of other belligerents, see Thierry Bonzon and Belinda Davis, "Feeding the Cities," in *Capital Cities at War: Paris, London, and Berlin, 1914–1919*, ed. J. M. Winter and J.-L. Robert (Cambridge: Cambridge University Press, forthcoming).

3. On the concerns of bourgeois reformers regarding the consumer seductions (e.g., music halls [*Tingeltangel*] and burlesque) luring factory workers, see Derek S. Linton, *Who Has the Youth, Has the Future: The Campaign to Save Young Workers in Imperial Germany* (Cambridge: Cambridge University Press, 1991). There is no German counterpart to the extensive work on the temptations that department stores and the like posed for the bourgeoisie in France and England. But see Warren G. Breckman, "Disciplining Consumption: The Debate about Luxury in Wilhelmine Germany, 1890–1914," *Journal of Social History* 24, no. 3 (spring 1991): 485–506.

4. There is a broad literature on the economics and culture of food in the Kaiserreich, on the crises of subsistence in the late nineteenth century, and on the pinch of inflation in the decade preceding the war. See the important work of Hans-Jürgen Teuteberg, for example, "Die Nahrung der Sozialen Unterschichten im

Späten 19. Jahrhundert," in *Ernährung und Ernährungslehre*, ed. Edith Heischkel-Artelt (Göttingen: Vandenhoeck und Ruprecht, 1976). On inflation before the war, which continued during and after the hostilities, see William C. Mathews, "The German Social Democrats and the Inflation: Food, Foreign Trade, and the Politics of Stabilization, 1914–1920" (Ph.D. diss., University of California, Riverside, 1982), chap. 1.

5. There is a rapidly growing literature on "wants" and "needs," pointing to the recurrent historical conflicts in defining each term, particularly in the context of discussing the welfare state. See, for example, Nancy Fraser, "Struggle over Needs: Outline of a Socialist-Feminist Critical Theory of Late-Capitalist Political Culture," in *Women, the State, and Welfare*, ed. Linda Gordon (Madison: University of Wisconsin Press, 1990), 199–225. On Germany specifically, see David Crew, "Bedürfnisse und Bedürftigkeit: Wolhfahrtsbürokratie und Wohlfahrtsempfänger in der Weimarer Republik, 1919–1933," *SoWi* 18, no. 1 (1989): 12–19; Alf Lüdtke, "Everyday Life, the Articulation of Needs and 'Proletarian Consciousness'—Some Remarks on Concepts," unpublished ms., 1977; and Michael Wildt, *Am Beginn der "Konsumgesellschaft": Mangelerfahrung, Lebenshaltung, Wohlstandshoffnung in Westdeutschland in den fünfziger Jahren* (Hamburg: Ergebnisse Verlag, 1994).

6. The class-specific consumer unions were perceived as special interest groups. Bourgeois housewives' associations spearheaded early consumer campaigns. Housewives' associations became stronger in the course of the war and were one of the direct beneficiaries of the new attention to consumers' interests after the war. See Renate Bridenthal, "'Professional' Housewives: Stepsisters of the Women's Movement," in *When Biology Became Destiny*, ed. Renate Bridenthal et al. (New York: Monthly Review Press, 1984), 153–73; and "Organized Rural Women and the Conservative Mobilization of the German Countryside in the Weimar Republic," in *Between Reform, Reaction and Resistance*, ed. L. E. Jones and J. N. Retallack (Providence, R.I.: Berg, 1993), 375–406.

7. The elections of 1903 and 1912, which threw widespread support to the Social Democratic Party, can be seen in part as the response of a broad population identifying their interests as urban consumers to combat state policies that deferred to Junker interests, protected German agricultural markets, and, thus, drove up the cost of German bread and meat. Surprisingly, compared to its counterparts elsewhere in Europe and in America, the Social Democratic Party in Germany engaged little in organizing buying cooperatives. See inter alia Gert-Joachim Glaessner, *Arbeiterbewegung und Genossenschaft: Entstehung und Entwicklung der Konsumgenossenschaften in Deutschland am Beispiel Berlins* (Göttingen: Vandenhoeck und Ruprecht, 1989). Party leaders did play some role in the War Commission for Consumer Interests during the course of hostilities.

8. This was so for much of the nineteenth century as well, although as Carola Lipp notes, from early on the notion of women as the traditional consumer was more perception than reality. See her "Frauenspezifische Partizipation an Hungerunruhen des 19. Jarhunderts. Überlegungen zu strukturellen Differenzen im Protestverhalten," in *Der Kampf um das Tägliche Brot: Nahrungsmangel, Versorgungspolitik und Protest, 1770–1990*, ed. Manfred Gailus and Heinrich Volkmann (Opladen: Westdeuscher, 1994), 203.

9. See Belinda Davis, "Reconsidering Habermas, Politics, and Gender: The Case of Wilhelmine Germany," in *Society, Culture, and the State in Germany, 1870–1930*, ed.

Geoff Eley (Ann Arbor: University of Michigan Press, in press), for a more developed discussion both of women in the public sphere and of women's citizenship and civil versus natural rights. On women's public personae, see Paula Hyman, "Immigrant Women and Consumer Protest: The New York City Kosher Meat Boycott of 1902," *American Jewish History* 70 (September 1980): 91–105.

10. It is notable that urban merchants, identifying themselves as consumers of a sort, joined in condemning the exploitative rural producer, and rural producers condemned speculation by merchants, perceived as a product of urban industrialized society. But public rhetoric consistently denied the legitimacy of such claims, intimating that one could not simultaneously be both a wronged consumer and a producer or distributor, at least when food was the commodity being consumed and produced.

Contemporaries explicitly identified street protesters as women, even though photographs, records of arrests, and other sources provide evidence that the crowds were composed of both men and women.

11. Berlin society, including trade union and Social Democratic Party leaders, roundly condemned workers—usually cast as male—who struck during the war years, although strikers demanded wage increases precisely because of the rising price of food. Of course, just as the corpus of consumers, defined even as those who procured food, was not made up exclusively of women, so was the factory workforce not made up exclusively of men. In fact, during the war, women rose to 50 percent and more of the labor force of many branches of industry, including even the heavy war industries, formerly the province of men only. For more detail, see Ute Daniel, *Arbeiterfrauen in der Kriegsgesellschaft* (Göttingen: Vandenhoeck und Ruprecht, 1989); as well as Charlotte Lorenz, *Die Gewerbliche Frauenarbeit während des Krieges* (Stuttgart: Deutsche Verlags-Anstalt, 1928).

12. Current historiography still regularly refers to women's bread riots in general, including those here under discussion—when they are discussed—as premodern and prepolitical in both character and effect. Work focusing specifically on food riots in late-eighteenth- and nineteenth-century France, England, and Germany provides a compelling corrective to this literature. See, for example, the recent collection *Der Kampf um das Tägliche Brot;* and Cynthia A. Bouton, *The Flour War: Gender, Class, and Community in Late Ancien Régime French Society* (University Park, Pa.: Penn State Press, 1993).

But there are important ways in which these war-era protests over food seem to be different from earlier riots. First, the sense that poor women consumers acted through their demonstrations (and even by standing quietly in line) as representatives for the interests, in some sense, of the larger urban communities is one important point of differentiation. Second, in terms of German precedents, the willingness of the bourgeois public to support the demands of the street for confiscation of farmers' goods—representing a serious if ostensibly temporary breach in the German government's role as protector of property—is remarkable. On the state's role as defender of property rights, see Alf Lüdtke, *Police and State in Prussia, 1815–1850* (Oxford: Oxford University Press, 1989), 49 passim.

13. Civilians' direct participation intensified in the fall of 1916, when the Supreme Army Command rapidly accelerated weapons production, forcing the entire adult noncombatant population into the war factories (men were legally bound to such

duty; authorities pressed women into service through propaganda and other indirect means of coercion).

14. The country was particularly deficient in indigenous fats (about 42 percent of its requirements were imported) and the phosphoric and nitrogenous fertilizers essential to domestic food production. See inter alia Avner Offer, *The First World War: An Agrarian Interpretation* (Oxford: Oxford University Press, 1989), 25, 63. Offer claims, investigating the whole of the country, that Germans suffered culturally, deprived of familiar foods, but that, throughout the war, sufficient calories in one form or another were available. I would argue that working-class and lower-middle-class Berliners at least had access to perilously few sources of calories for long periods in the second half of the war. But I agree that cultural aspects were extremely important as well.

15. On the question of precisely to what degree the blockade itself (as opposed to profiteering and mismanagement of supplies) actually was responsible for the ensuing shortages, see Joe Lee, "Administrators and Agriculture: Aspects of German Agricultural Policy in the First World War," in *War and Economic Development*, ed. J. M. Winter (Cambridge: Cambridge University Press, 1975), 229–38. See also George Yaney, *The World of the Manager: Food Administration in Berlin during World War I* (New York: Peter Lang, 1994). Officials were aware of Britain's plans for a blockade years before the war broke out, but failed to address the anticipated consequences for civilians.

16. *Vossische Zeitung,* 2 February 1915, cited in August Skalweit, *Die Deutsche Ernährungswirtschaft* (Stuttgart: Deutsche Verlagsanstalt, 1927), 28.

17. Authorities were mindful both of consumer riots over meat in Berlin in 1912 and of the prevailing feminized visage of the consumer. The 1912 riots were a consequence of the government tariffs on imported grain and meat, set in the interests of East Elbian Junkers, which greatly inflated the cost of meat for urban consumers, rendering it unaffordable for working-class Berliners. As a result of these riots, Berliner authorities acted for the first time to provide meat for residents. The city of Berlin brought in meat from outside the country and subsidized its sale, thereby defying the intent of imperial tariffs. But while protesters in the 1912 riot were effective in winning a positive response from municipal authorities, there was not the kind of support throughout Berlin society for these working-class consumers (commonly identified in sources as males) that was seen during the war. See on these riots Thomas Lindenberger, "Die Fleischrevolte am Wedding. Lebensmittelversorgung und Politik in Berlin am Vorabend des ersten Weltkrieges," in *Der Kampf um das Tägliche Brot*, 283–304.

18. See, for example, discussion of "the ten wartime missions of the housewife," which was published widely, including in the *Berliner Zeitung,* 17 January 1915. See Skalweit, *Die Deutsche Ernährungswirtschaft,* 28. As the war continued, propaganda was increasingly addressed as well to rural women, urging them to stay on the farm, to disclose production figures, and not to hoard, overeat, or fodder their goods.

19. Officials played simultaneously on several images of women: women as consumers, spies, adulterers (and other sexually vulnerable personae), and other figures suspected of treachery to both family and state. The pages of the weekly illustrated Berlin magazines *Ulk* and *Kladderadatsch* offer plentiful evidence of the prevalence of women figured in negative roles.

20. Geheimes Staatsarchiv Preussischer Kulturbesitz Zweigstelle Merseburg (GStAPK-M) 2.2.1. Rep. 197A, It 1a p. 171, letter from Prussian Interior Minister von Loebell to the Association for Prussian Doctors and to other important Berlin officials, 15 April 1915.

21. GStAPK-M 2.2.1. Rep. 197A, It 1a p. 108, letter from mayor of Lüdenscheid to Prussian Interior Minister von Loebell, 26 January 1915.

22. GStAPK-M 2.2.1. Rep. 197A, It 1a pp. 47–51, memorandum Prussian Interior Minister von Loebell to Sering, January 1915.

23. The notion of the "inner enemy" long preceded the war era. Arising at least as early as Bismarckian Germany, the term referred primarily to Social Democrats and, from the 1890s on, to Jews. Certainly the use of this term for soldiers' wives was not as widespread or as common as its use for Social Democrats or Jews, but records of oral discourse suggest regular reference to soldiers' wives as traitorous to the war effort and to the German people. Relatedly, while government propaganda first cast the blockade as an "economic war," compromising the well-being of civilians in unprecedented fashion, it was popular discourse that fashioned the situation as an "inner economic war," fought by "Germans" against the inner enemy (the latter came to designate a number of different populations).

The reports of plainclothes political police, who spied in the streets of the city to assess popular morale, provide a central source of evidence for the arguments here, along with the broad spectrum of the press, the correspondence and literature of associations and political parties, and government documents from municipal- to Reich-level, both civilian and military. Police reports obviously reflected the concerns and perspectives of these lower-middle-class civil servants—and indeed the argument here is based in part on the transformation in the course of the war in the way the political police represented the street scenes they observed. Moreover, my argument is largely based on the influence of these perceptions on government officials, by rendering this activity worthy of note, and by recommending particular courses of action. At the same time, the basic circumstances described and emphases placed by these police in their reports are confirmed by other sources.

24. There was also some resentment of hoarders—even when they "overprocured" on behalf of their families—because they had the means, which others lacked, to stockpile food. But the term, usually applied to middle- and upper-class women, was at least reported much less often than soldiers' wives.

25. LAP Pr. Br. Rep. 30, Berlin C, Tit. 95, Nr. 15808, pp. 199–201, Mood Report Schwarz, 11 December 1914.

26. LAP Pr. Br., Rep. 30, Berlin C, Tit. 95, Nr. 15810, p. 3, Mood Report Schulz, 1 April 1915.

27. LAP Pr. Br., Rep. 30, Berlin C, Tit. 95, Nr. 15808, p. 141, Report Jagow, 30 November 1914.

28. LAP Pr. Br., Rep. 30, Berlin C, Tit. 95, Nr. 15808, p. 229, Mood Report Diercks, 18 December 1914. The department store was normally the preserve of the bourgeoisie.

Another contrast that appears regularly in police reports is the juxtaposition of the "flurry of consumption" (*rege Kauflust*), which continued in department stores—now putatively frequented by soldiers' wives—and the difficult search for the most basic foods in market places and small shops in poorer quarters of the city.

29. At the same time, while the soldier's wife was the most prominent female consumer, other female consumers indeed counted among her victims.

30. Bundesarchiv Zweigstelle Potsdam (BA-P), Rep. 177, Nr. 13023, pp. 16–1, letter private citizen to Interior Ministry.

31. LAP Pr. Br., Rep. 30, Berlin C, Tit. 95, Nr. 15810, p. 61, Mood Report Diercks, 9 April 1915.

32. The change in the dominant representation of female consumers was astonishingly abrupt, though this is not to say that there were no references to a sympathetic female consumer before early 1915 or to say that there were no negative references to female consumers after that time.

Motherhood was part of this new representation of women consumers, as it had been earlier, but now mothers were seen as appropriately protecting their children. However, the positive characterization of food seekers explicitly as *Mütter* or *Familienmütter* (*mater familias*) was surprisingly rare. It is interesting that those who negatively characterized the mother with many children did not seem to assume that mothers would *naturally* provide for their children before themselves, though, of course, they condemned such women for not doing so. This scenario differs from those represented by Temma Kaplan and Dana Frank, who find tighter links between "woman," "consumer", and "mother" in the protests and collective action they examine, and who discover a specifically "female consciousness," which bound their subjects together as women. See Temma Kaplan, *Red City, Blue Period: Social Movements in Picasso's Barcelona* (Berkeley: University of California Press, 1992), 105–26; and Dana Frank, "Housewives, Socialists, and the Politics of Food: The 1917 New York Cost-of-Living Protests," *Feminist Studies* 11, no. 2 (summer 1985): 255–86. See also Anna Igra's critique of female consciousness in her "Neighborhood-Based Collective Action: The 1917 Anti–High Price Riots," unpublished ms.

33. LAP Pr. Br., Rep. 30, Berlin C, Tit. 95, Nr. 15809, pp. 14–15, Mood Report Dittmann, 14 February 1914.

34. The various populations looked for explanations for the shortage of food and protested their own innocence and goodwill, and, naturally, farmers did their own finger-pointing. See Robert G. Moeller, "Dimensions of Social Conflict in the Great War: A View from the Countryside," *Central European History* 14, no. 2 (1981): 142–68; and idem, *German Peasants and Agrarian Politics, 1914–1924: The Rhineland and Westphalia* (Chapel Hill: University of North Carolina, 1986), 43–67. Moeller looks particularly at the smaller farmers of the west of the country. The increasing acrimony between dwellers in city and countryside, as well as that among the various states and that between the capital and the rest of the country, created all the more intense pressure on Reich-level authorities, and these populations suggested very contradictory methods of recourse. See also Richard Bessel, *Germany after the First World War* (Oxford: Clarendon, 1993), and N. P. Howard, "The Social and Political Consequences of the Allied Food Blockade of Germany, 1918–1919," *German History* 11, no. 2 (1993): 161–188, for discussion of this issue in the postwar period.

35. LAP Pr. Br., Rep. 30, Berlin C, Tit. 95, Nr. 15820, p. 46, Mood Report Schade, 18 December 1916.

36. In fact, as more men were conscripted, more farms, most often family-run businesses, were in the hands of women exclusively. The conscription of men had a similar effect on retail businesses.

37. See, for example, H. von Gerlach, *Die Welt am Montag*, 6 April 1915; and Representative Emmanual Wurm, in a city council forum, quoted in LAP Pr. Br., Rep. 30, Berlin C, Tit. 95, Nr. 15809, pp. 157–60, Mood Report Dittmann, 5 March 1915.

38. See "Musste es dahin kommen?!" in the Social Democratic newspaper *Schwäbische Tagewacht* (Stuttgart), 30 March 1915; this sense was reflected in cities around the country. See also the liberal *Vossische Zeitung* (Berlin), 15 March 1915, relating "the consumer" and "we Germans."

39. Prof. Dr. C. L. Schleich, in *Berliner Tageblatt*, 17 January 1915; also cited in Skalweit, *Die Deutsche Ernährungswirtschaft*, 28.

40. See Skalweit, *Die Deutsche Ernährungswirtschaft*, 97.

41. Ernst Kaeber, *Berlin im Weltkriege: Fünf Jahre Städtischer Kreigsarbeit* (Berlin: de Gruyter, 1964), 199. This particular distinction was actually dropped in May and was replaced by price ceilings and rationing of numerous foods, following one upon the other in rapid succession. It seems to be the case that from the beginning of 1915, protesters generally greeted measures that regulated producers and merchants more enthusiastically than those that reinforced distinctions among consumers. Certainly the various hierarchies of distinction between heavy and light laborers and among the sick, the very young, and those designated for "normal" rations remained highly contentious throughout the war.

42. As suggested above, this challenge to the state to act on behalf of urban consumers was related to concerns and disaffections that existed before the war; but, at the same time, it was very much intensified by the immediate situation. It is worth noting the way in which political rhetoric, agenda, and strategy are so situationally specific. Mary McAuley notes that, in civil war–era St. Petersburg, protesters demanded a reintroduction of the free market to combat the food scarcity. This demand came in response to the new system of total government control of food supply and distribution, which was perceived to be failing in its efforts. See McAuley, "Bread without the Bourgeoisie," in *Party, State, and Society in the Russian Civil War,* ed. Dianne Koenker, William G. Rosenberg, and Ronald Grigor Suny (Bloomington: Indiana University Press, 1989), 158–79; and, more generally, idem, *Bread and Justice* (Oxford: Oxford University Press, 1992). (On the Russian case, see also Lars Lih, *Bread and Authority in Russia, 1914–1921* [Berkeley: University of California Press, 1990.]) This contrast between demands made in Germany and those made in Russia recalls the classic article by Renate Bridenthal and Claudia Koonz, "Beyond '*Kinder, Küche, Kirche*': Weimar Women in Politics and Work," in *When Biology Became Destiny: Women in Weimar and Nazi Germany*, ed. Renate Bridenthal et al. (New York: Monthly Review Press, 1984), 33–65. Correcting the notion that women are essentially politically conservative, Bridenthal and Koonz explain the immediate circumstances of women in the Weimar Republic and discuss the women's vision, the strategies that thereby seemed open to them.

43. LAP Pr. Br., Rep. 30, Berlin C, Tit. 95, Nr. 15809, p. 166, Mood Report Jagow, 6 March 15.

44. For the use of this juxtaposition, see, for example, "Kriegspreise," *Der Grundstein*, 5 January 1915; the author went on to claim that "the salesman had created the neediness of his fellow human." This rhetoric may be found much more widely than just in this Social Democratic paper.

45. Recorded in the Social Democratic newspaper *Mitteilungsblatt*, 10 March 1915,

clipping included in LAP Pr. Br., Rep. 30, Berlin C, Tit. 95, Nr. 15809, p. 174. Richard Bessel claims that it was enormous disenchantment with authorities' bungling intervention in the wartime market, among other things, that motivated significant protest, at least in the period of demobilization. See his "Mobilization and Demobilization in Germany, 1916–1919" (paper presented at Mobilizing for Total War, Dublin, July 1993) and idem, *Germany after the First World War*, 107. This seemingly contradictory motivation may well have been voiced by some sectors of the population, but it seems to me to be testimony to the degree to which the acceptance of and even express desire for intervention had become commonplace. It is clear that the Weimar constitution was framed under the presumption that such interventions were desirable and even demanded of the state in fulfillment of its new obligations. David Crew demonstrates nicely how it became clear as the Weimar years wore on that apparently unified demands for state subvention as well as intervention were based on different presumptions. see Crew, "'Wohlfahrtsbrot ist Bitteres Brot,'" *Archiv für Sozialgeschichte* 30 (1990): 217–45. I have attempted to trace how these different presumptions worked together throughout the war era while looking also at the conjunctural nature of political interests and alliances. See Davis, "Home Fires Burning" (Ph.D. diss., Univ. of Michigan, Ann Arbor, 1992).

46. "Das Pfund Butter: 2,80M," *Vossische Zeitung*, 17 October 1915.

47. From the conservative newspaper *Deutsche Kurier*, 1 April 1916, included in LAP Pr. Br., Rep. 30, Berlin C, Tit. 95, Nr. 15816, p. 10. The column goes on to assert, "[u]nfortunately we people cannot yet live entirely on air alone," establishing remarkably the editorial board's public identification with poorer urban consumers as victims of government policy on the "food question."

48. There were certainly enormous restraints on even willing public servants' ability to carry out policy based on this philosophy.

49. See Davis, "Reconsidering Habermas," for discussion of the contemporary sociology of crowds and the public sphere. In that vision, any traffic not continuously moving in the streets—such as in the form of shoppers waiting for hours before a food shop—automatically constituted an assembly; and assemblies were de facto political.

50. See Alf Lüdtke's study of the use of physical as well as symbolic violence by police in Prussia, *Police and State in Prussia, 1815–1850*. The degree to which the Prussian police were organized as a sort of paramilitary force, with a mandate to protect the state against its subjects, has long been argued. This Prussian tradition differs certainly from the Anglo-American tradition of the nineteenth and early twentieth centuries, in which police were ostensibly to serve and protect the people. The Prussian police were reorganized and their range of influence was extended under Wilhelm II. See, for example, Albrecht Funk, *Polizei und Rechtsstaat: Die Entwicklung des Staatlichen Gewaltmonopols in Preussen, 1848–1918* (Frankfurt am Main: Campus, 1986); and compare Ralph Jessen, *Polizei im Industrierevier: Modernisierung und Herrschaftspraxis im Westfälischen Ruhrgebiet 1848–1914* (Göttingen: Vandenhoeck and Ruprecht, 1991); and Elaine Glovka Spencer, *Police and the Social Order in German Cities: The Düsseldorf District, 1848–1914* (Dekalb: Northern Illinois University Press, 1992). As part of the reorganization, a corps of political police was created, which was to monitor and control the state's "inner enemies"; a corps of street police, which was to control public order, was also created. There was little love lost between the residents of working-class Berlin and the local patrolmen on the eve of the war (see on

this Thomas Lindenberger, "Strassenpolitik: Zur Sozialgeschichte der öffentlichen Ordnung in Berlin, 1900–1914" [Ph.D. diss., Technische Universität, Berlin, 1992], 126). Working-class women seemed to retain their dislike of the police throughout the war, even as the political police defended the needs of these women ever more vehemently to state authorities and increasingly offered evidence of their own difficulties with food scarcity and cost in the same breath. Indeed, police mood reports provide important evidence of near-mutinous activity by segments of the police force, though very different from the mutiny of sailors in October 1918. There is no study focusing on police activity during the war era, but this activity clearly warrants further study.

51. This grimly humorous description was a commonplace by late 1915. See, for example, LAP Pr. Br., Rep. 30, Berlin C, Tit. 95, Nr. 15819, p. 202, Mood Report Münn, 26 October 1916.

52. Working-class women were most prominent on the streets because the relocation of goods to wealthier neighborhoods meant shorter lines for richer women, who in any case were still sending servants to shop at this point in the war. Interestingly, wealthier women successfully employed more individualist strategies to achieve their ends, for example, calling on neighborhood police and otherwise threatening shopkeepers, or offering shopkeepers more than the posted price, for example, to be included on a special "customer list."

53. In this era, butter was sold almost exclusively through franchise shops. Chain dairies such as Bolle and Assmann had aroused mistrust for years.

54. See, for example, LAP Pr. Br., Rep. 30, Berlin C, Tit. 95, Nr. 15814, p. 97, Mood Report Hanff, 18 October 1915.

Radaulustig, literally "desirous of, or taking pleasure in, rows," is translated as "rabble-rousing" to suggest the qualities of willful provocation; but the term could also mean "looking for a fight," which suggests the creation of violent disturbance for its own sake. The term is employed frequently in police reports and the press, and the wider semantic range is relevant throughout.

55. They were conceived of as something like the brigands of revolutionary France were: see, for example, George Lefebvre, *The Great Fear of 1789* (New York: Pantheon, 1973).

56. LAP Pr. Br., Rep. 30, Berlin C, Tit. 95, Nr. 15814, pp. 29–30, Mood Report Sauer, 16.10.15. Notably, the central, damning clause regarding the "shameless exploitation" was stricken, probably by Sauer's superior, Sergeant Schwarz, before the report was passed on to Police Chief Jagow. (Of course, the original draft was filed as well as the final version, so presumably Jagow saw the clause.) In general, however, this opinion was articulated by police clearly and was widespread.

57. LAP Pr. Br., Rep. 30, Berlin C, Tit. 95, Nr. 15814, p. 95, Marginalia Schwarz on press clipping, 18 October 1915. *Anerkennung* is an interesting word; it means not only "acknowledgement" but also "approval." Thus police had ascribed to women "of little means" the power and stature to adjudicate on the satisfactory nature of the official act.

58. Poor women were in effect doubly disenfranchised, by virtue of both their gender and their income level.

59. LAP Pr. Br., Rep. 30, Berlin C, Tit. 95, Nr. 15813, p. 258, Mood Report Schwarz, 14 October 1915.

60. For example, military forays into Rumania and Ukraine were driven at least in part by domestic need for grain.

61. For a discussion of the consumer as citizen and patriot, and as the embodiment of a new German sovereignty in the course of the war, see Belinda Davis, "Bread and Democracy in World War I Germany," unpublished ms.; and compare Lizabeth Cohen, "Women as Citizen Consumers," unpublished ms., both presented at the conference "Consuming Politics," April 1993, New Brunswick, N.J.

62. Bismarckian and Wilhelmine social policy was characterized by a two-track system: one track was represented by the long-standing tradition of local-level, public/ private poor relief, often haphazard aid that stigmatized and marginalized its recipients; the other track was represented by Bismarck's policy of social insurance, Reich-level legislation that provided health insurance, workmen's compensation, and pension benefits. Although pathbreaking, the paternalistic social insurance was instituted precisely to maintain traditional relations of authority, in the face of Social Democratic demands for a far more radical redistribution of social, economic, and political power. See George Steinmetz's nuanced recent contribution, *Regulating the Social: The Welfare State and Local Politics in Imperial Germany* (Princeton: Princeton University Press, 1993).

63. On the idea of state support as a right, see, for example, Werner Abelshauser, ed., *Die Weimarer Republik als Wohlfahrtsstaat: Zum Verhältnis von Wirtschafts- und Sozialpolitik in der Industriegesellschaft* (Stuttgart: Kohlkammer, 1987).

Though there has been excellent work on the move from Wilhelmine social insurance to the Weimar welfare state, few have carefully examined the role of the war; and no studies have focused on the popular activities of working-class women or on the role of the consumer, as does this piece. See, for example, essays in Christoph Sachsse and Florian Tennstedt, eds., *Geschichte der Armenfürsorge in Deutschland* (Stuttgart: Kohlkammer, 1980); in Wolfgang Mommsen, ed., *The Emergence of the Welfare State in Britain and Germany, 1850–1950* (London: Croom Helm, 1981); and in Rudiger vom Bruch, ed., *Weder Kommunismus noch Kapitalismus: Bürgerliche Sozialreform in Deutschland vom Vormärz bis zur Ära Adenauer* (Munich: C. H. Beck, 1985). For works that bear more directly on the period of transition, see Young Sun Hong, "The Contradictions of Modernization in the German Welfare State: Gender and the Politics of Welfare Reform in First World War Germany," *Social History* 17, no. 2 (May 1992): 251–70; and Christoph Sachsse, "Social Mothers: The Bourgeois Women's Movement and German Welfare-State Formation, 1890–1929," in *Mothers of a New World: Maternalist Politics and the Origins of Welfare States*, ed. Seth Koven and Sonya Michel (New York: Routledge, 1993), 136–58. Both Sachsse and Hong focus primarily on transformations in the role played by bourgeois women and their associations from the Kaiserreich to the Weimar Republic.

64. See, for example, David Crew, "'Wohlfahrtsbrot ist Bitteres Brot,'" 217–45.

TEN

Making Up, Making Over
Cosmetics, Consumer Culture, and Women's Identity

Kathy Peiss

A painted face is a false face, a true falshood [sic], not a true face.
THOMAS TUKE, *DISCOURSE AGAINST PAINTING AND TINCTURING,* 1616

By changing the way you look . . . you can create a new you!
COSMOPOLITAN, 1991

In 1938 *Mademoiselle* magazine reported that the cosmetics firm Volupté had produced two new lipsticks for the market. These were "lipstick for types": one for "girls who lean toward pale-lacquered nails, quiet smart clothes and tiny strands of pearls"; the other "for the girl who loves exciting clothes, pins a strass pin big as a saucer to her dress, and likes to be just a leetle bit shocking." One had a "soft mat finish" while the other covered the lips "with a gleaming lustre." The names given to these lipsticks were, respectively, *Lady* and *Hussy*. As *Mademoiselle* put it, "Each of these two categories being as much a matter of mood as a matter of fact, we leave you to decide which you prefer to be."[1]

These products may not have fared well on the market, but the assumptions behind their promotion are remarkable. Social identities that had once been fundamental to women's consciousness, fixed in parentage, class position, conventions of respectability, and sexual codes, were now released from small swiveling cylinders. Not only could women choose these categories of identity, but for two dollars, they could enjoy both. "Lady" and "hussy" were no longer the moral poles of womanhood but rather "types" and "moods" defined largely by external signs. Products of a consumer culture, these lipsticks, trivial in themselves, underscore new relationships between cosmetics, appearance, and female identity in the twentieth century. For nineteenth-century Americans, being a lady meant forswearing visible cosmetics: the painted woman was a figure of deception and alterity, an inauthentic self and a debased social "other." By the 1930s, as this lipstick example makes clear, makeup had become integral to self-expression and the belief that identity was a purchasable style.

This essay focuses on changing cultural perceptions of the relationship between women's identity and appearance—the gendered self and self-presentation—and the effects of a commodity/consumer culture upon those perceptions. It explores the cultural and ideological construction of cosmetic practices, how commercially sold makeup problematized and signified women's identity.

In recent years, historians have debated the implications of twentieth-century American consumer culture for notions of personal and social identity. In Warren Susman's classic formulation, consumer culture transformed the self defined by "character" into one typified by "personality." By the early 1900s, the new apparatus of commerce—advertising agencies, mass communications, large-scale retailing, consumer credit, commercial leisure—fostered both a quantitative and qualitative change in Americans' relationship to goods. These changes reached deeply into the psyche. Where mid-nineteenth-century Americans had believed in the fixity of identity, a fundamental self rooted in a moral economy of hard work and thrift, by the 1920s, self had become largely a matter of merchandising and performance and was built around commodities, style, and personal magnetism. Historians since Susman have quarreled with the periodization of this formulation, finding "cultures of consumption" to exist in North America and Europe long before the early twentieth century. They argue with the distinction between character and personality, observing that definitions of the self through external markers—which purportedly characterize personality in the early twentieth century—were widespread in the Victorian era as well.[2]

Given several decades of feminist and postmodernist analysis, it is now apparent how much gender, and difference more generally, have shaped the conceptualization of identity in consumer culture. "Character" and "personality" contrast constellations of traits and values that have been deeply gendered: work/leisure, production/consumption, internal/external, natural/artificial, fixed/mutable, serious/superficial. Character appears less a matter of cultural consensus and more a cultural problem of the Victorian era, tied to the achievement, inscription, and essentializing of the social differences of gender, class, and race. If this is the case, what then does it mean that, in the early twentieth century, the traits and values associated with the second halves of these opposite pairs—all coded feminine—became so dominant in American cultural discourses?[3]

Among the central issues for us to explore, then, is the constitution of the gendered consumer in relation to other socially determined identities. Unfortunately, much of the foundational work on consumer culture naturalizes or overgeneralizes this question. To explain consumer behavior, scholars often rely on overarching psychological theories that simply assume a feminine actor. Feminist analyses that foreground gender frequently reduce the question to a debate over consumption's oppressive versus liberatory effects on women. Given the incipient state of the field, generalizations are not yet warranted. Buying a lipstick and buying a car, for instance, are different consumer acts occurring in distinct discursive and social contexts, although both involve, among other things, consumption, appearance, and identity. Historians will need to explore the distinctions among different forms of consumption and place consumption fully in context, before we can generally assess the effects of a consumer society on gender constitution and on women's lives.

This essay examines one specific consumer commodity, cosmetics, and the cultural meanings applied to powder and paint. Across time and cultures, cosmetics have been important means of expressing social status, commonality, and difference. In the twentieth century, a period of highly unstable and contested gender definitions, cosmetics—as mass-produced and mass-distributed commodities—became especially salient markers of normative female identity. This essay suggests some of the cultural processes through which that occurred.

COSMETICS AS A CULTURAL PROBLEM IN NINETEENTH-CENTURY AMERICA

In Western culture, the face, of all parts of the human body, has been marked as particularly meaningful, a unique site of expression, beauty, and character. The privileged position of the face as a sign of individual being was a commonplace of American thought in the nineteenth century. Believing in the commensurability of external appearance and the internal self, Americans held to a physiognomic paradigm, despite anxious perceptions that appearances might be deceiving. Physiognomic principles were closely wedded to a Romanticist moral aesthetic directed especially at female identity and beauty. In this view, physical beauty had "a representative and correspondent" relationship to spiritual beauty and moral goodness. Beauty thus originated less in visual sensation and formal aesthetics than in internal character. Writers specifically marked expressive eyes and transparent complexion as the critical media linking surface beauty to inner spirit.[4]

If beauty signified goodness, achieving beauty became a moral dilemma. Should a woman try to increase her beauty, and if so, how should she do it? The consensus in fiction and prescriptive literature in the pre–Civil War period was that beauty could be achieved only through moral improvement, a process that involved the spiritual and the physical body. By the 1830s, as Karen Halttunen has shown, a cult of sentimentality and sincerity advocated "moral cosmetics"—soap, exercise, and temperance—for the development of virtue, health, and beauty.[5]

The idealization of the "natural" face occurred, it should be noted, in a country that was already, in some sense, a consumer society. The middle classes were busily engaged in purchasing consumer goods, reading magazines and novels, taking in advertisements. Other places in which "private" and "public" met—the clothed body, the well-furnished parlor—were accepted, indeed celebrated, as sites of commodity culture. For nineteenth-century women, the clean, natural face was part of a consciously composed presentation of the self, in which artifice shaped the body to a fashionable silhouette and clothing was exuberantly ornamental.[6] The face, however, was understood to be outside fashion and consumption. It conveyed the fixity and essence of identity in contrast to the mutability, conformism, and social nature of dress. Still, women improved their faces (outside the realm of purchasable goods) through "complexion management"—pinching cheeks and biting lips, or wearing colored bonnet linings to enhance facial tints.[7] The "natural" thus must be seen as a culturally constructed category orienting standards of beauty, taste, and respectability.

Visible cosmetics entered into middle-class discourse as "corporeal hypocrisy." Symbolic of artifice, deception, and masking, they raised the value of "facial truth" required by the physiognomic paradigm. Americans contrasted skin-improving cosmetics, typically creams and lotions, with skin-masking paints, including powders and rouge. As one writer put it, "Paints must not be confounded with Cosmetics, which often really do impart whiteness, freshness, suppleness, and brilliancy to the skin. . . . these consequently assist Nature, and make amends for her defects." Paints, another said, masked nature's handiwork, hiding expression and truth behind an "encrusted mould," a "mummy surface."[8]

This typology—cosmetic and paint, nature and artifice—extended to the arena of manufacture and distribution. From at least the seventeenth century, skin-improving cosmetics were part of "kitchen-physic," the household manufacture of medicines and therapeutic substances long viewed as women's domain. These cosmetics were made in the Galenic tradition, using herbs and organic substances considered harmless. Handwritten recipe books, printed household manuals, and guides to beauty—all containing cosmetic recipes—were commonplace in the nineteenth century.[9]

Paints, in contrast, represented to many the entire class of proprietary cosmetics sold on the market by manufacturing chemists, patent medicine firms, and pharmacists. These frequently contained dangerous chemical compounds, including compounds of mercury, lead, and arsenic. The toxicity and commercialization of paints occasioned public concern and provoked anxiety over deceptive appearances and bodily dangers. Even when paints were made of relatively safe organic substances, people worried over such cosmetics' commodity form: paints, enamels, and powders represented quite literally larger fears about the corrosive effects of the market—the false colors of sellers, the superficial brilliance of advertisers, the masking of true value.[10]

In the postrevolutionary United States, paints also signified a discredited aristocratic culture of "high-style" gentility. In the eighteenth century, cosmetics use had been more a matter of class than of gender. Upper-class colonists of both sexes imitated the fashions of the English aristocracy by applying rouge, powder, and even beauty patches.[11] During and after the American Revolution, however, luxurious dry goods, decorative fashions, and imported cosmetics were attacked as patrician styles to be shunned in a republican society of manly citizens and virtuous domestic women. The transformation in attitudes toward self-presentation was most pronounced in men, for whom older styles of authority were newly defined as effeminate. By the 1830s, the democratization of politics had heightened the association between citizenship and rugged manliness. In such a climate, cosmetic practices among men became, at most, covert and unacknowledged.[12]

Women, too, were instructed to shun paints and artifice, but in the service of new notions of femininity. In early-nineteenth-century discourse, the feminine was identified with spiritual equality, domestic sovereignty, and a transcendent purity rooted in, but not limited to, sexual chastity. These views reinforced, and in turn were deepened by, the growing cultural authority of a middle class whose identity was structured, in large part, around essential gender/sexual difference.[13] This fixed, pre-existing feminine self was to be transparently represented, and indeed stabilized, through "natural" beauty.

Cosmetics continued to represent profound anxieties about women's nature and authenticity. Paint marked vices that for centuries had been associated with women—corrupt and uncontrolled sexuality, vanity, and deceit. "Oriental" Jezebel continued to be a point of reference for unacceptable female behavior in nineteenth-century Biblical commentary: painting the face with kohl and rouge triggered sermons on women's love of finery, their idolatry, and their objectionable sexuality.[14] Cosmetics were associated as well with illicit commerce, the merchandising of women's bodies in prostitution. In popular speech and song the stereotypical painted woman remained the prostitute, who brazenly advertised her immoral profession through rouge and eye paint. Newspapers, tracts, and other sources frequently mentioned, in a formulaic way, the "painted, diseased, drunken women, bargaining themselves away" in theaters, in public carriages, or in the streets.[15]

Still, the painted woman was in the nineteenth century a figure of accretions, a layering of earlier meanings with newer inflections. The earlier rhetoric of cosmetic practices frequently served to make cultural distinctions based on contemporary consumption styles and gender behavior *within* the middle and upper classes. By the Civil War, this language was increasingly directed against fast young ladies on the marriage market and middle-aged women seemingly more attentive to youth and fashion than maternity. A number of virulent attacks on fashionable women's appearance occurred in the 1860s and 1870s. Expressing anxiety over women's transgressive behavior, these articulated popular distaste for the rising "shoddy aristocracy" and nouveau riche (figure 26). The ultrafashionable woman, called by one author "a compound . . . of false hair, false teeth, padding of various kinds, paint, powder, and enamel," betrayed feminine nature by visiting the enameler's studio.[16] Such criticisms underscored and potentially enforced intraclass standards of genteel appearance, taste, and morality as they proscribed "selfish" female consumption.

Cosmetics not only marked symbolic distinctions between and within social classes but also reinforced racial typologies and hierarchies. The advocacy of the natural face masked the most widespread face-altering cosmetic practice in the nineteenth century, whitening the skin. Age-old anxiety over cosmetic deceit dovetailed with racial fears, particularly in the postemancipation advice literature. One cautionary tale about cosmetic washes containing lead or bismuth appeared repeatedly. The product was intended to whiten the skin but had the reverse effect when it came in contact with sulfur in the air. The setting for this story varied—a public lecture, a laboratory, a summer resort—but in each case the cosmetic-using woman was humiliated because her "lily white" complexion had been muddied and darkened.[17]

By the late nineteenth century, the linkage between cosmetics and racial identity, articulated increasingly in the languages of Darwinism and anthropology, served to mark boundaries of civilization and savagery. Face paint, which falsified beauty, hindered the progress of civilization by distorting the evolutionary process of sexual selection. One writer called visible cosmetics a "lingering taint of the savage and barbarous"; others ridiculed ultrafashionable American women, juxtaposing them with Pygmies, Hottentots, and other African peoples.[18] Such social classifications received reinforcement through common representational strategies. Smithsonian anthropologist Robert Shufeldt, for example, used photographs in his 1891 account of "Indian types of beauty"; the most beautiful posed in the guise of Victorian ladies, while those considered ugly appeared ethnographically, their seminaked bodies, frontal pose, and cosmetic paint conveying their "alien" and savage nature (figures 27 and 28).[19]

The dominant discourse on cosmetics, then, placed paint outside the truthful representation of personal and social identity, identifying cosmetics with disrepute and deceit, a debased female and non-European "other." This discourse was an effort to reinscribe the fixity and naturalness of social hierarchies by ensuring that external manifestations corresponded to inner being. The longstanding association of visible cosmetics with illicit sexuality and commerce, newly applied to nineteenth-century society, contributed to the bourgeois definition of the feminine. Even so, artifice and artfulness threatened to undermine this paradigm.

Figure 26. "Every One Recognizes Your Ability to Paint (Yourself)." Trade card, ca. 1870.

Figure 27. Robert W. Shufeldt, "A Belle of Laguna," 1891.

Figure 28. Robert W. Shufeldt, "Mohave Women," 1891.

MAKING UP FOR THE SHOW

In the post–Civil War decades, cultural tensions over female appearance and identity seem to have deepened substantially. Evidence of such anxiety abounds: warnings about prostitutes disguised as shoppers and saleswomen appearing to be "ladies"; advice to marriageable men on how to tell authentic beauties from fakes; stories of light-skinned octaroons passing into white society. Whether women's social status was quantitatively more fluid and unstable at this time would be difficult to establish, but certainly this perception was widespread.[20]

Scattered evidence in diaries and letters suggests that some nineteenth-century women embraced visible cosmetics and the potential for transgression and illusion they offered. During and after the Civil War, fashionable women, young and old, played with and subverted notions of natural beauty and appropriate female behavior. Ellen Ruggles Strong, a member of New York's social elite and wife of civic leader George Templeton Strong, provides one example. At various parties, philanthropic events, and hospital relief sites, Ellen could be seen, in diarist Mary Lydig Daly's words, "painted like a wanton." Her husband, however, clothed Ellen in the garb of true womanhood: "poor, little Ellen in her ignorance and simplicity," "a noble little girl." Although her own voice is missing, Ellen's skillful performance is not. Artfully, she portrayed the dutiful wife who appeared at hospitals and charity events, who gave up waltzing when her husband disapproved, and who shunned Tiffany's vanities as he watched. Out of his presence, she dabbled in the world of fashion, seductive young men, parties, and pleasures.[21] Her beauty secrets, unseen by men yet visible to women, were integral to her rendering of both parts.

This performance of identity—constituting the self through appearance and gesture—was fundamentally at odds with notions of fixed personal and social identity. While such performances may inherently constitute identity,[22] they became more visible and apparent as performances in the late nineteenth and early twentieth centuries. Increasingly incorporated into Americans' understanding of the self, notions of performance reconfigured the ways in which cosmetic practices were understood as well. What had been perceived as a falsifying, deceptive practice might instead be understood as dramatic enactment in a culture increasingly oriented to "looks," display, spectatorship, and consumption.[23]

The legitimation of visible cosmetics occurred first in contexts where women were consciously representing themselves to others, performing a role, or creating themselves as spectacles to be viewed. In the photographer's studio and the theater, we can see particular ways in which the physiognomic paradigm was undermined.

Photographic portrait taking became an occasion, as Alan Trachtenberg has put it, for "the making of oneself over into a social image," with the urban photographer's gallery a "new kind of city place devoted to performance." Patrons appeared dressed in their fanciest clothing, laden with jewelry, and they struck unnatural poses. Photographers began to teach their clients the art of self-portrayal. H. J. Rodgers' manual, for example, advised sitters on understanding their physiognomy, choosing appropriate fashions, and using cosmetics to enhance the face; the book included pages of cosmetic recipes.[24]

Although photographers praised the facticity of the photograph over the painted portrait, from the sitter's perspective the surface image of the photograph pulled in another direction, toward a critical assessment of appearance itself. The truth of the photograph could be quite painful, "too natural, to please any other than very beautiful sitters."[25] Given the disparity between self-image and photographic "truth," American women who might not wear cosmetics in their daily lives demanded to have their faces made up at the portrait studios. As the photograph became a popular commodity, it may have made manifest the tensions latent in the physiognomic paradigm by making beauty a more problematic category. What had once been a matter mainly for the imagination and the mirror was now externalized and fixed on the photographic plate. As "factual" representations of appearance, photographs measured the distance between ideal beauty and reality.

In the post–Civil War years, these measurements of appearance became even more palpable as actresses and professional "beauties" rose from women of questionable morality to celebrities and "stars." Although the United States had been enchanted by such female performers as Jenny Lind and Fanny Kemble in the antebellum period, women achieved a new prominence on the stage after 1860. While many of these were players in serious drama, the most visible and controversial were those who performed in burlesques and shows that combined sexual display with comic dialogue. Such figures as Adah Mencken and the British Blondes brought to the American stage a new kind of actress, who blurred the line between the performance of a theatrical role and the performance of her "real self." These women brought a new theatricality into everyday life, fostering a contentious debate over artifice and cosmetic effects. Their use of blonde hair dye and visible makeup became the popular rage, at least in New York.[26]

Female actresses were not only much talked about, they seem to have been incorporated into the private lives of Americans in new ways. By the 1860s, celebrity *carte de visite* photographs circulated widely. These images of retouched and idealized actresses were traded and placed in photograph albums, often on the same pages as pictures of family and friends. Significantly stage actresses were the first group to offer advertising testimonials for cosmetics. The new conceptual separation of prostitutes and actresses opened a space for the promotion of the use of makeup as a legitimate female cultural practice.[27]

The close relationship between makeup and performance began to justify the use of cosmetics more generally in the nineteenth century. Women wore makeup on occasions involving public or semipublic display, such as amateur theatricals, tableaux vivants, coming-out parties, and balls. The advice literature of the late nineteenth century distinguished between daytime and evening activities, permitting face powder and rouge in settings that involved a play-world of artificial light, spectacle, and pleasures. Artifice was allowable, beauty manuals now conceded, if used in the service of representing a woman's "true" identity. An old woman who used rouge to deceive a man into marriage was a "painted Jezebel," observed one advice book, but reddening the cheeks was a "fair stratagem" of the young woman if its use originated in "an innocent desire to please."[28] Here the older view of cosmetics was acknowledged but displaced by a new understanding of artifice based on the intentions and desires of the cosmetics consumer.

Connotations of women as tarnished merchandise continued to mark cosmetics: the prostitute remained the touchstone of condemnatory views of these commodities. But a critical new element was advanced in the late nineteenth century: that making up was preparation for women's legitimate public performances. This view implied a degree of agency, self-creation, and pleasure in self-representation. For the nascent beauty industry, this became the new paradigm of female appearance.

THE COSMETICS INDUSTRY AND THE MAKEOVER

In the late nineteenth century, a growing trade in cosmetics and beauty products, reinforced by the proliferation of magazines, advice literature, and advertising, began to intervene in the cultural discourse over the authenticity of the female face. Before that time, the cosmetics trade was small-scale and locally based. Typically a pharmacist or hairdresser would compound creams and lotions for sale to a familiar clientele. Some "patent cosmetics" were stocked by pharmacists and general stores, but there was little national distribution or advertising of cosmetic products.[29] By 1880 a spider's web of establishments—pharmaceutical houses, perfumers, beauty salons, drugstores, wholesale suppliers, the incipient mail order trade, and department stores—provided the infrastructure for beauty culture. This commercial nexus reached into every level of the social scale; by the early 1900s, beauty products were available to urban immigrants, African-Americans, and rural women.[30]

Commercial beauty culture converted complexion management from a largely private act to a public and visible ritual. Middle- and upper-class beauty parlors, like department stores, assiduously catered to their female clientele in the quality of their fixtures and the personal services provided by beauty operators. Even the cheaper salons created the experience of self-indulgence and sensuous pleasure, offering not only hairdressing but facial treatments and massage. Commercial beauty culture popularized the democratic and anxiety-inducing idea that beauty could be achieved by all women—if only they used the correct products and treatments. Initially beauty culturists were reticent about visible cosmetics, favoring "natural" methods of achieving beauty over paints. Until World War I, advertisements rarely promoted rouge or eyebrow pencils, even though drugstores and salons carried them.

Nevertheless, beauty culturists and cosmetics manufacturers evolved a language of metamorphosis for their services and products that spoke directly to the troubled relationship between appearance and identity. Before-and-after advertisements, instructions for makeup applications, and cosmetology manuals spoke of transformation, what women's magazines today call the makeover. Cosmetics not only remade external appearance, they became a crucial aspect of self-realization.

The notion of makeover resonated throughout the emergent cosmetics industry. A number of its leading female entrepreneurs had made *themselves* over as they pursued business success. Helena Rubinstein, for example, claimed for herself an aristocratic heritage and extensive scientific training. She in fact came from a petit bourgeois family in Austria; her training consisted of a year or two in medical school; the face cream formula that launched her business came from a pharmacist uncle. Elizabeth Arden, Rubinstein's greatest competitor, promoted an image of wealthy Anglo-Saxon gentility and hauteur for herself and her company. She began life, however, as Florence Nightingale Graham, born into a Canadian lower-middle-class family. Like many young women, she migrated to New York to find work and support herself. Starting out as a receptionist and beauty operator, she eventually became an independent salon owner and successful entrepreneur.[31]

In the 1910s and 1920s, the makeover promised both personal and social transformation, although its precise meaning varied within a market divided along the lines of class, race, and age. Arden and Rubinstein, for example, quietly urged their wealthy clientele to make up in the French style to become fashion leaders, to distinguish themselves from the less modern bourgeois women who scorned makeup or hid their makeup practices. Mass-market manufacturers, in contrast, depicted the makeover as the first step toward achieving upward mobility and personal popularity. They conceived of public arenas, from the workplace to the boardwalk, as performance sites where young women could succeed through manufactured beauty.

In promising transformation, the cosmetics industry blurred the distinction between the made-up face as *revealing* a woman's inner self and the made-up face *constituting* that self. The Armand complexion powder campaign exemplified the mixed message. This mass-market firm ran a series of advertisements in 1929 appealing to popular interest in psychology and beauty. Armand's advertising directed each woman to "find yourself," offering a free question-and-answer booklet written by a "famous psychologist and a noted beauty expert." However, individuality was readily submerged into a typology that coded personality in terms of facial appearance. Except for hairstyle and color, the faces of these women were hardly distinguishable, yet their personalities were classed with names—Sheba, Cleopatra, Cherie—that appear to be ethnic euphemisms (figure 29). By the mid-1920s companies packaged products on the basis of personality types defined largely by skin tone, eye color, or hair color.[32]

Cosmetic promotions found new ways to dislodge the sense of fixity and naturalism in the feminine. The early advertising for Pompeian face cream stressed conventional mother-daughter relationships, using the language of Victorian sentimentality and images that showed distinct differences in age and social role. By 1923, Pompeian was depicting the youthful modern mother. "You're getting younger every day!" observed the daughter, and indeed she was literally correct: mother had exactly the same face as her child. Maybelline advertisements broke the age-old association between eye make-up and "painted Jezebels" by promoting images of popular film actresses that were eroticized, yet within the realm of public acceptability. Advertising especially in confession and movie magazines, they urged young white working-class women to identify with these glamorous stars.[33]

By the early twentieth century, a mass cosmetics trade, supported by the coordinated efforts of advertising agencies, women's magazines, and professional beauty "experts," had validated a female identity signified by, and to some extent formed in, the marking and coloring of the face. Through this claim, which simultaneously prescribed feminine appearance and played upon the consumer's belief in her individuality, the cosmetics industry attempted to make its products necessary to American women's appearance and sense of self.

THE BEAUTY CULTURE OF THE "OTHER"

From the perspective of the late twentieth century, it may be hard not to view the aims and methods of commercial beauty culture in any but cynical terms. Decades of advertising and advice have touted the centrality of external beauty in women's successful negotiation of life and the role of cosmetics in enhancing self-esteem. For many feminists, these promises are simply manipulative and victimizing tactics to sell products.[34] The historical evidence suggests, however, that the cosmetics industry exploited already existing tensions in the relationship between appearance and female identity. Moreover, the specific rhetoric of cosmetic transformation, and the general promotion

Figure 29. "Which of These Alluring Types Are You?" Detail from
Armand Complexion Powder Ad Proof, 1929.

of beauty culture in the early twentieth century, spoke to genuine concerns and desires whose terms were bound up in the changing experiences of women. The proliferation of cosmetics in the consumer market coincided with women's new relationship to the public sphere: their expanding but contested participation in economic, political, and social activities formerly understood in cultural terms as masculine. Women's growing presence in the labor force generated anxiety that was frequently represented in bodily and sexual imagery. Indeed, a number of the new jobs open to women required particular attention to appearance and interpersonal behavior. Saleswomen, waitresses, secretaries, entertainers and others working in the clerical and service sectors transformed themselves into the "types" expected in these jobs. Even factory workers found themselves sorted into different kinds of labor based on the appearance of respectability, good grooming, and ethnic identity. Guidance counselors in high schools and colleges, orienting young people to the job market, offered vocational advice to women in part on the basis of attractiveness and other physical attributes. At the same time, working women brought cosmetic practices into their work cultures as a source of on-the-job pleasure and assertion: saleswomen, for example, exasperated department store managers with their excessive use of face powder.[35]

The social organization of sexuality and marriage similarly reinforced the importance of appearance in the early twentieth century. Dating and courtship increasingly occurred in a market context, in commercialized leisure and consumption activities where women could trade on their looks. The popular ideology of romantic love, articulated not only in mass-circulation magazines but in peer group cultures in schools and workplaces, promulgated notions of personal magnetism and fascination that, for women, merged with physical beauty.[36]

A closer look at the relationship of the cosmetics trade to specific communities of women should lead us to consider seriously the claims and concerns expressed by both producers and consumers of cosmetics. This is particularly the case for immigrant women, working-class women, and African-American women—the very groups against whom ideals of beauty had been defined in the nineteenth century. For women culturally defined as other, commercial beauty culture could become an arena in which issues not only of appearance but of personal, social, and even political identity might be staged and discussed.

In the early twentieth century, young immigrant and second-generation women, for example, signaled their new "American" status by adopting the conventions of external beauty promoted not only in cosmetics advertisements and beauty salons but in their interactions with peers. Cosmetics were often the grounds for intergenerational conflict, seen by young women as necessary for participation in social life but perceived by parents as sexually provocative. While many women used "respectable" amounts of powder and rouge, others embraced the theatricality of cosmetics. Some delighted in *showing* the artifice—making up their faces in restaurants or pulling powder puffs out of stocking tops at dance halls. Significantly, the most extreme cosmetics users in the early 1920s appear to have been working-class truants and delinquents, who wore thick layers of face powder and rouge, painted bow lips, and beaded eyelashes. Adopting an "artificial" facial appearance, they rejected the stigmatizing labels others placed on them, such as "problem girls" or "whores," and, imitating their movie idols, transformed themselves into romantic heroines.[37]

An even more telling example is the development of an African-American hair-care and cosmetics industry in the early 1900s, marketing to consumers who had been culturally denied the possibility of beauty in the nineteenth century.[38] Although white-owned patent medicine firms began to cultivate a Black consumer market in the 1880s and 1890s, such African-American entrepreneurs as Anthony Overton, Madame C. J. Walker, and Annie Turnbo Malone revolutionized the trade. The timing of their industry's development is notable: the industry took off in the period of disfranchisement and entrenched segregation in the South, worsening economic conditions, an expanding Black population in southern cities, and the beginnings of the great migration to the North.

The period was also significant for Black women's individual and collective response to decades of abuse, poverty, and discrimination. An important part of this response was the public denunciation of stereotypes of Black womanhood and the search for new, empowering identities. Although it is middle-class, educated African-American women who offer the fullest evidence of this response, women outside this group sought new modes of self-definition as well. An important dimension of this effort lay in the making over of appearance. As Azalia Hackley, author of a beauty manual for "colored girls," wrote: "The time has come to fight, not only for rights, but for looks as well."[39]

Debates over hair straighteners and skin bleaches—the most controversial of many beauty products used by African-American women—exemplify both the empowering and constraining meanings expressed through self-presentation. Many Black women reformers, political leaders, and journalists drew the conclusion that the use of these products was evidence of white aesthetic and psychological domination.[40] Yet white emulation, in a literal sense, seems an insufficient explanation for their popularity. Although some African-Americans indeed "passed" into white society, bleaches and straighteners held little possibility of effecting such a transformation.[41] More to the point, European aesthetic domination shaped status distinctions *among* African-Americans. Lighter skin, straight hair, and European features were believed advantageous for gaining job opportunities and good marriage partners. Still, careful observers noted a more complex valuation of color than

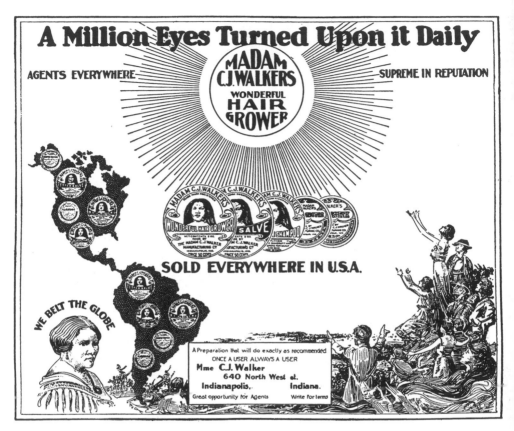

Figure 30. Madame C. J. Walker advertisement, 1919.

a simple hierarchy of whiteness. St. Clair Drake and Horace Cayton, in their study of Black Chicago in the 1940s, remarked: "When Negroes disapprove of 'blackness' they often mean a whole complex: dark-skin color, pronounced Negroid features and kinky hair."[42] It is this aesthetic complex, integral to white ideologies buttressing discrimination, and not an explicit desire to "look white" that African-American beauty culturists directly addressed. Gaining respect and dignity were the terms by which appearance became a basis of African-American commercial enterprise and consumption.

African-American beauty culturists made cosmetics central to the ideal of the "New Negro Woman." As consumers of beauty products, they argued, Black women could change the stereotyped representations that socially and sexually debased them. At the same time, evoking the Washingtonian emphasis on race pride and self-help, they called for public support of commercial beauty culture because these ventures empowered women as producers.

Figure 31. Madame C. J. Walker advertisement, 1925.

Trained to be salon owners, beauty operatives, and sales agents, African-American women would gain opportunities for economic advancement unavailable to female domestic or agricultural workers.

Madam C. J. Walker, perhaps the best-known African-American woman entrepreneur, tirelessly promoted this understanding of beauty culture (figures

30 and 31). Her own efforts to provide as a single mother, which had prompted her entry into the hair-care business, expanded into a larger "struggle . . . to build up Negro womanhood." She especially identified with poor Black women who toiled in the kitchen or the fields: "Don't think because you have to go down in the wash-tub that you are any less a lady." Beauty culture, Walker argued, offered economic emancipation for Black women subjected to a rigidly sex- and race-segregated labor market. Indeed, thousands of women, rural and urban, made a living or supplemented their income selling the "Walker System".[43]

Asserting that an attractive and well-groomed appearance would "glorify our womanhood," Walker studiously avoided the language of white emulation. Company advertising in the 1920s, after Walker's death, even further emphasized the central role of appearance in creating and expressing identity. A 1928 ad stated: "Radiate an air of prosperity and who is to know if your purse is lined with gold or not? Personal cleanliness, neatness, whitened teeth, luxurious hair, a flawless complexion and dainty hands—these are the things that impress others and pave the way for your success by building confidence." Individual success, however, could not be divorced from racial advancement. Amidst images of black businessmen, prosperous farms, and churches, it proclaimed, "Amazing Progress of Colored Race—Improved Appearance Responsible."[44]

Walker and other African-American entrepreneurs asserted that beauty products would effect personal and social transformation by lifting Black women from the cultural debasement represented in racist stereotypes of kinky hair and unkempt appearance. That is, cosmetics "performed" respectability and modernity. This position had limitations entrepreneurs and consumers of beauty culture never fully addressed in these years: they did not develop an explicit critique of white-defined beauty standards, nor did they come to terms with the effects of that aesthetic on the products and images promoted and consumed. At the same time, it is clear that African-American beauty culture signified a modern identity to many Black women and was integrated into their claims for the dignity and self-definition that had historically been denied them in American life.[45]

CONCLUSION

In this case study, the early-twentieth-century discourse on cosmetics, as articulated by producers and consumers of these commodities, shifted the burden of female identity from an essential, interior self to one formed in the marking and coloring of the face. Makeup contributed to the constitution of women's identity, no longer to its falsification. In the period from 1900 to 1930, making up became one of the tangible ways women in their everyday lives confirmed their identities as women: they *became* women in the application of blusher, mascara, and lipstick. These applications carried various and contested meanings for women.

If one effect of the cosmetics industry was to represent "woman" as a kind of merchandise or objectified spectacle, another was to destabilize nineteenth-century cultural hierarchies among women, open economic opportunities, and represent, however inadequately, new claims for cultural legitimacy. These commodities offered women a language through which they could articulate new demands, concerns, and desires: this in a period when women's relationships to the civic, economic, and social "public" realms were under renegotiation, a period when social differences of gender, race, ethnicity, and class were being challenged and redefined. In this context, external appearances could be manipulated to represent and mediate new notions of identity. Significantly, this possibility was seized not only by white middle-class women, the subjects of most studies of consumer culture, but also by immigrant, white working-class and African-American women as well.

NOTES

I am indebted to the Rutgers Center for Historical Analysis, which supported the research for and writing of this essay. My thanks to Peter Agree, Amy Stanley, Victoria de Grazia, David Kuchta, the participants of the Rutgers Center for Historical Analysis seminar, and volume contributors for their comments on earlier versions.

1. *Mademoiselle* 7, no. 1 (June 1938): 13.

2. Warren I. Susman, "'Personality' and the Making of Twentieth-Century Culture," in *Culture as History* (New York, 1984), 271–86. See also T. J. Jackson Lears, "From Salvation to Self-Realization: Advertising and the Therapeutic Roots of the Consumer Culture, 1880–1930," in *The Culture of Consumption*, ed. Richard Wightman Fox and T. J. Jackson Lears (New York, 1983), 1–38; Simon J. Bronner, ed., *Consuming Visions: Accumulation and Display of Goods in America, 1880–1920* (New York, 1989); William Leach, "Transformations in a Culture of Consumption: Women and Department Stores, 1890–1925," *Journal of American History* 71 (September 1984): 319–42; William Leach, *Land of Desire: Merchants, Power, and the Rise of a New American Culture* (New York, 1993); Lary May, *Screening Out the Past: The Birth of Mass Culture and the Motion Picture Industry* (New York, 1980). T. J. Jackson Lear's recent work takes issue with Susman's framework: see "Beyond Veblen: Rethinking Consumer Culture in America," in *Consuming Visions*, ed. Simon J. Bronner, 73–98.

3. Important theoretical contributions include: Joan Wallach Scott, *Gender and the Politics of History* (New York, 1988); Judith Butler, *Gender Trouble: Feminism and the Subversion of Identity* (New York, 1990). See also Andreas Huyssen, "Mass Culture as Woman: Modernism's Other," in *Studies in Entertainment: Critical Approaches to Mass Culture*, ed. Tania Modleski (Bloomington, Ind., 1986), 188–207.

4. The "physiognomic paradigm" is brilliantly explicated in Allan Sekula, "The Body and the Archive," *October*, no. 39 (winter 1986): 3–64. See also Joanne Finkelstein, *The Fashioned Self* (Philadelphia, 1991), 15–77. Primary sources include: Alexander Walker, *Beauty* (New York, 1844), xix; Wilson Flagg, *An Analysis of Female Beauty*

(Boston, 1833); Sir James Clark, *The Ladies' Guide to Beauty* (New York, 1858); *Etiquette for Ladies* (Philadelphia, 1841), 116, 126.

5. Karen Halttunen, *Confidence Men and Painted Women* (New Haven, 1982), esp. 56–91. For primary documentation, see *Godey's Ladies Book* 29 (July 1844): 32; Caroline Lee Hentz, "The Beauty Transformed," *Godey's Ladies Book* 21 (November 1840): 194–202; idem, "The Fatal Cosmetic," *Godey's Ladies Book* 18 (June 1839): 265–74; [Hannah Murray and Mary Murray], *The American Toilet* (New York, 1827).

6. On fashion in the "consumer revolution" of the eighteenth century, see Neil McKendrick, John Brewer, and J. H. Plumb, *The Birth of a Consumer Society: The Commercialization of Eighteenth-Century England* (Bloomington, Ind., 1982), 34–99; Jennifer Jones, "The Taste for Fashion and Frivolity" (Ph.D. diss., Princeton University, 1991). On nineteenth-century clothing fashion, see Lois W. Banner, *American Beauty* (Chicago, 1983); Claudia B. Kidwell and Margaret C. Christman, *Suiting Everyone: The Democratization of Clothing in America* (Washington, D.C., 1974). The commodification of the nineteenth-century home is treated in Clifford E. Clark Jr., *The American Family Home, 1800–1960* (Chapel Hill, 1986), 103–130; Kenneth L. Ames, "Meaning in Artifacts: Hall Furnishings in Victorian America," *Journal of Interdisciplinary History* 9 (summer 1978): 19–46; Karen Halttunen, "From Parlor to Living Room: Domestic Space, Interior Decoration, and the Culture of Personality," in *Consuming Visions: Accumulation and Display of Goods in America, 1880–1920,* ed. Simon J. Bronner (New York, 1989), 157–89. See also David Jaffee, "Peddlers of Progress and the Transformation of the Urban North, 1760–1860," *Journal of American History* 78 (September 1991): 511–35.

7. Mrs. S. A. Walker, *Female Beauty* (New York, 1846), 286–300, and color plates.

8. *The Book of Health and Beauty* (London, 1837), xviii, xvii; *Etiquette for Ladies,* 126.

9. Virginia Smith, "The Popularisation of Medical Knowledge: The Case of Cosmetics," *Society for the Social History of Medicine Bulletin,* no. 39 (1986): 12–15; Londa Schiebinger, *The Mind Has No Sex? Women in the Origins of Modern Science* (Cambridge, 1989), 112–16. For unpublished recipe books, see those of Mrs. Lowell and Mrs. Charles Smith, Garrison Family Papers, MS Group 60, Sophia Smith Collection, Smith College, Northampton, Massachusetts. Published household manuals and beauty guides are numerous; see the sources given in nn. 4, 8, and 17 and the extensive collection at the American Antiquarian Society, Worcester, Massachusetts. Bibliographic information on cookbooks may be found in Eleanor Lowenstein, *Bibliography of American Cookery Books, 1742–1860* (Worcester, Mass., 1972).

10. Lydia Maria Child, *Letters from New York,* 2d ser., 5th ed. (New York, 1848), 248–50; *Humbug: A Look at Some Popular Impositions* (New York, 1859), 37–42, 92. Cosmetic makers took their cue from the patent medicine trade, discussed in James Harvey Young, *The Toadstool Millionaires* (Princeton, 1961).

11. Gilbert Vail, *A History of Cosmetics in America* (New York, 1947), 34–38, 49–53, 74–78. The constellation of practices denoting gentility is discussed in Richard L. Bushman, "High Style and Vernacular Culture," *Colonial British America,* ed. Jack P. Greene and J. R. Pole (Baltimore, 1984), 345–83.

12. Vail, *A History of Cosmetics,* 95. For a general discussion, see also Kathy Peiss, "Of Men and Makeup: The Gendering of Cosmetics in Twentieth-Century America" (paper presented at the Material Culture of Gender/The Gender of Material Culture conference, Winterthur Museum, 11 November 1989). The history of Ameri-

can men's appearance remains to be written. For an important study of the European case, see David Kuchta, "Inconspicuous Consumption: Masculinity, Political Economy, and Fashion in England, 1550–1776" (Ph.D. diss., University of California, Berkeley, 1991).

13. On middle-class formation and gender, see especially Mary Ryan, *The Cradle of the Middle Class* (Cambridge, Mass., 1981); Christine Stansell, *City of Women* (New York, 1986), 68–75, 156–168; Nancy Cott, *Bonds of Womanhood* (New Haven, 1977). The emergence of a scientific discourse on sexual difference is discussed in Thomas Laqueur, *Making Sex: Body and Gender from the Greeks to Freud* (Cambridge, Mass., 1990); and Cynthia Eagle Russett, *Sexual Science: The Victorian Construction of Womanhood* (Cambridge, Mass., 1989).

14. 2 Kings 9:30–37; also Ezekiel 23:40–49. Religious criticism of cosmetics was most pronounced in Puritanism, which linked cosmetics use to adultery and witchcraft. See Annette Drew-Bear, "Cosmetics and Attitudes toward Women in the Seventeenth Century," *Journal of Popular Culture* 9 (summer 1975): 31–37. For an example of nineteenth-century "scientific" Biblical criticism on Jezebel, see John Peter Lange, *Commentary on the Holy Scriptures; Volume VI of the Old Testament* (New York, 1887), 99–108.

15. George G. Foster, *New York by Gaslight and Other Urban Sketches,* ed. Stuart M. Blumin (Berkeley, 1990), 154; Mary Ryan, *Women in Public* (Baltimore, 1990), 29; Marion S. Goldman, *Gold Diggers and Silver Miners: Prostitution and Social Life on the Comstock Lode* (Ann Arbor, 1981), 100. See also Stansell, *City of Women,* 187–88; Mariana Valverde, "The Love of Finery: Fashion and the Fallen Woman in Nineteenth-Century Social Discourse," *Victorian Studies* 32 (winter 1989): 169–88.

16. James D. McCabe, *Lights and Shadows of New York Life* (Philadelphia, 1872), 154; see also George Ellington, *The Women of New York* (1869; reprint, New York, 1972), 42–51, 82–90.

17. *Beauty: Its Attainment and Preservation* (New York, 1890), 232–33; Clark, *Ladies' Guide to Beauty,* iv–v; E. G. Storke, ed., *The Family and Householder's Guide* (Auburn, N.Y., 1859), 179.

18. Harry T. Finck, *Romantic Love and Personal Beauty* (New York, 1887), 327–29, 426, 452–59 (quote 458); Joseph Simms, *Physiognomy Illustrated or, Nature's Revelation of Character* (New York, 1891), 262–69, 505–31; Captain Mayne Reid, *Odd People* (Boston, 1864).

19. Robert W. Shufeldt, *Indian Types of Beauty,* pamphlet reprinted from *The American Field,* 1891, in the Department of Rare Books and Manuscripts, Kroch Library, Cornell University. See also Melissa Banta and Curtis M. Hinsley, *From Site to Sight: Anthropology, Photography, and the Power of Imagery* (Cambridge, Mass., 1986), 38–47.

20. For a brilliant discussion of this point in the context of legal history, see Amy Dru Stanley, "Conjugal Bonds and Wage Labor," *Journal of American History* 75 (1988): 471–500.

21. Cf. Harold Earl Hammond, ed., *Diary of a Union Lady, 1861–1865* (New York, 1962), 123, 321–22, 331–32; and Allan Nevins and Milton Halsey Thomas, eds., *The Diary of George Templeton Strong* (New York, 1952), 1:320, 317.

22. On this point, see Judith Butler, "Performative Acts and Gender Constitution: An Essay in Phenomenology and Feminist Theory," *Theatre Journal* 40 (December 1988): 519–31.

23. On this large cultural development, see Leach, "Transformations in a Culture of Consumption"; idem, *Land of Desire;* Rachel Bowlby, *Just Looking: Consumer Culture in Dreiser, Gissing, and Zola* (New York, 1985); Rosalind H. Williams, *Dream Worlds: Mass Consumption in Late-Nineteenth-Century France* (Berkeley, 1982); Robert C. Allen, *Horrible Prettiness: Burlesque and American Culture* (Chapel Hill, 1991).

24. Alan Trachtenberg, *Reading American Photographs* (New York, 1989), 14–70 (quote p. 40); see also William Welling, *Photography in America* (New York, 1978). H. J. Rodgers, *Twenty-Three Years under a Sky-Light* (Hartford, 1872); see also "Chip," *How to Sit for Your Photograph* (Philadelphia, [1872]).

25. Trachtenberg, *Reading American Photographs,* 24. See also *Photographic Art-Journal* 1 (August 1851): 212; Beaumont Newhall, *The Daguerreotype in America* (New York, 1968), 69, 77; Mrs. A. M. Richards, *Memories of a Grandmother* (Boston, 1854), 13–14.

26. On actresses' cultural influence, see Allen, *Horrible Prettiness;* Banner, *American Beauty,* 106–54; Tracy C. Davis, *Actresses as Working Women* (London, 1991). On the hair dye controversy, see also the *New York Times,* 22 November 1868, 3; 28 March 1869, 4. For contemporary commentary, see Olive Logan, *Apropos of Women and Theaters* (New York, 1869).

27. On the *carte de visite* craze, see *Humphrey's Journal* 13 (1 March 1862): 326–30; 14 (1 October 1862): 123–24; 16 (15 July 1864): 84; *Photographic News* 6 (9 May 1862): 225–26. My discussion of the personal use and idealization of actresses' images is based on an examination of photograph albums, Visual Arts Workshop, Rochester, New York, and the *cartes de visite* and stereograph collections, International Museum of Photography, George Eastman House, Rochester, New York. See also Elizabeth Anne McCauley, *A. A. E. Disderi and the Carte de Visite Portrait Photograph* (New Haven, 1985); Dan Younger, "Cartes-de-Visite: Precedents and Social Influences," *California Museum of Photography Bulletin* 6, no. 4 (1987): 4–5. Abigail Solomon-Godeau (in "The Legs of the Countess," *October* 39 [winter 1986]: 65–69, 77–78, 94) and Faye Dudden (personal communication) have suggested that actresses learned how to heighten their beauty in photographs through conventionalized pose, gesture, and makeup.

28. I. A. Mathews and Co., *Hints on Various Subjects Connected with Our Business* (Buffalo, 1856), 72–73. On makeup and performance, see Richard Hudnut, *Twentieth-Century Toilet Hints* (New York, 1899), 28, 50; *Personal Beauty* (New York, 1875), 47; "Laird's Bloom of Youth," leaflet in Cosmetics files, Warshaw Collection of Business Americana, National Museum of American History, Smithsonian Institution. See also Edith Wharton, *The House of Mirth* (New York, 1905); and Theodore Dreiser, *Sister Carrie* (New York, 1991), for descriptions of tableaux vivants and amateur theatricals.

29. There is little quantitative evidence on cosmetics manufacturing in the nineteenth century, since it tended to be subsumed in manufacturing censuses under such categories as perfumes and soaps. Wholesale drug catalogues from 1800 to 1900 show a significant expansion in cosmetics stock after 1865, and again in the 1890s. Cf. T. W. Dyott, *Approved Patent and Family Medicines* (Philadelphia, 1814); H. B. Foster's *Prices Current* (Concord, N.H., 1860); McKesson and Robbins, *Prices Current of Drugs and Druggists' Articles* (New York, 1872); Peter Van Schaack and Sons, *Annual Price Current* (Chicago, 1899). One can infer from the daybooks and formularies of several New York and New Jersey druggists circa 1850–1880 that they ordered some commercially prepared cosmetics and continued to compound their own. See Bryan

Hough, Daybook, 1856–1861; George E. Putney, Druggist's Invoice Book, 1857–1882; George H. White, Pharmacist's Book of Recipes, ca. 1857–1872, all in New Jersey Room, Alexander Library, Rutgers University, New Brunswick, N.J.

30. On the growth and organization of this industry, see Kathy Peiss, "Making Faces: The Cosmetics Industry and the Cultural Construction of Gender, 1890–1930," *Genders* 7 (spring 1990): 143–69; Banner, *American Beauty*; Margaret Allen, *Selling Dreams: Inside the Beauty Business* (New York, 1981).

31. Maxene Fabe, *Beauty Millionaire: The Life of Helena Rubinstein* (New York, 1972); Patrick O'Higgins, *Madame: An Intimate Biography of Helena Rubinstein* (New York, 1971); Alfred Allan Lewis and Constance Woodworth, *Miss Elizabeth Arden* (New York, 1972); Allen, *Selling Dreams*, 22–32.

32. Armand advertising proofs, Ayer Book 382, especially advt. no. 10039, 1929, N. W. Ayer Collection, National Museum of American History, Smithsonian Institution.

33. Cf. Pompeian advertisements in *Woman's Home Companion*, November 1909; and *Pictorial Review*, October 1923, 104; my thanks to Ellen Todd for her observations on the latter image. Maybelline advertising appeared in *Photoplay* and *True Story* in the 1920s.

34. For the most recent statement of this position, see Naomi Wolf, *The Beauty Myth* (New York, 1991).

35. See, for example, Lisa Fine, *The Souls of the Skyscraper* (Philadelphia, 1990), 62, 142, 175; Susan Porter Benson, *Counter Cultures: Saleswomen, Managers, and Customers in American Department Stores, 1890–1940* (Urbana, 1986), 139–40, 236–38; Alice Kessler-Harris, *Out to Work* (New York, 1982), 135–40; Dorothy Sue Cobble, *Dishing It Out* (Urbana, 1992), 122–31.

36. Kathy Peiss, *Cheap Amusements: Working Women and Leisure in Turn of the Century New York* (Philadelphia, 1986); Beth Bailey, *From Front Porch to Back Seat: Courtship in Twentieth-Century America* (Baltimore, 1989); Pamela Haag, "In Search of 'The Real Thing': Ideologies of Love, Modern Romance, and Women's Sexual Subjectivity in the U.S., 1920–1940," *Journal of the History of Sexuality* 2 (April 1992): 547–77.

37. On working-class women's use of cosmetics, see Peiss, *Cheap Amusements;* Marlou Belyea, "The Joy Ride and the Silver Screen: Commercial Leisure, Delinquency, and Play Reform in Los Angeles, 1900–1980" (Ph.D. diss., Boston University, 1983), 309–10; Mary Odem, "Single Mothers, Delinquent Daughters, and the Juvenile Court in Early-Twentieth-Century Los Angeles," *Journal of Social History* 25 (September 1991): 27–44. On immigrants and American style, see Andrew Heinze, *Adapting to Abundance: Jewish Immigrants, Mass Consumption, and the Search for American Identity* (New York, 1990); Elizabeth Ewen, *Immigrant Women in the Land of Dollars* (New York, 1985). For the influence of the motion pictures on popular style and appearance, see Herbert Blumer, *Movies and Conduct* (New York, 1933), 30–44.

38. The following discussion derives from my chapters on the African-American beauty industry in *Making Faces: Cosmetics and American Culture* (forthcoming). See also Gwendolyn Robinson, "Class, Race, and Gender: A Transcultural Theoretical and Sociohistorical Analysis of Cosmetic Institutions and Practices to 1920" (Ph.D. diss., University of Illinois, Chicago, 1984).

39. E. Azalia Hackley, *The Colored Girl Beautiful* (Kansas City, Mo., 1916), 36. For

a discussion of the new discourses on Black womanhood, see Hazel V. Carby, *Reconstructing Womanhood: The Emergence of the Afro-American Novelist* (New York, 1987), 95–120.

40. These criticisms appear in the radical press of the post–World War I period, including the *Messenger, Crusader,* and *Negro World,* as well as such "race papers" as the *New York Age.* The most nuanced analyses, however, came from the earlier black-female reform tradition. See, for example, Nannie Burroughs, "Not Color But Character," *Voice of the Negro* 1 (July 1904): 277–78; Fannie Barrier Williams, "The Colored Girl," *Voice of the Negro* 2 (June 1905): 400–403; Anna Julia Cooper, *A Voice from the South* (1892; reprint, New York, 1969), 75.

41. The cosmetic effects of bleach creams, for example, varied with the active ingredients. Some lightened blemishes and discolorations; others peeled the top layer of the skin, revealing the lighter layer below. However, the effect was a temporary one because exposure to the sun returned the skin to its original state. See Gerald A. Spencer, *Cosmetology in the Negro* (New York, 1944).

42. Horace Cayton and St. Clair Drake, *Black Metropolis* (New York, 1945), 503. On the continuing salience of color hierarchies in distributing opportunity and resources, see Verna Keith and Cedric Herring, "Skin Tone and Stratification in the Black Community," *American Journal of Sociology* 97 (November 1991): 760–779. See also Lawrence Levine's important discussion of color and the blues in *Black Culture and Black Consciousness* (New York, 1977) 284–93.

43. National Negro Business League, *Report of the Fifteenth Annual Convention* (Muskogee, Okla., 1914), 152; *Report of the Thirteenth Annual Convention* (Chicago, 1912), 154–55; *Report of the Fourteenth Annual Convention* (Philadelphia, 1913), 211–212. On Madam C. J. Walker's remarkable life, see A'Lelia Perry Bundles, *Madam C. J. Walker* (New York, 1991); Robinson, "Class, Race, and Gender," 377–411; Stanley Nelson and Associates, "Madam C. J. Walker: Two Dollars and a Dream" (video documentary, 1988). For contemporary commentaries, see F. B. Ransom, "Manufacturing Toilet Articles: A Big Negro Business," *Messenger* 5 (December 1923): 937; George S. Schuyler, "Madam C. J. Walker," *Messenger* 6 (August 1924): 251–58 passim.

44. "Amazing Progress of Colored Race," two-page Madam C. J. Walker advertisement, *Oklahoma Eagle,* 3 March 1928, clipping in box 262, f4, Barnett Collection, Chicago Historical Society, Chicago, Illinois.

45. See letters written to Madam C. J. Walker accompanying product orders in 1918, boxes 34–36, Madam C. J. Walker Collection (1910–1980), Indiana Historical Society, Indianapolis, Indiana. I am grateful to A'Lelia Bundles for granting me permission to see these records and to archivist Wilma Gibbs for her assistance.

ELEVEN

Nationalizing Women

The Competition between Fascist
and Commercial Cultural Models in Mussolini's Italy

Victoria de Grazia

This essay takes up the broad question of how the diffusion of modern consumption goods and habits intersects with changing definitions of national sovereignty and citizenship. By sovereignty, I intend the power assumed by or delegated to the state to exercise authority within its territorial boundaries, by citizenship, the duties and rights prescribed by law and custom for the inhabitants of this territory: which is to say, the claims the state can make on its subjects and, vice versa, the claims they are entitled to make on the state.

The far-flung literature on the subject suggests two diametrically different possibilities. One is that the diffusion on a mass scale of consumer goods and cultural artifacts and messages acts as a powerful force of integration. This process enhances central government authority and homogenizes collective identities by promoting a standard set of goods, a common commercial idiom, and a shared notion of political entitlement transcending regional, ethnic, and class cleavages. By and large, this interpretation derives from observation of the operations of mass consumption in the era of fordism, that is, the period roughly from 1900 to 1970. This period was characterized by large-scale standardized production, widening national markets, and institutional and redistributive reforms in the face of pressures for political and economic democracy.[1]

The other position treats mass consumption as a powerfully disaggregative force, one that subverts state authority and segments national publics. Operating on a transnational scale, with ever more differentiated appeals and an ever more diverse stock of goods, mass consumption would seem to engender a multiplicity of subjectivities. These have coalesced, around issues of gender, religion, and ethnicity, as the substrata of new forms of identity politics that defy control through conventional political appeals. This emphasis is consonant with the characteristics of a "postfordist consumption." The term is of course a very contemporary one, derived from the observation of trends such as the globalization of consumer production, the dropping of trade barriers, and the frenetic segmentation of markets that has been made possible by flexible production technologies and income redistribution and has resulted in new subnational and transnational collective identities.[2]

Whether these views on the effects of the spread of mass consumption diverge because they account for different time periods or because each focuses on a different facet of capitalist transformation is unclear, which suggests that we know very little about the operations of cultural meanings derived from mass consumption in constructing national identities. This essay, drawing on sources from Italy's experience of nation building between the two world wars, examines the efforts of an avowedly totalitarian regime to control consumer culture in order to define women's roles in Italian public life.[3] Though here I can only hint at the character of female collectivities that emerged as a result of this intervention, it appears that although the advent of mass consumption presented nation-states with new opportunities for mobilizing their citizens through the mass media and other artifacts of commercial culture, these same messages and goods also subjected collective identities to new centrifugal pressures. The tension between the centralizing and centrifugal tendencies of mass consumption was particularly notable with respect to female constituencies because of the peculiar ways in which their citizenship was constructed.

More generally, this essay suggests that in the era of mass consumption, it is difficult to conceive of the "imagined community" of the nation, to recall Benedict Anderson's phrase, without considering how political actors and social groups use the accumulation of goods typical of modern material culture to construct collective identities.[4] It also puts a different slant on how the nationalizing process in Europe has been conceptualized and narrated. It was the genial intuition of the German-American historian George Mosse that where authoritarian movements eventually took hold, notably in Germany, state authorities had played an especially active role in "nationalizing the masses." This particular form of building national citizenship was to compensate for the deficient growth of market and liberal-democratic institutions and had the effect of circumventing and eventually stunting the growth of a mature political system with parliamentary institutions and rational civic discourse at its center.[5] Eric Hobsbawm and Terence Ranger address a similar problematic in their volume *The Invention of Tradition,* particularly where they treat the instrumentalization of "mass-produced traditions" such as political rituals, buildings, and monument sites to forge new bonds of loyalty and new symbols of nationhood.[6] Such traditions had a double goal: to shore up community bonds weakened by the expansion of capitalist values and to absorb left-wing political formations. The historian of France Eugen Weber, though working within the framework of modernization theory, suggests a comparable picture: of the governmental institutions, market distribution networks, and cultural systems of an already fully formed state operating in tandem to convert (as Weber characterized the process) uncivilized peasants into modern Frenchmen.[7] In all of these analyses, it is assumed that market-generated cultural forms operated more or less in tandem with governmental and political processes, cementing identification around the central institutions of the nation-state and with the dominant political classes. By the same token, the authors construe citizenship largely in the terms that nineteenth-century state builders envisaged, as involving the transforming of refractory or apathetic male subjects into conscientious workers, prompt taxpayers, disciplined soldiers, and predictable voters.

This conceptualization offers a plausible enough account of the ambitions of nineteenth-century state builders in their "Weberian" endeavor to expose localist subcultures, entangled in parochial and obscure "webs of meaning," to the light of modern administrative rationality. But the explanatory virtues of such a schema surely fail before the modalities of sovereignty and citizenship typical of the post–World War I era. On the one hand, governments were faced with new subjects, the most conspicuous, leaving aside ever more insubordinate colonial peoples, being women. In the wake of the war, the problem of constituting women as citizens came to the fore, as it became necessary to recognize their participation in the war effort and to address the myriad complex issues attendant on an eventual extension of the suffrage, the discovery of the so-called demographic crisis, and the formulation of the first modern family policies. On the other hand, political elites and government demanded higher degrees of allegiance, in the face of new international pressures and domestic class cleavages, and they devised new modes of institutional integration through mass movements, corporatist institutions, and welfare-state programs, as well as through control of the emergent mass media—radio, cinema, and tabloids.

The state's attempts to exercise more control thus coincided not only with the challenge to extend citizenship rights but also with the threat of a loss of control over cultural forces that elites had formerly either ignored or regarded as readily manipulable, including leisure use, cinema spectatorship, fashion turnover, and goods consumption. Put in strongest terms, European states faced a crisis in the exercise of sovereignty. At the very moment that governing frameworks had to be reshaped to cope with mass social protest and to incorporate new social subjects, the tensions between the integrative and centrifugal powers of commodity flows became especially visible. Such tensions were all the more fraught as governments sought to organize culture and consumption according to rules more apt to running administrative bureaucracies than to managing market forces.

The awkward politics of the fascist regime with respect to "nationalizing women" suggests some of the salient dimensions of this crisis of sovereignty.

The fascist regime pretended to be the outgrowth of the Risorgimento democrat Giuseppe Mazzini's ambition to create a so-called ethical state, one that used political mobilization as opposed to social reform to convince the populace to identify with the national destiny. Hence, fascism claimed to be acting against corrupt vested interests and the congeries of particularisms proliferating as a result of the alleged agnosticism of liberal government during the Giolittian era (1901–1914). In contrast to its liberal predecessor, the fascist regime promised to build a whole and harmonious collectivity, the purposes of which, according to its avowedly Hegelian inspiration, were defined by a transcendent national state. Unlike Nazi totalitarianism, which held up the party as the supreme expression of racial unity, pretending to a complete and direct control over civil society, the fascist regime authorized the central state apparatus itself to organize the consent of the population. The new state was to operate by mobilizing a great range of fascist party, corporatist (mixed business and labor), and even private, voluntary institutions.

In principle, the regime's ambition to involve Italians of all ages and classes in the hierarchies of the state according to their newly defined duties and functions embraced women as well as men. Women's primary function was, of course, reproduction in the most basic biological sense. However, the female capacity to reproduce carried with it a real power of sorts, in view of the regime's orders to glorify the *stirpe*, or "racial stock." The fascist regime itself contemplated female citizenry as playing a more complex role on the stage of national history. At very least women had to be trained in child rearing (*puericultura*), and the brides of future elites needed education to share their consort's duties. In practice, the roles prescribed for women as mothers, welfare claimants, workers, and consumers were often at odds, and contradictory notions of rights and duties were the result. Family welfare reforms aggravated the tension between public allegiances and private and family loyalties. The Labor Charter of 1927 affirmed that citizenship was due only to those who worked. Yet government codes, contracts, and regulations restricted women's access to the labor market in the name of the health of the race. Political organizations mobilized women in public locations, whereas propaganda exhorted them to return to home and hearth. The National Fascist Party (PNF) incited women to worship the Duce at the same time that the Catholic church admonished them to adore God and to owe unswerving allegiance to their families.[8]

The tensions between the forms of recognition extended to women and the new constraints imposed on them are especially visible in the regime's effort to represent women not only in the party mass organizations but also in the new arenas of commercial culture. The dictatorship's overall politics toward an emerging consumer economy was double-sided. On the one hand, the fascist state was avowedly anticonsumption. By barring any effective union structure, it instituted a "low wage economy." It also tolerated high levels of unemployment. Autarchic tariffs and quotas, together with "battles" for import substitution, restricted foreign goods and raised the costs of staples such as cotton and wheat. As a result, some indices of consumer habit changed very little, such as caloric intake and shares of the family income spent on food and rent, and household amenities such as indoor plumbing, telephones, and basic appliances spread at a snail's pace. Indeed, as late as the early 1930s, a third of the national product was characterized as autoconsumption, indicating the huge number of families, as much as 40 percent of the population, whose livelihoods still depended on agriculture and who produced many goods and services for their self-support. This unremitting pressure on consumption, forcing households to be self-reliant, was of course consistent with traditionalist strategies aimed at pushing women out of the workforce and back into the home.

At the same time, the restructuring of the economy under the dictatorship was accompanied by changes in distributional structures and consumer purchasing patterns, changes that justify speaking of the emergence of a mass consumer culture in the interwar years. Italy's marginal position in Western markets exposed it to cultural and commodity flows from abroad, and its pinched domestic markets, with their underdeveloped distribution systems, left it wide open to the influences of foreign media and fashion influences, especially from the United States and France. This exposure was facilitated by the small increments of disposable income spent on consumer durables and mass leisure pastimes. Households with radios grew from perhaps one in thirty in the early 1920s to one in five in the late 1930s. Department stores were built in the centers of major towns. Cinema going became a common pastime for the urban lower classes. There was a burgeoning tabloid press of fashion, fan magazines, and novelettes for women. On the whole, consumption remained deeply stratified. Nonetheless, the consuming public for small amenities, as well as the new models of conduct, included urban working-class women as well as the leisured upper class, girls of the southern agro-towns, the migrant day laborers of the great Paduan rice fields, and the daughters of sharecroppers in Tuscany. By the early 1930s, agricultural experts dispatched to study farm families caught glimpses of the new ways of rural youth. Whereas the boys were becoming impassioned soccer fans, the girls were enthralled by fashion. In the Chianti Valley, teenagers who had acquired all of the latest embroidery and crocheting stitches from the commercial sewing schools at nearby Greve were observed crocheting, their needles clicking away, while they tended the sheep in the shade of the trees or gathered around the winter fire at night. On Saturday, the young women rushed to the town market to sell their handiwork in order to buy "Geegaws— wool and nylon stockings, ribbons, hairpins, combs, such, the likes of which they had never before even dreamed of."[9]

This proliferation of new cultural artifacts and consumer goods, however limited compared to that in far more urbanized and prosperous Great Britain or Germany, brought a regime with a totalizing concept of governmental prerogatives up against a new kind of public power: that associated with an emerging mass consumption, mainly identified with mass commercial culture. In the field of mass communications and commerce, the leading sites of invention lay abroad. In Italy itself, at least down to the early 1930s, the main points of production and dissemination of radio, cinema, and mass circulation magazines were the chief northern cities, Turin and Milan, rather than the political center, Rome, and the chief outlets of distribution were the capitals of the provinces, hugely distant from outlying rural towns and hamlets in terms of income and culture. In the towns, at least, leisure pastimes were open for the price of a ticket; they fed new notions of collectivity but also new perceptions of individuality. In the process, they challenged the symbolic order and spatial layout of nineteenth-century bourgeois society. But in equal measure they defied the organizing principles of fascist mass politics, with its emphasis on military-like hierarchies of rank and function and its ambition to monopolize public display and ritual. Men still appeared to be subject to integration within the state by means of extension of the rationalizing principles of Western bureaucratic power into the furthest recesses of civil society: the leisure-time sections, or *dopolavoro*, which numbered around ten thousand and had several million members, were model institutions in this regard.[10] But men's leisure was identified with well-defined physical spaces, schedules, and occupations and was thus more readily captured by bureaucratic agencies, whereas women's leisure tended to be bound up with the home and with the free-floating sociability of commercial cultural pastimes. To manipulate these pastimes thus entailed a more complex effort to establish control over the meanings of commercial cultural symbols.

To pursue this goal, the fascist dictatorship had to work within certain powerful cultural constraints. One limit was set by the class-based norms and individualist conceptions of self and society of the bourgeois social order. Under pressure, yet still intact, the social order's pervasive distinctions of rank and gender, inherited from Italy's liberal bourgeoisie and before that from aristocratic social relations, were manifest in all sorts of conventions of dress, physical movement, and social routine. The fascist elites were most reluctant to disturb these, for the socially parvenu rulers of fascist Italy had a vested interest in preserving the outer trappings of class and restoring the relations between the sexes turned topsy-turvy by the war. For the men in the fascist hierarchy, the old Italian art of cutting a *bella figura* included showing off their power to women as well as other men by physically dominating the old spaces of bourgeois sociability: the salon, the theater, the antechambers, not to mention the piazza. It also meant parading about in the company of their elegantly dressed wives and girlfriends. Not until the late 1930s, with the "reform of custom" undertaken by the fascist party to militarize Italian society, did the regime pretend to destroy the class-defined spaces of bourgeois society—and the "passé" habits displayed within them. The grounds were that these displays of luxurious living perpetuated the power of old elites and undermined the collective will of the New Fascist Era. In that context, the fascist party targeted the bourgeois female. "A creature of luxury," as propaganda liked to lambaste her, her conspicuous consumer mores were unwholesomely cosmopolitan, the rotten fruit of shopping sprees to Paris and cheating on the austerity programs of fascist autarchy.

Catholicism, meaning both church institutions, lay associations, and Catholic ideology, presented a far more complicated set of constraints. In violation of the church's fundamentalist vision of female chastity and public decorum, fascist officialdom put female youth on public display. Their purpose thereby was not only to demonstrate the fitness of the race but also to exercise a symbolic droit du seigneur over the young. (This purpose did not elude Pope Pius XI, who in 1928 first began to denounce gymnastic exhibitions and sports pageants as "modern paganism" and to denounce fascism itself as having a moral sensibility "weaker" than that of ancient Rome and, possibly, of the "even more corrupt towns" of ancient Greece.)[11] At the same time, the fascist government pandered to the fundamentalist prejudices of a still largely rural country, which were being revived with a veritable counterreformation spirit from the mid-1920s. Hence, the regime rallied to the church's cry of sexual danger, propagating society-wide the Catholic hierarchy's strictures against female nudity. By the late 1920s, major Italian churches had posted signs barring "immodest dress." Local political authorities acceded to Catholic pressure to enforce against women especially Article 794 of the Rocco Penal Code. This prohibited the exposure of "shameful nudity in public places" and "acts against public decency," on pain of one-month jail sentences and fines ranging from one hundred to two thousand lire. State authorities ordered all low-ranking female employees in public offices to wear black coverall aprons; northern textile managers barred factory girls from wearing short skirts.[12]

At the same time, the regime had an underhanded rival in a religious culture the origins of which lay in the premodern era. Church culture did not therefore abide by the divisions between private and public typical of modern secular states. With their injunctions to confront modernity by mastering desire and to nurture strong personal ideals while forswearing emancipation, Catholic organizations for women and girls, of which there were several thousand with perhaps a half million members in the late 1930s, defied the dichotomies of private and public, spirituality and politicking, and sentiment and reason, which made it so hard for fascism—a secular movement in a secular state—to engage female publics in a sustained way. The church organizations could afford to be syncretic if not contradictory; they could afford to tolerate multiple identities and loyalties (provided the over-riding ones were to the church). Hence, Catholic associationalism simultaneously coexisted with consumer culture and condemned it. Church organizations sponsored a vast parish-run movie circuit and popular magazines, such as *Famiglia cristiana,* that incited parish priests to enforce new codes of civic-religious morality. In the process, the basis was laid for what has more recently been characterized as the "latent hegemony" of Christian democratic political culture.[13] With two decades of experience responding to both the seduction of fascist secularism and the blandishment of mass consumption behind it, the church-affiliated party flourished after the war. In the post-1948 era and, at the head of all of the conservative ruling coalitions, it ably navigated Italy's passage through the choppy water of the first real consumer revolution, during the 1950s.

To show how fascism positioned itself with respect to bourgeois and Catholic conventions while trying to confront what was generally characterized as the "Americanization" of customs by means of the spread of commercial cultural idiom, this essay now turns to the regime's effort to redefine canons of female beauty and then to its attempts to manipulate fashion styles.

Since the turn of the century, first stage actresses, and later cinema actresses, had transformed standards of female beauty.[14] Circa 1910, the Dannunzian heroine Eleonora Duse taught women to affect La Duse's gestures, or *duseggiare;* thereafter the silent-cinema diva Lyda Borelli taught them to *borelleggiare*—to adopt languid poses, affected speech, and dress of a classicizing and orientalizing taste. By the early 1920s, Paris fashion and the U.S. movies introduced the boyish gamin or *garçonne.* By the 1930s, Hollywood stars—blond, muscular, leggy, toothy, with big smiles and visibly made-up—had made the whole body, not merely the face, the vehicle of physical expression, influencing the way Italian women had of "sitting, getting up, walking, pausing, and turning."[15]

This turnover of physical types, sped up by the turbine of commercial cultural production, was, understandably, a disturbing phenomenon. Long-standing mercantilist traditions held that the health of individual bodies contributed to the health of the entire nation. Thus when the Duce equated the health of individuals with the well-being of the nation, he subscribed to a time-worn metaphor.[16] The fascist head of state's concern over the physical preparedness of his female subjects was spurred by other factors as well. During the interwar years, comparisons among national female physiognomies multiplied. These were promoted by the Olympic Games, which began to include special women's events after the Great War and—together with international sports tournaments for women, held first at Amsterdam in 1928 and then at Prague in 1930—put female athleticism on show for the first time. The movies, photography, and advertising, by causing an ever wider and more intense circulation of images of attractive women, likewise stimulated comparisons of national female types, as well as sustained a more complex image of women's life cycle: in particular, they sustained an image in which birth was just one part of their life course, not the beginning of irreversible physical decline. An ever greater circulation of new beauty and personal products promoted a more diffuse culture of physicality, and this was quickly reinforced by new medical specializations in sports and plastic surgery. All in all, to define what female beauty is and to pass on who is beautiful or not is no small power. Men could thereby exorcise the influence that women allegedly exercised by manipulating their physical attractiveness. To be able to pass on whether a woman was pretty (or ugly) was also a way to relegate her to a subordinate role, as "an enchanting parenthesis in life," to use the Duce's expression. The regime sought to manipulate this lively awareness of female physicality in order to check the emancipatory impulses that stimulated and fed off of it, as well as to aggrandize itself by making female beauty, physical strength, and stylishness attributes of fascism's own exercise of national power.

To respond to the aesthetic disorder aggravated by the proliferation of American movies, tabloids, advertising plates, and commercial displays, the fascist propaganda machine—with Mussolini's approbation and, at times, his active intervention—championed new ideals of female beauty. The main enemy was a creature identified as the "crisis woman" (*la donna crisi*). False and alien, she was allegedly the product of Paris, Hollywood, and Italy's biggest cities, Milan and Rome. Originally, she was the invention of the small coterie of avowedly antimodernist intellectuals grouped around the Florentine journal *Il Selvaggio*. In 1931, this caricature was brought to national attention when Mussolini's press office ordered the press to eliminate "sketches of excessively thin and masculinized female figures who represent sterile female types."[17] Much could be said about the significance of the crisis woman. A common interpretation, which holds that she was condemned for being insufficiently maternal, hardly does justice to the fears that this "pale," "skeletal," and "transparent" creature seemed to elicit. Perhaps what was most disturbing about her was that she was out alone: erotic yet defying control, object of desire yet socially useless, a narcissist withholding her affections. "La donna e' mobile," as a popular song went:

> she drives your car,
> she's called the frail sex, but she's stronger by far.
> She's ever so changeable. Supposedly true,
> her memory is weak. Her thoughts not on you.
> She's madly in love with sports."[18]

The best course was to deeroticize and distance, if not to repress.

The imagery designed to defeat the crisis woman presented the "authentic Italian woman" under two guises. One was the nubile rural young woman;

346 VICTORIA DE GRAZIA

the other the mother. The former, with her rosy lips and cheeks, peasant dress, and rounded figure, ostensibly recalled the pristine beauty of rural Italy before its denizens were corrupted by licentious industry and town life. Too many commentators have misread her as a maternal figure. To look closer, there was nothing motherly about her. She was purely the invention of patriarchal desire, a procacious beauty, insolent yet submissive, her exuberant mien only restrained by the photographic gaze. The latter figure, the mother, was an oxymoron, at least from the point of view of aesthetic representation. Maternity was associated with beauty only with difficulty, pace Mussolini's dictum "maternity redounds to feminine beauty." Portrayals of motherhood were astonishingly impervious to images of the loveliness of the Virgin Mary. At one extreme, there was the objectification of the nurturing female, zooming in on the baby at the tit. At another, there was the utter effacement of the mother as person. Hired to publicize the annual Mothers and Children's Day, the eminent commercial poster master Marcello Dudovich, renowned as author of the famed Rinascente department store women (out shopping, bare armed, their faces glistening with desire), seemed stymied as he sought to find an appropriate iconography. Year in year out, his mothers were stylized like pillars of salt, back to the observer, their maternity signaled only by a single offspring to which they acted as props. The scant photographic evidence that we find of "prolific mothers" presents an aesthetically troubling scene: the youngest women, at forty, look ancient, their faces worn, their baggy black-aproned dresses drooping over sagging bosoms. No wonder these images were little circulated (see figures 32–35).

These official campaigns notwithstanding, Americanized images of female beauty proliferated in Italian commercial culture. The earliest nationwide beauty contest, that for the most beautiful secretary in Italy, was sponsored by Rizzoli Editor's weekly *Piccola* in 1929.[19] The first full-blown American-style contest, using the ever more familiar mass promotion techniques of American advertising, was held in 1939 by Count Visconti di Modrone's GVM pharmaceutical company to launch a new toothpaste. Under the slogan "A thousand lire for a smile," several dozen young women gathered at the northern resort town of Salsomaggiore for the finals. Although advertised as *Italian* beauties, their miens were very much like those of their Hollywood progenitors. The only real difference was not unsubstantial; fascist codes required that the face be the focus, not the body. In compensation, fascist iconography well tolerated images of the whole body. By the late 1930s, the dour militarized line-ups redolent of the official Nazi style had given way before Hollywood-like glossies of "sexy" girl cadres and *dopolavoro* kicklines.

The battle to refashion national dress codes presents a similar trajectory. Fashion was of course associated with aristocratic and bourgeois society, rather than Americanization. However, the great velocity of turnover of new models

Figure 32. Massing of mothers at a childcare clinic, 1929.

and the rapidity with which women of the lower classes—both peasant girls and urban working-class women—appropriated them were typical signs of the class and gender disorder that fascism's campaigns against the Americanization of national mores were intended to address. In the 1920s, fascist women seeking to testify to their loyalty to the regime by "nationalizing" dress devised a double agenda. The more conservative, including the one-time nationalist feminist Elisa Majer Rizzioli, the founder of the women's sections of the PNF, wanted to tame ostentatious dress (what was called "exaggerated luxury") to enable women as a sex to obtain greater freedom in public. The more parvenu and ambitious, rallied by Lydia De Liquoro, editor of the fashion magazine *Lidel,* wanted to restore internal hierarchies among women, thereby to ally old and new female elites under the fascist vanguard to the exclusion of the vulgar female masses. In the atmosphere of social restoration and antifeminism following the fascists' seizure of power, the latter course quickly won out.

Figure 33. Patriarchal selflessness: Marcello Dudovich's poster for
Mothers' and Children's Day, 1935.

Figure 34. Modern commercial selfhood: Gino Boccasile's *Grandi firme* girl dreaming of Garbo, 1937.

Figure 35. Dopolavoro kickline, Pirelli factory, 1938.

For the greater part of its rule, the regime delegated the process of giving meaning to changing fashion styles entirely to elite women. It could only gain by campaigns to buy national and to promote luxury display. The former promised to help the textile and clothing industries (which were plunged into deep and chronic crisis in the wake of the dictatorship's drastic revaluation of the lira in 1927). The latter promised to testify to the vitality of the dictatorship and to the harmonious social mixing of old and new wealth under its aegis. But starting in the second half of the 1930s, with the shift to autarchic economic strategies, the dictatorship tried to exercise firmer control over consumption habits. With the aim of rallying public support for austerity, fascist propagandists targeted "luxurious" women as enemies of state. Fascist women willingly went along with attacks on things foreign; it was harder for them to denounce the appearance of class difference in dress. In the wake of the League of Nations' sanctions against Italy in 1935, the attack on the idolization of things foreign—against "xenolatry"—slipped out of women's hands altogether. Henceforth, the battle to codify the meaning of female style became part and parcel of fascist party secretary Achille Starace's misogynist "reform of custom."

This was the context in which the regime sought to persuade its female subjects to embrace militaristic notions of rank in public appearances. In the context of my argument, this change involved replacing the subtle social distinctions and identities associated with access to an expanding market with the explicit hierarchy of functions ordained by state command. Before the onset of the Ethiopian campaign, fascist women had rarely worn uniforms. Down to World War II, even fascist inspectresses wore the outfits of the upper classes, that is, well-styled gabardine suits, graceful walking shoes, and perhaps an inconspicuous fur stole. The only respectable uniforms, if we except the polychrome regional costumes revived for arts and craft shows and as props for various events of state, were those of the *Crocerossine* (Red Cross nurses). This uniform had exceptional prestige, partly because the frontline nurses had performed heroically in World War I, but also because the outfits were worn by the Italian Red Cross's national patrons, the princesses of the House of Savoy. In 1935–1936, during the Ethiopian campaign, the PNF ordered its *visitatrici*, or "social assistants," to wear uniforms on duty, and the Fontana sisters, the doyennes of Italian high fashion, designed flattering dress uniforms of blue gabardine with white piqué blouses for the girls of good family attending the party's training school for female cadres at Orvieto. However, as late as 1938, Starace complained to Mussolini that his efforts to persuade women to dress in the Sardinian rough-wool (*orbace*) uniforms he recommended for men, had earned him nothing but ridicule.

Indeed, the maximum peacetime success of this effort suggested the fundamental tensions underlying it. It was only on 28 May 1939, on the occasion of the first gigantic gathering of "the female forces" of fascism, that the PNF was finally able to mount a national spectacle around women in which conventional signs of class distinction and social rank were effaced. The rally, passing over the parade route that led out of the Circus Maximus and moved along the restored Roman fora to culminate in Piazza Venezia, brought seventy thousand women to Rome. In the words of the official Stefani News Agency release, it was "the most total and thrilling demonstration ever of the party's efforts toward forming a full-blown fascist and imperial consciousness . . . among its female forces."[20]

Yet the representation of the event, if not the event itself, relayed an equivocal message. The wordy description, composed for and subsequently reproduced in one form or another in all of the Italian press, vacillated about what exactly was being represented. The rally incongruously kaleidoscoped fashion parade and military event.

> The antigas cohort passes and with it the first aid troops, gas masks around their necks, the packs flung over the shoulder. Rural housewives, all in costume. And from everywhere. Scarves and shawls; wide skirts cinched to display the grace of young bodies and robustness of maternal flanks; jackets and corsets and belts. The severe softness of Sardinia; the clamor of Basilicata, the explosion of colors of Emilia and Tuscany (red and sky blue predominate), flowered aprons and lace from Venetia; and clogs, sandals, kerchiefs. Harmonious and discordant colors; altogether in lock step . . . In their wake . . . the women workers' sections pass—in azure jumpsuits, walnut color, the outfits of the textile, artisan, and tobacco workers cohort. The leisure-time troops pick up the motifs of the sports groups. Then, the handsome ranks of the women professionals and artists, and, last, after a brief pause to allow for the faster pace, the speed cohorts: the young fascist bicyclists and motorists . . . Then the Red Cross nurses of the great wars for Africa and Spain pass, on tanks and ambulances, severe in dress and demeanor, faces to the Duce, then straight ahead, their blue veils lifting off their white headbands . . . The whole parade drawn up superbly by the horse-mounted young fascists . . .

One might argue that the shift between military and fashion was irrelevant: the marchers were still lodged in a traditional visual space, the objects of spectacle, the subjects of the male gaze. Yet the observer was led to highlight their nonuniformity, and by that means, to highlight what I read as a fundamental tension between the collectivist imagery of massed forces and the pursuit of exclusiveness and individuality typical of the workings of the modern fashion industry.[21] In the end, the reporter's rhetorical exuberance seemed to fail, as if his images of a feminine jamboree failed to yield the proper degree of disciplined conformity. To describe the parade's culminating moment, as the female cohorts passed by the automobile in which the Duce stood, his arm lifted in Roman salute, the press agent shifted images: to characterize the women as soldiers—males passing with a "jaunty, quick masculine step," and the Duce's face in response as "lit up with virile, satisfied pleasure." It was as if this design of the female "mass ornament," to refer to Siegfried Kracauer's method of observing representations of massed female figures in the 1920s, was too intractable, too volatile a subject for fascist rule.[22] The nation of fascism was most readily represented by the vision of fixed hierarchies, the gender of which were familiarly masculine.

If the foregoing analysis documents fascism's incapacity, despite its dictatorial powers and propagandistic skills, to create any stable axis of meaning around commercial cultural products, it still has not addressed what this clash over canons of physicality and dress meant for women's perceptions of themselves as individuals and as members of the national collectivity.

The attitudes of women toward wearing uniforms provide some evidence. Some women swore they would never wear them; not so much because they were fascist, but because they suggested a vulgar and conformist behavior, which is to say that uniforms grouped women with others for whom they had no regard—they were not exclusive. Besides which they were plain unflattering. This snobby dismissal of fascist dress implied of course that some other women may have regarded its leveling function as positive—which would not be at all surprising given the functions of fashion as an indicator of class status. Nonetheless, within the bourgeoisie, too, there were women, especially among the young, who appropriated the uniform as if it were a fashion ornament, transmogrifying it to display their individuality. Those who, like the Piedmontese Marquess Irene Giunti di Targiani, advocated the use of the uniform as a measure of discipline seemed quite rare: perhaps the marquess's considerable social clout added weight to her injunctions to young fascist social workers to throw off "their society dress" for the "uniform of discipline," to bury their "individual egoism" in the common cause.[23] The example of young Ida Cagossi—an Emilian and daughter of a working-class family living in Genova in the 1930s, who, as Vampa, would become a partisan leader in 1944—was perhaps more typical among very young women. She recalled how, at age eleven, her snappy black and white uniform fed her sense of what is sometimes called "protagonism": "Passing through the street that brought me to and from school, I was anxious to keep my black cape open over my uniform, letting it fall back over my shoulders to show off the various awards fastened to my white blouse. I walked chest out, with a firm step, and every time I crossed somebody's path, I peeked at my reflection in the shop mirrors, to check the effect produced."[24] In other words, the uniform itself, interpreted according to the canons of spectacle and dress of an increasingly competitive society, fed a sense of individuality, rather than group uniformity in the sense sought after by the regime. Pediatricians working with lower-class children reported similar attitudes—which they condemned. According to Luigi Maccone, a prominent Turinese doctor, doting families fed the overweening narcissism of even the smallest children, and this was only enhanced by the beauty contests and obsession with uniforms of the regime. Women writers, too, reflecting in positive terms on the character of the "1900 girl"—their cohort—highlighted this new self-absorption:

> More beautiful than our grandmothers because made healthier and stronger by her more intense activity, she doesn't conceal her anxiety to be admired; everything is a pretext and help. She's at the typewriter and knows her nails are shining; she's out driving and she knows that her attentive expression elicits glances; she caresses her children and she knows full well how sweet her gesture appears; she smokes a cigarette, her lovely lips pouting. At the most important moments of the day, thoughts about how she looks, worries about her appearance, never leave her.[25]

More evidence would need to be adduced to discuss this emergent culture of narcissism, to speculate about the mix of insecurity and vanity behind this quest after a new subject position. For now, we might want to accept, with the writer Maria Coppola, that this preoccupation with appearance, far from being debilitating, made her contemporaries more resilient and modern individuals. "The problems of aestheticism," she concluded, referring to her peers, the bourgeois "new woman" of the 1930s, "help make her brain more elastic."[26]

The question of how to categorize this cerebral elasticity—which is to say, the question of what it was used for—returns us to the issue of how to characterize the nodes of meanings arising through the agency of commercial culture. Were they transgressive? Did their discursive meanings break dominant codes? Did they constitute the basis of an antihegemonic or oppositional culture? Short of probing better the connections between individuality, personal autonomy, and political opposition, and between collective identity and national allegiance, it is premature to conclude with any one such conceptualization. It would be equally mistaken to suggest that commercial culture had generated the kind of "life-style feminism" associated with girl culture in the United States during the 1920s.[27] The Italian market was still too segmented, family, religious, and especially class identities were still too embracing, to contemplate the self-referential youth cultures arising in more advanced capitalisms of the interwar period, much less the proliferation of postmodern subcultural identities typical of the present. At least for the time being, commercial culture more likely attached to and reinforced a multiplicity of local girl-cultures.

If commercial culture did not lend itself to representing women in the national political culture, it nonetheless reinforced a shared national identity. Writing in the mid-1930s, the French anthropologist Marcel Mauss spoke of the shared "techniques of the body" that accrued as a result of education and emulation and that, displayed through physical gesture and movement, denoted a common belonging to a "national habitus."[28] He recognized that these techniques were becoming more mobile, under the influence of commercial culture—the case he remarked upon was the new gangly walk of young Parisian women, which he attributed to the influence of U.S. cinema. Under the fascist regime, various forces transformed appearance and gestuality: Italian young women became aware of their newness with respect to the past and a common identity as "we Italian women." However much the fascist regime tried to associate these changes with its rule, the effect, at best, was to strengthen a sense of nationness as opposed to nationalism, to construct what might be described as an anthropological female identity as opposed to a political one.

These conclusions, though perhaps disappointing in their tentativeness about the precise nature of women's collective identities under fascist rule, point to the different set of concerns explored here: namely, the incapacity of a fascist polity, despite its dictatorial powers and propagandistic skills, to dominate the production, much less to define the meaning, of commercial cultural products. Italian fascism was not unique in this respect. Detlev Peukert, drawing insight from the German historians' practice of "everyday life history," or *Alltagsgeschichte*, in his study of the Edelweiss pirates and other youth culture grouplets under a far more totalitarian system, namely, Nazi Germany, drew similar conclusions,[29] even if he did not tie them to any broader analysis of the consumerist aspects of capitalism under the Third Reich. It appears that young people, under the influence of mass culture, sometimes of U.S. provenance, had simply started marching to a different drummer. At the very apogee of Hitler's power, they could be found palavering in a language derived from commercial culture and insensible to the language of politics as it was remanipulated by the Nazis.

The continual struggle to appropriate and dominate the proliferation of goods and signs of an emerging mass consumer society and the paradoxes and resistances to which this struggle gave rise thus signaled the limits of a form of national sovereignty girded by autarchic economic policies and premised on incorporating citizens by means of a politics based on political mobilization. The implications for *systems* of political governance would of course not be visible until after the defeat of the Axis powers in 1945 and the subsequent reconstruction of European society according to more limited notions of sovereignty and new ideals of democratic citizenship. Yet well before these processes of commodification and expansion of market became identified with U.S. global hegemony, the conditioning exercised by international commodity movements on the capacity of states to mobilize civil society had become manifest. In that sense alone might we speak of emerging consumer cultures as subtly subversive of traditional forms of sovereignty. The point here then is not to backdate trends that are associated with contemporary consumer capitalism but to highlight the coexistence of as well as the conflict between the language of politics and the language of consumption. From that perspective, as early as the 1920s, women emerged as major protagonists of what in a present-day context is characterized as post-political citizenship; their presence in the public arena was defined not so much by the transformation of the political system as by notions of the self, of collective identity, and of entitlement associated with the diffusion of mass consumption.

NOTES

I am grateful to students and colleagues at the University of Connecticut at Storrs, and at Princeton, Cornell, and Columbia Universities for their comments on previous versions of this essay.

1. For a broad characterization of this view, framed in terms of modernization theory, see Reinhard Bendix, ed., *Nation-Building and Citizenship* (New York: John Wiley and Sons, 1964); see also Karl Deutsch, *Nationalism and Social Communism,* 2d ed. (Cambridge: MIT Press, 1966). For a discussion of the term "fordism," used to characterize an entire historical phase in a post-1970s perspective, see, for example, Scott Lash and John Urry, *The End of Organized Capitalism* (Cambridge, England: Polity Press, 1967).

2. The term "postfordist consumption" is advanced by Lash and Urry in their characterization of the features of postfordism. In addition to *The End of Organized Capitalism,* see their and other's contributions to Stuart Hall and Martin Jacques, eds., *New Times: The Changing Face of Politics in the 1990s* (London: Routledge, Chapman, and Hall, 1991). David Harvey, *The Condition of Postmodernity* (Oxford: Blackwell, 1991), offers a stimulating overview of the alternation of centrifugal and centralizing forces in capitalist accumulation. See also various contributions to this analysis by Arjun Appadurai: in particular "Disjuncture and Difference in the Global Cultural Economy," *Public Culture* 2, no. 3 (spring 1990): 1–24.

3. This essay reinterprets sources and themes presented in my recent *How Fascism Ruled Women: Italy, 1922–1945* (Berkeley: University of California Press, 1992) and my studies in progress on the process of Americanization in Europe: in particular "Cinema and Sovereignty: The Hollywood Challenge to European Cinemas, 1920–1960," *Journal of Modern History* 61, no. 1 (March 1989): 53–87.

4. Benedict Anderson, *Imagined Communities: Reflections on the Origin and Spread of Nationalism,* 2d ed., revised and extended (London: Verso, 1991). The importance that extrapolitical forces might have to shaping national identities is suggested in Gérard Noiriel, "La Question nationale come objet de l'histoire sociale," *Genèses* 4 (May 1991): 72–94. The role of nationalism in culture building in diverse national settings is discussed in Orvar Lofgren, "Materializing the Nation in Sweden and America," introduction to "Defining the National," a special issue of *Ethnos* 58, nos. 3–4 (1993): 161–96.

5. See George L. Mosse: *The Nationalization of the Masses* (New York: Meridien, 1975); also idem, *Nationalism and Sexuality* (New York: Fertig, 1985).

6. See especially Eric J. Hobsbawm, "Mass-Producing Traditions: Europe, 1870–

1914," in *The Invention of Tradition,* ed. Eric J. Hobsbawm and Terence Ranger, Canto Edition (Cambridge: Cambridge University Press, 1992), 266–308.

7. Eugen Weber, *Peasants into Frenchmen* (Stanford: Stanford University Press, 1976).

8. de Grazia, *How Fascism Ruled Women,* esp. 234–71.

9. *Mezzadri di Val di Pesa e del Chianti,* vol. 14 of *Studi e monografie: Monografie di famiglie agricole* (Rome: INEA, 1931), 63, cited in de Grazia, *How Fascism Ruled Women,* 121–22.

10. See Victoria de Grazia, *The Culture of Consent: The Mass Organization of Leisure in Fascist Italy* (New York: Cambridge University Press, 1981).

11. Cited from Sergio Giuntini, "La donna e lo sport in Lombardia durante il fascismo," unpublished paper presented at the conference of the Istituto Lombardo per la storia del movimento di liberazione in Italia, "Donna Lombarda (1860–1945)," Milan, April 1989; p. 8. See also de Grazia, *How Fascism Ruled Women,* 218.

12. de Grazia, *How Fascism Ruled Women,* 218, also 206 ff.

13. Renato Moro, "La 'modernizzazione' cattolica tra fascismo e postfascismo come problema storiografico," *Storia contemporanea* 19, no. 4 (August 1988): 625–716.

14. On the modernization of beauty canons after the turn of the century, see Michela De Giorgio, *Le italiane dall'Unità a oggi* (Rome: Laterza, 1992), esp. 147–208.

15. Luigi Santini, "Cinematografo: Riflessioni tra un tempo e l'altro," *Cordelia, 1934,* 134, cited in de Grazia, *How Fascism Ruled Women,* 211.

16. See especially Catherine Gallagher, "The Body versus the Social Body in the Work of Thomas Malthus and Henry Mayhew," in *The Making of the Modern Body,* ed. Catherine Gallagher and Thomas Laquer (Berkeley: University of California Press, 1987), 83–106.

17. Quoted in Natalia Aspesi, *Il lusso e l'autarchia: Storia dell'eleganza italiana, 1930–1944* (Milan: Rizzoli, 1982), 43. See also de Grazia, *How Fascism Ruled Women,* 212–13.

18. Cited in de Grazia, *How Fascism Ruled Women,* 201. For a contemporary example of the identification of the female with modernity and urbanism, see Patrice Petro, *Joyless Streets: Women and Melodramatic Representation in Weimar Germany* (Princeton: Princeton University Press, 1989), 39–78.

19. The very first local one dated back to 1911, the occasion being the universal exposition in honor of fifty years of Italian unity; that, however, was designed mainly for Roman consumption and drew becostumed girls from the city's neighborhoods.

20. Archivio Centrale di Stato, Presidenza Consiglio dei Ministri, 1937–1939, 1.7.7493, Grande Adunata delle Forze Femminili, 28 May 1939, Agenzia Stefani, n. 25, cited in de Grazia, *How Fascism Ruled Women,* 226.

21. This dynamic is still much debated. However, the German sociologist Georg Simmel's assessment from the perspective of the early twentieth century seems pertinent to the still highly stratified context of interwar Italy: "Fashion" (1904), *American Journal of Sociology* 62 (May 1957): 541–88; see too Fred Davis, *Fashion, Culture, and Industry* (Chicago: University of Chicago Press, 1992).

22. Siegfried Kracauer, "The Mass Ornament" (1927), *New German Critique* 5 (spring 1975): 67–76.

23. Irene Giunti di Targiani, *La donna nella famiglia, nel lavoro, nella vita sociale,*

Corso per visitatrici fasciste (Rome: Federazione dei fasci di combattimento dell'Urbe, delegazione provinciale fasci femminili, 1935), 6–7, 27. See also de Grazia, *How Fascism Ruled Women,* 264.

24. de Grazia, *How Fascism Ruled Women,* 159.

25. Ibid., 214, 218.

26. Maria Coppola, "La donna del millenovecento," *Cordelia, 1934,* 92. Cited in de Grazia, *How Fascism Ruled Women,* 214, 218.

27. Rayna Rapp and Ellen Ross, "The Twenties Backlash: Compulsory Heterosexuality, the Consumer Family, and the Waning of Feminism," in *Class, Race, and Sex: The Dynamics of Control,* ed. Amy Swerdlow and Hannah Lessinger (Boston: G. K. Hall, 1982), 93–107.

28. The role of commercial culture in transforming what Marcel Mauss calls "techniques du corp" is suggested in his essay "Notion de technique du corps" (1934), first published in *Journal de Psychologie* 32, nos. 3–4 (15 March–15 April 1936); reprinted in Marcel Mauss, *Sociologie et Anthropologie,* 4th ed. (Paris: Presses Universitaires de France, 1968), 365–68.

29. Detlev Peukert, *Inside Nazi Germany: Conformity, Opposition, and Racism in Everyday Life,* trans. Richard Deveson (New Haven: Yale University Press, 1987).

TWELVE

Deviant Pleasures?

Women, Melodrama, and Consumer Nationalism in West Germany

Erica Carter

This article uses a study of film melodrama as the starting point for an exploration of the changing relationship between femininity and consumption in 1950s West Germany. There are a number of reasons for choosing to focus on melodrama. First, as feminist film critics have convincingly demonstrated, melodrama has had a privileged relation to the female audience in the twentieth century: it is the "feminine" cinematic form par excellence.[1] Second, melodrama, with its focus on everyday life, intimate relationships, and the bourgeois family, has been located within film criticism as the dramatic mode for the "historic project"[2] of an ideological affirmation of the bourgeois family. In the bourgeois tradition, women's primary social role is a housewifely one, a role that involves, among other things, a competence in domestic consumption. It follows then that postwar melodrama, insofar as it promoted familial and thus housewifely values, is likely to have had an important relation to contemporary discourses of female consumption.

We will be concerned in what follows with three films from the early 1950s, a period in which West German economic policy, advertising, and marketing promoted domestic/familial as opposed to leisure/personal consumption as a route to national recovery. In what was for the majority of the population a time of austerity, the emphasis of consumer discourse was on thrift and rational domestic management, on saving for better days to come in the Federal Republic's much-vaunted but as yet barely perceptible economic miracle. In this context, housewives were seen to play a key role in the management and regulation of the familial (and by extension, it was argued, national) economy. Indeed, for one contemporary market analyst at least, the very survival of the free-market order was deemed "primarily" dependent on housewifely labor.[3] Woman's housewifely role within a reconstituted West German family was, then, promoted not only on moral, cultural and religious grounds but also as a route to economic stabilization. In the postwar transition to a consumer economy, it was deemed crucial that women be schooled in domestic consumption (saving, planning, shopping to feed and clothe the family) and encouraged to renounce—in the short term at least—the wayward pleasures of personal leisure consumption, from fast cars to fashionable dressing.[4]

The 1950s has been construed in much feminist history as a period in which, after a brief period of wartime autonomy (or, at least, a period of separation from men) women were "pushed back" into the home, more or less without resistance.[5] And on the surface, there is ample evidence to support this vision of 1950s West German womanhood as historically defeated: the gearing of employment policy under the first conservative administration, for instance, to the male breadwinner and the family wage;[6] the low levels of female participation in public politics;[7] the reluctance of the legislators to rewrite family and employment law in accord with constitutional guarantees of sexual equality;[8] and the establishment in 1953 of a Family Ministry with an explicit commitment to promoting housewifery as women's primary role.[9]

There is, however, always a paradox in official strategies for the reassertion of housewifery and domestic consumption as women's primary domain. On the one hand, the twentieth-century emergence of advanced consumer economies has seemed to confine women anew to the domestic arena, demanding as it does of housewives a whole new set of skills and competences, from managerial skill in the rational management of time and money in the consumption process through technical expertise in the handling of domestic technology to creative/aesthetic competence in the construction of the family home as a theater of leisure consumption. At the same time, as historians of consumer culture have regularly observed, mass consumption removes women from the domestic realm and produces new public forms for the social articulation of femininity. Hand in hand with an awareness of women's enlarged presence in public culture has gone, for example, an acknowledgement by twentieth-century commercial and governmental economic planners of the centrality of the female consumer to national markets and economies. Thus in 1950s West Germany, both market researchers and government policymakers identified housewives as the principal decision makers and arbiters of taste in domestic consumption—and, by extension, as key actors in national recovery.[10]

In the period under discussion here—1949 to the mid-1950s—it can be argued that consensus around economic development was constructed in part through appeals to national sentiment. The relatively untranslatable slogan of the period—"Wir sind wieder wer!" (We are someone again!)—is evocative of the way in which, following the defeat of German nationalism as a *political* force in 1945, national identification was visible again at the *cultural* level in the collective quest for personal and national prosperity.

Women's contradictory relation to what can tentatively be termed postwar "consumer nationalism" becomes clear, I will argue, in films of the period, where hegemonic femininity—the femininity of the bourgeois housewife—is positioned both in the subordinate familial role that nationalism traditionally affords to women and in a relation of superiority over class and ethnic/racial "others" to the nation—amongst whom, as we shall see, are included working-class women, Blacks, Americans, and diverse other figures of cultural deviance.

Each of the three films examined below presents a version of a crucial postwar feminine transition: the transformation, that is, of the female protagonist from luxury consumer to bourgeois housewife. *The Private Secretary* (*Die Privatsekretärin,* Paul Martin, 1953), a remake of a 1931 comedy classic by Wilhelm Thiele, stars one of the most popular screen couples of the 1950s, Sonja Ziemann and Rudolf Prack. The film centers on Gerda (Ziemann), a young secretary who comes to the city in search of fun and fast living, only to fall in love with, and have her appetites for luxury tamed by her bank-manager boss Erich Delbrück (Prack). In the second film, *Love without Illusion* (*Liebe ohne Illusion,* Erich Engel, 1955), Ziemann is similarly cast as a fun-loving and fashion-conscious young woman whose consumerist appetites are symptomatic of her more general tendency to socio-sexual transgression. In the role of Ursl, Ziemann plays an increasingly disconsolate housekeeper to her sister Christa (Heidemarie Hatheyer). Christa works as a doctor to support her disabled ex-actor husband, Walter (Curd Jürgens), but in doing so is shown to shirk all manner of wifely duties. Ursl steps in to fill the breach; she starts an affair with Walter. The liaison leads to near disaster; Ursl falls pregnant and seeks help from a backstreet abortionist, at whose hands she might have died without the last-minute intervention of her doctor sister. The film ends with reconciliation: Christa and Walter are reunited, the wayward Ursl restored to health and forgiven.

Love without Illusion, then, uses the figures of Ursl and Christa to play out familiar conflicts between two opposing contemporary models of femininity: the model of the professional working wife versus the fashionable, single and footloose consuming woman. In *Without You All Is Darkness* (*Ohne Dich wird es Nacht,* Curd Jürgens, 1956), by contrast, these two femininities are united in a single figure, Gina (Eva Bartók). Gina figures initially as a night-club glamour girl of dubious virtue, whose mercenary pursuit of luxury leads to her engagement to the unattractive but wealthy Arthur (Ernst Schröder). A moral transformation occurs in Gina after her encounter with Robert Kessler (Curd Jürgens), a lawyer whom some mysterious past affliction has driven to morphine addiction. Gina falls in love, marries Robert, and discards the role of fashionable temptress in favor of that of nurturant wife. In this capacity, she is able to cure Robert of his addiction: a signal, as in *The Private Secretary* and *Love without Illusion*, of the moral supremacy of housewifely femininity.

What I seek to show below is how these stories of the disavowal of consumer femininity—of its displacement by a more sober, housewifely femininity—are interwoven in each of the films with a narrative of national transformation: the story of West Germany's transition to a proto-American society of mass consumption.[11] What I offer, in other words, is not only a study of the way film handles representations of the consuming woman but a study, more particularly, of the way consumer femininities are defined in relation to other markers of cultural difference (specifically of ethnicity and nation). What that film-textual analysis in turn, I hope, illuminates is the need for any cultural study of gender and consumption to take account of the way gender is inflected and gains meaning from its insertion into other systems of representation—of class, "race," sexuality, or, in our case, the (German) "nation."

MELODRAMA AND EXCESS IN 1950s WEST GERMAN CINEMA

When Anglo-American film studies turned its attention to melodrama in the early 1970s, the initial focus was on melodrama's ideological function as "the dramatic mode for a historic project," which was to assert, suggests Christine Gledhill, "the centrality of the bourgeois family and the ascendancy and continued dominance of that class."[12] As feminist critics began to point out, however, it was through an exploration of family life and intimate relationships that melodrama traced the formation of the bourgeois individual. Melodrama's articulation of a bourgeois sensibility went hand in hand, in other words, with its exploration of patriarchal relations of gender.

Characteristic of much of this early criticism was the implicit belief that the issue of melodrama's ideological complicity (or otherwise) in bourgeois patriarchy could be resolved by text-centered analysis. In his early essay "Tales of Sound and Fury" (1972), film critic Thomas Elsaesser produced an influential account in this vein of melodrama's excessive style, its privileging of visual and aural cinematic qualities over narrative and dialogue as sources of meaning. Drawing on the work of a handful of melodramatic *auteurs* (Douglas Sirk, Max Ophuls, Vincent Minnelli, and so on), Elsaesser argued that those directors' foregrounding of mise-en-scène, music, gesture, and "dynamic space" over character and action located melodrama as the product of "a conscious use of style as meaning."[13] Focusing on 1950s Hollywood family melodrama, Elsaesser drew attention to the films' use of color, wide-screen, and deep focus to heighten their impact as spectacle; to the foregrounding of the rhythmic and musical qualities of speech as opposed to its status as dialogue; and to the "restless, and yet suppressed energy" suggested by acting style, lighting, composition, and decor, all of which contribute to "the feeling that there is always more to tell than can be said."[14]

It is this quality of stylistic excess that led Elsaesser and other critics to propose that melodrama has the potential to undermine its own narrative resolution and, thus, its affirmative ideological message. There is regularly in melodrama, it is claimed, a surplus of meaning that cannot be contained by the happy end. Thus in Elsaesser's essentially formalistic analysis, melodramatic form—in the hands of accomplished directors, at least—produces a protomodernist "open text," which releases the spectator from subordination to dominant meanings.

Though illuminating in their attention to textual detail, early film studies accounts of melodrama, in privileging formalist or psychoanalytic method,[15] tended to erase from view the historical dimensions of ideological contradictions. It is questionable, for example, whether the extravagance that is melodrama's stylistic hallmark releases meaning in every context from its anchorage in bourgeois systems of representation. In 1950s melodrama for instance, excess is most often figured precisely in terms of the protagonists' attachment to the markers of bourgeois prosperity: extravagant fashions, luxury homes, gourmet eating. What is thus at stake in the films' oscillation between excess and stability is not a disruption of established bourgeois order, but rather an exploration of the contradictions between two conflicting bourgeois models: the bourgeois family order on the one hand, mass participation in bourgeois affluence on the other.

Take for example Erich Engel's *Love without Illusion* (1955). The film tells the story of a ménage-à-trois: Heidemarie Hatheyer, the working wife, her sister, Sonja Ziemann, and husband, Curd Jürgens. Forced to work outside the home because of her ex-actor husband's disability (he returns from the war with a paralyzed arm), Hatheyer nonetheless displays an "unnatural" commitment to her profession. The imbalances in her identity—and, by extension, the imbalances in family life—are problematized in an early sequence in which the three discuss the issue over breakfast (a meal prepared, significantly, by the emasculated Jürgens). Hatheyer claims that she can control this existential division of her self by devoting 50 percent of her energy to work and the rest to marriage. Her assertion is rapidly undermined: we witness her returning late from work to a spoiled wedding anniversary dinner—she has, in any case, forgotten the occasion (figure 36)—and investing misplaced maternal energies in a sick young patient (the scene immediately follows one in which Jürgens has again retired to the kitchen to prepare her dinner). The disruption of domestic stability is further underlined by rapid crosscutting between Hatheyer's workplace and the marital home, where Ziemann, who has agreed to keep house for the couple, plays the bourgeois housewife in Hatheyer's stead.

Narrative logic points inexorably, then, to crisis in Hatheyer's marriage

Figure 36. Scene from *Love without Illusion*. Christa (Heidemarie Hatheyer), pictured here in her husband's arms, comes home late to a spoiled anniversary dinner.

and to Jürgens' and Ziemann's eventual adulterous liaison. In Hollywood melodrama of the same period, domestic crisis and illicit desire would perhaps have erupted in the very heart of the marital home (as they do, for example, to magnificent effect in Douglas Sirk's *Written on the Wind* [1956]). In *Love without Illusion,* by contrast, wayward desires are banished from the newly reconstructed bourgeois home. The film opens as the three partners in the love triangle move into a new apartment, and it is significant that all three are involved in the rituals that establish domestic order, from hanging curtains to choosing the proper crockery for breakfast (figures 37 and 38). Ziemann's constant carping at her sister's shirking of marital duties underlines the complicity of all three in the reconstitution of private life as the domain of bourgeois/patriarchal relations.

Adulterous desire, then, can find no outlet here; it must seek a more public milieu for its expression. The occasion presents itself when the threesome are invited to a Shrovetide (*Fasching*) party by Jürgens' unpleasantly fat and prosperous boss. Shrovetide is traditionally a season of permissible excess in Germany, a season not only of drinking and reveling but also of the abandonment of bourgeois etiquette and mores. It is the only occasion, for

Figures 37 (top) and 38. Scenes from *Love without Illusion*. The rituals that establish domestic order.

instance, when strangers may address each other in the familiar "Du" form
or be treated to such further gestures of intimacy as raspberries blown in the
face, unprompted insults, or spontaneous kissing. In *Love without Illusion*, the
possibility the season offers for an unleashing of surplus emotion is underscored by the party's setting. The huge hall where it takes place is bedecked
with streamers, sparkling with mirrors—a veritable fun-palace of leisure, pleasure, and consumption.

This is one of the few sequences in which the film approximates to the
stylistic extravagance Elsaesser observes in Hollywood melodrama. Unlike
their North American counterparts, early postwar West German examples
of the genre rarely made significant use of the stylistic techniques identified
by Elsaesser to situate the action in a context of emotional turbulence. The
films are black-and-white; tight framing ensures the privileging of character
and action over mise-en-scène; and narrative and dialogue take precedence
over sound and visual style. The party scene in *Love without Illusion*, however,
departs from the social realist tone of much of the rest of the film and employs at least some of the cinematic elements of stylistic excess. At the party's
opening, the camera pans the scene in long shot, establishing the dance hall
as a milieu for the pursuit of luxury and—permissible or illicit—pleasures.
The contrast with the spartan domesticity of the threesome's family home
could not be greater.

This division between the home as site of drab domestic realism and the
party hall as arena of fantasy and transgressive pleasure is mirrored by a shift
from realist costume to fancy dress. Hatheyer dresses as a flamenco dancer,
Ziemann as Harlequin, Jürgens as a stereotypical gypsy complete with a jaunty
scarf and an earring evocative of gender ambiguity. The gypsy costume in
particular, with its suggestion of a sexuality untrammeled by Germanic bourgeois norms, highlights Jürgens' potential for transformation from faithful
husband to wayward adulterer; and indeed, it is at the party that Jürgens and
Ziemann exchange the first kiss that will lead to their brief affair and her
unwanted pregnancy (figure 39).

Thus the party hall as "palace of consumption" becomes an arena of expression for desires repressed from the sober milieu of the bourgeois family home. This division of narrative space, between the home as the private
site of socio-sexual order and consumer culture as a public arena for the pursuit of illicit and excessive desires, is reproduced in other films of the period. In *Without You All Is Darkness*, the opening sequence, a long tracking
shot following the back of an unidentified man, establishes the shopping
street in which he walks as a place of mystery and vagrant desire. The man,
played by Curd Jürgens again, is soon identified as Robert the morphine
addict—a figure enslaved, then, precisely by his own transgressive desire. In
The Private Secretary, the city that draws the female protagonist, Sonja Ziemann, in search of a job, husband, and fortune is invested, like the shop-

Figure 39. Scene from *Love without Illusion*. The first adulterous kiss.

ping street in *Without You All Is Darkness,* with the power to lure its inhabitants down the wayward path of hedonistic consumption. Ziemann's desire for luxury consumption is figured in the film also as the desire for a life at large on city streets, hence, for example, one of many musical sequences featuring the film's theme tune, "Ich bin ja heut' so glücklich" (I'm So Happy Today). Here Ziemann's delight in a newfound job finds representation in a montage of brightly lit city streets, which provide a backdrop for the singing heroine as footloose and free-spending modern young woman.

THE CONSUMING WOMAN AS OUTSIDER TO THE NATION

As we shall see, the primary narrative drive in *The Private Secretary* is toward a taming of Gerda's newfound urban independence. The spectacle of woman in public space, it seems, is a source of narrative disruption and spectatorial anxiety. In all three films, however, commodified public space as arena of female desire is not the only source of trouble. At least equally unsettling, apparently, is the commodity orientation of the modern consuming woman.

In the early phase of West Germany's economic revival, from which these three films derive, the architects of the country's social market economy confronted a troubling contradiction in their own thinking. Committed on the one hand to laissez-faire liberalism, they were convinced on the other hand of the benefits of rational market management as a route to economic stability. Market regulation by means other than government intervention was thus identified as a priority, not only for manufacturers, via market research and advertising, but also for consumers, as key participants in market regeneration. The influence of microeconomic processes, that is, individual and family consumption practices, on economic stability at the macroeconomic level was repeatedly emphasized in official exhortations for price-conscious buying. In the absence of price controls, consumer attention to price was construed as important for inflation control and market competition; thus government and business alike promoted rational consumption as a route to both personal and national prosperity.

The discourse of rational consumption derived much of its popular attraction from its appeal to national sentiment. Nationalism has traditionally drawn much of its power from its appeal to historical memory; yet Germany's discredited recent past was no longer easily available as a focus for national identification. In addition, Germany's division into two separate states made it unclear where the boundaries of the German nation definitively lay. In the context of such uncertainties over West Germany's status as nation, the collective quest for prosperity arguably became a crucial focus of postwar national identification.[16]

In traditional German nationalisms (including under fascism), the family is situated as cornerstone of the "people's community" (*Volksgemeinschaft*), and women are positioned as mothers and breeders for the nation. In postwar West Germany, elements of this political nationalism were certainly evident, in pronatalist family policy, for instance, or retrogressive family law.[17] Yet, since nationalism was largely discredited as a political force, it tended to surface in a different guise, as a form of cultural nationalism inflected through economic rhetoric. Thus when government or big business called for rational consumption, they did so by evoking models drawn from traditional nationalism. Just as cultural nationalism had situated the family as linchpin to the nation, so too market analysts positioned the family as key unit of consumption and stressed the role of stable family structures in national reconstruction. And just as traditional nationalism had allotted domestic roles to women, so too did the movement for consumer rationalization, which specifically situated the rational housewife as the agent of national recovery.

In this context, women flaunting their enjoyment of extrafamilial leisure consumption were positioned not only as threats to domestic order but also as outsiders to the nation—threats to a very *German* project of rationally managed growth and mounting personal prosperity. Thus in all three of the films discussed here, the conjunction in the consuming woman of sexual allure with a commodification of the self, and with active desires for personal gratification, appears as transgressing patriarchal symbolic order. Fashion, for example, is encoded in all three films as a route to women's self-sufficiency. The heroine Gina (Eva Bartók) in *Without You All Is Darkness* works as a fashion illustrator, as does Ursl (Ziemann), the adulteress in *Love without Illusion,* whose descent through adultery to the status of fallen woman is emphasized by her turn to the equally dubious practice of fashion modeling.

Yet it is not only the clash between female leisure consumption and women's "proper" domestic role that is addressed in these films, but also the threat the consuming woman poses to (West) German-ness. In *Without You All Is Darkness,* Bartók is first seen in the bar where Jürgens procures his morphine (figure 40). Dressed in a white evening dress and glittering with diamonds, she is endowed with the radiance that, according to Richard Dyer, is linked in Hollywood glamour to "the transcendental rhetoric of popular Christianity": the glamorous star as modern image of the sacred. Dyer makes the observation in an important essay on white ethnicity, in which he links the codes of Hollywood glamour with the privileging of whiteness as cultural value.[18] The association between woman-as-spectacle and white ethnicity is similarly evident in 1950s German melodrama, yet the encoding is reversed—the glamour image is identified as duplicitous surface, which may conceal alien (non-German) identities. Thus in *Without You All Is Darkness,* there are clear xenophobic overtones in Jürgens' distrust of the commoditized female image. He jeers at Gina/Bartók—introduced to him as "Asiatic" (hence her heavy East European accent)—"From Asia? Aha! 'Mysterious' are you? 'Impenetrable'? 'Opaque'? . . ." Her status as an outsider in a national community rooted in patriarchal domestic order is further emphasized when Jürgens invites her for breakfast after both have spent a night in a bar with her husband-to-be, Arthur (Ernst Schröder). Her visual incongruity as dazzling consumer spectacle in domestic space (Jürgens' kitchen) is underlined, for spectators who haven't yet got the point, by her clumsy handling of Jürgens' old-fashioned coffee grinder. Her jewels get caught in the mechanism and prevent her performing even this simple task of everyday domestic labor (figure 41).

Much of the narrative of *The Private Secretary* circulates similarly around the contrast between naive young women who come to the city in pursuit of fine clothes and frivolous fun (paid for by a wealthy boyfriend/husband) and women who shun such dubious morality in favor of appropriate marriages and bourgeois order. When the heroine, Ziemann, confesses her desire for a wealthy man to her would-be husband, Rudolf Prack, he is sickened and almost deserts her. He relents but decides to test her virtue by offering her all the riches she desires if she will become his lover. (She refuses and becomes his wife.) As the German film critic Heide Schlüpmann argues, the postwar patriarch takes on a new role in *The Private Secretary* as the regulator of wayward consumer desire, which he successfully channels into a longing

Figure 40. Scene from *Without You All Is Darkness*. Bartók in the bar.

for marital propriety: "The fantasy of the good life is forced to give way to internalized etiquette."[19] In the film, Schlüpmann further observes, this domestication of consumer fantasy takes place via the disciplining of the female body. She notes how Sonja Ziemann—whose rather unconvincing talents as jazz dancer are displayed in earlier musical sequences—is schooled by Prack

Figure 41. Scene from *Without You All Is Darkness*. Bartók's jewels get caught in the coffee grinder.

in the stiffly stereotypical gestures of middle-class romance: the peremptory kiss, the plastic smile. A key sequence here is a long musical passage from Gerda's first date with her future husband. The song "Ich bin ja heut' so glücklich" features in the film as a leitmotiv in Gerda's moments of greatest pleasure. Here, it is allotted several minutes of screen time, in a musically eclectic arrangement that moves from German folk through polka to a German carol ("O Tannenbaum"). At the beginning of the musical sequence, Ziemann and Prack are happily dancing cheek to cheek. In the middle, the song switches incongruously to a syncopated sequence in which Ziemann breaks away from her partner to dance alone before an audience of lascivious men. Prack's self-conscious twirling with a *male* partner at this point highlights the ability of an alien musical form—jazz—to thwart heterosexual norms, not only by heightening women's capacity for independent bodily pleasure but also by opening up the possibility of mutual pleasuring by men.[20]

Ziemann's capacity for sexual independence is removed, however, as is the threat of Prack's exposure to homosexual embrace, when the music shifts again to a finale that incorporates alien and sexually threatening jazz elements into a stylistic hybrid of Broadway and German popular song. Restored to each other's arms, Prack and Ziemann now participate in a dance that

Figure 42. Publicity still from *The Private Secretary.* Ziemann and Prack: The
triumph of heterosexual coupledom.

celebrates the triumph of heterosexual coupledom, as the whole supporting cast hop and skip in pairs across the screen (figure 42).

Evident in this musical sequence are, on one level, the traces of a far larger
struggle between an American popular culture rendered especially alien by
its association with black ethnicity—through jazz, for instance—and German

folk or popular tradition. These few moments tell a whole cultural history, a story of how West Germany managed its encounter with an alien American consumerism by stripping mass cultural forms of their most fundamentally un-German elements. Hence the suppression from the finale of the musical traces of "roots," jazz. The perceived problem, of course, is the way jazz demands an encounter with the racial other, the American Black; and the debate the film references is a leftover from Weimar cultural critics and their descendants under National Socialism who denounced syncopation, jazz rhythm and dance as modernist, degenerate, and anti-German.[21]

What is most interesting from our perspective here is that the target of that moral crusade against American jazz is a woman, Sonja Ziemann. As lustful consuming woman, she is seen not only to transgress domestic order but, through her affiliation with Black American tradition, to threaten national identity. The female leisure consumer, it seems, is unamenable to confinement within either bourgeois marriage or stable ethnicity and must be disciplined.

RADICAL DIFFERENCE

What then can we conclude about the relation of these three examples of 1950s melodrama to the broader discursive field around femininity and consumption during that period? It would appear, first, that the stylistic excess identified by critics as a genre characteristic is evident in these films not so much in visual style as in the *character* of the excessive consuming woman. While stylistic excess can be read in classic Hollywood melodrama as a "symptom" of narrative anxiety, in these West German films, the same function is performed by character stereotype. The power of the stereotype lies precisely in its capacity to accommodate the surplus of affective energy that realist representation or social experience cannot contain.[22] In 1950s West German melodrama, this capacity to absorb affective excess seems often to be displayed precisely by the single consuming woman. Her association with the consumer world and the commodity form allows her to function as a vehicle for larger postwar anxieties about women's increased presence in the public world. The stereotype of the consuming woman sums up fears of the imbalance in gender relations produced by women's wartime independence, anxieties about women's increased postwar presence in the labor market and in consumer public space, and about their numerical preponderance over men.[23] At the same time, the consuming woman's attachment to the glamour image makes her a focus for national popular anxieties about Germany's swamping by an alien (American) consumerism: a fear articulated through the racist association of leisure consumption with the ethnic other (Eva Bartók as grasping "Eastern" female, the dancing body of Sonja Ziemann as the repository of black cultural tradition).

The displacement of stylistic excess in these films from the visual and aural levels of cinematic language to that of character has particular political
implications. If, as has been regularly suggested, the polysemy of visual and
aural signifiers in high melodrama makes the films resistant to ideological closure, the reverse seems true of the genre examples under scrutiny here.
Through the use of the character stereotype as repository of excess, spectatorial anxieties are displaced from mise-en-scène and sound onto primary figures of cultural difference (the ethnic other, the autonomous desiring
woman), who in the course of the narrative must be disciplined and regulated.

Writing in a different context—an illuminating study of authoritarian responses to homosexuality in contemporary Britain—the political theorist
Anna Marie Smith has produced a model for the analysis of the discursive
constitution of cultural difference that is especially pertinent to my discussion here. In Smith's terms, the "out" lesbian or gay man who publicly flaunts
her/his sexuality is positioned in New Right discourse as a figure of Derridean
"radical difference": "an irresolvable, non-neutralizable difference which is
prior to all coherence and regularity." Smith's further assertion that radical
difference "functions as the condition of possibility for any appearance
of closure" highlights the relevance of her argument to our consuming
woman.[24] Eva Bartók in *Without You All Is Darkness* and Sonja Ziemann in *The
Private Secretary* are both unassimilable, at least in their guise as luxury consumers, into bourgeois marriage and domestic order. But it is exactly this resistance to order that poses an *irresistible* challenge to their future husbands
(Rudolf Prack and Curd Jürgens), whose task becomes precisely that of containing the threat these women pose as figures of radical difference. Ziemann, as we have seen, is tamed by bodily regulation; Bartók's transformation is a moral one, from grasping adventuress to self-sacrificing wife.
Following a sermon (*Moralpredigt*) from Jürgens on the evils of a loveless marriage founded on personal greed, she breaks off her engagement to his col-
league and bar companion, Schröder. When Bartók later marries Jürgens,
her reconstitution as dutiful wife is registered both by her renunciation of
the glamour image and by her participation in domestic labor. In a second
kitchen scene, the camera's proprietal gaze (aligned here with that of husband Jürgens) lingers on Bartók washing and drying dishes, demurely
dressed this time in sexually unappealing—practical but feminine—trousers
and blouse (figure 43).

In feminist psychoanalytic and poststructuralist theory, "woman" is seen
to occupy a relation of fundamental negativity to dominant/phallocentric
cultural systems. She *is* a primary signifier of radical difference. Yet unlike
homosexuality (which is more resistant to assimilation), the threat of radical difference posed by femininity has historically been dealt with by women's
domestication within housewifely, maternal, and marital identities. In Anna
Marie Smith's terms, this is the result of an attempt to "divide radical dif-

Figure 43. Scene from *Without You All Is Darkness*. Bartók domesticated.

ference." and to transform some of its elements into "simple difference"—
difference stripped of some of its potency and cultural agency.[25] In postwar
melodrama, the passage from radical to simple difference is effected by the
transformation of the female protagonist from the consuming woman as
agent of desire to the bourgeois housewife as self-regulating agent of rational consumption. The genre seems constructed, then, at the textual level as
a vehicle for conservative restoration.

At this stage of my argument, however, the issue of the *effectivity* of that
ideological project must remain open. First, if Smith is correct in her Derridean analysis of textual difference, then ideological closure is in any case
impossible, given the tendency of language (in Derridean terms) towards a
play of difference that resists symbolic fixity or coherence. On the films discussed above, there is in this context a longer study to be done of the way in
which radical difference, though perhaps containable as long as it takes the
shape of consumer femininity, erupts back into the text in the shape of more
fundamentally unassimilable figures of the "other" and the "alien." When
for example the pregnant adulteress in *Love without Illusion* seeks help from
a backstreet abortionist, she is pictured on city streets, which, unlike the ordered space of domesticity that is the film's primary setting, bear the un-
mistakable scars of German history. The tenement walls she passes are rid-

Figure 44. Scene from *Love without Illusion*. The symbolic death of innocence: Ziemann loses her baby.

dled with bullet holes; the gloomy backyards and winding stairways are more reminiscent of 1930s documentary realism than of early 1950s images of prosperity. The stereotypically wild-eyed abortionist who opens the door to Ziemann is positioned, then, in two senses as an emblem of radical difference. First, her stark poverty reminds the spectator of the failure of an increasingly prosperous West Germany wholly to eradicate class hierarchies. Second, the visibility of the scars of war in this backstreet milieu force a recognition that postwar reconstruction has merely displaced, not yet obliterated, the traces of German violence in history. It is this, perhaps, that explains the vehemence of Ziemann's response to the abortionist's image. She screams, turns, runs, trips, and falls—and loses her baby. The fruits, it seems, of confrontation with the working-class other, who is also an emblem of a problematic past, are violence, tragedy, and the symbolic death of innocence, the unborn child (figure 44).

CONCLUSION

There are numerous other examples in which stereotypical figures of difference surface within the melodramatic narrative and pull against the narrative drive to stable meaning.[26] But merely registering this obsessive return to figures of otherness will not suffice as evidence of postwar melodrama's resistance to closure. Film-textual analysis cannot be the sole source for a history of consumer identity and female desire. Above I have begun to explore models of genre analysis that help situate West German melodrama in the historical context of postwar consumerism. There is, however, no space here to explore what is in fact a necessary component of this project, namely, the study of postwar melodrama and female spectatorship. Entirely absent from my discussion here, for instance, is the important question of textual positioning of the female spectator via the organization of point-of-view and the female gaze in postwar popular cinema. If, as I have implied, these films are directed towards the transformation of feminine identity, then we need an analysis of the mechanisms of identification and/or of the organization of visual perception that engage the attention of a female audience.[27] Equally central to the further development of the work begun here is a study of the empirical female audience. Though audience statistics for the period are sparse, there is evidence of a historical relation between gender and genre—of women's more powerful affiliation, that is, to melodrama—which needs further exploration. A study of the attachment of the female audience to melodrama must of course encompass more than merely quantitative evidence, but must range across the larger discursive field—from the star system to other popular media (advertising and women's magazines in particular)—in an attempt to grasp more fully the nature of the historical association between consumer culture, melodrama and femininity. The work presented above, then, is merely a starting point, and this "happy end" only a beginning.

NOTES

I would like to thank Betty Knight for help with typing.

1. See for example Ien Ang, *Watching Dallas: Soap Opera and the Melodramatic Imagination* (London, 1985); Pam Cook, "Melodrama and the Women's Picture," in *Gainsborough Melodrama*, ed. Sue Aspinall and Bob Murphy (London, 1983); Annette Kuhn, "Women's Genres: Melodrama, Soap Opera, and Theory," in *Home Is Where the Heart Is: Studies in Melodrama and the Women's Film*, ed. Christine Gledhill (London, 1987); Patrice Petro, *Joyless Streets: Women and Melodramatic Representation in Weimar Germany* (Princeton, 1989).

2. See Christine Gledhill, "Genre," in *The Cinema Book*, ed. Pam Cook (London, 1985), 74.

3. Karl-Christian Behrens, "Die Verbraucherin als Marktpartei," *Der Volkswirt* 44 (1954): 13–15.

4. There is a lengthy discussion of this point in my *How German Is She? Post-War West German Reconstruction and the Consuming Woman, 1945–1960* (Ann Arbor, forthcoming).

5. See for example Annette Kuhn, ed., *Frauen in der deutschen Nachkriegszeit*, vols. 1–2 (Düsseldorf, 1984–1986); Angela Delille and Andrea Grohn, eds., *Blick zurück aufs Glück: Frauenleben und Familienpolitik in den fünfziger Jahren* (Berlin, 1985); Angela Delille and Andrea Grohn, eds., *Perlonzeit: Wie die Frauen ihr Wirtschaftswunder erlebten* (Berlin, 1985).

6. Although Article 3 of the Basic Law (*Grundgesetz*) gave a constitutional guarantee of equal rights for women, those rights were not translated into equality at work during the 1950s. Until 1955 (when unequal pay for equal work was declared unconstitutional), wage settlements assumed reduced rates for women. Special labor legislation pertaining to women, which included restrictions on working time, also remained on the statute books for several postwar decades; and the very possibility of waged work for married women was limited by Paragraph 1360 of the Civil Code, which made their ability to work dependent on their husband's consent. For more detailed discussion of women and work in the 1950s, see Eva Kolinsky, *Women in West Germany: Life, Work, and Politics* (Oxford, 1989), 54 ff; also Delille and Grohn, eds., *Perlonzeit*, 22–33.

7. The proportion of women in the Bundestag, for instance, hovered at around 9 percent of the total number of seats throughout the decade.

8. See Kolinsky, *Women in West Germany*, 54 ff. The issue of equality in family law was hotly contested throughout the 1950s. In 1953, the Constitutional Court ruled that family law should be brought into line with Article 3 of the Basic Law, which stated: "Men and women have equal rights" (Männer und Frauen sind gleichberechtigt). The court ruling included a caveat, however: "Differentiations . . . which are grounded in differences in life circumstances [*Lebensumstände*] remain exempt from the prohibition on differentiation . . . Both spouses are to contribute to the best of their ability to supporting the family . . . the husband through work outside the family and financial provision, the wife through household management and care of the children." Thus, though it admitted the principle of sexual equality, the Constitutional Court gave its sanction to the legal inscription of sexual difference. The Adenauer government later attempted to drive through legislation that would, among other things, give decision-making authority in all marital affairs to husbands, invest sole parental authority in fathers, and enshrine in law the principle of a sexual division of labor—housewifery for women, waged work for men. However, the government's proposals met with powerful parliamentary opposition, not least from a cross-party women's lobby. The proposals were not enacted in law until 1957—and then in much diluted form.

9. The ministry was placed in the hands of the devout Catholic and avowed anti-Communist Franz-Joseph Wuermeling, for whom sexual equality represented no less than a "programmatic erosion" of "natural" differences. Wuermeling saw his task as that of transforming an economic and social order that was "essentially hostile" to the family, through such measures as housing programs, child allowances, tax incentives for large families, and so on (F.-J. Wuermeling, cited in Delille and Grohn, *Blick zurück aufs Glück*, 131).

10. For an elaboration of this argument, see Carter, *How German Is She?*

11. For more extensive discussion of responses to postwar Americanization, see Christopher W. E. Bigsby, ed., *Superculture: American Popular Culture in Europe* (London, 1985); Kaspar Maase, *Bravo Amerika: Erkundungen zur Jugendkultur der Bundesrepublik in den fünfziger Jahren* (Hamburg, 1992); Ralph Willett, *The Americanization of Germany, 1945–1949* (London, 1989).

12. Christine Gledhill, "Genre," 74.

13. Thomas Elsaesser, "Tales of Sound and Fury: Observations on the Family Melodrama (1972)," in *Home Is Where the Heart Is: Studies in Melodrama and the Women's Film*, ed. Christine Gledhill (London, 1987), 54.

14. Ibid., 53.

15. An argument analogous to Elsaesser's is made in psychoanalytic readings of the genre. In an early formulation of psychoanalytic approaches, Geoffrey Nowell-Smith, for example, read stylistic excess as the product of a form of Freudian conversion hysteria, in which "the energy attached to an idea that has been repressed returns converted into a bodily symptom." The symptom in melodrama is the extravagance of mise-en-scène, music, and sound, all of which bear witness to the repression that underpins bourgeois family identities and, thus, expose family ideology in its "shameless contradictoriness" (Geoffrey Nowell-Smith, "Minnelli and Melodrama (1977)," in *Home Is Where the Heart Is: Studies in Melodrama and the Women's Film*, ed. Christine Gledhill [London, 1987], 73).

16. The first major study in political science to register this shift was Gabriel A. Almond and Sidney Verba's *The Civic Culture: Political Attitudes and Democracy in Five Nations* (Princeton, 1963). See also the social-psychological work of Alexander Mitscherlich and Margarethe Mitscherlich in their *Die Unfähigkeit zu Trauern* (1967; reprint, München, 1977).

17. The measures taken by the Adenauer government included child allowances (from 1955 onwards, DM 25 monthly was paid for each child after the third, and the sum was increased to DM 40 in 1959) and tax relief for child dependents, which was placed on sliding scale after 1953 to favor larger families. On family law, see n. 8 above.

18. Richard Dyer, "White," *Screen* 29, no. 4 (1988): 63.

19. Heide Schlüpmann, "Deutsche Liebespaare," *frauen und film*, 35 (1983): 15.

20. This sequence underlines the ambiguity of the pleasures offered by jazz and rock 'n' roll to women. On one level, Gerda's escape from her boyfriend's arms simply positions her as an available sexual object for the other men present. At the same time, white women of the postwar generation have often commented on the way popular music since jazz has allowed them to enjoy the *independent* pleasure of absorption in their own dancing body. See for example the comments of Ziemann's contemporary, Rosemarie Kühn, interviewed in Maase, *Bravo Amerika*, 134.

21. On jazz under National Socialism, see Ekkehard Jost, "Jazz in Deutschland: Von der Weimarer Republik zur Adenauer-Ära," in *That's Jazz: Der Sound des 20. Jahrhunderts* (Darmstadt, 1988); Maase, *Bravo Amerika*, 55–61.

22. It is this that explains why the racist continues in his/her assertion that all Blacks are inferior, dirty, unwashed, and so on while allowing that his/her black neighbor is "not really of that kind." For specific comments on the textual function of stereotypes, see for example Steve Neale, "The Same Old Story: Stereotypes and Differ-

ence," *The Screen Education Reader: Cinema, Television, Culture,* ed. Manuel Alvarado, Edward Buscombe, and Richard Collins (London, 1983), 41–47.

23. The so-called woman surplus (*Frauenüberschuss*)—women outnumbered men by around three million—was the subject of intense public debate and popular anxiety throughout the early postwar period.

24. Anna Marie Smith, "A Symptomology of an Authoritarian Discourse: The Parliamentary Debates on the Prohibition of the Promotion of Homosexuality," *New Formations,* 10 (1990): 63.

25. Ibid.

26. One example is the regular appearance in early-1950s popular film of black stereotypes as both figures of fun and sources of narrative disruption. An example is Hans Grimm's 1953 film *Marriage Fanfares* (*Fanfaren der Ehe*), a comedy that prefigures Billy Wilder's *Some Like it Hot* (1959) in its use of cross-dressing and its focus on gender transformation. The film centers on two married couples, each with a small baby. The four protagonists are unemployed at the beginning of the film; but when the women find work, the men are forced to assume the role of mothers, and indeed to disguise themselves as women on a trip to the local baby clinic. The confusion around identity occasioned by their transvestism is further exacerbated when they snatch a black baby from the clinic, mistaking it as one of their own. The film at this point disintegrates into farce: the men are chased by frantic nurses and a distraught mother. The harum-scarum chase, following as it does on a moment of mistaken racial identity, positions the black baby (like the abortionist in *The Private Secretary*) as the source of a wholesale collapse of order and meaning.

27. A model example of such a study of an earlier period in German history is Petro, *Joyless Streets.*

THIRTEEN

Soft Sell

Marketing Rhetoric in Feminist Criticism

Rachel Bowlby

To begin, a message from our sponsor:

> Many commodities are strictly women's propositions, and the advertiser, to se-
> cure the largest returns, should know the foibles of the sex and base his cam-
> paign upon that knowledge.[1]

Taken from an American advertising textbook of 1916, and appealing to and
for a type of sexual differentiation reinforced and promoted by the expansion of marketing on both sides of the Atlantic during this period, this quotation still has a recognizable air. A vulnerable collective victim, "the sex"
with its special "foibles," is targeted by a quasi-militaristic masculine offensive, "his campaign." In this case, the author in fact goes on to suggest that
the sex's particular foibles are the result of occupational differences, rather
than being natural; he does not, for instance, suggest that marketing is only
directed to or against women, who are simply a particular case of an object
that might be any group. But in any case, the mutability of a sex's foibles,
and the fact that foibles are not confined to one sex, is no obstacle, rather
providing unlimited possibilities for successful operations and conquests on
the part of "the advertiser" whose sole concern is the maximization of profit,
"to secure the largest returns." Marketing doesn't depend in principle on
feminine foibles, as opposed to any others, but it has generally done pretty
well out of the kind of fruitful engagement suggested by the offering of
"strictly women's propositions."

This type of exploitation (in the most literal sense) has long been, in return, a ready target for feminist criticism. Sometimes consumerism has been
seen as the principal source of women's oppression in the twentieth century,
as a force which, by promoting a falsely feminine identity, distracts them from
what would otherwise be their true identities, as humans and/or as women.

Such criticisms echo and are sometimes explicitly linked to Marxist and other accounts of a deterioration of the collective identity of working-class communities through the baleful encroachments of consumer culture.[2] That this process has often been referred to in terms of "feminization" indicates the dominance of the quasi-sexual manipulation model of the opening quotation.

This is not the only line of reaction or resistance. Parallel to the operations of the rhetoric of marketing, there have in fact been two different constructions of the consumer to whom it appeals. In the first, of which the summary above is a version, the consumer is someone attacked by advertising as a powerless victim, her (or his) susceptibilities exploited in such a way that she or he is left with no effective choice. In the past this was usually a critical representation, whether from a liberal or a Marxist position, stressing the passive "feminization" of the consumer of whichever sex.

The second construction of the consumer represents him (or her) not as a victim, but as the advertiser's double, engaged in conscious planning and decision-making. The sharpest British personification of this second figure emerged by the 1960s with the magazine *Which?*, designed for the thinking consumer of economical household goods.[3] Instead of being seduced into unnecessary spending on worthless trinkets, this rational consumer is connoted as being a saver—of labor and time, as well as of money—and a sensibly functional person (she or he is more likely to buy a deodorant or a refrigerator than nail varnish or whiskey).

And despite appearances, not one but both of these models are implied in the types of response to consumerism described just now: one as the place of the consumer, who is deluded, the other as the place of the critic, who is not. For some time, then, the consumer has been a fairly hybrid being, half of it (more or less a feminine half) being that unhappy, or perhaps stupidly happy, victim of advertising's forces; and the other (more or less a masculine half) being a sober, rational sort of being who knows what he wants and makes the best possible decision based on the information available to get it. Meanwhile, although both these constructions remain in outline, they have undergone some extraordinary mutations of emphasis in the past few years.

The first, critical account has recently been given a more affirmative turn. Shopping is no longer seen as the despised symptom of patriarchal or capitalist alienation, but rather as part of a newly legitimate—politically acceptable—"postmodern" interest in pleasure and fantasy. Those days are gone when consumerism could be comfortably identified as oppressive or regressive without more ado, and from some safely assumed position of exteriority. This change is also criticized as being another weak acceptance of the status quo—a giving in on the part of the sex, and the other sex too, to a dominant order which has lately succeeded in pulling the wool or the lurex over a lot more critical eyes.

In tandem with this (but probably seated on a different and more old-fashioned bike), the rational consumer in Britain has undergone a massive diversification of influence, with the great extension of the use of the term "consumer" in everyday political language. The semantic territory of this figure has widened to the point where she or he has become synonymous with all sorts of other characters who might have been thought to have quite other concerns. In education, health, housing, water-drinking, egg-eating, voting and many other fields, we are all addressed as "consumers" now, and the term is assumed to imply individual rights and respect that are lacking for those who are merely regarded as parents, patients, voters, omelet eaters and so on. The consumer is fast becoming the model of citizenship itself.

A telling illustration of this is to be found in some recent remarks on behalf of Britain's National Consumer Council, arguing for consumer education as part of the new National Curriculum:

> Too many young people leave school knowing how to do algebra and geometry but with little or no knowledge of how to compare interest rates on different types of loans. They may be able to write an essay on Jane Austen—but unable to write a sensible letter of complaint. Throughout pupils' education, they should be encouraged to think of themselves as consumers, the council said.[4]

This takes up a long-established opposition between literature and other subjects as the irrelevant versus the practical or the socially useful. Austen's name probably serves better than those of many other writers regarded as great to conjure up the required image of trite gratuitousness, mere feminine society banter removed from the nitty-gritty of real-life problems. But what is interesting is that the "useful" or "socially relevant" side of the comparison should now be taken up not, for instance, by contemporary history or ethical questions, but by consumer rights and financial skills. The consumer the pupil is to be encouraged to think himself or herself is characterized simply by the capacity to demand for him/herself a decent service or product, epitomized in the unforgettable specification of the "sensible letter of complaint."

There has thus been an increasing use of and focus on languages of consumerism. Yet it is clear that the various types of the consumer imply different models of the mental processes of the person persuaded to buy, choose or want this or that. The consumer represented as the mindless credit-card junkie or the helpless victim of "subliminal" techniques is a rather different subject from the one construed as a savvy selector of the cheapest toothpaste or the best school for his child. These languages are not necessarily compatible, involving potential clashes between the "consuming passions" of the postmodern shopper and the reasonable rights of the citizen-consumer (though one "postmodern" representation would imply a third possibility, whereby the consumer is not passive *or* rational, pleasure-seeking *or* calculating, but either, alternately, according to mood or context).

Advertisers have been interested in subjectivity from a consciously prag-
matic point of view (to find out what will work as a persuasive tactic). Theorists of subjectivity have not been particularly interested in the techniques
of advertising or in the debates within marketing's special branch, already
established at the beginning of this century, "the psychology of advertising";
nor have they turned their attention to the models of subjectivity implied by
critics or advocates of consumerism. But despite this apparent separation,
models of marketing and the consumer do make an unacknowledged appearance in some writing about subjectivity in general, and not least in contemporary feminism.

Much feminist writing about subjectivity of the past few years has sought
to open up possibilities outside what it identifies as the political limits of psychoanalysis. Where psychoanalysis was brought in at an earlier moment to
rupture the Marxist centrality of class to the exclusion of other categories,
it is itself often perceived as being both monolithic and potentially unhis-
torical in its insistence on the primacy of sexual differentiation, and in a form
which necessarily makes femininity into an impossible derivative of what is
always a masculine norm. (I leave aside the details of this question, which I
have represented only from the point of view of critics of psychoanalysis.)

In place of this, models of identity are put forward now that seek to be
more flexible in their understanding of the ways in which identities, including
sexual identities, may be formed and may undergo changes. Class, gender
and race, as well as a variable range of other categories, are all seen to share,
though not necessarily equally, in the formation of identities. At the same
time, the identity of the subject is seen less as a forcible imposition, whereby
she is constrained either passively to take on or hopelessly to struggle against
something fundamentally negative, but rather as potentially desirable: enabling as much as it is constricting. The work of Michel Foucault is often
cited as the inspiration for such a conception of a multiplicity of identifica-
tions produced through the operation of numerous heterogeneous discourses that pull individuals in particular, provisional directions. The political edge is maintained by stressing that the possibilities are restricted by the
nature and number of discourses "available" for identification; and the need
for more or different ones is part of the argument. The aim is that no one
discourse or its corresponding mode of identity should be granted priority:
there can be many "femininities," for instance, though some, according to
political criteria that are given as a starting point, are deemed to be better
than others.

There is, however, a particular discourse which often does emerge as dominant in such descriptions, and that is none other than the discourse of marketing and consumption. To take one example, from Chris Weedon's *Feminist Practice and Poststructuralist Theory:*

Discourses, located as they are in social institutions and processes are continually competing with each other for the allegiance of individual agents . . .
Some forms of subjectivity are more readily available to the individual than
others and this will depend on the social status and power of the discourse in
question.

  The nature of femininity and masculinity is one of the key sites of discursive struggle for the individual and we need only look at a few examples of forms
of subjectivity widely on offer to realize the importance of this battle.[5]

Discourses behave here in a way that is identical to marketed products.
As with companies' attempts to secure brand loyalty, they are "competing"
for "the allegiance of individual agents." One factor in deciding whether a
discourse is picked up is its "social status," just as a prominent marketing
model of the consumer is based on her or his assumed need to be or appear
to be higher up the scale, whether this is represented negatively, as a fear of
falling ("keeping up with the Joneses") or positively, as a desire to rise (upward mobility). There is a perpetual "battle" (the military undertone of the
advertising "campaign") where what is being fought over is the capitulation
or resistance of the consumer as territory to be subdued on a "site" of struggle. By implication, discourses are not modified by the purchaser, but come
ready-made to be picked up and used as they are. Some are more readily
"available" than others, more "widely on offer."

  Does it make any difference to the argument to point to its hidden persuasions? The trouble arises not from the presence of this particular discourse—there is no a priori reason to think that it is more insidious than
any other—but from the fact that it is taken as not in need of the analysis
being given to other discourses and their processes of what Weedon calls "naturalization." Charged as it is, the discourse of marketing has been taken up
as neutral, and used as the framework within which to understand the operation of all discourses and the relations of subjects to them.

  Since the languages of marketing and consumerism have been making
their way into more fields of everyday life and talk than ever before, it becomes crucial to look out for them, not to take them as natural. But by the
same token, marketing cannot just be regarded as a weed which could simply be rooted out of the discursive garden. For one thing, it comes in many
shapes and forms, in varying degrees of intensity and distinguishability. For
another, like any other discourse, it did not spring up independently, but
developed out of a host of others—the military campaign and the planned
seduction are two—with which it still enters into complicated relations, and
from which it cannot wholly be separated.

  So there is no straightforward getting away from marketing—we could
not and need not stop using words like "offer" or "available." But there should
be no straightforward assumption of its normality, either. In the light of the
new pervasiveness of languages of marketing and consumption, far beyond

their first fields of application in advertising and shopping, it becomes all the more necessary to analyze the ways in which they work or sell. Feminists (who, by the way, are now a key target group for the marketers, interested in appealing to their particular foibles) shouldn't simply take on trust, as read, the language of advertising, which has never made any secret of having a special interest in the exploitation of women, but which, and by the same token, has always been most attractive to them too.

This is not simply a proposal that we should look carefully at the labels before committing ourselves to something that may turn out to be not what it seems at first. Instead, it seems to me that the question of whether or not you "buy" an argument is already part of the problem, suggesting that an argument is something comparable to a finished product, to be taken or rejected as is, according to whether it seems to satisfy our demand. The purchase of an interesting text extends beyond the first rapid glance.

All this too might indicate that there are more general questions to be asked about the rhetorics of feminist criticism: about the ways in which it does or does not "sell" what it is presenting as its version of feminism; about how it sets that apart from other versions of feminism or femininity to be rejected; about the mode of address to the readers, which varies from the academically authoritative to the cozily "women together." Sometimes, as with *The Feminine Mystique*, feminism has made its appeal precisely in the name of an alternative to a false femininity identified as imposed by consumerism. Some feminist sells are more conspicuous, some more soft than others. We can give them a hard critical look; we can enjoy them too. Feminist persuasions normally come without either guarantee or sell-by date: their effectiveness is as much up to their consumers as it is inherent in the quality of the offer.

NOTES

1. Henry Foster Adams, *Advertising and its Mental Laws* (New York: Macmillan, 1916), p. 317. In alluding to a desirable combination of psychological research and economic application—the need to "know the foibles of the sex" in order "to secure the largest returns"—the quotation nicely summarizes the striking new development in advertising which is also indicated by the "mental laws" of the book's title. From the 1890s onwards, and with increasing momentum, the rapidly developing enterprises of advertising and marketing entered into various forms of alliance with the academic discipline of psychology, which was also undergoing expansion and consolidation at the time. As the Adams quotation suggests, understanding the minds of potential buyers was henceforth considered to be essential for understanding what would persuade them to buy; and the buyer's sex was taken to be one of the fundamental differentials, whether innate or socially determined, in assessing the likely propensities of particular minds. See further, "Make Up Your Mind: Scenes from the

Psychology of Selling and Shopping," in Rachel Bowlby, *Shopping with Freud* (London and New York: Routledge, 1993), pp. 94–119.

2. It is no accident, given the differences of history and of forms of cultural analysis, that the most obvious example of the first type of critique, in terms of sex, should be American—Betty Friedan's *The Feminine Mystique* (1963)—and of the second, in terms of class, British—Richard Hoggart's *The Uses of Literacy* (1957). For more on the first in this context see "'The Problem with No Name': Rereading Friedan's *The Feminine Mystique*," in Rachel Bowlby, *Still Crazy After All These Years: Women, Writing and Psychoanalysis* (London and New York: Routledge, 1992), pp. 76–94.

3. The American equivalent, *Consumer Reports*, has a much longer history, as would befit the earlier development on that side of the Atlantic of a consumer culture involving the mass production of brand-name goods. The first issue of *Consumers Union Reports* was published in 1936; and against the grain of the usual differences between Britain and the United States, in its early years it was concerned with cooperative consumer action to pressure manufacturers to improve factory working conditions as well as with the quality of the goods produced and sold.

4. Ngaio Crequer, "Pupils 'need lessons to be consumers,'" *The Independent*, 8 August 1989.

5. Chris Weedon, *Feminist Practice and Poststructuralist Theory* (Oxford: Basil Blackwell, 1987), pp. 97, 98.

Gender and Consumption
in Historical Perspective
A Selected Bibliography

Ellen Furlough

This bibliography includes studies significant to the history of consumption, consumer culture, and gender. It contains histories of consumption and consumer culture, as well as theoretical and conceptual works that offer important perspectives on these topics. Many, indeed most, of these historical and conceptual works do not directly engage questions of gender. By contrast, the sections that follow—on sites of consumption, marketing and design, spectatorship and reception, production of representations, domesticity, sexuality, appearance, and politics and ideologies of consumption—generally use gender as a primary category of analysis. These categories suggest the variety of perspectives on practices of consumption framed by feminist research. The items of bibliography included in each category range historically from the Middle Ages to the contemporary era. Most are Western; some seek a global perspective.

The studies also come from a wide variety of academic disciplines, from history to literature, cultural studies, art history, and film. This attention to gender and consumption across and within many disciplines both points to the importance and salience of the subject and demonstrates the range of recurrent themes, for example, that of the "consuming woman" as target of commercial solicitation and a source of social disturbance, as well as a subject negotiating her own pleasures and desires. This bibliography is limited in that it does not include works in languages other than English (with a few exceptions) or unpublished papers and dissertations. The bibliography is not, therefore, meant to be comprehensive but is instead a selective guide to further reading and research.

CONCEPTUALIZATIONS

These works represent a range of theoretical perspectives on consumer culture, mass culture and modernity, the workings of social distinctions in relation to consumption, the politics of consumption, the effects of a global cultural economy, the meanings of material culture, and theories of signification associated with the commodity form. Many of these works variously engage a central problem within studies of consumption and mass consumerism, namely, how to interpret the effects of consumer capitalism, and in particular its cultural dimensions. Ever since Karl Marx theorized the peculiar and fetishistic qualities of the commodity, theorists have differed on its implications. This bibliography presents a wide variety of interpretations, from Veblen's notions of conspicuous and invidious consumption, to theories (most associated with the Frankfurt School but also elaborated by later writers) that disagree as to whether commodities saturated capitalist society, further binding workers as producers and buyers to capitalism, or whether commodities contained and helped express utopian dimensions of human dreams, aspirations, and pleasure.

Adorno, Theodor W. "Veblen's Attack on Culture." In *Prisms*. Translated by Samuel Weber and Shierry Weber. 73–94. Cambridge: MIT Press, 1981.

Adorno, Theodor W., and Max Horkheimer. *Dialectics of Enlightenment*. New York: Continuum, 1991.

Appadurai, Arjun. "Disjuncture and Difference in the Global Cultural Economy." *Public Culture* 2, no. 3 (spring 1990): 1–24.

Appadurai, Arjun, ed. *The Social Life of Things: Commodities in Cultural Perspective*. Cambridge: Cambridge University Press, 1986.

Bataille, Georges. *Visions of Excess: Selected Writings, 1927–1939*. Edited by Alan Stoekel. Minneapolis: University of Minnesota Press, 1985.

Baudrillard, Jean. *Selected Writings*. Edited by Mark Poster. Stanford: Stanford University Press, 1988.

Benjamin, Walter. "The Work of Art in the Age of Mechanical Reproduction." In *Illuminations: Essays and Reflections*. Edited by Hannah Arendt and translated by Harry Zohn. New York: Schocken Books, 1988.

Bourdieu, Pierre. *Distinction: A Social Critique of the Judgement of Taste*. Cambridge: Harvard University Press, 1984.

———. *Outline of a Theory of Practice*. New York: Cambridge University Press, 1977.

Braudel, Fernand. *Afterthoughts on Material Civilization and Capitalism*. Translated by Patricia M. Ranum. Baltimore: Johns Hopkins University Press, 1977.

———. *Civilization and Capitalism, 15th–18th Centuries*. Vol. 1, *The Structures of Everyday Life;* Vol. II, *The Wheels of Commerce*. Translated by Siân Reynolds. New York: Harper and Row, 1982.

Campbell, Colin. *The Romantic Ethic and the Spirit of Modern Consumerism*. Oxford: Basil Blackwell, 1987.

Csikszentmihalyi, Mihaly, and Eugene Rochberg-Halton. *The Meaning of Things: Domestic Symbols and the Self*. New York: Cambridge University Press, 1981.

Culture and History 7 (summer 1990). Special issue entitled "Approaches to the History of Consumerism."

Debord, Guy. *The Society of the Spectacle.* 1967. Reprint, Detroit: Black and Red, 1983.

De Certeau, Michel. *The Practice of Everyday Life.* Translated by Steven Rendall. Berkeley: University of California Press, 1984.

Douglas, Mary, and Baron Isherwood. *The World of Goods: Towards an Anthropology of Consumption.* New York: W. W. Norton, 1979.

Ewen, Stuart. *All Consuming Images: The Politics of Style in Contemporary Culture.* New York: BasicBooks, 1988.

Falk, Pasi. *The Consuming Body.* London: Sage, 1994.

Featherstone, Mike. *Consumer Culture and Postmodernism.* London: Sage, 1991.

Halbwachs, Maurice. *La Classe ouvrière et les niveaux de vie: Recherches sur la hierarchie des besoins dans les sociétés industrielles contemporaines.* Paris: Félix Alcan, 1912.

———. *L'Evolution des besoins dans les classes ouvrières.* Paris: Félix Alcan, 1933.

Hall, Stuart, and Martin Jacques, eds. *New Times: The Changing Face of Politics in the 1990s.* London: Routledge, Chapman, and Hall, 1991.

Haug, Wolfgang Fritz. *Commodity Aesthetics, Ideology, and Culture.* Translated by Susan Brown and Karen Kramer. New York: International General, 1987.

Hebdige, Dick. *Hiding in the Light: On Images and Things.* London: Routledge, 1989.

———. *Subculture: The Meaning of Style.* New York: Methuen, 1979.

Hirsch, Fred. *The Social Limits to Growth.* Cambridge: Harvard University Press, 1976.

Hirschman, Albert O. *Rival Views of Market Society and Other Recent Essays.* New York: Viking, 1986.

Huyssen, Andreas. *After the Great Divide: Modernism, Mass Culture, Postmodernism.* Bloomington: Indiana University Press, 1987.

Jameson, Frederic. "Postmodernism and Consumer Society." In *The Anti-Aesthetic: Essays in Postmodern Culture,* edited by Hal Foster, 111–125. Port Townsend, Washington: Bay Press, 1983.

Kornai, Janos. *The Socialist System: The Political Economy of Communism.* Princeton: Princeton University Press, 1992.

Kracauer, Siegfried. *The Mass Ornament: Weimar Essays.* Edited, translated, and with an introduction by Thomas Y. Levin. Cambridge: Harvard University Press, 1995.

Lefebvre, Henri. *Everyday Life in the Modern World.* Translated by Sacha Rabinovitch. 1962. Reprint, New Brunswick, N.J.: Transaction Publishers, 1994.

Leiss, William. *The Limits to Satisfaction: An Essay on the Problem of Needs and Commodities.* Toronto: University of Toronto Press, 1976.

Marx, Karl. *Capital: A Critique of Political Economy.* Vol. 1, chaps. 1–3. Translated by Ben Fowkes. 1867. Reprint, New York: Penguin Classics, 1990.

Mauss, Marcel. *The Gift: The Form and Reason for Exchange in Archaic Societies.* 1924. Reprint, New York: W. W. Norton, 1990.

McCracken, Grant. *Culture and Consumption: New Approaches to the Symbolic Character of Consumer Goods and Activities.* Bloomington: Indiana University Press, 1988.

Miller, Daniel. *Material Culture and Mass Consumption.* Oxford: Basil Blackwell, 1987.

Patten, Simon N. *The New Basis of Civilization.* 1907. Reprint, Cambridge: Harvard University Press, 1968.

Preteceille, Edmond, and Jean-Pierre Terrail. *Capitalism, Consumption, and Needs.* Translated by Sarah Matthews. Oxford: Basil Blackwell, 1985.

Quimby, Ian, ed. *Material Culture and the Study of Material Life.* New York: W. W. Norton, 1978.

Rutz, Henry J., and Benjamin S. Orlove, eds. *The Social Economy of Consumption.* Monographs in Economic Anthropology, no. 6. Lanham, Maryland: University Press of America, 1989.

Scitovsky, Tibor. *The Joyless Economy: An Inquiry into Human Satisfaction and Consumer Dissatisfaction.* New York: Oxford University Press, 1976.

Sombart, Werner. *Luxury and Capitalism.* Translated by W. R. Dittmar. 1913. Ann Arbor: University of Michigan Press, 1967.

Theory, Culture, and Society 1, no. 3 (1983). Special issue entitled "Consumer Culture."

Veblen, Thorstein. *The Theory of the Leisure Class: An Economic Study in the Evolution of Institutions.* 1899. Reprint, New York: New American Library, 1953.

Williams, Raymond. "Advertising: The Magic System." In *Problems in Materialism and Culture,* 170–195. London: Verso, 1980.

Willis, Susan. "I Shop Therefore I Am: Is There a Place for Afro-American Culture in Commodity Culture?" In *Changing Our Own Words: Essays on Criticism, Theory, and Writing by Black Women,* edited by Cheryl A. Wall, 173–195. New Brunswick, N.J.: Rutgers University Press, 1989.

HISTORICAL PERSPECTIVES

These works document and analyze the emergence of a modern, capitalist consumer culture. While the whole issue of periodization is open to debate, much of the historical literature has argued for its emergence during the early modern period (ca. 1500–1800) in (primarily) British, then American, commercial institutions, patterns of representation, and cultural forms. Other works study the widening forms and increasing velocity of the dissemination of goods and services, as well as changing attitudes, cultural meanings, and behaviors associated with the consolidation of consumer capitalism and mass markets in the nineteenth and twentieth centuries.

Agnew, Jean-Christophe. *Worlds Apart: The Market and the Theater in Anglo-American Thought, 1550–1750.* Cambridge: Cambridge University Press, 1986.

Asendorf, Christoph. *Batteries of Life: On the History of Things and Their Perception in Modernity.* Translated by Don Reneau. Berkeley: University of California Press, 1993.

Barker-Benfield, G. J. *The Culture of Sensibility: Sex and Society in Eighteenth-Century Britain.* Chicago: University of Chicago Press, 1992.

Breen, T. H. "Baubles of Britain: The American and Consumer Revolutions of the Eighteenth Century." *Past and Present* 119 (1988): 73–104.

———. "Narrative of Commercial Life: Consumption, Ideology, and Community on the Eve of the American Revolution." *The William and Mary Quarterly.* 3d ser., vol. 50, no. 3 (July 1993): 471–501.

Brewer, John, and Roy Porter, eds. *Consumption and the World of Goods.* London: Routledge, 1993.

Briggs, Asa. *Victorian Things.* Chicago: University of Chicago Press, 1989.

Bronner, Simon J., ed. *Consuming Visions: Accumulation and Display of Goods in America, 1880–1920*. New York: W. W. Norton, 1989.

Brooks, John. *Showing Off in America: From Conspicuous Consumption to Parody Display*. Boston: Little, Brown, 1981.

Brown, Gillian. *Domestic Individualism: Imagining the Self in Nineteenth-Century America*. Berkeley: University of California Press, 1990.

Carson, Cary, Ronald Hoffman, and Peter J. Albert. *Of Consuming Interests: The Style of Life in the Eighteenth Century*. Charlottesville: University of Virginia Press, 1994.

Clunas, Craig. *Superfluous Things: Material Culture and Social Status in Early Modern China*. Urbana: University of Illinois Press, 1991.

Coffin, Judith G. "Credit, Consumption, and Images of Women's Desires: Selling the Sewing Machine in Nineteenth-Century France." *French Historical Studies* 18, no. 3 (spring 1994): 749–83.

Cross, Gary. *Time and Money: The Making of Consumer Culture*. New York: Routledge, 1993.

de Grazia, Victoria. "Mass Culture and Sovereignty: The American Challenge to European Cinemas, 1920–1960." *Journal of Modern History* 61 (March 1989): 53–87.

Drakulic, Slavenka. *How We Survived Communism and Even Laughed*. New York: Harper-Collins, 1993.

Dyer, Christopher. "The Consumer and the Market in the Later Middle Ages." *Economic History Review* 42 (1989): 305–27.

Edsforth, Ronald. *Class Conflict and Cultural Consensus: The Making of a Mass Consumer Society in Flint, Michigan*. New Brunswick, N.J.: Rutgers University Press, 1987.

Ewen, Stuart, and Elizabeth Ewen. *Channels of Desire: Mass Images and the Shaping of American Consciousness*. 2d. ed. Minneapolis: University of Minnesota Press, 1992.

Fine, Ben, and Ellen Leopold. *The World of Consumption*. New York: Routledge, 1993.

Fitzgerald, Robert. *Roundtree and the Marketing Revolution, 1862–1969*. New York: Cambridge University Press, 1995.

Fox, Richard Wightman, and T. J. Jackson Lears, eds. *The Culture of Consumption: Critical Essays in American History, 1880–1980*. New York: Pantheon Books, 1983.

Fraser, Hamish. *The Coming of the Mass Market, 1850–1914*. Hamden, Conn.: Archon Books, 1981.

Freccero, Carla. "Economy, Woman, and Renaissance Discourse." In *Refiguring Woman: Perspectives on Gender and the Italian Renaissance*, edited by Marilyn Migiel and Juliana Schiesari, 192–208. Ithaca: Cornell University Press, 1991.

Harris, Neil. "The Drama of Consumer Desire." In *Yankee Enterprise: The Rise of the American System of Manufactures*, edited by Otto Mayr and Robert C. Post, 189–216. Washington, D.C.: Smithsonian Institution Press, 1981.

Horowitz, Daniel. *The Morality of Spending: Attitudes toward the Consumer Society in America, 1875–1940*. Baltimore: Johns Hopkins University Press, 1985.

Lears, T. J. Jackson. *Fables of Abundance: A Cultural History of Advertising in America*. New York: BasicBooks, 1994.

Lemire, Beverly. *Fashion's Favourite: The Cotton Trade and the Consumer in Britain, 1660–1800*. Oxford: Oxford University Press, 1991.

Loeb, Lori Anne. *Consuming Angels: Advertising and Victorian Women*. New York: Oxford University Press, 1994.

Marchand, Roland. *Advertising the American Dream: Making Way for Modernity*. Berkeley: University of California Press, 1985.

McKendrick, Neil, John Brewer, and J. H. Plumb. *The Birth of a Consumer Society: The Commercialization of Eighteenth-Century England.* Bloomington: Indiana University Press, 1982.

Mintz, Sidney. *Sweetness and Power: The Place of Sugar in Modern History.* New York: Viking Penguin, 1985.

Mort, Frank, and Peter Thompson. "Retailing, Commercial Culture, and Masculinity in 1950s Britain: The Case of Montague Burton, the 'Tailor of Taste.'" *History Workshop Journal,* no. 38 (autumn 1994): 106–27.

Mukerji, Chandra. *From Graven Images: Patterns of Modern Materialism.* New York: Columbia University Press, 1983.

Nasaw, David. *Going Out: The Rise and Fall of Public Amusements.* New York: BasicBooks, 1993.

Olney, Martha L. *Buy Now, Pay Later: Advertising, Credit, and Consumer Durables in the 1920s.* Chapel Hill: University of North Carolina Press, 1991.

Pinkus, Karen. *Bodily Regimes: Italian Advertising under Fascism.* Minneapolis: University of Minnesota Press, 1995.

Richards, Thomas. *The Commodity Culture of Victorian England: Advertising and Spectacle, 1851–1914.* Stanford: Stanford University Press, 1990.

Saisselin, Rémy G. *The Bourgeois and the Bibelot.* New Brunswick, N.J.: Rutgers University Press, 1984.

Schama, Simon. *The Embarrassment of Riches: An Interpretation of Dutch Culture in the Golden Age.* New York: Alfred Knopf, 1987.

Schor, Juliet. *The Overworked American: The Unexpected Decline of Leisure.* New York: BasicBooks, 1991.

Schudson, Michael. *Advertising: The Uneasy Persuasion.* New York: BasicBooks, 1984.

Strasser, Susan. *Satisfaction Guaranteed: The Making of the Mass Market.* New York: Pantheon, 1989.

Susman, Warren. *Culture as History: The Transformation of American Society in the Twentieth Century.* New York: Pantheon, 1984.

Tedlow, Richard S. *New and Improved: The Story of Mass Marketing in America.* New York: BasicBooks, 1990.

Teuteberg, Hans-Jürgen. *European Food History: A Research Review.* New York: St. Martin's Press, 1992.

Thirsk, Joan. *Economic Policy and Projects: The Development of a Consumer Society in Early Modern England.* Oxford: Clarendon Press, 1978.

Walton, Whitney. *France at the Crystal Palace: Bourgeois Taste and Artisan Manufacture in the Nineteenth Century.* Berkeley: University of California Press, 1992.

Weatherill, Lorna. *Consumer Behavior and Material Culture in Britain, 1660–1760.* London: Routledge, 1988.

Williams, Rosalind H. *Dream Worlds: Mass Consumption in Late Nineteenth-Century France.* Berkeley: University of California Press, 1982.

SITES OF CONSUMPTION:
DISTRIBUTION, RETAILING, AND SHOPPING

These studies analyze the ways in which public spaces of consumption and leisure, such as department stores, shops and shopping centers, amusement parks, arcades, and nickelodeons, have gendered the meanings and practices of consumers. One line of analysis, most often focused on department stores, has tended to categorize these institutions as rationalized institutions of capitalist distribution and leisure, as "women's palaces" that promote commercial enticements based on new consumer aesthetics and identities. Retailing institutions, especially, have been understood to construct and solicit women's desires for consumer goods, desires that can either be channeled toward "appropriate" consumer buying or spin out of control as "kleptomania." Several recent analyses have built upon theories of the pleasures and even liberating aspects of shopping and leisure, especially for women, and other studies have extended this logic to the subversive potential of "oppositional shopping"—switching price tags, stealing merchandise, and so on. Many of these studies draw upon literature associated with theories of public space and public culture, theories that are most often associated with the work of Jürgen Habermas, which is not included here.

Abelson, Elaine S. *When Ladies Go A-Thieving: Middle-Class Shoplifters in the Victorian Department Store.* New York: Oxford University Press, 1989.

Adburgham, Alison. *Shops and Shopping: 1800–1914: Where and in What Manner the Well-Dressed English Woman Bought Her Clothes.* 1964. Reprint, London: Barrie and Jenkins, 1989.

Allen, Jeanne. "Palaces of Consumption as Women's Club: En-Countering Women's Labor History and Feminist Film Criticism." *Camera Obscura,* no. 22 (January 1990): 150–58.

Austin, Regina. "'A Nation of Thieves': Consumption, Commerce, and the Black Public Sphere." *Public Culture* 7, no. 1 (fall 1994): 225–48.

Benson, Susan Porter. *Counter Cultures: Saleswomen, Managers, and Customers in American Department Stores, 1890–1940.* Urbana: University of Illinois Press, 1986.

Bowlby, Rachel. *Shopping with Freud.* London: Routledge, 1993.

Buck-Morss, Susan. "The Flâneur, the Sandwichman, and the Whore: The Politics of Loitering." *New German Critique* 13, no. 39 (fall 1986): 99–140.

Camhi, Leslie. "Stealing Femininity: Department Store Kleptomania as Sexual Disorder." *Differences* 5, no. 2 (spring 1993): 27–50.

Chaney, David. "The Department Store as a Cultural Form." *Theory, Culture, and Society* 3 (1983): 22–31.

Davis, Dorothy. *A History of Shopping.* London: Routledge and Kegan Paul, 1966.

Davis, Shane Adler. "'Fine Cloths on the Altar': The Commodification of Late-Nineteenth-Century France." *Art Journal* 48 (spring 1989): 85–89.

Laermans, Rudi. "Learning to Consume: Early Department Stores and the Shaping of Modern Consumer Culture (1860–1914)." *Theory, Culture, and Society* 10, no. 4 (November 1993): 79–102.

Leach, William. *Land of Desire: Merchants, Power, and the Rise of a New American Culture.* New York: Pantheon Books, 1993.

McBride, Theresa. "A Woman's World: Department Stores and the Evolution of Women's Employment, 1870–1920." *French Historical Studies* 10 (fall 1978): 664–83.

Melosh, Barbara. "Sex and Shopping: Critiques of Leisure and Consumption." In *Engendering Culture: Manhood and Womanhood in New Deal Public Art and Theater.* Washington, D.C.: Smithsonian Institution Press, 1991.
Miller, Michael B. *The Bon Marché: Bourgeois Culture and the Department Store, 1869–1920.* Princeton: Princeton University Press, 1981.
Morris, Meaghan. "Things to do with Shopping Centres." In *Grafts: Feminist Cultural Criticism,* edited by Susan Sheridan, 193–225. London: Verso, 1988.
Nasaw, David. *Going Out: The Rise and Fall of Public Amusements.* New York: BasicBooks, 1993.
O'Brien, Patricia. "The Kleptomania Diagnosis: Bourgeois Women and Theft in Late Nineteenth-Century France." *Journal of Social History* 17 (1983): 65–77.
Pasdermadjian, Hrant. *The Department Store: Its Origins, Evolution, and Economics.* 1949. Reprint, New York: Arno Press, 1976.
Peiss, Kathy. *Cheap Amusements: Working Women and Leisure in Turn-of-the-Century New York.* Philadelphia: Temple University Press, 1986.
Rabinovitz, Lauren. "Temptations of Pleasure: Nickelodeons, Amusement Parks, and the Sights of Female Sexuality." *Camera Obscura,* no. 23 (May 1990): 71–89.
Reekie, Gail. *Temptations: Sex, Selling, and the Department Store.* Sydney: Allen and Unwin, 1993.
Shields, Rob. *Lifestyle Shopping: The Subject of Consumption.* London: Routledge, 1992.
Whittemore, Leila. "Getting the Goods Together: Consumer Space and Gender in Nineteenth-Century Paris." *Architecture Research Criticism* 5 (1994): 14–25.
Wolff, Janet. "The Invisible Flâneuse: Women and the Literature of Modernity." *Theory, Culture, and Society* 2, no. 3 (1985): 37–46.
Zola, Émile. *The Ladies' Paradise.* Introduction by Kristin Ross. Berkeley: University of California Press, 1992.

MARKETING AND DESIGN

These studies take as their starting point the enjoining of business history and cultural history. Most seek to understand the ways in which commercial institutions have used merchandising techniques (advertising, display windows, trade shows) and design strategies (for homes, automobiles, and cigarettes) as purveyors of gendered images intended to instruct, cajole, and solicit consumers. We see in these studies, for example, how advertisements touted the "newness" and allure of consumer goods and helped to construct the idealized body and the need for appropriate cosmetics. Merchandising techniques sold both the goods and the meanings constructed in relation to those goods. These studies suggest how display and advertising became information and discuss the ways design fostered the purchase and use of material goods.

Banks, Jane, and Patricia R. Zimmerman. "The Mary Kay Way: The Feminization of a Corporate Discourse." *Journal of Communication Inquiry* 11 (1987): 85–97.
Barthel, Dianne. *Putting on Appearances: Gender and Advertising.* Philadelphia: Temple University Press, 1988.

Coffin, Judith G. "Credit, Consumption, and Images of Women's Desires: Selling the Sewing Machine in Nineteenth-Century France." *French Historical Studies* 18, no. 3 (spring 1994): 749–83.

————. "Production, Consumption, and Gender: The Sewing Machine in France." In *Gender and the Reconstruction of European Working-Class History.* Edited by Laura Frader and Sonya Rose. Ithaca: Cornell University Press, 1995

Coward, Rosalind. *Female Desires: How They are Sought, Bought, and Packaged.* New York: Grove Press, 1985.

Eckert, Charles. "The Carole Lombard in Macy's Window." *Quarterly Review of Film Studies* 3, no. 1 (winter 1978): 1–21.

Fitzgerald, Robert. *Rowntree and the Marketing Revolution, 1862–1969.* New York: Cambridge University Press, 1994.

Forty, Adrian. *Objects of Desire: Design and Society from Wedgwood to IBM.* New York: Pantheon Books, 1986. No

Fox, Bonnie J. "Selling the Mechanized Household: Seventy Years of Ads in *Ladies Home Journal.*" *Gender and Society* 4 (March 1990): 25–40. No

Frederick, Christine McGoffey. *Selling Mrs. Consumer.* New York: The Business Course, 1929.

Furlough, Ellen. "Selling the American Way in Interwar France: Prix Uniques and the Salons des Arts Ménagers." *Journal of Social History* 26, no. 3 (spring 1993): 491–519.

Goffman, Erving. *Gender Advertisements.* 1976. Reprint, New York: Harper and Row, 1979.

Goings, Kenneth W. *Mammy and Uncle Mose: Black Collectibles and American Stereotyping.* Bloomington: Indiana University Press, 1994.

Hayden, Dolores. *The Grand Domestic Revolution: A History of Feminist Designs for American Homes, Neighborhoods, and Cities.* Cambridge: MIT Press, 1981. No

Jackson, Peter. "Black Male: Advertising and the Cultural Politics of Masculinity." *Gender, Place, and Culture: A Journal of Feminist Geography* 1, no. 4 (1994): 49–59.

Jordon, William Chester. *Women and Credit in Pre-Industrial and Developing Societies.* Philadelphia: University of Pennsylvania Press, 1993.

Loeb, Lori Anne. *Consuming Angels: Advertising and Victorian Women.* New York: Oxford University Press, 1994.

Notar, Beth. "Of Labor and Liberation: Images of Women in Current Chinese Television Advertising." *Visual Anthropology Review* 10, no. 2 (fall 1994): 29–44.

Peiss, Kathy. "Making Faces: The Cosmetics Industry and the Cultural Construction of Gender, 1890–1930." *Genders* 7 (March 1990): 143–69. No

Pieterse, Jan N. "Blacks in Advertising." In *White on Black: Images of Africa and Blacks in Western Popular Culture,* 188–210. New Haven: Yale University Press, 1992.

Reekie, Gail. "Impulsive Women, Predictable Men: Psychological Constructions of Sexual Difference in Sales Literature to 1930." *Australian Historical Studies* 97 (October 1991): 359–77.

Scharf, Virginia. *Taking the Wheel: Women and the Coming of the Motor Age.* New York: Macmillan, 1991. No - ordered

Schudson, Michael. "Women, Cigarettes, and Advertising in the 1920s: A Study in the Sociology of Consumption." In *Mass Media between the Wars: Perceptions of Cultural Tension, 1918–1941,* edited by Catherine L. Covert and John D. Stevens, 71–84. Syracuse: Syracuse University Press, 1984. No

Seiter, Ellen. *Sold Separately: Children and Parents in Consumer Culture.* New Brunswick, N.J.: Rutgers University Press, 1993.
Silverberg, Miriam. "Advertising Every Body: Images from the Japanese Modern Years." In *Choreographing History*, edited by Susan Leigh Foster, 129–48. Bloomington: Indiana University Press, 1995.
Silverman, Debora. *Selling Culture: Bloomingdale's, Diana Vreeland, and the New Aristocracy of Taste in Reagan's America.* New York: Pantheon Books, 1986.   N O
Simpson, Amelia. *Xuxa: The Mega-Marketing of Gender, Race, and Modernity.* Philadelphia: Temple University Press, 1993.
Weems, Robert E., Jr. "The Revolution Will Be Marketed: American Corporations and Black Consumers during the 1960s." *Radical History Review*, no. 59 (spring 1994): 94–107.   No
Wernick, Andrew. "(Re-)Imaging Gender: The Case of Men." In *Promotional Culture: Advertising, Ideology, and Symbolic Expression.* London: Sage Publications, 1991.
Williamson, Judith. *Decoding Advertisements: Ideology and Meaning in Advertising.* London: Marion Boyars, 1978.

SPECTATORSHIP AND RECEPTION

These studies explore the "consuming subject" of film, television, and popular literature. The gendering of this consuming subject, the spectator, has been the object of considerable debate. While analyses initially posited the spectator as a male, and specifically a voyeuristic and fetishistic male, more recent studies have insisted that both women and men are and have been spectators and that both actively "consume" media images and discourses. Some of these references also explore questions of pleasure and identification, and the related "subversive" possibilities (cross-dressing, masquerade, lesbian and black spectatorship) within film, television, and literature. These analyses have opened up the interpretative potential of gender for understanding both the audience and the media images themselves.

Allen, Jeanne. "The Film Viewer as Consumer." *Quarterly Review of Film Studies* 5, no. 4 (fall 1980): 481–501.
Blumer, Herbert. *Movies and Conduct.* New York: Macmillan, 1933.
Butler, Cheryl B. "The *Color Purple* Controversy: Black Woman Spectatorship." *Wide Angle* 13, nos. 3–4 (July–October 1991): 62–71.
Camera Obscura, nos. 20–21 (May–September 1989). Special issue entitled "The Spectatrix."
De Lauretis, Teresa. *Alice Doesn't: Feminism, Semiotics, Cinema.* Bloomington: Indiana University Press, 1984.
———. "Film and the Visible." In *How Do I Look: Queer Film and Video*, edited by Bad Object-Choices, 223–64. Seattle: Bay Press, 1991.
Doane, Mary Ann. *The Desire to Desire: The Woman's Film of the 1940s.* Bloomington: Indiana University Press, 1987.
———. *Femmes Fatales: Feminism, Film Theory, Psychoanalysis.* New York: Routledge, 1991.

————. "Film and the Masquerade: Theorizing the Female Spectator." *Screen* 23 (September–October 1982): 74–88.

Doane, Mary Ann, Patricia Mellencamp, and Linda Williams, eds. *Re-vision: Essays in Feminist Film Criticism.* Frederick, Maryland: University Publications of America, 1984.

Gamman, Lorraine, and Margaret Marshment, eds. *The Female Gaze: Women as Viewers of Popular Culture.* London: Women's Press, 1988.

Hansen, Miriam. "Adventures of Goldilocks: Spectatorship, Consumerism, and Public Life." *Camera Obscura*, no. 22 (January 1990): 51–72.

————. *Babel and Babylon: Spectatorship in American Silent Film.* Cambridge: Harvard University Press, 1991.

Herzog, Charlotte Cornelia, and Jane Marie Gaines. "Puffed Sleeves before Tea-Time: Joan Crawford, Adrian, and Women Audiences." *Wide Angle* 6, no. 4 (1985): 24–33.

hooks, bell. "The Oppositional Gaze: Black Female Spectators." In *Black American Cinema*, edited by Manthia Diawara, 288–302. New York: Routledge, 1993.

Joyrich, Lynn. "All That Television Allows: TV Melodrama, Post-Modernism, and Consumer Culture." *Camera Obscura*, no. 16 (January 1988): 129–54.

Modleski, Tania. *Loving with a Vengeance: Mass-Produced Fantasies for Women.* New York: Methuen, 1984.

————. "Time and Desire in the Woman's Film." *Cinema Journal* 23, no. 3 (spring, 1984): 19–30.

Modleski, Tania, ed. *Studies in Entertainment: Critical Approaches to Mass Culture.* Bloomington: Indiana University Press, 1986.

Mulvey, Laura. *Visual and Other Pleasures* (Bloomington: Indiana University Press, 1989).

Perec, Georges. *Things: A Story of the Sixties.* 1st U.S. ed. Translated by Andrew Leak. Boston: D. Godine, 1990.

Petro, Patrice. *Joyless Streets: Women and Melodramatic Representation in Weimar Germany.* Princeton: Princeton University Press, 1989.

————. "Mass Culture and the Feminine: The 'Place' of Television in Film Studies." *Cinema Journal* 25, no. 3 (spring, 1986): 5–21.

Pribram, E. Diedre, ed. *Female Spectators: Looking at Film and Television.* London: Verso, 1988.

Radway, Janice. *Reading the Romance: Women, Patriarchy, and Popular Literature.* Chapel Hill: University of North Carolina Press, 1984.

Waldman, Diane. "Film Theory and the Gendered Spectator: The Female or the Feminist Reader?" *Camera Obscura*, no. 18 (September 1988): 80–94.

Weiss, Andrea. *Vampires and Violets: Lesbians in Film.* New York: Penguin Books, 1993.

Wicke, Jennifer. *Advertising Fictions: Literature, Advertisement, and Social Reading.* New York: Columbia University Press, 1988.

PRODUCTION OF REPRESENTATIONS

In various ways and through studies of diverse sites—soap operas, burlesque, literature, modern art, magazines, and film—the books and articles here all have shifted analytical attention away from an understanding of images as reflections of "reality" and toward one where images are part of complicated systems of representation. As such, most of these studies analyze the ways images work to construct femininity and masculinity and how, in turn, notions of gender have shaped the "culture industries" themselves. Some of these references document the ways the culture industries have produced, and given power to, normative and gendered representations of, for example, consumer desire, romance, beauty, domesticity, and modern glamour. Other studies explore the alternative and utopian dimensions that these representations make available to a mass audience.

Allen, Robert. *Horrible Prettiness: Burlesque and American Culture.* Chapel Hill: University of North Carolina Press, 1991.
————. *Speaking of Soap Operas.* Chapel Hill: University of North Carolina Press, 1985.
Bowlby, Rachel. *Just Looking: Consumer Culture in Dreiser, Gissing, and Zola.* New York: Methuen, 1985.
————. *Shopping with Freud.* London: Routledge, 1993.
Clark, Danae. "Commodity Lesbianism." *Camera Obscura*, nos. 25–26 (January–May 1991): 181–201.
Copeland, Edward. "Jane Austen and the Consumer Revolution." In *The Jane Austen Companion*, edited by J. David Grey, A. Walton Litz, and Brian Southam, 77–92. New York: Macmillan, 1986.
De Lauretis, Teresa. "Sexual Indifference and Lesbian Representation." *Theatre Journal* 40 (1988): 155–77.
Doane, Mary Ann. "The Economy of Desire: The Commodity Form in/of the Cinema." *Quarterly Review of Film and Video* 11, no. 1 (1989): 23–33.
Dyer, Gary R. "The 'Vanity Fair' of Nineteenth-Century England: Commerce, Women and the East in the Ladies' Bazaar." *Nineteenth-Century Literature* 46 (1991): 196–222.
Ewen, Stuart, and Elizabeth Ewen. *Channels of Desire: Mass Images and the Shaping of American Consciousness.* 2d ed. Minneapolis: University of Minnesota Press, 1992.
Fischer, Lucy. "Two-Faced Women: The 'Double' in Women's Melodrama of the 1940s." *Cinema Journal* 23, no. 1 (fall 1983): 24–43.
Fiske, John. "Women and Quiz Shows: Consumerism, Patriarchy, and Resisting Pleasures." In *Television and Women's Culture: The Politics of the Popular*, edited by Mary Ellen Brown, 134–43. London: Sage, 1990.
Freccero, Carla. "Talking Commodities: Woman in a Renaissance Text." *Rethinking Marxism* 3, nos. 3–4 (fall–winter 1990): 238–50.
Gaines, Jane. "The Queen Christina Tie-Ups: Convergence of Show Window and Screen." *Quarterly Review of Film and Video* 11, no. 1 (1989): 35–60.
————. "The Showgirl and the Wolf." *Cinema Journal* 20, no. 1 (fall 1980): 53–67.
————. "Women and Representation: Can We Enjoy Alternative Pleasure?" In *American Media and Mass Culture: Left Perspectives*, edited by Donald Lazere, 357–72. Berkeley: University of California Press, 1987.
Gledhill, Christine, ed. *Home Is Where the Heart Is: Studies in Melodrama and the Woman's Film.* London: British Film Institute, 1987.

Goings, Kenneth W. *Mammy and Uncle Mose: Black Collectibles and American Stereotyping.* Bloomington: Indiana University Press, 1994.

Griggers, Cathy. "A Certain Tension in the Visual/Cultural Field: Helmut Newton, Deborah Turbeville, and the *Vogue* Fashion Layout." *Differences* 2, no. 2 (summer 1990): 76–104.

Haralovich, Mary Beth. "Sitcoms and Suburbs: Positioning the 1950s Homemaker." *Quarterly Review of Film and Video* 11, no. 1 (1989): 61–83.

Kaplan, E. Ann. "Feminist Film Criticism: Current Issues and Problems." *Studies in Literary Imagination* 19 (1986): 7–20.

———. *Women and Film: Both Sides of the Camera.* New York: Methuen, 1983.

Kirby, Linda. "Gender and Advertising in American Silent Film: From Early Cinema to the Crowd." *Discourse* 13, no. 2 (spring–summer 1991): 3–20.

Kracauer, Siegfried. "The Mass Ornament." 1927. *New German Critique* 5 (spring 1975): 67–76.

Kuhn, Annette. *The Power of the Image: Essays on Representation and Sexuality.* New York: Routledge and Kegan Paul, 1985.

Lavin, Maud. *Cut with the Kitchen Knife: The Weimar Photomontages of Hannah Hoch.* New Haven: Yale University Press, 1993.

Leonard, Garry. "Women on the Market: Commodity Culture, 'Those Lovely Seaside Girls,' and 'Femininity' in Joyce's *Ulysses.*" *Joyce Studies Annual* 2 (1991): 27–68.

Maayan, Myriam D. "The 'Feminine' in Contemporary French Critical Discourse on the Consumer Society and Utilitarianism." *Contemporary French Civilization* 16, no. 2 (summer–fall 1992): 242–61.

Marling, Karal Ann. *As Seen on TV: The Visual Culture of Everyday Life in the 1950s.* Cambridge: Harvard University Press, 1994.

Mattelart, Michele. "Women and the Cultural Industries." *Media, Culture, and Society* 4, no. 2 (April 1982): 133–51.

McCracken, Ellen. *Decoding Women's Magazines: From "Mademoiselle" to "Ms."* New York: St. Martin's Press, 1992.

McRobbie, Angela. "Settling Accounts with Subcultures: A Feminist Critique." In *Culture, Ideology, and Social Process: A Reader,* edited by Tony Bennett, 112–24. London: The Open University, 1981.

McRobbie, Angela, and Mica Nava, eds. *Gender and Generation.* New York: Macmillan, 1984.

Mizejewski, Linda. *Divine Decadence: Fascism, Female Spectacle, and the Making of Sally Bowles.* Princeton: Princeton University Press, 1992.

Mulvey, Laura, and Peter Wollen. "The Discourse of the Body." In *Looking On: Images of Femininity in the Visual Arts and Media,* edited by Rosemary Betterton, 211–16. London: Pandora, 1987.

Nava, Mica. *Changing Cultures: Feminism, Youth, and Consumerism.* London: Sage Publications, 1992.

Parsi, Peter. "'Black Bart' Simpson: Appropriation and Revitalization in Commodity Culture." *Journal of Popular Culture* 27, no. 1 (summer 1993): 125–42.

Passerini, Luisa. "The Ambivalent Image of Woman in Mass Culture." In *A History of Women in the West.* Vol. 5, *Toward a Cultural Identity in the Twentieth Century,* edited by Françoise Thébaud, 324–42. Cambridge: Harvard University Press, 1994.

Petro, Patrice. *Joyless Streets: Women and Melodramatic Representation in Weimar Germany.* Princeton: Princeton University Press, 1992.

Quarterly Review of Film and Video 11, no. 1 (1989). Special issue entitled "Female Representation and Consumer Culture," edited by Jane Gaines and Michael Renov.

Radner, Hilary. *Feminine Culture and the Pursuit of Pleasure.* New York: Routledge, 1994.

Rapp, Rayna, and Ellen Ross. "The 1920s: Feminism, Consumerism, and Political Backlash in the United States." In *Women in Culture and Politics: A Century of Change,* edited by Judith Friedlander, Blanche Wiesen Cook, Alice Kessler-Harris, and Carroll Smith-Rosenberg, 52–61. Bloomington: Indiana University Press, 1986.

Roper, Michael. "Product Fetishism and the British Company Man, 1945–1985." In *Manful Assertions: Masculinities in Britain since 1800,* edited by John Tosh and Michael Roper, 190–211. London: Routledge, 1991.

Ross, Kristin. *Fast Cars, Clean Bodies: Decolonization and the Reordering of French Culture.* Cambridge: MIT Press, 1995.

Silverberg, Miriam. "Remembering Pearl Harbor, Forgetting Charlie Chaplin, and the Case of the Disappearing Western Woman: A Picture Story." *Positions* 1, no. 1 (spring 1993): 24–76.

Spigel, Lynn, and Denise Mann, eds. *Private Screenings: Television and the Female Consumer.* Minneapolis: University of Minnesota Press, 1992.

Studlar, Gaylyn. "The Perils of Pleasure: Fan Magazine Discourse as Women's Commodified Culture in the 1920s." *Wide Angle* 13, no. 1 (1991): 6–33.

Todd, Ellen Wiley. *The 'New Woman' Revisited: Painting and Gender Politics on Fourteenth Street.* Berkeley: University of California Press, 1993.

Tuchman, Gaye, Arlene Kaplan Daniels, and James Benet, eds. *Hearth and Home: Images of Women in the Mass Media.* New York: Oxford University Press, 1978.

Waldman, Diane. "'At Last I Can Tell It to Someone!': Feminine Point of View and Subjectivity in the Gothic Romance Film of the 1940s." *Cinema Journal* 23, no. 2 (winter 1983): 29–40.

Walters, Suzanna Danuta. *Lives Together/Worlds Apart: Mothers and Daughters in Popular Culture.* Berkeley: University of California Press, 1993.

Whiting, Cécile. *Pop Art, Mass Culture, and the Gendered Object.* Cambridge: Cambridge University Press, forthcoming.

Williamson, Judith. *Consuming Passions: The Dynamics of Popular Culture.* London: Marion Boyars, 1985.

Wilson, Christopher P. "The Rhetoric of Consumption: Mass-Market Magazines and the Demise of the Gentle Reader, 1880–1920." In *The Culture of Consumption: Critical Essays in American History, 1880–1920,* edited by Richard Wightman Fox and T. J. Jackson Lears, 39–64. New York: Pantheon Books, 1983.

Winship, Alec. *'Woman Becomes an Individual': Femininity and Consumption in Women's Magazines, 1954–1969.* Women's Series, no. 65. Birmingham, U.K.: Centre for Contemporary Cultural Studies.

Winship, Janice. *Inside Women's Magazines.* London: Pandora, 1987.

DOMESTICITY, HOUSEHOLD, AND FAMILY

The books and articles in this section analyze the historical development of a family economy in which women, as housekeepers and homemakers, have been primarily responsible for the purchase, use, and display of domestic goods. Some argue that the home is a primary site for women's oppression, the locus of the "feminine mystique" or "domestic ideal" that depended upon women's unceasing labor as consumers, itself a product of a gendered division of labor under capitalism. Others emphasize the ways domestic consumer goods, in their symbolic and material aspects, constructed and communicated social relations and distinctions, as well as private familial meanings. These works have thus tended to stress women's creative activities, skills (aesthetic and managerial), status, and even power as consumers within a domestic, familial context. Still others have focused on the labor of housework and have evaluated the impact of new technologies and products, notably consumer durables, on that labor.

Becker, Gary S. "A Theory of the Allocation of Time." In *Gender and Economics*, edited by Jane Humphries, 113–137. Brookfield, Vt.: E. Elgar, 1995.

Blee, Kathleen. "Family Patterns and the Politicization of Consumption Relations." *Sociological Spectrum* 5 (1985): 295–316.

Carter, Erica. "Intimate Outscapes: Problem-Page Letters and the Remaking of the 1950s German Family." In *Becoming Feminine: The Politics of Popular Culture*, edited by Leslie G. Roman and Linda K. Christian-Smith, 60–75. London: Falmer Press, 1988.

Cheal, David. "Women Together: Bridal Showers and Gender Membership." In *Gender in Intimate Relationships*, edited by Barbara J. Risman and Pepper Schwartz, 86–93. Belmont, Calif.: Wadsworth Publishing Company, 1989.

Cohen, Lizabeth. "Embellishing a Life of Labor: An Interpretation of the Material Culture of American Working-Class Homes, 1885–1915." *Journal of American Culture* 3 (1984): 752–75.

Conrad, Christophe, and Armand Triebel. "Family Budgets as a Source for Comparative Social History: Western Europe-USA, 1889–1937." *Historical Social Research* (Historische Sozialforschung) 35 (1985): 45–66.

Cowan, Ruth Schwartz. *More Work for Mother: The Ironies of Household Technology from the Open Hearth to the Microwave*. New York: BasicBooks, 1983.

Davidoff, Leonore, and Hall, Catherine. *Family Fortunes: Men and Women of the English Middle Class, 1780–1850*. Chicago: University of Chicago Press, 1987.

Delphy, Christine. "Sharing the Same Table: Consumption and the Family." In *Close to Home: A Materialist Analysis of Women's Oppression*. Amherst: University of Massachusetts Press, 1984.

Dolin, Tim. "*Cranford* and the Victorian Collection." *Victorian Studies* 36, no. 2 (winter 1993): 179–206.

Duchen, Claire. "Occupation Housewife: The Domestic Ideal in 1950s France." *French Cultural Studies* 2 (February 1991): 1–11.

Ferber, Marianne A., and Bonnie A. Birnbaum. "The 'New Home Economics': Retrospects and Prospects." *Journal of Consumer Research* 4, no. 1 (June 1977): 19–28.

Formanek-Brunell, Miriam. *Made to Play House: Dolls and the Commercialization of American Girlhood, 1830–1930*. New Haven: Yale University Press, 1993.

Friedan, Betty. *The Feminine Mystique*. New York: Dell Publishers, 1963.

Frost, Robert. "Machine Liberation: Inventing Housewives and Home Appliances in Interwar France." *French Historical Studies* 18, no. 1 (spring 1993): 109–30.

Gonzalez de la Rocha, Mercedes. "Economic Crisis, Domestic Reorganization and Women's Work in Guadalajara, Mexico." *Bulletin of Latin American Research* 7, no. 2 (1988): 207–24.

Gordon, Jean, and Jan McArthur. "American Women and Domestic Consumption, 1800–1920: Four Interpretive Themes." *Journal of American Culture* 8, no. 3 (1985): 35–46.

Halttunen, Karen. "From Parlor to Living Room: Domestic Space, Interior Decoration, and the Culture of Personality." In *Consuming Visions: Accumulation and Display of Goods in America, 1880–1920,* edited by Simon J. Bronner, 157–89. New York: W. W. Norton, 1989.

Haralovich, Mary Beth. "Sitcoms and Suburbs: Positioning the 1950s Homemaker." *Quarterly Review of Film and Video* 11, no. 1 (1989): 61–83.

Hardyment, Christina. *From Mangle to Microwave: The Mechanization of Household Work.* New York: Basil Blackwell, 1988.

Heinze, Andrew. *Adapting to Abundance: Jewish Immigrants, Mass Consumption, and the Search for American Identity.* New York: Columbia University Press, 1990.

Jewell, K. Sue. *From Mammy to Miss America and Beyond: Cultural Images and the Shaping of U.S. Policy.* New York: Routledge, 1992.

Levine, Susan. "Workers' Wives: Gender, Class, and Consumerism in the 1920s United States." *Gender and History* 3 (spring 1991): 45–64.

Matthews, Glenna. *Just a Housewife: The Rise and Fall of Domesticity in America.* New York: Oxford University Press, 1987.

May, Elaine Tyler. *Homeward Bound: American Families in the Cold War Era.* New York: BasicBooks, 1988.

May, Martha. "'The Good Manager': Married Working-Class Women and Family Budget Studies, 1895–1915." *Labor History* 25, no. 3 (summer 1984): 351–72.

McKendrick, Neil. "Home Demand and Economic Growth: A New View of the Role of Women and Children in the Industrial Revolution." In *Historical Perspectives: Studies in English Thought and Society in Honour of J. H. Plumb,* edited by Neil McKendrick, 152–210. London: Europa, 1974.

Miller, Barbara Diane. "Gender and Low Income Household Expenditures in Jamaica." In *The Social Economy of Consumption,* edited by Henry J. Rutz and Benjamin S. Orlove, 379–98. Lanham, Maryland: University Press of America, 1989.

Nolan, Mary. "'Housework Made Easy': The Taylorized Housewife in Weimar Germany's Rationalized Economy." *Feminist Studies* 16, no. 3 (fall 1990): 549–77.

Pumphrey, Martin. "The Flapper, the Housewife, and the Making of Modernity." *Cultural Studies* 1, no. 2 (May 1987): 179–94.

Scott, Joan Wallach, and Louise A. Tilly, "Women in the Family Consumer Economy," in *Women, Work, and Family.* 2d ed. New York: Methuen, 1987.

Shammas, Carole. *The Pre-Industrial Consumer in England and America.* Oxford: Clarendon Press, 1990.

Smith, Bonnie. *Ladies of the Leisure Class: The Bourgeoises of Northern France in the Nineteenth Century.* Princeton: Princeton University Press, 1981.

Strasser, Susan. *Never Done: A History of American Housework.* New York: Pantheon Books, 1982.

Tebbutt, Melanie. *Making Ends Meet: Pawnbroking and Working-Class Credit.* New York: St. Martin's Press, and Leceister Univ. Press, 1983.

Thompson, Alistair. "Domestic Drudgery Will Be a Thing of the Past: Co-Operative Women and the Reform of Housework." In *New Views of Co-Operation,* edited by Stephen Yeo, 108–27. London: Routledge, 1988.

Thompson, James. "Jane Austen's Clothing: Things, Property, and Materialism in Her Novels." *Studies in Eighteenth-Century Culture,* no. 13 (1984): 217–31.

Vickery, Amanda. "Women and the World of Goods: A Lancashire Consumer and Her Possessions, 1751–1781." In *Consumption and the World of Goods,* edited by John Brewer and Roy Porter, 274–301. New York: Routledge, 1993.

Walton, Whitney. "Feminine Hospitality in the Bourgeois Home of Nineteenth-Century Paris." *Proceedings of the Western Society for French History,* no. 14 (1987): 197–203.

Weatherill, Lorna. "A Possession of One's Own: Women and Consumer Behavior in England, 1660–1." *Journal of British Studies* 25, no. 2 (1986): 131–56.

Weinbaum, Batya, and Amy Bridges. "The Other Side of the Paycheck: Monopoly Capital and the Structure of Consumption." *Monthly Review* 28, no. 3 (July–August 1976): 88–103.

Wildt, Michael. "Plurality of Taste: Food and Consumption in West Germany during the 1950s." *History Workshop Journal,* no. 39 (1995): 23–41.

SEXUALITY

From a range of disciplinary perspectives and approaches, the works in this section address the mutually constitutive relationship between sexuality and consumption. Included are studies of the images of sexuality within consumer culture, advertising, "sexual science," and various fetishistic discourses, as well as studies of practices, such as cross-dressing and kleptomania, that link sexuality and consumer goods. Most of these studies argue for an understanding of sexuality as socially constructed and historically specific, and they analyze the ways in which ideals and practices of consumption forge sexualities.

Apter, Emily, and William Pietz, eds. *Fetishism as Cultural Discourse.* Ithaca: Cornell University Press, 1993.

Bailey, Peter. "Parasexuality and Glamour: The Victorian Barmaid as Cultural Prototype." *Gender and History* 2, no. 2 (summer 1990): 148–72.

Birkin, Lawrence. *Consuming Desire: Sexual Science and the Emergence of a Culture of Abundance, 1871–1914.* Ithaca: Cornell University Press, 1988.

Camhi, Leslie. "Stealing Femininity: Department Store Kleptomania as Sexual Disorder." *Differences* 5, no. 1 (spring 1993): 27–50.

Clark, Danae. "Commodity Lesbianism." *Camera Obscura,* nos. 25–26 (January–May 1991): 181–201.

Haug, Wolfgang Fritz. *Critique of Commodity Aesthetics: Appearance, Sexuality, and Ad-*

vertising in Capitalist Society. Translated by Robert Bock. Minneapolis: University of Minnesota Press, 1986.

Kuhn, Annette. *The Power of the Image: Essays on Representation and Sexuality.* London: Routledge and Kegan Paul, 1985.

Rabinovitz, Lauren. "Temptations of Pleasure: Nickelodeons, Amusement Parks, and the Sights of Female Sexuality." *Camera Obscura,* no. 23 (May 1990): 71–89.

Robertson, Jennifer. *Same Sex/Different Gender: The Cultural Politics of Cross-Dressing in Japan.* Berkeley: University of California Press, 1994.

Weiss, Andrea. *Vampires and Violets: Lesbians in Film.* New York: Penguin Books, 1993.

Weston, Kath. "Do Clothes Make the Woman? Gender, Performance Theory, and Lesbian Eroticism." *Genders* 17 (fall 1993): 1–21.

Wilson, Elizabeth. "Deviant Dress." *Feminist Review* 35 (summer 1990): 67–76.

APPEARANCE: BODIES, CLOTHING, AND BEAUTY

The books and articles listed here indicate a lively interest in intersections of personal appearance, consumer culture, and consumer products. Some of these works emphasize the ways women and men have been trained into norms of appearance. Some studies have argued that, for women especially, the use of consumer goods to express these norms—of fashion, style, and beauty—has led to fashion enslavement, a decorative dependency, and a crippling narcissism. Such studies believe that most women have been unwilling or unable to conform to the "fashion system" and other cultural norms related to appearance. Other studies have shifted emphasis from the normative to the expressive possibilities of appearance-oriented commercial goods such as clothing and makeup. These goods can be seen as vehicles for creativity, pleasure, and critical reinterpretations of gender norms. Fabricating one's appearance is deemed playful, performative, and potentially subversive of the gender system.

Ash, Juliet, and Elizabeth Wilson, eds. *Chic Thrills: A Fashion Reader.* Berkeley: University of California Press, 1993.

Banner, Lois W. *American Beauty.* New York: Alfred Knopf, 1983.

Barber, Bernard, and Lyle S. Lobel. "'Fashion' in Women's Clothes and the American Social System." *Social Forces* 32 (1952): 124–31.

Barthes, Roland. *The Fashion System.* Translated by Matthew Ward and Richard Howard. New York: Hill and Wang, 1983.

Benedict, Ruth. "Dress." *Encyclopedia of Social Sciences.* Vol. 5. New York: Macmillan, 1931.

Bordo, Susan. *Unbearable Weight: Feminism, Western Culture, and the Body.* Berkeley: University of California Press, 1993.

Cordwell, Justine M., and Ronald A. Schwartz, eds. *The Fabrics of Culture: An Anthropology of Clothing and Adornment.* The Hague: Mouton, 1979.

Craik, Jennifer. *The Face of Fashion: Cultural Studies in Fashion.* London: Routledge, 1994.

Dalby, Lisa. *Kimono: Fashioning Culture.* New Haven: Yale University Press, 1993.

Davis, Fred. *Fashion, Culture, and Industry.* Chicago: University of Chicago Press, 1992.

Featherstone, Mike. "The Body in Consumer Culture." *Theory, Culture, and Society* 1, no. 1 (1982): 18–33.

Finkelstein, Joanne. *The Fashioned Self.* Philadelphia: Temple University Press, 1991.

Gaines, Jane, and Charlotte Herzog. *Fabrications: Costume and the Female Body.* New York: Routledge, 1990.

Garber, Marjorie. *Vested Interests: Cross Dressing and Cultural Anxiety.* New York: Routledge, Chapman, and Hall, 1992.

Horowitz, R. Tamar. "From Elite Fashion to Mass Fashion." *Archives Européenes de sociologie* 16, no. 2 (1975): 283–95.

Jacobeit, Sigrid. "Clothing in Nazi Germany." In *Marxist Historiography in Transformation: East German Social History in the 1980s,* edited by Georg G. Iggers, translated by Bruce Little, 227–45. New York: Berg, 1991.

Jones, Eric L. "The Fashion Manipulators: Consumer Tastes and British Industries, 1660–1800." In *Business Enterprise and Economic Change: Essays in Honor of Harold F. Williamson,* edited by Louis P. Cain and Paul J. Uselding, 198–226. Kent, Ohio: Kent State University Press, 1973.

Kidwell, Claudia Brush, and Valerie Steele, eds. *Men and Women: Dressing the Part.* Washington, D.C.: Smithsonian Institution Press, 1989.

Kidwell, Claudia B., and Margaret C. Christman. *Suiting Everyone: The Democratization of Clothing in America.* Washington, D.C.: The Smithsonian Institution Press, 1974.

Lakoff, Robin Tolmach, and Raquel L. Scherr. *Face Value: The Politics of Beauty.* London: Routledge and Kegan Paul, 1984.

Lemire, Beverly. *Fashion's Favourite: The Cotton Trade and the Consumer in Britain, 1660–1800.* Oxford: Oxford University Press, 1991.

Lipovetsky, Gilles. *The Empire of Fashion: Dressing Modern Democracy.* Translated by Catherine Porter. Princeton: Princeton University Press, 1994.

MacCannell, Dean, and Juliet Flower MacCannell. "The Beauty System." In *The Ideology of Conduct: Essays on Literature and the History of Sexuality,* edited by Nancy Armstrong and Leonard Tennenhouse, 206–238. New York: Methuen, 1987.

Mandel, Ruth. "Turkish Headscarves and the 'Foreigner Problem': Constructing Difference through Emblems of Identity." *New German Critique* 46 (winter 1989): 27–46.

McKendrick, Neil. "The Commercialization of Fashion." In *The Birth of a Consumer Society: The Commercialization of Eighteenth-Century England,* by Neil McKendrick, John Brewer, and J. H. Plumb, 34–99. Bloomington: Indiana University Press, 1982.

Nag, Dulali. "Fashion, Gender, and the Bengali Middle Class." *Public Culture* 3, no. 2 (spring 1991): 93–114.

O'Neill, John. "The Consumer Body." In *Five Bodies: The Human Shape of Modern Society.* Ithaca: Cornell University Press, 1985.

Perrot, Philippe. *Fashioning the Bourgeoisie: A History of Clothing in the Nineteenth Century.* Translated by Richard Bienvenu. Princeton: Princeton University Press, 1994.

Roach, Mary Ellen, and Joanne Bubolz Eicher. *Dress, Adornment, and the Social Order.* New York: Wylie, 1965.

Roberts, Mary Louise. "Samson and Delilah Revisited: The Politics of Women's Fashions in 1920s France." *American Historical Review* 98, no. 3 (June 1993): 657–84.

Robertson, Jennifer. *Same Sex/Different Gender: The Cultural Politics of Cross-Dressing in Japan*. Berkeley: University of California Press, 1994.

Roche, Daniel. *The Culture of Clothing: Dress and Fashion in the Ancien Régime*. Translated by Jean Birrell. New York: Cambridge University Press, 1994.

Schneider, Jane. "The Anthropology of Cloth." *Annual Review of Anthropology* 16 (1987): 409–48.

———. "Peacocks and Penguins: The Political Economy of European Cloth and Colors." *American Ethnologist* 5 (August 1978): 413–47.

Shapiro, Susan C. "Sex, Gender, and Fashion in Medieval and Early Modern Britain." *Journal of Popular Culture* 20, no. 4 (spring 1987): 113–28.

Silverman, Kaja. "Fragments of a Fashionable Discourse." In *Studies in Entertainment: Critical Approaches to Mass Culture*, edited by Tania Modleski, 139–52. Bloomington: Indiana University Press, 1986.

Simmel, Georg. "Fashion." 1904. *American Journal of Sociology* 62 (May 1957): 541–88.

Steele, Valerie. *Fashion and Eroticism: Ideals of Feminine Beauty from the Victorian through the Jazz Age*. New York: Oxford University Press, 1985.

Turner, Bryan S. *The Body and Society: Explorations in Social Theory*. Oxford: Basil Blackwell, 1984.

Weston, Kath. "Do Clothes Make the Woman?: Gender, Performance Theory, and Lesbian Eroticism." *Genders* 17 (fall 1993): 1–21.

Wilson, Elizabeth. *Adorned in Dreams: Fashion and Modernity*. Berkeley: University of California Press, 1985.

———. "Deviant Dress." *Feminist Review* 35 (summer 1990): 67–76.

Wilson, Elizabeth, and Lou Taylor. *Through the Looking Glass: A History of Dress from 1860 to the Present Day*. London: BBC Books, 1991.

Young, Iris Marion. "Women Recovering Our Clothes." In *Throwing Like a Girl and Other Essays in Feminist Philosophy and Social Theory*. Bloomington: Indiana University Press, 1990.

Zdatny, Steven. "Fashion and Class Struggle: The Case of Coiffure." *Social History* 18, no. 1 (January 1993): 53–72.

POLITICS AND IDEOLOGIES OF CONSUMPTION

The studies in this section all deal with the historical problem of how to analyze the ways consumption has been both political (that is, has articulated or challenged relations of power) and ideological. Some works explore the ways women and men have organized politically around issues of consumption, for example, in trade unions, consumer cooperatives, the workplace, and consumer leagues. Others study how the products of commercial culture have been used to buttress or to expose the ideological and political contradictions within political regimes. Still others analyze the gendered implications of consumer modernity. All offer compelling investigations suggesting that consumption and consumer culture are neither neutral nor apolitical.

Brown, Clair. "Consumption Norms, Work Roles, and Economic Growth, 1918–80." In *Gender in the Workplace,* edited by Clair Brown and Joseph A. Pechman, 13–59. Washington, D.C.: The Brookings Institution, 1987.

Carter, Erica. "Alice in the Consumer Wonderland: West German Case Studies in Gender and Consumer Culture." In *Gender and Generation,* edited by Angela McRobbie and Mica Nava, 185–214. London: Macmillan, 1984.

Cohen, Lizabeth. *Making a New Deal: Industrial Workers in Chicago, 1919–1939.* New York: Cambridge University Press, 1990.

de Grazia, Victoria. *How Fascism Ruled Women: Italy, 1922–1945.* Berkeley: University of California Press, 1992.

Frank, Dana. *Purchasing Power: Consumer Organizing, Gender, and the Seattle Labor Movement, 1919–1929.* Cambridge: Cambridge University Press, 1994.

Friedan, Betty. *The Feminine Mystique.* New York: Dell Publishers, 1963.

Furlough, Ellen. "Women and Cooperation." In *Consumer Cooperation in France: The Politics of Consumption, 1834–1930.* Ithaca: Cornell University Press, 1991.

Gaffin, Jean. "Women and Cooperation." In *Women in the Labor Movement: The British Experience,* edited by Lucy Middleton, 113–42. London: Croom Helm, 1977.

Glickman, Lawrence. "Inventing the 'American Standard of Living': Gender, Race, and Working-Class Identity, 1880–1925." *Labor History* 34, nos. 2–3 (spring–summer 1993): 221–35.

Golden, Lester. "The Women in Command: The Barcelona Women's Consumer War of 1918." *UCLA Historical Journal* 6 (1985): 5–32.

Hinton, James. "Militant Housewives: The British Housewives League and the Attlee Government." *History Workshop Journal,* no. 38 (autumn 1994): 129–56.

Hyman, Paula H. "Immigrant Women and Consumer Protest: The New York City Kosher Meat Boycott of 1902." *American Jewish History,* no. 70 (September 1980): 88–98.

McAuley, Mary. "Bread without the Bourgeoisie." In *Party, State, and Society in the Russian Civil War: Explorations in Social History,* edited by Dianne P. Koenker, William G. Rosenberg, and Ronald Grigor Suny, 158–80. Bloomington: Indiana University Press, 1989.

Rapping, Elaine. "Tupperware and Women." *Radical America* 14, no. 6 (November–December 1980): 39–49.

Silverberg, Miriam. "The Modern Girl as Militant." In *Recreating Japanese Women, 1600–1945,* edited by Gail Lee Bernstein, 239–66. Berkeley: University of California Press, 1991.

Wolfe, Allis Rosenberg. "Women, Consumerism, and the National Consumers' League in the Progressive Era, 1900–1923." *Labor History* 16, no. 3 (summer 1975): 378–92.

NOTES ON CONTRIBUTORS

Leora Auslander teaches European history at the University of Chicago. Her book entitled *Taste and Power: Furnishing Modern France* is forthcoming from the University of California Press. She is currently working on citizenship and everyday life in France and Germany in the twentieth century.

Susan Porter Benson is Associate Professor of History and Director of the Women's Studies Program at the University of Connecticut. She is the author of *Counter Cultures: Saleswomen, Managers, and Customers in American Department Stores, 1890–1940* (1986). Her article here is drawn from the forthcoming *Household Accounts: Working-Class Family Economies in the United States, 1919–1941.*

Sue Bowden is Senior Lecturer in Economics at the University of Sheffield and the author of numerous essays on consumption in interwar England. She is coauthor of *The Motor Vehicle Industry* (1995). She is currently working on postwar productivity and industrial performance in Europe.

Rachel Bowlby is Professor of English at Sussex University. She is the author of *Just Looking: Consumer Culture in Dreiser, Gissing, and Zola* (1985), *Virginia Woolf: Feminist Destinations* (1988), *Still Crazy after All These Years* (1992), and *Shopping with Freud* (1993). She is currently working on a history of supermarkets.

Erica Carter is a Research Fellow in German Studies at the University of Warwick in England. Her most recent publication is *How German Is She? Post-War West German Reconstruction and the Consuming Woman, 1945–1960* (forthcoming).

Belinda Davis is Assistant Professor of History at Rutgers University. The author of various essays on early-twentieth-century Germany, she is currently finishing a book on political culture and popular politics in World War I Berlin.

Victoria de Grazia is Professor of History and Director of the Institute for Research on Women and Gender at Columbia University. Her writings include
The Culture of Consent in Fascist Italy (1981), *How Fascism Ruled Women: Italy,
1922–1945* (1992), and essays on Americanization and consumer society in
Europe, which is the subject of her current research.

Ellen Furlough is Associate Professor of History at Kenyon College and author
of *Consumer Cooperation in France: The Politics of Consumption, 1834–1930*
(1991). Her current research focuses on French consumer culture, in particular tourism and vacations.

Anna R. Igra teaches history at Carleton College. Her dissertation completed
at Rutgers University is entitled "Other Men's Wives and Children: Anti-Desertion Reform in New York, 1900–1935."

Jennifer Jones is Assistant Professor at Rutgers University and is currently working on a book on women's roles as producers and consumers in Parisian fashion culture, 1650–1789.

David Kuchta is Lecturer in the Humanities at the University of California,
San Diego, and is the author of the forthcoming *English Masculinity and the
Politics of Consumption, 1550–1850.*

Avner Offer is Professorial Fellow and Reader in Recent Social and Economic
History at Nuffield College, University of Oxford. He is the author of *The
First World War: An Agrarian Interpretation* (1989) and is currently working on
a comparative study of the coming of mass consumption to England and the
United States.

Kathy Peiss teaches history at the University of Massachusetts at Amherst. She
is the author of *Cheap Amusements: Working Women and Leisure in Turn-of-the-
Century New York* (1986) and coeditor of *Passion and Power: Sexuality in History* (1989). Her book entitled *Making Faces: Cosmetics and American Culture* is
forthcoming from Basic Books.

Erika Rappaport is Assistant Professor of History at Florida International University. Her book on the history of gender and commercial culture in Victorian and Edwardian London is forthcoming from Princeton University
Press.

Abigail Solomon-Godeau is Associate Professor of Art History at the University
of California, Santa Barbara. In addition to numerous articles and catalogue
essays, she is author of *Photography at the Dock: Essays on Photographic History,
Institutions, and Practices* (1991) and *Male Trouble: A Crisis in Representation,*
forthcoming from Thames and Hudson.

ART CREDITS

1. François Boucher, *La Marchande de modes*, 1746. Stockholm, National Museum. Reproduced by permission of the National Museum.

2. "Promenade de la gallerie du Palais-Royal," ca. 1789. Musée Carnavalet. Photo courtesy of the Photothèque des Musées de la Ville de Paris.

3. *Les Belles Marchandes*, 1784. Musée des Arts Décoratifs. Reproduced by permission of the Musée des Arts Décoratifs.

4. Almanach, *Les Délices de Paris*, 1804. Musée des Arts Décoratifs. Reproduced by permission of the Musée des Arts Décoratifs.

5. *The Courtier's Calling* (London, 1675), frontispiece. Reproduced by permission of the British Library.

6. *An Essay in Defence of the Female Sex* (London, 1696), frontispiece. Reproduced by permission of the British Library.

7. F. Nivelon, *Rudiments of Genteel Behavior* (London, 1737), plate 1 for men. Reproduced by permission of the British Library.

8. F. Nivelon, *Rudiments of Genteel Behavior* (London, 1737), plate 1 for women. Reproduced by permission of the British Library.

9. Nicolas Emmanuel Péry, "Comment trouves-tu la nouvelle mode, Fany?" from the series *Les Cocottes*, lithograph, ca. 1850. Cabinet des Estampes, Bibliothèque Nationale. Reproduced by permission of the Bibliothèque Nationale.

10. Octave Tassaert, *Le Piano*, lithograph by François Le Villain, ca. 1830. Cabinet des Estampes, Bibliothèque Nationale. Reproduced by permission of the Bibliothèque Nationale.

11. Achille Devéria, *Le Roman du jour/The fashionable novel*, lithograph, 1829. Cabinet des Estampes, Bibliothèque Nationale. Reproduced by permission of the Bibliothèque Nationale.

12. Eugène le Roux, untitled lithograph, 1848. Cabinet des Estampes, Bib-

liothèque Nationale. Reproduced by permission of the Bibliothèque Nationale.

13. Charles Landelle, *Aujourd'hui/Today,* lithograph, 1850. Cabinet des Estampes, Bibliothèque Nationale. Reproduced by permission of the Bibliothèque Nationale.

14. Becquier and Bettanier, *Les Cocottes en 1867,* lithograph, 1867. Cabinet des Estampes, Bibliothèque Nationale. Reproduced by permission of the Bibliothèque Nationale.

15. Grandville (Jean-Ignace-Isidore Gérard), *Venus at the Opera,* wood engraving. From Grandville, *Un Autre Monde: Transformations, visions, incarnations . . . et autre choses* (Paris, H. Fournier, 1844). Reproduced by permission of the Bibliothèque Nationale.

16. Octave Tassaert, "Il y a des gens qui diraient: je vous remércie," from the series *Les Amants et les époux,* lithograph, 1829. Cabinet des Estampes, Bibliothèque Nationale. Reproduced by permission of the Bibliothèque Nationale.

17. Achille Devéria, *Le Rêve,* lithograph by Lemercier, 1829. Cabinet des Estampes, Bibliothèque Nationale. Reproduced by permission of the Bibliothèque Nationale.

18. *La Belle de New-York,* anonymous lithograph, ca. 1830. Cabinet des Estampes, Bibliothèque Nationale. Reproduced by permission of the Bibliothèque Nationale.

19. Anonymous wet plate stereo carte, ca. 1855. Réserve Libre, Cabinet des Estampes, Bibliothèque Nationale. Reproduced by permission of the Bibliothèque Nationale.

20. Nicolas Maurin, "J'en veux, j'en veux encore," lithograph, ca. 1830. Cabinet des Estampes, Bibliothèque Nationale. Reproduced by permission of the Bibliothèque Nationale.

21. Anonymous lithograph, ca. 1830s. Réserve Libre, Bibliothèque Nationale. Reproduced by permission of the Bibliothèque Nationale.

22. Alexandre Quinet and Paul Baudry, untitled academy, wet plate photograph, ca. 1855. Cabinet des Estampes, Bibliothèque Nationale. Reproduced by permission of the Bibliothèque Nationale.

23. Octave Tassaert, "Vous nous le paierez," from the series *Boudoirs et mansardes,* lithograph, 1828. Cabinet des Estampes, Bibliothèque Nationale. Reproduced by permission of the Bibliothèque Nationale.

24. Octave Tassaert, "Ah, mes belles dames . . . ," from the series *Les Amants et les époux,* lithograph, 1828. Cabinet des Estampes, Bibliothèque Nationale. Reproduced by permission of the Bibliothèque Nationale.

25. Albert (or Wilhelm) Teichel, *Une chambre de rats,* lithograph, 1851. Cabinet des Estampes, Bibliothèque Nationale. Reproduced by permission of the Bibliothèque Nationale.

26. "Every One Recognizes Your Ability to Paint (Yourself)," trade card, ca. 1870. Author's collection.

27. Robert W. Shufeldt, "A Belle of Laguna," *Indian Types of Beauty* (1891), Shufeldt N3662, Division of Rare and Manuscript Collections, Carl A. Kroch Library, Cornell University. Reprinted by permission of the Division of Rare and Manuscript Collections, Cornell University Library.

28. Robert W. Shufeldt, "Mohave Women," *Indian Types of Beauty* (1891), Shufeldt N3663, Division of Rare and Manuscript Collections, Carl A. Kroch Library, Cornell University. Reprinted by permission of the Division of Rare and Manuscript Collections, Cornell University Library.

29. "Which of These Alluring Types Are You?" Detail from Armand Complexion Powder Ad Proof, 1929. Photo no. 89-14353. N. W. Ayer Collection. Reprinted by permission of N. W. Ayer Collection, Archives Center, National Museum of American History, Smithsonian Institution, Washington, D.C.

30. Madame C. J. Walker Advertisement, *The Crisis* 18 (March 1919): 256.

31. Madame C. J. Walker Advertisement, *The Messenger* 7 (May 1925): 212.

32. "Un gruppo di mamme," *Maternità ed infanzia* (1929). Reproduced courtesy of the National Library of Florence.

33. Marcello Dudovich, "Giornata della Madre ed Infanzia, 1935," in *Pubblicità d'Italia,* nos. 17–18 (1938). Reproduced courtesy of the National Library of Florence.

34. Gino Boccasile, cover, *Le grandi firme,* 29 April 1937. Reproduced courtesy of the National Library of Florence.

35. Montage of Pirelli workers, *I dopolavoro aziendali in Italia* (1938). Reproduced courtesy of the National Library of Florence.

36–39. Stills from *Love without Illusion.* Reprinted by permission of the Stiftung Deutsche Kinemathek.

40–41. Stills from *Without You All Is Darkness.* Reprinted by permission of the Stiftung Deutsche Kinemathek.

42. Publicity Still from *The Private Secretary.* Reprinted by permission of the Stiftung Deutsche Kinemathek.

43. Still from *Without You All Is Darkness.* Reprinted by permission of the Stiftung Deutsche Kinemathek.

44. Still from *Love without Illusion.* Reprinted by permission of the Stiftung Deutsche Kinemathek.

INDEX

88–89; as fordist unit of consumption,
156; individuation's tension with, 19,
96–99, 102–4, 110n77, 111n80, 153–54;
market's linkage with, 164–65, 166,
180–81n4; modern reconstruction of,
197–99, 208n50–51; producer to
consumer transition in, 8–9, 151–52,
157–59, 161n13, 189; workplace's
differentiation from, 15, 82–83, 166. *See
also* Consumer households
Family law: West German, 360, 368, 378n8,
379n17. *See also* Domestic relations courts
(New York City)
Family Ministry (West Germany), 360, 378n9
Farmers (Germany), food shortage
responsibility of, 289, 292–93, 303n10,
306n34, 306n36
Farwell, Beatrice, 116
Fascist regime (Italy): anticonsumption
agenda of, 340–41; Catholic constraints
on, 343–44; consumer culture's tension
with, 278, 283, 355–56; cultural constraints on, 342–43; fashion agenda
of, 346, 347, 351–53; female beauty
campaign of, 345–46; political mobilization model of, 282–83, 340. *See also*
Italian women; Italy
Fashion: on credit, 172; domesticity's
compatibility with, 37–38, 46; English vs.
French, 60, 64, 73n12, 73n14; expanded
class participation in, 30, 33, 37;
expenditures on, 30–31, 42, 53n64,
257–58; fascist regime's agenda on, 346,
347, 351–53; female production of,
40–42; inconspicuous consumption
dynamic of, 55, 72; individuality/exclu-
siveness of, 352, 357n21; masculine
renunciation of, 12, 54–56, 60, 62–65, 71,
73n2, 73–74n17, 75n32, 75n34; morality
and, 41–42; as necessaries vs. luxuries,
176–77, 187n80; physical lust and, 11,
42–43, 45; physiological/psychological
linkages to, 11–12, 35–37. *See also*
Marchandes de modes
Favardin, Patrick, 90
Female agency, defined, 180–81n4
Female beauty. *See* Beauty
Female body, 370–71, 379n20. *See also*
Feminine image
Female identity: African-American expression of, 327–29, 336n40–41; appearance

and, 311–12, 313, 320, 323–24, 328–29,
354, 355; cosmetic signification of,
281–82, 311, 324, 329–31; the face as,
314, 323–24; as fixed, 315; as performance, 320–22, 334n27. *See also* Identity
Female spectatorship, 280–81, 377
Feminine image: censorship of, 134–35;
commodity's coupling with, 113–15, 129;
decontextualization of, 131; male
spectator of, 123; patriarchal production
of, 114–15; photographic dissemination
of, 143–44; as signifier of modernity, 12,
115, 116–17, 125–26, 147n20. *See also*
Femininity
The Feminine Mystique (Friedan), 386, 387n2
Femininity: consumption's identification
with, 1, 7, 13, 14, 27, 60; defined, 145n3;
deserted wives' lack of, 193–94; fashion
production's ties to, 40–41; fetishized
image of, 129, 131, 133; iconographic
dominance of, 115–16, 117; interdepen-
dent discourses of, 144–45; lithographic
stereotypes of, 141–42; mass culture's
association with, 120, 147n20; opposing
contemporary models of, 361–62;
political construction of, 65–66, 67–68,
75n43; psychoanalytic discourse on, 384;
threat of, 13, 47–48, 374–75. *See also*
Female identity; Feminine image;
Women
Feminist criticism: consumption/con-
sumerism issues of, 7, 275–76, 281,
381–82, 387n2; on melodrama, 362–63;
rhetorics of, 386; on subjectivity, 384–85
Feminist Practice and Poststructuralist Theory
(Weedon), 384–85
Financial Times (England), 267, 273n96
Findlen, Paula, 107n29
Flâneurs, 91. *See also* Dandyism
Floyd, Vivian, 177, 178
Flugel, J. C., 55–56, 73n2
Fontana sisters, 351
Food shortage (Berlin): and broadening
class identification, 293–95, 299,
303–4n12–13, 308n47; farmers'
responsibility for, 289, 292–93, 303n10,
306n34, 306n36; middlemen's impact
on, 288, 302n7; propaganda response to,
290, 304n17–19; and rationing/redistrib-
ution measures, 294, 307n41; state
intervention and, 294–95, 307n42,

83–85, 87. *See also* Appliances; Collecting;
    Fashion; Household expenditures
Gordon, Linda, 197, 198, 208n51
Graham, Florence Nightingale (pseud.
    Elizabeth Arden), 323
Gramont, Elisabeth de, 89
Grandville. *See* Gérard, Jean-Ignace-Isidore
Great Depression, 18, 193, 206n21, 218
Great Reform Act of 1832 (England), 55
Green, Nicholas, 144
Grimm, Hans, 380n26
Grisette (young shop girls), 29, 42–44, 49n14,
    141
GVM (pharmaceutical company), 346

Habermas, Jürgen, 17
Hackley, Azalia, 327
Halbwachs, Maurice, 23n19, 153
Hall, Catherine, 56, 164
Hallmann, Mr. and Mrs. Edward (litigants),
    177–78
Halttunen, Karen, 313
Hansen, Miriam, 281
Hard, William, 202
Hardyment, Christina, 264
Hatheyer, Heidemarie, 361, 363, 366
Haug, W. F., 113, 114–15
Haussmann, Baron, 91
Hebberd, Robert W., 202, 210n70
Heinze, Andrew, 197, 205n3
Helen Hall Papers, 237n6
Hennequin, Mme, 96, 97
Hertzberg, Max, 195
Hill-McCue Bill (1915, New York), 210n70
Hirschman, Albert, 277
Hitler, Adolf, 278
Hobsbawm, Eric, 338
Hochschild, Arlie, 233, 234
Hoggart, Richard, 387n2
Hollywood, 364, 366, 369, 373
Home and Gardens, 267, 273–74n97
Homosexuality, 374
Hoover, Herbert, 159
Household. *See* Family
Household appliances. *See* Appliances
Household expenditures: of British middle
    class, 262, 263 table 13; class patterns of,
    23n19, 153–54; of Italian women, 341;
    male authority over, 165–66, 169,
    184n36; in U.S. vs. Europe, 157–58,
    161n13; women's management of,

222–23; of working-class households,
    152–53, 154, 228, 256–57. *See also*
    Appliances
Household management movement (U.S.),
    156
Household-production theory, 246
Housewives. *See* Wives
Housework: class equalization of, 157;
    technology's alleviation of, 244–45,
    266–67, 281; women's dislike of, 231–32;
    by working-class husbands, 214, 230,
    232–34, 242n119. *See also* Appliances;
    Electricity
Husbands: credit/expenditure authority of,
    164, 165–66, 172, 173, 184n36; debt
    liability of, 169, 170, 176–79; as
    normative breadwinner, 189. *See also*
    Breadwinning; Deserters; Male wage
    earners

Ibsen, Henrik, 154
Ideal Home, 267
Identity: consumption's formation of,
    279–83, 287, 301n1, 337–39, 342, 356n2,
    356n4; multiple discourses shaping,
    384–85; performances of, 320–22,
    334n27; racial, 316, 327–30, 336n41. *See
    also* Collective identities; Female identity;
    Individuality
Igra, Anna, 155
Illinois, 210n69–70
Imagerie d'epinal, 120
Imagined community, 338
Immigrants: and American gender norms,
    189, 194, 205n3; anti-desertion reformers
    on, 194, 196–97; as cosmetics users,
    326–27; gender transgressions by,
    214–15, 225–26, 227, 232, 234–35,
    242n119; reform movement's criticism
    of, 196–97. *See also* Anti-desertion
    movement; Breadwinning
Immortality, collectors' goal of, 87–88, 89,
    92, 108n43
Income. *See* Wages/income
Inconspicuous consumption. *See* Masculine
    renunciation
Individuality: bourgeois women's expression
    of, 96–101, 111n80, 153–54; collective
    action's relation to, 276–77, 352–54,
    357n21; family's tension with, 19, 96–99,
    102–4, 110n77, 111n80, 153–54; as male

Compositor:	Integrated Composition Systems
Text:	10/12 Baskerville
Display:	Baskerville
Printer and binder:	Thomson-Shore, Inc